London

"All you've got to do is decide to go and the hardest part is over.

So go!"

TONY WHEELER, COFOUNDER – LONELY PLANET

STEVE FALLON, DAMIAN HARPER, LAUREN KEITH, MASOVAIDA MORGAN, TASMIN WABY

Contents

Plan Your Trip 4

Explore London 70

Understand London 361

Survival Guide 409

London Maps 435

KIEV.VICTOR/SHUTTERSTOCK ©

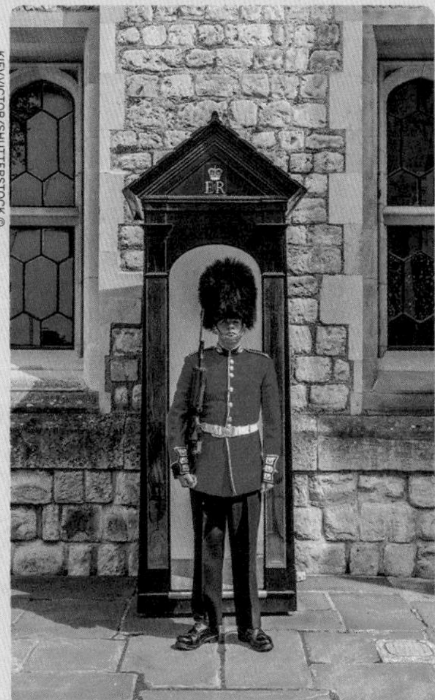

Tower of London (p137)
The Queen's Guards in red are world famous.

COVID-19

We have re-checked every business in this book before publication to ensure that it is still open after the COVID-19 outbreak. However, the economic and social impacts of COVID-19 will continue to be felt long after the outbreak has been contained, and many businesses, services and events referenced in this guide may experience ongoing restrictions. Some businesses may be temporarily closed, have changed their opening hours and services, or require bookings; some unfortunately could have closed permanently. We suggest you check with venues before visiting for the latest information.

ETORRES/SHUTTERSTOCK ©

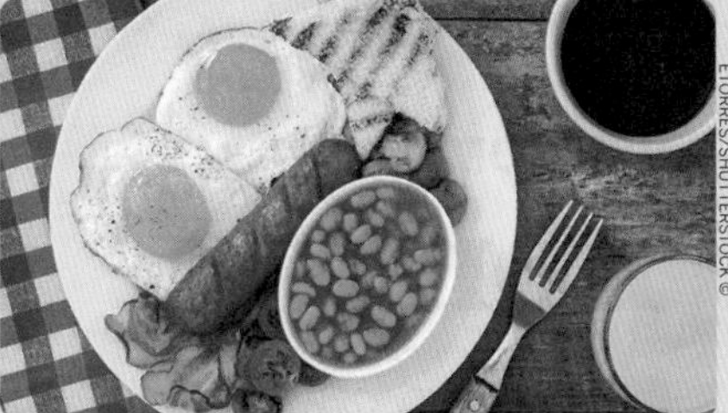

Full English breakfast (p47)
Begin your day with this traditional morning feast.

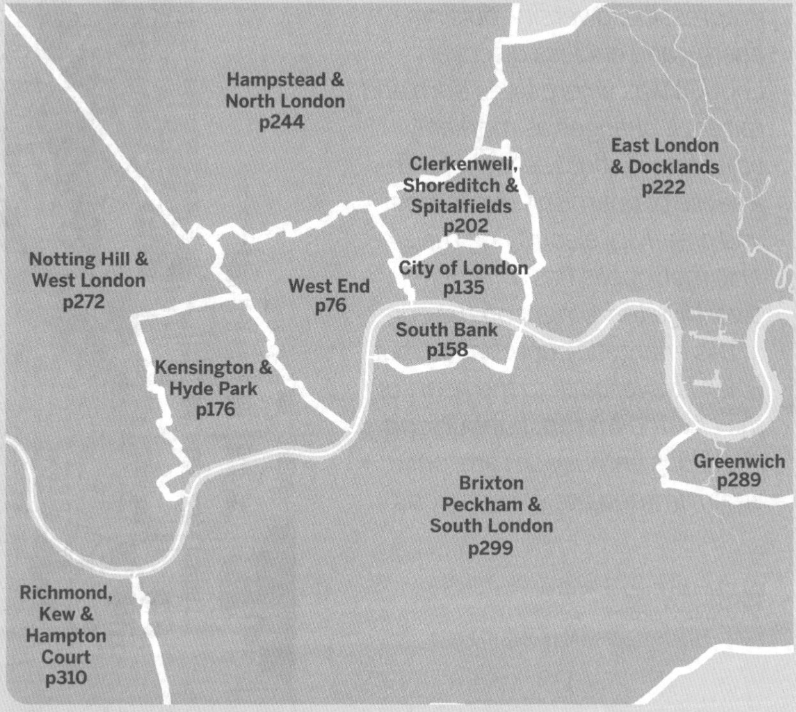

Right: The Gherkin skyscraper (p385)

ARCHITECT NORMAN FOSTER; ALEXANDER SPATARI/GETTY IMAGES ©

WELCOME TO London

A city of wide-open parkland, riverside pubs, leafy squares, irrepressible diversity, pulsing energy and endless discovery, London was where I was born and raised. It changes as markedly as its four distinct seasons, with a sense of optimism, excitement and creativity electrifying the air. This metropolis has a life of its own: I live today right on the edge of this energetic conurbation, but when I travel back to the heart of the city, the frisson, hubbub and infectious enthusiasm are, once again, immediate companions.

By Damian Harper, Writer
damian.harper
For more about our writers, see p480

London's Top Experiences

1 LONDON'S BIG COLLECTIONS

London's museums are not just world class, they exist in a class of their own. Not only are most of them free, many are housed in some of London's finest architecture, stuffed with riveting exhibits and solve, at a stroke, debates about how to entertain the kids. There's also a museum for almost every niche interest,

3DF MEDIASTUDIO/SHUTTERSTOCK ©

ARCHITECT NORMAN FOSTER : ALEX SEGRE/SHUTTERSTOCK ©

British Museum

Britain's most visited attraction (pictured left), you could spend a lifetime exploring this vast and hallowed gathering of artefacts, art and age-old antiquity and still make daily discoveries, . Whatever your approach, make sure you glimpse the Rosetta Stone (pictured right), key to deciphering hieroglyphics, and the museum's other-worldly mummies. p81

ELROCE/SHUTTERSTOCK ©

ANTON_IVANOV/SHUTTERSTOCK ©

Natural History Museum

With its architecture straight from a Gothic fairy tale, the Natural History Museum is an astonishing work of curatorial imagination. Kids are the target audience, but adults aren't far behind. Winter brings its own magic, when the glittering ice rink by the East Lawn swarms with skaters. p182

Victoria & Albert Museum

The world's leading collection of decorative arts has something for everyone, from Islamic textiles to antique Chinese statues, photography, fashion, works by Raphael and modern design classics such as iMacs and Nike shoes. And don't overlook the incredible museum architecture. p178

2 LIVING HISTORY

Whichever way you wend in London, you'll be bumping into the city's dazzling and imposing past, whether it's hanging on a Beefeater's every word at the Tower of London, getting lost in the historic maze at Hampton Court Palace or walking in amazed silence around the sublime magnificence of Westminster Abbey. And remember, there's always more history right round the next corner.

ALEXANDER CHAIKIN/SHUTTERSTOCK ©

JOHN HARPER/GETTY IMAGES ©

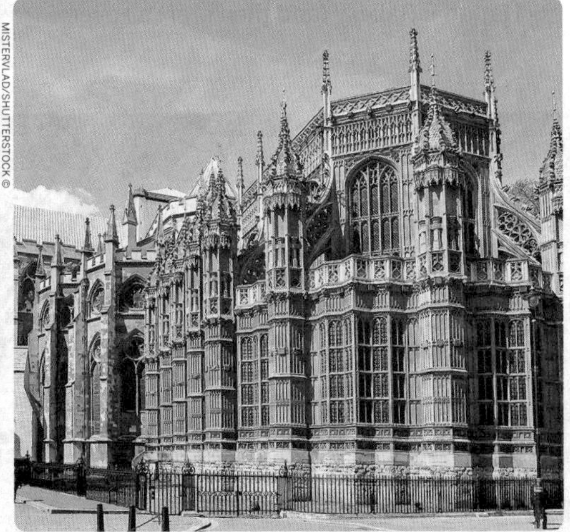

MISTERVLAD/SHUTTERSTOCK ©

Tower of London

Few buildings in the UK are as steeped in history, legend and superstition as this fabulous fortress (pictured above left). There's the world's largest diamond, free tours from magnificently attired Beefeaters, a dazzling array of weaponry, and a palpable sense of history at every turn. p137

Westminster Abbey

Medieval ecclesiastic fans will be in seventh heaven at this awe-inspiring abbey, (pictured top and above) a hallowed place of coronation for England's sovereigns. Among highlights, you will find Poet's Corner, the Coronation Chair, a 900-year-old garden, and royal sarcophagi. p78

Hampton Court Palace

The magnificent Tudor palace, so coveted by Henry VIII, was extended in the 17th century by Christopher Wren. Don't miss the Tudor kitchens and do leave time for the sumptuous gardens, the legendary maze (and the ghost stories). p312

3 DIVE INTO THE ARTS

If art floats your boat, you need to drop anchor in one of London's superlative collections and go walkabout. There's something for every taste and sensibility, from Renaissance masterpieces to cutting-edge conceptual art and all aesthetic points in between. It's hard just knowing where to kick off, or where to finish: you could spend the entire day at the National Gallery (and then start all over again).

Tate Modern

A vast shrine to modern and contemporary art, the much-loved Tate Modern (pictured right) enjoys a triumphant position on the River Thames. Housed in the former Bankside Power Station, the museum is a vigorous statement of modernity, architectural renewal and accessibility. The permanent collection is free and new exhibition spaces host installations and performance art. p160

ARCHITECTS HERZOG & DE MEURON ; RON ELLIS/SHUTTERSTOCK ©

PHILIP BIRD LRPS CPAGB/SHUTTERSTOCK ©

COWARDLION/SHUTTERSTOCK ©

National Gallery

A bravura performance (pictured left) and one not to be missed, this roll-call of some of the world's most outstanding artistic compositions has highlights that include works by Leonardo da Vinci, Michelangelo, Gainsborough, Constable, Turner, Monet, Renoir and Van Gogh. p91

Tate Britain

On the other side of the river from its modern sibling, the Tate Britain (pictured top) houses a mesmerising collection of British art, dating from 1500 to the present day. Highlights include resplendent pieces by JMW Turner and a sublime selection of Pre-Raphaelite works. p92

4 GO GREEN

With eight million trees and a staggering 47% of London given over to green space, London's urban parkland is virtually second to none. It's also the place to see locals at ease and in their element. You can find Europe's largest parkland (Richmond Park) here as well as a host of extensive Royal Parks and small, tidy and specialist pockets of flora such as the Chelsea Physic Garden.

STEFAN-KADAR/SHUTTERSTOCK ©

PAJOR PAWEL/SHUTTERSTOCK ©

BRIAN MINKOFF/SHUTTERSTOCK ©

Kew Gardens

Kew Gardens (pictured above left) is loved by Londoners for its 19th-century Palm House and other Victorian glasshouses, its conservatories, tree-canopy walkway, architectural follies and mind-boggling variety of plants. Kids will have a blast in the play areas. p316

Kensington & Hyde Park

Hyde Park (pictured above) ranges across 142 hectares; throw in Kensington Gardens and you have even more space to roam and everything you could want: a central setting, a royal palace, deck chairs, boating, concerts, galleries and magnificent trees. p176

Greenwich Park

A delightful mix of expansive lawns and beautiful trees in the home of the Meridian (pictured top). Clamber up to the Royal Observatory and gaze out onto some of the most amazing views that London has to offer. p292

5 LONDON EATS

London has long been a shining light of culinary excellence, with a kaleidoscope of cuisines unrivalled in Europe. The capital is particularly strong in Indian and other Asian flavours, but don't miss the opportunity of trying traditional or Modern British cuisine, either in a good gastropub or one of the finer restaurants. For those with a sweet tooth, an afternoon tea or a treat from the capital's many cake shops is a must.

Fresh flavour

Modern British Food needs to be on your culinary list and the nation's capital can quickly point you in the direction of the very best chefs. Adorned with two Michelin stars, Dinner by Heston Blumenthal is a superb choice. p193

Afternoon Tea

For *the* quintessential English experience, afternoon tea is a must. For full-on indulgence, make a reservation at the Foyer and Reading Rooms at Claridge's (dress smart). p120

London's Food Markets

London's wholesome food markets will overwhelm you with aroma, taste and texture and endless selections of street food, food stalls and something for everyone. p50

6 ROYAL DUTY

London pulls out some serious stops to crowd-please with its unrivalled collection of royal sights. Whether you are waiting for the Changing of the Guard, eyeballing the dazzling Crown Jewels at the Tower of London or swooning among the State Rooms at Buckingham Palace, the city has pageantry and the monarchy covered. Some sights (the State Rooms at Buckingham Palace) are seasonal, but most are year round.

Buckingham Palace

At the heart of London, the Queen Mother of all London's palaces with the crowd-pulling Changing of the Guard (pictured above). You can visit the State Rooms and the gardens between July and September. p85

Windsor Castle

A melange of architectural styles, this magnificent, ancient and imposing fortress lords it over the town of Windsor. If you missed the Buckingham Palace spectacular, the castle has its own Changing of the Guard. p328

Kensington Palace

Princess Diana's former palatial home, this stately and stunning royal palace is the highlight of Kensington Gardens, with the astonishing Albert Memorial a very short walk away. p187

7 NIGHTS OUT

No trip to London would be complete without an evening of *Mamma Mia!*, *Les Misérables* or *The Phantom of the Opera*, but you could pretty much say the same about all of London's theatres, while a visit to one of the city's characterful pubs is a mandatory occasion (and longer opening hours have cemented pubs as the cornerstone of a good night out across the capital).

COWARDLION/SHUTTERSTOCK ©

CKTRAVELS.COM/SHUTTERSTOCK ©

West End Shows

The West End is synonymous with musicals, but if musicals don't float your boat, there's theatre, dance, opera, small gigs, big-ticket concerts or live jazz at venues such as Ronnie Scott's. p76

Shakespeare's Globe

Claim a Bard's-eye view of the stage at the recreated Shakespeare's Globe (pictured top left) for an unusual Elizabethan-style experience. p162

Pubs

London minus its pubs, such as the Lamb & Flag, would be like Paris sans cafes. Pub culture is a part of London's DNA, and the pub is the best place to see local people in their element. p124

8 GREAT ESCAPES

I WEI HUANG/SHUTTERSTOCK ©

JOE DANIEL PRICE/GETTYIMAGES ©

PHAUSTOV/SHUTTERSTOCK ©

Shake off the crowds and you'll find that London has a bountiful choice of tranquil retreats, wild heathland and pastoral settings. What better way to explore the city's less built-up side? If you want to go the whole hog, day trips to Oxford and Cambridge are packed with collegiate history and picture-postcard charm, while if it's pebble beaches and sunshine you hanker for, head south to Brighton.

Hampstead Heath

Wild, hilly, carefree heathland, woodland and meadows is the ultimate escape. There's perhaps no better rambling territory in the capital and the views over London from the top of Parliament Hill (London's highest open space; pictured left) are priceless. p255

Petersham Meadows

A verdant oasis of pastoral England alongside the Thames, these beautiful meadows are yet another reason to visit Richmond. p319

Oxford

Just over an hour away by train and steeped in tradition and learning, the university town of Oxford (pictured left) is perhaps the ultimate day trip for history seekers, museum enthusiasts and fans of sublime college architecture. p333

What's New

Ever-changing and restless, it's an almost impossible task to capture what's novel about London. COVID-19 may have stilled the wind in the city's sails, but with architectural transformation, public art initiatives, an increasingly cashless city, an evolving restaurant scene, and a metropolis reflecting on its new status as a capital of a nation outside the EU, London is still evolving.

Veganism on a Roll

Veganism is rampant in the Big Smoke, with London recently topping the list of world cities with the most vegan restaurants (152). Huge numbers of restaurants also have vegan choices, even sausage-roll specialists Greggs recently introduced a much-loved vegan roll.

Medicine: The Wellcome Galleries at the Science Museum

Covering an area that could accommodate 1500 hospital beds, the £24 million medicine galleries are a major development and feature at the Science Museum, forming the world's largest galleries dedicated to medicine, with over 3000 objects on display, including the world's first MRI scanner.

King's Cross Redevelopment

Regeneration of once-derelict King's Cross continues apace. It's rapidly becoming one of London's coolest areas. See www.kingscross.co.uk/the-story-so-far.

Europe's Largest Shopping Centre

A £600-million extension has made Westfield, in Shepherd's Bush, one of Europe's largest shopping centres. Shops include a scintillating Tesla showroom and the excellent Kidzania (p242), where children can play as grown-ups!

Silo

Flaunting scrupulous sustainability credentials and innovative excellence, the world's first zero-waste restaurant, uber-ethical Silo (p235) – which opened on the coast in Brighton in 2014, but dates to 2011 and Australia – recently moved to Hackney

LOCAL KNOWLEDGE

WHAT'S HAPPENING IN LONDON

Damian Harper, Lonely Planet writer

The ceaseless Brexit chatter that filled the streets of London for years eventually made way for the latest angles on mask-wearing and elbow bumps (when anyone was *actually* on the streets of lockdown London in 2020). But property prices still animate dinner party conversation, along with knife crime, vehicle emissions, global warming and of course, coronavirus. And you won't stop Londoners talking about rising rents, transport woes and vanishing pubs. But there's path-breaking optimism too: London is becoming a vegan paradise and with 66 Michelin-star restaurants, food is again the talk of the town, while more and more road-users are hopping on their bikes and leaving the car at home!

Wick. Furniture, plates and fittings are all recycled or upcycled.

Japan House

A handsome and evocative celebration of Japanese art, culture and design, this superbly chic two-floor space (p285) – topped by a Japanese restaurant – on Kensington High St is a delightful new arrival.

Sober London

As millennials eschew the grain and the grape – getting drunk is no longer cool – temperate nightlife is growing, with expanding no-alcohol options at pubs and bars, booze-free establishments, and lengthening lists of alcohol-free drinks.

Bikes for All

More and more competitors to the Santander (Boris Bike) public-bicycle-hire schemes, both push and electric (including Lime, Freebike), are taking to the streets.

Illuminated Bridges

Bridges are being lit up at night as part of the Illuminated River art installation (https://illuminatedriver.london). This new public art commission aims to light up 14 bridges along the river at night, allowing Londoners and visitors the chance to see the river and its crossings in an entirely new light.

Garden at 120

Adding to London's mushrooming number of vantage points to admire city panoramas, this roof garden (p146) is the largest in town, with superb vistas of some of London's most cutting-edge and iconic skyscrapers.

Cashless London

The shift toward a cashless city was further accelerated by the COVID-19 pandemic, with cash withdrawals in London falling by 40% between 2019 and 2021. A growing bevy of restaurants and bars are now cash-free.

Museum of the Home

Shut for three years and an £18.1 million redevelopment, the ivy-clad brick almshouses of the former Geffrye Museum reopened in mid 2021 as the Museum of the Home (p204). Rooms have been furnished as they were in 18th and 19th centuries, with evocative attention to detail.

Wild Swimming

Wild Swimming has become a national craze, and London is no exception. If you want to join the flow, follow the crowds into the waters of Hampstead Heath ponds, Parliament Hill Lido, the Serpentine Lido and even Queen Victoria Docs.

Holocaust Gallery

In 2021 the Imperial War Museum opened a £30.5 million pair of new and thought-provoking galleries, Second World War and The Holocaust, cataloguing, displaying and contextualising the Holocaust over two floors within the cataclysmic 20th century conflict.

LISTEN, WATCH & FOLLOW

For inspiration and up-to-date news, visit www.lonelyplanet.com/england/london/articles

Insta @prettylittlelondon Idyllic and evocative photos of London.

Insta @londonist.com London through and through.

Secret London (https://secretldn.com) Off-radar London.

London on the Inside (https://londontheinside.com) Up-to-the-minute London.

FAST FACTS

Food Trend veganism

Number of rides daily on the Tube up to five million

Percentage of green space 47%

Pop 9 million

LONDON ENGLAND

≈ 400 people per sq km

Need to Know

For more information, see Survival Guide (p409)

Currency
Pound sterling (£)

Language
English

Visas
There are several different short-stay visas, depending on the nature of your visit. For stays of up to six months, Australian, Canadian, NZ and US visitors, among others, don't need visas.

Money
ATMs are widespread. Major credit cards are accepted everywhere. Change money at post-offices, which don't charge a commission.

Mobile Phones
Unless your international roaming charges are good, buy a local SIM card once in the UK. Now that Britain has left the EU, it's likely international roaming charges will return for EU providers.

Time
London is on GMT/UTC; during British Summer Time (BST; late March to late October) clocks are one hour ahead of GMT/UTC.

Tourist Information
Visit London (www.visitlondon.com) has info on special events, tours, accommodation, eating, theatre, shopping etc.

Daily Costs

Budget: Less than £85
- ➡ Dorm bed: £12–30
- ➡ Market-stall snack or supermarket sandwich: £3.50–5
- ➡ Many museums: free
- ➡ Standby theatre tickets: 10p–£25
- ➡ Santander Cycles daily rental fee: £2

Midrange: £85–200
- ➡ Double room: £100–200
- ➡ Two-course dinner with glass of wine: £35
- ➡ Temporary exhibitions: £12–18
- ➡ Theatre tickets: £15–60

Top end: More than £200
- ➡ Four-star or boutique hotel room: more than £200
- ➡ Three-course dinner in top restaurant with wine: £60–90
- ➡ Black cab trip: £30
- ➡ Top theatre tickets: £65

Advance Planning

Three months before Book accommodation, dinner reservations, and tickets for top shows and must-see temporary exhibitions.

One month before Check websites such as *Time Out* (www.timeout.com/london) for fringe theatre, live music and festivals, and book tickets.

A few days before Check the weather online through the Met Office (www.metoffice.gov.uk).

Useful Websites

Lonely Planet (www.lonelyplanet.com/england/london) Destination info, hotel bookings, traveller forum and more.

Time Out London (www.timeout.com/london) Entertainment listings; free every Tuesday.

Londonist (www.londonist.com) Info on London and everything that happens in it.

Transport for London (www.tfl.gov.uk) Essential tool for staying mobile in the capital.

London Evening Standard (www.standard.co.uk) London's main newspaper; free at Tube stations.

Met Office (www.metoffice.gov.uk) Weather forecasts.

WHEN TO GO

Summer means peak season, long days, festivals and crowds. Spring and autumn are cooler. Winter is cold and wet, with short days.

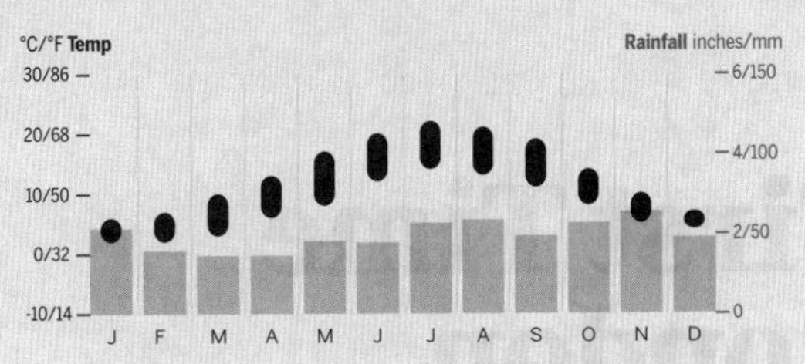

Arriving in London

Heathrow Airport Trains, the Tube and buses to London from around 5am to before midnight (night buses run later and 24-hour Tube trains run Friday and Saturday) cost £5.10 to £25, taxis £50 to £100. Heathrow Express (p410) runs to Paddington train station in 15 minutes (from around 5am to between 11pm and midnight).

Gatwick Airport Trains to London (4.30am to 1.35am) cost £10 to £20; 24/7 hourly buses from £10; taxis £100.

Stansted Airport Trains to London (5.30am to 12.30am) cost £19.40; 24/7 buses £7 to £10; taxis £130.

Luton Airport Trains to London (7am to 10pm) from £16.70; 24/7 buses £7 to £11; taxis £110.

London City Airport DLR trains to central London (5.30am to 12.15am Monday to Saturday, 7am to 11.15pm Sunday) from £3.30; taxis £30 to £60.

St Pancras International Train Station In central London; connected by Underground to rest of city.

For much more on **arrival** see p410

Digital London

There are scores of cool apps for travellers. Here are some of our favourite free ones – from inspirational to downright practical. Many museums and attractions also have their own.

Streetmuseum Historical images (photographs, paintings, drawings etc) superimposed on modern-day locations.

CityMapper Great app giving you all the options for getting from A to B (on foot, by public transport, bike or cab).

TubeMap Features a Tube map offline, and a full interactive route service when connected.

Gett Summons the nearest black cab right to the curb.

Bolt, Kabbee or Free Now For minicabs or ride-shares at competitive prices.

London Live Bus Countdown Real-time route finder and bus arrivals for a stop of your choice.

Santander Cycles Find a 'Boris bike', a route and a place to return it.

For much more on **getting around** see p413

Sleeping

Accommodation in London can be painfully expensive, and you'll almost always need to book well in advance. Decent hostels are easy to find but aren't as cheap as you might hope. Hotels range from no-frills chains to the world's ritziest establishments, such as the Ritz itself. B&Bs are often better value and more atmospheric than hotels.

Useful Websites

Visit London (www.visitlondon.com) Huge range of listings; official tourism portal.

London Town (www.londontown.com) Last-minute offers on boutique hotels and B&Bs.

London Bed & Breakfast (www.londonbb.com) B&B in private homes across the city.

Lonely Planet (lonelyplanet.com/england/london/hotels) Recommendations and bookings.

For much more on **sleeping** see p344

First Time London

For more information, see Survival Guide (p409)

Checklist

➡ Make sure your passport is valid for at least six months past your arrival date.

➡ Arrange travel insurance and inform your debit-/credit-card company of your travel plans.

➡ Book tickets for popular plays, shows or festivals to avoid disappointment.

➡ Reserve hotel rooms well in advance.

What to Pack

➡ A small umbrella (yes, the rumours about the weather are true).

➡ Good walking shoes – the city is best explored on foot.

➡ UK plug adaptor.

➡ A few extra layers – it can be cool, even in summer.

➡ A small day pack.

Top Tips for Your Trip

➡ An Oyster Card is a cheaper and convenient way to use public transport, but you can also pay by contactless credit or debit card (ie with the wi-fi symbol on the card).

➡ A growing number of bars and restaurants are cashless.

➡ Walk – it's the best way to discover central London.

➡ For West End performances at bargain prices, opt for standby tickets (which you buy on the day at the venue) or last-minute tickets from the booth on Leicester Sq. The TodayTix app is very handy.

➡ To treat yourself to fine dining without breaking the bank, opt for lunch rather than dinner, or try for pre- or post-theatre dinner deals.

➡ Book tickets online to save money and skip queues.

➡ Download apps such as Gett (for black cabs): for minicabs, try Bolt, Kabbee or Free Now.

What to Wear

London fashion is vibrantly and ethnically eclectic, so you're unlikely to stand out, whatever your sartorial choice. Many top-end restaurants, bars and clubs will insist on smart attire, so avoid trainers (sneakers) and flip-flops. Style is pretty relaxed elsewhere, although Londoners usually make an effort in the evenings, whether they're kitted out in cool T-shirts or more formal gear. Unless you're carrying an umbrella, always wear a jacket that can repel a shower. And wrap up warm in winter.

Be Forewarned

➡ Terrorist attacks have afflicted London in recent years, but risks to individual visitors are remote. Report anything suspicious to the police by calling ☎999 (emergency) or 101 (non emergency).

➡ Keep an eye on your handbag/wallet/device in bars, nightclubs and crowded areas like the Underground.

➡ Watch out for cyclists when crossing the road.

➡ If catching a cab post-clubbing, get a black taxi or licensed minicab.

Money

Most Londoners use cashless contactless payments with a credit or debit card (with the wi-fi symbol); for purchases over £30, you'll need a four-digit PIN.

For more information, see p421.

Taxes & Refunds

Value-added tax (VAT) is a 20% sales tax levied on most goods and services. Restaurants must always include VAT in prices, but the same requirement doesn't apply to hotel-room prices. It's possible for visitors to claim a refund of VAT paid on goods while on holidays (p422). You must live outside the EU and be heading back home.

Tipping

Hotels Pay a porter £1 per bag; gratuity for room staff is at your discretion.

Pubs Not expected unless table service is provided, then £1 for a round of drinks is sufficient. If you tip at the bar, staff will assume you must be American.

Restaurants Service charge is always included in the bill. If not (it pays to check!), 10% is fine for decent service, but 15% is best for good service.

Taxis Londoners generally round the fare up to the nearest pound only.

ROBERTO LA ROSA/SHUTTERSTOCK ©

Etiquette

Although largely informal in their everyday dealings, Londoners do observe some (unspoken) rules of etiquette.

Strangers Unless asking for directions, Londoners generally won't start a conversation at bus stops or on Tube platforms.

Queues Locals don't tolerate queue jumping.

Tube Stand on the right and pass on the left while riding an Underground escalator.

Bargaining Haggling over the price of goods (but not food) is OK in markets, but nonexistent in shops.

Punctuality It's poor form to be more than 10 minutes late for drinks or dinner. If you're late, keep everyone in the loop.

Apologise The British love apologising. If you bump into someone on the Tube, say sorry.

Staying Connected

➡ Virtually every London hotel provides free wi-fi.

➡ Numerous cafes and restaurants offer free wi-fi to customers, as do cultural venues such as the Barbican or the Southbank Centre.

➡ Open-air and street wi-fi access is available in areas across London. Users have to register, but there's no charge.

➡ Major train stations, airport terminals and over 260 Underground stations and 79 Overground stations (ticket halls, walkways and platforms) also have wi-fi (usually free; see https://tfl.gov.uk/campaign/station-wifi).

Getting Around

For more information, see Transport (p410)

The cheapest way to get around London is with an **Oyster Card** (https://oyster.tfl.gov.uk/oyster/entry.do) or a UK contactless card (foreign cardholders should check for contactless charges first).

Tube

(London Underground) The most efficient way of getting around town. Trains operate between around 5.30am and 12.30am on weekdays and 24 hours on Friday and Saturday on five lines (plus a section of the London Overground East London Line). The DLR and Overground network are ideal for more distant parts of the city.

Train

Trains run from a number of stations to more distant destinations in and around London.

Bus

The London bus network is very extensive and efficient; while bus lanes free up traffic, buses can still be slow going.

Taxis

Black cabs are available around the clock, but aren't cheap. Gett is a handy black cab app.

Rideshare

Apps like Bolt, Kabbee, Kapten or Free Now allow you to book a ride quickly and can save you money.

Bicycle

Santander Cycles are great for shorter journeys around central London.

Key Phrases

Black cab London's signature taxi. Despite the name, they're not all black!

Boris bike A colloquialism that has stuck for the red Santander-branded bikes for hire all across London. Nicknamed after former mayor – and current Prime Minister – Boris Johnson (the new types are dubbed Sadiq Cycles, after current mayor Sadiq Khan).

Contactless Payment card (debit or credit) that can be used to make quick (and reduced fare) payments without signature or chip and PIN; used in the same way as an Oyster Card.

DLR Docklands Light Railway, an overground, driverless train in East London.

Minicab A taxi that cannot be hailed in the street and must be pre-booked over the phone, in person with the dispatcher (offices generally have an orange flashing light) or through apps such as Bolt.

Oyster Card Smart-card ticket for London's transport network.

Night Tube London's underground all-night service, running 24 hours on Friday and Saturday across five underground lines plus a section of the London Overground East London Line.

The Tube London's underground metro system.

Key Routes

Bus Route 15 This 'heritage' bus route uses the classic Routemaster double-decker buses to the Tower of London, St Paul's, the Strand and Trafalgar Sq.

Bus Route 9 Another 'heritage' classic Routemaster double-decker bus passing Somerset House, Trafalgar Sq, Piccadilly, Hyde Park Corner, Knightsbridge and Kensington High St.

Bus Route 24 Heading from Pimlico past Victoria to Westminster Abbey, Downing St, Trafalgar Sq and Hampstead Heath.

Tube: Piccadilly Line This Tube line stops at some of London's key sights and neighbourhoods – Piccadilly Circus, Covent Garden, Hyde Park Corner and Knightsbridge – and also runs from all Heathrow airport terminals.

How to Hail a Taxi

➡ Vacant black cabs, either at taxi ranks or driving, have a 'For Hire' sign lit up.

➡ Handy black cab apps include Gett; for minicabs, try Bolt, Kabbee, Kapten or Free Now.

TOP TIPS

➡ Get an Oyster Card and return it when you leave to recoup the £5 deposit, along with any remaining credit; or use contactless.

➡ Eschew the Tube within Zone 1 unless going from one end to the other: cycling, walking or the bus will be cheaper/quicker.

➡ Check www.tfl.gov.uk or advanced notices in Tube stations for weekend engineering works and line closures.

➡ Santander Cycles (p415) are good for short trips. Get a rental bike for longer trips.

➡ The Citymapper app plans your journeys.

When to Travel

➡ Rush hour is between 6.30am and 9.30am and from 4pm to 7pm.

➡ Travelling at these times can be uncomfortably crowded: think seat races, face-in-armpit standing, toe-treading and frayed nerves.

➡ Tube fares are more expensive at rush hour.

➡ Weekends are notorious for engineering works, when entire Tube lines or sections shut down. Replacement bus services are usually in place, but they take longer, so plan ahead.

➡ On Sunday to Thursday nights, the Tube stops running around 12.30am. The Night Tube operates a 24-hour service on Friday and Saturday nights, covering the Central, Jubilee, Victoria, Northern and Piccadilly lines and a section of the London Overground East London Line, with trains running roughly every 10 to 15 minutes. Night Tube fares are standard off-peak.

➡ Night buses cover all of London, but some services only run every half-hour. Check times before leaving.

Travel Etiquette

➡ Have your ticket or card ready before you go through the gate. Londoners are well practised at moving through ticket barriers without breaking stride.

➡ On escalators, stand on the right-hand side and use the left if you want to walk down. Failure to observe this can cause consternation and tutting among other users, especially during rush hour.

➡ Take your rucksack off at rush hour to avoid sweeping off somebody's newspaper, tablet or child.

➡ Give up your seat for people less able to stand than you – people with reduced mobility have priority over the seats closest to the doors on the Tube.

➡ Cars will almost always stop for pedestrians at zebra crossings without a traffic light; remember to look right first!

Tickets & Passes

➡ The cheapest and most convenient way to pay for public transport is to use a contactless card; an Oyster Card, a smart card on which you can store credit, is also good value and handy. The card works on the entire transport network and can be purchased from all Tube and train stations and some shops.

➡ Contactless cards can be used instead of Oyster Cards (they benefit from the same 'smart-fare' system); just check for international fees with your card issuer.

➡ Oyster Cards will work out whether to charge you per journey, for a return or for a day Travelcard.

➡ You need to pay a £5 deposit per Oyster Card, which you will get back when you return the card, along with any remaining credit. You can order an Oyster card online and have it posted to you to beat the queues.

➡ Paper tickets are still available but are more expensive than contactless or Oyster Card fares, and you need to queue each time.

For much more on **getting around** see p413

Perfect Days

Day One

West End (p76)

First, visit **Westminster Abbey** for a sublime intro to the city's (and nation's) history, or join the crowds at **Buckingham Palace** for the **Changing the Guard**. Walk up the Mall to **Trafalgar Sq** for its architectural grandeur and views down Whitehall. Art lovers can dive into the **National Gallery** to discover its outstanding collection of European paintings.

Lunch Brasserie Zédel (p114) concocts a *superbe* French ambience.

South Bank (p158)

With your pre-booked ticket for the **London Eye**, walk across pedestrian Hungerford Bridge to the South Bank and enjoy a 30-minute revolution in the city skies and superb views, notably of the **Houses of Parliament**. Afterwards stroll along the river and head into the bowels of the **Tate Modern** for some grade-A art. Aim your smartphone camera at **St Paul's Cathedral** on the far side of the elegant **Millennium Bridge**.

Dinner Grills or more complex dishes at Skylon (p170).

South Bank (p158)

Depending on what mood you're in, you might catch a performance at **Shakespeare's Globe**. 'Groundling' (standing) tickets can be bought last minute but book ahead for seats. Otherwise, join the post-work crowds in the pubs around **London Bridge** for real ales and deeply seasoned, historical ambience.

Day Two

City of London (p135)

London's finance-driven Square Mile is home to the sprawling and ancient **Tower of London**. Spend the morning watching the Beefeaters and resident ravens preen and strut, then marvel at the **Crown Jewels**. When you're finished, admire the iconic **Tower Bridge** from the banks of the Thames or through the glass floors of the walkways connecting the two towers.

Lunch BrewDog Tower Hill (p153) has tempting dishes and craft beers.

West End (p76)

Hop on a double-decker bus for city views and head to the **British Museum** for superlative shots of world culture. Choose one of the excellent introductory tours or rent an audio guide so as not to feel overwhelmed. Round off the afternoon with an afternoon tea at **Tea & Tattle** across the road.

Dinner Head to Hakkasan Hanway Place (p111) for Cantonese delicacies.

West End (p76)

If you fancy soaking up the atmosphere, stroll through **Chinatown** and **Soho** and make your way to **Leicester Square** for people-watching. There are literally dozens of pubs, bars and cocktail lounges along the way from which to choose.

US2112/SHUTTERSTOCK ©

Greenwich Meridian (p292)

LITTLE_DESIRE/SHUTTERSTOCK ©

Blue water lily in Kew Gardens (p316)

Day Three

Greenwich (p289)

Hop on a boat from any central London pier and make your way down to Greenwich with its world-renowned architecture and links to time, the stars and space. Start your visit at the legendary **Cutty Sark**, a star clipper during the tea-trade years, and pop into the **National Maritime Museum**.

Lunch Goddards at Greenwich (p297) for traditional English pie and mash.

Greenwich (p289)

Stroll up through **Greenwich Park** all the way to the **Royal Observatory**. The views of **Canary Wharf**, the business district across the river, are stunning. Inside the observatory, straddle the **Greenwich Meridian** and find out about the incredible quest to solve the longitude problem. Walk back down to Greenwich, admire the **Painted Hall** and the **Old Royal Naval College**, before settling down for a pint at the **Trafalgar Tavern**.

Dinner Polpo (p208) for tasty Italian-style tapas in a picturesque street.

Clerkenwell, Shoreditch & Spitalfields (p202)

Head back to central London on the DLR from Greenwich and treat yourself to dinner in one of the fine restaurants dotting this part of town. There are plenty of clubs if you fancy a boogie after dinner, otherwise opt for a beautifully crafted cocktail at **Zetter Townhouse Cocktail Lounge**.

Day Four

Richmond, Kew & Hampton Court (p310)

Head to **Kew Gardens** bright and early to make the most of the morning: so much more than a botanical garden, it's one of London's most beautiful experiences. Families shouldn't miss the treetop walkway, while plant lovers will go weak at the knees in the Victorian **Palm House** and **Princess of Wales Conservatory**.

Lunch Glasshouse (p324) for fine gastronomy.

Kensington & Hyde Park (p176)

Hop on the Tube to **Knightsbridge**. Keen shoppers will want to stroll down Old Brompton Rd and browse through **Harrods**, the amazing department store. Culture vultures should save some calories to tackle the nearby **Victoria & Albert Museum**, the **Natural History Museum** or the **Science Museum**; each is brilliant.

Dinner Dishoom (p280) for some of the finest Indian cuisine in town.

Notting Hill & West London (p272)

If the pubs around Knightsbridge and South Kensington Tube stations are too staid for you, hop over to **Notting Hill** where the crowds are livelier and the nightlife more eclectic. If you just fancy sitting down with a good film, you're in luck: Notting Hill has some of the coolest independent cinemas in London: see what's on at the iconic **Electric Cinema**.

Month By Month

TOP EVENTS

Chelsea Flower Show, May

Trooping the Colour, June

Wimbledon Lawn Tennis Championships, June

Notting Hill Carnival, August

Guy Fawkes Night, November

January

New Year kicks off with a big bang at midnight. London is in the throes of winter, with short days: light appears at 8am and is all but gone by 4pm.

London International Mime Festival

Held across the month, this festival (www.mimelondon.com) is a must for lovers of originality, playfulness, physical talent and the unexpected.

London Art Fair

More than 130 major galleries participate in this contemporary art fair (www.londonartfair.co.uk), one of the largest in Europe, with thematic exhibitions, special events and the best emerging artists.

February

February is chilly and wet. It's Chinese New Year, plus locals lark about with pancakes on Shrove Tuesday.

Chinese New Year

In late January or early February, Chinatown fizzes, crackles and pops in this colourful street festival, which includes a Golden Dragon parade, feasting and partying.

BAFTAs

The British Academy of Film and Television Arts (BAFTA; www.bafta.org) rolls out the red carpet mid-February to hand out its annual cinema awards. Expect plenty of celebrity glamour.

March

Spring is in the air, trees begin to blossom and daffodils emerge across parks and gardens.

Head of the River

Some 400 crews take part in this colourful annual boat race, held over a 6.8km course on the Thames, from Mortlake to Putney.

St Patrick's Day Parade & Festival

Top festival for the Irish in London, held on the Sunday closest to 17 March, with a colourful parade through central London and other festivities in and around Trafalgar Sq.

April

Warmer days bring a lighthearted vibe. British Summer Time starts late March, moving clocks forward an hour, so it's now light until 7pm. Some sights previously shut for winter reopen.

Oxford & Cambridge Boat Race

Crowds line the banks of the Thames to see the famous universities going oar-to-oar from Putney to Mortlake. Dates vary, due to each university's Easter breaks; check the website (www.theboatraces.org).

(Top) Trooping the Colour (p30)
(Bottom) Guy Fawkes night fireworks (p82)

CHRISPICTURES / SHUTTERSTOCK ©

MELINDA NAGY / SHUTTERSTOCK ©

London Marathon

Some 40,000 runners – most running for charity – pound through London in one of the world's biggest road races (www.virginmoneylondonmarathon.com), heading from Blackheath to the Mall.

Underbelly Festival

Housed in a temporary venue on the South Bank and running annually for over a decade, this festival of comedy, circus, cabaret, music and general family fun (www.underbellyfestival.com) has become a spring favourite. Events run through to September.

May

Days are warming up and the locals enjoy two bank holidays (the first and the last weekends of May).

London Tweed Run

Charmingly eccentric British event (www.tweedrun.com) that sees cyclists dressing up in their finest tweeds and brogues to pedal past famous London landmarks, stopping for tea and picnicking en route.

Chelsea Flower Show

The world's most renowned horticultural event (p192) attracts green-fingered and flower-mad gardeners. Talks, presentations and spectacular displays from the cream of the gardening world.

June

Peak season begins with long, warm days (it's light until 10pm), the arrival of Wimbledon and other alfresco events.

Trooping the Colour

The Queen's official birthday (www.trooping-the-colour.co.uk) is celebrated with much flag-waving, parades, pageantry and noisy flyovers. The Royal Family usually attends in force.

London WNBR (World Naked Bike Ride)

Cyclists take to the streets of London dressed only in their birthday suits to celebrate body freedom, protest against car culture, highlight cyclists' vulnerability and fight for rights for bicycle users.

London Festival of Architecture

This month-long celebration of London's built environment (www.londonfestivalofarchitecture.org) explores the significance of architecture and design and how London has become a centre for innovation in these fields.

Meltdown

Southbank Centre hands over the curatorial reins to a contemporary music legend (eg Grace Jones, Patti Smith, Guy Garvey) to pull together a program of concerts, talks and films mid-June (www.facebook. meltdownfest).

(Top) Notting Hill Carnival (p277)

(Bottom) Pride London (p

VIKTOR KOVALENKO/ SHUTTERSTOCK ©

HELLOTICA / SHUTTERSTOCK ©

Royal Academy Summer Exhibition

Running through to August, this exhibition (p104) at the Royal Academy of Arts showcases works submitted by artists from all over Britain and the world, distilled to a thousand or so pieces.

Open Garden Squares Weekend

Over a weekend, 200 plus gardens that are usually inaccessible to the public fling open their gates (www.opensquares.org).

Wimbledon Lawn Tennis Championships

For two weeks a year, the quiet South London village of Wimbledon falls under a sporting spotlight as the world's best tennis players gather to battle for the championships.

July

This is the time to munch on strawberries, drink in beer gardens and join in the numerous outdoor activities, including big music festivals.

Pride London

The gay community paints the town pink (and rainbow) in this annual extravaganza (www.prideinlondon.org), featuring talks and live events, and culminating in a huge parade across London.

Wireless

One of London's top music festivals, with an emphasis on dance and R&B, Wireless (www.wirelessfestival.co.uk) in Finsbury Park. Extremely popular and tickets can sell out on the spot (depending on the line-up).

BBC Promenade Concert (the Proms)

Starting in mid-July, the Proms offers two months of outstanding classical concerts (www.bbc.co.uk/proms) at various prestigious venues, centred on the Royal Albert Hall.

Lovebox

Two-day music extravaganza (www.loveboxfestival.com) in Gunnersbury Park created by dance duo Groove Armada. Its raison d'être is dance music, but there are plenty of other genres too, including indie, pop and hip hop.

August

School's out for summer. Hugely popular Notting Hill Carnival takes place on the last weekend of the month, a bank holiday.

Summer Screen at Somerset House

For a fortnight Somerset House turns its stunning courtyard into an open-air cinema (p106), screening an eclectic mix of film premieres, cult classics and popular requests.

Great British Beer Festival

Organised by CAMRA (Campaign for Real Ale), this boozy festival (www.gbbf.org.uk) cheerfully cracks open casks of ale from the UK and abroad at Olympia exhibition centre.

Notting Hill Carnival

Europe's biggest, and London's most vibrant, outdoor carnival (p277) celebrates Caribbean London, featuring music, dancing and costumes over the summer bank-holiday weekend.

September

Autumn begins. A lovely time to be in town, with comedy festivals and a chance to look at London properties normally shut to the public.

Totally Thames Festival

Celebrating the River Thames, this cosmopolitan festival (www.totallythames.org) brings fairs, street theatre, music, food stalls, fireworks and river races, culminating in the superb Night Procession.

Greenwich Comedy Festival

This week-long laugh fest – London's largest comedy festival – brings big names and emerging acts to the National Maritime Museum.

Open House London

For a weekend in mid-September the public is invited in to see over 800 heritage buildings throughout the capital that are normally off-limits (www.openhouselondon.org.uk).

October

It's getting colder, but parks are splashed with gorgeous autumnal colours. Clocks go back

to winter time the last weekend of the month.

London Cocktail Week

Seven-day mixology celebration (https://drinkup.london/cocktailweek; festival pass £10, cocktails £6) across 300 London bars plus access to a dedicated Cocktail Village. Cheers!

London Film Festival

The city's premier film event (www.bfi.org.uk/lff) attracts big names and shows more than 100 British and international films before their cinema release. Masterclasses are given by world-famous directors.

Dance Umbrella

London's annual festival of contemporary dance (www.danceumbrella.co.uk) features two weeks of performances by British and international dance companies at venues across London.

November

Nights are getting longer. Enjoy the last of the parks' autumn colours and relax by an open fire in a pub afterwards.

Guy Fawkes Night (Bonfire Night)

Bonfire Night commemorates Guy Fawkes' foiled attempt to blow up Parliament in 1605. Bonfires and fireworks light up the night on 5 November. Primrose Hill, Highbury Fields, Alexandra Palace, Clapham Common and Blackheath have some of the best displays.

Lord Mayor's Show

In accordance with Magna Carta (1215), the newly elected Lord Mayor of the City of London travels by state coach from Mansion House to the Royal Courts of Justice to take an oath of allegiance to the Crown – nowadays with floats, bands and fireworks (www.lordmayorsshow.london).

London Jazz Festival

Musicians from around the world swing into town for 10 days of jazz (www.efglondonjazzfestival.org.uk). World influences are well represented, as are more conventional styles.

December

Christmas approaches and a festive mood reigns. Days are at their shortest. Christmas Day is quiet, with all shops and museums closed and the tube network shut.

Lighting of the Christmas Tree & Lights

A celebrity is called upon to switch on all the festive lights that line Oxford, Regent and Bond Sts, and a towering Norwegian spruce is set up in Trafalgar Sq.

With Kids

London is a terrific place for young ones. The city's museums will enthral all age groups, and you'll find theatre, dance and live music performances ideal for older kids and teens. Playgrounds and parks, city farms and nature reserves are perfect for either toddler energy-busting or relaxation.

ANTON_IVANOV/SHUTTERSTOCK ©

Madame Tussauds wax museum (p107)

Museums

London's museums are nothing if not child-friendly. There are dedicated children or family trails in virtually every museum. Additionally, you'll find plenty of activities such as storytelling at the National Gallery (p91), thematic backpacks to explore the British Museum (p81), pop-up performances at the Victoria & Albert Museum (p178), family audio guides at the Tate Modern (p160), and arts and crafts workshops at Somerset House (p106), where kids can dance through the fountains in the courtyard in summer. The Science Museum (p186) has a marvellous interactive area downstairs called 'the Garden', where tots can splash around with water; however, some kids never get beyond the fantastic shop at the museum. Older kids will be thrilled with the flight simulators at the Science Museum too.

In winter (November to January), a section by the East Lawn of the Natural History Museum (p182) is transformed into a glittering and highly popular ice rink; book your slot well ahead (www.ticketmaster.co.uk). Somerset House also sparkles with a fantastic ice rink in winter; more rinks can be found at Hampton Court Palace (p312), the Tower of London (p137) and other sights.

Museum & Attraction Sleepovers

What better fun than sleeping at the feet of a dinosaur? Museum sleepovers are very popular and must be booked at least a couple of months in advance.

Natural History Museum

Snooze under the watchful eye of the blue whale in the Hintze Hall, having first explored the museum's (p182) darkest nooks and crannies with only a torch to light your way. Monthly; adults welcome too!

Science Museum

Astronights for kids aged seven to 11 give young ones the chance to enjoy hands-on workshops, science shows and activities and to explore and stay overnight in the museum (p186).

British Museum

Sleepovers give kids aged eight to 15 the chance to bed down next to Egyptian sculpture at the British Museum (p81).

Best for Kids

There is so much to see and do that you won't know where to start.

V&A Museum of Childhood

Dressing-up boxes, toys from times gone by and interactive **play areas** (Map p462, C4; 020-8983 5200; www.museumofchildhood.org.uk; Cambridge Heath Rd, E2; admission free; 10am-5.45pm; ; Bethnal Green).

Natural History Museum

Dinosaurs, animals, more dinosaurs, planet Earth and mind-boggling facts and discoveries – all fascinating stuff at this superlative museum (p182).

London Transport Museum

Twenty London Transport buses and trains are on display and available for climbing on and general child-handling at this museum (p417).

Greenwich Park & Royal Observatory

First there is the park (p292), which you need to gambol through to get to the observatory (p291); then there are the Astronomy Galleries and the Planetarium, which kids will marvel at, as well as the camera obscura.

ZSL London Zoo

Want to see your kids saucer-eyed with wonder in London's largest menagerie? Well, you can do that here (p248).

Kidzania

For kids aged four to 14, the opportunity to test real grown-up skills in a city (p287) run by young ones!

Horniman Museum

An aquarium, a hands-on music room, natural history galleries and huge grounds – this museum (p302) offers endless fun.

Best for Teenagers

London punches above its weight when it comes to entertaining blasé teenagers.

ArcelorMittal Orbit's Slide

This 178m-long corkscrewing slide (p229) is one of London's most adrenalin-inducing experiences, with superb views.

Science Museum

The sensational displays about space, information technology, flying and more will have teenagers enthralled at the Science Museum (p186).

Tate Modern

The Drawing Bar at Bloomberg Connects at this modern art museum (p160) has digital sketch pads where teens can express their inner Rothko.

Madame Tussauds

With its celebrity waxworks this museum (p107) is selfie heaven, be it with Luke Skywalker, Dua Lipa or Captain America.

London Film Museum

The James Bond car collection steals the show, but there is plenty more film memorabilia (p102) to enjoy here.

London Transport Museum

The A to Zs and nuts and bolts of London transport (p417) told in fun fashion. The museum also stages Hidden London tours (from 14 years) taking you down into secret shelters and disused tunnels across London (book early).

HMS Belfast

This light cruiser (p164) served in WWII and the Korean War. Amazing displays bring those history lessons to life.

Changing the Guard

Soldiers in bearskin hats and red uniforms, military orders and all the pomp at

ALEXEY FEDORENKO/SHUTTERSTOCK ©

Hyde Park (p184)

the Changing the Guard (p104) – everyone will gape.

Best for Rainy Days

Plans rain-checked by London's famously unpredictable weather? In addition to myriad museums and galleries, here are some ideas to stay warm and dry.

BFI IMAX Cinema

Documentaries and blockbusters in 3D for a different cinema experience (p175).

Queens Ice & Bowl

Get your skates on and go spinning around the rink (p288), or have the kids aim for a strike in the bowling alley.

West End Matinee Show

The West End (p126) has plenty of plays and musicals children will love, from *Matilda* to *The Curious Incident of the Dog in the Night-Time*. Tickets are often available on the day.

Best for Outdoor Fun

Treetop Walkway

Go underground and then up 18m into the canopy for an unforgettable encounter with nature at Kew Gardens (p316).

Mayfield Lavender

Wander among the lavender flowers in a magically beautiful **landscape** (☎07503 877707; www.mayfieldlavender.com; 1 Carshalton Rd, Banstead, SM7; adult/child £4/free; ⏲9am-6pm Jun-Aug; 🚻; 🚌166) 🍃.

London's Parks

Let your young ones loose on one of London's myriad parks, sit back and watch them scamper about (p197).

Hampton Court Palace Maze

It takes the average visitor 20 minutes to find the centre of the maze (p313) – can your kids beat that? Look out for summer events such as jousting and falconry too.

NEED TO KNOW

Transport Under-16s travel free on buses, under-11s travel free on the Tube and under-5s go free on trains. Steps and escalators mean some stations are hard to access with buggies (strollers) – buses are a safer bet. Transport for London has accessible-transport details (www.tfl.gov.uk/transport-accessibility).

Walking The best way to see London is by walking – public transport can be crowded and hot in summer.

Like a Local

Local life envelops you in London, but you might only notice it in fleeting snatches. This big city's residents are pragmatic about crowds and elbows: Londoners will wait for late-opening nights before slipping into museums to avoid the masses, but swarm to parks as soon as the sun pops out.

ALENA VEASEY/SHUTTERSTOCK ©

Borough Market (p163)

Drinking Like a Local

Londoners, and the British in general, get bad press for binge drinking. But most drinking in London is actually warmly affable, gregarious and harmless fun. Londoners drink at the 'local' – shorthand for the 'pub around the corner'. Prices may be high but generosity is commonplace and drinkers always step up to buy a round. Despite the fickle weather, alfresco drinking is popular, be it in beer gardens, on patios or strewn out along pavements.

Dining Like a Local

As a rule of thumb, Londoners will dine at their local fish-and-chip shop or enjoy Sunday roast at their local gastropub rather than trek across town for dinner, but they'll readily go out for a meal further afield for special occasions. You'll also find them piling on the peri-peri sauce at Nando's, enjoying a fry-up (full English breakfast) at a 'greasy spoon' (a no-frills cafe), wolfing down sweat-inducing curries, heading to Chinatown for dim sum or queuing outside food trucks that dot the city for a hot takeaway lunch. Food markets are incredibly popular, be they the gourmet kind such as Borough Market (p163) or smaller farmers markets across town.

Idiosyncratic delicacies you'll find Londoners tucking into include chip butties (fries in a sandwich), Marmite (a love-it-or-loathe-it yeast extract spread) on toast or pie and mash with liquor (parsley sauce).

Taking to the Park

London has some of the world's most beautiful, and ample, urban green spaces, and locals swarm en masse to the park the minute the sun pops out, to read a book, play football, rule over a picnic or barbecue, or just chat with friends on the grass. Join them at lunchtime when office workers come out for their fix of sunlight or at weekends for fun and games.

Sightseeing Like a Local

Londoners habitually head off the beaten track, taking the back route into their local park, exploring London's wilder fringes or making shortcuts such as following Regent's Canal (p252) across North London. Go exploring in zones 2 and 3 and see what you find. Many Londoners bide their time till late-night openings for central London museums, when there are smaller crowds, and save 'regular hour' visits for special exhibitions.

Londoners are also well tuned to special events such as Open House London (p383) and candlelit evening openings of house museums, which shine a different and special light on historic interiors.

Local Obsessions

Property

Owning a property is a national obsession in the UK, but is made particularly difficult in London, where prices are stratospheric. Talks of unaffordable housing, renting versus buying, mortgage deals, putting in an offer, being gazumped, DIY, garden size and the Brexit effect are classic Sunday lunch fodder.

North vs South

The existential divide between 'Norff' and 'Saff' of the river remains as wide as ever. Each camp swears by its side. For Londoners, the main difference is that South London is less accessible by Tube (which means that house prices are generally lower, although this is about to change with the extension of the northern line). North of the river, East vs West is a further feud. But for visitors, the debate is moot: London is London, with the same amazing array of sights, restaurants, bars and markets.

The Weather (& Whether It'll Hold Out for Saturday's Barbecue)

More than wet, cold or grey, London's weather is fickle and unpredictable. This causes Londoners all sorts of angst about their barbecue/picnic/beer-garden plans from April to September, when it's supposed to be spring/summer but plans can be upended by unseasonal showers/cold snaps/high winds/sleet.

Public Transport

London has a world-class public transport network, but Londoners like nothing more than to moan about their commute to work. Grievances range from delays due to improbably long red lights/signal failure/leaves on track/the wrong kind of snow (all real-life examples) to the horribly high fares. Londoners can also argue endlessly about the definitive route from A to B.

Politics

Britain has a tradition of rabble-rousing – see the rather combative style of debate in the House of Commons. While Londoners may be reticent at first, once their teeth are stuck in they won't let a political debate go; so if you like politics, you'll find company.

Football

Passions run high when it comes to the beautiful game, and rivalries between London's three major teams (Arsenal, Chelsea and Tottenham Hotspur) are real. The capital has other clubs in the Premier League, including West Ham and Crystal Palace, each with equally devoted supporters.

NEED TO KNOW

Santander Cycles (p415) Bike-sharing is fun, cheap, practical and definitively local, and there are docking stations everywhere.

Oyster Cards Londoners who travel by public transport use this smart card as well as contactless credit and debit cards, which net excellent discounts and avoid queues for tickets.

Routemaster heritage bus 15 This bus line is excellent for sightseeing, so grab a seat upstairs.

For Free

London may be one of the world's most expensive cities, but it doesn't have to cost the earth. Many sights and experiences are free or cost next to nothing.

IACOMINO FRIMAGES/SHUTTERSTOCK ©

Changing of the Guard (p86)

Sights

Watching the Changing the Guard (p104) and visiting the Houses of Parliament (p87) to witness debates are both free. For one weekend in September, Open House London (p383) opens the doors to over 800 buildings for free.

Museums & Galleries

The permanent collections of state-funded museums and galleries are free. They include the Victoria & Albert Museum (p178), Tate Modern (p160), British Museum (p81) and National Gallery (p91). The supreme Horniman Museum (p302) is also free.

Views

Ascend to Level 10 of Switch House at Tate Modern, the Sky Garden (p146) atop the 'Walkie Talkie' or gaze out over London from One New Change (p157) or Garden at 120 (p146).

Concerts

Some churches offer free lunchtime classical-music concerts. Try St Martin-in-the-Fields (p102), St James's Piccadilly (p98), Temple Church (p105) and St Alfege Church (p294).

Walks

Roam Hampstead Heath (p255) in North London, follow the Thames along the South Bank or Richmond, or stroll around compact West End.

NEED TO KNOW

Websites For ideas, visit www.londonforfree.net or www.skintlondon.com.

Discount cards Buy the London Pass (www.londonpass.com) if you want to see a lot in a short time.

Wi-fi access Many cafes and bars offer customers free wi-fi.

Newspapers *Time Out*, the *Evening Standard* and *Metro* are free.

Children Under-11s travel free on buses and Underground, under-fives free on trains.

Under the Radar

The COVID-19 pandemic meant that resourceful and innovative London had to contend with an unpredictable downturn and cater to an entirely different breed of traveller: the domestic tourist. It stepped up to the challenge and learned a few things along the way.

ALEX SEGRE / SHUTTERSTOCK ©

Hampstead Heath (p255)

Lockdown London

Lockdown had a profound effect on travel psychology in the Big Smoke, as everywhere. Even if COVID-19 becomes manageably endemic or possibly even a thing of the past, the powerful impact of lockdown and social-distancing on the travel psyche may be long-lasting. There may also be an explosion of so-called 'revenge travel' – unleashing pent-up travel yearnings – which could see London deluged in visitors, making up for lost time.

The Staycationers

COVID-19 spawned a wave of London staycationers who took to exploring – and genuinely discovering – their home city. The trend may continue as international travel uncertainties remain.

Social-distancing has conditioned human behaviour. British home-buyers and renters sought out properties with gardens and travel behaviour has been similarly modified as people discover quieter and less crowded spaces, to celebrate nature and London's wilder expanses.

The long-term effects of all this are uncertain, but prepare for a transformation of the travel landscape, with more visitor congestion and potential overtourism at some sights, but less visitors elsewhere. An oversimplification perhaps, but expect to see a drift from window-shopping along Oxford Street and Regent Street to travellers decamping to **Kew Gardens** (Royal Botanic Gardens, Kew; www.kew.org; Kew Rd, TW9; adult/child £17.50/5.50; 10am-7pm Apr-Sep, to 6pm Mar & Oct, closes earlier rest of year; Kew Pier, Kew Bridge, Kew Gardens) or wild swimming in the ponds at **Hampstead Heath** (www.cityoflondon.gov.uk/things-to-do/green-spaces/hampstead-heath; Hampstead Heath or Gospel Oak), jogging along the Thames, counting cows in **Petersham Meadows** (Richmond, Richmond) or visiting London's best beer gardens.

Outside town, the intensifying lure of domestic beach side destinations such as Brighton has seen staycationers migrating *en masse* to the East Sussex town for rays, fish and chips and ice cream. Beyond Brighton, the south England coastline awaits splendid exploration.

Hiking London

Hikers are on a roll. The closure of gyms during lockdown prompted a nationwide rummage for cobwebby hiking boots. Reports point to an 8% jump in British people who identify as ramblers (up to 24% from 16% in 2018). Some hikers were also motivated by the disruption of their overseas holiday-making and an increasingly mainstream sustainable travel ethos. Being unscripted, rambling can make your journey more individual and rewarding.

Wilder London

Rambles through wilder areas such as **Wimbledon Common** (020-8788 7655; www.wpcc.org.uk; Wimbledon, Wimbledon, Wimbledon) and **Richmond Park** (0300 061 2200; www.royalparks.org.uk/parks/richmond-park; 7am-dusk; Richmond) are growing in popularity, as are night hikes or cycles across London, which let you encounter a city transformed by empty streets.

London's Waterways

Treks along London's waterways such as the **Regent's Canal** (https://canalrivertrust.org.uk/enjoy-the-waterways/canal-and-river-network/regents-canal) or the **Grand Union Canal** dramatically bring into focus different aspects of the city. The **Thames Path** is the queen of London waterside hikes. The entire trail from Woolwich to the river's source in the Cotswolds is 184 miles (294 Km) in length, but stick to the London trail and you will pass an eye-catching crop of London's sights in slow motion along the way, including the Thames Barrier, Greenwich and Canary Wharf, Tower Bridge and the Tower of London, the Tate Modern, South Bank, the London Eye, the Houses of Parliament, Battersea Park and beyond. A string of ancient riverside pubs provides liquid nourishment.

Cycling

The growing London boom in cycling is creating a new dynamic on the roads, too. In 2020, London's population of cyclists grew by a massive 120%, part of a pre-existing drift towards more sustainable forms of transport but largely motivated by the closing of gyms during lockdown. It is perhaps too early to say whether increased cycling will be a COVID-19 blip or a long-term behavioural change, though patterns suggest the bicycle is winning the nation's hearts. Join them by hopping on a **Santander Cycle** (0343 222 6666; www.tfl.gov.uk/modes/cycling/santander-cycles).

Green London

Already experiencing rapid growth pre-COVID-19, sustainable travel is expanding massively to meet the needs of more environmentally-conscious travellers.

Zero-Carbon London?

In 2018, the London Mayor Sadiq Khan revealed ambitious targets to create a zero-carbon city with at least 50 per cent green space by 2050. Tree-planting projects and greening measures will see the enhancement of London's urban woodland and parks, further encouraging the propagation of wildlife...

NEED TO KNOW

Kayaking London (www.kayakinglondon.com) For waterborne expeditions along the Thames and canals.

Wild Swimming Go for a dip in Hampstead Heath (p39) Ponds.

Climbing Clamber on to the huge roof of the **O2** (www.theo2.co.uk/upattheo2; O2 Arena, Greenwich Peninsula, SE10; from £30; North Greenwich) in the Greenwich Peninsula.

City Farms Head to **Mudchute** (020-7515 5901; www.mudchute.org; Pier St, E14; admission free; 9am-5pm; ; DLR Mudchute) FREE Come face to face with cows, sheep, pigs, llamas and alpacas on the Isle of Dogs.

Dark Sky London Fans of planetary observation can check out updates on stargazing in and around London on https://darksky.london/.

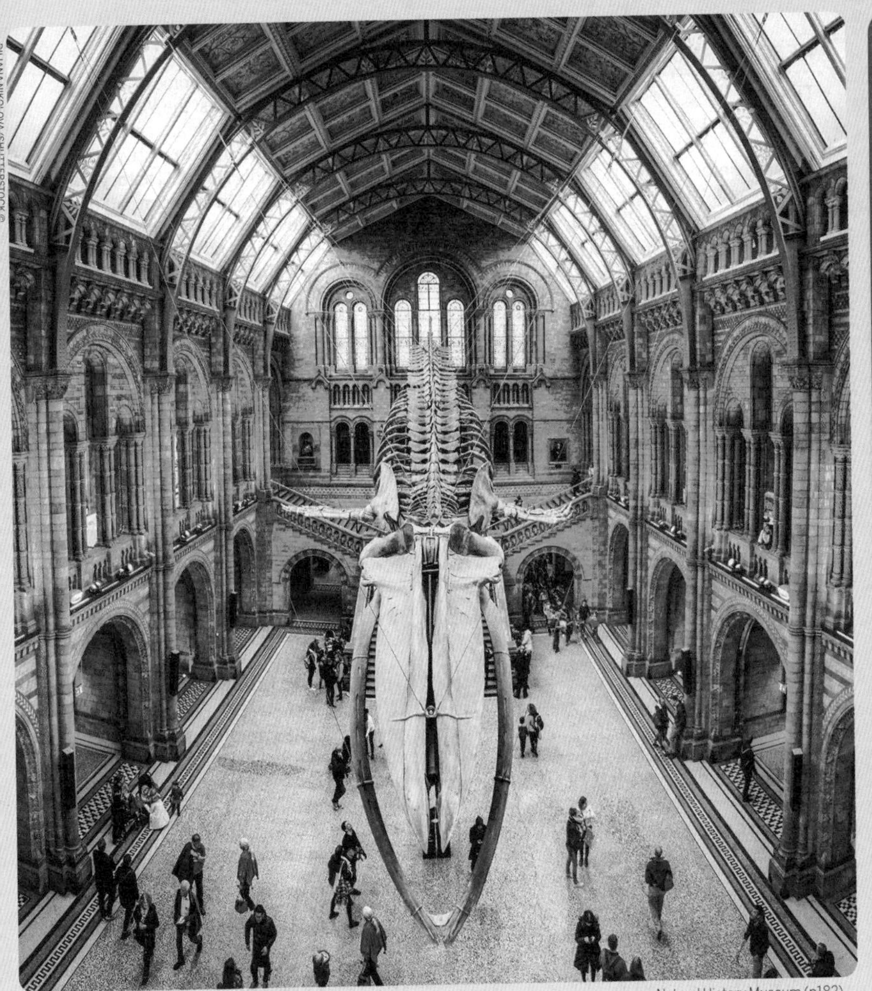

Natural History Museum (p182)

Museums & Galleries

London's reputation for world-class museums and galleries definitely precedes it. Housed in historically – and architecturally – fascinating buildings, many have collections of the world's treasures (yes, it's controversial) on display. There is a trinity of top-name museums awaiting you in South Kensington, plus a good concentration in the West End, with others scattered across London.

NEED TO KNOW

Tickets

➡ Permanent collections at national museums (eg British Museum, National Gallery, Victoria & Albert Museum) are free; temporary exhibitions cost extra and should be booked ahead.

➡ Smaller private museums charge entrance fees, typically £5 to £10.

➡ Art galleries are usually free or have a small admission fee.

Opening Hours

National collections are generally open 10am to about 6pm, with one or two late nights a week; evenings are an excellent time to visit museums as there are far fewer visitors.

Dining

Many of the top galleries also have fantastic restaurants (eg Wallace Collection, Somerset House), worthy of a visit in their own right.

Useful Websites

Most London museums – especially the most visited ones such as the British Museum, National Gallery and Victoria & Albert Museum – have sophisticated and comprehensive websites.

Museum Crush (www.museumcrush.org) Reams of museum and gallery information.

Visit London (www.visitlondon.com) Check 'what's on this weekend' for up-to-date exhibition openings and pop-up museum or gallery experiences

The Heavy Hitters

London's most famous museums are all central, easy to get to and – best of all – free (donations gratefully received of course)!

The **National Gallery** (p88) on Trafalgar Sq displays masterpieces of Western European art from the 13th to the early 20th centuries, with everyone represented from Leonardo da Vinci and Rembrandt to Turner and Van Gogh. Just behind the gallery, the **National Portrait Gallery** has closed for refurbishment and isn't scheduled to reopen until late 2023. A 15-minute (1.2km) walk north leads to the **British Museum** (p81) in Bloomsbury, housing an astonishing assembly of antiquities representing 7000 years of human civilisation.

South Kensington is the home of three of London's leading museums: the **Victoria & Albert Museum** (p178), with its vast range of historical exhibits from the decorative arts, and the family-friendly **Natural History Museum** (p181) and **Science Museum** (p186).

Modern-art lovers will enjoy **Tate Modern** (p160) on South Bank. And a short river cruise away, **Tate Britain** (p92) is home to British artworks across the centuries.

Private Galleries

London's vibrant artistic scene is on display at the 1500 private galleries across the city. Mayfair has long been strong in the more traditional schools of art, while more intellectually and creatively adventurous finds are exhibited in gallery spaces in Spitalfields, Hoxton and Hackney Wick. Time your visit for one of the major up-and-coming art fairs like **Moniker International Art** (www.monikerartfair.com) and **The Other Art Fair** (www.theotherartfair.com) to have the pick of the new artists to buy from.

A Night at the Museum

Many museums open late once or even twice a week, but several museums organise special nocturnal events to extend their range of activities and to present the collection in a different light.

Museums with special nocturnal events or late-night opening hours:

British Museum (p81) Open to 8.30pm on Friday.

British Library (p246) Galleries open to 8pm on Tuesday.

Sir John Soane's Museum (p95) Book an evening tour illuminated by candlelight.

Tate Britain – Open to 10pm on select Fridays.

Tate Modern – Open to 10pm Friday and Saturday.

Courses, Talks & Lectures

Museums and galleries are excellent places to pick up specialist skills from qualified experts in their field. If you'd like to learn a new skill, brush up on an old one, or attend a fascinating lecture – there are many to choose from. Venues include the British Library (p246), British Museum (p81), **Dulwich Picture Gallery** (p302), National Gallery (p91), Tate Britain (p92), Tate Modern (p160) and Victoria & Albert Museum .

Museums & Galleries by Neighbourhood

West End (p81) British Museum, National Gallery, Tate Britain, Churchill War Rooms and many others.

City of London (p147) Museum of London, Guildhall Art Gallery, Barbican Arts Centre, Bank of England Museum and Dr Johnson's House.

South Bank (p160) Tate Modern, Hayward Gallery and other smaller museums and galleries.

Kensington & Hyde Park (p176) Victoria & Albert Museum, Natural History Museum, Science Museum, Saatchi Gallery, Serpentine Gallery and others.

Clerkenwell, Shoreditch & Spitalfields (p204) Museum of the Home, Dennis Severs' House and St John's Gate.

East London & Docklands (p224) Museum of London Docklands, Ragged School Museum, Whitechapel Gallery and others.

Hampstead & North London (p250) Wellcome Collection, London Canal Museum, Kenwood House, British Library, Vagina Museum, Freud Museum, Jewish Museum and others.

AVOIDING THE CROWDS

Unfortunately, queues, crowds and bag searches are all part of the London experience. The busiest times tend to be on weekend afternoons and during school holidays. Even during these times, though, you can duck the worst of the crowds by arriving right on opening time or during the late evening sessions. Weekday afternoons are best at the Natural History Museum, as school groups tend to visit in the mornings.

Notting Hill & West London (p274) Design Museum, Museum of Brands, Leighton House and William Morris Society.

Greenwich (p294) National Maritime Museum, Royal Observatory, Ranger's House.

Brixton, Peckham & South London (p301) Imperial War Museum, Horniman Museum, Florence Nightingale Museum.

Richmond, Kew & Hampton Court (p312) Cumberland Art Gallery at Hampton Court Palace and Wimbledon Lawn Tennis Museum.

Victoria & Albert Museum (p178)

Best Museums

British Museum (p81) Supreme collection of international artefacts and an inspiring testament to human creativity over seven millennia.

Tate Modern (p160) A feast of modern and contemporary art, housed within a transformed riverside power station.

National Gallery (p88) One of the world's great art collections.

Science Museum (p186) Popular with kids, both small and big.

Natural History Museum (p182) A cathedral to the natural world.

Victoria & Albert Museum (p178) Eclectic collection of decorative arts in what is affectionately known as 'the nation's attic'.

Best Small Museums

Museum of the Home (p204) A fascinating journey through British living rooms from the 17th century onwards.

Sir John Soane's Museum (p95) The atmospheric home of the 19th-century architect showcasing his collection of art and antiquities.

Shakespeare's Globe (p162) As much as you'll ever need to know about the Bard and his work.

London Transport Museum (p417) Everything from horse-drawn omnibuses to the still-under-construction Crossrail project.

Viktor Wynd Museum of Curiosities, Fine Art & Natural History (p226) Highly eclectic collection of strange and disturbing ephemera.

Old Operating Theatre Museum & Herb Garret (p164) Delve into the pre-anaesthetic, pre-antiseptic days of medicine.

Dulwich Picture Gallery (p302) Lots of classic paintings from the Old Masters.

Best Small Galleries

Kenwood House (p249) Spectacular collection of art from the 17th to 19th century in an equally wonderful setting.

Guildhall Art Gallery (p147) Eclectic City of London collection above a Roman amphitheatre.

Whitechapel Gallery (p226) A groundbreaking gallery that continues to challenge with excellent exhibitions.

Saatchi Gallery (p191) Cutting-edge, ultra-cool shrine to contemporary art.

Photographers' Gallery (p101) Photography as an art form in a splendid building.

House of Illustration (p251) Charity-run gallery started by Quentin Blake.

Newport Street Gallery (p302) Damien Hirst's personal art collection.

Best House Museums

Dennis Severs' House (p206) A quirky time capsule that sends you back to an 18th-century Huguenot house.

Charles Dickens Museum (p97) The Victorian novelist's only London house.

18 Stafford Terrace (p274) A comfortable middle-class Victorian family brought back to life.

Apsley House (p189) No 1 London: home to the Duke of Wellington for 35 years.

Leighton House (p274) Byzantine gem on the cusp of Holland Park.

Keats House (p255) The setting that inspired some of Keats's most memorable poetry.

Best Specialist Museums

Imperial War Museum (p301) Devoted to Britain's military history, with a must-see WWI section.

Churchill War Rooms (p94) The nerve centre of Britain's war effort during WWII.

Science Museum (p186) Spellbinding A to Z of gizmos, devices, contraptions and thingamabobs.

Design Museum (p275) Devoted to the role of design in everyday life.

Museum of London Docklands (p230) The story of the river and the trade that made London prosper.

Horniman Museum (p302) Natural history on display in this small but family-friendly South London musuem.

Curries on display at Camden Market (p254)

Dining Out

London's hospitality scene is now up there with the best dining destinations, but it pays to do your research; there is a lot of mediocre eating here too. London's strongest asset is its incredible diversity: from street-food markets to high-end dining with epic views – and global cuisines from Afghan to Zambian – it's an A to Z of foodie experiences.

NEED TO KNOW

Opening Hours

Most restaurants serve lunch between noon and 2.30pm and dinner between 6pm and 11pm. Brasserie-type establishments and chains tend to have continuous service from noon to 11pm.

Price Ranges

The following price ranges refer to a main course.

£	less than £15
££	£15–25
£££	more than £25

Reservations

It always pays to make a reservation, especially on weekends or if you're in a group (but note the new 'credit card required to book' policy many popular places have adopted). Some restaurants run multiple sittings, with allocated time slots (generally two hours).

Tipping

Most restaurants automatically add a 'discretionary' service charge (usually 12.5%) onto the bill. If you feel the service wasn't adequate, you can ask for it to be removed, but you won't find many Londoners prepared to make a fuss. If there's no service charge on your bill, it's best to add at least 10% (ideally in cash to your server).

Haute Cuisine, Low Prices

➡ Many high-end restaurants offer good-value set-lunch menus.

➡ À la carte lunches are usually less expensive than dinners.

➡ Some West End and South Bank restaurants offer pre- or post-theatre menus.

BYO

BYO (bring your own) is common among budget establishments; some charge corkage (£1 to £5 per bottle of wine).

Specialities

ENGLISH FOOD

England might have given the world baked beans on toast, mushy peas and chip butties (fried potatoes between slices of buttered white bread), but that's not the whole story. When well prepared – be it a Sunday lunch of roast beef and Yorkshire pudding (batter baked until fluffy, eaten with gravy) or a cornet of fish and chips sprinkled with salt and malt vinegar – English food has its charms. And the hungover masses will attest to the restorative powers of a full English breakfast after a big night out.

Modern British food has come of age, propelled into the spotlight by writer chefs like Fergus Henderson and Jamie Oliver championing traditional (and sometimes underrated) ingredients such as root vegetables, smoked fish, shellfish, game, salt-marsh lamb, sausages, black pudding, offal, less common cuts of meat and bone marrow.

WINE & CHEESE

If English cuisine was once the butt of jokes, English wine raised a comical eyebrow. This is changing: locally produced sparkling wine has garnered international attention, and is now served at state banquets in Buckingham Palace and in first class on British Airways. Even the Champagne house Taittinger is on board having acquired a vineyard in the chalky seaside region of Kent with plans to produce its first release here in 2023. Local producers to look out for include Wiston Estate, Furleigh Estate, Theale Vineyard, Ridgeview, Bolney Estate and Hambledon.

The cold and wet climate lends itself to particular hardy white-grape varieties, many of which are quite obscure. Alongside Chardonnay you'll see the likes of Bacchus, Madeleine Angevine, Seyval Blanc, Pinot Blanc, Reichensteiner and Müller-Thurgau. Some good Pinot Noir is also being produced.

British cheese has never had an image problem. Stilton is the most famous, but look out for Stinking Bishop and the blues from Wensleydale, Derby, Dorset and Shropshire. The king of the crumbly hard cheeses is aged cheddar, but Cheshire, Lancashire and Caerphilly all have their own distinctive varieties.

Eating by Neighbourhood

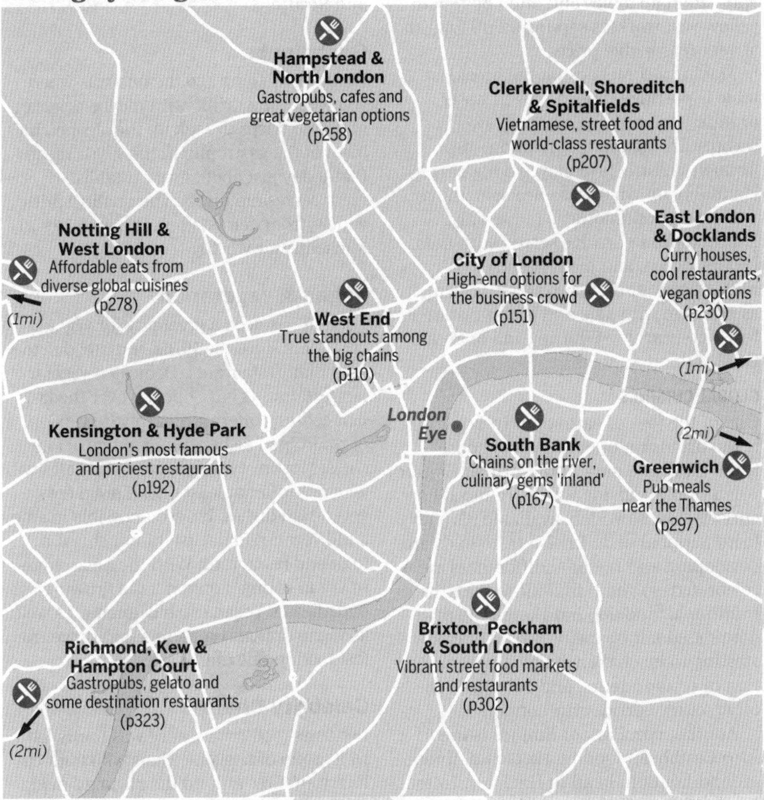

Hampstead & North London
Gastropubs, cafes and great vegetarian options (p258)

Clerkenwell, Shoreditch & Spitalfields
Vietnamese, street food and world-class restaurants (p207)

Notting Hill & West London
Affordable eats from diverse global cuisines (p278)
(1mi)

East London & Docklands
Curry houses, cool restaurants, vegan options (p230)
(1mi)

City of London
High-end options for the business crowd (p151)

West End
True standouts among the big chains (p110)

London Eye

Kensington & Hyde Park
London's most famous and priciest restaurants (p192)

South Bank
Chains on the river, culinary gems 'inland' (p167)

Greenwich
Pub meals near the Thames (p297)
(2mi)

Brixton, Peckham & South London
Vibrant street food markets and restaurants (p302)

Richmond, Kew & Hampton Court
Gastropubs, gelato and some destination restaurants (p323)
(2mi)

Great places to sample British wine and cheese in London include Neal's Yard Dairy (p132), Borough Market (p163) and Paxton & Whitfield (p129).

SEAFOOD

Many visitors to England comment that for islanders, Brits seem to make surprisingly little of their seafood, with the exception of the ubiquitous – and institutionalised – fish and chips. But modern British restaurants have started to cast their nets wider, and many offer local specialities such as Dover sole, Cornish oysters, Scottish scallops, smoked Norfolk eel, Atlantic herring and mackerel. Top-of-the-line restaurants specialising in seafood abound, and fish-and-chips counters trading in battered cod, haddock and plaice are everywhere.

DESSERTS

Leave room for the sweet course! England does a tasty dessert, and establishments serving British cuisine revel in these indulgent treats. Favourites include bread-and-butter pudding, sticky toffee pudding, the alarmingly named spotted dick (steamed suet pudding with currants and raisins), Eton mess (a very photogenic concoction of meringue, cream and strawberries), and seasonal musts such as Christmas pudding (a steamed pudding with candied fruit and brandy) and fruity crumbles (rhubarb, apple, or berries...).

BREAKFAST OR BRUNCH

Brits have always been big on breakfast – and proudly invented one, the Full English. It's something of a protein overload, but it's so simple you cannot really get it wrong. A typical plate will include bacon, sausages, baked beans in tomato sauce, eggs (fried or scrambled), mushrooms, tomatoes and toast (maybe with Marmite). You'll find countless brightly lit 'caffs' (cafes; also nicknamed 'greasy spoons') tightly packed with laminate tables and often busy with yellow-vest workers serving a Full English at very reasonable prices.

Making a comeback on the breakfast table is porridge (boiled oats in water or milk, served hot), dished up sweet or savoury. Instagram and London's new 'brunch' culture have played a big part in glamming up what was once something you ate at grandmother's house only. Expect to find porridge served with nuts, berries, cocoa, and plant-based or dairy milk, or something more savoury such as porridge with kale and bacon inspired by Hugh Fearnley-Whittingstall or Yotam Ottolenghi.

GLOBAL CUISINES

One of the joys of eating out in London is the profusion of cuisines to choose from. Since the days of the British Empire when Indian cuisine was introduced here, curry is now so widely available it's a de facto national dish. British taste buds are developing and regional differences are celebrated, so you'll find more than the traditional vindaloo out there. The male-dominated landscape of Brick Lane is starting to be challenged by a new generation of restaurateurs, and Tooting is the other 'curry corridor' in London.

Another corollary of Empire is the Afro-Caribbean food markets and diners around London: head to Hackney, Tottenham and Brixton for tangy jerk chicken or jollof rice.

Asian cuisine is everywhere, though you'll more readily find Chinese and Japanese (including ready-made sushi chains), with really good Thai, Vietnamese and Korean requiring a little more research.

Food from the Mediterranean and the Middle East has made a huge impact on London's dining culture, with a stronger focus on fresh seasonal ingredients, simple dishes, robust flavours and sharing plates.

Baltic, Nordic and continental European restaurants – Lithuanian, Scandinavian, French, Italian, German – are all represented both at the budget and higher end of the market. And in the last decade Eastern European dining has made its mark with pirogi, pelmeni or a hearty borscht: mainly in neighbourhoods where Polish, Bulgarian and Russian communities are found (check out Shepherd's Bush and Stratford).

Gastropubs

While not so long ago the pub was where you went for a drink, with maybe a packet of potato crisps to soak up the alcohol, the birth of the gastropub in the 1990s means that today just about every establishment serves full meals. The quality varies widely, from defrosted-on-the-premises to Michelin-star-worthy.

Vegan & Vegetarian

London has been a great city for vegetarian diners since the 1970s, initially due to its Indian restaurants. Dedicated vegetarian restaurants have opened over the last half century, offering a herbivore version of traditional dishes from a range of cuisines. Most restaurants, pubs and cafes will generally offer at least one, if not a few, vegetarian dishes. It's even possible to enjoy a full vegetarian degustation menu at a high-end restaurant. With the huge surge in vegan eating, London has a growing list of dedicated vegan establishments, as well as vegan options on menus that range from fast food to fine dining.

Celebrity Chefs

London's food renaissance was partly led by a group of telegenic chefs who built culinary empires around their names, made famous by their TV shows. Gordon Ramsay is the most (in)famous of the lot, and his London venues are still standard-bearers for top-quality cuisine. Other big names include Jamie Oliver, Nigella Lawson and Heston Blumenthal – whose mad-professor-like experiments with food have earned him an international reputation.

Coffee

The quality of coffee and cafes in the capital is still pretty erratic. What was a nonexistent coffee scene a decade ago has been replaced with a steady rise in postage stamp-sized cafes doing excellent coffee and pastries. These are often run by Australians and New Zealanders bringing their third-wave coffee culture and smashed avocado on sourdough with them. Large coffee chains are ubiquitous but typically mediocre, with a sometimes nonchalant approach to cleaning table areas.

Above: Traditional British roast dinner (p52)

Right: English Shropshire blue cheese

BARMALINI/SHUTTERSTOCK ©

Food Markets

London's food markets come in three broad categories: food stalls that are part of a broader mixed market and appeal to visitors keen to soak up the atmosphere – Old Spitalfields (p219) and Camden (p254); specialist food and farmers markets, which sell local and/or organic produce and artisanal products – Borough (p163) and Broadway (p242) are prime examples; and then there are the many colourful general street markets where the barrow boys will upsell that bowl of juicy fresh mangoes in a perfect Cockney accents or Jamaican patois – head to Brixton (p309), Ridley Road (p225), Portobello Road (p276), especially if you're self-catering.

Trends

Street-food markets Open air, shipping container or inside a larger complex, hawker-style street food markets are everywhere including the West End (p116). Some also sell booze and turn into a de facto party in the evening.

Credit card required when booking One has to assume a punishing number of no-shows is behind the move to taking a credit card at booking and threatening a charge if the correct number of diners does not appear at the allotted time. Stressful for whoever is making the booking.

No reservations Some smaller high-turnover restaurants favour walk-ins over bookings. If you're not there early, you're asked to form an orderly queue. Some places will run a telephone wait list so hungry diners can hole up at a nearby pub or bar until a table is available.

Know your region It's no longer 'Chinese food' you're craving, but Dongbei or Xinjiang; and forget 'Indian' and choose a Gujarati, Goan or Punjabi menu.

Allergies and food intolerances Most (but not all) London restaurants are on board with menu substitutions and special dietary requests. Food labelling has improved too.

Healthy buffets A new breed of buffet-style restaurant has popped up in London, where you can eat a feast of vegetarian (and vegan) dishes at a reasonable price. Look out for the Tibits (www.tibits.co.uk) and Natural Kitchen (www.naturalkitchen.co.uk) franchises.

Family-Friendly Chains

While the usual comfort-eating fast-food chains can be found all over the capital, London also boasts some excellent home-grown franchises. They're usually pretty good value, especially if a meal deal or set-price (or kids' menu) is on offer. You'll find these chains in pretty much every central London neighbourhood. Table manners are still required from the little ones!

Busaba Eathai (www.busaba.com) Thai food served without fuss among beautiful, modern Asian decor.

Carluccio's (www.carluccios.com) Upmarket but ubiquitous Italian with excellent service.

Franco Manca (www.francomanca.co.uk) Wood-fired sourdough pizza.

Giraffe (www.giraffe.net) Global cuisine and all-day brunch.

Honest Burgers (www.honestburgers.co.uk) Hamburgers made with quality British produce.

Masala Zone (www.masalazone.com) Indian chain that specialises in *thalis* (a meal made up of several small dishes).

Nando's (www.nandos.co.uk) Ever-popular for its peri-peri chicken and off-the-scale trademark spicy sauces; order at the till.

Pret a Manger (www.pret.co.uk) Affordable sandwich chain with a good selection of fillings; it has recently launched dedicated Veggie Pret shops.

Real Greek (www.therealgreek.com) Beautifully presented mezze and souvlaki, perfect for sharing between friends.

Tas (www.tasrestaurants.co.uk) Established chain of Turkish restaurants with a roll call of stews, grills and meze.

Wagamama (www.wagamama.com) Japanese noodle place with rapid turnover; ideal for a quick meal.

Wahaca (www.wahaca.com) Working the Mexican street-food angle in fresh, colourful settings.

Lonely Planet's Top Choices

St John (p208) The original nose-to-tail British restaurant.

Palomar (p113) Stunning Israeli/Levantine food in an atmosphere of culinary theatre.

Clove Club (p210) From Dalston supper club to stupendous Michelin-starred restaurant.

Kiln (p113) Exceptional Thai in the West End, served tapas-style.

Best by Budget

£

Padella (p167) Handmade-pasta specialists in Borough Market.

Hook Camden Town (p261) Sustainable fish and chips with homemade sauces.

Beijing Dumpling (p112) West End specialist in soup dumplings.

Breddos Tacos (p208) A former food van doing perhaps London's best tacos.

Seven Dials Market (p116) Street food, drinks and music in the West End.

££

Glasshouse (p324) Michelin-starred Modern European restaurant in Kew.

Duck & Waffle (p151) Stunning views and playful fusion cuisine.

Palomar (p113) Excellent Jerusalem-style dishes for sharing in Soho.

Ottolenghi (p264) Islington's legendary Mediterranean cafe and bakery.

£££

Clove Club (p210) Adventurous Shoreditch restaurant rated among the very best in the world.

City Social (p152) Jason Atherton's contemporary dishes do well to compete with the extraordinary views.

Five Fields (p196) Chelsea restaurant serving inventive British fare.

Gymkhana p120) Plaudit-winning British Raj–style Indian restaurant in the West End.

Dinner by Heston Blumenthal (p193) A supreme fusion of perfect British food, eye-catching design and celeb stature.

Best by Cuisine

British

Spring (p117) Skye Gyngel's delightful dishes in the gorgeous Somerset House.

Launceston Place (p193) Magnificent food, presentation and service.

Rabbit (p196) Hop to King's Rd for seasonal British cuisine.

Andrew Edmunds (p114) Soho classic that still delivers great Modern British.

Battersea Pie Station (p116) Cold pork pies in the heart of Covent Garden.

Simpsons Tavern (p151) As old-school as they come with traditional pub grub.

Chinese

Hakkasan Hanway Place (p111) Superlative subterranean Cantonese den in the West End.

Yauatcha (p115) Glamorous dim sum and great for people-watching.

Mamalan (p303) Beijing street food in Brixton.

Bar Shu (p113) Authentic Sichuan that will sear your taste buds.

Beijing Dumpling (p112) Cheap and not always cheerful but great for dumplings.

French

Gordon Ramsay (p196) The TV chef's signature restaurant; one of only two in London with three Michelin stars.

Chez Bruce (p305) Timeless elegance on the edge of Wandsworth Common.

Pied à Terre (p111) London Francophile classic with an updated vegan menu.

Chez Lindsay (p323) A bit of Brittany in Richmond.

Indian

Quilon (p110) London's most inventive Indian cuisine.

Dishoom (p280) With multiple outlets, consistently good dishes and service.

Café Spice Namasté (p231) The best of the East End's celebrated subcontinental restaurants.

Gymkhana (p120) Splendid club-style Raj environment and top cuisine.

Tamarind (p119) High-end contemporary Indian with tandoor at its heart.

Italian

Padella (p167) Cheap and flavourful home-made pasta in Borough Market.

Locanda Locatelli (p119) London's most renowned Italian restaurant.

Polpo (p208) Serves *cicchetti* – 'tapas' like the Venetians make it.

Trullo (p264) Italian-style charcoal grills in Islington.

River Cafe (p282) Another famous name, drawing legions of loyal fans to Fulham.

Vegan

Temple of Seitan (p233) Expect weekend queues for these seitanic burgers and 'chicken'.

Wulf & Lamb (p196) Elegant, delicious, and entirely plant-based.

Tibits (p170) You pay by the grams at this fresh vegetarian and vegan franchise.

Vegetarian

Gate (Hammersmith) (p281) Offers an inventive meat-free, flavour-filled menu.

Gate (Clerkenwell) (p208) Another branch, with plenty of Indian and Middle Eastern influences.

Mildreds (p112) Soho stalwart with vegan dishes too.

Sagar (p111) South Indian vegetarian food as light as it is tasty.

Best Sunday Roast

Anchor & Hope (p169) Flying the gastropub flag on South Bank for over a decade.

Empress (p235) Choice East End spot with an excellent modern British menu.

Hawksmoor Spitalfields (p213) There's nowhere better to loosen a belt-notch on Sunday.

Swan at the Globe (p169) Lively Thames-side pub with an excellent kitchen.

Smokehouse (p264) A light-filled back-street pub serving gourmet roasts.

Best for Views

City Social (p152) Wow-factor views from the City to the Shard and beyond.

Skylon (p170) The same views in reverse, from South Bank to the City skyline.

Coq d'Argent (p153) Rooftop French restaurant in the financial district.

Duck & Waffle (p151) Hearty British dishes round the clock at the top of Heron Tower.

Ivy Asia (p152) Views of St Paul's at this late-night Asian restaurant bar.

Peckham Levels (p304) Street food and sunset views over South London.

Best Afternoon Tea

Foyer & Reading Room at Claridge's (p120) The last word in classic art-deco elegance.

Delaunay (p116) Viennese-style afternoon teas complete with *gugelhupfs* (fruit scones) and Sachertorte.

Oscar Wilde Lounge (p115) Take tea in one of London's most over-the-top rooms.

Orange Pekoe (p323) Specialises in teas and does all-day cream tea.

Tea & Tattle (p111) In a bookshop near the British Museum.

Sketch (p121) Sink into the plush pink banquettes and get your camera out.

Best Food Markets

Borough Market (p163) Foodscapes, free tastings and glorious takeaways.

Broadway Market (p242) The East End foodies' weekly event.

Portobello Road Market (p276) A global atlas of street food.

Maltby Street Market (p303) Perfect for lazing an afternoon away at quirky food stalls.

Market Hall Victoria (p196) Something for everyone, including vegans.

Best Destination Restaurants

Dinner by Heston Blumenthal (p193) Molecular gastronomy at its very best.

Gordon Ramsay (p196) Where Ramsay's culinary credentials reside.

Glasshouse (p324) Kew Gardens does Modern European.

Petersham Nurseries Cafe (p324) A bucolic day out in Richmond.

Chiltern Firehouse (p119) Michelin-starred chef Nuno Mendes in Marylebone.

Best Gelato

Gelateria Danieli (p323) Handmade ice cream with seasonal flavours, such as Christmas pudding.

Ruby Violet (p261) Next-level flavours.

Chin Chin Labs (p261) Liquid-nitrogen ice cream: weird and utterly wonderful.

Gelupo (p112) All natural ingredients, right in central London.

Bar Open

You need only glance at William Hogarth's pictures Gin Lane *or the happier* Beer Street *from 1751 to realise that Londoners have always had a special relationship with alcohol. Today there is still no shortage of places to enjoy a drink, from speakeasy-style cocktail bars to all-night clubs, with a growing number of alcohol-free options for those who like their nightlife sober.*

NEED TO KNOW

Opening Hours

Pubs traditionally open at 11am or noon and close at 11pm, with an earlier closing on Sunday. Some bars and pubs open later and remain open until around 2am or 3am on weekends. Clubs generally open at 10pm on the weekend and close between 3am and 7am.

Costs

Many clubs are free or cheaper during the week. If you want to go to a famous club on a Saturday night, expect to pay up to £25 for entry (cover charge). Some are cheaper if you arrive earlier in the evening.

Tickets & Guest Lists

Queuing in the cold at 11pm can be frustrating; arrive early and/or book tickets for bigger events if you can't bear being left in limbo. Some clubs allow you to sign up on their guest list beforehand; check ahead on their websites.

Dress Code

London's clubs are generally relaxed. Upmarket clubs in areas such as Kensington will have a stronger dress code: so dress to impress (no denim or trainers). The further east you go, the more creative the outfits, but door policies are less unforgiving.

What's On

Check listings in *Time Out* (www.timeout.com/london) but word of mouth (or the modern equivalent, social media) is often your best source of intel on what's happening this week in London's nightlife.

Fabric nightclub (p214)

The Pub

The pub (public house) is at the heart of British life and is one of the capital's great social levellers. Virtually every Londoner has a 'local' and finding one to call your own will make your visit to the UK all the more special.

Pubs in central London often turn into after-work drinking dens, busy from 5pm onwards with the post-work crowd during the week. In residential areas, pubs come into their own at weekends, when long lunches turn into sloshy afternoons and groups of friends settle in for the night. Many also run popular quizzes on week nights. Others entice punters through the doors with music, comedy and even spoken-word events. Some have a reputation for the quality of their food; you'll need to book at the best.

You can order almost any beverage you like in a pub: beer, wine, soft drinks, spirits and sometimes hot drinks too. Some specialise in craft beer from local microbreweries, including real ale, fruit beers, organic ciders and other rarer beverages. Modernised 'gastropubs' (food-focused pubs) will often have a strong wine list too.

In winter, pubs get cosy with mulled wine or cider; in summer, beer gardens are popular, and the must-have drink of Pimm's and lemonade can be bought by the jug.

WEATHERSPOONS

Due in no small part to its cut-price beers, the JD Weatherspoons pub franchise has become a hit among austerity drinkers in London. Many of its pubs are in interesting historic buildings, the latest to join the fold is a Grade II–listed building on the Strand, a former Lloyds bank. Each 'Spoons' also has a unique carpet celebrating its location, a fact detailed in a Tumblr blog that then became a book published by Penguin, *Spoon's Carpets: An Appreciation*.

CRAFT BEER & BIG BREWERIES

Pubs generally serve a good selection of lager (highly carbonated and drunk cool or cold) and a smaller selection of real ales or 'bitter' (still or only slightly gassy, drunk at room temperature, with strong flavours).

The best-known British lager brand is the forgettable Carling, though you'll find everything from the mainstream Fosters and Stella Artois to Czech lagers like Budvar and Pilsner Urquell.

Fuller's is the last big-brand brewery left in London, so its London Pride is understandably popular. Greenwich-based Meantime was sold to international Asahi. Other major labels on offer in London pubs include Truman's Runner, Landlord from Timothy Taylor, Samuel Smith's ales, Spitfire from Shepherd Neame, Directors from Courage, Adnams' Ghost Ship and Old Peculiar from Theakston.

Once considered something of an old man's drink, real ale has enjoyed a renaissance among young Londoners, riding tandem with their love of craft beers. Staff at bars that serve a good selection of real ales and craft beers are often hugely knowledgeable, just like a sommelier in a restaurant, so ask them for recommendations if you're not sure what to order.

Stout, the best known of which is Irish Guinness, is a slightly sweet, dark beer with a distinct flavour that comes from malt that is roasted before fermentation.

Like everywhere else in the known world microbreweries have increased exponentially in the past decade or so – from nine here in 2006 to 130 today. Craft beers/breweries to look out for include Beavertown, Brixton Brewery, Fourpure, London Fields Brewery, the Five Points Brewing Company, Redchurch, Crate Brewery, Hackney Brewery, the Kernel and East London Brewing Company.

For an afternoon tasting new brews, head out on a self-guided tour of Bermondsey Beer Mile (p306).

London's Bar Scene

In the space left between pubs and clubs, bars are a popular alternative for a London night out. Generally staying open later than pubs but closing earlier than clubs, they tempt those who are keen to kick on past 11pm but don't want to pay a cover charge or stay out until dawn. Many bars will have a DJ on weekends and sometimes a small dance floor too. Drinks tend to be more expensive than typical pub prices, but table service is sometimes part of the deal.

Cocktail bars have undergone a renaissance in pub-focused London. With clever and amusing cocktail names and often a dimly lit speakeasy vibe, some also mix up an excellent mocktail too. Specialist wine, whisky, gin, craft beer, cider and no-alcohol bars have also been sprouting up around the city. Do your research if you want to indulge a niche drinking interest, and you'll no doubt find it here.

Clubbing

When it comes to clubbing, London is up there with the best of them. You'll probably know what kind of night you're after: famous superclubs such as Fabric (p214) or Ministry of Sound (p308), or something smaller and sweatier like XOYO (p216), with the hottest new DJ talent. You're going to find everything from thumping techno, indie rock, Latin, ska, pop, dubstep, grime, minimal electro, R&B or hip hop, pretty much any night of the week in London.

Thursdays are a big night, with some Londoners willing to work through a hangover, but serious office workers will mob the clubs on Fridays to blow off their stresses. Saturdays are the busiest for serious all-night-and-day clubbing. Sundays often see surprisingly good events throughout London, popular with hospitality workers who traditionally have Mondays off.

There are clubs in central London still, but many are moving further out; revellers make the most of the Night Tube on weekends as well as night buses. The East End, especially Shoreditch, Dalston and Hackney, is defined by makeshift clubs in bar basements and former shops. Camden Town still favours the indie and rock crowd, while King's Cross has a bit of both. The gay party crowd mainly gravitates south of the river, especially Vauxhall, although it retains a toehold in the West and East Ends.

Cabaret

After years of low-profile parties with high-glitter gowns, the cabaret scene has burst into the mainstream over the last couple of decades, showering London with nipple tassels, top hats, corsets and some of the best parties in town. Subsequently, the alternative cabaret scene has become overwhelmingly mainstream, and some club-night organisers raised prices to ward off the voyeurs. Prepare to pay up to £25 for some (but not all) of the city's best cabaret nights – and make sure you look like a million dollars.

Expect anything from male burlesque contests to girls on roller skates hosting tea

Drinking by Neighbourhood

parties. Bethnal Green Working Men's Club (p237) is a true working men's club that nonetheless hosts quirky cabaret nights. RVT (p308) is the kooky kingpin of London's queer cabaret scene and home to the legendary Duckie, the flagship rock 'n' roll night every Saturday.

Sober Nightlife

Londoners have been embracing the sobriety movement with glee, which means there's plenty to do after dark without boozing. From escape rooms to spoken-word performances, pay-as-you-please stand-up comedy nights, night kayaking, and the occasional sober rave (www.morninggloryville.com), there's no need to stay in just because you don't want a hangover when you're travelling.

Art aficionados will love the late hours at the art galleries and museums. Some run weekly – Tate Modern (p160); Royal Academy of Arts (p104); National Gallery (p91); the Wellcome Collection (p252) – and some are monthly or just for special events, such as the British Museum (p81), the V&A (p178) and Whitechapel Gallery (p226). Late-night events can include DJs, live performances and dancing: just a regular party, but without sticky carpets and toilet queues. Most large bookshops are also open at night, some with excellent cafes attached for a late-night refreshment too.

Many pubs and bars in London now stock an increasing list of nonalcoholic drinks to choose from, including alcohol-free craft beers from Brew Dog (p283), CBD (cannabidiol) drinks from brands like Green Monkey (www.greenmonkey.co.uk) and Little Rick (www.littlerick.co.uk), and sophisticated mocktails.

Lonely Planet's Top Choices

Holly Bush (p267) Cosy Georgian pub tucked away in genteel Hampstead.

Magritte Bar (p126) Age-old elegance in Mayfair's Beaumont Hotel.

Netil360 (p238) Rooftop eyrie with expansive views and rounds of croquet.

City Barge (p324) Steeped in London history, it's a destination pub.

Oriole (p153) Global themed cocktails and beguiling decor.

Best Pubs

George Inn (p170) Dickens-era pub with a cobble courtyard in summer.

White Cross (p325) Great old riverside pub in Richmond.

Lamb & Flag (p124) Just about everyone's West End favourite, so expect a scrum.

Cat & Mutton (p240) Simultaneously traditional and hip, and always up for a party.

Mayflower (p309) Venerable riverside pub with an American connection.

Fox & Anchor (p214) Traditional Victorian boozer with an early license for market workers.

Best Cocktails

Zetter Townhouse Cocktail Lounge (p213) An antique-filled lounge tucked away in Clerkenwell.

High Water (p237) Welcoming Dalston bar devising its own delectable concoctions.

Satan's Whiskers (p237) Friendly crew swizzling up a storm in Bethnal Green.

Artesian (p125) The re-energised flagship cocktail bar at the Langham Hotel.

Lyaness (p172) A soft modern fit-out and run by an award-winning mixologist.

Cocktail Trading Co (p217) Classy and cool, with killer cocktails.

Unique Experiences

Seabird (p172) Restaurant and bar with big views and oysters to accompany the cocktails.

Bar Pepito (p258) Pocket-sized Andalusian bar dedicated to lovers of sherry.

Crate Brewery (p239) Canal-side drinking with pizzas in industrial Hackney Wick.

American Bar (p124) Mayfair hotel bar with art deco ambience.

Bethnal Green Working Men's Club (p237) Burlesque, cabaret, retro nights, glitter and grunge.

Nickel Bar (p153) Gatsby vibes in this vaulted lobby of The Ned, with torchlight jazz and piano.

Best Beer Gardens

Windsor Castle (p282) Come summer, regulars abandon the Windsor's historic interior for the chilled-out garden.

Queen Elizabeth Hall Roof Garden (p174) Summer-only but an 'urban meadow' with London views.

Edinboro Castle (p266) A festive Camden boozer in which to stretch out a summer evening.

Garden Gate (p267) Sip on a Pimm's amid the Hampstead greenery.

People's Park Tavern (p239) Rambling beer garden with minigolf and the tree-lined avenues of Victoria Park next door.

Tap on the Line (p325) Nestled into a train station with a sunny courtyard.

WILLY BARTON/SHUTTERSTOCK ©

Royal Albert Hall (p187)

Showtime

Since a young bard from Stratford-upon-Avon set up shop here in the Elizabethan era, London has been entertaining its residents with energetic, talent-driven theatre, comedy, dance and opera. Want live music? Passionate new bands play divey backrooms at the local pub or catch the world's top artists at London's best (or sometimes worst) music venues.

Theatre

Going to the theatre is very much a must-do London experience, but like with many of the best things in London, life belongs to the organised. For famous productions subscribe to their newsletter for alerts on the next ticket release to get good seats at the best price. Last-minute tickets are almost always more expensive.

Blockbuster shows like *Hamilton* or *Harry Potter & the Cursed Child* sell out quickly, you're then left with buying from a third-party reseller such as **TodayTix** (www.todaytix.com/x/london). Some productions do have last-minute ticket sales or ballots (check their websites).

The peak theatre district (40+ theatres) is in the West End (p72), where you'll find everything from old-school classics (often starring well-known actors), raise-the-roof musicals, and new drama, as well as ballets, opera and long-running shows – sometimes reborn with a fresh new direction (*Les Misérables,* for example).

Beyond the West End established institutions such as the National Theatre (p174), the Barbican Centre (p156), the Old Vic (p174) and Shakespeare's Globe (p174) put on world-class shows and classics remastered for the modern age.

Highly regarded smaller theatres are moving audiences with incredible new works. Many go on to have a run in the West End, or Broadway. Look at the performance schedule for the Almeida (p268), Bridge Theatre (p174), Young Vic (p174), Bush Theatre (p284), Donmar Warehouse (p127), Hackney Empire (p241), and the Arcola (p241).

Finally, if you hadn't suffered option paralysis already... you could also take a punt (and pay a lot less) at smaller theatre productions at the Vaults (p175), Riverside Studios (p285), King's Head Theatre (p268) or Hampstead Theatre (p270). Families may love the major shows from *Matilda* to the *Lion King*, but child-focused theatre companies Unicorn Theatre (p175) and the Puppet Theatre Barge (p284) are other more affordable options.

Classical Music

With multiple world-class orchestras and ensembles, astonishing venues and reasonable ticket prices, even the most critical classical-music buff should find something to enjoy. Wigmore Hall (p127), Royal Festival Hall (p174), Barbican Centre (p156), Royal Albert Hall (p198), Kings Place (p251) and Handel & Hendrix (p109) all maintain a strong roster of classical performances.

Beyond these major venues you'll see flyers and social media advertisements for smaller performances often in churches and bespoke venues: **Multi-Story Orchestra** (www.multi-story.org.uk) performs in a Peckham carpark. The **Proms** is a famous orchestral festival running for eight summer weeks at the Royal Albert Hall (p198) and Cadogan Hall (p198).

Opera

With one of the world's leading opera companies at the Royal Opera House (p127) in Covent Garden, the English National Opera (p128) based at the London Coliseum and plenty of other smaller players and events, London keeps opera lovers satisfied. It's not just the classics that get attention: new productions grappling with contemporary themes are regularly staged. In summer, Holland Park (p284) is the venue for opera under the stars. And, yes, opera is expensive to produce and so, consequently, are the tickets.

NEED TO KNOW

Purchasing Tickets

➡ Book well ahead for popular shows. Buy directly from the venue.

➡ Last-minute standby tickets are limited. Third party re-sellers and apps like TodayTix are your best bet.

➡ Don't buy tickets from random strangers online; it's almost always a scam.

➡ Ticket touts have been thwarted by technology.

Standing Tickets

➡ Shakespeare's Globe (p174) offers 700 standing tickets (£5) for every performance. There really is nowhere to sit.

➡ Limited cut-price standing tickets are available for a host of major shows, including *Hamilton*.

Cheap Tickets

➡ Midweek matinees are often cheaper than evening performances; the audience is mainly retirees.

➡ The National Theatre (p174) also does live streaming to London cinemas for popular shows.

➡ Buy discounted tickets up to two days in advance for West End productions from Tkts Leicester Square.

Useful Websites & Apps

Time Out (www.timeout.com/london) Free weekly magazine with up-to-date theatre and entertainment listings.

Bach Track (www.bachtrack.com/city/london) Lists classical performances, opera and dance.

London Theatre (www.londontheatre.co.uk) Musicals, plays, drama and fringe theatre in London.

Songkick (www.songkick.com) Syncs your Spotify data to make gig recommendations.

Dice (https://dice.fm) Download for information on indie events and shows.

Dance

The Royal Ballet, arguably the best classical ballet company in Britain, is based at the Royal Opera House (p127) in Covent Garden. The English National Ballet (p393) often performs at the London Coliseum, especially at Christmas and in summer. In north London, Sadler's Wells (p218) is famous for its more contemporary and experimental choreography. **Dance Umbrella Festival** (www.danceumbrella.co.uk) is a multicultural contemporary performance festival that takes place in October.

Live Music

Despite Bristol and Birmingham muscling in, London is still a hot spot for musical talent. London's beautiful old churches, theatres and music halls are chosen by many well-known artists for a more intimate setting, but these shows are also quick to sell out. Look out for gigs at Union Chapel (p270), O2 Academy Brixton (p309), Roundhouse (p269), Electric Ballroom (p269) and Hammersmith Apollo (p284).

In summer, London (and indeed Britain) is bursting with large bacchanalian music festivals (with international acts the main draw), plus street food, booze, and party zones. Many of these hyper-well-organised events, such as **British Summer Time** (www.bst-hydepark.com), take over a city park for a weekend. The festivals market is saturated, and competition for headliners, park venues and punters is stiff, which means tickets rarely sell out quickly.

Inspired by the success of artists like Stormzy, there is a generation of self-publishing lounge-room producers who also love to get out and perform. Check out established venues such as Ronnie Scott's (p127) and 606 Club (p198), or Dalston's Vortex Jazz Club (p241) and Cafe Oto (p241), but most of London's hip hop, rap, grime, spoken word, jazz, blues, and R&B gigs are advertised by social media. Dig online or ask other musicians.

Comedy

Londoners have a remarkable sense of humour (a survival strategy no doubt), and comedy shows flourish in the capital. Most acts have their eyes on the critical Edinburgh Festival season, which means from April to July new material is usually being tried out on unsuspecting audiences. You may well catch the next Phoebe Waller-Bridge before his or her genius is applauded around the globe. Check the winners list of the **Edinburgh Comedy Awards** (www.comedyawards.co.uk) for the best new shows to catch this year.

Film

London has a strong film-making and film-watching culture. Cinema venues range from the super-sized BFI IMax (p175) to the quirky and boutique Rio Cinema (p241). Cinemas such as the Prince Charles (p126) have cheap tickets, run mini-festivals and screen popular singalong classics. For back-catalogue classics, turn to the BFI Southbank (p174). The BFI (British Film Institute) also runs the biggest film event of the year, the **London Film Festival** (www.bfi.org.uk/lff; ⌚Oct). Many major premieres are held in Leicester Sq, the priciest part of London for cinema tickets.

One of London's most exciting cinema experiences is a must-do if the stars align for you. Secret Cinema (www.secretcinema.org) sees the world of screen classics recreated in real life. Audiences are asked to dress in character and immerse themselves into the set before watching the film. And as phones and camera are banned, the whole experience remains a secret for the duration of each production.

Showtime by Neighbourhood

West End (p126) Packed with theatres, opera houses, classical-music concert halls, small live-music venues, comedy clubs and cinemas.

City of London (p156) Barbican Centre and church concerts.

South Bank (p173) Some of London's best-known and most prestigious theatres.

Kensington & Hyde Park (p198) Royal Albert Hall, the Royal Court Theatre and some smaller music venues.

Clerkenwell, Shoreditch & Spitalfields (p218) Sadler's Wells, live music and comedy.

East London & Docklands (p240) Independent theatres, cinemas and live-music venues.

Hampstead & North London (p268) One word: Camden! Indie rock, jazz, blues, traditional music, folk dancing, comedy and theatre.

Notting Hill & West London (p284) Cinemas, live music and summer opera.

Brixton, Peckham & South London (p309) Live-music venues at the local to international acts at O2 Academy Brixton.

Lonely Planet's Top Choices

Royal Opera House (p127) London's pre-eminent stage for opera and classical dance.

Wigmore Hall (p127) A story-book concert hall with excellent acoustics.

Southbank Centre (p165) Concerts, recitals, musicals – you name it – the Southbank Centre has it.

Barbican Centre (p156) Architecturally significant centre for culture, from music and dance to theatre and film.

Shakespeare's Globe (p174) Shakespeare, as it would have been 400 years ago.

Royal Albert Hall (p198) Sit back and imagine you're in Victorian London.

Best Theatre

Almeida (p268) Classics redone and new productions that often go on to the West End.

Old Vic (p174) A heavy hitter in London's theatrical scene.

Young Vic (p174) Finding new audiences and tackling new content.

Donmar Warehouse (p127) Consistently delivers thought-provoking productions.

Royal Court Theatre (p199) Forward-thinking, promoting new voices.

Best Music Venues

Roundhouse (p269) Camden's large-yet-intimate heritage-listed performance venue.

Union Chapel (p270) One of London's most atmospheric venues.

Eventim Apollo (p284) A venue of legendary status still getting great acts.

Wilton's (p240) Victorian music hall with an eclectic program.

Cadogan Hall (p198) Chelsea home of the Royal Philharmonic Orchestra.

Cafe Oto (p241) Intimate music venue for serious connoisseurs.

Best Comedy

Soho Theatre (p128) Stages local and foreign talent.

Comedy Store (p127) Hosts the most famous improvisation outfit in town.

Angel Comedy (p269) Pay-what-you-feel shows every night of the week at the Camden Head and the Bill Murray.

Museum of Comedy (p128) Free Monday-night comedy in the West End.

Best Dance

Sadler's Wells (p218) Top-drawer international and UK contemporary dance.

Royal Opera House (p127) The Royal Ballet, the nation's largest ballet company, is based here.

English National Ballet (p393) Touring company based at the London Coliseum.

The Place (p128) The very birthplace of modern British dance.

Best Church Concerts

St Martin-in-the-Fields (p102) Excellent classical-music concerts, many by candlelight.

Westminster Abbey (p78) Evensong and the city's finest organ concerts.

St Paul's Cathedral (p143) Evensong at its most evocative.

St Alfege Church (p294) Free lunchtime concerts on Thursdays and most Saturdays.

SERENAROSSI/SHUTTERSTOCK ©

Portobello Road Market (p276)

Treasure Hunt

Whether you're hunting for something unique to cherish or want to live out a rags-to-riches-montage fantasy, London is a fabulous shopping destination. You'll find everything here from vintage stores to all the international fashion labels. Iconic London shopping landmarks include Camden Market, Portobello Road, Rough Trade, Harrods, Hamleys and Fortnum & Mason.

Designers

London fashion houses you can't miss include Vivienne Westwood, Stella McCartney, Karen Miller, Alexander McQueen, Paul Smith and Burberry. Also look out for the next generation of UK designers like Molly Goddard, Christopher Kane and Mimi Wade, and the deconstructed look by Jamie Wei Huang and Vinti Andrews.

Markets

Perhaps the biggest draw for visitors is the capital's famed markets. A treasure trove of small designers, unique jewellery, original framed photographs and artworks, and outstanding vintage pieces: the perfect antidote to the climate-controlled shopping centres or same-same high streets. Camden (p254) has a '90s grunge vibe, Old Spitalfields (p219) is undercover and eclectic, and Portobello Road (p276) is nestled among gorgeous architecture. Brick Lane's Sunday Upmarket (p218) is a must-see (but weekends only).

Vintage Treasures

Vintage apparel is about more than finding offbeat and original outfits; it's now part of

Shopping by Neighbourhood

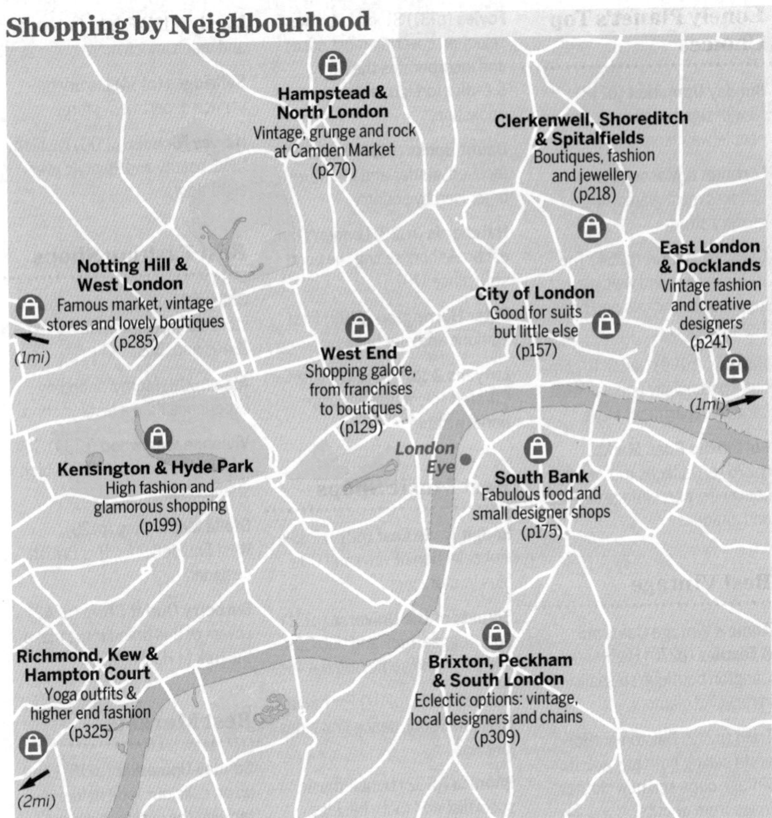

the mainstream carbon-conscious shopping habit. London has plenty of upmarket vintage boutiques. Some of it is imported en masse from the USA and Canada to feed Londoner's thirst for winter coats, Hawaiian shirts and boiler suits. There are still plenty of charity shops to dive into – in more salubrious areas like Marylebone, Chelsea, Kensington and Richmond you'll find quality designer pieces, though jaw-dropping bargains are a thing of the past.

Big Chains

Major fashion chains are a staple of shopping centres and high streets, leaving small independents struggling to pay the rent. You won't have any trouble finding the global fast-fashion brands like H&M, Uniqlo and Zara, plus home-grown chains such as Karen Millen and Topshop in most London neighbourhoods.

NEED TO KNOW

Opening Hours

➡ Shops open from 9am or 10am to 6pm or 7pm Monday to Saturday and noon to 5pm Sundays.

➡ West End stores and major shopping centres open to 9pm on Thursday and Friday nights.

Tax & Refunds

➡ A 20% value-added tax (VAT) is included in the advertised prices of most goods, excluding kids' clothes and food.

➡ When leaving the country, non-EU visitors can recoup VAT on purchases made in stores displaying a 'tax free' sign.

➡ For more info, see www.gov.uk/tax-on-shopping/taxfree-shopping.

Lonely Planet's Top Choices

Sunday Upmarket (p218) New designers, street food and people-watching.

Fortnum & Mason (p129) Britain's most glamorous grocery store

Camden Market (p254) The 1990s is alive and well: piercings, leather jackets and band T-shirts abound.

Harrods (p199) Garish to some but a perennially popular West London department store.

Portobello Road Market (p276) An eclectic mix of arty souvenirs, plus vintage clothes and antiques.

Best Vintage

Annie's Vintage Costume & Textiles (p270) High-end Islington boutique specialising in recycled glamour.

Traid (p242) Dalston not-for-profit selling both top-notch vintage duds and new clothes made from offcuts.

Atika (p220) A massive selection of just about everything.

Beyond Retro (p242) London vintage empire with a rock 'n' roll heart.

Rellik (p287) Classic designer cast-offs from the 1950s to the 1990s.

Best Bookshops

John Sandoe Books (p199) Gorgeous bookshop stuffed with gems.

Foyles (p131) Stocks a brilliant selection covering most bases and incorporates the Grant & Cutler foreign-language bookshop.

Daunt Books (p133) Travel focused, guides and literature, organised by country.

Hatchards (p129) London's oldest bookshop, selling the good stuff since 1797.

Peter Harrington (p199) First editions and rare books.

Lutyens & Rubinstein (p285) Curated selections of exceptional writing.

Best Music Shops

Rough Trade East (p219) Excellent selection of vinyl and CDs, plus in-store gigs.

Sounds of the Universe (p131) Soul, reggae, funk and dub CDs and vinyl, and some original 45s.

Honest Jon's (p287) For reggae, jazz, funk, soul, dance and blues junkies.

Phonica (p132) Dance-music specialist and more besides.

Reckless Records (p132) Secondhand vinyl in Soho since 1984.

Best Department Stores

Fortnum & Mason (p129) A world of food in luxurious historic surroundings.

Harrods (p199) Enormous, overwhelming and indulgent, with a world-famous food hall.

Liberty (p131) Fabric, fashion and much, much more.

Selfridges (p134) Luxury full-service department store.

Harvey Nichols (p200) Fashion, food, beauty and lifestyle over eight floors.

Best Fashion Shops

Collectif (p220) Spitalfields store taking inspiration from the 1940s and '50s.

Aida (p219) More a shopping experience than a fashion shop.

Vivienne Westwood (p134) Still leading the way for bold fashion statements.

Stella McCartney (p129) West End outlet for this British designer.

Burberry Outlet Store (p242) Lovers of this brand must make the trek to Hackney.

Best Markets

Sunday Upmarket (p218) Load up on delicious food before tackling the designer stalls.

Camden Market (p254) From authentic antiques to tourist tat – and everything in between.

Portobello Road Market (p276) Classic Notting Hill sprawl, perfect for vintage everything.

Old Spitalfields Market (p219) Major labels rub shoulders with vintage and antiques stalls.

Broadway Market (p242) Locally made produce plus street food, dotted with craft stalls.

Active London

For the 2012 Summer Olympics, East London's sports infrastructure was vastly improved, adding to the already world-famous venues scattered around the city. There are also surprisingly large tracts of green space in the city, where you'll see locals working up a sweat at a Parkrun. And cycling, both for commuting and pootling around the city's landmarks, has become a popular activity supported by cycle lanes and better signage.

Swimming

With two 50m pools and a 25m diving pool, the London Aquatics Centre (p243) at Queen Elizabeth Olympic Park is London's best facility for swimmers. The city is also blessed with many lovely art deco–era lidos (public outdoor swimming pools), though many are summer-only. For those who prefer their swimming a little more wild (and a lot more memorable), head to the famous all-year-round swimming ponds at Hampstead Heath (p271) or the Serpentine Lido (p201) in Hyde Park.

Cycling

London is criss-crossed by dedicated cycle paths from canalside towpaths (these can be rather busy on weekends) to longer routes through parks and commons. Central London is flat and surprisingly compact, making two-wheeled exploration a great way to experience the city. The easiest way to do this is to take advantage of the many Santander Cycles (p415) self-service docking stations scattered around the city; or sign up for one of the new commercial schemes like JUMP (www.jump.com) bikes.

Cycling enthusiasts should head to the Lee Valley VeloPark (p243) for the experience of riding on the Olympic velodrome and attached kids (big and smaller kids) will enjoy the BMX park (bike hire and helmet included).

Tennis

Wimbledon (p322) becomes the centre of the sporting universe for a fortnight in June/July when the world's most famous tennis tournament gets underway. Obtaining tickets is far from straightforward. You need to apply for the ballot or plan for an overnight queuing adventure (we'll spare you the details here – look online for intel). To view or visit Centre Court at other times of the year, head to the Wimbledon Lawn Tennis Museum (p322).

Canoeing, Rafting & Boating

Options range from gentle cruises on the Thames to white-water rafting, kayaking, hydrospeeding and tubing sessions at the **Lee Valley White Water Centre** (www.gowhitewater.co.uk). **Kayaking London** (www.kayakinglondon.com) and **Moo Canoes** (www.moocanoes.com) offer river and canal adventures, a unique way to experience London.

There's also fast-paced Thames Rockets (p175) speed boating on the Thames; hot tub or BBQ boats around Canary Wharf with **Skuna Boats** (www.skunaboats.com; adult/teen £45/35, private hire £225); canal trips from Camden with London Waterbus Company (p415); or you can hire a rowboat from Richmond Bridge Boat Hire (p326) and paddle about on the river at your leisure. If you just want to spectate, head to the Oxford Cambridge Boat Race (p319) in late March/early April for peak posh Britain.

NEED TO KNOW

Opening Hours

As a rule, most gyms open very early, usually from 6am and stay open until at least 9pm (some are 24 hour). Gated parks are generally open from dawn to dusk.

Tickets

Tickets for sporting events need to be booked well in advance. Check websites for individual teams, specific venues or events such as The Ashes for details on how to get tickets.

Cricket

On a long summer's day, there's nothing more English than to pack a picnic and enjoy the thwack of leather on willow. The English Cricket Board website (www.ecb.co.uk) has complete details of match schedules and tickets. Neighbourhood parks will generally have a couple of local teams playing it out in their tell-tale whites. International test matches are played at Lord's (p253) and the Oval (p309). Tickets sell via a ballot for major events, but you should be able to get tickets to lower-stakes games and enjoy the very polite atmosphere, with decent views of the hallowed turf.

Football

Football is at the very heart of British sporting culture, with about a dozen league teams in London. At the time of research, five London teams were in the Premier League (www.premierleague.com): Arsenal, Chelsea, Crystal Palace, Tottenham Hotspur and West Ham United. The competition runs from August to May.

It's difficult for visitors to secure tickets to matches (they are usually all snapped up by season-ticket holders) but with bigger stadiums (and more expensive ticket prices suppressing demand) you may get lucky on a League Cup games. If not, consider taking a tour at **Wembley** (☎0800 169 9933; www.wembleystadium.com; tours adult/child £19/12; ⓤWembley Park), Tottenham Hotspur Stadium (p259), London Stadium (p230), Arsenal Emirates Stadium (p256) or Stamford Bridge (p276) instead.

Ice Skating

A combined ice rink and bowling venue, Queens Ice & Bowl (p288) has skating year-round and disco nights on ice. In winter months, skating is hugely popular with Londoners and outside ice rinks sparkle at Somerset House (p106), the Natural History Museum (p182), the Tower of London (p137), Hampton Court Palace (p312) and Hyde Park's Winter Wonderland (p200).

Active London by Neighbourhood

West End (p76) Grab a Santander Cycle and explore major sites by bike.

Kensington & Hyde Park (p200) Jogging, horse riding, cycling, swimming, boating and tennis in Hyde Park itself.

Clerkenwell, Shoreditch & Spitalfields (p202) Play minigolf in the Old Truman Brewery.

East London & Docklands (p242) Myriad activities in Olympic Park; climbing in Mile End; canoeing on the canal.

Hampstead & North London (p244) Home to Lord's and Arsenal Emirates Stadium, plus strolling or swimming at Hampstead Heath.

Notting Hill & West London (p272) Chelsea Football Club, Queens Ice & Bowl and kayaking in Little Venice.

Brixton, Peckham & South London (p299) Cricket at the Oval, plus major parks to play in.

Greenwich (p289) Climb the O2 roof with Up at the O2, or walk the riverfront back into town.

Richmond, Kew & Hampton Court (p310) World-famous Wimbledon tennis and Twickenham Rugby Stadium, plus boating at Richmond.

Lonely Planet's Top Choices

Wimbledon (p67) Enter the ballot or camp overnight to secure a ticket to the prestigious Grand Slam lawn tennis tournament

Lord's (p253) Tour the venerable stadium or settle in for a day of leather on willow and jugs of Pimms in the sunshine.

Hampstead Heath Ponds (p271) Whether it's the women's, men's, or mixed pond you're in for a memorable wild swim.

London Aquatics Centre (p243) Channel your inner Michael Phelps or Katie Ledecky in the city's actual Olympic pool.

Somerset House (p106) Magical spot for winter ice skating.

Will to Win (p201) Tennis with racquet hire, lawn bowls, and an outdoor gym: sweat it out in central London.

Best Swimming

London Aquatics Centre (p243) Olympic pools encased in a beautiful shell.

London Fields Lido (p243) Restored East End complex with 1930s charm.

Hampstead Heath Ponds (p271) Single-sex and mixed bathing ponds for freshwater dips among the greenery.

Serpentine Lido (p201) Cordoned-off swimming in Hyde Park's lake.

Porchester Spa (p288) Gorgeous art deco complex with a 30m indoor pool.

Best for Families

Kidzania (p287) A mini-world of imaginative play that children will remember for a lifetime.

Diana, Princess of Wales Memorial Playground (p188) Outstanding playground in central London.

ArcelorMittal Orbit (p229) Head to the top for epic London views then take a 178m slide to the ground.

Queens Ice & Bowl (p288) Great rainy-day option for kids and parents who love ice skating and bowling, who doesn't?

London Aquatics Centre (p243) Inflatable aqua-play course for kids over eight.

Best Stadium Tours

Lord's (p253) The hallowed 'home of cricket', with a fascinating museum.

Wembley Stadium (p66) The city's landmark national stadium, used for football matches and mega concerts.

Twickenham Rugby Stadium (p321) London's famous rugby union stadium, used for international test matches.

Tottenham Hotspur Stadium (p259) Guided tours of Spurs' state-of-the-art stadium.

London Stadium (p230) Built as the centrepiece stadium for the 2012 Olympics and now home to West Ham United FC.

Arsenal Emirates Stadium (p256) Offers both self-guided tours or tours led by former Arsenal FC players.

LGBTIQ+

The city of Oscar Wilde, Virginia Woolf and Elton John will not disappoint LGBTIQ+ visitors, with everything in queer culture from the highbrow to underground parties. London's gay, lesbian and transgender communities are visible and loving life. Laws protecting broader identities and lifestyles do exist but be warned, not all Londoners are open-minded or enlightened.

Gay Bars & Clubs

A number of venues have closed their doors in recent times – due, in part, to gentrification of traditionally gay and 'upcoming' neighbourhoods pushing up rents and bringing in corporate money.

While there are some specific LGBTIQ+ clubs, more often promoters hold specialist nights at established venues. This means that a spot that was full of shirtless ripped dudes one night may well be full of goths the next.

Gay venues are dotted across the city today, so whether you fancy a quiet pint in an old-fashioned boozer, a pumping club at which to dance till dawn, cabaret, karaoke, or a leather fetish club, you'll need to do your homework.

Lesbian Hang-Outs

The lesbian scene has few venues of its own – She Soho (p122) on Old Compton St being a notable exception – most gay bars are overwhelmingly male. That said, the hipper, younger venues – such as the Glory (p215), Bethnal Green Working Men's Club (p237) and Dalston Superstore (p238) – tend to be much more mixed, and there are regular women's nights held at establishments straight and gay, especially in the East End.

Legal Rights

Protection from discrimination is enshrined in law and same-sex couples have the right to marry. Unfortunately, homophobia does exist in the UK, and anti-gay violence occurs with increased regularity. However, it would be extremely surprising (not to mention illegal) for same-gender couples to strike any problems when booking a double bed in a hotel or, indeed, dealing with any service provider. Do report homophobic crimes to the police (☎101 for non emergencies). For confidential advice contact **Switchboard LGBT+ Helpline** (☎0300 330 0630; https://switchboard.lgbt).

Gay & Lesbian by Neighbourhood

West End (p76) Centred on Old Compton St, Soho's gay village still has the best concentration of venues for a guaranteed night out.

East London & Docklands (p222) Hackney and Tower Hamlets have an alternative, diverse and mixed scene, some old-school gay venues as well as LGBTIQ+-friendly nights. Check local media for listings.

Brixton, Peckham & South London (p73) Vauxhall and Clapham have good-natured scenes from cabaret at the iconic RVT (p308) to weekend clubbing or weeknight line dancing at Two Brewers (p309). Ride 'em cowboy.

Best Events

Pride (p32) One of the world's largest LGBTIQ+ parades, complete with floats, stalls and performers.

Fringe! (www.fringefilmfest.com) Queer film and arts festival, held in various venues in November.

Best Bars & Pubs

Yard (p123) A rare indoor-outdoor venue in the middle of gay Soho.

Glory (p215) One of London's most eclectic venues, where weird is a term of genuine endearment.

Two Brewers (p309) Long-standing Clapham bar serving a local South London crowd.

Duke of Wellington (p123) Nothing flashy here, just an unpretentious gay boozer attracting a beardy crowd.

Old Ship (p240) Unassuming and cosy corner pub in Limehouse.

Best for Lesbians

She Soho (p122) London's only dedicated lesbian bar, in the heart of the gay strip.

Ku Bar (p124) Party girls head down the stairs for the weekly Ruby Tuesdays takeover.

Dalston Superstore (p238) Regular women's nights readjust the gender balance of this female-friendly hipster hang-out.

Royal Vauxhall Tavern (p308) Monthly *Butch, Please!* nights, plus a whole host of drag kings and other lesbian performers.

Glory (p215) A mixed crowd of hip young things head to this bastion of kooky camp.

Best Club Nights

Bethnal Green Working Men's Club (p237) Merging pop, punk, and cabaret in the hedonistic monthly Cookie Jar Party.

Heaven (p125) Love it or hate it, G-A-Y is where seemingly half of Soho heads on Saturday.

Royal Vauxhall Tavern (p308) Tagged London's 'flagship rock 'n' roll honky-tonk', Duckie is the club's legendary queer performance night.

Eagle (p308) Horse Meat Disco is the long-standing Sunday nighter for dudes old enough to know better.

Best Historical & Cultural Sites

Gay's the Word (p131) Bookshop that's been a bastion of gay culture since 1979.

Hampstead Heath (p255) Legendary cruising ground, with popular single-sex bathing ponds immortalised in Hollinghurst's *The Line of Beauty*.

Cadogan Hotel, Sloane St, Knightsbridge Site of Oscar Wilde's arrest in 1895; has reopened as a hotel.

52 Tavistock Sq, Bloomsbury The house where Virginia Woolf was living when she wrote *Orlando*, inspired by Vita Sackville-West.

Admiral Duncan, 54 Old Compton St, Soho Gay pub that was the site of a homophobic bombing in 1999, killing three patrons.

Best Clubs

Heaven (p125) London's most famous gay club has been reeling them in since the late '70s.

Dalston Superstore (p238) Diner by day, subterranean nightclub after dark.

Eagle (p308) Blokey, beardy and a bit beary, this is a cracker of a late-night venue.

Royal Vauxhall Tavern (p308) Themed party nights, cabaret, drag shows, open stage and all kinds of wacky shenanigans.

Ku Bar (p124) After Soho's bars close, the Ku beckons.

NEED TO KNOW

Free Press

Boyz (www.boyz.co.uk) Monthly magazine covering the bar, club and sauna scenes.

QX (www.qxmagazine.com) A weekly mag devoted mainly to men's venues.

Pride Life (www.pridelife.com) Quarterly news and lifestyle magazine, also online.

Attitude (www.attitude.co.uk) Monthly gay men's lifestyle glossy.

Gay Times (www.gaytimes.co.uk) Long-standing monthly gay men's mag.

Diva (www.divamag.co.uk) Monthly lesbian magazine.

Online Resources

60by80 (www.60by80.com) Gay travel information.

Time Out London LGBT (www.timeout.com/london/lgbt) Bar, club and events listings.

Explore London

LONDON'S TOP EXPERIENCES

Left: Big Ben (p87)

Neighbourhoods at a Glance

❶ West End p76

The West End encompasses many of London's most iconic locations, buildings and museums, notably Trafalgar Square, Piccadilly Circus, Buckingham Palace, Westminster Abbey and the British Museum – not to mention theatres, parks, shopping and nightlife.

❷ City of London p135

London's historic core is usually packed with office workers on weekdays but eerily quiet at weekends. The current millennium has seen a profusion of daring skyscrapers sprout, a visual contrast to famous sites Tower of London and St Paul's Cathedral.

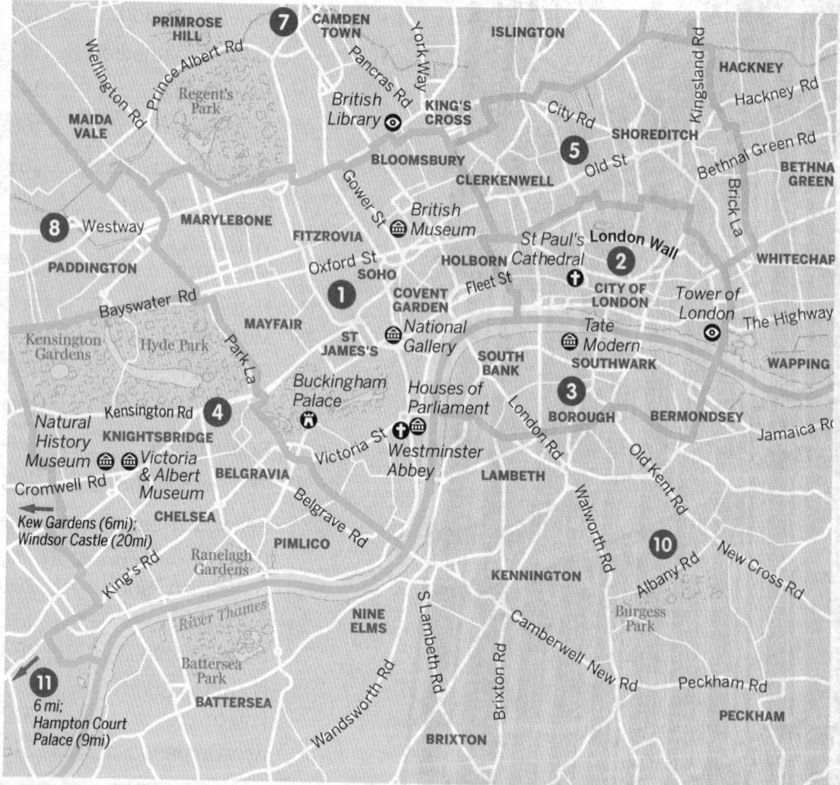

❸ South Bank p158

South Bank is a must-visit area for art lovers, theatre goers and architecture buffs, with the newly updated Tate Modern and iconic brutalist buildings to explore.

❹ Kensington & Hyde Park p176

Well-groomed Kensington is among London's handsomest neighbourhoods. It has three fine museums – V&A, Natural History Museum, Science Museum – plus excellent dining and shopping, graceful parklands and grand period architecture.

❺ Clerkenwell, Shoreditch & Spitalfields p202

Historic city-fringe neighbourhoods best known for culture and nightlife. Shoreditch and Hoxton long ago replaced Soho and Camden as London's hippest party spots.

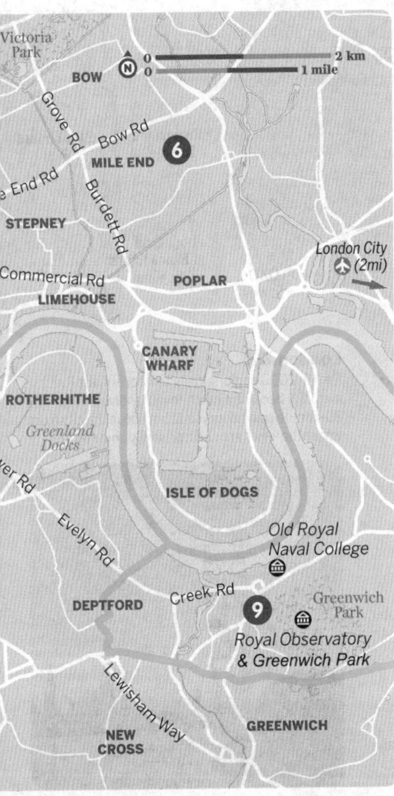

❻ East London & Docklands p222

Interesting museums and galleries, excellent pubs, canalside dining, punctuated by street art and vintage stores.

❼ Hampstead & North London p244

Head east from Camden's famous market and unrivalled music scene to check out the transformed King's Cross Station area. Then take in the green spaces at Hampstead Heath and Regent's Park.

❽ Notting Hill & West London p272

Come for Portobello Road Market, the Design Museum, historic cinemas, lush parkland, grand mansions and imposing churches. Stay for the superb pubs and clubs, diverse shopping and global eats.

❾ Greenwich p289

Regal historic Greenwich complements its riverside village feel with grand architecture, bustling weekend markets, grassy parklands and cosy riverside pubs.

❿ Brixton, Peckham & South London p299

In Brixton and Peckham, Afro-Caribbean haunts bump up against pocket-sized eating and drinking venues. Sample suburban Clapham and Battersea for local life, and Dulwich Village for country-hamlet vibe.

⓫ Richmond, Kew & Hampton Court p310

Visit London's leafy, riverside region to get lost in Kew Gardens, deer-spot in Richmond Park, traipse around Wimbledon Common and down a pint waterside as the sun sets on the Thames.

The River Thames

A FLOATING TOUR

London's history has always been determined by the Thames. The city was founded as a Roman port nearly 2000 years ago and over the centuries since then many of the capital's landmarks have lined the river's banks. A boat trip is a great way to experience the attractions.

There are piers dotted along both banks at regular intervals where you can hop on and hop off the regular services to visit places of interest. The best place to board is Westminster Pier, from where boats head downstream, taking you from the City of Westminster, the seat of government, to the original City of London, now the financial district (and dominated by a growing band of skyscrapers). Across the river, the once shabby and neglected South Bank now bristles with as many top attractions as its northern counterpart, including the slender Shard.

In our illustration we've concentrated on the top highlights you'll enjoy from a waterborne

KIEVVICTOR / SHUTTERSTOCK ©

St Paul's Cathedral

Though there's been a church here since AD 604, the current building rose from the ashes of the 1666 Great Fire and is architect Christopher Wren's masterpiece. Famous for surviving the Blitz intact and for the wedding of Charles and Diana, it's looking as good as new after a major clean-up for its 300th anniversary in 2011.

Somerset House

This grand neoclassical palace was once one of many aristocratic houses lining the Thames. The huge arches at river level gave direct access to the Thames until the Embankment was built in the 1860s.

London Eye

Built in 2000 and originally temporary, the Eye instantly became a much-loved landmark. The 30-minute spin takes you 135m above the city from where the views are unsurprisingly amazing.

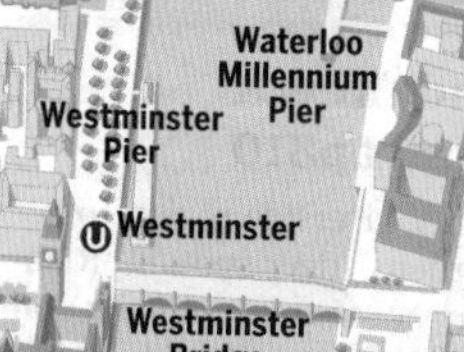

Houses of Parliament

Rebuilt in neo-Gothic style after the old Palace of Westminster burned down in 1834. The most famous part of the British parliament is the clocktower. Generally known as Big Ben, it's named after Benjamin Hall, who oversaw its construction.

VERDOONIE / BUDGETTRAVEL ©

vessel. These are, from west to east, the ❶ **Houses of Parliament**, the ❷ **London Eye**, ❸ **Somerset House**, ❹ **St Paul's Cathedral**, the ❺ **Tate Modern**, ❻ **Shakespeare's Globe**, the ❼ **Tower of London** and ❽ **Tower Bridge**.

In addition to covering this central section of the Thames, boats can also be taken upstream as far as Kew Gardens and Hampton Court Palace, and downstream as far as Greenwich and the Thames Barrier.

BOAT HOPPING

Thames Clippers' hop-on/hop-off services are aimed at commuters but are equally useful for visitors, operating every 15 minutes on a loop from piers at Westminster, Embankment, Waterloo, Blackfriars, Bankside, London Bridge and the Tower. Those with Oyster Cards get a discount off the boat ticket price.

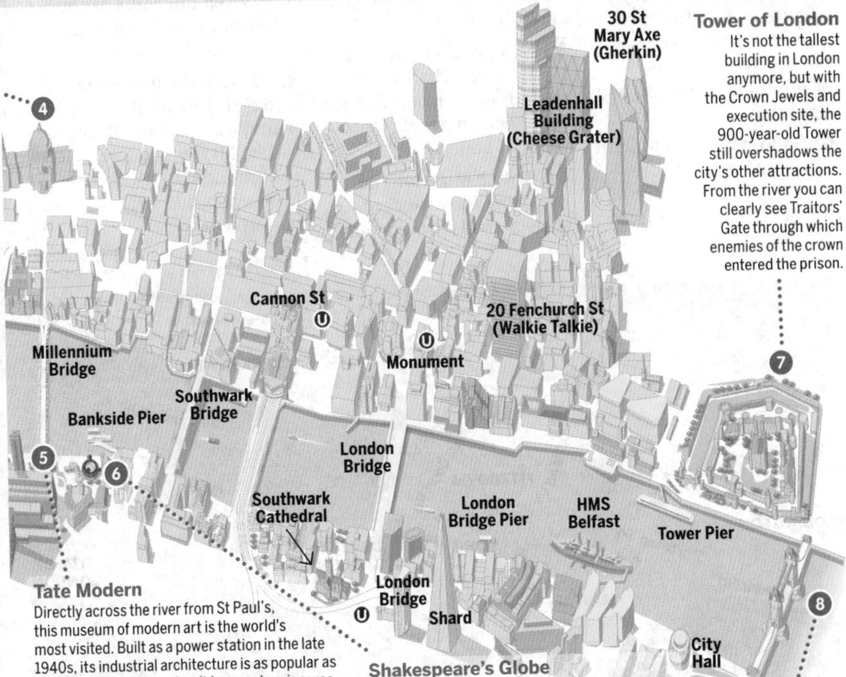

30 St Mary Axe (Gherkin)

Leadenhall Building (Cheese Grater)

Cannon St

20 Fenchurch St (Walkie Talkie)

Monument

Millennium Bridge

Southwark Bridge

Bankside Pier

London Bridge

Southwark Cathedral

London Bridge Pier

HMS Belfast

Tower Pier

London Bridge

Shard

City Hall

Tower of London

It's not the tallest building in London anymore, but with the Crown Jewels and execution site, the 900-year-old Tower still overshadows the city's other attractions. From the river you can clearly see Traitors' Gate through which enemies of the crown entered the prison.

Tate Modern

Directly across the river from St Paul's, this museum of modern art is the world's most visited. Built as a power station in the late 1940s, its industrial architecture is as popular as its artworks, while a splendid new extension was completed in 2016.

Shakespeare's Globe

The reconstructed Globe stands on the river a few hundred metres from where the original stood (and burnt down in 1613 during a performance). The life's work of American actor Sam Wanamaker, the theatre runs a hugely popular season from April to October each year.

Tower Bridge

It might look as old as its namesake neighbour but one of the world's most iconic bridges was only completed in 1894. Not to be confused with London Bridge upstream, this one's famous raising bascules allowed tall ships to dock at the old wharves to the west and are still lifted up to 1000 times a year.

CLAUDIO DIVIZIA / SHUTTERSTOCK ©

PRES PANAYOTOV / SHUTTERSTOCK ©

West End

WESTMINSTER | BLOOMSBURY & FITZROVIA | ST JAMES'S | SOHO & CHINATOWN | COVENT GARDEN & LEICESTER SQUARE | WHITEHALL | HOLBORN & THE STRAND | MARYLEBONE | MAYFAIR

Neighbourhood Top Five

1 Westminster Abbey (p78) Defending the 'great' in Great Britain – the church of coronations, royal burials, weddings and pageantry.

2 Soho (p100) Queuing to eat at a pocket-sized restaurant, or spilling out of a rowdy pub at all hours, in what was once a den of vice and iniquity.

3 St James's Park (p99) Hiring a deckchair in the city's most manicured green space and enjoying regal views of London.

4 British Museum (p81) Exploring the history of ancient civilisations going back seven millennia at this excellent (though somewhat controversial) museum.

5 Covent Garden Piazza (p102) Hitting all the British boutiques, from Ted Baker to Doc Martens, before celebrating the neighbourhood's amazing street performers.

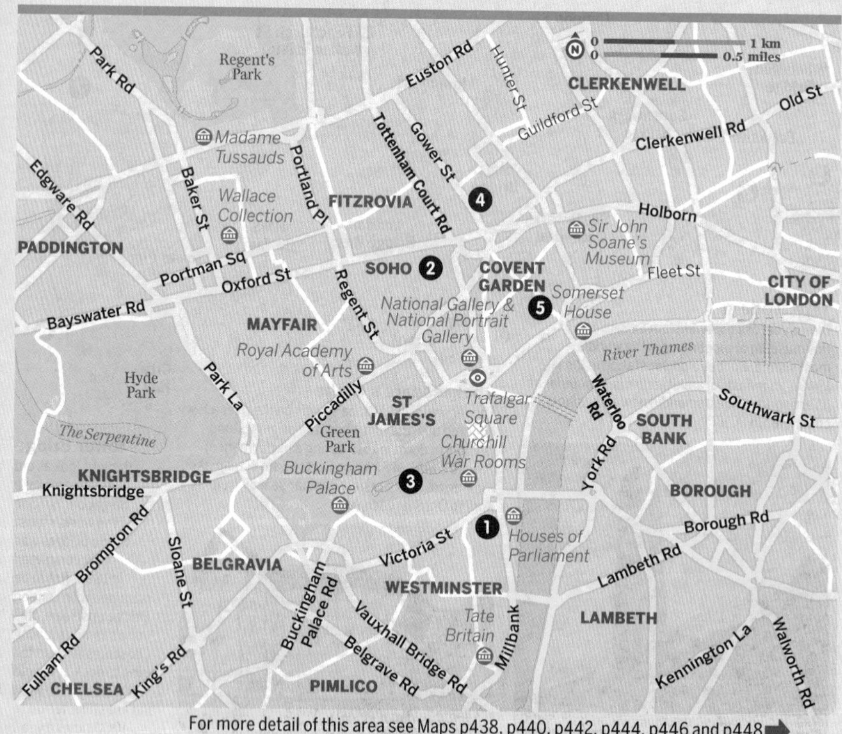

For more detail of this area see Maps p438, p440, p442, p444, p446 and p448

Explore the West End

The West End packs in a lot when it comes to sights, eating, shopping and entertainment. Allow up to a half-day for each of the big museums – the British Museum (p81) and the National Gallery (p91), and at least a couple of hours for places like Westminster Abbey (p78) and Buckingham Palace (p85) – the latter only open in summer).

The West End throngs with big-city energy night and day – enjoy it by walking around and taking it all in. You'll find atmospheric spots to have a breather or a bite to eat while people-watching at **Lincoln's Inn Fields**, St James's Park (p99) and Soho Sq (p100).

At night, the Westminster area is quiet, as is the region around St James's. Instead, head to Soho (p100) to hop between pubs, bars and restaurants, or into the streets around Covent Garden Piazza (p102) filled with theatregoers.

Local Life

Eating out Soho is unrivalled when it comes to eating out. Stalwarts like Andrew Edmunds (p114) are complemented by exciting new dining spots along with new classics such as Polpo (p115), Kricket Soho (p115) and Palomar (p113).

Late-night openings Be it catching the latest exhibition or enjoying the permanent collections without the weekend crowds, many Londoners make the best of late-night openings at the National Gallery (p91) and the British Museum (p81), and the less-frequent ones at Tate Britain (p92) and Sir John Soane's Museum (p95).

Shopping Pushing beyond the retail frenzy of Oxford St, Londoners know where their favourite designers can be found in the backstreets of Marylebone, Covent Garden and Soho.

Getting There & Away

Underground Almost every Tube line goes through the West End, so you'll have no difficulty getting here. The Tube is also good for getting from one end of the West End to the other.

Walking The West End is relatively compact, and it's cheaper and often more interesting to walk. Stick to backstreets to avoid the crowds and photograph your own architectural or style gems.

Bicycle Cycling is great for quick journeys, with Santander Cycles docking stations all over the West End, but beware of clueless pedestrians and one-way streets.

Lonely Planet's Top Tip

The West End is surprisingly good for budget travellers as many of London's most important museums are here (British Museum, National Gallery, Tate Britain) as well as lesser-known ones (Sir John Soane's Museum, Wallace Collection) – all with free entry. You'll also find two verdant royal parks to relax in, plus the city's smallest (Green Park) and the prettiest (St James's Park). And, as the West End is reasonably compact, you can cycle or walk – it's often quicker than the bus or Tube.

Best Eating

- Kiln (p113)
- Palomar (p113)
- Spring (p117)
- Bar Shu (p113)
- Seven Dials Market (p116)

For reviews, see p110.

Best Drinking & Nightlife

- Lamb & Flag (p124)
- Artesian (p125)
- Sketch (p121)
- Magritte Bar (p126)

For reviews, see p121.

Best Entertainment

- Royal Opera House (p127)
- Prince Charles Cinema (p126)
- Ronnie Scott's (p127)
- Wigmore Hall (p127)
- Donmar Warehouse (p127)

For reviews, see p126.

TETRA IMAGES/GETTY IMAGES ©

TOP EXPERIENCE

MARVEL AT WESTMINSTER ABBEY

Westminster Abbey is such an important commemoration site that it's hard to overstress its symbolic value or imagine its equivalent anywhere else in the world. Except for Edward V (murdered) and Edward VIII (abdicated), every English sovereign has been crowned here since William the Conqueror in 1066. Sixteen royals have been married here and many are buried here.

A Regal History

Though a mixture of architectural styles, the Abbey is considered the finest example of Early English Gothic. The original church was built in the 11th century by King Edward the Confessor (later a saint), who is buried in an elaborate tomb behind the High Altar. King Henry III (r 1216–72) began work on the new building but didn't complete it; the Gothic nave was finished by King Richard II in 1388. Henry VII's huge and magnificent Lady Chapel was added in 1516.

The Abbey was initially a monastery for a dozen Benedictine monks, and many of the building's features attest to this collegial past, including the octagonal Chapter House, the Quire and the College Garden. In the 1530s, King Henry VIII separated the church in England from Rome and dissolved the monasteries. The king became head of the Church of England and the Abbey acquired its 'royal peculiar' status, meaning it is administered directly by the Crown and exempt from any ecclesiastical jurisdiction.

DON'T MISS

- Tomb of the Unknown Warrior
- Scientists' Corner
- Cosmati Pavement and the High Altar
- Lady Chapel
- Queen's Diamond Jubilee Galleries
- Poets' Corner

PRACTICALITIES

- Map p448, D4
- 020-7222 5152
- www.westminster-abbey.org
- 20 Dean's Yard
- adult/child £24/10, half-price Wed 4.30pm
- 9.30am-3.30pm Mon, Tue, Thu & Fri, to 6pm Wed, to 3pm Sat May-Aug, to 1pm Sat Sep-Apr
- U Westminster

North Transept, Sanctuary & Quire

The North Transept is often referred to as **Statesmen's Aisle**: politicians (notably prime ministers) and eminent public figures are commemorated by large marble statues and imposing marble plaques here.

At the western end of the nave is the **Tomb of the Unknown Warrior**, killed in France during WWI and laid to rest here in 1920. The grave was filled in with soil from the battlefield and covered with a slab of black Belgian marble. More than 3300 people are buried at Westminster Abbey, but this is the only grave on the floor that is not allowed to be walked on.

Chapels & Chair

Henry VII's magnificent Perpendicular Gothic-style **Lady Chapel**, in the easternmost part of the Abbey, is the most spectacular, with its fan vaulting on the ceiling, colourful banners of the Order of the Bath and dramatic oak stalls with carved misericord seats. Behind the chapel's altar is the elaborate sarcophagus of Henry VII and his queen, Elizabeth of York.

The sanctuary is surrounded by smaller chapels. Behind the tomb of Henry VII is the **Royal Air Force Chapel**, with a stained-glass window commemorating the force's finest hour, the Battle of Britain (1940), and the nearly 1500 RAF aircrew who died fighting. A stone plaque on the floor marks the spot where Oliver Cromwell's body lay for two years from 1658 until the Restoration, when it was disinterred, hanged and beheaded.

There are two small chapels on either side of the Lady Chapel with the tombs of famous monarchs: on the north side is where **Queen Elizabeth I** and her half-sister **Queen Mary I** (also known as 'Bloody Mary') rest. Two bodies, believed to be those of King Edward V and his brother, the so-called **Princes in the Tower** who were allegedly murdered in the Tower of London by their uncle Richard III in 1483, were buried here almost two centuries later in 1674. On the south side is the tomb of **Mary Queen of Scots**, beheaded on the orders of her cousin Queen Elizabeth I in 1587.

Shrine of St Edward the Confessor

At the heart of the Abbey is the beautifully tiled sanctuary, the stage for coronations, royal weddings and funerals. Architect George Gilbert Scott designed the ornate **High Altar** in 1873. In front of the altar is the **Cosmati Pavement** from 1268. It has intricate designs of small pieces of stone and glass

TAKE A BREAK

Not far from the Abbey, the Vincent Rooms (p110) is an excellent spot for modern European cuisine at very reasonable prices. It's operated by the talented hospitality students of Westminster Kingsway College.

In 2011 Prince William married Catherine Middleton at Westminster Abbey. The couple decorated the Abbey with live trees and 30,000 flowers, most of which came from Windsor Great Park in Surrey. The bride wore a gown by British designer Sarah Burton, of luxury fashion brand Alexander McQueen. William and Kate's elaborately scrawled marriage certificate is now on display in the Queen's Diamond Jubilee Galleries.

inlaid into plain marble, which symbolise the universe at the end of time (an inscription claims the world will end after 19,683 years!).

At the entrance to the lovely **Chapel of St John the Baptist** is a sublime translucent alabaster *Virgin and Child*, placed here in 1971 after the original statuette was lost or destroyed during the Reformation.

The most sacred spot in the Abbey is the access-restricted **shrine of St Edward the Confessor**, which lies behind the High Altar (and has great views of the Cosmati Pavement through holes in the wall). King Edward, long considered a saint before he was canonised, was the founder of the Abbey, and the original building was consecrated a few weeks before his death in 1066. Henry III added a new shrine with Cosmati mosaics in the mid-12th century where the sick prayed for healing – and also chipped off a few souvenirs to take home.

Verger-led tours (£7 after admission) of the Abbey lasting 1½ hours include a visit to the shrine; access is kept to a minimum to protect the fragile 13th-century flooring.

South Transept & Nave

The south transept contains the incredible **Poets' Corner**, where many of England's finest writers are buried or memorialised. Famous names you'll find on the plaques include Geoffrey Chaucer, Charles Dickens, Thomas Hardy, Alfred Tennyson, Samuel Johnson, Rudyard Kipling, William Shakespeare, Jane Austen, the Brontë sisters and Philip Larkin.

A New Abbey Museum

Opened in 2018, the **Queen's Diamond Jubilee Galleries** (an additional £5) are a new museum and gallery space located in the medieval triforium, the arched gallery above the nave. Among its exhibits are the death masks and wax effigies of generations of royalty, armour and stained glass. Highlights include the graffiti-inscribed chair used for the coronation of Mary II, the beautifully illustrated manuscripts of the *Litlyngton Missal* from 1380 and the 13th-century Westminster Retable, England's oldest surviving altarpiece.

Rising above the bustle of the Abbey below, these galleries are much quieter and less visited than the central nave and very much worth the extra ticket price, as they boast the best views of the Abbey.

Outer Buildings & Gardens

Parts of the Abbey complex are free to visitors, including the Cloisters, Chapter House and the 900-year-old College Garden, though if you only see these, you won't get a sense of the grandeur of the Abbey.

The octagonal **Chapter House** dates from the 1250s and was where the monks would meet for daily prayer and their job assignments, before Henry VIII's suppression of the monasteries some three centuries later. To the right of the entrance to the Chapter House is what's claimed to be the oldest door in Britain – it's been there since the 1050s. Used as a treasury, the crypt-like **Pyx Chamber** dates from about 1070 and takes its name from boxes that held gold and silver to be tested for purity to make coins, which now takes place in Goldsmiths' Hall in the City of London.

One of the original gardens within Westminster Abbey, the lovely 900-year-old **College Garden** (off Great College St; ⌚10am-4pm Tue-Thu) FREE was used for growing medicinal herbs and foods for the Abbey's monks.

Unlike in the Abbey, photography is allowed in most of these areas.

CLAUDIO DIVIZIA/SHUTTERSTOCK ©

TOP EXPERIENCE

FIND THE WORLD AT THE BRITISH MUSEUM

The country's most visited attraction, the British Museum draws in 5.8 million people each year. It's an exhaustive and exhilarating stampede through world cultures over many millennia, with 90 galleries of over 80,000 objects spanning the globe and reaching far into the past (only 1% of the collection's eight million pieces can fit into the display cases at any given time).

History & the Great Court

The museum was founded in 1753 when physician and collector Sir Hans Sloane sold his 'cabinet of curiosities' for the then-princely sum of £20,000, raised by national lottery. The collection opened to the public for free in 1759, and the museum has since kept expanding its collection through judicious acquisitions, bequests and controversial imperial plundering.

Past the entry hall is the gasp-worthy **Great Court**, covered with a spectacular glass-and-steel roof designed by architect Norman Foster in 2000. In its centre is the **Reading Room**, currently closed, where Karl Marx researched and wrote *Das Kapital;* Virginia Woolf and Mahatma Gandhi were also cardholders.

Ancient Egypt, Middle East & Greece

The most prized item in the museum is the **Rosetta Stone** (room 4), the key to deciphering Egyptian hieroglyphics. Nearby is the enormous bust of ancient Egyptian pharaoh **Ramesses II**.

Assyrian treasures from ancient Mesopotamia include the hulking **winged bulls from Khorsabad** (room 10), at 16 tonnes the heaviest object in the museum. Behind it are the exquisite **lion hunt reliefs from Nineveh** (room 10) dating

DON'T MISS

- Rosetta Stone
- Mummy of Katebet
- Parthenon sculptures
- Winged bulls from Khorsabad
- Sutton Hoo Ship Burial artefacts
- Mildenhall Treasure
- Lewis Chessmen

PRACTICALITIES

- Map p444, E6
- 020-7323 8000
- www.britishmuseum.org
- Great Russell St
- admission free
- 10am-5.30pm, to 8.30pm Fri
- Tottenham Court Rd or Russell Sq

The British Museum

A HALF-DAY TOUR

The British Museum, with almost eight million items in its permanent collection, is so vast and comprehensive that it can be daunting for the first-time visitor. To avoid a frustrating trip – and getting lost on the way to the Egyptian mummies – set out on this half-day exploration, which takes in some of the museum's most important sights. If you want to see and learn more, join a tour, grab an audio guide (£7) or download the free app.

A good starting point is the ❶ **Rosetta Stone**, the key that cracked the code to ancient Egypt's writing system. Nearby treasures from Assyria – an ancient civilisation centred in Mesopotamia between the Tigris and Euphrates Rivers – including the colossal ❷ **Winged Bulls from Khorsabad**, give way to the ❸ **Parthenon Sculptures**, high points of classical Greek art that continue to influence us today. Be sure to see both the sculptures and the

Winged Bulls from Khorsabad
This awesome pair of alabaster winged bulls with human heads once guarded the entrance to the palace of Assyrian King Sargon II at Khorsabad in Mesopotamia, a cradle of civilisation in present-day Iraq.

Parthenon Sculptures
The Parthenon, a white marble temple dedicated to Athena, was part of a fortified citadel on the Acropolis in Athens. There are dozens of sculptures and friezes with models and interactive displays explaining how they all once fitted together.

Ancient Greece & Rome
3
Lion Hunt Reliefs from Nineveh
2
West Stairs
1
4
South Stairs
Audio Guides Desk
Main Entrance
Great Court
Reading Room
Great Court Shop
China, India & Southeast Asia
Information Desk
North America
Ticket Desk (Temporary Exhibitions)

GROUND FLOOR

Rosetta Stone
Written in hieroglyphic, demotic (cursive ancient Egyptian script used for everyday) and Greek, the 762kg stone contains a decree exempting priests from tax on the first anniversary of young Ptolemy V's coronation.

PHOTOS.COM / GETTY IMAGES ©

Bust of Pharaoh Ramesses II
The most impressive sculpture in the Egyptian galleries, this 725kg bust portrays Ramesses the Great, scourge of the Israelites in the Book of Exodus, as great benefactor.

NATALYA OKOROKOVA / SHUTTERSTOCK ©

monumental frieze celebrating the birth of Athena. En route to the West Stairs is a huge ❹ **Bust of Pharaoh Ramesses II**, just a hint of the large collection of ❺ **Egyptian mummies** upstairs. (The earliest, affectionately called Ginger because of wispy reddish hair, was preserved simply by hot sand.) The Romans introduce visitors to the early Britain galleries via the rich ❻ **Mildenhall Treasure**. The Anglo-Saxon ❼ **Sutton Hoo Ship Burial** and the medieval ❽ **Lewis Chessmen** follow.

EATING OPTIONS

Court Cafe At the northern end of the Great Court; takeaway counters with salads and sandwiches; communal tables.

Gallery Pizzeria Out of the way off room 12; quieter; children's menu available.

Great Court Restaurant Upstairs overlooking the former Reading Room; sit-down meals.

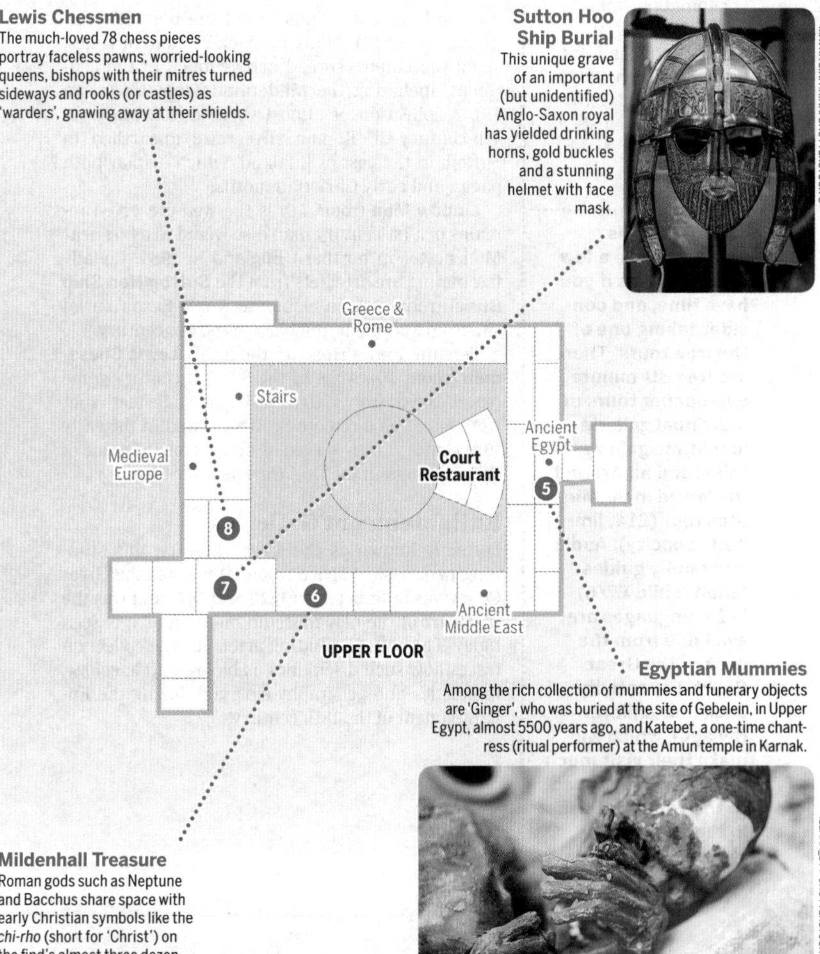

Lewis Chessmen
The much-loved 78 chess pieces portray faceless pawns, worried-looking queens, bishops with their mitres turned sideways and rooks (or castles) as 'warders', gnawing away at their shields.

Sutton Hoo Ship Burial
This unique grave of an important (but unidentified) Anglo-Saxon royal has yielded drinking horns, gold buckles and a stunning helmet with face mask.

Egyptian Mummies
Among the rich collection of mummies and funerary objects are 'Ginger', who was buried at the site of Gebelein, in Upper Egypt, almost 5500 years ago, and Katebet, a one-time chantress (ritual performer) at the Amun temple in Karnak.

Mildenhall Treasure
Roman gods such as Neptune and Bacchus share space with early Christian symbols like the *chi-rho* (short for 'Christ') on the find's almost three dozen silver bowls, plates and spoons.

TAKE A BREAK

The British Museum is vast, so you'll need to recharge. **Abeno** (Map p444; 020-7405 3211; www.abeno.co.uk; 47 Museum St; mains £13-21; noon-10pm; Holborn) is nearby for scrumptious savoury pancakes and other dishes from Japan.

For something more traditional, enjoy a cream tea at Tea & Tattle (p111), which is just across the road from the Great Russell St entrance.

The museum is huge, so make a few focused visits if you have time, and consider taking one of the free tours. There are free 30-minute Eye-opener tours of individual galleries, lunchtime gallery talks, and an Around the World in 90 Minutes tour (£14, limited capacity). Audio and family guides (adult/child £7/6) in 10 languages are available from the desk in the Great Court. For activity packs for children (by age), which will make their visit much more engaging, head to the Families Desk in the Great Hall.

from the 7th century BCE, which influenced Greek sculpture. Such antiquities are all the more significant after the Islamic State's bulldozing of Nimrud, Iraq, in 2015.

A major highlight of the museum is the **Parthenon sculptures** (room 18). The 80m-long marble frieze is thought to be of the Great Panathenaea, a festival in honour of the Greek goddess Athena held every four years.

The star of the show is the **Ancient Egypt collection** on Level 3. It comprises sculptures, fine jewellery, papyrus texts, coffins and mummies, including the beautiful and intriguing **Mummy of Katebet** (room 63).

Roman & Medieval Britain

Also on Level 3 are finds from Britain and Europe (rooms 40 to 51). Many go back to Roman times, when the empire spread across much of the continent, including the **Mildenhall Treasure** (room 49), a collection of almost three dozen pieces of 4th-century-CE Roman silverware unearthed in Suffolk in the east of England, which display both pagan and early Christian motifs.

Lindow Man (room 50) is the well-preserved remains of a 1st-century man discovered in a bog near Manchester in northern England in 1984. Equally fascinating are artefacts from the **Sutton Hoo Ship Burial** (room 41), an elaborate Anglo-Saxon burial site from Suffolk dating back to the 7th century.

Perennial favourites are the lovely **Lewis Chessmen** (room 40), some of the 82 12th-century game pieces carved from walrus tusk and whale teeth that were found on a remote Scottish island in the early 19th century. They served as models for the game of Wizard Chess in the first *Harry Potter* film.

Enlightenment Galleries

Formerly known as the King's Library, this stunning neoclassical space (room 1) just off the Great Court was built between 1823 and 1827 and was the first part of the new museum building as it is seen today. Through fascinating artefacts, the collection traces how such disciplines as biology, archaeology, linguistics and geography emerged during the Enlightenment of the 18th century.

LUKASZ PAJOR/SHUTTERSTOCK ©

TOP EXPERIENCE

FEEL ROYAL AT BUCKINGHAM PALACE

Built in 1703 for the Duke of Buckingham and then purchased by King George III, the palace has been the Royal Family's London lodgings since 1837 when Queen Victoria moved in. Commoners can get a peek at the State Rooms – a mere 19 of the palace's 775 rooms – from mid-July to September when Her Majesty is on holiday in Scotland.

State Rooms

The tour starts in the **Grand Hall** at the foot of the monumental **Grand Staircase**, commissioned by King George IV in 1828. It takes in architect John Nash's Italianate **Green Drawing Room**, the **State Dining Room** (all red damask and Regency furnishings), the **Blue Drawing Room** (which has a gorgeous fluted ceiling by Nash) and the **White Drawing Room**, where foreign ambassadors are received.

Admission includes entry to a themed special exhibition (royal couture during the Queen's reign, growing up at the palace etc) in the enormous **Ballroom**, built between 1853 and 1855, and these displays are often the main reason for a visit. The **Throne Room** is rather anticlimactic, with his-and-her pink chairs monogrammed 'ER' and 'P'.

Picture Gallery & Gardens

The 47m-long **Picture Gallery** features works by artists such as Anthony van Dyck, Rembrandt, Rubens, Canaletto, Nicolas Poussin, Antonio Canova and Johannes Vermeer.

Wandering the **gardens** at the end of the tour is another highlight – in addition to admiring some of the 350 or so species of flowers and plants, you'll get beautiful views of the palace and a peek at its famous lake. For an idea of the garden's full size (16 hectares), you'll need to join the three-hour State Rooms & Garden Highlights Tour.

DON'T MISS

- White Drawing Room
- Rotating exhibition in the Ballroom
- Picture Gallery
- Palace gardens
- Royal Mews

PRACTICALITIES

- Map p448, A4
- %0303 123 7300
- www.rct.uk/visit/the-state-rooms-buckingham-palace
- Buckingham Palace Rd
- adult/child/under 5yr £26.50/14.50/free, incl Royal Mews & Queen's Gallery £49/26.50/free
- 9am-6pm mid-Jul–end Sep
- U Green Park or St James's Park

TAKE A BREAK

Make a booking at The Other Naughty Piglet (p110) for a fixed-price lunch menu (two courses £18) of small-plate-style dining in this open-plan bistro, inside The Other Palace Theatre. Fish, meat and wine are all strong features of the seasonal menu.

Four royal babies have been christened in the palace's Music Room – the Prince of Wales (Prince Charles), the Princess Royal (Princess Anne), the Duke of York (Prince Andrew) and the Duke of Cambridge (Prince William) – with water brought from the River Jordan, where Jesus is said to have been baptised.

Queen's Gallery

Since the reign of King Charles I, the Royal Family has amassed a priceless collection of paintings, sculpture, ceramics, furniture and jewellery, and the small **Queen's Gallery** (Map p448; www.rct.uk/visit/the-queens-gallery-buckingham-palace; South Wing, Buckingham Palace, Buckingham Gate; adult/child £13.50/6.70; ⏲10am-5.30pm, from 9.30am mid-Jul–Sep; Ⓤ St James's Park or Green Park) showcases some of the palace's treasures on a rotating basis.

Originally on the site of the gallery, in the South Wing of Buckingham Palace, was a conservatory designed by Welsh architect John Nash. It was converted into a chapel for Queen Victoria in 1843, destroyed in a 1940 air raid and reopened as a gallery in 1962. A £20-million renovation for Queen Elizabeth II's Golden Jubilee in 2002 added three times more display space.

Royal Mews

Southwest of the palace, the **Royal Mews** (Map p448; www.rct.uk/visit/royalmews; Buckingham Palace Rd; adult/child £13/7.50; ⏲10am-5pm Apr-Oct, to 4pm Mon-Sat Feb, Mar & Nov; Ⓤ Victoria) started life as a falconry but is now a working stable looking after the Royal Family's immaculately groomed horses, along with the opulent vehicles the monarch uses for transport. The Queen is well known for her passion for horses; she names every steed that resides at the mews.

Highlights include the enormous and opulent Gold State Coach of 1762, used for every coronation since that of King George IV in 1821; the 2014 Diamond Jubilee State Coach (the newest in the fleet); and the stunning 1820s stables where you might spot some of the Windsor Greys or Cleveland Bays.

Changing of the Guard

The pageantry of soldiers in red uniforms and bearskin hats parading down the Mall and into Buckingham Palace is madly popular with tourists. The 45-minute ceremony (www.royal.uk/changing-guard; Buckingham Palace, Buckingham Palace Rd; ⏲11am Mon, Wed, Fri, Sun Aug-May, 11am daily Jun & Jul; Ⓤ St James's Park or Green Park) FREE swaps out the Old Guard (Foot Guards of the Household Regiment) with the New Guard on the forecourt, and ends with a full military band. The pomp and circumstance can feel far away when you're in row 15, trying to watch through a forest of selfie sticks, so get here at least 45 minutes before the main event. Check the calendar online (www.changing-guard.com/dates-buckingham-palace.html), as the ceremony is sometimes cancelled due to bad weather or road closures.

TOP EXPERIENCE

EXPLORE THE HOUSES OF PARLIAMENT

Both the elected House of Commons and the House of Lords, who are appointed or hereditary, sit in the sumptuous Palace of Westminster, a neo-Gothic confection dating from the mid-19th century (with a few sections that survived a catastrophic fire in 1834). A visit here is a journey to the very heart of British democracy.

Towers

The most famous feature of the Houses of Parliament is the Clock Tower, officially named the Elizabeth Tower to mark the Queen's Diamond Jubilee in 2012 but commonly known as **Big Ben** (www.parliament.uk/visiting/visiting-and-tours/tours-of-parliament/bigben; Bridge St). Big Ben is actually the 13.7-tonne bell hanging inside and is named after Benjamin Hall, the first Commissioner of Works when the tower was completed in 1859. On the southern end, at the base of the Victoria Tower, the tallest tower at the palace, is the **Sovereign's Entrance**, which is used by the Queen.

Westminster Hall

One of the most interesting features of the Palace of Westminster, the seat of the English monarchy from the 11th to the early 16th centuries, is **Westminster Hall**. Originally built in 1097, it is the oldest surviving part of the complex; the awesome hammer-beam roof was added between 1393 and 1401 and is the largest medieval timber roof in northern Europe. The only other part of the original palace to survive the devastating 1834 fire is the **Jewel Tower** (☎020-7222 2219; www.english-heritage.org.uk/visit/places/jewel-tower; Abingdon St; adult/child £5.40/3.30; ⏲10am-6pm Apr-Sep, to 5pm Oct, to 4pm Sat & Sun Nov-Mar), built in 1365 and used to store the monarch's valuables.

DON'T MISS

- Westminster Hall's hammer-beam roof
- The 'Tudor Gothic' interior
- Elizabeth Tower & Big Ben
- Sovereign's Entrance
- Joining a tour

PRACTICALITIES

- Map p448, E4
- ☎tours 020-7219 4114
- www.parliament.uk
- Parliament Sq
- guided tour adult/child £26.50/11.50, audio-guide tour £19.50/free
- Ⓤ Westminster

1

2

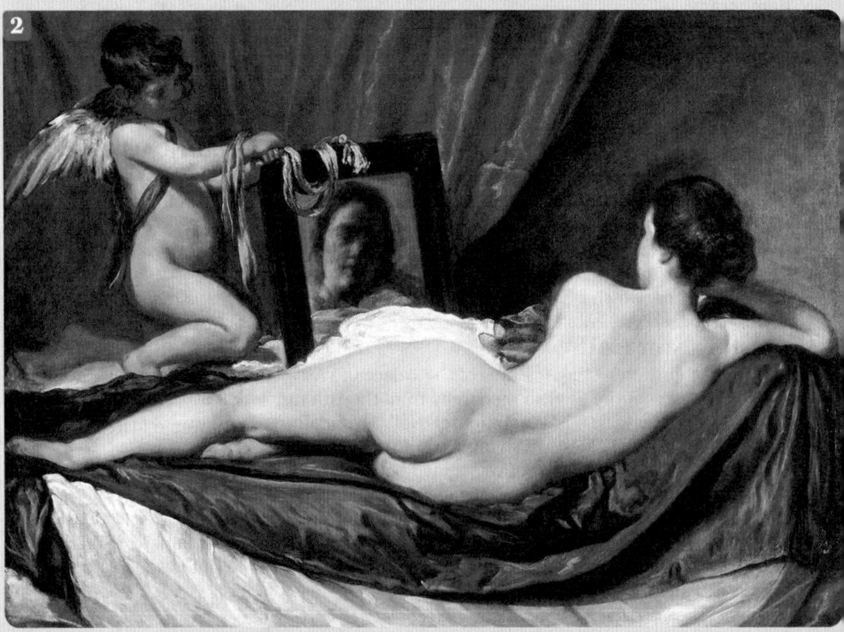

1. *The Fighting Temeraire* by John William Turner **2.** *The Rokeby Venus* by Diego Velázquez **3.** *Sunflowers* by Vincent Van Gogh

National Gallery Masterpieces

The National Gallery's collection spans seven centuries of European painting in a whirl of 2300-odd tableaux displayed in sumptuous, airy galleries. All are masterpieces, but some stand out for their sheer beauty and brilliance.

Venus & Mars, Botticelli

Venus, goddess of love, upright and alert, stares intently at Mars, god of war, fast asleep after they've made love. The message: make love not war, because love conquers all.

Sunflowers, Van Gogh

This instantly recognisable masterpiece, one of four by the great Dutch post-impressionist, depicts 14 sunflowers at different stages of life. The main colour – yellow – is applied thickly, a bold new 'sculptural' approach to painting.

Rokeby Venus, Velázquez

A a rare subject during the Spanish Inquisition, a self-absorbed Venus is gazing at herself – and us – in a mirror held by her son Cupid.

Arnolfini Portrait, Van Eyck

This is history's first bourgeois portrait, an early example of the use of oils and a revolutionary way to create space by painting light. It shows a rich Bruges merchant and his wife, who, despite looking pregnant, is making a fashion statement with her voluminous attire.

Hay Wain, Constable

A horse-drawn wagon in the middle of a river is a romantic portrayal of England on the eve of the Industrial Revolution. Flecks of white paint ('Constable snow') reflect and create movement – a foretaste of impressionism.

Fighting Temeraire, Turner

Painted by JMW Turner in his 60s, this magnificent painting shows the ghostly ship Temeraire, a hero of Trafalgar, being towed to a ship-breaking yard in Rotherhithe. The sun goes down, the moon comes up; her world is ending and the age of industrialisation approaches.

TAKE A BREAK

Take afternoon tea in a riverside House of Commons room for an additional £30 (£15 for children). The House of Commons Members' Dining Room is sometimes open to the public too.

Better yet, consider booking lunch at the elegant Skylon (p170) in Southbank Centre with floor-to-ceiling window views of the Thames and skyline.

When Parliament is in session, visitors are welcome to attend debates. It's not unusual to have to wait for hours to access the chambers. The best (and busiest) time to watch a debate is during Prime Minister's Question Time at noon on Wednesday.

The debating style in the Commons is quite combative, but not all debates are flamboyant argumentative duelling matches – many are rather boring and long-winded.

Westminster Hall was used for coronation banquets in medieval times and served as a courthouse until the 19th century. The trials of William Wallace (1305), Thomas More (1535), Guy Fawkes (1606) and King Charles I (1649) took place here. In the 20th century, monarchs and Prime Minister Winston Churchill lay in state here after their deaths.

House of Commons

The House of Commons is where Members of Parliament (MPs) propose and discuss new legislation and grill the prime minister and other ministers.

The layout of the Commons Chamber is based on St Stephen's Chapel in the original Palace of Westminster. The chamber, designed by architect Giles Gilbert Scott, replaced the one destroyed by a 1941 bomb.

Although the Commons is a national assembly of 650 MPs, the chamber only has seating for 437. Government members sit to the right of the Speaker and Opposition members to the left.

House of Lords

The House of Lords is visited via the amusingly named Strangers' Gallery. The intricate 'Tudor Gothic' interior led its architect, Augustus Welby Pugin, to an early death from overwork and nervous strain in 1852.

The House of Lords contains Lords Spiritual, bishops of the Church of England, and Lords Temporal, who are appointed and hereditary.

Most (in fact 85%) of the 814 lords are life peers (appointed for their lifetime); among them are 186 'crossbench' members not affiliated to the main political parties. Hereditary peers number 92 as of 2020 and there are 26 bishops. Some 73% of the members of the House of Lords are men.

Tours

Visitors are welcome on Saturdays year-round and some weekdays during parliamentary recesses (Easter, summer and Christmas). Choose either a **self-guided audio tour** (adult/child £19.50/free) in one of nine languages (75 minutes) or a more comprehensive **90-minute guided tour** of both chambers, Westminster Hall and other historic buildings (English only).

A **60-minute child-focused tour** is also available (book this family-friendly tour early as numbers are limited). Check the changing schedules online. Tickets are sold from the office in front of Portcullis House on Victoria Embankment. UK residents can also approach their MPs to arrange a free tour.

ELROCE/SHUTTERSTOCK ©

TOP EXPERIENCE
MASTER THE ARTS AT THE NATIONAL GALLERY

With more than 2300 European paintings in its collection, this is one of the world's richest art galleries, with seminal paintings from the 13th to the mid-20th century, including works by Leonardo da Vinci, Michelangelo, Titian, Vincent van Gogh and Auguste Renoir.

The modern Sainsbury Wing on the gallery's western side, the newest part of the building, houses the oldest paintings, dating from 1200 to 1500. Here you will find largely religious works commissioned for private devotion, such as the stunning *Wilton Diptych* (alcove of room 51), as well as more unusual masterpieces such as Sandro Botticelli's *Venus & Mars* (room 58) and Jan van Eyck's *Arnolfini Portrait* (room 63). Leonardo da Vinci's *Virgin of the Rocks* (room 66) is a visual and technical masterpiece.

Works from the High Renaissance (1500–1600) embellish rooms 2 to 14, where Michelangelo, Titian, Raphael, Correggio, El Greco and Bronzino hold court; Rubens, Rembrandt and Caravaggio grace rooms 15 to 32 (1600–1700). Notable here are two self-portraits by Rembrandt (at age 34 and at 63, in room 22) and the beautiful *Rokeby Venus* by Diego Velázquez in room 30.

Many visitors flock to the eastern part of the gallery (1700–1930), where works by British artists such as Thomas Gainsborough, John Constable and JMW Turner, and seminal impressionist and post-impressionist masterpieces by Van Gogh, Renoir and Claude Monet await. Before you leave, don't miss the astonishing floor mosaics in the main vestibule.

DON'T MISS

- *Venus & Mars* by Sandro Botticelli (room 58)
- *Arnolfini Portrait* by Jan van Eyck (room 63)
- *Wilton Diptych* (alcove of room 51)
- *Rokeby Venus* by Diego Velázquez (room 30)
- *Sunflowers* by Vincent van Gogh (room 41)

PRACTICALITIES

- Map p438, B7
- 020-7747 2885
- www.nationalgallery.org.uk
- Trafalgar Sq
- admission free
- 10am-6pm Sat-Thu, to 9pm Fri
- Charing Cross

I WEI HUANG/SHUTTERSTOCK ©

TOP EXPERIENCE

FIND NATIONAL TREASURES AT TATE BRITAIN

The older and more venerable of the two Tate siblings celebrates British works from 1500 to the present, including those from Blake, Hogarth, Gainsborough, Barbara Hepworth, Whistler, Constable and Turner, as well as vibrant modern and contemporary pieces from Lucian Freud, Francis Bacon and Henry Moore.

The stars of the show at Tate Britain are, however, the light-infused visions of JMW Turner – 300 oil paintings and about 30,000 sketches and drawings bequeathed to the nation. The collection at Tate Britain constitutes a sweeping celebration of his work, including classics such as *The Scarlet Sunset* and *Norham Castle, Sunrise.*

There are also seminal works from Constable, Gainsborough and Reynolds, as well as the Pre-Raphaelites, including William Holman Hunt's *The Awakening Conscience,* John William Waterhouse's *The Lady of Shalott, Ophelia* by John Everett Millais and Edward Burne-Jones' *The Golden Stairs.* Look out also for Francis Bacon's *Three Studies for Figures at the Base of a Crucifixion.*

The prestigious and often controversial Turner Prize for contemporary art returned in late 2020 after a stint at Turner Contemporary in Margate.

DON'T MISS

- *The Scarlet Sunset* by JMW Turner
- *Three Studies for Figures at the Base of a Crucifixion* by Francis Bacon
- *Ophelia* by John Everett Millais
- *The Awakening Conscience* by William Holman Hunt

PRACTICALITIES

- Map p448, E7
- ☎020-7887 8888
- www.tate.org.uk/visit/tate-britain
- Millbank
- admission free
- 🕙10am-6pm
- Ⓤ Pimlico

PRETTYAWESOME/SHUTTERSTOCK ©

TOP EXPERIENCE
LOSE YOURSELF IN TRAFALGAR SQUARE

Trafalgar Square is the true centre of London, where rallies and marches take place, tens of thousands of revellers usher in the New Year and locals congregate for anything from pop-up open-air cinema to political protests.

It is dominated by the 52m-high **Nelson's Column**, which honours Admiral Horatio Nelson, who died leading the British fleet's heroic victory over Napoleon in 1805, and is ringed by four large **bronze lions** and many splendid buildings, including the National Gallery (p91) and St Martin-in-the-Fields church (p102). Here, too, is the latest (and no doubt zany) **Fourth Plinth**, a pedestal spotlighting a piece of modern art that is swapped out every 18 months. In March 2020, the 13th piece was revealed. By the British artist Heather Phillipson, the latest sculpture – a giant, unstable dollop of whipped cream topped with a cherry, a fly and a drone that's apparently filming onlookers – is titled *The End*.

Fountains were included in the square's designs to reduce the number of people who gather in the area and to deter riots. In case anything got out of hand, a small **police box** with a direct line to Scotland Yard and narrow windows to view the whole square was built in the southeast corner and is often called London's smallest police station.

DON'T MISS

- Nelson's Column
- Bronze lions
- Fourth Plinth sculpture
- London's smallest police station

PRACTICALITIES

- Map p438, B7
- U Charing Cross or Embankment

JOHN HARPER/GETTY IMAGES ©

TOP EXPERIENCE
VISIT THE CHURCHILL WAR ROOMS

In late August 1939, with war appearing imminent, the British cabinet and chiefs of the armed forces decided to move underground into a converted basement below what is now the Treasury. On 3 September Britain was at war.

The bunker served as nerve centre of the war cabinet until the end of WWII in 1945: here chiefs of staff ate, slept and plotted Hitler's downfall, believing they were protected from Luftwaffe bombs (it turns out the 3m slab of concrete above them would have crumpled had the area taken a direct hit).

The **Cabinet War Rooms** have been left much as they were on 15 August 1945. Many rooms have been preserved, including the room where the War Cabinet met 115 times; the Transatlantic Telegraph Room, with a hotline to US President Roosevelt; the converted broom cupboard that was Churchill's office-bedroom (though he slept here only three times); and the all-important Map Room, which was the operational centre.

The superb multimedia **Churchill Museum** in the centre doesn't shy away from its hero's foibles – it portrays the heavy-drinking Churchill as having a legendary temper, being a bit of a maverick and, on the whole, a pretty lousy peace-time politician. It does focus on his strongest suit: his stirring speeches.

DON'T MISS

- Map Room
- Anecdotes from former War Rooms staff
- Extracts from Churchill's famous speeches
- Churchill's office-bedroom
- The film footage of Churchill's funeral

PRACTICALITIES

- Map p448, D3
- ☎020-7416 5000
- www.iwm.org.uk/visits/churchill-war-rooms
- Clive Steps, King Charles St
- adult/child £23/11.50
- ⌚9.30am-6pm
- Ⓤ Westminster

TOP EXPERIENCE

DISCOVER SIR JOHN SOANE'S MUSEUM

This little museum is one of the most atmospheric and fascinating in London. The building is the bewitching home of architect Sir John Soane (1753–1837), which he left brimming with surprising personal effects and curiosities.

A professor of architecture at the Royal Academy, Soane designed the Bank of England, among other buildings. In his work, he drew on classical ideas picked up while on an 18th-century grand tour of Italy. After his marriage, Soane built his house-museum at No 12 Lincoln's Inn Fields, and eventually bought the one next door at No 13.

The heritage-listed house is itself a main part of the attraction. It has a canopy dome that brings light right down to the crypt, a colonnade filled with statuary and a picture gallery. This is where Soane's choicest artwork is displayed, including paintings by Canaletto and the original *A Rake's Progress,* William Hogarth's set of satirical cartoons of late-18th-century London lowlife. Among Soane's more unusual acquisitions are the sarcophagus of the Egyptian Pharaoh Seti I and his precious Model Room, located in his private apartment on the 2nd floor of the house.

The hour-long **Highlights Tour** (£15), which includes the private apartments and Model Room, is pre-bookable online.

DON'T MISS

- *A Rake's Progress* by William Hogarth
- Sarcophagus of Pharaoh Seti I
- *Riva degli Schiavoni, Looking West* by Canaletto
- Model Room

PRACTICALITIES

- Map p438, E2
- 020-7405 2107
- www.soane.org
- 13 Lincoln's Inn Fields
- admission free
- 10am-5pm Wed-Sun
- Holborn

SIGHTS

Westminster

WESTMINSTER ABBEY CHURCH

See p78.

HOUSES OF PARLIAMENT HISTORIC BUILDING

See p87.

ST MARGARET'S CHURCH CHURCH

Map p448 (020-7654 4840; www.westminster-abbey.org/st-margarets-church; 9.30am-3.30pm Mon-Fri, to 1.30pm Sat, 2-4.30pm Sun; Westminster) Adjacent to Westminster Abbey is St Margaret's Church, the House of Commons' place of worship since 1614, where windows commemorate churchgoers Caxton and Milton, and Sir Walter Raleigh is buried by the altar. It can look insubstantial alongside the vast abbey, but it was constructed next to the abbey run by Benedictine monks to serve the spiritual needs of the common people. It is the third church dedicated to St Margaret to stand at this spot since the end of the 11th century.

WESTMINSTER CATHEDRAL CHURCH

Map p448 (020-7798 9055; www.westminstercathedral.org.uk; Victoria St; adult/child tower £6/3, treasury £5/2.50, combined £9/4.50; church 7am-7pm Mon-Fri, from 8am Sat & Sun, bell tower & treasury 9.30am-5pm Mon-Fri, to 6pm Sat & Sun; Victoria) With its distinctive candy-striped red-brick and white-stone tower features, John Francis Bentley's 19th-century Cathedral of the Most Precious Blood, the mother church of Roman Catholicism in England and Wales, is a splendid example of neo-Byzantine architecture. Although construction started here in 1895 and worshippers began attending services seven years later, the church ran out of money and the sparse interior remains largely unfinished, although some radiant mosaics dazzle from the altar and side chapels.

The **Chapel of the Blessed Sacrament**, to the left of the main altar, is ablaze with Eastern Rite mosaics and ornamented with 100 types of marble; the arched ceiling of the **Lady Chapel** on the other side of the main altar is also richly presented. Some other areas of the church remain unfaced brick.

The highly regarded stone bas-reliefs of the **Stations of the Cross** (1918) by Eric Gill and the marvellously sombre atmosphere make this a welcome haven from the traffic outside. The views from the viewing gallery 64m (210ft) up in the 83m (272ft) **bell tower** – thankfully, accessible by lift – are impressive. The church plate and ecclesiastical objects on display in the **Treasury** are a delight and there's a **cafe** near the Baptistery to the right as you enter. Several Masses are held daily, including one in Latin (usually at 10.30am), and one accompanied by the cathedral's choir (at 5.30pm or 6pm); check the website for the details.

SUPREME COURT LANDMARK

Map p448 (020-7960 1900; www.supremecourt.uk; Parliament Sq; 9.30am-4.30pm Mon-Fri; Westminster) FREE The Supreme Court, the highest court in the UK, was the Appellate Committee of the House of Lords until 2009. It is now housed in the neo-Gothic Middlesex Guildhall (1913) on Parliament Sq. There's a permanent exhibition looking at the work and history of the court as well as the building's history on the lower ground floor. There's a self-guided tour booklet (£1) or guided tours (adult/child £7/free) at 11am, 2pm and 3pm on Friday.

During the Supreme Court's summer recess (August to early September), there are also tours at 11am and 2pm on most weekdays. Members of the public are welcome to observe cases when the court is sitting (11am to 4pm Monday, 10.30am to 4pm Tuesday to Thursday). For who or what's on trial, ask for a list at reception, or go to the 'Current Cases' section of the Supreme Court website.

Bloomsbury & Fitzrovia

BRITISH MUSEUM MUSEUM

See p81.

ALL SAINTS MARGARET STREET CHURCH

Map p444 (020-7636 1788; www.allsaintsmargaretstreet.org.uk; 7 Margaret St; 7am-7pm Mon, Tue, Thu & Fri, from 8.30am Wed, from 11am Sat; Oxford Circus) In 1859 architect William Butterfield completed one of the country's most supreme examples of High Victorian Gothic architecture, with extraordinary tiling and sumptuous stained glass. All Saints was selected by the head of English Heritage in 2014 as one of the top 10 buildings in the UK that have changed the face of the nation, a list that included Westminster Abbey and Christ Church in Oxford.

CHARLES DICKENS MUSEUM

MUSEUM

Map p444 (☎020-7405 2127; www.dickensmuseum.com; 48-49 Doughty St; adult/child £9.50/4.50; ⏰10am-5pm Tue-Sun, plus Mon in Dec; 📶; ⓤRussell Sq or Chancery Lane) The prolific writer Charles Dickens lived with his growing family in this handsome four-storey Georgian terraced house for a mere 2½ years (1837–39), but this is where his work really flourished, as here he completed *The Pickwick Papers*, *Nicholas Nickleby* and *Oliver Twist*. Each of the dozen rooms, some restored to their original condition, contains various memorabilia, including the study where you'll find the desk at which Dickens wrote *Great Expectations*.

Though many places in London claim to have a Dickens connection, this address is his sole surviving residence in town. The house was saved from demolition, and the museum opened in 1925.

The charming **Garden Cafe** is free to visit, without requiring admission to the museum. One night a month the museum is open until 8pm (check the calendar on the website), with the last admission at 7pm.

ST GEORGE'S HANOVER SQUARE

CHURCH

Map p440 (☎020-7629 9874; www.stgeorgeshanoversquare.org; St George St; ⏰8am-4pm Mon, Tue, Thu & Fri, to 6pm Wed, to noon Sun; ⓤOxford St) Built in 1724 as one of 50 churches projected by Queen Anne's Act of 1710, St George's has hosted more than a few society weddings over the years; among those married here were Lady Hamilton, Shelley, Disraeli, George Eliot and, in 1886, the 26th president of the USA, Theodore Roosevelt. It's also the church referred to in the song 'Get Me to the Church on Time' in the musical *My Fair Lady*.

Inside there's a reredos carved by Grinling Gibbons and an altarpiece of the *Last Supper* attributed to William Kent.

POLLOCK'S TOY MUSEUM

MUSEUM

Map p444 (☎020-7636 3452; www.pollockstoys.com; 1 Scala St; adult/child £7/4; ⏰10am-5pm Mon-Sat; ⓤGoodge St) Aimed at adults as much as (older) kids, this museum is simultaneously creepy and mesmerising. You walk in through its shop, laden with excellent wooden toys and various games, and start your exploration by climbing up a rickety narrow staircase, where displays begin with mechanical toys, puppets and framed dolls from Latin America, Africa, India and Europe.

PETRIE MUSEUM OF EGYPTIAN ARCHAEOLOGY

MUSEUM

Map p444 (UCL; ☎020-7679 2884; www.ucl.ac.uk/culture/petrie-museum; University College London, Malet Pl; ⏰1-5pm Tue-Sat; ⓤGoodge St) FREE With some 80,000 artefacts, this is one of the most impressive collections of Egyptian and Sudanese archaeology in the world. The old-fashioned displays in glass cases and outdated presentation don't really do much to highlight them, though. University College London runs free weekly public tours of this, the Grant Museum of Zoology and the UCL Art Museum.

ST GEORGE'S BLOOMSBURY

CHURCH

Map p444 (☎020-7242 1979; www.stgeorgesbloomsbury.org.uk; Bloomsbury Way; ⏰1-4pm; ⓤHolborn or Tottenham Court Rd) One of a half-dozen designed by Nicholas Hawksmoor, this superbly restored church (1730) is distinguished by its classical portico of Corinthian capitals and a steeple (visible in William Hogarth's satirical painting *Gin Lane*) inspired by the Mausoleum of Halicarnassus (now Bodrum in Turkey). The statue atop the steeple is of King George I in Roman dress, while lions and unicorns scamper about its base. Guided tours of the church (£5) must be booked ahead.

FOUNDLING MUSEUM

MUSEUM

Map p444 (☎020-7841 3600; https://foundlingmuseum.org.uk; 40 Brunswick Sq; adult/child £9.50/free; ⏰10am-5pm Tue-Sat, from 11am Sun; ⓤRussell Sq) Thomas Coram established the Foundling Hospital in 1739 for children abandoned or handed over by their mothers; when it closed in 1953 it had been the home of 27,000 children. The museum in its place traces the history

LITERARY BLOOMSBURY

Bloomsbury's beautiful squares were once colonised by the so-called Bloomsbury Group, a coterie of artists and writers that included Virginia Woolf and EM Forster, whose intricate love affairs were as fascinating as their books. Charles Dickens, Charles Darwin, William Butler Yeats and George Bernard Shaw also lived in this district, as attested by the many blue plaques you'll spot around the 'hood.

Bedford Square (Map p444; ⓤTottenham Court Rd) was home to many London publishing houses until the 1990s, when they were swallowed up by multinational conglomerates, and relocated. They included Jonathan Cape, Chatto and the Bodley Head (set up by Woolf and her husband Leonard), and were largely responsible for perpetuating interest in the Bloomsbury Group by churning out seemingly endless collections of associated letters, memoirs and biographies.

Today Bloomsbury contains some excellent streetscapes, speciality stores, bookshops and cafes, while remaining relatively undeveloped.

of the hospital and the children who lived here; particularly moving is the collection of amulets left behind by mothers for their children to remember them by. The Georgian interior also contains a wonderful art gallery.

ST PANCRAS CHURCH — CHURCH

Map p444 (☎020-7388 1461; http://stpancraschurch.org; cnr Euston Rd & Upper Woburn Pl; ⊙8am-6pm Mon-Fri, 7.30-11.30am & 5.30-7pm Sun; ⓤEuston) This striking Greek Revival church has a tower designed to imitate the Temple of the Winds in Athens, a portico with six Ionic columns and a wing decorated with caryatids like the Erechtheion on the Acropolis. When it was completed in 1822 this was the most expensive new church to have been built in London since St Paul's Cathedral. Head to the atmospheric Crypt Gallery to see the latest art exhibition or drop in to a free lunchtime recital on a Thursday (1.15pm).

WIENER LIBRARY — MUSEUM

Map p444 (☎020-7636 7247; www.wienerlibrary.co.uk; 29 Russell Sq; ⊙10am-5pm Mon & Wed-Fri, to 7.30pm Tue; ⓤRussell Sq) FREE The Wiener Library was established by German Alfred Wiener in 1933 to document the rise of anti-Semitism in his home country, from which he had fled in the face of Nazi persecution. It's the world's oldest institution dedicated to the study of the Holocaust. Now a public library and research institute, it contains over a million items relating to one of history's darkest periods. Free one-hour public tours are held on Tuesdays at 1pm.

GRANT MUSEUM OF ZOOLOGY — MUSEUM

Map p444 (www.ucl.ac.uk/culture/grant-museum-zoology; Rockefeller Bldg, University College London, 21 University St; ⊙1-5pm Mon-Sat; ⓤEuston Sq) FREE This fascinating and little-known museum contains 68,000 specimens from the animal kingdom, including many that are extinct or critically endangered. Items of particular interest include the very rare skeleton of a quagga (an extinct South African zebra), the bones of a dodo and a Tasmanian tiger (an extinct dog-like striped marsupial), plus a riveting collection of bisected animal heads. The Micrarium displays back-lit microscope slides framing more than 20,000 tiny objects, including the hair of a woolly mammoth.

⊙ St James's

BUCKINGHAM PALACE — PALACE

See p85.

TATE BRITAIN — GALLERY

See p92.

ST JAMES'S PICCADILLY — CHURCH

Map p448 (☎020-7734 4511; www.sjp.org.uk; 197 Piccadilly; ⊙8am-8pm; ⓤPiccadilly Circus) The only church (1684) Christopher Wren built from scratch and one of a handful established on a new site (most of the other London churches are replacements for those destroyed in the Great Fire), this simple building substitutes what some might call the pompous flourishes of Wren's most famous churches with a warm and elegant accessibility. The baptismal font portraying Adam and Eve on the shaft and the altar reredos are by Grinling Gibbons.

This is a wonderfully sociable and charitable church; it houses a counselling service, provides a night shelter for the homeless in winter (they can sleep in the pews), stages lunchtime and evening concerts, and hosts a **food market** (10am to 3.30pm Monday and Tuesday) and an **arts and crafts fair** (10am to 6pm Wednesday to Saturday) in the forecourt. Note the arresting bronze Statue of Peace in the garden. It costs £1800 per day to run this generous church. Consider leaving a donation, however small.

ST JAMES'S PARK — PARK

Map p448 (www.royalparks.org.uk/parks/st-jamess-park; The Mall; ⏲5am-midnight; Ⓤ St James's Park or Green Park) At 23 hectares, St James's is the second-smallest of the eight royal parks after Green Park. But what it lacks in size it makes up for in grooming, as it is the most manicured green space in London. It has brilliant views of the London Eye, Westminster, St James's Palace, Carlton House Terrace and Horse Guards Parade; the picture-perfect sight of Buckingham Palace from the **Blue Bridge** spanning the central lake is the best you'll find.

The lake brims with ducks, geese, swans and other waterfowl – including the famous **pelicans**, introduced to the park in 1664 as a gift from the Russian Ambassador to King Charles II. The pelicans are fed fresh fish between 2.30pm and 3pm near Duck Island cottage.

The brightly coloured flower beds – scarlet geraniums, red tulips and yellow wallflowers – near Buckingham Palace were added in 1901 as a memorial to Queen Victoria. You can rent **deckchairs** during daylight hours from March to October (per hour/day £2/10) to make lounging around more comfortable.

BURLINGTON ARCADE — HISTORIC BUILDING

Map p448 (www.burlingtonarcade.com; 51 Piccadilly; ⏲9am-7.30pm Mon-Sat, 11am-6pm Sun; Ⓤ Green Park) Flanking Burlington House, which is home to the Royal Academy of Arts (p104), is this delightful arcade, built in 1819. Today it is a shopping precinct for the wealthy, and is most famous for the Burlington Beadles, uniformed guards who patrol the area keeping an eye out for such offences as running, chewing gum, whistling, opening umbrellas or anything else that could lower the tone. (The fact that the arcade once served as a brothel is kept quiet.)

Running perpendicular to it between Old Bond and Albemarle Sts is the more recent 1880 Royal Arcade.

CLARENCE HOUSE — PALACE

Map p448 (☎0303 123 7300; www.rct.uk/visit/clarence-house; Cleveland Row; adult/child £11.30/6.80; ⏲10am-4.30pm Mon-Fri, to 5.30pm Sat & Sun Aug only; Ⓤ Green Park) Five ground-floor rooms of Clarence House, the official residence of Charles, the Prince of Wales, and his consort, Camilla, the Duchess of Cornwall, are open to the public on 45-minute guided tours for one month in summer. The highlight is the late Queen Mother's small art collection, including one painting by playwright Noël Coward and others by WS Sickert and Sir James Gunn. The house was originally designed by John Nash in the early 19th century but has been modified a lot since.

SPENCER HOUSE — HISTORIC BUILDING

Map p448 (☎020-7514 1958; www.spencerhouse.co.uk; 27 St James's Pl; adult/child £15.50/12.50; ⏲10am-4.30pm Sun; Ⓤ Green Park) Just outside the borders of Green Park is Spencer House, completed in the Palladian style in 1766 for the first Earl Spencer, an ancestor of the late Princess Diana. The Spencers moved out in 1927 and their grand family home was used as an office, until Lord Rothschild stepped in and returned it to its former glory in 1987 with an £18-million restoration. Visits to the eight lavishly furnished state rooms designed by John Vardy and James 'Athenian' Stuart are by guided tour only.

The 18th-century gardens are open only between 2pm and 5pm on a couple of Sundays in summer; consult the 'What's On' section of the website for details.

GREEN PARK — PARK

Map p448 (www.royalparks.org.uk/parks/green-park; ⏲5am-midnight; Ⓤ Green Park) At 19 hectares, Green Park is the smallest of the eight royal parks. It has huge plane and oak trees and undulating meadows, and it's never as crowded as its neighbour, the more manicured St James's Park. It was once a duelling ground and, like Hyde

Park (p184), served as a vegetable garden during WWII.

It famously has no flower beds as they were banned by Queen Catherine of Braganza after she learned her philandering husband Charles II had been picking posies for his mistresses. Or so the story goes...

GUARDS MUSEUM MUSEUM

Map p448 (☎020-7414 3428; www.theguardsmuseum.com; Wellington Barracks, Birdcage Walk; adult/child £8/free; ⏲10am-4pm; ⓤSt James's Park) Take stock of the history of the five regiments of foot guards (Grenadier, Coldstream, Scots, Irish and Welsh Guards) and their role in military campaigns from Waterloo onwards at this little museum in Wellington Barracks. There are uniforms, oil paintings, medals, curios and memorabilia that belonged to the soldiers. Perhaps the biggest draw is the huge collection of toy soldiers for sale in the shop. Don't miss the adjoining Royal Military Chapel flattened by a bomb in June 1944.

If you found the crowds at the Changing the Guard (p104) ceremony overwhelming and didn't see much, get here at 10.30am on any day of the change to see the soldiers of the New Guard muster and get into formation outside the museum, be inspected 20 minutes later, and depart just before 11am for their march over to Buckingham Palace to relieve the Old Guard.

INSTITUTE OF CONTEMPORARY ARTS ARTS CENTRE

Map p448 (ICA; ☎020-7930 3647; www.ica.art; Nash House, The Mall; £5, Tue free; ⏲noon-9pm Tue-Sun; 📶; ⓤCharing Cross) Housed in a Regency building designed by John Nash along the Mall, the untraditional ICA is where Picasso and Henry Moore had their first UK shows. Since then the ICA has been on the cutting (and controversial) edge of the British arts world, with an excellent range of experimental and progressive films, music nights, photography, art, lectures, multimedia works and book readings. There's also the licensed ICA Cafe Bar and a small bookshop.

⊙ Soho & Chinatown

SOHO AREA

Map p440 (ⓤTottenham Court Rd or Leicester Sq) In a district that was once pastureland, the name Soho is thought to have evolved from a hunting cry. While the centre of London nightlife has shifted east, and Soho has recently seen landmark clubs and music venues shut down, the neighbourhood definitely comes into its own in the evenings and remains a proud gay district. You'll be charmed by the area's vitality during the day too.

At Soho's northern end, leafy **Soho Square** is the area's back garden. It was laid out in 1681 and originally called King's Sq; a statue of Charles II stands in its northern half. In the centre is a tiny half-timbered mock-Tudor cottage built as a gardener's shed in the 1870s. The space below it was used as an underground bomb shelter during WWII.

South of the square is **Dean Street**, lined with bars and restaurants. No 28 was the home of Karl Marx and his family from 1851 to 1856; they lived here in extreme poverty as Marx researched and wrote *Das Kapital* in the Reading Room of the British Museum.

Old Compton Street is the epicentre of Soho's gay village. It's a street loved by all, gay or other, for its great bars, risqué shops and general good vibes.

Seducer and heartbreaker Casanova and opium-addicted writer Thomas de Quincey lived on nearby **Greek Street**, while the parallel **Frith Street** housed Mozart at No 20 for a year from 1764.

PICCADILLY CIRCUS SQUARE

Map p440 (ⓤPiccadilly Circus) Architect John Nash had originally designed Regent St and Piccadilly in the 1820s to be the two most elegant streets in London but, restrained by city planners, he couldn't fully realise his dream. He may be disappointed, but suitably astonished, by Piccadilly Circus today: a traffic maelstrom, deluged by visitors and flanked by high-tech advertisements.

Piccadilly Circus has become a postcard for the city, buzzing with the liveliness that makes it exciting to be in London. 'Piccadilly' was named in the 17th century for piccadills, the stiff collars that were the must-have accessory at the time (and were the making of a nearby tailor's fortune), while 'Circus' comes from the Latin word for ring or circle.

At the centre of Piccadilly Circus stands the famous aluminium statue mistakenly called **Eros** as it actually portrays his twin

SEX, DRUGS & ROCK 'N' ROLL: THE HISTORY OF SOHO

Soho's character was moulded by successive waves of immigration. Residential development started in the 17th century, after the Great Fire of 1666 had levelled much of the city. Greek and Huguenot refugees, and later the 18th-century influx of Italian, Chinese and other artisans and radicals into Soho, replaced the bourgeois residents, who moved into neighbouring Mayfair. During the following century, Soho was little more than a slum, beset by cholera and squalor. Despite its difficulties, the cosmopolitan vibe attracted writers and artists, and the overcrowded area became a centre for entertainment, with restaurants, taverns and coffee houses springing up. The squalor also helped incubate radical ideas: Karl Marx lived in shocking poverty at 28 Dean St between 1851 and 1856.

The 20th century was even more raucous, when a fresh wave of European immigrants settled in, making Soho a bona-fide bohemian enclave for the two decades after WWII. Ronnie Scott's famous jazz club, originally in Gerrard St, provided Soho's soundtrack from the 1950s, while the likes of Jimi Hendrix, the Rolling Stones and Pink Floyd had early gigs at the legendary Marquee club, which used to be on Wardour St. Soho had a long-held reputation for seediness, but when the hundreds of prostitutes who served the Square Mile were forced off the streets and into shop windows, it became the city's unofficial red-light district and a centre for porn, strip joints and bawdy clubs. LGBTIQ+ liberation soon followed, and by the 1980s Soho was the hub of London's gay scene, as it remains today. Despite the gentrification that is changing the face of Soho, it retains a real sense of community, best absorbed on a weekend morning when Soho almost feels like a village.

brother, Anteros. To add to the confusion, the figure is officially the 'Angel of Christian Charity' and dedicated to the philanthropist and social reformer Lord Shaftesbury. The sculpture was at first cast in gold but later replaced by newfangled aluminium, the first outdoor statue in that lightweight metal.

REGENT STREET — STREET

Map p440 (UPiccadilly Circus or Oxford St) The handsome border dividing the trainer-clad clubbers of Soho from the Gucci-heeled hedge-fund managers of Mayfair, Regent St was designed by John Nash as a ceremonial route linking Carlton House, the Prince Regent's long-demolished town residence, with the 'wilds' of Regent's Park. Nash had to downsize his plan and build the thoroughfare on a curve, but Regent St is today a well-subscribed shopping street lined with some lovely listed buildings.

Its anchor tenant is undoubtedly Hamleys, London's premier toy and game store. Regent St is also famous for its Christmas light displays, which get glowing with great pomp earlier and earlier (or so it seems) each year (usually around mid-November). The street is closed to traffic each Sunday in July for the so-called Summer Streets celebration.

PHOTOGRAPHERS' GALLERY — GALLERY

Map p440 (020-7087 9300; https://thephotographersgallery.org.uk; 16-18 Ramillies St; adult/child £5/free; 10am-6pm Mon-Sat, to 8pm Thu, 11am-6pm Sun; UOxford Circus) FREE With six galleries over five floors, an excellent cafe and a shop brimming with prints and photography books, the Photographers' Gallery is London's largest public gallery devoted to photography. It has awarded the prestigious Deutsche Börse Photography Foundation Prize, which is of major importance for contemporary photographers, annually since 1997. Admission is free after 5pm.

Past winners of the Deutsche Börse award have included Richard Billingham, Luc Delahaye, Andreas Gursky and Juergen Teller and, more recently, Richard Mosse and Trevor Paglen.

Covent Garden & Leicester Square

NATIONAL GALLERY — GALLERY

See p91.

TRAFALGAR SQUARE — SQUARE

See p93.

LONDON TRANSPORT MUSEUM

MUSEUM

Map p438 (☎020-7379 6344; www.ltmuseum.co.uk; Covent Garden Piazza; adult/child £18/free; ⏰10am-6pm; 👪; Ⓤ Covent Garden) Housed in Covent Garden's former flower-market building, this captivating museum looks at how London developed as a result of better transport. It's stuffed full of horse-drawn omnibuses, vintage Underground carriages with heritage maps, and old double-decker buses (some of which you can clamber through, making this something of a kids' playground). The **gift shop** also sells great London souvenirs such as retro Tube posters and pillows made from the same fabric as the train seats.

COVENT GARDEN PIAZZA

LANDMARK

Map p438 (☎020-7420 5856; www.coventgarden.london; Ⓤ Covent Garden) London's wholesale fruit-and-vegetable market until 1974 is now mostly the preserve of visitors, who flock here to shop among the quaint Italian-style arcades, eat and drink in the myriad cafes and restaurants, browse through eclectic market stalls in the Apple Market, toss coins at street performers on the West Piazza and traipse through the fun London Transport Museum.

The open square in front of St Paul's Church (nicknamed the Actors' Church) has long been a place of performance: even Samuel Pepys' diary from 1662 mentions an Italian puppet play with a character named Punch. The best views of the action today are from the upper terrace of the Punch & Judy pub.

An old painted noticeboard with rules and charges for vendors can still be found lurking in one of the alleys on the northern side, and black-and-white photos of Covent Garden's days as a food traders' market line the walls of the narrow passages.

The kitsch is hauled out for the quirky Rent Ceremony, in which the chairman and trustees strut around the piazza, accompanied by a town crier and live band, to pay Covent Garden's landlord the yearly rent of five red apples and five posies of flowers. It usually takes place in June.

ST PAUL'S CHURCH

CHURCH

Map p438 (☎020-7836 5221; http://actorschurch.org; Bedford St; ⏰8.30am-5.30pm Mon-Fri, 9am-1pm Sun, hours vary Sat; Ⓤ Covent Garden) When the Earl of Bedford commissioned Inigo Jones to design Covent Garden Piazza, he asked for a simple church 'not much better than a barn'; the architect responded by producing 'the handsomest barn in England'. Completed in 1633, St Paul's Church has long been known as the Actors' Church for its associations with all the nearby theatres.

Inside are memorials to the likes of Charlie Chaplin, Noël Coward, Peter O'Toole, Vivien Leigh and even Boris Karloff, who was born William Henry Pratt in Lewisham in 1887. The first Punch and Judy show took place in front of St Paul's in 1662; note the pub of that name with the balcony opposite.

ST MARTIN-IN-THE-FIELDS

CHURCH

Map p438 (☎020-7766 1100; www.stmartin-in-the-fields.org; Trafalgar Sq; ⏰8.30am-6pm Mon-Fri, from 9am Sat & Sun; Ⓤ Charing Cross) This parish church to the Royal Family is a delightful fusion of neoclassical and baroque styles. It was designed by architect James Gibbs, completed in 1726 and served as a model for many wooden churches in New England, USA. The church is well known for its excellent classical music concerts, many by candlelight (£9 to £32), and its links to the Chinese community (with services in English, Mandarin and Cantonese).

The wonderful **Cafe in the Crypt** hosts two-hour jazz evenings (£8 to £15; £3.50 standing tickets if concert sold out) at 8pm on Wednesday; there are also free lunchtime concerts at 1pm on Monday, Tuesday and Friday. The **shop** offers brass rubbing, an activity adored by the Victorians, in which paper is placed over a brass etching and coloured over with a wax crayon so you can take your own copy away (from £4.50).

In 2006 refurbishment excavations unearthed a 1.5-tonne limestone Roman sarcophagus from about 410 CE in the churchyard – a significant find, as this area was far outside the bounds of Roman Londinium.

LONDON FILM MUSEUM

MUSEUM

Map p438 (☎020-7202 7040; www.londonfilmmuseum.com; 45 Wellington St; adult/concessions/family £14.50/9.50/38; ⏰10am-6pm; Ⓤ Covent Garden) Dedicated solely to the

INNS OF COURT

Clustered around Holborn and just off Fleet St are the Inns of Court, with quiet alleys, open spaces and a serene atmosphere. All London barristers must work from within one of the four inns, and a roll-call of former members includes the likes of Oliver Cromwell, Charles Dickens, Mahatma Gandhi and Margaret Thatcher. It would take a lifetime working here to grasp all the intricacies of their arcane protocols, most of which originated in the 13th century. It's best just to soak up the dreamy ambience of the alleys and open spaces.

Lincoln's Inn (Map p438; 020-7405 1393; www.lincolnsinn.org.uk; Lincoln's Inn Fields, Serle St; grounds 7am-7pm Mon-Fri, chapel 9am-5pm Mon-Fri; Holborn) still has some original 15th-century buildings. It's the oldest and most attractive of the bunch, with a 17th-century chapel and pretty landscaped gardens.

Gray's Inn (Map p438; 020-7458 7800; www.graysinn.org.uk; Grays Inn Rd; garden noon-2.30pm Mon-Fri, chapel 11am-6pm Mon-Fri; Chancery Lane) was largely rebuilt after German bombs levelled it during WWII.

Middle Temple (p105) and **Inner Temple** (p105) both sit between Fleet St and Victoria Embankment. The former is the better preserved, while the latter is home to the intriguing 12th-century **Temple Church** (p105).

British film industry, the London Film Museum has a heavy focus on the James Bond franchise. You'll see 007 vehicles (more than two dozen on display) including James Bond's submersible Lotus Esprit (from *The Spy Who Loved Me*), the iconic Aston Martin DB5, Goldfinger's Rolls Royce Phantom III and Timothy Dalton's Aston Martin V8 (from *The Living Daylights*). Other exhibits display more personal curios, such as Bond's various passports.

LEICESTER SQUARE — SQUARE

Map p440 (Leicester Sq) Surrounded by cinemas that host regular film premieres (if you're there at the right time, there will be crowds by the red carpet), Leicester Sq is a heaving central hub of bars, restaurants and tourist shops. In addition to a statue of William Shakespeare, there's a summer splash fountain for kids and a pop-up Christmas market in winter.

Whitehall

CHURCHILL WAR ROOMS — MUSEUM

See p94.

NO 10 DOWNING STREET — HISTORIC BUILDING

Map p448 (www.number10.gov.uk; 10 Downing St; Westminster) The official office of British leaders since 1735, when King George II presented No 10 to 'First Lord of the Treasury' Robert Walpole, this has also been the prime minister's London residence since the late 19th century. For such a famous address, No 10 is a small-looking Georgian building on a plain-looking street, hardly warranting comparison with the White House, for example. Yet it is actually three houses joined into one and boasts roughly 100 rooms plus a 2000-sq-metre garden.

The street was cordoned off with a large gate during Prime Minister Margaret Thatcher's time, so you won't see much. After an IRA mortar attack in 1991, the stout wooden door was replaced with a blast-proof steel version (which cannot be opened from the outside).

Unsurprisingly, you'll find that access to Downing St is restricted unless you're a head of state, but a few lucky souls who get drawn in the ballot can take a peek inside during Open House London and Open Garden Squares Weekend (www.opensquares.org).

BANQUETING HOUSE — PALACE

Map p448 (020-3166 6000; www.hrp.org.uk/banqueting-house; Whitehall; adult/child £7.50/free; 10am-5pm; Westminster) Banqueting House is the sole surviving section of the Tudor Whitehall Palace (1532) that once stretched most of the way down Whitehall before burning to the ground in a 1698 conflagration. Designed by Inigo Jones in 1622 and refaced in Portland stone in the 19th century, Banqueting House was England's first purely Renaissance building and resembled no other structure in the country at the time. Don't miss the **Undercroft** cellar.

In a huge, virtually unfurnished hall on the 1st floor there are nine ceiling panels painted by Peter Paul Rubens in 1635. They were commissioned by Charles I and celebrate the 'benefits of wise rule' and the *Union of England and Scotland Act* (1603).

A bust outside commemorates the date 30 January 1649, when Charles I, accused of treason by Oliver Cromwell during the Civil War, was executed here on a scaffold built against a 1st-floor window. When the monarchy was reinstated with Charles' son crowned as Charles II, it became something of a royalist shrine. Look to the **clock tower** opposite at Horse Guards Parade – the number 2 (the time of the execution) has a black background.

Tickets are marginally cheaper online, but check the closure schedule online as Banqueting House sometimes closes for functions.

THE CENOTAPH MEMORIAL

Map p448 (Whitehall; Ⓤ Westminster or Charing Cross) The Cenotaph, completed in 1920 by Edwin Lutyens and fashioned from Portland stone, is Britain's most important memorial to the men and women of Britain and the Commonwealth killed during the two world wars. The Queen and other public figures lay poppies at its base on Remembrance Sunday, the second Sunday in November.

The word 'cenotaph' derives from the Greek words *kenos* ('empty') and *taphos* ('tomb').

HORSE GUARDS PARADE HISTORIC SITE

Map p448 (off Whitehall; Ⓤ Westminster or Charing Cross) In a more accessible version of Buckingham Palace's Changing of the Guard (p88), the horse-mounted troops of the Household Cavalry swap soldiers here at 11am from Monday to Saturday and at 10am on Sunday. A slightly less ceremonial version takes place at 4pm when the dismounted guards are changed. On the Queen's official birthday in June, the **Trooping the Colour** (www.householddivision.org.uk/trooping-the-colour; Horse Guards Parade) parade takes place here.

During the reigns of King Henry VIII and his daughter Queen Elizabeth I, jousting tournaments were staged here. The

TOP EXPERIENCE
EXPLORE THE ROYAL ACADEMY OF ARTS

Britain's oldest society devoted to fine arts was founded in 1768 and moved to Burlington House a century later. Its collection of drawings, paintings, architectural designs, photographs and sculptures by past and present Royal Academicians, such as Sir Joshua Reynolds, John Constable, Thomas Gainsborough, JMW Turner, David Hockney and Tracey Emin, has been dominated by men historically, but things are slowly changing.

Highlights of the permanent collection are displayed in the **John Madejski Fine Rooms** on the 1st floor (accessible on free guided tours only).

The famous **Summer Exhibition** (adult/child £18/free; ⌚10am-6pm mid-Jun–mid-Aug), which has showcased contemporary art for sale by unknown as well as established artists for nearly 250 years, is the academy's biggest annual event.

Burlington House's courtyard piazza has lights and fountains displaying the astrological star chart of Sir Joshua Reynolds, the RA's first president, on the night he was born. The courtyard hosts temporarily installed statues and outdoor works by contemporary artists.

In 2018 the academy expanded into neighbouring 6 Burlington Gardens.

DON'T MISS

- Summer Exhibition
- John Madejski Fine Rooms
- Themed family activity packs

PRACTICALITIES

- Map p448, B1
- ☎020-7300 8000
- www.royalacademy.org.uk
- Burlington House, Piccadilly
- admission free
- ⌚10am-6pm daily, to 10pm Fri
- Ⓤ Green Park

parade ground and its buildings were built in 1745 to house the Queen's so-called Life Guards. Here you'll also find the **Household Cavalry Museum** (Map p448; 020-7930 3070; www.householdcavalrymuseum.co.uk; Horse Guards Parade; adult/child £9/7; 10am-6pm Apr-Oct, to 5pm Nov-Mar).

Holborn & The Strand

SIR JOHN SOANE'S MUSEUM MUSEUM

See p95.

★TEMPLE CHURCH CHURCH

Map p438 (020-7353 3470; www.templechurch.com; King's Bench Walk; adult/child £5/3; 10am-4pm Mon, Tue, Thu & Fri, 2-4pm Wed, hours & days vary; Temple) This magnificent church was built by the secretive Knights Templar, an order of crusading monks founded in the 12th century to protect pilgrims travelling to and from Jerusalem. Today the sprawling oasis of fine buildings and pleasant, traffic-free green space is home to two Inns of Court: Inner Temple and Middle Temple. A key scene of *The Da Vinci Code* by Dan Brown was set here.

The Temple Church has a distinctive design and is in two parts: the Round (consecrated in 1185 and believed to have been modelled after the Church of the Holy Sepulchre in Jerusalem) adjoins the Chancel (built in 1240), which is the heart of the modern church. Both parts were badly damaged by a bomb in 1941. The church's most obvious points of interest are the life-size stone effigies of nine 13th-century knights lying on the floor of the Round. In 1214–15, the church was the site of vital negotiations for the Magna Carta. It's one of just four round churches left in England.

ROYAL COURTS OF JUSTICE HISTORIC BUILDING

Map p438 (020-7947 6000; www.justice.gov.uk/courts; 460 The Strand; 9am-4.30pm Mon-Fri; Temple) FREE Where the Strand joins Fleet St, you'll see the entrance to this gargantuan melange of Gothic spires, pinnacles and burnished Portland stone, built in 1874. It is a public building and you're allowed to sit in on court proceedings; the daily 'cause list' of cases to be heard is both on the website and posted on signboards in the reception of the Great Hall.

The building was designed by aspiring cathedral builder GE Street; see his statue in the Great Hall. Apparently the job took so much out of him that he died of a stroke shortly before its completion. The statues at the top represent Christ in Majesty, King Solomon and King Alfred the Great. You can also enter the building from the northern side on Carey St, which offers better views of the awesome interior.

MIDDLE TEMPLE HISTORIC BUILDING

Map p438 (020-7427 4800; www.middletemple.org.uk; Middle Temple Lane; grounds 10am-4pm Mon-Fri; Temple) From the Strand, look for a studded black door labelled 'Middle Temple Lane', opposite Bell Yard and the Royal Courts building, and you'll find yourself in the sprawling complex surrounding the Temple Church and the Elizabethan Middle Temple Hall. The church was originally planned and built by the secretive Knights Templar in the mid-12th century; the hall was pieced together bit by bit after being blown to smithereens during WWII. There are wonderful gardens and courtyards at every turn.

On weekends enter from Tudor St to the east. Tours of the Middle Temple are available (£8 to £12), but you will need to book ahead.

INNER TEMPLE HISTORIC BUILDING

Map p438 (020-7797 8208; www.innertemple.org.uk; King's Bench Walk; grounds 6am-8pm, gardens 12.30-3pm Mon-Fri; Temple) Duck under the archway at Old Mitre Court (47 Fleet St) and you'll find yourself in the Inner Temple, a sprawling complex of some of the finest buildings on the river, including 17th-century terrace houses and Temple Church.

Forty-five-minute guided tours (£12) of the Inner Temple can be arranged. Check the website for details.

ST CLEMENT DANES CHURCH

Map p438 (020-7242 8282; https://stclementdanesraf.org; The Strand; 9am-4pm Mon-Fri, to 3pm Sat, 9.30am-3pm Sun; Temple) Christopher Wren designed the original church here in 1682, but only the walls and a steeple added by James Gibbs in 1719 survived bombing in 1941; the church was subsequently rebuilt as a memorial to

TOP EXPERIENC

FIND A FOUNTAIN AT SOMERSET HOUSE

Passing beneath the arched entrance fronting this splendid Palladian masterpiece, it's hard to believe that the magnificent **Edmond J Safra Fountain Court**, with its 55 dancing fountains, was a car park for tax collectors until a spectacular refurbishment in 2000. William Chambers designed the house in 1775 for royal societies and it now contains two galleries.

In the North Wing near the Strand entrance, the **Courtauld Gallery** displays a wealth of 14th- to 20th-century art, including masterpieces by Rubens, Botticelli, Cézanne, Degas, Renoir, Seurat, Manet, Monet, Léger and others. Look out for Manet's *Le Déjeuner sur l'herbe* and *Bar at the Folies-Bergère;* Seurat's *The Bridge at Courbevoie;* Gauguin's *Nevermore;* and a delightful collection of medieval and Renaissance art on the ground floor.

The **Embankment Galleries** in the South Wing host temporary exhibitions (photography, media, design and fashion); prices and hours vary, so check online.

The Safra Fountain Court hosts open-air live performances and Summer Screen films in summer, and ice skating in winter. Children love cavorting through the fountains in the court on warm summer days.

DON'T MISS

- Ice skating in winter
- Open-air cinema in summer
- South Wing riverside terrace
- Courtauld Gallery (when it reopens)

PRACTICALITIES

- Map p438, E5
- ☎020-7845 4600
- www.somersethouse.org.uk
- The Strand
- courtyard 7.30am-11pm
- Temple

Allied airmen. An 'island church' named after the Danes who colonised Aldwych in the 9th century, St Clement Danes today is the chapel of the Royal Air Force (RAF), and there are some 800 slate badges of different squadrons set into the nave pavement.

The statue in front of the church contentiously commemorates the RAF's Sir Arthur 'Bomber' Harris, who led the bombing raids that obliterated Dresden and killed up to 25,000 civilians during WWII.

Should you pass the church at 9am, noon, 3pm, 6pm or 9pm, you may hear the bells chiming a vaguely familiar tune. It's the 18th-century English nursery rhyme that incorporates the names of London churches starting: 'Oranges and lemons, say the bells of St Clements', with the soothing final lines being: 'Here comes a candle to light you to bed/Here comes a chopper to chop off your head/Chop, chop, chop, chop, the last man's dead!'. Night-night, kids.

TWO TEMPLE PLACE GALLERY

Map p438 (☎020-7836 3715; www.twotempleplace.org; 2 Temple Pl; 10am-4.30pm Mon & Thu-Sat, to 9pm Wed, 11am-4.30pm Sun mid-Jan–mid-Apr; Temple) FREE This neo-Gothic house built in the late 1890s for William Waldorf Astor, of hotel fame and once the richest man in America, showcases art from UK museum collections outside the capital. Visit as much to see the opulent house (it's astonishing) as the collections on display, but note it's only open for a few months each year for its winter exhibition.

STAPLE INN HISTORIC BUILDING

Map p438 (www.stapleinn.co.uk; Staple Inn; Chancery Lane) The half-timbered shopfront facade is the main interest at Staple Inn (1580), the last of eight Inns of Chancery whose functions were superseded by the Inns of Court (p103) in the 18th century. The buildings, mostly postwar reconstructions, are now occupied by offices and law chambers and aren't open to the public, though you can have a look around the courtyard.

THE STRAND
STREET

Map p438 (Ⓤ Charing Cross or Temple) In the late 12th century, nobles built houses of stone with gardens along the 'shore' (ie strand) of the Thames. The Strand linked Westminster, the seat of political power, with the City, London's centre of trade. It became one of the most prestigious places to live in London and in the 19th century Disraeli pronounced it the finest street in Europe. Some of these buildings are now fine hotels and restaurants; modern times have added offices and souvenir shops.

Other Strand addresses include **Twinings** (Map p438; ☎020-7353 3511; www.twinings.co.uk; 216 The Strand; ⏰9.30am-7pm Mon-Fri, 10am-5pm Sat, 11am-5pm Sun; Ⓤ Temple) – a teashop opened by Thomas Twining in 1706 and thought to be the oldest company in the capital still trading on the same site – and the stamp- and coin-collectors' titan **Stanley Gibbons** (Map p438; ☎020-7836 8444; www.stanleygibbons.com; 339 The Strand; ⏰9am-5.30pm Mon-Fri, from 9.30am Sat; Ⓤ Covent Garden or Charing Cross).

Marylebone

★MADAME TUSSAUDS
MUSEUM

Map p446 (☎0870 400 3000; www.madame-tussauds.com/london; Marylebone Rd; adult/child 4-15yr £35/30; ⏰10am-6pm; Ⓤ Baker St) It may be kitschy and pricey, but Madame Tussauds makes for a fun-filled day. There are photo ops with your dream celebrity (be it Daniel Craig, Lady Gaga, Benedict Cumberbatch or Audrey Hepburn), the Bollywood gathering (sparring studs Hrithik Roshan and Salman Khan) and the Royal Appointment (the Queen, Harry and Meghan, William and Kate). Book online for much cheaper rates and check the website for seasonal opening hours.

If you're into politics, get up close and personal with Donald Trump who stands uncomfortably close to Vladimir Putin, while Luke Skywalker and Han Solo enthusiasts can turn to the Star Wars experience, which features a host of its key heroes and villains in iconic settings.

The place is pretty commercial, with shops and spending opportunities in each of the dozen rooms. But the Spirit of London

TOP EXPERIENCE

TIME HOP AT THE WALLACE COLLECTION

The Wallace Collection is an enthralling glimpse into 18th-century aristocratic life. The sumptuously restored Italianate mansion – worth the visit in itself – houses a treasure trove of 17th- and 18th-century paintings, porcelain, artefacts and furniture collected by generations of the same family and bequeathed to the nation by the widow of Sir Richard Wallace (1818–90) on the condition it remain displayed in the same fashion.

Among the many highlights are paintings by Rembrandt, Delacroix, Titian, Rubens, Poussin, Velázquez and Gainsborough in the stunning Great Gallery; look out for the *Laughing Cavalier* by Frans Hals. Particularly rich is its collection of rococo paintings, such as the strangely titillating *The Swing* by Jean-Honoré Fragonard, and furniture, paintings and porcelain that belonged to French Queen Marie-Antoinette. There's also an astonishing array of armour and weapons, both medieval and Renaissance and from Europe and Asia. The sweeping staircase is deemed one of the best examples of French interior architecture anywhere in the world.

DON'T MISS

- Great Gallery
- Marie-Antoinette's furniture, paintings and porcelain
- The *Laughing Cavalier* by Frans Hals
- *The Swing* by Jean-Honoré Fragonard

PRACTICALITIES

- Map p446, C3
- ☎020-7563 9500
- www.wallacecollection.org
- Hertford House, Manchester Sq
- admission free
- ⏰10am-5pm
- Ⓤ Bond St

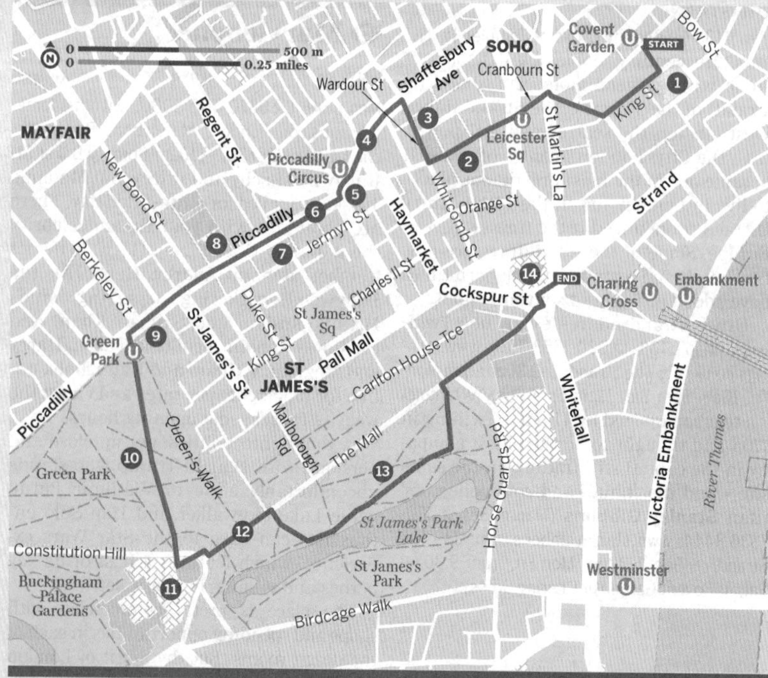

Neighbourhood Walk
Unmissable West End

START COVENT GARDEN TUBE STATION
END TRAFALGAR SQ
LENGTH 2.5 MILES; 1½ HOURS

Stroll through the heart of the West End, from Covent Garden's chic shopping streets to Trafalgar Square, via Chinatown and leafy St James's Park.

First, head south to busy 1 **Covent Garden Piazza** (p102) and enjoy the street performers along James St and opposite St Paul's Church. Follow King and Garrick streets west; turn left onto Cranbourn St to reach 2 **Leicester Square** (p103), where films premiere. At the square's western end turn right into Wardour St; you'll soon come to the Oriental gates of 3 **Chinatown** (Map p440, G5; www.chinatown.co.uk; Wardour St; Ⓤ Leicester Sq) on your right. The area is especially attractive around Chinese New Year, when hundreds of lanterns adorn the streets.

Turn left on 4 **Shaftesbury Avenue**, where you'll find some of the West End's most prestigious theatres. At the avenue's end is buzzy 5 **Piccadilly Circus** (p100), full of shops, tourists and traffic.

Make your way west along 6 **Piccadilly**, which gives just a hint of the aristocratic St James's and Mayfair neighbourhoods nearby. Pop into 7 **St James's Piccadilly** (p98), the only church Wren built from scratch. Further along on the right, you'll see stately Burlington House, home of the 8 **Royal Academy of Arts** (p104), while on the southern side of the road is the landmark 9 **Ritz** (p349) hotel.

Turn left into quiet 10 **Green Park** (p99), with stunning oak trees and old-style street lamps. 11 **Buckingham Palace** (p85) is at the bottom of the park, past the beautiful Canada Gates.

Walk down the grandiose red-asphalt 12 **Mall**; on the right is well-manicured 13 **St James's Park** (p99). Views of Buckingham Palace and the Horse Guards Parade are stunning from the pedestrian Green Bridge over the lake. At the end of the Mall is 14 **Trafalgar Square** (p93), dominated by Nelson's Column and the National Gallery.

taxi ride through the city's history is great, educational fun, and the new Search for Sherlock Holmes (£5 extra) is theatrical.

The museum has a long and interesting history, which started when the French artist and model-maker Marie Tussaud (1761–1850) made death masks of people guillotined during the French Revolution. She came to London in 1803 and exhibited around 30 wax models in nearby Baker St, providing visitors with their only glimpse of the famous and infamous before photography became widespread.

SHERLOCK HOLMES MUSEUM — MUSEUM

Map p446 (☎020-7224 3688; www.sherlock-holmes.co.uk; 221b Baker St; adult/child £15/10; ⏰9.30am-6pm; Ⓤ Baker St) Arthur Conan Doyle's classic detective novels have been boosted by the popularity of the *Sherlock* TV series, and fans of the books trek here to elbow their way over three floors of fusty, reconstructed Victoriana, which even the most dedicated can see in about 30 minutes. But just as many would-be visitors baulk at the queues and the extortionate entry fee and opt to peruse the gift shop or take a photo with the costumed door guardian instead.

In fact, even the address of the museum itself is a work of fiction. Originally occupying 215–229 Baker St was the Abbey National Bank down the road, where a secretary had the full-time job of responding to fan mail. When the bank moved out in 2002, Royal Mail agreed to deliver post addressed to Sherlock Holmes to the museum, even though it's located between 237 and 241 Baker St.

Mayfair

MARBLE ARCH — MONUMENT

Map p446 (Ⓤ Marble Arch) Designed by John Nash in 1828, this huge white arch was moved here next to Speakers' Corner from its original spot in front of Buckingham Palace in 1851. If you're feeling anarchic, walk through the central portal, a privilege reserved by (unenforced) law for the Royal Family and the ceremonial King's Troop Royal Horse Artillery.

Lending its name to the neighbourhood, the arch contains three rooms (inaccessible to the public) and was a police station from 1851 to 1968 (two doors access the interior), large enough to accommodate 100 policemen who could rush to nearby Speaker's Corner if trouble was a-brewing.

A ground plaque on the traffic island between Bayswater and Edgware Rds indicates the spot where the infamous Tyburn Tree, a three-legged gallows, once stood. An estimated 50,000 people were executed here between 1196 (the first recorded execution) and 1783, many having been dragged from the Tower of London. During the 16th century many Catholics were executed for their faith, and it later became a place of Catholic pilgrimage.

To the west of the arch stands a magnificent outsized bronze sculpture of a horse's head called *Still Water*, created by Nic Fiddian-Green in 2011.

HANDEL & HENDRIX IN LONDON — MUSEUM

Map p446 (☎020-7399 1953; http://handelhendrix.org; 25 Brook St; adult/child £10/5; ⏰11am-6pm Tue-Sat; Ⓤ Bond St) George Frederick Handel lived in this 18th-century Mayfair building for 36 years until his death in 1759. This is where he composed some of his finest works, including *Water Music, The Messiah, Zadok the Priest* and *Fireworks Music*. The house at No 23, now incorporated into the museum, was home to American guitarist Jimi Hendrix (1942–70), who lived there for less than a year from 1968.

Early editions of Handel's operas and oratorios, portraits of musicians and singers who worked with Handel, and musical instruments are in the composer's music and composition rooms on the 1st floor; musicians regularly come to practise so you may be treated to a free concert. On the 2nd floor are Handel's bedroom (where he died) and dressing room; there's also a shop here. The volunteer staff are very knowledgeable. Ticketed events at the house include plays, concerts and recitals.

The 3rd floor is devoted to Hendrix, with a brief but comprehensive exhibition, photo gallery and record room. Most fetching is the fully restored 1960s-style bedroom Hendrix shared with his girlfriend Kathy Etchingham, complete with vintage turntable and television set, overflowing ashtrays and an overhead canopy made from an Indian shawl.

EATING

With neighbourhoods as diverse as Soho, Mayfair, Bloomsbury and Marylebone, the West End is a difficult area to encapsulate, but many of the city's most eclectic, fashionable and, quite simply, best restaurants are here. As with most things in London, it pays to be in the know: there's a huge concentration of mediocre places to eat along the main tourist drags, while the best eating experiences are frequently tucked away on backstreets and are not at all obvious. Some of the best require bookings, others are walk-in-only establishments.

Westminster & St James's

5TH VIEW — BISTRO £

Map p440 (020-7851 2433; www.5thview.com; 5th fl, Waterstones Piccadilly, 203-206 Piccadilly; mains £10-12; 9am-9.30pm Mon-Sat, noon-5pm Sun; ; Piccadilly Circus) The views of Westminster from the top floor of Waterstones bookshop on Piccadilly are worth the stairs (OK, there's a lift too). Add a relaxed dining room and you have a bit of a secret spot for a meal and escape from the bustle on the streets below. Afternoon tea (one/two people £16/30) is served from 3pm to 6pm Monday to Saturday and noon to 5pm Sunday.

KAHVE DÜNYASI — CAFE £

Map p440 (020-8287 9063; www.kahvedunyasi.co.uk; Unit 3, 200 Piccadilly; snacks £4-5.50; 7.30am-10pm Mon-Fri, 8am-10.30pm Sat, 9am-9.30pm Sun; ; Piccadilly Circus) An exotic alternative to the ubiquitous coffee chains nearby, Istanbul import Kahve Dünyası brews up authentic Turkish coffee, creamy *sahlep* (a hot milky drink made from dried wild-orchid tubers), pistachio-based desserts, real *lokum* (Turkish delight) and mastic ice cream.

VINCENT ROOMS — MODERN EUROPEAN ££

Map p448 (020-7802 8391; www.thevincentrooms.co.uk; Westminster Kingsway College, Vincent Sq; 2/3 courses £17/21; noon-3pm Mon-Fri, 6-9pm Tue-Thu in term time; Victoria) Care to be a guinea pig for student chefs at Westminster Kingsway College, where such celebrity chefs as Jamie Oliver and Ainsley Harriott were trained? Service is eager to please, the atmosphere in both the Brasserie and the Escoffier Room smarter than expected, and the food (including veggie options) ranges from wonderful to exquisite – at very affordable prices.

THE OTHER NAUGHTY PIGLET — BISTRO ££

Map p448 (020-7592 0322; www.theothernaughtypiglet.co.uk; The Other Palace Theatre, 12 Palace St; small plates £10-12; noon-2.15pm Tue-Sat & 5.15-9.15pm Mon-Sat; ; Victoria) On the 1st floor of The Other Palace Theatre and roomier than Naughty Piglets, its elder sibling in Brixton, this unpretentious open-kitchen restaurant is a pleasure, tempting with seasonally opportunistic dishes such as smoked eel, rhubarb, ginger and coriander. Lunch and pre-theatre set menus, offered Tuesday to Saturday, are great value (two/three courses £18/22).

CAFE MURANO — ITALIAN ££

Map p448 (020-3371 5559; www.cafemurano.co.uk; 33 St James's St; mains £18-28; noon-3pm & 5.30-11pm Mon-Sat, 11.30am-4pm Sun; Green Park) The setting may seem demure at this superb restaurant from Michelin-starred chef Angela Hartnett (a protégé of Gordon Ramsay), but when producing sublime northern Italian dishes such as venison with celeriac and *agrodolce* ('sweet-and-sour') onion there's no need to follow the whims of fashion. The set menus are excellent value (two/three courses £20/24), with reasonably priced wines suggested as accompaniments.

QUILON — INDIAN £££

Map p448 (020-7821 1899; www.quilon.co.uk; 41 Buckingham Gate; mains £18-35; noon-2.30pm & 6-11pm Mon-Fri, 12.30-3.30pm & 5.45-11pm Sat, 12.30-3.30pm & 6-10.30pm Sun; ; St James's Park) Specialising in the cuisines of Goa and Kerala, this Michelin-starred restaurant might serve the best and most inventive Indian food in London. While the restaurant itself in posh St James's is unremarkable, the dishes can't be ignored: how about crispy *idlis* (rice cakes) with black chickpeas, lentil crisps, tomato, cucumber, carrot, and ginger chutney with spicy crispy vegetables?

Vegetables and seafood are richly represented.

Bloomsbury

TEA & TATTLE CAFE ££

Map p444 (07722 192703; www.teaandtattle.com; 41 Great Russell St; afternoon tea for 1/2 £19/38; 9am-6pm Mon-Fri, noon-4pm Sat; ; Tottenham Court Rd) Below Arthur Probsthain, a family-run bookshop specialising in Oriental and African art and culture since 1903, you'll find this intimate, chatty, timber-floored little tearoom – an ideal place to recuperate after either the British Museum or Oxford St. If you're not committed to a full afternoon tea (including sandwiches, scones and cake), you can order components individually.

NORTH SEA FISH RESTAURANT FISH & CHIPS ££

Map p444 (020-7387 5892; http://northseafishrestaurant.co.uk; 7-8 Leigh St; mains £14-22; noon-2.30pm Tue-Sat, 5-10pm Mon-Sat, 5-9.30pm Sun; Russell Sq) Since 1977 the North Sea has set out to cook fresh fish and potatoes – a simple ambition in which it succeeds admirably. Jumbo-sized plaice, halibut, sole and other fillets are delivered daily, deep-fried or grilled, and served with plenty of chips. The original takeaway counter, an alternative to the simply furnished sit-down restaurant, is generally open 30 minutes longer each night.

Fitzrovia

SAGAR INDIAN £

Map p444 (020-7631 3319; www.sagarveg.co.uk; 17a Percy St; mains £6-11; noon-3pm & 5.30-10.45pm Mon-Thu, noon-11pm Fri & Sat, to 10pm Sun; ; Tottenham Court Rd) This branch of a mini-chain specialises in vegetarian dishes from the southern Indian state of Karnataka. It's cheap, filling and of a fine standard. Try the *masala dosa*, an enormous lentil pancake with spicy potato filling. Thalis (steel trays with a selection of small dishes) are £17 to £18.

PASSYUNK AVENUE AMERICAN £

Map p444 (020-3960 2251; www.passyunk.co.uk; 80 Cleveland St; £11-12; 11.30am-11.30pm Mon-Thu, to midnight Fri & Sat, to 10.30pm Sun; Great Portland St) A pocket of pure Americana on a quiet street in Fitzrovia, Passyunk Avenue is a classic dive bar straight outta Philadelphia. The walls are draped with sports paraphernalia, but what people come for is the Philly cheesesteak – the city's iconic sandwich – and they don't leave disappointed.

The South Philly fries, sprinkled with oregano and parmesan cheese, are also amazing.

RAGAM SOUTH INDIAN £

Map p444 (020-7636 9098; www.ragamindian.co.uk; 57 Cleveland St; mains £9-11; noon-3pm & 6-11pm; ; Goodge St) If it ain't broke, don't fix it, and tiny Ragam hasn't been messing with the fundamentals – affordable, excellent dishes – since 1985. It hardly merits a glance from the outside, looking like a rather uninspiring hole-in-the-wall, but never judge a book by its cover: the dosas (£6.95 to £7.95) are supreme, and there are plenty of vegetarian choices.

ROKA JAPANESE ££

Map p444 (020-7580 6464; www.rokarestaurant.com; 37 Charlotte St; mains £17-26; noon-3.30pm & 5.30-11.30pm Mon-Fri, 12.30-4pm & 5.30-11.30pm Sat, 12.30-4pm & 5.30-10.30pm Sun; ; Goodge St) This stunner of a Japanese restaurant mixes casual dining on wooden benches with *robatayaki* (charcoal-grilled) titbits from the central range, augmented by sushi and cocktails. It has modern decor, dominated by grey steel glass, with floor-to-ceiling windows.

PIED À TERRE FRENCH £££

Map p444 (020-7636 1178; www.pied-a-terre.co.uk; 34 Charlotte St; lunch menus from £33, 10-course tasting menu £105; noon-2.30pm Mon-Fri & 6-11pm Mon-Sat; ; Goodge St) This petite and elegant Michelin-starred French restaurant, a stayer on London's dining scene, presents plenty of Francophile favourites (such as skate wing in browned butter sauce) but is unafraid to experiment (super-fresh prawns may be diced for a tartare including yuzu, samphire and quinoa). It's also making a serious pitch to non-meat eaters, with one vegan and two vegetarian menus.

HAKKASAN HANWAY PLACE CHINESE £££

Map p444 (020-7927 7000; https://hakkasan.com; 8 Hanway Pl; mains £39-49; noon-3pm & 5.30-10.30pm Mon-Wed, noon-3pm & 5.30-11pm Thu & Fri, noon-11pm Sat, to 10.30pm Sun; ; Tottenham Court Rd) Inaugurating glamorous Cantonese dining in London in 2001,

Hakkasan now has offspring throughout Asia, the Middle East and the US, yet it still puts everything into the original, tucked away in Fitzrovia's Hanway Pl. Classic dim sum include king-crab dumplings with peppercorn sauce, while the wider menu offers simple, perfect dishes such as stir-fried ribeye with lily bulb and black bean.

Set menus ranging from £33 to £120 per person can be wonderful ways to sample the range of the talented Cantonese chefs behind the fancy, lacquered dining room.

LIMA PERUVIAN £££

Map p444 (020-3002 2640; www.limalondongroup.com/fitzrovia; 31 Rathbone Pl; mains £24-26; noon-2.30pm daily, 5.30-10.30pm Mon-Sat, to 9.30pm Sun; ; Tottenham Court Rd) Peru's capital has one of the hottest food scenes in the world, and this namesake restaurant brings that colour, zest and simple deliciousness to London. It's almost mandatory to start with a ceviche (perhaps the classic bream in 'tiger's milk' with sweet potato and toasted Peruvian corn) before wondering if anything could be better than the 18-hour-braised suckling piglet.

Soho & Chinatown

HOPPERS SOUTH INDIAN £

Map p440 (020-3319 8110; www.hopperslondon.com; 49 Frith St; mains £10-11; noon-2.30pm & 5.30-10.30pm Mon-Thu, noon-10.30pm Fri & Sat; Tottenham Court Rd) All bare brick and spice-box tones, this snug Sri Lankan is the real deal: serving bowl-shaped *hoppers* (fermented-rice pancakes) alongside *karis* (curries) of black pork, aubergine and other star ingredients, *paneer* (fresh cheese) with chilli and butter, and the wonderful *sambols* (chutneys) that adorn the island's cuisine. Bookings are taken only for larger groups; at peak times, leave your number.

The £19.50 lunch menu includes a starter, *hopper*, *kari* and *sambol*.

BEIJING DUMPLING CHINESE £

Map p440 (020-7287 6888; www.facebook.com/beijingdumpling; 23 Lisle St; mains £9-11; noon-11.30pm Mon-Sat, to 10.30pm Sun; Leicester Sq) You can see the stars of the show before you even walk in, as tiny dough pockets ready to be made into *xiaolongbao* (soup dumplings) are kneaded at speed behind the steamy front window: do not leave without ordering a basket or three. Though the surroundings are no-frills, nearly every dish is top-notch. Service can be gruff but efficient.

MILDREDS VEGETARIAN £

Map p440 (020-7494 1634; www.mildreds.co.uk; 45 Lexington St; mains £12-13; 11am-11pm Mon-Sat, to 10pm Sun; ; Oxford Circus or Piccadilly Circus) One of the West End's most enduringly popular vegetarian restaurants, Mildreds is crammed at lunchtime: you can't be shy about sharing a table in the sky-lit dining room. Expect the likes of pumpkin gnocchi (boiled and fried) with pumpkin sauce and *pangrattato* (fried breadcrumbs), halloumi and harissa burgers, and Levantine Chick'n kebabs. There are also vegan and gluten-free options.

So popular has Mildreds become, there are now branches in Dalston, Camden and King's Cross.

KOYA BAR JAPANESE £

Map p440 (www.koya.co.uk; 50 Frith St; mains £11-15; 8.30am-10.30pm Mon-Wed, to 11pm Thu & Fri, 9.30am-11pm Sat, to 10.30pm Sun; Tottenham Court Rd or Leicester Sq) Arrive early if you don't want to queue at this informal but excellent Japanese eatery with counter seating. Londoners come here for their fill of authentic udon noodles (served hot or cold, in soup or with a cold sauce), efficient service and very reasonable prices. The Hiyashi Saba (udon noodles with chunks of smoked mackerel and watercress) is excellent.

GELUPO GELATERIA £

Map p440 (020-7287 5555; www.gelupo.com; 7 Archer St; 1/2/3 scoops £4/5/6; 11am-11pm Mon-Thu, to midnight Fri & Sat, noon-11pm Sun; ; Piccadilly Circus) The queue outside Gelupo can stretch down the street on summer weekend evenings, and it's no wonder: this is central London's most authentic *gelateria*. All the ingredients are natural and the servings are generous. Go for traditional flavours such as pistachio or bitter chocolate or try original creations such as bergamot, ricotta or fig and walnut.

PIZZA PILGRIMS

PIZZERIA £

Map p440 (☎020-7287 8964; www.pizzapilgrims.co.uk; 11 Dean St; pizza £9-11; ⏲11.30am-10.30pm Mon-Wed, 11am-11pm Thu, 11.30am-11.30pm Fri & Sat, noon-9.30pm Sun; ✎; Ⓤ Tottenham Court Rd) One of our favourite places for pizza in the very heart of Soho, PP serves 12-inch Neapolitan-style pizzas with delectably crispy crusts. There are a half-dozen standards on offer plus a guest pizza introduced each month.

Pizza Pilgrims is very vegetarian-friendly, it offers plenty of sides, bespoke topping, and beer, wine and cocktails to cater to most tastes.

BONE DADDIES RAMEN BAR

NOODLES £

Map p440 (☎020-7287 8581; www.bonedaddiesramen.com; 31 Peter St; dishes £11-13; ⏲noon-10pm Mon, to 11pm Tue-Wed, to 11.30pm Thu-Sat, to 9.30pm Sun; 📶; Ⓤ Tottenham Court Rd) For a bowl of sustaining ramen noodles, you couldn't do better than Bone Daddies on Peter St. This is the original of an ever-expanding chain.

Choose your 'foundation' – be it noodles in broth or a salad – and then add a topping or two (*chashu* pork, pulled chicken, bean sprouts etc).

CEVICHE

PERUVIAN £

Map p440 (☎020-7292 2040; www.cevichefamily.com; 17 Frith St; mains £9-15; ⏲noon-3pm Mon-Fri, 5-11pm Mon-Thu, 5-11.30pm Fri, noon-11.30pm Sat, to 10pm Sun; 📶; Ⓤ Tottenham Court Rd) This colourfully decorated bodega serves some of the most authentic Peruvian food in town.

Start with *cancha* (large crunchy corn kernels) and move on to one of the signature dishes – ceviche (fish or shellfish marinated in lime juice with chillies, onion and coriander) or *lomo saltado* (steak stir-fry). Salads with quinoa and palm hearts are excellent.

The long back bar is the perfect spot to try a pisco sour made with Peru's indigenous firewater.

★BAR SHU

CHINESE ££

Map p440 (☎020-7287 6688; http://barshurestaurant.co.uk; 28 Frith St; mains £11-23; ⏲noon-11pm Sun-Thu, to 11.30pm Fri & Sat; Ⓤ Piccadilly Circus or Leicester Sq) You might think Bar Shu – adorned with slatted blinds, latticed woodwork and tasselled lanterns – was a sweet-and-sour honeytrap for Soho tourists; but you'd be missing out on possibly the best Sichuan food to be found in London.

The *ma-po* tofu ('pockmarked grandmother's tofu', reputedly Chairman Mao's favourite) is the best we've ever had: all funky fermented beans, chilli oil, pork and fresh bean curd.

There's a wide disparity in dish pricing: while simple choices such as the *ma-po* or 'ants climbing trees' (a classic stir-fried cellophane-noodle dish) come in at around £10, you'll be in for a shock if you order sea cucumber, abalone or crab without checking the prices first.

★PALOMAR

ISRAELI ££

Map p440 (☎020-7439 8777; www.thepalomar.co.uk; 34 Rupert St; mains £14-16; ⏲noon-2.30pm & 5.30-11pm Mon-Sat, 12.30-3.30pm & 6-9pm Sun; 📶; Ⓤ Piccadilly Circus) Packed and praised from the day it opened, Palomar is a wonderful Israeli/Levantine restaurant with the look of a 1930s diner and the constant theatre of expert chefs whipping up magic behind the central zinc bar.

Unusual dishes such as date-glazed octopus with harissa will blow you away, as will slow-cooked Tel Aviv seafood and beetroot labneh with parsley vinaigrette.

It's usually possible to get one or two of the 16 bar stools at shortish notice for lunch, but book further ahead for a table in the 40-seat dining room, or for dinner. Chefs interact unaffectedly with the diners, adding to the whole experience.

★KILN

THAI ££

Map p440 (www.kilnsoho.com; 58 Brewer St; dishes £4.50-14; ⏲noon-3pm & 5-11pm Mon-Thu, noon-11pm Fri & Sat, to 10pm Sun; Ⓤ Piccadilly Circus) Crowned the UK's best restaurant in 2018, this tiny Thai grill cooks up a storm in its long, narrow kitchen, overseen by diners on their stools. The short menu rides the small-plates wave and works best with a few friends so you can taste a much greater variety of what's on offer.

The beef-neck curry is phenomenal, as are the hugely popular claypot-baked glass noodles.

LONDON'S BEWILDERING POSTCODES

The 20 *arrondissements* in Paris spiral clockwise from the centre in a lovely, logical fashion. Not so London's postcodes. Look at a map and you may be thinking: why does SE23 border SE6? We headed to London's Postal Museum (p207) to find out.

When they were introduced in 1858, the postcodes were fairly clear, with all the compass points represented, along with an east and west central (EC and WC). But not long afterwards NE was merged with E and S with SE and SW, and problems began.

The real convolution came during WWI when a numbering system was introduced for inexperienced post sorters (regular employees were off fighting in 'the war to end all wars'). No 1 was the centre of each zone, but other numbers related to the alphabetical order of the postal districts' names. Thus anything starting with a letter near the beginning of the alphabet, like Chingford in East London, would get a low number (E4), even though it was miles from the centre at Whitechapel (E1), while Poplar, which borders Whitechapel, got E14.

It wasn't designed to confuse regular punters, but it does.

MORTIMER HOUSE KITCHEN — MEDITERRANEAN ££

Map p444 (020-7139 4401; www.mortimerhouse.com/restaurant; 37-41 Mortimer St; mains £21-26; 7.30am-11.30pm Mon-Thu, to midnight Fri, 9am-midnight Sat, to 6pm Sun; Goodge St or Oxford Circus) Tranquil isn't a word ever applied to Soho, even in this slightly less-trafficked part, but somehow this restaurant channels Great Gatsby-style zen and confidence in its art-deco-flavoured dining room. The Med meets the Middle East on its menu, hopscotching from salsify with *chermoula* sauce and tahini and beetroot *tortelli* with smoked burrata. Service is stellar.

10 GREEK ST — MODERN EUROPEAN ££

Map p440 (020-7734 4677; www.10greekstreet.com; 10 Greek St; mains £20-26; noon-2.30pm Mon-Sat, 5.30-10pm Mon & Tue, 5.30-10.30pm Wed-Sat, noon-11pm Sun; ; Tottenham Court Rd) This confidently undemonstrative bistro is making quite a splash with food that marries top-quality British and Mediterranean produce and techniques seamlessly and pleasurably (expect temptations such as prawns with lentils, *salsa verde* and lardons, or hake with hispi cabbage, chorizo and Jerusalem artichoke). Desserts such as lemon granita with curd and blackberries maintain the standard. Service is excellent.

Bookings are taken for lunch but not dinner.

BRASSERIE ZÉDEL — FRENCH ££

Map p440 (020-7734 4888; www.brasseriezedel.com; 20 Sherwood St; mains £15-18; 11.30am-midnight Mon-Sat, to 11pm Sun; ; Piccadilly Circus) This restaurant in the renovated art-deco ballroom of a former hotel may be the most French brasserie north of Calais. Favourites include *choucroute alsacienne* (sauerkraut with sausages and charcuterie) and *steak haché* (chopped steak) with pepper sauce and *frites*. Set menus (£11/14 for two/three courses) and *plats du jour* such as rabbit with mustard offer value and variety.

The attached **Bar Américain** is a classic art-deco spot for a pre-dinner cocktail (from £10).

ANDREW EDMUNDS — BRITISH ££

Map p440 (020-7437 5708; www.andrewedmunds.com; 46 Lexington St; mains £18-20; noon-3.30pm & 5.30-10.45pm Mon-Fri, 12.30-3.30pm & 5.30-10.45pm Sat, 1-4pm & 6-10.30pm Sun; Oxford Circus or Piccadilly Circus) This charismatic little restaurant, operating from the same Georgian town house since 1985, is exactly the sort you might wish still abounded in Soho. Offering two floors of wood-panelled bohemia, and a handwritten menu of Modern British cooking (such as cold roast sirloin with salsify dressing or warm ox tongue with gem lettuce and mustard), it's enduringly popular so reservations are essential.

The excellent wine list offers plenty of enticing bargains.

YAUATCHA — CHINESE ££

Map p440 (020-7494 8888; www.yauatcha.com; 15-17 Broadwick St; mains £15-30, dim sum £8-10; noon-1am Mon-Sat, to midnight

Sun; ⓤTottenham Court Rd or Oxford Circus) London's glamorous Michelin-starred dim sum restaurant has a ground-floor dining room that's a blue-bathed oasis of calm from the chaos of Berwick Street Market; downstairs is smarter, with constellations of 'star' lights. Lobster dumplings with *tobiko* (flying-fish roe) exemplify the refined dim sum, while spicy steamed bass with pickled chilli is just one of the more substantial options.

The Soho Lunch (£28 per person for at least two) is a great-value introduction to its divine dim sum. Unusually, Yauatcha also produces delicate cakes, macarons and other sweet delights.

POLPO VENETIAN ££

Map p440 (☎020-7734 4479; www.polpo.co.uk; 41 Beak St; small plates £4-9; ⊙11.30am-11pm Mon-Sat, to 10.30pm Sun; ; ⓤOxford Circus or Piccadilly Circus) Cicchetti – Venetian bar snacks akin to tapas – are all the rage in their watery homeland's backstreet *bàcari* (wine bars), and ebullient Polpo brings a lovely selection to London. Larger plates include clams with *fregole* (Sardinian couscous) and parsley, and there's a good range of classic cocktails and Italian wines. Polpo now has three new London locations and another in Brighton.

As coincidental as it may seem, the Venetian painter Canaletto lived at 41 Beak St for two years from 1749.

KRICKET SOHO INDIAN ££

Map p440 (☎020-7734 5612; https://kricket.co.uk; 12 Denman St; small plates £8-14; ⊙noon-2.30pm & 5.15-10.30pm Mon-Sat; ; ⓤPiccadilly Circus) Another in the cooking-as-theatre genre (chefs sweat in an open kitchen behind a long, narrow bar, watched by stool-perched diners), Kricket turns out innovative sharing plates influenced by many Indian regions. There are more veggie than meat options (the corn roti with Mangalorean mushrooms are superb); booths and a second dining room are available for those less keen on the bar.

Cocktails (mostly £9.50) are also very good.

BARRAFINA TAPAS ££

Map p438 (☎020-7440 1456; www.barrafina.co.uk; 10 Adelaide St; basic tapas £4-7, larger plates £9-17; ⊙noon-3pm & 5-11pm Mon-Sat; ⓤEmbankment or Leicester Sq) With no reservations, you may need to get in line for an hour or so at this restaurant that produces some of the best tapas in town. Divine mouthfuls are served on each plate, from the prawns with roasted *piquillo* pepper to the Iberian pork ribs and chargrilled artichokes, so you may think it worth the wait.

There's a maximum group size of four and a couple of tables on the pavement.

GAUTHIER SOHO FRENCH £££

Map p440 (☎020-7494 3111; www.gauthiersoho.co.uk; 21 Romilly St; 3-course lunch with/without wine £38/32; ⊙noon-2.30pm & 6.30-9.30pm Tue-Thu, noon-3pm & 6.30-10pm Fri & Sat; ; ⓤLeicester Sq) Alexis Gauthier's temple of gastronomy is housed over two floors of a handsome Regency townhouse where you have to buzz for entrance. Evening meals are a delight but pricey at £60/70 for three/four courses. Do what we did and treat yourself to a luxurious weekday lunch for half the price. Vegan chef Alexis Gauthier ensures plenty of plant-based choices.

Try the truffle risotto to start, perhaps followed by Norfolk quail with pressed savoy cabbage and *pommes boulangère* ('baker's potatoes').

POLLEN STREET SOCIAL EUROPEAN £££

Map p440 (☎020-7290 7600; www.pollenstreetsocial.com; 8-10 Pollen St; mains £41-44; ⊙noon-2.30pm & 6-10.30pm Mon-Sat; ⓤOxford Circus) Chef Jason Atherton's cathedral to haute cuisine (Michelin-starred within six months of opening) is a worthy splurge, especially for those in search of the best produce in these islands. It's expensive, but if you fancy trying Braehead pheasant with chestnut gnocchi or roasted Cornish cod with salt-baked vegetables without overspending, the three-course lunch menu (£40) is excellent value.

OSCAR WILDE LOUNGE TEAHOUSE £££

Map p440 (☎020-7406 3310; www.hotelcaferoyal.com/afternoontea; 68 Regent St; afternoon tea £55, with champagne from £65; ⊙noon-5.30pm; ⓤPiccadilly Circus) An extravagant gilt-and-parquet jewellery box within the Hotel Café Royal, the Oscar Wilde Lounge – dating from 1865 and named after its most famous habitué – is literally a brilliant spot for afternoon tea. Historically patronised by an extraordinary cast of celebrities including David Bowie and Elizabeth Taylor, it serves sandwiches, scones and dainties of the classic British afternoon tea.

Covent Garden & Leicester Square

DELAUNAY COUNTER CAFE £

Map p438 (020-7499 8558; www.thedelaunay.com/counter; 55 Aldwych; soups & sandwiches £7.50-8.50; 7am-8.30pm Mon-Fri, from 10.30am Sat, 11am-5.30pm Sun; Temple or Covent Garden) The informal sibling of the grand Mitteleuropean Delaunay next door, the Counter goes full Vienna with Sachertorte (dark-chocolate iced cake filled with apricot jam), *Wiener Kaffee* (double espresso and whipped cream) and Stiegl Austrian beer. Also offering savouries such as borscht soup or chicken-schnitzel sandwiches, it's ideal therapy after shopping with the crowds in Covent Garden.

★SEVEN DIALS MARKET STREET FOOD £

Map p438 (www.sevendialsmarket.com; Earlham St; 11am-11pm Mon-Sat, noon-10.30pm Sun; Covent Garden) In a former banana warehouse (thus the banana motif) and reminiscent of New York's famous Chelsea Market, this two-storey indoor street-food collective delivers everything from vegan tacos at Club Mexicana to Japanese soul food at the tiny outpost of Brixton's Nanban. Sun streams through the glass skylights by day, live music gets the party vibe going at night.

SHORYU JAPANESE £

Map p440 (www.shoryuramen.com; 9 Regent St; mains £10-14.50; 11.15am-midnight Mon-Sat, to 10.30pm Sun; ; Piccadilly Circus) The first of a small empire of ramen bars in the UK, Shoryu is busy, friendly and efficient, but has a no-bookings policy. Fantastic *tonkotsu* (pork-broth ramen) is the best choice here, sprinkled with *nori* (dried, pressed seaweed), spring onion, *nitamago* (soft-boiled eggs) and sesame seeds. Steamed buns filled with roast pork, fried chicken and other treats are also excellent.

Veggie and gluten-free ramen is available, as well as a range of sake, Korean soju, Japanese whisky and beer.

BATTERSEA PIE STATION BRITISH £

Map p438 (020-7240 9566; www.batterseapie.co.uk; lower ground fl, 28 The Market, Covent Garden; mains £7-10; 11am-7.30pm Mon-Fri, 10am-8pm Sat, 11am-7pm Sun; Covent Garden) This small, white-tiled cafe has a terrific choice of pies to satisfy all levels of hunger, from careful nibblers to voracious teens. Meat is all free-range, flavours are classic and rich (steak-and-kidney, mushroom-and-chicken), and traditional sides such as stiffly mashed potatoes and liquor (parsley sauce) are all done well. Cold pork pies also feature.

DELAUNAY EUROPEAN ££

Map p438 (020-7499 8558; www.thedelaunay.com; 55 Aldwych; mains £19-26; 7am-11pm Mon-Fri, from 8am Sat, 9am-10pm Sun; ; Temple or Covent Garden) This immaculate spot channels the majesty of the grand cafes of Central Europe. Schnitzels, sausages and fish take pride of place on the menu, which is rounded out with Alsatian *tarte flambée* (thin-crust 'pizzas' with crème fraiche, onions and bacon lardons) and a rotating *Tagesteller* (dish of the day). The more relaxed Delaunay Counter is next door.

IVY MARKET GRILL EUROPEAN ££

Map p438 (020-3301 0200; https://theivymarketgrill.com; 1a Henrietta St; mains £15-25, 2-/3-course theatre menu £18/21; 8am-12.30am Mon-Sat, to 11.30pm Sun; ; Covent Garden) Another offshoot of one of London's most venerable celeb-spotting venues, this outpost has a lovely front terrace full of greenery, traditional interior with lots of wood and brass lanterns, and high-end comfort food like shepherd's pie, fish and chips and steak tartare. Breakfast merges into brunch (on weekends) then all-day dining, and there's even a dedicated vegan menu.

A fine traditional afternoon tea is served daily from 3pm to 5pm (£27/20 with/without champagne).

NATIONAL CAFÉ CAFE ££

Map p438 (020-7747 2525; www.nationalgallery.org.uk/visiting/eat-and-drink; ground fl, National Gallery, Trafalgar Sq; 2-/3-course set lunch £20/25; 9.30am-8.30pm Mon-Thu, to 10pm Fri, to 6pm Sat & Sun; Charing Cross) A good spot for a meal at the National Gallery, accessible either internally or from St

Martin's Pl, this cafeteria-cum-cafe-restaurant offers both self-serve light meals for those on the go and a proper sit-down bistro with extended hours that's as popular with locals as with museum-goers. Come for breakfast, lunch, afternoon tea (3pm to 5.30pm daily; £32/23 with/without champagne) or dinner.

Basic 'grab-and-go' sandwiches, pastries and hot drinks are available from 8am weekdays and 9am weekends.

J SHEEKEY SEAFOOD £££

Map p438 (020-7240 2565; www.j-sheekey.co.uk; 28-32 St Martin's Ct; mains £27-36; noon-3pm & 5pm-midnight Mon-Sat, noon-3.30pm & 5.30-10.30pm Sun; ; Leicester Sq) A jewel of the Covent Garden dining scene, this incredibly smart restaurant was opened by 1890s fishmonger Josef Sheekey on the permission of Lord Salisbury (who wanted somewhere to eat after the theatre). It has four elegant, discreet and spacious wood-panelled rooms in which to savour the riches of the sea, cooked simply but exquisitely. Set menus for two/three courses are £25/30.

The adjoining **Atlantic Bar** (noon-midnight Mon to Sat, to 10.30pm Sun), popular with pre- and post-theatregoers for its oysters and shellfish, is another highlight.

BALTHAZAR BRASSERIE £££

Map p438 (020-3301 1155; https://balthazarlondon.com; 4-6 Russell St; mains £21-33; 7.30am-11.30pm Mon-Thu, to midnight Fri, 9am-midnight Sat, to 11pm Sun; ; Covent Garden or Temple) Few are disappointed by the mostly French fare on offer – mussels, *salade niçoise*, duck confit – at this handsome brasserie, where there's the odd nod to *les rosbifs* ('roast beefs', or Britons) in the way of the rack of lamb (though it's made with aubergine and flageolet beans). Fabulous zinc bar and yummy bakery treats are on offer at the adjacent *boulangerie*.

The excellent-value weekday set lunch (two/three courses for £20/23) is also available from 5pm to 6.30pm and from 10pm till closing Monday to Saturday.

RULES BRITISH £££

Map p438 (020-7836 5314; https://rules.co.uk; 35 Maiden Lane; mains £29-30; noon-11.30pm Mon-Sat, to 10.30pm Sun; ; Covent Garden) Established in 1798, this posh and very British establishment lays claim to being London's oldest restaurant. The menu is inevitably meat-oriented – Rules specialises in classic game cookery, serving up tens of thousands of birds between mid-August and January from its own estate in the High Pennines of northwest England – but fish dishes are also available.

Puddings are traditional: tarts, crumbles, sticky toffees and treacles with lashings of custard.

Holborn

★KANADA-YA JAPANESE £

Map p438 (020-7240 0232; www.kanada-ya.com; 64 St Giles High St; mains £11-13; noon-3pm & 5-10.30pm Mon-Sat, to 8.30pm Sun; Tottenham Court Rd) In the debate over London's best ramen, we're still voting for this one. With no reservations taken, queues can get impressive outside this tiny and enormously popular canteen, where ramen cooked in *tonkotsu* (pork-bone broth) draws in diners from near and far. The noodles arrive at just the right temperature and hardness, steeped in a delectable broth and rich flavours.

HOLBORN DINING ROOM MODERN BRITISH ££

Map p438 (020-3747 8633; https://holborndiningroom.com; 252 High Holborn; mains £20-26; 7am-10.30pm Mon-Fri, from 7.30am Sat & Sun; Holborn) This masculine-feeling brasserie attached to the Rosewood London (p349) – all reclaimed oak, antique mirrors and leather banquettes – serves up such delights as roast Suffolk pork belly, curried mutton pie and shrimp burger. But you'd be perfectly justified simply fronting up to the huge copper-topped bar to try one of 500-plus gins and 30 tonics on offer.

★SPRING BRITISH £££

Map p438 (020-3011 0115; www.springrestaurant.co.uk; New Wing, Somerset House, Lancaster Pl; mains £29-33, 2-/3-course lunch £29/32; noon-2.30pm & 5.30-10.30pm Mon-Sat; Temple) White walls, ball chandeliers and columns are offset by the odd blossom in this restored Victorian drawing room in Somerset House (p106). Award-winning Australian chef Skye Gyngell leads a team dedicated to sustainability – no single-use plastic and an early-evening scratch menu (£25 for three courses) using food that would otherwise be wasted. Desserts are legendary.

Marylebone

ETHOS VEGETARIAN £

Map p444 (020-3581 1538; www.ethosfoods.com; 48 Eastcastle St; lunch & dinner plate £8-12; 8am-10pm Mon-Fri, from 11am Sat, 11am-5pm Sun; ; Oxford Circus) More than 40 meat-free and vegan dishes inspired by global cuisines are laid out for self-service in this airily designed restaurant that charges by weight at lunch and dinner (breakfast is à la carte). Dairy-free, gluten-free and refined-sugar-free requirements aren't forgotten, and you can choose takeaway if need be.

YALLA YALLA LEBANESE £

Map p444 (020-7637 4748; www.yalla-yalla.co.uk; 12 Winsley St; mains £13-15; 11.30am-11pm Mon-Sat, noon-8pm Sun; ; Oxford Circus) A delightful respite from the lawless pavements of Oxford St, this exuberantly decorated and welcoming restaurant focuses on high-quality Lebanese classics: shawarma (spiced chicken slices with accompaniments), *fattoush* (bread salad), baba ganoush (smoky aubergine dip) and the like. If you have a proper appetite, the three-course Lebanese Feast Menu for two or more is abundantly generous (£30 per person).

GOLDEN HIND FISH & CHIPS £

Map p446 (020-7486 3644; www.goldenhindrestaurant.com; 71a-73 Marylebone Lane; fish £11-15; noon-3pm Mon-Fri & 6-10pm Mon-Sat; Bond St) Proudly owned by a succession of Italian and Greek Londoners since founded by M Esposito in 1914, this chippie retains a classic interior, vintage fryer and chunky wooden tables where labourers rub elbows with suits over excellent fish and chips. It has a liquor licence, although you may be more tempted by the bring-your-own-bottle (BYO) policy, with corkage at just £2 per person.

ROTI CHAI INDIAN ££

Map p446 (020-7408 0101; www.rotichai.com; 3 Portman Mews S; small plates £5-8; noon-10.30pm Mon-Sat, 12.30-9pm Sun; ; Marble Arch) With a bustling open kitchen that's never shy of flavour, Roti Chai does a roaring trade in Bombay-style *bhel puri* (puffed rice with tamarind), *dhokla* (Gujarati steamed chickpea cake) and Bengali *macher jhol* (fish in *kasundi* mustard sauce) in the sociable upstairs section. The basement dining room (noon to 2.30pm during the week, dinner only on weekends) offers more options (mains £12 to £15).

28-50 INTERNATIONAL ££

Map p446 (020-7486 7922; www.2850.co.uk/marylebone; 15-17 Marylebone Lane; mains £18-28; noon-10.30pm Mon-Wed, to 11pm Thu-Sat, to 10pm Sun; Bond St) This intimate, triangular wine bar and restaurant with floor-to-ceiling windows near Oxford St is a favourite of clued-in shoppers and concertgoers (Wigmore Hall is around the corner). Dishes are unfussy but always excellent, such as the slow-roasted lamb shoulder, seared tuna in an Asian broth, or fish pie with curried leeks. Solo diners can comfortably eat at the long bar.

The wine lists are excellent, with special bottles for those with the means to splash out.

WALLACE RESTAURANT EUROPEAN ££

Map p446 (020-7563 9505; www.peytonandbyrne.co.uk/venues/wallace-restaurant; Hertford House, Manchester Sq; mains £20-24; 3-course set menu £35; 10am-5pm Sun-Thu, to 11pm Fri & Sat; Bond St) Run by an outfit with broader catering experience, the Wallace Collection's (p107) cafe-restaurant is a notch above what you'd expect from a museum. Equally good for a daytime coffee and pastry, an evening drink or a more substantial French-inspired meal, it's in the covered, candy-pink-and-white central courtyard. Even potted plastic bay and Japanese maple trees don't detract from the civilised atmosphere.

Afternoon tea is served daily between 2.30pm and 4.30pm. It's £19 per person, or £27 if you'd like a glass of bubbles with your coronation chicken sandwiches.

FISHWORKS SEAFOOD ££

Map p446 (020-7935 9796; www.fishworks.co.uk; 89 Marylebone High St; mains £22-28, 2-course set lunch £18; noon-10.30pm; Baker St) The emphasis here is on the freshest seafood: entry is via the attached fishmongers (9am to 10pm Monday to Saturday, from 10am Sunday). There are some nice English specialities to try such as Dover sole, Devon scallops, Dartmouth crab and Colchester oysters, but you'll also find seafood delights from across the pond or the Mediterranean, including lobster, tuna steak and Italian-style fish soup.

LOCANDA LOCATELLI ITALIAN £££

Map p446 (☎020-7935 9088; www.locandalocatelli.com; 8 Seymour St; mains £28-33; ⊙noon-3pm daily, 6-11pm Mon-Thu, to 11.30pm Fri & Sat, to 10.15pm Sun; 📶; UMarble Arch) This quietly glamorous restaurant in an otherwise unremarkable Marble Arch hotel remains one of London's best Italian establishments, and you're likely to see some famous faces being greeted by revered chef Giorgio Locatelli. The restaurant is renowned for its pasta dishes, and the mains include five fish dishes, five meat ones, and even two for vegans. Booking is essential.

CHILTERN FIREHOUSE MODERN EUROPEAN £££

Map p446 (☎020-7073 7676; www.chilternfirehouse.com; 1 Chiltern St; mains £32-42; ⊙7-10.30am, noon-3pm & 5.30-10.30pm Mon-Fri, 8am-3pm Sat & Sun, 6-10.30pm Sat, to 10pm Sun; 📶; UBaker St or Bond St) In-house restaurant of the hotel of the same name, itself occupying a beautiful red-brick firehouse from 1889, this splendidly dapper eatery offers opportunities to celeb-spot while enjoying the famed cooking of head chef Nuno Mendes. It's wildly popular, so book well ahead to enjoy dishes such as glazed hake with leek hearts and crab bisque flavoured with Chinese XO sauce.

Mayfair

MOMO MOROCCAN ££

Map p440 (☎020-7434 4040; www.momoresto.com; 25 Heddon St; mains £21-24; ⊙noon-1am Mon-Sat, to midnight Sun; 📶; UPiccadilly Circus) Overflowing with cushions and lamps, and staffed by tambourine-playing waiters, this atmospheric Moroccan restaurant has warm service and dishes as exciting as you dare to be. After the mezze, eschew the ubiquitous tagine (stew cooked in a clay pot) and couscous, and tuck into *pastilla* (sweet pigeon pie) or octopus with salt-baked beetroot. Two-/three-course set lunch (£29/39) offered for groups of nine or more.

There's outside seating on this quiet backstreet in the warmer months.

EMBER YARD GRILL ££

Map p440 (☎020-7439 8057; www.saltyardgroup.co.uk/ember-yard; 60 Berwick St; mains £13-20; ⊙noon-midnight Mon-Sat, to 10pm Sun; UOxford Circus) The *parillas* of Spain, *asadors* of the Basque country and barbeques of Italy inspire the food at this stylish restaurant, decked out in polished timber, and fitted with a basement bar lined with genuinely comfy stools. Beyond smaller bites such as charred octopus and chorizo with *alioli* are more substantial wood-grilled plates such as pork ribs glazed with quince paste.

Something called a 'siesta menu' (presumably a scaled-back selection focusing on charcuterie and cheese) is offered on weekdays between 3pm and 5pm.

TAMARIND INDIAN ££

Map p446 (☎020-7629 3561; www.tamarindrestaurant.com; 20 Queen St; mains £18-27; ⊙noon-2.30pm & 5.30-10.30pm; ✎; UGreen Park) A mix of refined classics from various Indian regions and innovations such as vegetable-and-kale *seekh* kebab stuffed with black-fig chutney, Tamarind has won plenty of plaudits and a loyal clientele. The set lunches are £25/30 for two/three courses, while you'll need to settle in a little longer to enjoy the tasting menu (£69 or £59 for the vegetarian version).

BRICIOLE ITALIAN ££

Map p446 (☎020-7723 0040; http://briciole.co.uk; 20 Homer St; mains £13-17; ⊙11.30am-10.45pm Mon-Sat, noon-10.30pm Sun; UEdgware Rd) 'Crumbs' is an inviting corner trattoria with a cafe and deli out front and a cosy dining room out back. The food isn't overly complex: Palermo-style meatballs in sweet-and-sour onions, barbecued rib-eye, pork ribs stewed with greens and plenty of pasta. But, of course, simplicity and deliciousness are the cornerstones of real Italian food, and the prices are very reasonable.

EL PIRATA SPANISH ££

Map p446 (☎020-7491 3810; www.elpirata.co.uk; 5-6 Down St; tapas £4.95-8.95, mains £18-20; ⊙noon-11.30pm Mon-Fri, 6-11.30pm Sat; UGreen Park or Hyde Park Corner) Its bemusing name notwithstanding, this quality, split-level Spanish restaurant offers over 50 tapas, traditional mains such as grilled lamb chops and daily specials such as *huevos rotos especiales* (eggs with potatoes, prawns, chorizo and chilli). The indecisive can choose from two set tapas menus for two or more (both £25 per person) and there's a great selection of Spanish wines.

★FOYER & READING ROOM AT CLARIDGE'S BRITISH £££

Map p446 (☎020-7107 8886; www.claridges.co.uk; Brook St; afternoon tea £70, with champagne £80-90; ⏰7am-11pm Mon-Sat, from 8am Sun, afternoon tea 2.45-5.30pm; 📶; Ⓤ Bond St) Refreshing the better sort of West End shopper since 1856, the jaw-dropping Foyer and Reading Room at Claridge's (p350), refulgent with art-deco mirrors and a Dale Chihuly glass sculpture, really is a memorable dining space. Refined food is served at all mealtimes, but many choose to nibble in best aristocratic fashion on the finger sandwiches and pastries of a classic afternoon tea.

Smart attire is always required.

GREENHOUSE FRENCH £££

Map p446 (☎020-7499 3331; www.greenhouserestaurant.co.uk; 27a Hay's Mews; 4-course set menu £110, tasting menus £125-145; ⏰noon-1.45pm Tue-Fri, 6.30-9.45pm Tue-Sat; 📶; Ⓤ Green Park) Reached through a wonderful sculpture-filled garden, twin-Michelin-starred Greenhouse is a mainstay of Mayfair luxury dining. The tasting menus are only for the intrepid and truly hungry. Bear in mind that this place doles out so many extras – from *amuses-gueules* (appetisers) and sorbets between courses to petits fours – you'll never get up.

NOBU JAPANESE £££

Map p446 (☎020-7447 4747; www.noburestaurants.com/london-old-park-lane; 1st fl, Metropolitan Hotel, 19 Old Park Lane; mains £26-45; ⏰noon-2.30pm daily, 6-10.30pm Mon-Wed, 6-11pm Thu-Sat, 6-10pm Sun; 📶; Ⓤ Hyde Park Corner) Book well in advance to chew and view at one of London's greatest celebrity magnets. The food is Japanese-Peruvian (with a heavy emphasis on the former) and signature dishes include the black cod with miso and the Wagyu cooked and served on a *toban yaki* (ceramic plate). From the decor to the service, everything is perfectly pitched.

KITTY FISHER'S MODERN BRITISH £££

Map p446 (☎020-3302 1661; www.kittyfishers.com; 10 Shepherd Market; mains £27-29; ⏰noon-2.30pm & 6-9.30pm Mon-Sat; Ⓤ Green Park) Taking pride of place in Mayfair's 18th-century Shepherd Market (historically one of London's red-light districts), this cosy dining room is named after the 18th-century courtesan painted by Joshua Reynolds. Now a handsomely furnished, twin-roomed restaurant, it serves quality British fare such as monkfish with cauliflower and curried butter, or partridge with celeriac and pickled pear. The wine list is excellent.

LE BOUDIN BLANC FRENCH £££

Map p446 (☎020-7499 3292; www.boudinblanc.co.uk; 5 Trebeck St; mains £23-32; ⏰noon-3pm & 6-11pm Mon-Sat, to 10.30pm Sun; 📶; Ⓤ Green Park) Surely this is one of the best French bistros in London, with meat dishes such as confit duck leg or Dover sole cooked to perfection, sauces perfectly executed and portions generous. The *frites* are so much more than just chips, the room transports diners to Paris, and a list of over 500 wines keeps this place perennially popular. Book ahead.

★GYMKHANA INDIAN £££

Map p448 (☎020-3011 5900; www.gymkhanalondon.com; 42 Albemarle St; mains £17-38, 4-course menus £40; ⏰noon-2.30pm & 5.30-10.15pm Mon-Sat; 📶🖉; Ⓤ Green Park) The rather sombre setting at this serious Indian fine-dining establishment is intended to invoke the 'good old days' of the British Raj – lazily whirling fans in oak ceilings, period cricket photos and hunting trophies – but the food is anything but dull. Seven-course tasting meat/vegetarian menus are offered (£85/80), and the bar, reminiscent of a 17th-century East India punch-house, opens until 1am.

SEXY FISH JAPANESE £££

Map p446 (☎020-3764 2000; www.sexyfish.com; Berkeley Sq House, Berkeley Sq; mains £21-38; ⏰noon-2am Mon-Sat, to 1am Sun; Ⓤ Green Park) The high-level Japanese restaurant and DJ bar Mayfair never knew it needed, Sexy Fish is pure flamboyance, with art by Damien Hirst and Frank Gehry, a lurid colour scheme and an enormous aquarium. The food is expensive but fantastic, featuring lobster with chilli, pomelo and coconut, super-fresh sashimi, or *robata*-grilled lamb chops with miso and *gochujang* (Korean chilli paste).

The bar offers the full à la carte menu, has DJs every night from Wednesday to Saturday, and apparently contains the largest Japanese whisky collection in the world.

PARK CHINOIS CHINESE £££

Map p446 (☎020-3327 8888; https://parkchinois.com; 17 Berkeley St; mains £28-55; ⏰noon-3pm Mon-Fri, to 4pm Sat & Sun, 6pm-2am Mon-Sat, to midnight Sun; Ⓤ Green Park) This opulent restaurant and club south of Berkeley Sq serves refined dim sum and other Chinese fare daily in the glitzy ground-floor **Salon de Chine**. From 6pm Tuesday to Saturday, you can also head underground to the extravagant **Club Chinois**, where DJs, cabaret and other entertainment await, the full menu is served, and the Wave Bar mixes up excellent cocktails.

The house band, playing upstairs from 7.45pm each night, is subsidised by adding a slightly cheeky £10 per person to the bill, while diners in the Club Chinois can expect their contribution to rise to £25.

DRINKING & NIGHTLIFE

Even though the famous clubs have slowly disappeared (a few pockets of decadence remain), the West End buzzes with excitement almost every night of the week, with revellers heading to theatre shows, excellent restaurants, late-night bookshops, and the myriad pubs and bars from Soho to Leicester Sq.

St James's

★SKETCH COCKTAIL BAR

Map p440 (☎020-7659 4500; www.sketch.london; 9 Conduit St; ⏰7am-2am Mon-Fri, 8am-2am Sat, 8am-midnight Sun; Ⓤ Oxford Circus) Merrily undefinable, Sketch has all at once a two-Michelin-starred restaurant, a millennial-pink dining room lined with nonsensical cartoons by British artist David Shrigley, a mystical-forest-themed bar with a self-playing piano, and toilets hidden inside gleaming white egg-shaped pods. We don't know what's happening either, but we're here for it.

RIVOLI BAR COCKTAIL BAR

Map p448 (☎020-7493 8181; www.theritzlondon.com/dine-with-us/rivoli-bar; Ritz London, 150 Piccadilly; ⏰11.30am-11.30pm Mon-Sat, noon-10.30pm Sun; 📶; Ⓤ Green Park) You may not quite need a diamond as big as the Ritz (p349) to drink at this art-deco marvel, but it might help. All camphor wood, illuminated Lalique glass, golden-ceiling domes and stunning cocktails, the bar is a gem. Unlike in some other parts of the Ritz, dress code here is smart casual (this laxity does not extend to trainers).

Caviar, oysters, and more substantial classics such as tuna niçoise and oxtail shepherd's pie are available between 11.30am and 10.30pm (£36 to £375).

DUKES LONDON COCKTAIL BAR

Map p448 (☎020-7491 4840; www.dukeshotel.com/dukes-bar; Dukes Hotel, 35 St James's Pl; ⏰2-11pm Mon-Sat, 4-10.30pm Sun; 📶; Ⓤ Green Park) Superb martinis and a gentlemen's-club-like ambience are the ingredients of this classic bar, where white-jacketed masters mix up perfect preparations. James Bond fans should make a pilgrimage here: author Ian Fleming used to frequent the place, where he undoubtedly ordered his drinks 'shaken, not stirred'. Smokers can ease into the secluded **Cognac and Cigar Garden** to enjoy cigars purchased here.

The dress code is smart casual, and hotel guests can linger slightly longer at closing time.

Bloomsbury & Fitzrovia

LAMB PUB

Map p444 (☎020-7405 0713; www.thelamblondon.com; 94 Lamb's Conduit St; ⏰11am-11pm Mon-Wed, to midnight Thu-Sat, noon-10.30pm Sun; Ⓤ Russell Sq) Its curved mahogany bar topped with etched-glass 'snob screens' (swivelling panels concealing genteel Victorian drinkers from bar staff and other workers) and its walls hung with antique lithographs, the Lamb seems the Platonic ideal of a London pub. Enjoy your Young's bitter on the deep-green upholstered banquettes, or in the walled beer garden in fine weather.

QUEEN'S LARDER PUB

Map p444 (☎020-7837 5627; www.queenslarder.co.uk; 1 Queen Sq; ⏰11.30am-11pm Mon-Fri, noon-11pm Sat, noon-10.30pm Sun; Ⓤ Russell Sq)

This cheery local favourite takes its name from Queen Charlotte, who previously stored food here for her husband George III, during his nearby treatment for insanity. The food today is *very* English (think Spam with chips and beans) and served daily from noon to 3pm, while the snug bar is augmented by a few outside tables and an upstairs dining room.

MUSEUM TAVERN PUB

Map p444 (020-7242 8987; 49 Great Russell St; 11am-11.30pm Mon-Thu, to midnight Fri & Sat, noon-10.30pm Sun; ; Holborn or Tottenham Court Rd) Inaugurated in 1723, this storied pub has refreshed scholars from the British Museum's Reading Room including Karl Marx, George Orwell, Sir Arthur Conan Doyle and JB Priestley. Handsomely adorned with original late-Victorian etched glass, lead lighting and woodwork, it's popular with academics, students and travellers alike. It also serves pub classics from pies and burgers to a Sunday roast.

Sunday roasts and week-round pub fare will set you back around £11 to £14.

LONDON COCKTAIL CLUB COCKTAIL BAR

Map p444 (020-7580 1960; www.londoncocktailclub.co.uk/goodge-street; 61 Goodge St; 4.30pm-midnight Mon-Sat; Goodge St) Pendant bar lights, bright clutter, graffitied walls and raucous atmosphere give a New York vibe to this snug basement saloon just north of Oxford St. If you prefer to drink seated, arrive early or hire the private booth: it gets pretty packed. The cocktail menu is about the length of the Brooklyn Bridge, with plenty of house specials.

Monday nights are great value: two cocktails for £12 all night.

Soho & Chinatown

SWIFT COCKTAIL BAR

Map p440 (020-7437 7820; www.barswift.com; 12 Old Compton St; 3pm-midnight Mon-Sat, to 10.30pm Sun; Leicester Sq or Tottenham Court Rd) A favourite Soho drinking spot, Swift has a sleek, candlelit upstairs bar for walk-ins seeking a superior cocktail before dinner or the theatre, and a bookings-only downstairs bar (open from 5pm) offering more than 250 whiskies, art-deco-inspired sofas, and live blues and jazz from 9pm on Fridays and Saturdays. Bar snacks include oysters and olives.

SHE SOHO LESBIAN

Map p440 (020-7437 4303; www.she-soho.com; 23a Old Compton St; 4-11.30pm Mon-Thu, to midnight Fri & Sat, to 10.30pm Sun; Leicester Sq) This intimate basement bar has DJs, comedy, drag-king cabaret, burlesque, live music and party nights, all in addition to a generally friendly and unpretentious atmosphere. It's open till 3am on the last Friday and Saturday of the month, and everybody is welcome, although women are given preference and men need a female chaperone.

FRENCH HOUSE PUB

Map p440 (020-7437 2477; www.frenchhousesoho.com; 49 Dean St; noon-11pm Mon-Sat, to 10.30pm Sun; Leicester Sq) This legendary, twin-storied bohemian boozer has quite a history: it was the meeting place of the Free French Forces during WWII and de Gaulle is said to have drunk here often, while Dylan Thomas, Peter O'Toole and Francis Bacon all measured their length on the wooden floor at least once. Expect to share space with media and theatre types enjoying liquid lunches.

Sip on Ricard, French wine or Kronenbourg, and socialise with the quirky locals (a practice encouraged by the house's 'no music, no machines, no television and no mobile phones' policy). Francophile food such as oysters, *rillettes* and rabbit with mustard (mains around £16) is served from 12.30pm to 3.30pm Monday to Friday, plus 6pm to 9.30pm Tuesday to Thursday.

EXPERIMENTAL COCKTAIL CLUB CHINATOWN COCKTAIL BAR

Map p440 (www.chinatownecc.com; 13a Gerrard St; 6pm-3am Mon-Sat, to midnight Sun; ; Leicester Sq or Piccadilly Circus) Deliberately obscure in its nondescript location, the ECC is a sensational cocktail bar behind an unmarked, faded-grey door in Chinatown. Soft lighting, mirrors, bare-brick walls and distressed furnishings match the sophisticated cocktails, rare spirits and vintage champagne on offer. Half the space is open to those without reservations (only accepted by email), and there's a £5 cover charge after 11pm.

YARD GAY

Map p440 (020-7437 2652; www.yardbar.co.uk; 57 Rupert St; 2-11.30pm Mon & Tue, from noon Wed & Thu, noon-midnight Fri & Sat, to 10.30pm Sun; Piccadilly Circus) This Soho favourite attracts a cross-section of the good, the bad and the beautiful. Fairly attitude-free, it's perfect for pre-club drinks or just an evening out. Grab a seat in the upstairs loft bar or join the friendly crowd in the open-air courtyard bar (heated in season) below.

BAR TERMINI BAR

Map p440 (07860 945018; http://bar-termini-soho.com; 7 Old Compton St; 10am-11.30pm Mon-Thu, to 1am Fri & Sat, to 10.30pm Sun; Leicester Sq or Tottenham Court Rd) Cool, assured and expertly staffed, this tiny Soho cafe-bar is perfect for a negroni (the speciality), house cocktail (mostly £12) or top-notch coffee, sandwich or charcuterie plate. You won't need long to ponder alternative drink choices (only three wines and one beer are offered) and it's wise to book a table (one-hour slots are available from noon).

TWO FLOORS BAR

Map p440 (020-7439 1007; www.twofloors.com; 3 Kingly St; noon-11.30pm Mon-Thu, to midnight Fri & Sat, to 10.30pm Sun; ; Oxford Circus or Piccadilly Circus) This chilled Soho spot has managed to stay off the lager-lout radar screen by eschewing outdoor signage. The Pacific bar on the main floor has a long zinc bar and tables but, as suckers for anything Polynesian (grass skirts, poi, aloha), we head straight downstairs to the Tiki bar for a 'poco loco' or a zombie (£8.50 to £10).

Enter from Kingly St or Kingly Ct.

CAHOOTS COCKTAIL BAR

Map p440 (020-7352 6200; www.cahoots-london.com; 13 Kingly Ct; 5pm-1am Mon-Wed, 4pm-2am Thu, to 3am Fri, 1pm-3am Sat, 3pm-midnight Sun; Oxford Circus) Tricked up to look like a disused Underground station, Cahoots is a retro cocktail bar channelling the spirit of London during WWII and its aftermath. Cocktails such as the 'Vera Lynn' (gin, apple juice, pear purée, ginger, elderflower, lime and pepper) are presented with period flair, and live jazz and swing are regular diversions. It's best to book in advance.

Cahoots is not the easiest place to find; you can also enter from Beak St.

VILLAGE GAY

Map p440 (020-7478 0530; www.villagesoho.co.uk; 81 Wardour St; 4pm-2am Mon-Thu, to 3am Fri & Sat, to 11.30pm Sun; Piccadilly Circus) Ever since opening its doors in 1991, the Village has been up for a party any night of the week. There are karaoke nights, go-go-dancers and DJs on the weekend, and half-price cocktails from 4pm to 7pm daily. And if you can't wait until the club's open to strut your stuff, there's a dance floor downstairs – complete with pole, of course.

DOG & DUCK PUB

Map p440 (020-7494 0697; www.nicholsonspubs.co.uk; 18 Bateman St; 11.30am-11pm Mon-Wed, to 1am Thu-Sat, noon-10.30pm Sun; Tottenham Court Rd) With a fine array of real ales and some stunning Victorian glazed tiling and pressed-tin ceilings adorning its intimate interior, the Dog & Duck has attracted an eclectic crowd since opening its doors around 1734 – including John Constable, Dante Gabriel Rossetti, George Orwell and Madonna. Intriguing pies such as boar and chorizo and wild game reward the curious.

G-A-Y LATE CLUB

Map p440 (020-7437 0479; www.g-a-y.co.uk; 5 Goslett Yard; 11pm-3am Sun-Thu, from 10.30pm Fri & Sat; Tottenham Court Rd) This hugely popular lesbian and gay bar and club with a late licence plays pop and other nonsense (imagine Donna Summer's 'Last Dance') till the wee hours.

DUKE OF WELLINGTON GAY

Map p440 (020-7439 1274; www.dukeofwellingtonsoho.co.uk/london; 77 Wardour St; noon-midnight Mon-Sat, to 11.30pm Sun; ; Leicester Sq) This twin-floored pub off Old Compton St attracts a beardy, fun-loving gay crowd, welcoming friendly comers of all persuasions. A classic jumping-off point for wilder Soho nights, it spills onto the pavement in the warmer months, hosting free DJ after-parties when 'divas' such as Mariah Carey and Celine Dion are performing in town.

Covent Garden & Leicester Square

★LAMB & FLAG PUB

Map p438 (020-7497 9504; www.lambandflagcoventgarden.co.uk; 33 Rose St; 11am-11pm Mon-Sat, noon-10.30pm Sun; Covent Garden) Perpetually busy, the pint-sized Lamb & Flag is full of charm and history: there's been a public house here since at least 1772, when it was known as the Cooper's Arms and infamous for staging bare-knuckle boxing matches. Rain or shine, you'll have to elbow your way through the merry crowd drinking outside to get to the bar.

The main entrance is at the top of tiny, cobbled Rose St, but it's also accessible from the backstreet donkey path called Lazenby Ct that will temporarily transport you back to Dickensian London. Watch your head.

TERROIRS WINE BAR

Map p438 (020-7036 0660; www.terroirswinebar.com; 5 William IV St; noon-11pm Mon-Sat; ; Charing Cross) This food-friendly wine bar near Charing Cross has a fantastic selection of Old and New World wines, with plenty by the glass and available for takeaway. Food isn't an afterthought either, with small plates such as burrata with clementine, radicchio and pine nuts augmented by a couple of mains (perhaps lamb rump with black-cabbage pesto and aubergine) and charcuterie platters.

SALISBURY PUB

Map p438 (020-7836 5863; 90 St Martin's Lane; 11am-11pm Mon-Thu, to midnight Fri & Sat, to 10.30pm Sun; Leicester Sq) Brave the crowds at this centrally located pub established in 1899, just to see the beautifully etched and engraved windows and other Victorian features that have somehow escaped the developer's hand. It has a vast range of beers, including lots of cask ales and some rarer continental lagers.

KU BAR GAY

Map p440 (020-7437 4303; www.ku-bar.co.uk; 30 Lisle St; noon-3am Mon-Sat, to midnight Sun; Leicester Sq) Ku is a three-tiered pleasure palace near Leicester Sq, with a cocktail bar and lounge above ground playing pop videos on wall-hung screens, and a proper, pumping nightclub below, open from 10pm.

Holborn & The Strand

★AMERICAN BAR COCKTAIL BAR

Map p438 (020-7836 4343; www.fairmont.com/savoy-london/dining/americanbar; Savoy Hotel, The Strand; 11.30am-midnight Mon-Sat, from noon Sun; ; Temple, Charing Cross or Embankment) Home of the Lonely Street, Concrete Jungle and other house cocktails named after iconic songs collected in the 'Savoy Songbook', the seriously dishy American Bar is a London icon, with soft blue furniture, gleaming art-deco lines and live piano jazz from 6.30pm nightly. Cocktails start at £20 and peak at a stupefying £5000 (for the Sazerac, containing cognac from 1858).

Named for serving 'American-style' drinks (now known as cocktails), it's the oldest cocktail bar in London. The dress code is smart casual.

CRAFT BEER CO CRAFT BEER

Map p438 (020-7240 0431; www.thecraftbeerco.com/covent-garden; 168 High Holborn; noon-midnight Sun-Wed, to 1am Thu-Sat; Tottenham Court Rd) Incongruously carved out of a corner of a leisure centre, this branch of a nine-strong chain boasts 15 cask pumps from UK microbreweries, as well as 30 keg lines and a range of 100-plus beers in bottles and cans from around the world. Don't worry if the bar looks rammed; there's usually table space in the basement.

RADIO ROOFTOP BAR BAR

Map p438 (020-7395 3440; https://radiorooftop.com/london; 10th fl, ME London, 336-337 The Strand; 7am-1am Mon-Wed, to 2am Thu-Sat, to midnight Sun; Temple or Covent Garden) This stunner of an art-deco bar (cocktails £17) offers gorgeous views, especially of the Thames, South Bank and Trafalgar Sq, from the open-air terrace on the 10th floor of the ME London (p349) hotel. It also does food at all hours, including a £30 buffet breakfast, 'brunch' (lunch, really) of burgers, eggs and sandwiches, and all-day dining focused on sharing plates.

Non-guests can't stay in the bar beyond 11pm.

HOLBORN WHIPPET PUB

Map p438 (☎020-3137 9937; www.holbornwhippet.com; 25-29 Sicilian Ave; ⏰noon-11pm Mon-Sat; ⓤHolborn) Sitting at the north-western entrance to the marble-enriched Edwardian pedestrian arcade Sicilian Ave, the Whippet is a snug modern pub with an emphasis on small-producer craft beers: typically around 10 from the tap and five from casks. Pop-up kitchens such as LIU Xiaomian, specialising in hot-and-numbing noodles from Chongqing, serve lunch here from Tuesday to Friday.

PRINCESS LOUISE PUB

Map p438 (☎020-7405 8816; 208 High Holborn; ⏰11am-11pm Mon-Fri, from noon Sat, noon-6.45pm Sun; ⓤHolborn) The gorgeous ground-floor saloon of this Sam Smith's pub, dating from 1872, boasts pressed-tin ceilings, handsome tiling, etched mirrors and 'snob screens', and a stunning central horseshoe bar. The original Victorian wood partitions provide plenty of private nooks, and typical pub food is served from noon to 2.30pm Monday to Friday, and 6pm to 8.30pm Monday to Thursday (mains £8 to £12).

HEAVEN GAY

Map p438 (☎020-7930 2020; www.heavennightclub-london.com; Villiers St; ⏰11pm-5am Mon, to 4am Thu & Fri, 10.30pm-5am Sat; ⓤEmbankment or Charing Cross) Encouraging hedonism since 1979, when it opened on the site of a former roller disco, this perennially popular mixed/gay bar under the Charing Cross arches hosts excellent gigs and club nights, and has hosted New Order, the Birthday Party, Killing Joke and many a legendary act. Monday's mixed party Popcorn offers one of the best weeknight's clubbing in the capital.

The celebrated G-A-Y takes place here on Thursday (G-A-Y Porn Idol), Friday (G-A-Y Camp Attack) and Saturday (plain ol' G-A-Y).

GORDON'S WINE BAR WINE BAR

Map p438 (☎020-7930 1408; https://gordonswinebar.com; 47 Villiers St; ⏰11am-11pm Mon-Sat, noon-10pm Sun; ⓤEmbankment or Charing Cross) Quite possibly the oldest wine bar in London (it opened in 1890), cavernous, candlelit and atmospheric Gordon's is a victim of its own success – it's relentlessly busy, and unless you arrive before the office crowd does, forget about landing a table. Nibble on cheese, bread and olives with your plonk – there's even a vegan/organic wine list.

Warm weather increases the available space, as tables are set out on Watergate Walk.

BAR POLSKI BAR

Map p438 (☎020-7831 9679; www.facebook.com/barpolskilondon; 11 Little Turnstile; ⏰4-11pm Mon, 12.30-11pm Tue-Thu, to 11.30pm Fri, 6-11pm Sat; ⓤHolborn) With around 60 different Polish spirits on offer – from hazelnut- and wheat-flavoured vodkas to *slivowica* (plum brandy) – every devotee of strong liquor should find something to their taste at this tucked-away little bar. For around £8 to £10 there's great Polish food like *bigos* (hunter's stew of sauerkraut and smoked meats) and *pierogis* (dumplings), but the triangular, tiled interior lacks atmosphere.

Marylebone

★ARTESIAN COCKTAIL BAR

Map p446 (☎020-7636 1000; www.artesian-bar.co.uk; Langham Hotel, 1c Portland Pl; ⏰11am-1am Mon-Wed, to 2am Thu-Sat, to midnight Sun; 📶; ⓤOxford Circus) For a dose of colonial glamour with a touch of Oriental elegance, the sumptuous (often crowded) bar at the Langham hits many marks. Its cocktails (from £20) have won multiple awards, and the bar itself has been acclaimed the world's best. Its name acknowledges the 110m-deep well beneath the hotel and, metaphorically, the immaculately designed 'source of indulgence' to be found within.

PURL COCKTAIL BAR

Map p446 (☎020-7935 0835; www.purl-london.com; 50-54 Blandford St; ⏰5-11.30pm Mon-Thu, to midnight Fri & Sat; ⓤBaker St or Bond St) Purl is a fabulous underground drinking den – decked out in overstuffed vintage furniture in intimate nooks, and adorned with antique wood, stripped bricks and mementoes of glorious past epochs like the silent-film era. Foams, aromas, unlikely garnishes and bespoke glassware give cocktails old and new an air of discovery, while subdued lighting and conversation add to the mysterious air.

It's all seated, across a variety of rooms and alcoves, and booking several days ahead is recommended – aim for Wednesday if you like live jazz.

GOLDEN EAGLE PUB

Map p446 (020-7935 3228; 59 Marylebone Lane; 11am-11pm Mon-Sat, noon-10.30pm Sun; Bond St) If you are seriously into singalongs, head for this attractive free house in Marylebone, where the keys of the old 'goanna' (piano) get tickled by Tony 'Fingers' Pearson from 8.30pm to 11.15pm every Tuesday, Thursday and Friday. With no kitchen to distract from the boozing and singing, it can be lots of fun.

Mayfair

★MAGRITTE BAR COCKTAIL BAR

Map p446 (020-7499 1001; www.thebeaumont.com/dining/american-bar; Beaumont, Brown Hart Gardens; 11.30am-midnight Mon-Sat, to 11pm Sun; ; Bond St) Sip a bourbon or a classic cocktail in the 1920s art-deco ambience of this stylish bar at the hallmark Beaumont (p349) hotel. It's central, glam and like a private members' club, but far from stuffy. Only a few years old, the Magritte Bar feels like it's been pouring drinks since the days of the flapper and the jazz age.

10° AT GALVIN AT WINDOWS BAR

Map p446 (020-7208 4021; www.galvinatwindows.com; 28th fl, London Hilton on Park Lane, 22 Park Lane; 11am-1am Mon-Wed, to 2am Thu-Sat, to 11pm Sun; ; Hyde Park Corner) From the 28th floor of the Park Lane Hilton, this swish bar boasts delightful views, especially during the golden sunset hour to which '10°' refers. Cocktail prices reach similar heights, but the drinks are expertly made and to be enjoyed in leather seats in exuberantly colourful yet elegant surrounds. Hanging greenery and small eats from the excellent restaurant complete the catalogue of pleasures.

From Bellini Sunday lunches (£55 per person) to three-course pre-theatre menus (£35), there are a number of ways to enjoy the Galvin at Windows' kitchen at a discount. A smart-casual dress code applies.

CONNAUGHT BAR COCKTAIL BAR

Map p446 (020-7499 7070; www.the-connaught.co.uk/mayfair-bars/connaught-bar; Connaught Hotel, Carlos Pl; 11am-1am Mon-Sat, to midnight Sun; ; Bond St) Drinkers who know their stuff single out the travelling martini trolley for particular praise, but almost everything mixed at the silver-and-platinum-toned bar at this iconic Mayfair hotel, built as the Coburg in 1815, gets the nod. You'll enjoy lavish art-deco design, faultless service and some of the best drinks in town. Classic and reimagined cocktails range from £12 to £21.

Food, including oysters, caviar and truffled pasta (mains £28 to £31), is served from 11am to 3.30pm and again in the evening, and dress code is smart casual.

PUNCHBOWL PUB

Map p446 (020-7493 6841; www.punchbowllondon.com; 41 Farm St; 11.30am-11pm Mon-Sat, to 10pm Sun; ; Green Park) The Grade II–listed Punchbowl, one of Mayfair's oldest pubs, is split between the public bar, a more formal dining room and a reservations-only club. Retaining many of its original 18th-century features (wood panels, cornicing etc), it attracts a young and moneyed crowd sipping cask ales, fine wines and whisky rather than pints of gassy lager.

Pub classics and snacks are served in the pub (small plates £5 to £8), while the dining room aspires to greater things in dishes such as bass with crab-crushed potatoes, wilted spinach and *sauce américaine* (mains £16 to £27).

ENTERTAINMENT

The West End not only has the lion's share of London's theatres (plus two opera houses), it's also home to an eclectic mix of cinemas and comedy clubs, and the doyen of jazz clubs, Ronnie Scott's.

★PRINCE CHARLES CINEMA CINEMA

Map p440 (020-7494 3654; www.princecharlescinema.com; 7 Leicester Pl; Leicester Sq) The last independent theatre in the West End, Prince Charles Cinema is universally loved for its show-anything attitude. Singalongs and quote-a-longs (*Frozen*, *Elf* and *The Rocky Horror Picture Show* are perennial faves), all-nighter movie marathons (including PJ parties), and anniversary and special-format screenings regularly grace its listings. Arriving in costumed character is encouraged.

DONMAR WAREHOUSE THEATRE

Map p438 (020-3282 3808; www.donmarwarehouse.com; 41 Earlham St; Covent Garden) The 250-seat Donmar Warehouse is London's 'thinking person's theatre'. With new artistic director Michael Longhurst, works in progress are more provocative and less celebrity-driven than traditional West End theatre. The 2020 program includes works from playwrights like Caryl Churchill and Nina Segal.

ROYAL OPERA HOUSE OPERA

Map p438 (020-7304 4000; www.roh.org.uk; Bow St; gift shop & cafe from 10am; Covent Garden) Opera and ballet have a fantastic setting on Covent Garden Piazza, and a night here is a sumptuous affair. Although the program has modern influences, the main attractions are still the classic productions with their world-class performers. A three-year, £50-million revamp finished in October 2018, with new areas open to the non-ticketed public for the first time, including the cafe and bar.

Discounted tickets (just 49 of them) for the week ahead go on sale on Fridays at 1pm in an event called **Friday Rush**. Half-price standby tickets are occasionally available four hours before the performance.

If you want a peek behind the curtain, sign up for a **guided tour**. The popular 1¼-hour Backstage Tour (adult/child £15/11.50) takes you behind the scenes to imagine the preparation, excitement and histrionics before a performance in this inspiring venue. Photography is not allowed.

★WIGMORE HALL CLASSICAL MUSIC

Map p446 (020-7935 2141; www.wigmore-hall.org.uk; 36 Wigmore St; Bond St) Wigmore Hall, built in 1901 as a piano showroom, is one of the best and most active classical-music venues in town, with more than 460 concerts a year. This isn't just because of its fantastic acoustics, beautiful Arts and Crafts–style cupola over the stage and great variety of concerts, but also because of the sheer quality of the performances.

The Sunday-morning concerts at 11.30am (which are followed by coffee or sherry) and the lunchtime events at 1pm on Mondays (broadcast live on BBC Radio 3) are excellent value (adult/concession £16/14).

★RONNIE SCOTT'S JAZZ

Map p440 (020-7439 0747; www.ronniescotts.co.uk; 47 Frith St; 6pm-3am Mon-Sat, noon-4pm & 6.30pm-midnight Sun; Leicester Sq or Tottenham Court Rd) Ronnie Scott's jazz club opened in 1959 and became widely known as Britain's best, hosting such luminaries as Miles Davis, Charlie Parker, Ella Fitzgerald, Count Basie and Sarah Vaughan. The club continues to build upon its formidable reputation by presenting a range of big names and new talent. Book in advance, or come for a more informal gig at **Upstairs @ Ronnie's**.

PICTUREHOUSE CENTRAL CINEMA

Map p440 (0871 902 5747; www.picturehouses.com/cinema/Picturehouse_Central; Shaftesbury Ave; adult/child £16.90/7.90; Piccadilly) A beautifully designed, multiscreen cinema in the buzzing heart of Piccadilly Circus, Picturehouse Central is pure style from the moment you walk in and are met with the grand, red-tiled staircase illuminated by a cascade of lights. There's a downstairs cafe for anyone with a ticket, and upstairs there's a members' bar and roof terrace, with great views of the streets below.

POETRY CAFÉ PERFORMING ARTS

Map p438 (020-7420 9888; https://poetrysociety.org.uk/poetry-cafe; 22 Betterton St; 11am-10pm Mon-Sat; Covent Garden) Covent Garden's renovated Poetry Café is a favourite for lovers of verse. It has almost daily readings and performances by established poets, open-mic evenings and writing workshops. Vegetarian and vegan dishes include soups, stews and sandwiches.

COMEDY STORE COMEDY

Map p440 (0844 871 7699; www.thecomedystore.co.uk; 1a Oxendon St; Piccadilly Circus) This is one of the first (and some say one of the best) comedy clubs in London. The Comedy Store Players take the stage on Wednesday and Sunday nights, with the wonderful Josie Lawrence, a veteran of the scene, plus special guest comedians. On Thursdays, Fridays and Saturdays, Best in Stand Up features the best of London's comedy circuit.

NOVELTY AUTOMATION ARCADE

Map p444 (www.novelty-automation.com; 1a Princeton St; 10 tokens for £8; ⏲11am-6pm Tue, Wed, Fri & Sat, noon-8pm Thu; Ⓤ Holborn) This eccentric homemade arcade is full of coin-operated satirical machines that combine vintage seaside charm with the trials and tribulations of modern times. Games include building your own reactor ('Free edible nuclear waste every time!'), papping celebrities with a flying drone, and using a crane to dredge a lake of coins and sneaking them into the City of London without being spotted by regulators.

THE PLACE DANCE

Map p444 (☎020-7121 1100; www.theplace.org.uk; 17 Duke's Rd; Ⓤ Euston Sq) The birthplace of modern British dance is one of London's most exciting cultural venues, still concentrating on challenging and experimental choreography. Behind the late-Victorian terracotta facade you'll find a 300-seat theatre, an arty, creative cafe atmosphere and a dozen training studios. Tickets usually cost from £15.

ENGLISH NATIONAL OPERA OPERA

Map p438 (ENO; ☎020-7845 9300; www.eno.org; St Martin's Lane; Ⓤ Leicester Sq) The English National Opera is celebrated for making opera modern and more accessible, as all productions are sung in English. It's based at the impressive London Coliseum, built in 1904 and lovingly restored a century later. The **English National Ballet** also holds regular performances at the Coliseum. Tickets range from £12 to £125.

Backstage tours of the London Coliseum are bookable online (adult/concession £10/£8).

ST JOHN'S, SMITH SQUARE CLASSICAL MUSIC

Map p448 (☎020-7222 1061; www.sjss.org.uk; Smith Sq; Ⓤ Westminster or St James's Park) In the heart of Westminster, this eye-catching church was built by Thomas Archer in 1728 under Queen Anne's *New Churches in London and Westminster Act* (1710), which aimed to build 50 new churches for London's rapidly growing metropolitan area. After receiving a direct hit during WWII, it was rebuilt in the 1960s as a classical-music venue and is renowned for its excellent acoustics. Check the website for upcoming concerts and other events.

Although they never did build all 50 churches, St John's, along with a dozen others, saw the light of day. Unfortunately, with its four corner towers and monumental facades, the structure was much maligned for the first century of its existence thanks to rumours that Queen Anne likened it to a footstool. Today it is considered a masterpiece of English baroque. The brick-vaulted Footstool Restaurant in the crypt is a delightful choice for sustenance or a coffee.

SOHO THEATRE COMEDY

Map p440 (☎020-7478 0100; https://sohotheatre.com; 21 Dean St; tickets £8-25; Ⓤ Tottenham Court Rd) The Soho Theatre has developed a superb reputation for showcasing new comedy-writing talent and comedians. It also hosts top stand-up and sketch-based comedians, plus cabaret.

CURZON SOHO CINEMA

Map p440 (www.curzoncinemas.com; 99 Shaftesbury Ave; tickets £8-17; 📶; Ⓤ Leicester Sq or Piccadilly Circus) The Curzon Soho is one of London's best cinemas with a broad program of the best of British, European, US and world indie films, regular Q&As with directors, shorts and mini festivals, plus a cafe on the ground floor with free wifi and cakes to die for, and an ultra-comfortable bar upstairs.

MUSEUM OF COMEDY COMEDY

Map p444 (www.museumofcomedy.com; The Undercroft, St George's Church, Bloomsbury Way; ⏲5-10pm Mon-Sat, 1-10pm Sun; Ⓤ Holborn or Tottenham Court Rd) FREE Although the 'museum' is not worth crossing town for, it is free to enter. Book tickets to see established British comedians working new material, or better still, drop in for a drink and to watch newcomers at the free Monday Club performances. It also runs comedy-writing courses.

AMUSED MOOSE SOHO COMEDY

Map p440 (☎020-7287 3727; www.amusedmoose.com; Karma Sanctum Hotel, 20 Warwick St; Ⓤ Piccadilly Circus or Oxford Circus) The peripatetic Amused Moose can often be found pitched up at a Soho hotel, such as the Karma Sanctum. Shows are 'audience-friendly', so don't be afraid to sit in the front row. Big-name comedians sometimes do 'secret' gigs here to practise for TV or larger audiences, and if you can't make it north to Scotland, you'll find Edinburgh Fringe previews here.

SHOPPING

The West End's shopping scene hardly needs a formal introduction. Oxford St and Regent St are busy with the big chains from Primark to H&M to Zara. Covent Garden is also beset with well-known labels, but the shops are smaller and counterbalanced by independent boutiques and vintage stores. Soho is the spot for vinyl and book stores, and some arty independents where you'll find excellent souvenirs.

Westminster & St James's

★FORTNUM & MASON DEPARTMENT STORE

Map p448 (020-7734 8040; www.fortnumandmason.com; 181 Piccadilly; 10am-9pm Mon-Sat, 11.30am-6pm Sun; Green Park or Piccadilly Circus) With its classic eau-de-Nil (pale green) colour scheme, the 'Queen's grocery store' (established in 1707) refuses to yield to modern times. Its staff – men and women – still wear old-fashioned tailcoats, and its glamorous food hall is supplied with hampers, marmalade and speciality teas. Stop for a spot of afternoon tea at the **Diamond Jubilee Tea Salon**, visited by Queen Elizabeth II in 2012.

HATCHARDS BOOKS

Map p448 (020-7439 9921; www.hatchards.co.uk; 187 Piccadilly; 9.30am-8pm Mon-Sat, noon-6.30pm Sun; Green Park or Piccadilly Circus) The UK's oldest bookshop dates back to 1797, and has been cramped into this Georgian building for more than 200 years. Holding three royal warrants, Hatchards has a solid supply of signed editions plus a strong selection of first editions on the ground floor.

WATERSTONES PICCADILLY BOOKS

Map p440 (020-7851 2433; www.waterstones.com; 203-206 Piccadilly; 9am-9.30pm Mon-Sat, noon-5pm Sun; Piccadilly Circus) The chain's megastore is the largest bookshop in Europe, with helpful, knowledgeable staff and regular author readings, signings and discussions. The store spreads across eight floors, with a fabulous rooftop-bar-restaurant, 5th View (p110). Don't expect to escape within the hour.

STELLA MCCARTNEY FASHION & ACCESSORIES

Map p448 (www.stellamccartney.com; 23 Old Bond St; 10am-6.30pm Mon-Sat, noon-6pm Sun; Bond St) Stella McCartney is known for her sharp tailoring, floaty designs, accessible style and ethical approach to fashion (no leather, fur or modern slavery). This recently refurbished space showcases the designer's current collections in the West End's luxury-designer hub. Depending on your devotion and wallet, you'll feel at ease or like a trespasser.

PENHALIGON'S PERFUME

Map p448 (020-7629 1416; www.penhaligons.com; 16-17 Burlington Arcade; 9am-6.30pm Mon-Fri, from 9.30am Sat, noon-6pm Sun; Piccadilly Circus or Green Park) Follow your nose through the historic Burlington Arcade (p99) to this classic British perfumery. Attendants enquire about your favourite smells, take you on an exploratory tour of the shop's signature range, and help you discover new scents in their traditional perfumes, home fragrances and bath and body products. Everything is produced in England, with prices to match.

PAXTON & WHITFIELD FOOD & DRINK

Map p448 (020-7930 0259; www.paxtonandwhitfield.co.uk; 93 Jermyn St; 10am-6.30pm Mon-Sat, 11am-5pm Sun; Piccadilly Circus or Green Park) With modest beginnings as an Aldwych stall in 1742 and purveying a dizzying range of fine cheeses, this black-and gold-fronted shop holds two royal warrants.

Whatever your cheese leanings, you'll find the shop well supplied with hard and soft cheeses as well as blue and washed-rind examples.

TAYLOR OF OLD BOND STREET BEAUTY

Map p448 (020-7930 5321; www.taylorold bondst.co.uk; 74 Jermyn St; 9am-6pm Mon-Sat; Green Park or Piccadilly Circus) Plying its trade since the mid-19th century, this shop supplies the 'well-groomed gentleman' with every sort of razor, shaving brush and scent of shaving soap imaginable – not to mention oils, soaps and other bath products.

POP-UP SHOPPING

Taking a commendable stand against tacky souvenirs, **We Built This City** (☎020-3642 9650; www.webuilt-thiscity.com; ⊙10am-7pm Mon-Wed, to 8pm Thu-Sat, 11am-6.30pm Sun) sells locally themed merchandise that the recipient might actually want – most of which Londoners would happily put in their own homes, too. Gorgeous framed prints line the walls and celebrate London's neighbourhoods and the city's creativity. Check the website for its latest pop-up address.

Bloomsbury & Fitzrovia

★LONDON REVIEW BOOKSHOP — BOOKS

Map p444 (☎020-7269 9030; www.londonreviewbookshop.co.uk; 14 Bury Pl; ⊙10am-6.30pm Mon-Sat, noon-6pm Sun; ⓊHolborn) The flagship bookshop of the *London Review of Books* fortnightly literary journal doesn't put faith in towering piles of books and slabs on shelves, but offers a wide range of titles in a handful of copies only. It often hosts high-profile author talks, and there's a charming cake store where you can leaf through your new purchases.

JAMES SMITH & SONS UMBRELLAS — FASHION & ACCESSORIES

Map p438 (☎020-7836 4731; www.james-smith.co.uk; 53 New Oxford St; ⊙10am-5.45pm Mon, Tue, Thu & Fri, from 10.30am Wed, 10am-5.15pm Sat; ⓊTottenham Court Rd) Nobody makes and stocks such elegant umbrellas (not to mention walking sticks and canes) as this place.

It's been fighting the British weather from the same address since 1857, and London's ever-present drizzle means they'll hopefully be here for years to come. Prices reflect the quality employed to produce each item. The beautiful old-school signage is worth a photo stop alone.

BLADE RUBBER STAMPS — ARTS & CRAFTS

Map p444 (☎020-7831 4242; www.bladerubberstamps.co.uk; 12 Bury Pl; ⊙10.30am-6pm Mon-Sat, 11.30am-4.30pm Sun; ⓊHolborn) This specialist stationery shop stocks just about every wooden-handled rubber stamp you care to imagine: from London icons like phone boxes and the Houses of Parliament to landscapes, planets, rockets and Christmas stamps. You can have one made to your design or DIY with a stamp-making kit. They make excellent lightweight gifts!

ATLANTIS BOOKSHOP — BOOKS

Map p444 (☎020-7405 2120; www.theatlantisbookshop.com; 49a Museum St; ⊙10.30am-6pm Mon-Sat; ⓊHolborn) A stone's throw from the British Museum, this bookshop has been running for almost a century and specialises in the occult. The shop stocks a variety of magic-related literature and items, including rare editions of books, magic ware (eg crystal balls, wands, cauldrons and the like) and tarot cards. It regularly acts as a venue for book launches, talks and other such events.

JARNDYCE — BOOKS

Map p444 (☎020-7631 4220; www.jarndyce.co.uk; 46 Great Russell St; ⊙11am-5.30pm Mon-Fri; ⓊTottenham Court Rd) Named after a court case in Charles Dickens' *Bleak House,* this antiquarian bookshop is opposite the British Museum in a building dating from the early 18th century.

It specialises in literature from around that time period and later, particularly the 19th century – Dickens is a speciality – and is packed with other affordable curiosities and surprises.

FOLK — FASHION & ACCESSORIES

Map p444 (www.folkclothing.com; 49 & 53 Lamb's Conduit St; ⊙11am-7pm Mon-Fri, 10am-6pm Sat, noon-5pm Sun; ⓊHolborn) Independent London-based brand offering simple but strikingly styled casual clothes, often in bold colours and with a handcrafted feel.

Head for No 49 for Folk's own line of menswear and to nearby No 53 for womenswear.

PERSEPHONE BOOKS BOOKS

Map p444 (☎020-7242 9292; www.persephonebooks.co.uk; 59 Lamb's Conduit St; ⏰10am-6pm Mon-Fri, 11am-5pm Sat, noon-4pm Sun; Ⓤ Russell Sq) Specialising in lesser-known literature by mostly women writers from the mid-20th century, Persephone Books has carved out an interesting and valuable niche.

The works range from memoirs and diaries to novels and short stories, and each comes with a bespoke grey jacket and bookmark.

GAY'S THE WORD BOOKS

Map p444 (☎020-7278 7654; www.gaystheword.co.uk; 66 Marchmont St; ⏰10am-6.30pm Mon-Sat, 2-6pm Sun; Ⓤ Russell Sq) The UK's first and only specifically gay and lesbian bookstore, this London institution has been selling LGBTIQ+ works since 1979. It has a superb selection and a genuine community spirit, bolstered by weekly and monthly discussion groups.

WATERSTONES BLOOMSBURY BOOKS

Map p444 (☎020-7636 1577; www.waterstones.com; 82 Gower St; ⏰9.30am-9pm Mon-Fri, to 8pm Sat, noon-6pm Sun; Ⓤ Euston Sq) Beautiful branch of the giant bookshop chain in a gorgeous 19th-century terracotta building in the heart of London university land.

Soho

★FOYLES BOOKS

Map p440 (☎020-7434 1574; www.foyles.co.uk; 107 Charing Cross Rd; ⏰9.30am-9pm Mon-Sat, noon-6pm Sun; Ⓤ Tottenham Court Rd) London's most legendary bookshop, where you can find even the most obscure titles. Once synonymous with chaos, Foyles got its act together and now this carefully designed store is a joy to explore. The cafe is on the 5th floor, plus a small gallery for art exhibitions. Grant & Cutler, the UK's largest foreign-language bookseller, is on the 4th floor.

HAMLEYS TOYS

Map p440 (☎0371 704 1977; www.hamleys.com; 188-196 Regent St; ⏰10am-9pm Mon-Fri, from 9.30am Sat, noon-6pm Sun; 👪; Ⓤ Oxford Circus) The biggest and oldest toy emporium in the world, Hamleys houses six floors of fun for kids of all ages, from the basement's Star Wars and Harry Potter collections up to Lego World, a sweet shop and tiny cafe on the 5th floor. Staff on each level have opened the packaging and are playing with everything from boomerangs to bubbles. Kids will happily spend hours here planning their Santa letters.

LIBERTY DEPARTMENT STORE

Map p440 (☎020-7734 1234; www.libertylondon.com; Regent St, entrance on Great Marlborough St; ⏰10am-8pm Mon-Sat, 11.30am-6pm Sun; 📶; Ⓤ Oxford Circus) One of London's most recognisable shops, Liberty department store has a white-and-wood-beam Tudor Revival facade that lures shoppers in to browse luxury contemporary fashion, homewares, cosmetics and accessories, all at sky-high prices.

Liberty is also known for its fabrics and has a full haberdashery department; a classic London gift or souvenir is a Liberty fabric print, especially in the form of a scarf.

★SOUNDS OF THE UNIVERSE MUSIC

Map p440 (☎020-7734 3430; https://soundsoftheuniverse.com; 7 Broadwick St; ⏰10am-7.30pm Sat, 11.30am-5.30pm Sun; Ⓤ Oxford Circus or Tottenham Court Rd)
Outlet of the **Soul Jazz Records** label: explorers of wild, wonderful and often forgotten corners of black music who bring back gems for their legendary compilations.

Vinyl fetishists will love the many brilliant, previously rare reissues on sale.

SISTER RAY MUSIC

Map p440 (☎020-7734 3297; www.sisterray.co.uk; 75 Berwick St; ⏰10am-8pm Mon-Sat, noon-6pm Sun; Ⓤ Oxford Circus or Tottenham Court Rd) Another stalwart of the Soho record-shop scene, specialising in a collection that BBC 1's John Peel would have been proud of: innovative, experimental and indie music. Staff are knowledgeable, and the tunes are banging (that means good, not painful).

RECKLESS RECORDS MUSIC

Map p440 (☎020-7437 4271; www.reckless.co.uk; 30 Berwick St; ⏰10am-7pm; Ⓤ Oxford Circus or Tottenham Court Rd) This small independent record store has hardly changed since it opened in 1984. Even this far into the 21st century, Reckless is still stuffed with people rifling through secondhand records and CDs. The shopfront was shown on the album cover of iconic British band Oasis, *(What's the Story) Morning Glory?*, on display in the front window.

PHONICA MUSIC

Map p440 (☎020-7025 6070; www.phonicarecords.co.uk; 51 Poland St; ⏰11.30am-7.30pm Mon-Wed & Sat, to 8pm Thu & Fri, noon-6pm Sun; Ⓤ Tottenham Court Rd or Oxford Circus) Uber-cool, yet a fairly chill vinyl store stocking mainly house, electro and hip-hop. Dig deeper and there's remastered reggae, dub, jazz and rock heading to the clubs and house parties of London.

AGENT PROVOCATEUR CLOTHING

Map p440 (☎020-7439 0229; www.agentprovocateur.com; 6 Broadwick St; ⏰11am-7pm Mon-Sat, noon-5pm Sun; Ⓤ Oxford Circus) For women's lingerie designed to be worn and seen, and certainly not hidden, pull up to wonderful Agent Provocateur, started by Joseph Corré, son of British fashion designer Vivienne Westwood. Its sexy and playful corsets, and bras and nighties for all shapes and sizes, exude confident and positive sexuality.

GOSH! BOOKS

Map p440 (☎020-7437 0187; www.goshlondon.com; 1 Berwick St; ⏰10.30am-7pm; Ⓤ Piccadilly Circus) Gosh! pack a big pow into this small space filled with prints, graphic novels, manga and children's books and games. Comics have taken over the basement, where super-fans can geek out over vintage editions and back issues.

Covent Garden & Leicester Square

★STANFORDS BOOKS

Map p438 (☎020-7836 1321; www.stanfords.co.uk; 7 Mercer Walk; ⏰9am-8pm Mon-Sat, noon-6pm Sun; Ⓤ Leicester Sq or Covent Garden) Trading since 1853, this grandaddy of travel bookshops and seasoned seller of maps, guides and globes is a destination in its own right. Polar explorer Ernest Shackleton, Victorian missionary David Livingstone and writer and presenter Michael Palin have all shopped here. In 2019 Stanfords left the iconic Long Acre building it had been housed in since 1901 and moved around the corner to its new address.

★FORBIDDEN PLANET COMICS

Map p438 (☎020-7420 3666; https://forbiddenplanet.com; 179 Shaftesbury Ave; ⏰10am-7pm Mon & Tue, to 7.30pm Wed, Fri & Sat, to 8pm Thu, noon-6pm Sun; Ⓤ Tottenham Court Rd) Forbidden Planet is a trove of comics, sci-fi, horror and fantasy literature, as well as action figures and toys, spread over two floors. It's an absolute dream for anyone into manga comics, off-beat genre titles, and sci-fi and fantasy memorabilia.

NEAL'S YARD DAIRY FOOD

Map p438 (☎020-7240 5700; www.nealsyarddairy.co.uk; 17 Shorts Gardens; ⏰10am-7pm Mon-Sat; Ⓤ Covent Garden) A fabulous, fragrant cheese house that would fit in somewhere in rural England, this place is proof that Britain can produce top-quality cheeses in most classes. There are more than 70 varieties of English and Irish cheeses that the shopkeepers will let you taste, including independent farmhouse brands. Condiments, pickles, jams and chutneys are also on sale.

CAMBRIDGE SATCHEL COMPANY FASHION & ACCESSORIES

Map p438 (☎020-3077 1100; www.cambridgesatchel.com; 37 Neal St; ⏰10am-8pm Mon-Fri, to 7pm Sat, 11am-6pm Sun; Ⓤ Covent Garden) Colourful Cambridge Satchel Company is the perfect place to pick up a British-made leather bag, passport holder or steamer trunk for your next adventure. Items can be personally embossed in-store, which takes just 15 minutes.

MOLTON BROWN BEAUTY

Map p438 (☎020-7240 8383; www.moltonbrown.co.uk; 18 Russell St; ⏰10am-7pm Mon-Sat, 11am-6pm Sun; Ⓤ Covent Garden) Made in England with rare, exotic ingredients from around the globe, fabulously fragrant natural-beauty brand Molton Brown is *the* toiletries choice for boutique hotels, posh restaurants and first-class airline bathrooms. No matter where you're going on your trip, its 'London via the World' range of soaps, lotions and perfumes is bound to take your travels even further.

WATKINS BOOKS

Map p438 (☎020-7836 2182; https://watkinsbooks.com; 19-21 Cecil Ct; ⊙10.30am-6.30pm Mon-Wed & Fri, 11am-7.30pm Thu & Sat, noon-7pm Sun; ⓤLeicester Sq) More books than you can shake a dreamcatcher at on subjects as wide-ranging as the afterlife, tarot, the Kabbalah, shamanism, spirituality, astrology, Tibetan Buddhism and more. If you have even the mildest interest in the occult, you could find yourself here for hours. Tarot and astrology readings can be booked here too, or sign up for a self-help course.

TED BAKER FASHION & ACCESSORIES

Map p438 (☎020-7836 7808; www.tedbaker.com; 9-10 Floral St; ⊙10.30am-7.30pm Mon-Sat, noon-6pm Sun; ⓤCovent Garden) The one-time Glasgow-based tailor shop has grown into a superb brand of clothing for both men and women. Ted's forte is its formal wear, with beautiful dresses for women (lots of daring prints and exquisite materials) and sharp tailoring for men. The casual collections (denim, beachwear etc) are popular too.

BENJAMIN POLLOCK'S TOYSHOP TOYS

Map p438 (☎020-7379 7866; www.pollocks-coventgarden.co.uk; 1st fl, 44 Market Bldg, Covent Garden Piazza; ⊙10.30am-6pm Mon-Wed, to 6.30pm Thu-Sat, 11am-6pm Sun; 👪; ⓤCovent Garden) This traditional toyshop is stuffed with the things that kids of all ages love: Victorian paper theatres, wooden marionettes, finger puppets and antique teddy bears (which look far too fragile to cuddle, much less play with).

Marylebone

★DAUNT BOOKS BOOKS

Map p446 (☎020-7224 2295; www.dauntbooks.co.uk; 83 Marylebone High St; ⊙9am-7.30pm Mon-Sat, 11am-6pm Sun; ⓤBaker St) An original Edwardian bookshop, with oak panels, galleries and gorgeous skylights, Daunt is one of London's loveliest bookshops. There are several Daunt outlets but none as gorgeous. Browse its travel, general fiction and nonfiction titles over two floors.

BEATLES STORE GIFTS & SOUVENIRS

Map p446 (☎020-7935 4464; www.beatlesstorelondon.co.uk; 230 Baker St; ⊙10am-6.30pm; ⓤBaker St) Fab Four guitar picks, Abbey Road fridge magnets, Ringo T-shirts, mop-top mugs, Magical Mystery Tour bags, Yellow Submarine Christmas lights, *Help!* posters, alarm clocks…the whole Beatles shebang. Other artistes (from Bowie and Queen to Nirvana and Jimi Hendrix) are represented in its sister shop **It's Only Rock 'n' Roll** across the street.

CATH KIDSTON FASHION & ACCESSORIES

Map p446 (☎020-7935 6555; www.cathkidston.com; 51 Marylebone High St; ⊙10am-6pm Mon-Tue, to 7pm Wed-Sat, 11am-7pm Sun; ⓤBaker St) British homewares and fashion designer Cath Kidston's signature floral prints and vintage-inspired fashion are immediately recognisable and dotted around the city. There's a great selection of travel-related products, as well as delightful London-branded gift items for souvenirs.

CADENHEAD'S WHISKY SHOP & TASTING ROOM DRINK

Map p446 (☎020-7935 6999; www.whiskytastingroom.com; 26 Chiltern St; ⊙10.30am-6.30pm Mon-Thu, from 11am Fri, 10.30am-6pm Sat; ⓤBaker St) Scotland's oldest independent bottler of pure, non-blended whisky from local distilleries, this shop is a joy for anyone with a passion for *uisge-beatha* (water of life; the Scots Gaelic word for whisky). All bottled whiskies derive from individually selected casks, without any filtrations, additions or colouring. Regular whisky tastings are held downstairs.

Mayfair

★VIVIENNE WESTWOOD FASHION & ACCESSORIES

Map p440 (☎020-7439 1109; www.viviennewestwood.com; 44 Conduit St; ⊙10am-6pm Mon-Wed, Fri & Sat, to 7pm Thu, noon-5pm Sun; ⓤBond St or Oxford Circus) The fashion doyenne of the punk and new-wave aesthetic, Westwood has always had a reputation for being controversial and political. She continues to design collections as bold, innovative and provocative as ever, featuring 19th-century-inspired bustiers, wedge shoes, tartan and sharp tailoring.

SELFRIDGES DEPARTMENT STORE

Map p446 (☎0800 123 400; www.selfridges.com; 400 Oxford St; ⏰9am-10pm Mon-Sat, 11.30am-6pm Sun; Ⓤ Bond St) Set in a grandiose column-flanked Grade II–listed structure, Selfridges has been innovating since its doors opened in 1909. Its wacky, ever-changing window displays draw a crowd of its own, especially at Christmas. Inside, an unparalleled food hall, sprawling cosmetics stations and the usual department-store essentials are topped by a rooftop **restaurant** with delicious city views.

BURBERRY FASHION & ACCESSORIES

Map p440 (☎020-3402 1500; www.burberry.com; 21-23 New Bond St; ⏰10am-7pm Mon-Sat, noon-6.30pm Sun; Ⓤ Bond St) The first traditional British brand to reach the heights of fashion, Burberry is known for its innovative take on classic pieces (eg brightly coloured trench coat and khaki pants with large and unusual pockets), its brand check pattern, and a tailored, groomed look.

GINA SHOES

Map p446 (☎020-7499 7539; www.gina.com; 119 Mount St; ⏰10am-6pm Mon-Wed, Fri & Sat, to 7pm Thu, noon-5pm Sun; Ⓤ Bond St) Beyond the quality of leather and fabrics and gorgeously chic styling, a frequent motif of these beautifully made and elegant British couture women's slingbacks, stilettos, trainers, flat sandals and platforms is the glittering Swarovski crystals. You'll be singing 'Diamonds on the Soles of Her Shoes' as prices start from around £485.

MULBERRY FASHION & ACCESSORIES

Map p446 (☎020-7491 3900; www.mulberry.com; 50 New Bond St; ⏰10am-7pm Mon-Sat, noon-6pm Sun; Ⓤ Bond St) Mulberry bags, famous for their quality leather and craftsmanship, are a massive status – sorry, style – statement. The brand has followed in the footsteps of other British design titans like Burberry and modernised itself in recent years.

GRAYS ANTIQUES ANTIQUES

Map p446 (www.graysantiques.com; 58 Davies St; ⏰10am-6pm Mon-Fri, 11am-5pm Sat; Ⓤ Bond St) Some 200 specialist stallholders selling antique jewellery, costumes, military collectables, Oriental works and much more can be found in two buildings, the main one on Davies St and an adjoining one on Davies Mews. Make sure you head to the basement of the Mews building where the River Tyburn still runs through a channel in the floor. Not all dealers open on Saturday.

City of London

Neighbourhood Top Five

❶ **Tower of London** (p137) Stepping through a treasury of history, past the colourful Beefeaters, spectacular Crown Jewels, soothsaying ravens and armour fit for a *very* large king.

❷ **St Paul's Cathedral** (p143) Walking in awed reverence below the mighty dome of London's most beloved building before climbing all 528 steps to the top.

❸ **Museum of London** (p150) Exploring the city's lengthy history and many incarnations through intriguing artefacts, interactive displays and recreated streetscapes.

❹ **Sky Garden** (p146) Marvelling at London's ultramodern architecture from the penthouse urban jungle atop the 'Walkie Talkie' building.

❺ **City Social** (p152) Elevating dinner to new heights with Michelin-starred cuisine in an art-deco-inspired 24th-floor lookout.

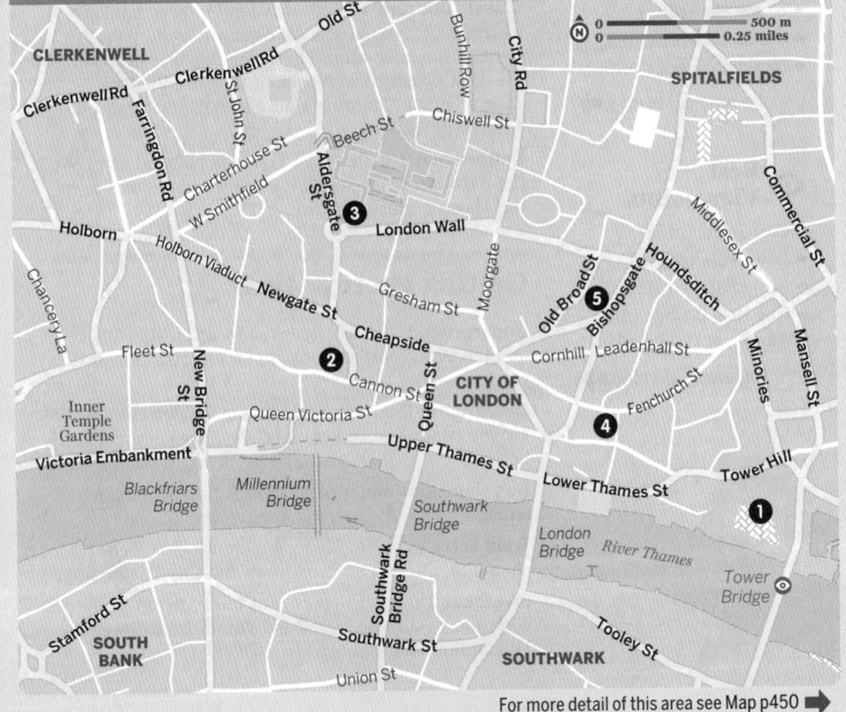

For more detail of this area see Map p450

Lonely Planet's Top Tip

Designed by French architect Jean Nouvel, One New Change (p157) is a shopping centre housing mainly high-street brands, but take the lift to the 6th floor and an open viewing platform will reward you with up-close views of the dome of St Paul's Cathedral and out over London.

Best Eating

- City Social (p152)
- Duck & Waffle (p151)
- Simpsons Tavern (p151)

For reviews, see p151.

Best Drinking & Nightlife

- Oriole (p153)
- Nickel Bar (p153)
- Viaduct Tavern (p155)
- Merchant House (p155)

For reviews, see p153.

Best Viewpoints

- City Social (p152)
- Sky Garden (p146)
- Sushi Samba (p152)
- One New Change (p157)
- Garden at 120 (p146)

For reviews, see p146.

Explore the City of London

For its small size, the City of London – also known as the Square Mile – punches well above its weight for must-see attractions. Start with the heavyweights, the Tower of London and St Paul's Cathedral (p143), allowing at least half a day for each. You can combine other sights with wanders through the City's lesser-known alleyways and quiet corners – Christopher Wren's dozens of churches make peaceful stops.

More than half a million people work in the City of London, but only about 7400 live here. To appreciate its industrious buzz, visit on a weekday when everything is open. The neighbourhood largely empties in the evening as workers retreat to the suburbs. Weekends have traditionally been quiet – and are a brilliant time for nearly people-free explorations, a rarity in a world-class metropolis – but that's slowly changing as bars and restaurants catch on and adjust their hours beyond the nine to five.

Local Life

Meals with a view Every London skyscraper now seems to come affixed with a high-altitude bar or restaurant, and we aren't complaining. Duck & Waffle (p151) is the loftiest.

Classic boozers Though they tend to keep bankers' hours, the City's old-school restaurants and pubs are some of the most atmospheric and historic in town. The best places to step back in time are Viaduct Tavern (p155), Counting House (p153), and Simpsons Tavern (p151).

Culture hub The City isn't London's cultural core, but the Barbican Centre (p156) is a powerhouse of innovative theatre, music and art.

Getting There & Away

Underground The City is served by seven Tube lines and the DLR; most stations are on the District and Circle lines.

Overground From Liverpool St, the London Overground heads east to Bethnal Green, Hackney and beyond.

Bus Numerous routes pass through the City's main streets.

Train Services run to Moorgate, Liverpool St, Fenchurch St, Cannon St, Blackfriars and City Thameslink.

Riverboat Thames Clippers runs boats east to Woolwich and west to Battersea and Putney from Tower Millennium Pier and Blackfriars Pier.

TOP EXPERIENCE

TACKLE THE TOWER OF LONDON

HARDYUNO/GETTY IMAGES ©

With a history as bloody as it is fascinating, the Tower is London's most absorbing sight. Begun during the 11th-century reign of William the Conqueror, this royal fortress is in fact a castle containing 22 towers, and has served as a palace, observatory, armoury, mint, zoo, prison and execution site.

Tower Green

The buildings to the west and the south of this verdant patch have always accommodated Tower officials. The current constable has a flat in Queen's House, built in 1540. But what looks at first glance like a peaceful, almost village-like slice of the Tower's inner ward is actually one of its bloodiest.

Scaffold Site

Those 'lucky' enough to have met their fate here (rather than suffering the embarrassment of execution on Tower Hill while being observed by thousands of jeering and cheering onlookers) included two of Henry VIII's wives, Anne Boleyn and Catherine Howard; 16-year-old Lady Jane Grey, who fell foul of Henry's daughter Mary I after her family attempted to have her crowned queen; and Robert Devereux, Earl of Essex, once a favourite of Elizabeth I. Just west of the scaffold site is **Beauchamp Tower** (1280, pronounced 'beach-em'), where high-ranking prisoners left behind unhappy inscriptions and other graffiti. In total, 22 people are known to have been executed within the Tower grounds, including 11 German spies killed by firing squad during WWI and WWII.

DON'T MISS

- A Yeoman Warder tour
- Crown Jewels
- Armour collection in the White Tower
- Ravens

PRACTICALITIES

- Map p450, G4
- ☎ 020-3166 6000
- www.hrp.org.uk/tower-of-london
- Petty Wales
- adult/child £28.90/14.40
- ⏲ 9am-4.30pm Tue-Sat, from 10am Sun & Mon
- Ⓤ Tower Hill

TAKE A BREAK

Within the Tower walls, the **New Armouries Cafe** serves British standards in a self-serve cafeteria-style setting. BrewDog Tower Hill (p153) is a short walk away, dishing up pizzas, burgers and salads that are best washed down with a craft beer brewed on-site.

The iconic Yeomen Warders, dressed in their signature red-trimmed navy uniform, have been guarding the Tower of London since the 15th century. Though their roles today are mostly ceremonial, they must have served at least 22 years in the British Armed Forces to qualify for the job. Hearing the Warders' stories is a highlight of visiting. Entertaining 45-minute-long tours leave from the bridge near the main entrance every 30 minutes until 3.30pm (2.30pm in winter). Make this your first stop before exploring the Tower on your own; it's included in the price of your entry ticket.

Chapel Royal of St Peter ad Vincula

On the northern edge of Tower Green is the 16th-century Chapel Royal of St Peter ad Vincula (St Peter in Chains), a rare surviving example of ecclesiastical Tudor architecture. Those buried here include three queens (Anne Boleyn, Catherine Howard and Lady Jane Grey) and two saints (Thomas More and John Fisher). A third saint, Philip Howard, was also interred here before his body was moved to Arundel in southern England.

Crown Jewels

To the east of the Chapel Royal and north of the White Tower is **Waterloo Barracks**, home of the Crown Jewels, which are in a very real sense priceless. Visitors file past film clips of the jewels and their role through history (including footage of Queen Elizabeth II's coronation in 1953) before reaching the vault itself. The queue to get in can be extremely long.

Once inside, you'll be dazzled by lavishly bejewelled sceptres, orbs and crowns. Two moving walkways take you past crowns and other coronation regalia, including the platinum crown of the late Queen Mother, Elizabeth, which is set with the 106-carat Koh-i-Nûr (Persian for 'Mountain of Light') diamond, and the Sovereign's Sceptre with Cross topped with the drop-shaped 530-carat Great Star of Africa diamond (also known as Cullinan I). Photography is prohibited, so if you want a second (or third) peek, double back to the beginning of the walkways.

A bit further on, exhibited on its own, is the centrepiece: the Imperial State Crown, set with 2868 diamonds (including the 317-carat Second Star of Africa, also known as Cullinan II), sapphires, emeralds, rubies and pearls. It's worn by the monarch at the State Opening of Parliament. At the exit, note the bizarre custom-built boxes used to transport the Crown Jewels from the Tower to state functions.

White Tower

At the heart of the site is the oldest building left standing in the whole of London. Constructed from stone as a fortress in the 1070s, the White Tower was the original Tower of London – its current name arose after Henry III whitewashed it in the 13th century. Standing just 27m high, it's not exactly a skyscraper by modern standards, but in the Middle Ages it would have dwarfed the wooden huts surrounding the castle walls and intimidated the peasantry.

Most of its interior is given over to the **Royal Armouries** collection of cannons, guns, suits of chain mail, and armour for men and horses. Some of the most remarkable exhibits in the **Line of Kings** are Henry VIII's suits of armour, including one made for him when he was a dashing 24-year-old and another when he was a bloated 50-year-old with a waist measuring 129cm. Among a late-17th-century parade of carved wooden horses and heads of historic kings, look out for the giant-like 2m suit of armour once thought to have been made for John of Gaunt, the Duke of Lancaster, and next to it the tiny child's suit of armour likely designed for James I's young son, the future Charles I.

On the top floor, you'll find the block and axe used to execute Simon Fraser at the last public beheading on Tower Hill in 1747, and the damaged Windsor back chair upon which German spy Josef Jakobs was shot by firing squad in 1941, the Tower's last execution. In the next room, you can try your hand at various interactive displays, including archery and swordsmanship.

Chapel of St John the Evangelist

This unadorned 11th-century chapel, with its vaulted ceiling, rounded archways and 14 stone pillars, is a fine example of Norman architecture and was also used as a national record office. Elizabeth of York, wife of grief-stricken Henry VII, lay in state here for 12 days, having died after complications during childbirth on her 37th birthday in 1503. Daily chapel tours start here at 10.45am, 12.45pm and 2.15pm.

Bloody Tower

Directly opposite Traitors' Gate, through which prisoners were transported by boat, is the huge portcullis of the Bloody Tower (1225). It takes its nickname from the princes in the Tower – 12-year-old Edward V and his younger brother, Richard – who were held here and later thought to have been murdered to annul their claims to the throne. The blame is usually laid (notably by Shakespeare) at the feet of their uncle, Richard III. A small exhibition recreates the study of explorer Sir Walter Raleigh – a repeat prisoner here – and looks at torture at the Tower, with gruesome replica devices like the Rack and the Scavenger's Daughter.

Medieval Palace

The Medieval Palace complex is composed of three towers. The entrance is via **St Thomas's Tower** (built 1275–79), where there's a reconstructed hall and bedchamber from the time of Edward I. Adjoining **Wakefield Tower** (1220–40) was built by Edward's father, Henry III. It has been furnished with a replica throne and other decor to give an impression of how it might have looked. During the 15th-century Wars of the Roses between the Houses of York and Lancaster, Henry VI is said to have been murdered as he knelt in prayer in this tower. A plaque on the chapel floor commemorates this Lancastrian king. There's a display on torture in the basement of this tower, but it's accessed from a separate entrance. The main route, however, continues through **Lanthorn Tower** (1220–38), residence of medieval queens.

Wall Walk

The huge inner wall of the Tower was added by Henry III from 1220 to improve the castle's defences. The Wall Walk allows you to tour its eastern and northern edge and the towers that punctuate it. Start at the southeastern **Salt Tower**, probably built to store saltpetre for gunpowder but, as the historic graffiti demonstrates, also used to house prisoners such as St Henry Walpole.

The walk continues through the **Broad Arrow Tower** and **Constable Tower**, containing small displays on weapons and the Peasants' Revolt. The **Martin Tower**, which housed the Crown Jewels from 1669 to 1841, contains an exhibition

Tower of London

TACKLING THE TOWER

Although it's usually less busy in the late afternoon, don't leave your assault on the Tower until too late in the day. You could easily spend hours here and not see it all. Start by getting your bearings on one of the Yeoman Warder (beefeater) tours; they are included in the cost of admission and are highly entertaining. The 1 **Scaffold Site** is directly in front of the 2 **Chapel Royal of St Peter ad Vincula**, where three queens and two saints are buried.

The building immedi-ately to the east is Waterloo Barracks, where the 3 **Crown Jewels** are housed. These are the absolute highlight of a Tower visit, so keep an eye on the entrance and pick a time to visit when it looks relatively quiet. Once inside, take things at your own pace. Slow-moving travelators shunt you past the dozen or so crowns that are the treasury's centrepieces, but feel free to double-back for a second or even third pass.

Allow plenty of time for the 4 **White Tower**, the core of the whole complex, starting with the exhibition of royal armour. As you continue onto the 1st floor, keep an eye out for 5 **Chapel of St John the Evangelist**.

The famous 6 **ravens** can be seen in the courtyard south of the White Tower. Next, visit the 7 **Bloody Tower** and the torture displays in the dungeon of the Wakefield Tower. Head next through the towers that formed the 8 **Medieval Palace**, then take the 9 **East Wall Walk** to get a feel for the castle's mighty battlements. Spend the rest of your time poking around the many other fascinating nooks and crannies of the Tower complex.

BEAT THE QUEUES

➡ Buy tickets online, avoid weekends and aim to be at the Tower first thing in the morning, when queues are shortest.

➡ The London Pass (www.london pass.com) allows you to jump the queues and visit the Tower (plus some other 80 attractions) as often as you like.

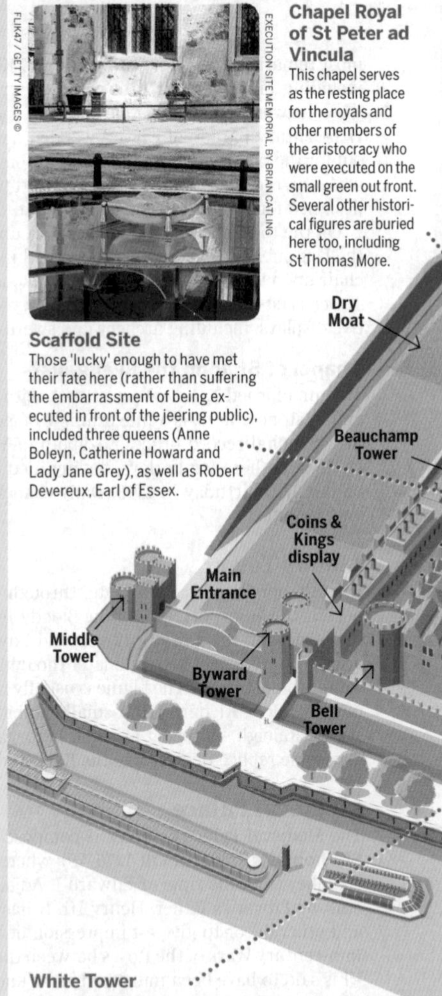

Chapel Royal of St Peter ad Vincula

This chapel serves as the resting place for the royals and other members of the aristocracy who were executed on the small green out front. Several other histori-cal figures are buried here too, including St Thomas More.

Scaffold Site

Those 'lucky' enough to have met their fate here (rather than suffering the embarrassment of being ex-ecuted in front of the jeering public), included three queens (Anne Boleyn, Catherine Howard and Lady Jane Grey), as well as Robert Devereux, Earl of Essex.

White Tower

Much of the White Tower is given over to the Royal Armouries collection of weapnry and armour. Look for the virtually cuboid suit made to match Henry VIII's bloated 49-year-old body, complete with an oversized armoured codpiece to protect, ahem, the crown jewels.

St John's Chapel

The White Tower's unadorned 11th-century chapel is a fine example of Norman architecture and was also used as a national record office.

JOSEPH M. ARSENEAU / SHUTTERSTOCK ©

Crown Jewels

When it's not being worn for state ceremonies, the monarch's bling is kept here.Look out for the Sovereign's Sceptre with Cross, topped with the drop-shaped 530-carat Great Star of Africa diamond (also known as Cullinan I), the largest part chiselled off from the biggest diamond in the world.

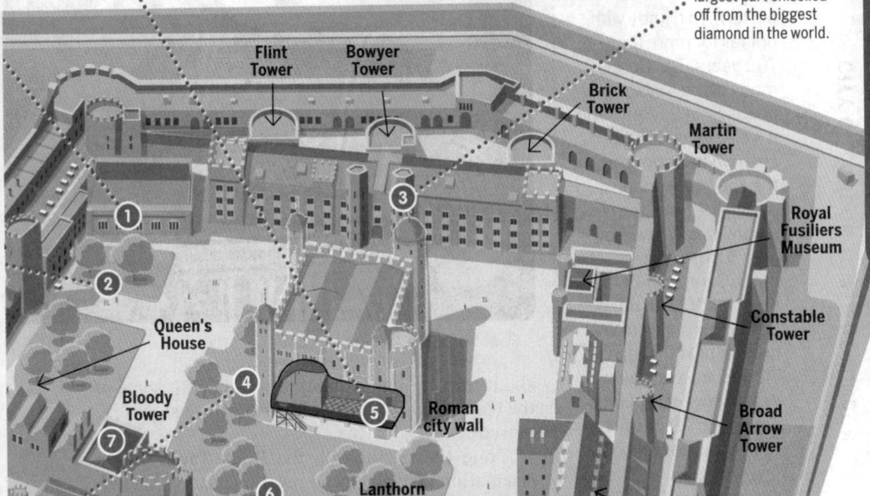

Flint Tower
Bowyer Tower
Brick Tower
Martin Tower
Royal Fusiliers Museum
Constable Tower
Broad Arrow Tower
New Armouries
Well Tower
Salt Tower
Cradle Tower
Lanthorn Tower
Roman city wall
Queen's House
Bloody Tower
Wakefield Tower
Traitors' Gate & St Thomas's Tower
River Thames
1
2
3
4
5
6
7
8
9

Medieval Palace

This part of the Tower complex was begun around 1220 and was home to England's medieval monarchs. Look for the recreations of the bedchamber of Edward I in St Thomas's Tower (1275-79) and the throne room of his father, Henry III in the Wakefield Tower.

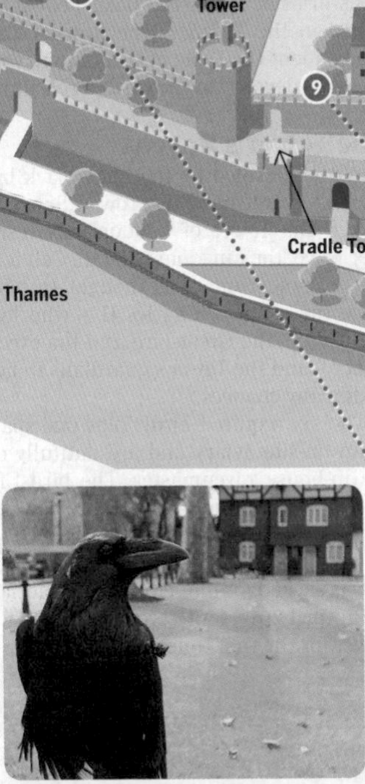

CRISTIAN SANTINON / SHUTTERSTOCK ©

Ravens

This stretch of green is where the Tower's half-dozen ravens are kept, fed on raw meat and blood-soaked biscuits. According to legend, if the ravens depart the fortress, the Tower and the monarchy will fall.

Wall Walk

Follow the inner ramparts along the Tower's eastern and northern fortifications. Each of the seven towers along the way has themed displays, covering everything from the royal menagerie to the Tower during WWI.

CEREMONY OF THE KEYS

Said to be the oldest military ceremony in the world, the elaborate locking of the Tower's main gates has been performed nightly without fail for more than 700 years. The Ceremony of the Keys begins precisely at 9.53pm, and it's all over by 10.05pm. Even when a bomb hit the Tower of London during the Blitz, the ceremony was delayed by only 30 minutes. Tickets to the Ceremony of the Keys cost £1 and must be booked online (www.hrp.org.uk) far ahead. Tickets are available a year in advance, but it's not rare to see the first 10 months are sold out.

MARCHING ORDERS

If you can't get tickets for the Ceremony of the Keys, two other traditions can be more readily seen. The Tower is officially unlocked at 9am daily by a Yeoman Warder accompanied by four armed regimental guards. At 2.45pm daily, soldiers of the Queen's Guard, who protect the Crown Jewels, march from Waterloo Barracks to the Byward Tower to collect the secret password for after-hours entry to the Tower from the Chief Yeoman Warder – it's called the Ceremony of the Word.

Beefeater at the Tower of London

about the original coronation regalia with some of the older crowns on show (their precious stones removed).

Along the north wall, the **Brick Tower** has a fascinating display on the royal menagerie, including stories of a tethered polar bear that swam and fished in the Thames. The **Bowyer Tower** has exhibits about the Duke of Wellington, while the **Flint Tower** is devoted to the castle's role during WWI.

The Tower's Ravens

Don't be alarmed by the huge black birds you see circling overhead at the Tower. Superstition has it that if the Tower of London's six resident ravens ever leave, the kingdom will fall. Call it silly, but the 350-year-old rumour is thought to have persisted since the reign of Charles II – who lived through the plague, the Great Fire *and* the execution of his father – and the Tower's guardians today still aren't taking any chances.

The six required birds, plus one spare, are kept in an on-site aviary and are dutifully cared for by the in-house ravenmaster. The birds' feathers are clipped to keep them around the Tower, but the ravens can still fly; one was found in Greenwich and was returned by a member of the public, and another was sacked for munching on TV aerials.

In April 2019, four raven chicks were born at the Tower for the first time in 30 years.

TOP EXPERIENCE

MARVEL AT ST PAUL'S CATHEDRAL

PETER ADAMS/GETTY IMAGES ©

Sir Christopher Wren's gleaming grey-domed masterpiece is the City of London's most magnificent building. Built between 1675 and 1710 after the Great Fire destroyed its predecessor, St Paul's was the first triple-domed cathedral in the world. Its vast, climbable cupolas still soar triumphantly over Ludgate Hill, offering sublime London panoramas, and some of the country's most celebrated citizens are interred in its crypt.

Interior

At a time of anti-Catholic fervour, it was controversial to build a Roman-style basilica rather than using the more familiar Gothic style. St Paul's interiors were more reflective of Protestant tastes, being relatively unadorned, with large clear windows. The statues and mosaics seen today were added later.

In the north aisle of the vast nave, you'll find the grandiose **Duke of Wellington Memorial** (1912), which took 54 years to complete. The Iron Duke's horse Copenhagen originally faced the other way, but it was deemed unfitting that a horse's rear end should face the altar. In contrast, beneath the dome is a quote from the elegant epitaph written for Wren by his son: *Lector, si monumentum requiris, circumspice* (Reader, if you seek his monument, look around you).

In the north transept chapel is William Holman Hunt's celebrated painting *The Light of the World* (1851–53), which depicts Christ knocking at a vine-covered door that, symbolically, can only be opened from within. In the heart of the cathedral, you'll find the spectacular **quire** (or chancel) – its ceilings and arches dazzling with colourful mosaics – and the **high altar**. The ornately carved **choir stalls** by

DON'T MISS

- Climbing the dome
- Quire ceiling mosaics
- Tombs of Vice Admiral Nelson and the Duke of Wellington in the crypt
- American Memorial Chapel

PRACTICALITIES

- Map p450, C2
- 020-7246 8357
- www.stpauls.co.uk
- St Paul's Churchyard
- adult/child £20/8.50
- 8.30am-4.30pm Mon-Sat
- St Paul's

TAKE A BREAK

For an on-site pick-me-up, visit the cafe or tearoom in the crypt. If you prefer not to eat in church, Ivy Asia (p152) dishes up OTT fusion plates with views of the cathedral through its floor-to-ceiling windows. Cheaper chain restaurants can be found in the One New Change (p157) shopping centre.

Audioguides are included in the ticket price but it's worth signing up for two guided tours of St Paul's to visit usually off-limits areas. Free 1½-hour guided tours cover similar ground as the audioguide, with the bonus of accessing the quire for a better look at the ceiling mosaics. These tours can't be booked online or in advance, so check in at the tour desk as soon as you arrive. The Triforium Tour (£8) runs much less frequently but allows you to descend the Geometric Staircase (the Divination Stairwell from the *Harry Potter* films), take in the BBC-exclusive view of the nave (usually reserved for camera crews), see Wren's original oak model of St Paul's and visit the astounding library (closed for renovations until at least spring 2021).

Dutch-British sculptor Grinling Gibbons on either side of the quire are exquisite, as are the ornamental **wrought-iron gates**, separating the aisles from the altar, by French Huguenot Jean Tijou (both men also worked on Hampton Court Palace).

Walk around the altar, with its massive gilded oak **baldacchino** (canopy) with barley-twist columns, to the **American Memorial Chapel**, commemorating the 28,000 Americans based in Britain who lost their lives during WWII. Note the Roll of Honour book (turned daily), symbols of each state in the stained glass, and American flora and fauna in the carved wood panelling.

In the north quire aisle, Henry Moore's abstract *Mother and Child: Hood* sculpture stands next to Bill Viola's *Mary*, a video companion to his poignant installation in the south quire called *Martyrs (Earth, Air, Fire, Water)*, which depicts four figures being overwhelmed by natural forces. Back towards the central dome is an **effigy of John Donne** (1572–1631), metaphysical poet and one-time cathedral dean, which survived the Great Fire; look for the scorch marks where the flames licked the statue.

Dome

Wren wanted to construct a dome that was imposing on the outside but not disproportionately large on the inside. The solution was to build it in three parts: a plastered brick inner dome, a nonstructural lead outer dome and a brick cone between them holding it all together, one inside the other. This unique structure, inspired by St Peter's Basilica in the Vatican, made the cathedral Wren's tour de force. He originally wanted mosaics to decorate the interior of the dome, but the sober grey monochrome tones of Sir James Thornhill's **scenes from the life of St Paul** were deemed more appropriately Protestant.

Victorian-era **mosaics** were added in the space between the arches and the start of the dome, depicting the four evangelists (Matthew, Mark, Luke and John) and the four major prophets (Isaiah, Ezekiel, Daniel and Joshua).

Climb up the 528 stairs, thankfully in three stages, to access the cathedral's galleries. The first 257 steps lead to the **Whispering Gallery**, 30m above the floor, which was closed at time of research but expected to reopen in summer 2021.

Heading up another 119 steps brings you to the **Stone Gallery**, an outdoor viewing platform 53m above the ground, obscured by pillars and other safety measures. The remaining 152 iron steps to the **Golden Gallery** are steeper and narrower than

ST PAUL'S CATHEDRAL

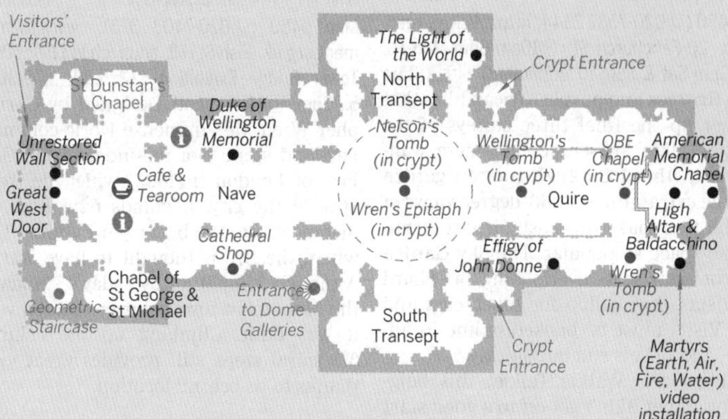

Cathedral Floor & Crypt

below but are worth the effort. From here, 85m above London, you can enjoy superb 360-degree views of the city.

Crypt

On the eastern side of both the north and south transepts are stairs leading down to the crypt and the **OBE Chapel**, where services are held for members of the Order of the British Empire. The crypt has memorials to around 300 of Britain's great and good, including Florence Nightingale, TE Lawrence (better known as Lawrence of Arabia) and Winston Churchill. Those actually buried here include the Duke of Wellington, Vice Admiral Horatio Nelson, Christopher Wren and painters Joshua Reynolds, John Everett Millais, JMW Turner and William Holman Hunt. On the surrounding walls are plaques in memory of those from the Commonwealth who died in various conflicts during the last century.

Also in the crypt are the cathedral's cafe, tearoom, gift shop and toilets.

Churchyard & Surrounds

A **statue of Queen Anne** (the reigning monarch when St Paul's was built) stands at the cathedral steps, her gilded crown, sceptre and orb glinting in the sun. The figures at her feet represent Britannia, North America, France and Ireland. Made by sculptor Louis Auguste Malempré in 1886, it's a replica of the Francis Bird original from 1712.

Outside the north transept, the simple, squat and round **People of London Memorial** honours the 32,000 civilians killed (and 50,000 seriously injured) during WWII.

SIGHTS

ST PAUL'S CATHEDRAL CATHEDRAL

See p143.

TOWER OF LONDON HISTORIC SITE

See p137.

★SKY GARDEN VIEWPOINT

Map p450 (☎020-7337 2344; https://skygarden.london; 20 Fenchurch St; ⏰10am-6pm Mon-Fri, 11am-9pm Sat & Sun; Ⓤ Monument) FREE The ferns, fig trees and purple African lilies that clamber up the final three storeys of the 'Walkie Talkie' skyscraper are mere wallflowers at this 155m-high rooftop garden – it's the extraordinary 360-degree views of London that make this vast, airport-terminal-like space so popular. The Sky Garden has front-row seats overlooking the Shard and vistas that gallop for miles east and west. Visits must be booked online in advance, and tickets run out quickly.

Dubbed the 'Walkie Talkie', this bulging skyscraper didn't get off to a good start when it opened in 2014, as its highly reflective windows melted the plastic bodywork of several cars parked below, and it was named 'the worst new building in the UK' in the 2015 Carbuncle Cup.

The garden space includes a restaurant, a brasserie and three bars with varying opening times. If tickets have sold out, you can reserve a table at one of them to gain access, though you will have to order something.

GARDEN AT 120 VIEWPOINT

Map p450 (www.thegardenat120.com; 120 Fenchurch St; ⏰10am-9pm Mon-Fri Apr-Sep, to 6.30pm Oct-Mar; Ⓤ Bank) FREE London's largest roof garden, the Garden at 120 is a blossoming 15th-floor pocket park paradise. Its mid-rise vantage point gives a unique perspective on nearby skyscrapers, with up-close views of the Walkie Talkie, Gherkin and the Lloyd's Building. Booking isn't required, making this a good alternative if you can't get into the Sky Garden.

ST MARY ALDERMARY CHURCH

Map p450 (☎020-7248 9902; Bow Lane; ⏰7.30am-4.30pm Mon-Fri; 📶; Ⓤ Mansion House) A Christoper Wren reconstruction, the church of St Mary Aldermary (1682) is unusual for the architect: it was built in Gothic style, and it's the only surviving church in the City of London of this type. Be prepared to spend some time gawping at the ceiling of the columned nave, covered in gleaming white plaster fan vaulting that's offset by the polished wood pews and medieval-style blood-red floor tiles. **Host Cafe** livens up the scene from its espresso bar in the apse.

MONUMENT TO THE GREAT FIRE OF LONDON MONUMENT

Map p450 (☎020-7403 3761; www.themonument.org.uk; Fish St Hill; adult/child £5/2.50, incl Tower Bridge Exhibition £12/5.50; ⏰9.30am-5.30pm; Ⓤ Monument) Designed by Christopher Wren, this immense Doric column of Portland stone is a reminder of the Great Fire of London in 1666, which destroyed 80% of the city. It stands 62m high, the distance from the bakery in Pudding Lane where the fire is thought to have started. Although Lilliputian by today's standards, the Monument towered over London when it was built. Climbing up the column's 311 spiral steps still provides great views thanks to its central location.

ST STEPHEN WALBROOK CHURCH

Map p450 (☎020-7626 9000; www.ststephenwalbrook.net; 39 Walbrook; ⏰10am-4pm Mon, Tue & Thu, 11am-3pm Wed, 10am-3.30pm Fri; Ⓤ Bank) St Stephen Walbrook (1679) is one of Wren's finest parish churches and, as it was his first experiment with a dome, a forerunner to St Paul's Cathedral. Sixteen pillars with Corinthian capitals support the coffered dome, and the modern travertine marble altar is by sculptor Henry Moore.

GUILDHALL HISTORIC BUILDING

Map p450 (☎020-7332 1313; www.cityoflondon.gov.uk/guildhallgalleries; Guildhall Yard; ⏰10am-4.30pm May-Sep; Ⓤ Bank) FREE Guildhall has been the City's seat of government for more than 800 years. The Great Hall dates from the early 15th century and is positively Hogwartsian in its Gothic grandeur, with pointy arched windows and 27m-high ceilings. It's the only remaining secular structure to have survived the Great Fire of 1666, although it was severely damaged both then and during the Blitz of 1940.

Inside it's hung with the banners and shields of London's 12 principal livery companies, or guilds, which used to wield immense power. The lord mayor and two sheriffs are still elected annually in the vast open hall. Statues and memorials of Winston Churchill, Admiral Nelson, the Duke of Wellington and both Prime

Ministers William Pitt (the Elder and the Younger) line the walls.

In the upper gallery, at the western end, are statues of the biblical giants Gog and Magog, traditionally considered to be guardians of the City; today's figures replaced similar 18th-century statues destroyed in the Blitz. Guildhall's stained glass was also blown out during the bombing, and a modern window in the southwestern corner depicts the city's history: look for London's most famous lord mayor, Richard 'Dick' Whittington, with his famous cat, a scene of the Great Fire and even the Lloyd's of London building.

To visit, enter through the reception of the City's modern administration block.

GUILDHALL ART GALLERY GALLERY

Map p450 (☎020-7332 3700; www.cityoflondon.gov.uk/guildhallgalleries; Guildhall Yard; ⊙10am-5pm Mon-Sat, noon-4pm Sun; UBank) FREE The City of London has had centuries to acquire an impressive art collection, which it's shown off since 1885. The original gallery was destroyed in the Blitz, and when the site was redeveloped in 1985, the remains of a **Roman amphitheatre** (c 70 CE) were discovered, so the gallery was redesigned to incorporate the ruins. The 4500-piece collection is particularly strong on London scenes and Victorian art, including significant Pre-Raphaelite works by John Everett Millais and Dante Gabriel Rossetti.

Taking over an entire gallery wall is American artist John Singleton Copley's *Defeat of the Floating Batteries at Gibraltar* (1791), which depicts a 1782 British victory. This immense oil painting was removed to safety just three weeks before the gallery was hit by a German bomb in 1941.

Nearly half of the gallery's collection consists of scenes in London, from great Venetian painter Canaletto's *The Monument from Gracechurch St* to 1960s visions of Smithfield Market and Leadenhall Market by Jacqueline Stanley. New works continue to be purchased on the themes of money, trade and capitalism, historically the City's chief concerns.

While only a few remnants of the stone walls lining the eastern entrance of the Roman amphitheatre still stand, they're imaginatively fleshed out with a black-and-fluorescent-green outline of the missing seating, and computer-meshed images of spectators and gladiators. Black markings on the square outside Guildhall indicate the extent and scale of the stadium, which could seat up to 6000 spectators.

Free tours leave at 12.15pm, 1.15pm, 2.15pm and 3.15pm on Tuesdays, Fridays and Saturdays.

LEADENHALL MARKET MARKET

Map p450 (www.leadenhallmarket.co.uk; Gracechurch St; ⊙public areas 24hr; UBank) The ancient Romans had their forum on this site, but this covered shopping arcade harks back to the Victorian era, with cobblestones underfoot and 19th-century ironwork linking its shops, restaurants and pubs. The market appears as Diagon Alley in *Harry Potter and the Philosopher's Stone*, and the optician's shop with a blue door on Bull's Head Passage was used as the entrance to the Leaky Cauldron in *Harry Potter and the Goblet of Fire*.

BANK OF ENGLAND MUSEUM MUSEUM

Map p450 (☎020-3461 5545; www.bankofengland.co.uk/museum; Bartholomew Lane; ⊙10am-5pm Mon-Fri; UBank) FREE This surprisingly interesting museum explores the evolution of money and the history of the venerable Bank of England, founded in 1694 by a Scotsman. Its centrepiece is a reconstruction of architect John Soane's original Bank Stock Office. Don't miss the chance to get your hands on a hefty 13kg solid-gold bar, worth more than £570,000.

POSTMAN'S PARK PARK

Map p450 (www.postmanspark.org.uk; King Edward St; USt Paul's) This serene patch of green, north of what was once London's General Post Office, contains the unusual **Memorial to Heroic Self-Sacrifice**, a loggia with 54 ceramic plaques commemorating deeds of bravery by ordinary people who died saving the lives of others, unveiled in 1900. It was the brainchild of artist George Frederic Watts (1817–1904). His wife, Mary, oversaw the project after his death, but the memorial was all but abandoned when she died in 1938.

Only one plaque has been added since then, dedicated to Leigh Pitt, who died in 2007 while trying to rescue a nine-year-old boy from drowning in a canal in southeast London.

BARBICAN ARCHITECTURE

Map p450 (☎020-7638 4141; www.barbican.org.uk; Silk St; UBarbican) The architectural value of this sprawling post-WWII brutalist housing estate divides Londoners, but the Barbican remains a sought-after living space as well as the City's preeminent cultural centre. Public spaces include a quirky conservatory and the Barbican Centre (p156) theatres, cinema and two art galleries: **Barbican Art Gallery** (☎020-7638 8891; www.barbican.org.uk; Level 3 Barbican Centre, Silk St; ⏲noon-6pm Mon & Tue, to 9pm Wed-Fri, 10am-9pm Sat, to 6pm Sun; 📶; U Barbican) and **The Curve** (☎020-7638 8891; Level 1 Barbican Centre; ⏲11am-8pm Sat-Wed, to 9pm Thu & Fr) FREE. Navigating the Barbican, designed to be a car-free urban neighbourhood, requires reliance on a network of elevated paths that didn't quite come to fruition. Find your bearings on an **architecture tour** (adult/child £12.50/10).

The whole site makes for a fascinating stroll, especially around the fountain-studded central lake, with ample seating and cafes with outdoor terraces.

Built on a huge bomb site abandoned after WWII and opened progressively between 1969 and 1982, the complex is named after a Roman fortification built to protect ancient Londinium, the scant remains of which can be seen in the southwest section of the estate. The estate incorporates 17th-century poet John Milton's parish church, **St Giles' Cripplegate** (Map p450; ☎020-7638 1997; www.stgilescripplegate.com; Fore St; ⏲11am-4pm Mon-Fri; U Barbican).

BARBICAN CONSERVATORY — GARDENS

Map p450 (☎0845 120 7500; www.barbican.org.uk; Level 3 Barbican Centre, Upper Frobisher Cres; ⏲noon-5pm Sun; U Barbican) FREE The definition of a concrete jungle, this glass-topped conservatory is a surprisingly lush urban rainforest inside the brutalist Barbican, London's second-largest after Kew Gardens (p316). More than 2000 species of plants, along with fish, birds and terrapins, reside in this space, originally designed to hide the theatre's six-storey-high rigging system. Check the website for dates of gardener-led tours (adult/child £12.50/10) and afternoon teas (£35).

TOWER BRIDGE EXHIBITION — MUSEUM

Map p450 (☎020-7403 3761; www.towerbridge.org.uk; Tower Bridge; adult/child £9.80/4.20, incl Monument £12/5.50; ⏲9.30am-5pm; U Tower Hill) The inner workings of Tower Bridge can't compare with its exterior magnificence, but this geeky exhibition

TOP EXPERIENCE
WITNESS TOWER BRIDGE IN ACTION

It doesn't matter from where you first glimpse Tower Bridge, with two neo-Gothic towers rising gracefully from either side of the Thames: London's emblematic river crossing is astonishing. Draped with curved suspension struts, painted in patriotic red, white and blue for Queen Elizabeth II's silver jubilee, the city's most easterly bridge was finished in 1894. On completion, its steam-driven bascule mechanism could raise the bridge's roadway in three minutes, allowing ships to pass underneath.

You can still witness Tower Bridge in action: it lifts as often as 10 times a day (check online for times) but is now electrically powered. The best spot to see it raised is at the 11m-long glass walkways of the **Tower Bridge Exhibition**, 42m above the river. Views plunge into the Thames, outshining the story of the bridge's construction, which is also recounted here.

Designed by Horace Jones and tweaked by engineer John Wolfe Barry, the bridge was made entirely from British materials, including Glaswegian steel, Portland stone and Cornish granite. Sadly Jones never saw the bridge completed, dying in 1887, a year into its construction.

DON'T MISS

- View from the upper walkways
- Glass floor
- Victorian Engine Rooms
- Footage of the bridge lifting for the first time
- Seeing it in action yourself

PRACTICALITIES

- Map p450, A7
- ☎020-7403 3761
- www.towerbridge.org.uk
- Tower Bridge
- U Tower Hill

tries to bridge that gap with details of the construction and access to the Victorian steam-powered machinery that once raised the bascules. Archive footage at the start of the exhibition shows the bridge lifting for the first time, and girders in the South Tower show the bridge's original drab chocolate-brown paint job. Walking on the **glass floors** 42m above the River Thames is a highlight.

SMITHFIELD MARKET — MARKET

Map p450 (☎020-7248 3151; www.smithfieldmarket.com; Charterhouse St; ⏲2-10am Mon-Fri; ⓤFarringdon) Smithfield is central London's last surviving meat market, and though most of the transactions today are wholesale, visitors are invited to shop too; arrive before 7am to see it in full swing. The market has been at this location since the 12th century, but the current colourful building was designed in 1868 by Horace Jones, who also designed Leadenhall Market (p147) and Tower Bridge. City of London guides run 1½-hour **tours** (£12.50) monthly at 6.45am.

Smithfields is at a developmental crossroads: the area is being rebranded as the Cultural Mile corridor, which runs between Farringdon and Moorgate. The market itself is looking to move to Dagenham in East London, pending the Parliament's permission. Part of the vast market complex is already abandoned, and the Museum of London (p150) is planning to relocate to the semi-derelict General Market section by 2024.

ST DUNSTAN IN THE EAST — RUIN

Map p450 (St Dunstan's Hill; ⏲24hr; ⓤMonument) Bombed to bits in the Blitz, the atmospheric ruins of 12th-century St Dunstan's have been left to the elements, resulting in a beautifully sombre public garden sprouting below the miraculously intact steeple and amidst the church's surviving blackened walls, with ivy crawling through the skeletal windows.

ROYAL EXCHANGE — HISTORIC BUILDING

Map p450 (☎020-3861 6500; www.theroyalexchange.co.uk; btwn Cornhill & Threadneedle St; ⓤBank) Founded by 16th-century merchant Thomas Gresham as a centre to trade stocks, the Royal Exchange was officially opened by Queen Elizabeth I in 1571. Today's colonnaded neoclassical building is the third on the site, built in 1844. It ceased functioning as a financial institution in the 1980s and now houses upmarket retailers and a plush bar-restaurant from Fortnum & Mason (p129).

ST BRIDE'S — CHURCH

Map p450 (☎020-7427 0133; www.stbrides.com; St Bride's Ave, Fleet St; ⏲8am-6pm Mon-Fri, 10am-3.30pm Sat, to 6.30pm Sun; ⓤBlackfriars) Printing presses on Fleet St fell silent in the 1980s, but St Bride's is still referred to as the 'journalists' church'; a moving memorial in the north aisle honours journalists who died whilst working. Designed by Christopher Wren in 1672, St Bride's had his tallest steeple at 71m. Its distinctive layers are said to have inspired the design of the tiered wedding cake.

In the 11th-century crypt, dense information boards present the history of the church and the journalistic background of Fleet St. There's also a section of Roman pavement from 180 CE. Ninety-minute guided tours (£6) depart at 2.15pm on Tuesdays between January and November.

ALL HALLOWS BY THE TOWER — CHURCH

Map p450 (☎020-7481 2928; www.ahbtt.org.uk; Byward St; ⏲8am-6pm Mon-Fri, 10am-5pm Sat & Sun; ⓤTower Hill) The oldest church in the City, All Hallows has been a place of worship since 675 CE. It was spared in the Great Fire, but much of today's building is from the 1957 post-Blitz reconstruction, though the bombing did uncover a Saxon-era arch. The museum in the crypt has a number of curious artefacts, including a slab of 2nd-century tessellated Roman pavement and a historic church register documenting the marriage of John Quincy Adams, the sixth US president.

On the ground floor, don't miss the beautiful 17th-century font cover by master woodcarver Grinling Gibbons. Free 20-minute tours run from 2pm to 4pm most weekdays from April to October.

ST MARY-LE-BOW — CHURCH

Map p450 (☎020-7248 5139; www.stmarylebow.co.uk; Cheapside; ⏲7am-6pm Mon-Fri; ⓤSt Paul's or Bank) It's said that a true Cockney is born within earshot of the Bow bells, and they ring out from the delicate steeple at St Mary-le-Bow, designed by Christopher Wren. Completed in 1673, the church was badly damaged during WWII and wasn't reconsecrated until 1964 when the beautiful stained-glass windows were added. You can grab a cuppa at Café Below in the crypt.

ST BARTHOLOMEW THE GREAT CHURCH

Map p450 (☎020-7600 0440; www.greatstbarts.com; W Smithfield; adult/child £5/4.50; ⌚8.30am-5pm Mon-Fri, 10.30am-4pm Sat, 8.30am-8pm Sun; U Barbican) Dating from 1123, St Bartholomew the Great is one of London's oldest churches. The Norman arches and profound sense of history lend this holy space an ancient calm, and it's even more atmospheric when entered through the restored 13th-century half-timbered gatehouse. The church was originally part of an Augustinian priory but became the parish church of Smithfield in 1539 when Henry VIII dissolved the monasteries.

Painter William Hogarth was baptised here, and the young American statesman Benjamin Franklin worked as an apprentice printer in what is now the Lady Chapel. The church has been the set for many films and TV productions, including *Four Weddings and a Funeral, Shakespeare in Love* and *Sherlock Holmes*. Look out for the astonishingly macabre Damien Hirst gilded bronze statue of St Bartholomew with his flayed skin (2006).

DR JOHNSON'S HOUSE MUSEUM

Map p450 (☎020-7353 3745; www.drjohnsonshouse.org; 17 Gough Sq; adult/child £7/3.50; ⌚11am-5pm Mon-Sat; U Chancery Lane) This 16th-century Georgian pile is one of the few surviving in the City, and it was the home of Samuel Johnson, author of the first serious English dictionary and the man who famously proclaimed, 'When a man is tired of London, he is tired of life'. The preserved interior contains antique furniture and artefacts from Johnson's life, including a copy of the first edition of the dictionary from 1755 and the 18th-century front door with a spiked iron bar to deter child thieves.

LONDON MITHRAEUM RUIN

Map p450 (☎020-7330 7500; www.londonmithraeum.com; 12 Walbrook; ⌚10am-6pm Tue-Sat, noon-5pm Sun; U Cannon St) FREE It takes a little stagecraft to bring these ruins to life, but it's amazing what low lighting and Latin chanting can do. This Roman temple was dedicated to the all-male cult of Mithras, a little-understood religion; what you see today is a sympathetic reconstruction of the temple after it was uprooted in the 1950s for display up the road. A well-presented dis-

TOP EXPERIENCE

TIME HOP AT THE MUSEUM OF LONDON

Tracing the history of this place to its ancient roots, the entertaining and educational Museum of London meanders through the city's various incarnations.

The first gallery, **London Before London**, sheds light on the small settlements along the Thames. It's followed by **Roman London**, which shows reconstructed rooms (seek out the incredibly intact Bucklersbury mosaic) and engrossing archaeological finds. After a glimpse of the real Roman city wall from the window, head into **Medieval London** for artefacts from Saxon Lundenwic and onto **War, Plague & Fire**, with depictions of the 1666 fire that forever altered the city.

Downstairs, **Expanding City** documents London's transformation into a centre of empire and industry, though the 1750s debtors' cell shows that not all benefitted. Take a spin through the suitably Dickensian mock-up of a Victorian street and recreated Vauxhall Pleasure Gardens in **People's City**; other highlights include a 1908 taxi, a 1928 art-deco lift from Selfridges and a fascinating multimedia display on the suffragettes. **World City** brings the timeline up to date with Beatles memorabilia, remnants of race riots and gay-rights marches, and the 2012 Olympics kit.

DON'T MISS

- Roman-era Bucklersbury mosaic
- 1750 debtors' cell
- Victorian Walk
- Art-deco lift from Selfridges

PRACTICALITIES

- Map p450, D1
- ☎020-7001 9844
- www.museumoflondon.org.uk
- 150 London Wall
- admission free
- h10am-6pm
-
- U Barbican

play case near the entrance shows intriguing fragments of Roman life in London.

For guaranteed timed entry, book online in advance. All floors have step-free access.

BEVIS MARKS SYNAGOGUE SYNAGOGUE

Map p450 (020-7621 1188; www.bevismarks.org.uk; Bevis Marks; adult/child £5/2.50; 10.30am-2pm Mon, Wed & Thu, to 1pm Tue & Fri, to 12.30pm Sun; Aldgate) Completed in 1701, this Grade I-listed Sephardic synagogue was the first to be built in Britain after Oliver Cromwell allowed Jews to return in 1657, and it's the only synagogue in Europe that has had regular services for more than 300 years. Its resemblance to a Protestant church is not coincidental; the architect, Joseph Avis, was a Quaker and took his cue from Wren's City churches. Tours, included with admission, take place at 11am on Sunday and 11.30am on Wednesday and Friday.

EATING

London's financial heart caters for a well-to-do crowd, and it can be tough to find cheap eats. Take the sting out of the price with discounted set lunches at high-end restaurants. Many old-school restaurants are closed on weekends and some even after the weekday lunch rush. Bloomberg Arcade is a promising new foodie corridor. Chain restaurants populate One New Change (p157) and Leadenhall Market (p147).

SIMPSONS TAVERN BRITISH £

Map p450 (020-7626 9985; www.simpsonstavern.co.uk; Ball Ct, 38½ Cornhill; mains £9.75-15.80; 8.30-10.30am Tue-Fri & noon-3.30pm Mon-Fri; Bank) 'Old school' doesn't even come close to describing Simpsons, a City institution since 1757. Huge portions of traditional British grub are served to diners in dark-wood and olive-green booths. Save space for the tavern's famous stewed-cheese dessert.

CITY CÀPHÊ VIETNAMESE £

Map p450 (www.citycaphe.com; 17 Ironmonger Lane; mains £5.25-8; 11.30am-4.30pm Mon-Fri; ; Bank) Don't be put off by the long lunchtime queue of office workers stretching out the door; the Vietnamese street-food specialists at City Càphê quickly dispense steaming bowls of pho, *bún huế* (noodle soup) and tasty *bánh mì* (filled baguettes) as efficiently as a Hanoi hawker. Cash only under £15.

CAFÉ BELOW CAFE £

Map p450 (020-7329 0789; www.cafebelow.co.uk; St Mary-le-Bow, Cheapside; mains £10.50-15.50; 7.30-10am & 11.30am-2.30pm Mon-Fri; Mansion House) The delightful Norman crypt below the Wren-rebuilt St Mary-le-Bow (p149) is now an atmospheric cafe-restaurant offering fresh seasonal meals for breakfast and lunch, such as a twice-baked goat's cheese soufflé and pan-fried sea bream. In summer, tables are set up outside in the shady courtyard.

★DUCK & WAFFLE BRITISH ££

Map p450 (020-3640 7310; www.duckandwaffle.com; Heron Tower, 110 Bishopsgate; mains £14-44; 24hr; ; Liverpool St) London tends to have an early bedtime, but Duck and Waffle is the best restaurant that's ready to party all night. Survey the kingdom from the highest restaurant in town (on the 40th floor) over a helping of the namesake dish: a fluffy waffle topped with a crispy leg of duck confit and a fried duck egg, drenched in mustard-seed maple syrup.

MIYAMA JAPANESE ££

Map p450 (020-7489 1937; www.miyama-restaurant.co.uk; 17 Godliman St; mains £13.50-30; 11.30am-2.30pm & 5.45-9.30pm Mon-Fri; St Paul's) There's a sense of a well-kept secret about this authentic Japanese restaurant, tucked away in a basement of a nondescript building (enter from Knightrider St). Come at midday for the good-value set-menu lunch that could include sashimi, tempura, tonkatsu and teriyaki, and sit at the sushi or teppanyaki bar for culinary drama.

HAWKSMOOR GUILDHALL BRITISH ££

Map p450 (020-7397 8120; https://thehawksmoor.com; 10 Basinghall St; steak from £22; 7-10.30am, noon-3pm & 5-10.30pm Mon-Fri; Bank) Parquet floors, maroon leather seating and rich wood panelling create a clubby atmosphere in this subterranean steakhouse, one of a handful in a London-founded chain. There's a decent-value set lunch menu (two/three courses £25/28), but the breakfasts are legendary. Plates come piled high with bacon, eggs, sausage, black pudding, short-rib bubble and squeak, and the signature grilled bone marrow.

KYM'S CHINESE ££

Map p450 (☎020-7220 7088; www.kymsrestaurant.com; 19 Bloomberg Arcade; mains £14-29; ⊙noon-2.30pm & 5.30-11pm Mon-Sat; Ⓤ Cannon St) Centred on a 5m-high artificial cherry-blossom tree, this highly stylised Andrew Wong restaurant, more informal than his Michelin-starred spot (p197) in Pimlico, is a celebration of Chinese roasting techniques. Don't miss the Three Treasure dish, which assembles the best mains in one: crispy pork belly, Iberico *char siu* (pork in hoisin sauce) and soy chicken, each with its own dipping sauce.

FORTNUM'S BAR & RESTAURANT BRITISH ££

Map p450 (☎020-7734 8040; www.fortnumandmason.com/stores/the-royal-exchange-london; Courtyard, Royal Exchange; mains £14-38; ⊙7am-11pm Mon-Fri; 🖉; Ⓤ Bank) The august Royal Exchange (p149) provides a fitting setting for this bar-restaurant from Fortnum & Mason (p129), London's poshest department store.

Oysters and caviar are served by suited staff from the pale-green oval-shaped bar, and fancied-up favourites such as calves' liver and bacon, savoury pies and the catch of the day sate diners in the courtyard seating area.

COPPA CLUB BRITISH ££

Map p450 (☎020-8016 9227; www.coppaclub.co.uk; 3 Three Quays Walk; mains £12.95-24.95; ⊙7.30am-11pm Mon-Thu, to midnight Fri, 9am-midnight Sat, to 10.30pm Sun; Ⓤ Tower Hill) With enviable Tower Bridge views, the riverside terrace at this all-day restaurant is the spot to nab.

In winter, outdoor tables are encased in geodesic dome igloos (book well ahead). The food is often only so-so, but it's the best option with immediate proximity to the Tower of London.

★**CITY SOCIAL** BRITISH £££

Map p450 (☎020-7877 7703; www.citysociallondon.com; Tower 42, 25 Old Broad St; mains £26-37; ⊙noon-2.30pm & 6-10.30pm Mon-Fri, 5-10.30pm Sat; Ⓤ Bank) City Social pairs sublime skyscraper views from its 24th-floor digs with delicate Michelin-starred cuisine.

The interior is all art deco–inspired low-lit glamour. If you don't want to splash out on the full menu, opt for the bar, **Social 24**, which has longer hours and a compelling menu of nibbles (don't miss the goat's-cheese churros with locally sourced truffle-infused honey).

Bookings are essential; expect airport-style security before you can get in the lift.

BOB BOB CITÉ FRENCH £££

Map p450 (☎020-3928 6600; www.bobbobcite.com; Leadenhall Bldg, 122 Leadenhall St; mains £19.50-45; ⊙noon-3pm & 5.30pm-midnight Tue-Thu, to 12.30am Fri & Sat; Ⓤ Bank) Three floors up the Cheesegrater building is the second outpost of the restaurant that made the 'press for champagne' button a quintessential over-the-top London experience.

This pleasure palace is kitted out to the nines, with a dot-matrix ticker tape that loops around the walls and illuminates with your table number when the button is pushed. Make sure and check your credit limit before you order.

IVY ASIA ASIAN £££

Map p450 (☎020-3971 2600; www.theivyasia.com; 20 New Change; mains £13.50-48; ⊙11.30am-2.30am Mon-Sat, to 12.30am Sun; Ⓤ St Paul's) Newly opened Ivy promises to inject some late-night life into this part of the City, and it's well on its way with a nightly resident DJ, an extensive range of Japanese whiskies and OTT menu items like black-truffle dumplings that come sprinkled in gold leaf.

The glowing green floor is made from semiprecious stones, and St Paul's gleams through the huge windows.

SUSHI SAMBA FUSION £££

Map p450 (☎020-3640 7330; www.sushisamba.com; Heron Tower, 110 Bishopsgate; mains £13-65; ⊙11.30am-1.30am Sun-Tue, to 2am Wed-Sat; Ⓤ Liverpool St) One floor below Duck & Waffle, Sushi Samba is a vivacious blend of Japanese, Brazilian and Peruvian cuisine that dishes up spot-on sushi rolls, churrasco and ceviche in equal turn.

It's more than a tad overpriced, but once you step outside to the 38th-floor terrace, the highest outdoor dining space in Europe, you'll be content to splurge on a little more for the experience.

COQ D'ARGENT

FRENCH £££

Map p450 (020-7395 5000; www.coqdargent.co.uk; 1 Poultry; mains £24-43; 7.30-10am, 11.30am-3pm, 5.30-11pm Mon-Fri, noon-4pm & 5.30-11pm Sat, noon-4pm Sun; Bank)
On the rooftop of the candy-striped building at the busy Bank junction is this phenomenal French restaurant, with an extensive (and expensive) wine list and all the trimmings you'd expect from a smart City eatery.

The biggest draw is the year-round terrace, lush in summer and aprés-ski-style in winter, providing mid-rise views of neighbouring skyscrapers and the grand Royal Exchange. Enter through the pedestrian-only Bucklersbury Passage.

DRINKING & NIGHTLIFE

Once the after-work crowd clears out, parts of the City can feel like a ghost town after dark, though more pubs and bars are staying open late and even pouring pints on weekends. For a late drink, look to the rooftop bars perched high atop the City's skyscrapers or head to Duck & Waffle (p151), one of the few places in town open 24/7.

★ORIOLE

COCKTAIL BAR

Map p450 (020-3457 8099; www.oriolebar.com; E Poultry Ave; 6pm-2am Tue-Sun, to 11pm Mon; Farringdon) Down a darkened alley through the eerie evening quiet of Smithfield Market is an unlikely spot for one of London's best cocktail bars, but the journey of discovery is the theme at speakeasy-style Oriole.

The cocktail menu, divided into Old World, New World and the Orient, traverses the globe, with out-of-this-world ingredients including clarified octopus milk, strawberry tree curd and slow-cooked chai palm.

Book in advance to spend less time waiting with the bouncer. There's a cover charge after 9pm when live music is on (£10 Friday and Saturday, £7 Wednesday and Thursday) that goes directly to the musicians.

★NICKEL BAR

COCKTAIL BAR

Map p450 (020-3828 2000; www.thened.com/restaurants/the-nickel-bar; 27 Poultry; 8am-2am Mon-Fri, 9am-3am Sat, to midnight Sun; ; Bank) There's something *Great Gatsby*–ish about the Ned (p351) hotel: the elevated jazz pianists, the vast verdite columns, the classy American-inspired cocktails. Of all the public bars inside this magnificent former banking hall, the Nickel Bar soaks up the atmosphere best. Inspired by the glamorous art-deco saloons and the ocean-liner-era elegance, this is timeless nightcap territory.

CLOUDM

BAR

Map p450 (020-3519 4830; www.citizenm.com/cloudm-tower-of-london; 40 Trinity Sq, citizenM Tower of London; 7am-1am Mon-Fri, 3pm-1am Sat, to midnight Sun; ; Tower Hill)
Settle into the sleek mod furniture at this hotel bar (p351), where floor-to-double-height-ceiling bookcases and pop-art portraits of the Queen overlook the Tower of London just across the street.

The standard drinks menu doesn't stray into groundbreaking territory, but the wrap-around outdoor balcony provides unforgettable sundowner views and Instagram moments.

BREWDOG TOWER HILL

BREWERY

Map p450 (020-7929 2545; www.brewdog.com; 21 Great Tower St; noon-11pm Sun-Wed, to midnight Thu-Sat; ; Tower Hill) The ubiquitous but delicious Scottish brewery recently opened this new outpost half-buried under an office block just steps from the Tower of London.

The 33 craft-beer taps, featuring BrewDog's own beers – some of which are brewed on-site – as well as the greatest hits from other brewers, ensure the place never goes dry. Three shuffleboard tables keep drinkers occupied until the wee hours.

COUNTING HOUSE

PUB

Map p450 (020-7283 7123; www.the-counting-house.com; 50 Cornhill; 8am-11pm Mon-Fri, 11am-11pm Sat, to 9pm Sun; ; Bank)
With its grand wooden staircase and painted ceilings edged with gold-coloured crown moulding, this pub, part of the Fuller's chain, is still every bit as dignified as when it opened as Prescott's Bank in 1893.

Suited City folk eagerly crowd around the elegantly curved central bar under the domed skylight for the range of traditional cask ales and speciality pies that have become its trademark.

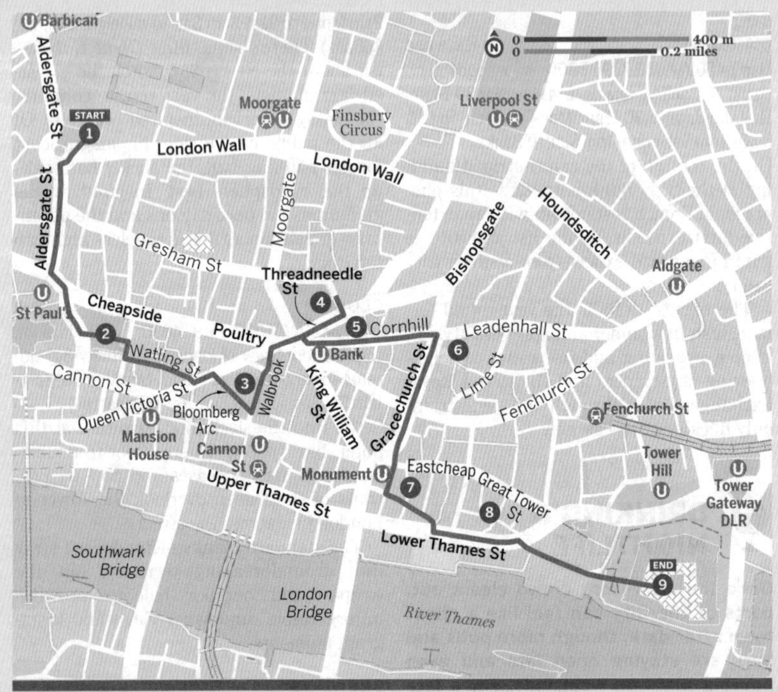

Neighbourhood Walk
London from the Romans to the Recent

START MUSEUM OF LONDON
END TOWER OF LONDON
LENGTH 1.2 MILES; THREE HOURS

Today's City of London is about the same size as Roman Londinium, and this walk saunters through many of the key stages of the area's history.

Start at the 1 **Museum of London** (p150) for an overview of the city's past and present. Exit the museum and head to Aldersgate St and continue south onto Cheapside. These roads were once London's markets, indicated by street names such as Milk St and Honey Lane. Still a hub of commerce, the modern 2 **One New Change** (p157) shopping centre has arguably the City's richest view of St Paul's Cathedral; take the lift up to the public roof terrace for a free peek.

Leave the shopping centre on Bread St, turn left on Watling St and then cross Queen Victoria St into Bloomberg Arcade. Left on Walbrook is the 3 **London Mithraeum** (p150), a Roman cult temple dedicated to the bull-slaying god Mithras. Make your way to the Bank junction, pausing to admire the imposing Bank of England – and visiting the 4 **Bank of England Museum** (p147) if it's open – before ducking into the 5 **Royal Exchange** (p149) for a Fortnum & Mason cuppa. East on Cornhill is the splendid 19th-century 6 **Leadenhall Market** (p147), roughly where the Roman forum once stood. Meander past the shops used as Diagon Alley in *Harry Potter*.

Head south on Gracechurch St to the 7 **Monument to the Great Fire of London** (p146), climbing 311 stairs to the top before the views snatch your breath away again. Leave via Monument St and turn left at St Dunstan's Hill, where the bombed-out 8 **St Dunstan in the East** (p149) church stands as a stark reminder of the Blitz.

Head down the hill and then turn left on Lower Thames St, and in a few minutes you'll bump into the moat guarding the 9 **Tower of London** (p137).

In 2019, the pub opened 15 four-star hotel rooms (doubles from £244) on the upper floors that used to be a gentlemen's club.

SEARCYS AT THE GHERKIN — BAR

Map p450 (☎0330 107 0816; https://searcysatthegherkin.co.uk; 30 St Mary Axe; ⏰11am-11pm Mon-Sat, 10am-4pm Sun; Ⓤ Aldgate) The top two floors of the iconic Gherkin skyscraper were once reserved as a private members' club, but now anyone dressed to impress is invited up. Cocktails in the 40th-floor bar under the oculus roof with 360-degree views of the City are a sight to behold. On Sundays, Helix, the restaurant on the 39th floor, is open for a sky-high brunch.

Advance booking is required.

VIADUCT TAVERN — PUB

Map p450 (☎020-7600 1863; www.viaducttavern.co.uk; 126 Newgate St; ⏰10am-11pm Mon-Fri, noon-9pm Sat; 📶; Ⓤ St Paul's) Opened in 1869, the Viaduct Tavern is one of the only remaining Victorian gin palaces in the City, with etched-glass panes, blood-red embossed vines crawling along the ceiling, and even the old cashier's booth where drink tokens were purchased (because the bar staff weren't trusted with cash). The tavern still specialises in gin, and a selection of house-made infusions beckons from behind the bar.

The Viaduct is said to be one of London's most haunted pubs, perhaps not a surprise given its proximity to the notorious, now demolished Newgate Prison; there are still jail cells in the pub's basement.

14 HILLS — BAR

Map p450 (☎020-3981 5222; https://14hills.co.uk; 120 Fenchurch St; ⏰11.30am-midnight Mon-Thu, to 1.30am Fri & Sat, to 5pm Sun; Ⓡ Fenchurch St, Ⓤ Monument) Growing from the roots of the newly opened Garden at 120 (p146) one floor up, this 14th-floor jungle bar has no outside space but is planted with more than 2500 trees, shrubs and ferns, and boasts gorgeous London views. Its menu takes a fresh approach to delicious cocktails, using house-made ingredients such as cacao-nibs syrup, oregano tincture and lavender-infused gin.

There's also a food menu of British favourites with a French twist.

TRADING HOUSE — BAR

Map p450 (☎020-7600 5050; www.thetradinghouse.uk.com; 89-91 Gresham St; ⏰noon-11pm Mon & Tue, to 1am Wed-Fri; Ⓤ Bank) Formerly the Bank of New Zealand, this magnificent Grade II–listed building has reincarnated as a whimsical mock Victorian-era trading outpost stuffed with mounted zebra heads and decadent taxidermied birds under a high barrel-vaulted ceiling. The cocktails, inspired by 'the world's most eclectic cultures', are priced as low as £7.95 – a bargain for this part of town – so it won't break the bank to study up.

BLACKFRIAR — PUB

Map p450 (☎020-7236 5474; www.nicholsonspubs.co.uk; 174 Queen Victoria St; ⏰10am-11pm Mon, Thu & Fri, to midnight Tue, noon-10.30pm Wed, 9am-11pm Sat, noon-10.30pm Sun; Ⓤ Blackfriars) Built in 1875 on the site of a Dominican monastery (hence the name and the corpulent chap above the door), this much-loved pub was famously saved from demolition in the 1960s by poet Sir John Betjeman. The monastic-themed friezes date from a 1905 art-nouveau makeover. The small dining room serves pub grub, and drinkers often spill out the doors soon after 5pm.

MERCHANT HOUSE — COCKTAIL BAR

Map p450 (www.merchanthouse.bar; 13 Well Ct; ⏰3pm-1am Mon-Fri, 4pm-1am Sat; Ⓤ Mansion House) This well-hidden bar, on a seemingly forgotten alleyway off pedestrian-only Bow Lane, has some 600 whiskies, 400 rums and 400 gins. Don't worry about a novel-size drink list, though: instead, the master mixologists will whip up a custom concoction based on your alcohol of choice and one of five taste palettes, such as umami, tropical, coastal or smoke.

For personalised service, book into **The Brig**, dubbed London's smallest bar. For £65 per person per hour, couples or small groups can get their own private bartender and all drinks included.

Merchant House's rum-centric sister bar, **Black Parrot** (Map p450; ☎020-3802 4451; https://blackparrotbar.co.uk; 8 Bride Ct; ⏰3pm-midnight Mon-Sat; Ⓡ City Thameslink, Ⓤ Blackfriars), is also hidden away, down a small lane near City Thameslink station, and is equally worth tracking down.

CITY OF LONDON DISTILLERY COCKTAIL BAR

Map p450 (020-7936 3636; www.cityoflondondistillery.com; 22-24 Bride Lane; 2-11pm Mon-Sat; City Thameslink, Blackfriars) The first gin distillery to be opened in the City for nearly 200 years, this small-batch micro-distillery has brought back the art of 'mother's ruin'.

Sip on a classic G&T while peeking at the shiny vats behind glass windows at the back of the bar, or if you can't choose just one, opt for a gin flight. The distillery also runs tours and gin-making classes. To take some of the tipple home with you, pick up a bottle on your way out.

GOBPSY COCKTAIL BAR

Map p450 (www.thegobpsy.com; 142 Fenchurch St; noon-midnight Mon-Wed, to 1am Thu & Fri; Monument) The unpronounceable Gobpsy takes its speakeasy status seriously. There's no signage at street level, so be ready to duck into a totally ordinary working barbershop and descend the stairs into this 1920s-themed drinking den.

The delightful cocktails come in quirky containers, such as a glass cigar pipe and a raspberry-eyed skull topped with candy floss. In true City fashion, it's shuttered on weekends.

JAMAICA WINE HOUSE PUB

Map p450 (020-7929 6972; www.jamaicawinehouse.co.uk; St Michael's Alley; 11am-11pm Mon-Fri; Bank) The 'Jampot' does double duty as a historic wood-lined pub with a basement wine bar.

It stands on the site of London's first coffee house (1652), frequented by diarist Samuel Pepys. Reached by a narrow alley off Cornhill, the art-nouveau red sandstone building from 1869 still has a number of classic features, such as the glowing street-lamp sign and a 19th-century coffee-bean roaster.

YE OLDE CHESHIRE CHEESE PUB

Map p450 (020-7353 6170; Wine Office Ct, 145 Fleet St; noon-11pm Mon-Sat; City Thameslink, Blackfriars) Rebuilt in 1667 after the Great Fire, this is one of London's most famous – and most crowded – pubs. It has strong literary connections, with Mark Twain, Sir Arthur Conan Doyle and Charles Dickens on the list of regulars who have frequented it.

The gloomy interior, narrow passageways and convoluted layout add to its appeal, but surly staff and tight quarters will force you to move on quickly.

LAMB TAVERN PUB

Map p450 (020-7626 2454; www.lambtavernleadenhall.com; 10-12 Leadenhall Market; 11am-11pm Mon-Fri, from noon Sat; Monument) At the central crossroads of Victorian iron-trussed Leadenhall Market, the Lamb Tavern is an old-school boozer owned by the Young's pub chain.

There's an upstairs, reached by a rickety metal spiral staircase, but the relatively small interior pushes convivial after-work drinkers out onto the market's cobblestoned lanes.

EL VINO WINE BAR

Map p450 (020-7353 6786; www.elvino.co.uk; 47 Fleet St; 10am-10pm Mon, to 11pm Tue-Fri, noon-11pm Sat; City Thameslink, Blackfriars) Started in 1879, this venerable institution is where barristers, solicitors and other legal types from the Royal Courts of Justice across the way come to let their hair down. The old-school wood-lined flagship wine bar (one of five in a small chain) has one of the best wine lists in the City.

ENTERTAINMENT

BARBICAN CENTRE PERFORMING ARTS

Map p450 (020-7638 8891; www.barbican.org.uk; Silk St; box office 10am-9pm Mon-Sat, noon-8pm Sun; Barbican) You'll get as lost in the astounding program as you will in the labyrinthine brutalist building of the Barbican Centre.

Home to the **London Symphony Orchestra**, the **BBC Symphony Orchestra** and the **Royal Shakespeare Company**, the Barbican Centre is the City's premier cultural venue. It hosts concerts, theatre and dance performances, and screens indie films and Hollywood blockbusters at the cinema on Beech St.

LONDON'S CITY CHURCHES

Before the Great Fire in 1666, the Square Mile had 111 churches wedged into its narrow streets, but 86 of them including old St Paul's were lost in the inferno, and more were later shattered in the Blitz. Today, in the shadow of rebuilt St Paul's Cathedral, 47 centuries-old stone churches, many also designed by St Paul's architect Sir Christopher Wren, have survived the odds and remain integral pieces of the financial district's fabric. Sandwiched between modern high-rises, these churches remain peaceful oases in the City's relentless hustle.

St Mary Aldermary (p146) Built in 1682, this church is not only one of the most architecturally impressive, with its immaculate fan-vaulted ceiling, but also one of the most forward-thinking: get a good cuppa from the coffee shop in the apse.

St Vedast-alias-Foster (Map p450; 020-7606 3998; www.vedast.org.uk; 4 Foster Lane; 8am-5.30pm Mon-Fri, 11am-4pm Sat; St Paul's) Easy to hurry past at ground level, it's worth seeking out for the hidden alleyway garden and 17th-century-style plaster ceiling detailed with gold and varnished aluminium leaf.

Holy Sepulchre (Map p450; 020-7236 1145; https://hsl.church; Holborn Viaduct; noon-2pm Tue & Thu, 11am-3pm Wed; City Thameslink, St Paul's) Connected via a tunnel to the notorious Newgate Prison, the church rung a heavy bell, preserved in glass under the impressive coffered ceiling, to mark the execution of a prisoner. It's also the burial place of John Smith, of Pocahontas fame.

St Nicholas Cole Abbey (Map p450; www.stnickschurch.org.uk; 114 Queen Victoria St; 7am-4.30pm Mon-Fri; Mansion House) Pick your next sightseeing stop at the brilliant cafe inside this church, the first of Wren's to be rebuilt after the Great Fire.

SHOPPING

Unless you're shopping for business attire, the City doesn't hold much purchasing appeal, and most shops are closed on weekends. The Royal Exchange (p149) is home to some high-end boutiques and jewellery dealers.

ONE NEW CHANGE — SHOPPING CENTRE

Map p450 (020-7002 8900; www.onenewchange.com; 1 New Change; 10am-6pm Mon-Wed & Sat, to 8pm Thu & Fri, noon-6pm Sun; St Paul's) This modern, multilevel shopping centre is filled with places to eat for all budgets and all the usual chain-store suspects – and is thankfully open on weekends. Whether or not you're indulging in some retail therapy, get the lift to the 6th-floor public roof terrace for unbeatable views of St Paul's Cathedral.

LONDON SILVER VAULTS — ANTIQUES

Map p450 (020-7242 3844; https://silvervaultslondon.com; 53-64 Chancery Lane; 9am-5.30pm Mon-Fri, to 1pm Sat; Chancery Lane) For one of London's oddest shopping experiences, pass through security and descend 12m into the windowless subterranean depths of the London Silver Vaults, which house the largest collection of silver for sale in the world. The 30-odd independently owned shops, each entered through thick bank-safe-style doors, offer vintage Victorian and Georgian silver, cufflinks, candleholders, goblets and much more.

Despite its Chancery Lane address, the entrance is on Southampton Buildings.

South Bank

LONDON BRIDGE & BERMONDSEY ST | BANKSIDE & SOUTHWARK | WATERLOO

Neighbourhood Top Five

1 **Tate Modern** (p160) Getting a grip on modern art by exploring this magnificent collection housed inside a former power station with spectacular city views.

2 **Borough Market** (p163) Stimulating your taste buds on a gastronomic tour of the many flavours of London at this gourmet market and its surrounding bars and restaurants.

3 **Shakespeare's Globe** (p162) Grabbing a Bard's-eye view of Elizabethan theatrics at this authentic re-creation of the 16th-century original.

4 **Southbank Centre** (p165) Losing yourself in the concrete corridors of this brutalist arts complex, Europe's largest.

5 **Leake Street Arches** (p165) Admiring spray-painted street art in a tunnel opened by Banksy, before diving into an immersive installation in an abandoned railway arch.

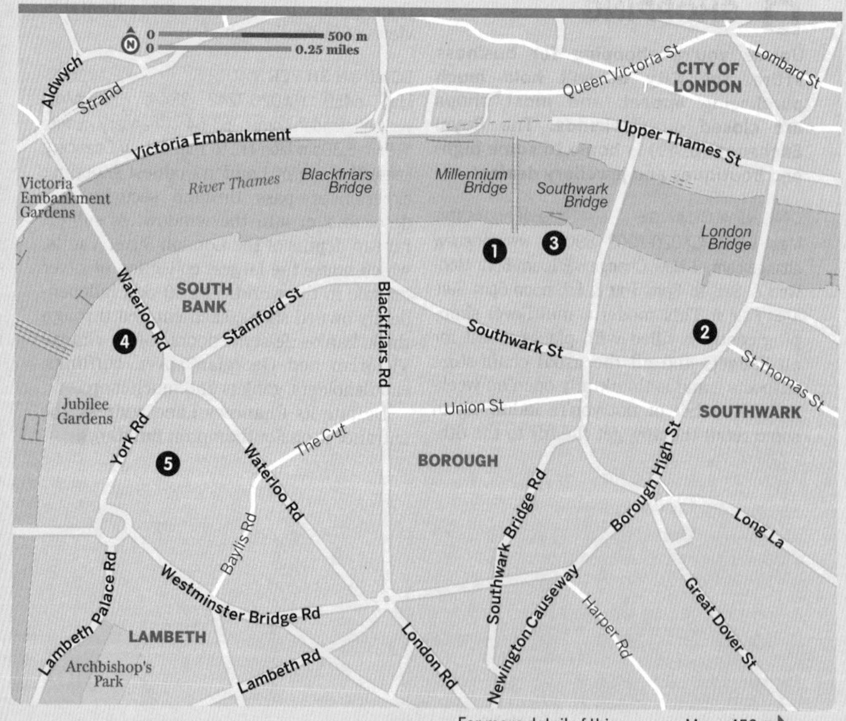

For more detail of this area see Map p452

Explore South Bank

Thanks to the huge drawcard sights that stretch along the riverside between Westminster Bridge and Tower Bridge, South Bank is a tourist-friendly and heavily visited neighbourhood.

Make time for the theatre; South Bank stages it all in its myriad performance spaces. Seeing a show in the authentically reconstructed Shakespeare's Globe (p162) is sure to be a big tick off the bucket list. The huge Southbank Centre (p165) complex is Europe's largest arts venue, and Christmas Day might be the only quiet time in its calendar.

It pays to book in advance for South Bank's higher-end bars and restaurants, especially those with views, as seats go quick. However, some popular restaurants, notably Padella (p167), have rebelled against this and don't take reservations at all.

Local Life

Neighbourhood local The views are grand, but the riverside is clogged with chains. Instead, head inland for locally loved backstreet boozers, such as Kings Arms (p173).

Hotel bars Londoners aren't staying overnight, but you'll sure find them at hip hotel watering holes, such as Lyaness (p172) and Hoxton's Seabird (p172).

Abandoned arches London's once derelict railway arches are undergoing huge regeneration projects: seek out street art in the Leake Street Arches (p165) or follow the still-in-progress Low Line (p173) to the restaurants in the Old Union Yard Arches and Flat Iron Square (p167).

Getting There & Away

Underground The Jubilee Line is the main artery through South Bank, with stations at Waterloo, Southwark, London Bridge and Bermondsey, but the area can also be reached on the Bakerloo, Northern and Waterloo & City lines.

Train National Rail services head to London Bridge, Waterloo and Blackfriars.

Bus In addition to a number of other services, the RV1 bus runs between Tower Gateway and Covent Garden through South Bank and Bankside, linking all the main sights.

Riverboat Thames Clippers boats stop at London Bridge City Pier, Bankside Pier and London Eye Pier.

Lonely Planet's Top Tip

Exploring South Bank on foot is best; if you're pressed for time, allocate at least half a day to walk from Westminster Bridge to London Bridge along the River Thames, with stops at the London Eye, Southbank Centre, Tate Modern, Shakespeare's Globe and Borough Market.

Best Eating

- Arabica Bar & Kitchen (p168)
- Padella (p167)
- Skylon (p170)
- Anchor & Hope (p169)
- Casa do Frango (p168)

For reviews, see p167.

Best Drinking & Nightlife

- Lyaness (p172)
- George Inn (p170)
- Kings Arms (p173)
- Seabird (p172)
- Scootercaffe (p173)

For reviews, see p170.

Best Theatres

- Shakespeare's Globe (p174)
- National Theatre (p174)
- Bridge Theatre (p174)
- Old Vic (p174)
- Young Vic (p174)

For reviews, see p174.

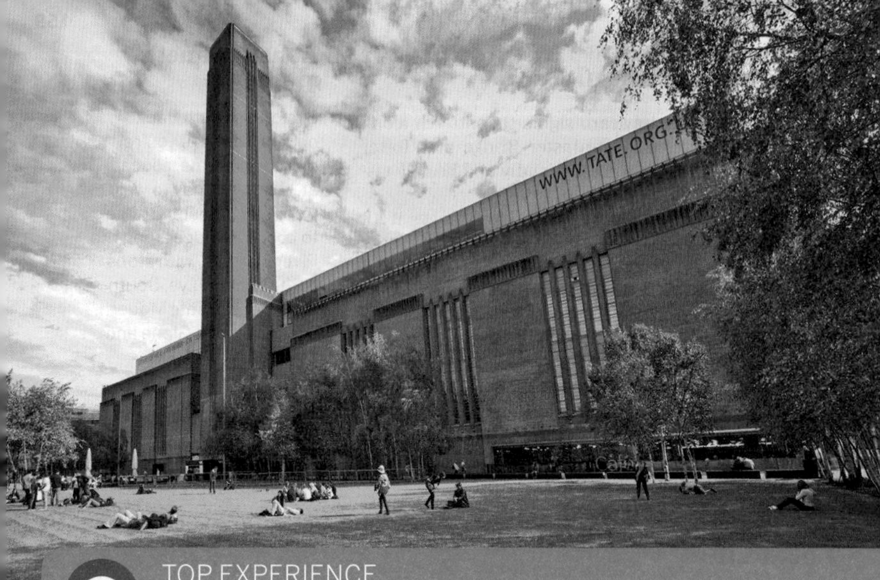

JOHN HARPER/GETTY IMAGES ©

TOP EXPERIENCE

FIND THE FUTURE OF ART AT TATE MODERN

Tate Modern is a phenomenally successful modern- and contemporary-art gallery housed in an imposing former power station on the riverside. The 10-storey Blavatnik Building extension, opened in 2016, increased exhibition space by 60%.

Natalie Bell Building

The original gallery lies inside what was once the boiler house for the Bankside Power Station. Now called the Natalie Bell Building in recognition of a local community activist, it's an imposing sight: a 200m-long building made of 4.2 million bricks. Don't miss the views of the Thames and St Paul's Cathedral from the 6th-floor cafe.

Turbine Hall

The first space to greet you as you pour down from the side entrance at Holland St is the astounding 3300-sq-metre Turbine Hall. Originally housing the power station's huge electricity generators, this vast area has become the commanding venue for large-scale installations and temporary exhibitions. The annual commission aims to make art more accessible and has led to popular and often interactive pieces, such as Kara Walker's *Fons Americanus*, a 13m-tall working fountain that highlights the history of the slave trade; a full-on playground of three-person swings installed by Danish art collective Superflex; and a maze of geometric gardens called *Empty Lot* by Abraham Cruzvillegas, which took soil from parks around London and watered it for six months to see if anything grew. Note that if you enter from the riverside doors, you'll end up on the more muted level 1, but stairs lead down to the main floor of the Turbine Hall.

DON'T MISS

- Turbine Hall
- 10th-floor Viewing Level of the Blavatnik Building
- View of St Paul's Cathedral from the 6th-floor cafe in the Natalie Bell Building
- Floors of free displays

PRACTICALITIES

- Map p452, D3
- 020-7887 8888
- www.tate.org.uk
- Bankside
- admission free
- h10am-6pm Sun-Thu, to 10pm Fri & Sat
- (wi-fi)
- U Southwark

Blavatnik Building

The Tate Modern extension that opened in 2016 echoes the original building in appearance: it is also constructed of brick, although these are slightly lighter and have been artistically laid out in a lattice to let light in (and out – the building looks stunning after dark).

The interior is stark, with raw, unpolished concrete vaguely reminiscent of brutalist buildings, and the exhibition space is fantastic, giving the collection the room it deserves to shine.

Viewing Level

Take the lift to level 10 for sweeping panoramic views of the city. The combination indoor-outdoor space means it's still worth a visit in bad weather.

Permanent Collection

Tate Modern's permanent collection is free to visit and is arranged by both theme and chronology on levels 2 and 4 of the Natalie Bell Building and on levels 0, 3 and 4 of the Blavatnik Building. The emphasis in the latter is on art from the 1960s onwards.

More than 60,000 works are on constant rotation, which can be frustrating if you'd like to see one particular piece, but keeps it thrilling for repeat visitors. Helpfully, you can check the excellent website (www.tate.org.uk/search) to see whether a specific work is on display – and where.

Curators have at their disposal paintings by Georges Braque, Henri Matisse, Piet Mondrian, Andy Warhol, Mark Rothko and Jackson Pollock, as well as pieces by Joseph Beuys, Barbara Hepworth, Damien Hirst, Rebecca Horn and Claes Oldenburg.

A great place to begin is the **Start Display** on level 2 of the Natalie Bell Building: this small, specially curated taster features some of the best-loved works in the collection and gives visitors useful pointers for understanding modern art.

Special Exhibitions

With the opening of the Blavatnik Building, Tate Modern has increased the number of special exhibitions it hosts. You will find the exhibits on level 3 of the Natalie Bell Building and level 2 of the Blavatnik Building; all are subject to admission charges, which vary by exhibition.

Past special exhibitions have included retrospectives on Andy Warhol, Henri Matisse, Edward Hopper, Frida Kahlo, Roy Lichtenstein, August Strindberg, Nazism and 'Degenerate art', and Joan Miró.

TAKE A BREAK

Borough Market (p163), a 10-minute walk east along the river, is a gourmet feast, crammed with interesting things to eat and drink. All-vegetarian Tibits (p170) offers innovative platefuls paid for by the weight.

For the most scenic of culture trips, take the RB2 riverboat service between Bankside Pier (Map p452; www.thamesclippers.com; one way adult/child £8.70/4.35) **outside Tate Modern and Millbank Pier near its sister museum, Tate Britain (p92).**

TOURS

Three free 45-minute tours run every day through Tate Modern's permanent exhibitions, providing an introduction to the gallery before moving on to a specific section. These talks start at noon, 1pm and 2pm on level 4 of the Natalie Bell Building.

GIMAS/SHUTTERSTOCK ©

TOP EXPERIENCE
CATCH A PLAY AT SHAKESPEARE'S GLOBE

Unlike other venues for Shakespearean plays, Shakespeare's Globe was designed to resemble the original Globe Theatre as closely as possible, from the materials used in construction to the open-air stage that exposes viewers to London's changeable skies. Seeing a play here is experiencing Shakespeare's work at its best and most authentic.

Authentic Reconstruction

Despite Shakespeare's popularity, the original Globe Theatre, demolished by the Puritans in 1644, was almost a distant memory when American actor Sam Wanamaker came searching for it in 1949. He began fundraising for a memorial theatre, and work started in 1987. Sadly, Wanamaker died four years before the theatre opened in 1997.

The aim in reconstructing the Globe was to make it as close to the original as possible. It is built with 600 oak pegs, specially fired Tudor-style bricks and thatch from Norfolk. The plaster contains goat hair, lime and sand, as it did in Shakespeare's time.

Visiting Shakespeare's Globe

To go behind the scenes, join the informative guided tours which depart half-hourly and last approximately 40 minutes. Tours include access to an exhibition about Shakespeare, theatre in the 17th century and life in Bankside. You can also see costumes and props used in performances, and get an insight into how stunts (some very gory!) were done in Shakespeare's time. Best of all, of course, is taking in a play (p174): a groundling ticket, standing under the open-air 'wooden O', costs just £5.

DON'T MISS

- Buying a groundling ticket and enjoying a show for just £5
- Authentic theatre architecture
- Guided tour and exhibition access

PRACTICALITIES

- Map p452, E3
- 020-7401 9919
- www.shakespeares-globe.com
- 21 New Globe Walk
- tour adult/child £17/10
- box office 10am-6pm
- Blackfriars or London Bridge

TOP EXPERIENCE

TASTE THE WORLD AT BOROUGH MARKET

For a thousand years, a market has existed at the southern end of London Bridge, making this still-busy ancient gathering point a superb spectacle. Overflowing with small shops, food stalls cooking in close quarters and wholesale greengrocers catering to London's top-end restaurants, Borough Market makes a delicious lunch stop, afternoon grazing session or pure dinner-party inspiration. The market is committed to sustainability and supporting small-scale food producers.

Gourmet Stalls

The market specialises in high-end fresh (and often local) products. You'll find an assortment of fruit and vegetable stalls, cheesemongers, butchers, fishmongers and bakeries, as well as delis and gourmet stalls selling spices, nuts, preserves and condiments. This gastronomic ensemble makes for an eye-catching and mouth-watering display, and plenty of visitors stroll through with their cameras at the ready.

Food Stalls

Once you're too hungry to continue window-shopping (and sampling), grab some grub from one of the many takeaway stalls. Choose anything from sizzling gourmet German sausages to Ethiopian curries, Caribbean stews, falafel wraps, and raclette cheese melted over cured meats and potatoes. Save room for dessert from the cake stalls; walking out without a treat will be a challenge. Many of the takeaway food stalls cluster in **Green Market**, the area closest to Southwark Cathedral (p171).

DON'T MISS

➡ Lunching at one – or several – of the takeaway food stalls

➡ Looking through the greengrocers' goods

➡ People-watching with a drink in hand outside one of the market's many pubs or cafes

PRACTICALITIES

➡ Map p452, F4

➡ https://boroughmarket.org.uk

➡ 8 Southwark St

➡ full market 10am-5pm Wed & Thu, to 6pm Fri, 8am-5pm Sat, limited market 10am-5pm Mon & Tue

➡ London Bridge

SIGHTS

London Bridge & Bermondsey St

BOROUGH MARKET MARKET

See p163.

SHARD VIEWPOINT

Map p452 (0844 499 7111; www.theviewfromtheshard.com; Joiner St; adult/child from £25/20; 10am-9pm; London Bridge) Puncturing the skies above London, the dramatic splinter-like form of the Shard has become an icon of the city and is one of the tallest buildings in Europe. The scene from the 244m-high viewing platforms on floors 69 and 72 is like none other in town, but it comes at an equally lofty price; book online in advance for a potential discount. Premium tickets come with a good-weather guarantee, meaning you might be able to return for free.

To take in the view for less, visit one of the building's restaurants or bars; you'll pay half the viewing-platform ticket price for a cocktail at Aqua Shard (p171), where the views are still spectacular.

HMS BELFAST MUSEUM

Map p452 (www.iwm.org.uk/visits/hms-belfast; Queen's Walk; adult/child £19/9.50; 10am-4pm; London Bridge) HMS *Belfast* is a magnet for kids of all ages. This large, light cruiser – launched in 1938 – served in WWII, helping to sink the Nazi battleship *Sand* shelling the Normandy coast on D-Day, and in the Korean War. Its 6-inch guns could bombard a target 12 miles distant. Displays offer great insight into what life on board was like, in peacetime and during military engagements. Excellent audioguides, included in the admission fee, feature anecdotes from former crew members.

OLD OPERATING THEATRE MUSEUM & HERB GARRET MUSEUM

Map p452 (020-7188 2679; www.oldoperatingtheatre.com; 9a St Thomas St; adult/child £6.50/3.50; 2-5pm Mon, from 10.30am Tue-Fri, noon-4pm Sat & Sun; London Bridge) This unique museum, 32 steps up a spiral stairway in the tower of St Thomas Church (1703), is the unlikely home of Britain's oldest surviving operating theatre. Rediscovered in 1956, the attic was used by the apothecary of St Thomas' Hospital to store medicinal herbs. The museum looks back at the horror of 19th-century medicine, all pre-anaesthetic and pre-antiseptic. You can browse the natural remedies, including snail water for venereal disease, and recoil at the fiendish array of amputation knives and blades.

WHITE CUBE BERMONDSEY GALLERY

Map p452 (020-7930 5373; www.whitecube.com; 144-152 Bermondsey St; 10am-6pm Tue-Sat, from noon Sun; London Bridge) FREE The newest and largest of the White Cube galleries, this spot impresses with its large exhibition spaces, which lend themselves to monumental pieces or expansive installations using several mediums. White Cube is the brainchild of Jay Jopling, dealer to the stars of the Brit Art movement. He made his reputation in the 1990s by exhibiting then unknown artists such as Tracey Emin, Damien Hirst and Antony Gormley.

LONDON BRIDGE EXPERIENCE & LONDON TOMBS MUSEUM

Map p452 (020-7403 6333; www.thelondonbridgeexperience.com; 2-4 Tooley St; adult/child £28.95/22.50; 10am-6pm Mon-Fri, from 9.30am Sat & Sun; London Bridge) In the vaults beneath London Bridge, this historical if somewhat tacky attraction takes you on a whistle-stop tour of London's dark past. Things ratchet up from a tame museum to full-on haunted house as you descend past a series of 14th-century tombs and plague pits – real ones – while animatronic rodents and costumed and bloodied actors frighten the bejesus out of unsuspecting groups. Book tickets online in advance to jump the queue and save on the hefty entry fee.

CROSSBONES GARDEN GARDENS

Map p452 (020-7403 3393; www.crossbones.org.uk; cnr Union St & Redcross Way; noon-2pm Wed-Fri; Borough) This peaceful, if slightly ramshackle, garden is an unconsecrated burial ground where those living on the margins of society were buried until 1853. It's estimated that some 50,000 people were buried here over the centuries, most of them women (who worked as prostitutes) and children. Volunteers have fought for decades to preserve the site from development and transform it into a garden of remembrance in honour of the 'outcast dead'.

Bankside & Southwark

TATE MODERN GALLERY

See p160.

SHAKESPEARE'S GLOBE THEATRE

See p162.

MILLENNIUM BRIDGE BRIDGE

Map p450 (Ⓤ Blackfriars) The elegant steel, aluminium and concrete Millennium Bridge staples the south bank of the Thames, in front of Tate Modern, to the north bank, at Peter's Hill below St Paul's Cathedral. The low-slung frame designed by Sir Norman Foster and Anthony Caro looks spectacular, particularly when lit up at night, and the view of St Paul's from South Bank has become one of London's iconic images.

Waterloo

LEAKE STREET ARCHES AREA

Map p452 (http://leakestreetarches.london; Leake St; Ⓤ Waterloo) A grungy road under Waterloo station seems an unlikely place to find art, theatre and restaurants, but Leake St is the latest of London's railway arches to get the redevelopment treatment. Opened by famous street artist Banksy in 2008, the walls of the 200m-long **Leake Street Tunnel** are covered from floor to ceiling with some seriously impressive spray-painted works, and new taggers turn up daily. Banksy's work is long gone, but you can watch today's artists painting over what was put up yesterday.

Restaurant options include Vietnamese from Banh Bao Brothers and Polish from Mamuśka, plus board games and beer at Draughts. Enter from Lower Marsh or York Rd.

HAYWARD GALLERY GALLERY

Map p452 (☎020-3879 9555; www.southbankcentre.co.uk/venues/hayward-gallery; Belvedere Rd; ⏰11am-7pm Mon, Wed, Sat & Sun, to 9pm Thu; Ⓤ Waterloo) Part of the Southbank Centre, the Hayward Gallery hosts a changing roster of contemporary art in a 1960s brutalist building. It doesn't have a permanent collection; instead, it puts on three to four exhibitions a year. A huge refurbishment was completed in 2018, restoring the 66 glass-pyramid skylights to let natural light in for

TOP EXPERIENCE

VISIT MUSIC'S HOME AT SOUTHBANK

Southbank Centre, a concrete complex sprawling over 7 hectares constructed for the 1951 Festival of Britain, is Europe's largest centre for performing and visual arts. It's easy to get lost in the tangle of venues, which present more than 1200 events a year.

The glass and Portland stone facade of the **Royal Festival Hall** (p174) is more approachable than its 1970s neighbours. It is one of London's leading music venues, and even if you're not here for a gig, you can relax at the aptly named **Riverside Terrace Cafe** or step back into the 1950s at **Skylon** (p170). Track down the **singing lift** that serenades at every stop.

To the north, **Queen Elizabeth Hall** (p174) is an austere brutalist icon, albeit with a playful daffodil-yellow staircase that leads up to the **roof garden** (p174), which opens as a cafe-bar in the warmer months. Music tops the annual program here, with gigs, chamber orchestras, dance performances and opera year-round. In 2018 it emerged from a three-year refurb.

The 1968 **Hayward Gallery**, a leading contemporary-art exhibition space, is another recently renovated brutalist beauty. It doesn't have a permanent collection, so check to see what's on before you go.

DON'T MISS

- A performance at the Royal Festival Hall
- The singing lift
- Queen Elizabeth Hall roof garden
- Hayward Gallery exhibition

PRACTICALITIES

- Map p452, A4
- ☎020-3879 9555
- www.southbankcentre.co.uk
- Belvedere Rd
- h10am-11pm
-
- Ⓤ Waterloo

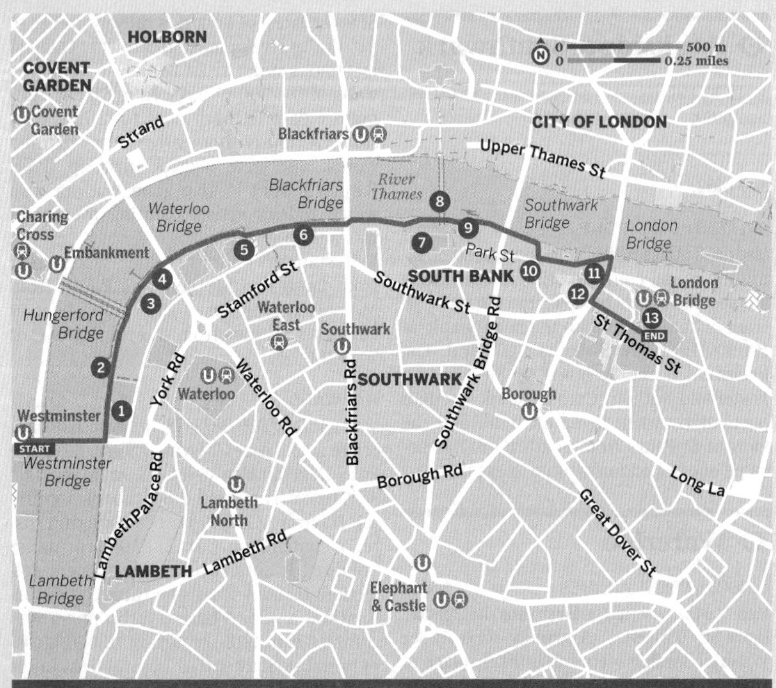

Neighbourhood Walk
South Bank Stroll

START WESTMINSTER TUBE STATION
END THE SHARD
LENGTH 3.1 MILES; 3½ HOURS

From Westminster Tube station, cross Westminster Bridge and go down the eastern stairs to reach South Bank and the colonnaded ❶ **County Hall** (Map p452, A5; Westminster Bridge Rd; Ⓤ Westminster or Waterloo), the seat of London's local government from 1922 to 1986. The ❷ **London Eye** (p168) gracefully rotates next to it, and this stretch of the River Thames is always heaving with visitors, ice-cream vans, street performers and Londoners on a lunchtime run. Push on east past the ❸ **Southbank Centre** (p165) and pause to admire the acrobatics of local teenagers at the graffitied Undercroft skatepark underneath the ❹ **Queen Elizabeth Hall** (p174). Carry on strolling along the river, past the indie shops of ❺ **Gabriel's Wharf** (p175) and ❻ **Oxo Tower Wharf** (p175).

A few minutes after passing under Blackfriars Bridge, you'll emerge in front of the imposing ❼ **Tate Modern** (p160), a power station turned contemporary-art gallery. Leading to the north bank is the ❽ **Millennium Bridge** (p165), a steel suspension bridge with beautiful views of St Paul's Cathedral. Just 100m east of the Tate Modern is the magnificently rebuilt ❾ **Shakespeare's Globe** (p162). Walk under Southwark Bridge, which is beautifully lit at night, past the perennially busy ❿ **Anchor Bankside** (p172) pub, and down the maze of streets leading to ⓫ **Southwark Cathedral** (p171).

Spreading around the railway arches is ⓬ **Borough Market** (p163), London's premier gourmet products market (and one of its oldest), at its busiest on Fridays and Saturdays. Lording over everything in this area, though, is the dramatic form of the ⓭ **Shard** (p164), one of the tallest buildings in Europe and a modern London icon.

the first time, among other improvements. Ticket prices vary by exhibition.

ROUPELL ST STREET

Map p452 (Roupell St; ⓤWaterloo) The backstreets of Waterloo hide some amazing architecture. Roupell St is an astonishingly pretty row of low-rise workers' cottages, all sooty bricks and brightly painted doors, dating back to the 1820s. The street is so uniform it looks like a film set. The same architecture extends to Theed and Whittlesey Sts, which run parallel to Roupell St to the north.

SEA LIFE LONDON AQUARIUM AQUARIUM

Map p452 (www.visitsealife.com/london; County Hall, Westminster Bridge Rd; adult/child £29/23; ⏲10am-4pm Mon-Wed & Fri, from 11am Thu, 10am-5pm Sat & Sun; 👪; ⓤWaterloo or Westminster) Mostly geared towards kids, the Sea Life London Aquarium includes a shark tunnel, ray lagoon and gentoo penguin enclosures that will keep little ones enraptured for hours. Feeds and talks are scheduled throughout the day, and you can even dive into the shark tank. Booking tickets online in advance will net a small discount and give guaranteed entry. Opening times vary throughout the year, with longer hours during summer, weekends and school holidays, so check before you go.

LONDON DUNGEON AMUSEMENT PARK

Map p452 (☎0333 321 2001; www.thedungeons.com/london; County Hall, Westminster Bridge Rd; adult/child £30/24; ⏲10am-4pm Mon-Wed & Fri, from 11am Thu, 10am-6pm Sat, to 5pm Sun; ⓤWaterloo or Westminster) A scary tour of London's gruesome history awaits. Expect darkness, sudden loud noises, flashing lights, squirts of unspecified liquid and unpleasant smells as you shuffle through themed rooms where actors, often covered in fake blood, tell creepy stories and goad visitors. It's spooky, interactive and fun if you like jumping out of your skin. Pre-booking tickets online is essential. It takes around 90 minutes to work your way through. Not suitable for young children.

EATING

The presence of Borough Market (p163) established South Bank's foodie credentials long ago, and now even more restaurants are setting up shop on the market fringes and side streets. Tooley St and Bermondsey St also have meals for all tastes. Sadly, the prime riverside real estate is mostly reserved for bland chains.

London Bridge & Bermondsey St

★PADELLA ITALIAN £

Map p452 (www.padella.co; 6 Southwark St; dishes £4-12.50; ⏲noon-3.45pm & 5-10pm Mon-Sat, noon-3.45pm & 5-9pm Sun; ✎; ⓤLondon Bridge) Come hungry for the best pasta this side of Italy. Padella is a small, energetic bistro specialising in handmade noodles, inspired by the owners' extensive culinary adventures. The portions are small, which means that you can (and should!) have more than one dish. The queue is always long; download the WalkIn app to join it virtually and head to the pub.

The dishes on offer are often switched up, but the menu mainstay of *pici cacio e pepe* is a must.

FLAT IRON SQUARE FOOD HALL £

Map p452 (☎020-3179 9800; www.flatironsquare.co.uk; Flat Iron Sq; ⏲noon-midnight Mon-Sat, 10.30am-10pm Sun; ✎; ⓤLondon Bridge) This industrial-chic food court weaves through seven railway arches and has commandeered the surrounding outdoor space to offer a foodie hub for the indecisive. Want to dine on *gyoza*, pizza, pad thai, buttermilk chicken or Mediterranean salads? No need to pick just one. Flat Iron also hosts events, including vintage markets and themed nights. Hours and prices vary for individual traders.

VINEGAR YARD STREET FOOD £

Map p452 (www.vinegaryard.london; 72-82 St Thomas St; ⏲noon-10pm Mon-Fri, from 11am Sat & Sun; ⓤLondon Bridge) Equal parts street food market, bar, vintage shopping and art installation, Vinegar Yard wants to be all things to all people, and it accomplishes it seamlessly. The huge outdoor space is a major draw, a rarity for somewhere so central, but there's indoor space too for when the weather isn't cooperating. Hungry visitors will find delicious oferings of Lebanese and Italian street food, Indian inspired burgers and more. A flea market takes over every weekend.

WATCH HOUSE

CAFE £

Map p452 (☎020-7407 6431; www.thewatchhouse.com; 199 Bermondsey St; sandwiches from £4.95; ⏰7am-6pm Mon-Fri, from 8am Sat & Sun; ✎; Ⓤ Borough) Saying that Watch House nails the sandwich doesn't do justice to this tip-top cafe. But don't expect to get a seat in the barely 2.5-sq-metre space; it's in a wonderfully restored 19th-century watch-house once used by guards patrolling the graveyard of St Mary Magdalen.

★ARABICA BAR & KITCHEN

MIDDLE EASTERN ££

Map p452 (☎020-3011 5151; www.arabicabarandkitchen.com; 3 Rochester Walk, Borough Market; dishes £6-14; ⏰noon-10.30pm Mon-Fri, from 9am Sat, 10am-9.30pm Sun; ✎; Ⓤ London Bridge) Set in a brick-lined railway arch, Arabica specialises in classic Middle Eastern favourites served mezze-style, so round up a group to sample and share as many of the small plates as possible. Stars of the menu include creamy baba ganoush, made with perfectly smoked aubergine and saffron yoghurt, and charcoal-grilled lamb kebab.

CASA DO FRANGO

PORTUGUESE ££

Map p452 (www.casadofrango.co.uk; 32 Southwark St; dishes £6-10; ⏰noon-3pm & 5-10.30pm Mon-Thu, noon-11pm Fri & Sat, to 10pm Sun; Ⓤ London Bridge) Forget your notions of Nando's: Casa do Frango kicks peri-peri up a notch in its cool plant-filled upstairs space steps away from Borough Market (p163). Frango, Algarvian-style charcoal-grilled chicken brushed with peri-peri sauce, is the star of the menu, which also includes regionally flavoured sharing plates. Seek out the hidden door to the dimly lit speakeasy for after-dinner drinks.

TEXAS JOE'S

BARBECUE ££

Map p452 (☎020-3759 7355; www.texas-joes.com; 8-9 Snowsfields; mains £10-22; ⏰noon-10pm Mon-Thu, to 11pm Fri & Sat, to 9pm Sun; Ⓤ London Bridge) Started by an expat from Dallas, Texas Joe's brings big Lone Star attitude and authenticity to a Bermondsey backstreet. Huge hunks of meat are smoked round the clock and then doled out with white bread, pickles and pots of zingy barbecue sauce. Add on side dishes such as bone marrow and bacon-wrapped jalapeños to enter true food-induced narcosis.

TOP EXPERIENCE

SEE THE CITY FROM THE LONDON EYE

It's hard to imagine South Bank without the London Eye (officially named the Coca-Cola London Eye after its current sponsor), the world's largest cantilevered observation wheel, which began twirling in 2000 to mark the turn of the millennium. It was originally a temporary attraction, intended to be dismantled after five years, but its unceasing popularity has ensured its longevity. Standing 135m tall in a fairly flat city, it has fundamentally altered London's skyline and is visible from various viewpoints.

A ride – or 'flight' as it is called here – in one of the wheel's 32 glass-enclosed eye-shaped pods takes a gracefully slow 30 minutes and, weather permitting, you can see 25 miles (as far as Windsor Castle) in every direction from the top. Don't let poor weather put you off: the close-up views of the Houses of Parliament, just across the river, are the highlight of the ride. Interactive tablets provide multilingual information about landmarks as they come up in the skyline.

Tickets aren't cheap, and it's worth booking in advance for a slight discount, plus a 15-minute time slot for entry. Two-for-one entry is sometimes available on www.daysoutguide.co.uk.

DID YOU KNOW?

➡ The London Eye is the focal point of the capital's New Year's Eve fireworks, for which it is rigged with thousands of fireworks.

PRACTICALITIES

➡ Map p452, A4

➡ www.londoneye.com

➡ near County Hall

➡ adult/child £28/23

➡ ⏰10am-8.30pm, shorter hours in winter

➡ Ⓤ Waterloo or Westminster

EL PASTOR

MEXICAN ££

Map p452 (www.tacoselpastor.co.uk; 7a Stoney St; tacos £6.75-10.50; ⊙noon-3pm & 5-11pm Mon-Fri, noon-4pm & 6-11pm Sat, noon-4pm Sun; ⓤLondon Bridge) Decent Mexican food has strangely been missing from London's food scene, but fortunately a few places have stepped up to fill the void. Step through the plastic flaps into this taco temple and order a few plates (portions are tiny) or bigger sharers. The mezcal (an agave spirit similar to tequila) menu is twice the size of the food menu.

No reservations; expect to queue.

TAPAS BRINDISA

TAPAS ££

Map p452 (☎020-7357 8880; www.brindisatapaskitchens.com; 18-20 Southwark St, SE1; dishes £5-16; ⊙10am-11.30pm Mon-Fri, from 8.30am Sat, 10am-10pm Sun; ⓤLondon Bridge) On the corner of Borough Market and busy Southwark St is one of London's first tapas bars, which has grown into an *español* empire across the city. Tables spill onto the pavement as punters order plate after plate of Spanish classics: croquetas, *pan con tomate* (bread with tomato), *jamón ibérico* (cured ham) and whole octopus legs.

RABOT 1745

FUSION ££

Map p452 (☎020-7378 8226; www.hotelchocolat.com; 2-4 Bedale St; mains £15-21; ⊙noon-10pm Tue-Fri, from 9am Sat; ⓤLondon Bridge) Started by the founders of Hotel Chocolat who restored a cacao plantation on the Caribbean island of St Lucia, Rabot 1745 dishes up an intriguing mix of British plates with flavours of the West Indies. Every dish has cacao of some sort – white chocolate mash, meat marinated in cacao nibs, 70% ganache on the burger – and somehow it all works perfectly.

CASSE-CROÛTE

FRENCH ££

Map p452 (☎020-7407 2140; www.cassecroute.co.uk; 109 Bermondsey St; mains from £20; ⊙noon-10pm Mon-Sat, to 4pm Sun; ⓤLondon Bridge) So typical is the French interior of this bistro that you'll have to keep reminding yourself that you are in London and not in Paris. The daily changing menu, written on a chalkboard only in French, is quintessential hearty countryside fare, from *lapin à la moutarde* (rabbit in mustard sauce) to *île flottante* (a soft-set meringue in vanilla custard). Reservations recommended.

GARRISON PUBLIC HOUSE

GASTROPUB ££

Map p452 (☎020-7089 9355; www.thegarrison.co.uk; 99-101 Bermondsey St; mains £16-32; ⊙8am-11pm Mon-Thu, to midnight Fri, 9am-midnight Sat, to 10.30pm Sun; 📝; ⓤLondon Bridge) Bermondsey St's classiest pub grub is served inside the Garrison's traditional green-tiled exterior, at tables with mismatched seats of antique and distressed wood. The menu is mostly British but looks to Western Europe for inspiration, and there's always at least one solid veggie option on offer.

Bankside & Southwark

★ANCHOR & HOPE

GASTROPUB ££

Map p452 (☎020-7928 9898; www.anchorandhopepub.co.uk; 36 The Cut; mains £12.40-19.40; ⊙5-11pm Mon, from 11am Tue-Sat, 12.30-3.15pm Sun; ⓤSouthwark) Started by former chefs from nose-to-tail pioneer St John (p208), the Anchor & Hope is a quintessential gastropub: elegant but not formal, serving utterly delicious European fare with a British twist. The menu changes daily, but it could include grilled sole served with spinach, or roast rabbit with green beans in a mustard-and-bacon sauce. Bookings taken for Sunday lunch only.

BALA BAYA

JEWISH ££

Map p452 (☎020-8001 7015; https://balabaya.co.uk; Arch 25, Old Union Yard Arches, 229 Union St; mains £11-18; ⊙noon-3pm & 5-10pm Mon-Fri, 10.30am-4pm & 6-10pm Sat, 10.30am-4pm Sun; 📝; ⓤSouthwark) 🍃 This two-level arch is a love letter to Tel Aviv, with a whitewashed curving Bauhaus-inspired interior and a menu full of fresh and sustainably sourced ingredients, meaning fantastic choices for veggies and vegans. With an Israeli chef at the helm, expect playful takes on Mediterranean favourites: the caramelised cauliflower pita topped with tahini is a lunchtime must.

SWAN AT THE GLOBE

GASTROPUB ££

Map p452 (☎020-7928 9444; www.swanlondon.co.uk; 21 New Globe Walk; mains £16.50-25; ⊙8am-11.30pm Mon-Wed, to midnight Thu, to 12.30am Fri, 10am-12.30am Sat, to 11pm Sun; ⓤBlackfriars or London Bridge) You can't get a pre-theatre meal closer to Shakespeare's Globe (p174) than this – and an excellent one at that. But even if you're not stopping in for a show, book into the Swan to savour thoughtful British cuisine, such as game-and-porcini-mushroom pie, in delightfully refined surrounds with elevated river views.

TIBITS VEGETARIAN ££

Map p452 (020-7202 8370; www.tibits.co.uk; 124 Southwark St; plates priced by weight; 7.30am-10pm Mon-Wed, to 11pm Thu & Fri, 11.30am-11pm Sat, to 10pm Sun; ; Blackfriars, Southwark) This all-vegetarian cafe puts a hip spin on cafeteria-style dining. A rotating selection of innovative veggie and vegan dishes are laid out along a DIY service counter, where you can load up on helpings of salad, curry, risotto and more, and then your plate is weighed at the till. Its location and relaxed atmosphere make it a perfect post–Tate Modern refuelling stop.

BALTIC EASTERN EUROPEAN ££

Map p452 (020-7928 1111; www.balticrestaurant.co.uk; 74 Blackfriars Rd; mains £14.50-19; 5.30-11.15pm Mon, noon-3pm & 5.30-11.15pm Tue-Sat, noon-4.30pm & 5.30-10.30pm Sun; Southwark) In a bright and airy, high-ceilinged dining room with glass roof and wooden beams, Baltic is travel on a plate: dumplings and blini, pickle and smoke, rich stews and braised meat. From Polish to Georgian, the flavours are authentic and the dishes beautifully presented. The wine and vodka lists are equally extensive. Pre-theatre and set lunches are good value.

Waterloo

LOWER MARSH MARKET STREET FOOD £

Map p452 (020-7620 1201; www.lowermarshmarket.com; Lower Marsh; market 9am-5pm Mon-Sat, food traders noon-2pm Mon-Fri; Waterloo) This food and bric-a-brac market has become a fixture on the once shabby Lower Marsh road, giving it a sense of community. Food tents sell dishes ranging from curry to falafel, and quality is generally good. Despite its proximity to the river, the market sees more local office workers than visitors. On Saturdays, expect more clothing and craft stalls than cuisine.

OXO TOWER BRASSERIE EUROPEAN ££

Map p452 (020-7803 3888; www.harveynichols.com/restaurant/the-oxo-tower/brasserie; Oxo Tower Wharf, Bargehouse St; mains £14.50-26; noon-10pm Sun-Wed, to 11pm Thu-Sat; ; Waterloo) The mid-'90s conversion of the iconic Oxo Tower with this 8th-floor brasserie – the first from luxe department store Harvey Nichols – helped spur much of South Bank's dining renaissance. The stunning glassed-in terrace provides a front-row seat to stellar city views, though you'll pay for it handsomely. Fish dishes usually comprise half the menu; vegetarians are well catered for too. Bookings essential.

★**SKYLON** EUROPEAN £££

Map p452 (020-7654 7800; www.skylon-restaurant.co.uk; 3rd fl, Royal Festival Hall, Southbank Centre, Belvedere Rd; mains £16.50-34; noon-11pm Mon-Fri, 11.30am-3pm & 5-11pm Sat, 11.30am-10.30pm Sun; ; Waterloo) Named after the original structure in this location for the 1951 Festival of Britain, Skylon brings the 1950s into the modern era, with retro-futuristic decor (trendy then, trendier now) and a season-driven menu of contemporary British cuisine. But its biggest selling point might be the floor-to-ceiling windows that bathe you in magnificent views of the Thames and the city.

Booking is advised. Children under 10 eat free.

DRINKING & NIGHTLIFE

You won't go thirsty in South Bank. Chain pubs with average offerings but stellar views are plonked along the river; find more authentic backstreet boozers further inland. A number of superb rooftop bars have sprouted up in convenient intervals near the waterfront.

London Bridge & Bermondsey St

★**GEORGE INN** PUB

Map p452 (020-7407 2056; www.nationaltrust.org.uk/george-inn; 77 Borough High St; 11am-11pm Mon-Thu, to midnight Fri & Sat, noon-10.30pm Sun; London Bridge) This magnificent galleried coaching inn is the last of its kind in London. The building, owned by the National Trust, dates from 1677 and is mentioned in Charles Dickens' *Little Dorrit*. In the evenings, the picnic benches in the huge cobbled courtyard fill up (no reservations); otherwise, find a spot in the labyrinth of dark rooms and corridors inside.

RAKE

PUB

Map p452 (☎020-7407 0557; www.facebook.com/TheRakeSE1; 14 Winchester Walk; ⏰noon-11pm Mon-Thu, from 11am Fri, 10am-11pm Sat, noon-10pm Sun; ⓊLondon Bridge) Run by the founders of hop emporium Utobeer (p175), Rake has an astonishing selection of suds, including rare brews impossible to find anywhere else in town. Guided by the helpful bar staff, you can't go wrong. It's a teensy place, and it's always busy; the decking outside is especially popular.

AQUA SHARD

BAR

Map p452 (☎020-3011 1256; www.aquashard.co.uk; 31st fl, Shard, 31 St Thomas St; ⏰10.30am-1am Sun-Thu, to 3am Fri & Sat; ⓊLondon Bridge) If you want a view from the Shard (p164) for the price of a cocktail, find your way up to the 31st floor and into this gorgeous three-storey bar and restaurant. The lofty ceiling adds awe to the London panoramas shining through the high sloping glass walls. Only the restaurant takes bookings, so expect a wait if you come at peak drinking hours.

CHAPTER 72

CAFE

Map p452 (www.chapter-72.com; 72 Bermondsey St; ⏰7am-7.30pm Mon & Tue, to 10pm Wed-Fri, 9am-10pm Sat, to 7.30pm Sun; ⓊLondon Bridge) Named the best local coffee shop in SE1 in 2018, this cafe-cocktail bar can do anything with espresso, and it's so dedicated to coffee that it even runs an espresso-martini masterclass. Try the Dark Arts negroni, which is spiked with Tia Maria and can come served in a sharing teapot. After-hours coffee-lovers can even order a decaffeinated espresso martini.

214 BERMONDSEY

BAR

Map p452 (☎020-7403 6875; www.two1four.com; 214 Bermondsey St; ⏰5-11pm Mon-Wed, to midnight Thu, to 1.30am Fri & Sat, 4-10.30pm Sun; ⓊLondon Bridge) Something of a speakeasy but with none of the pretentiousness, this bar hidden below the Flour & Grape restaurant lists more than 100 gins, served splashed with its own house-made craft tonic or expertly fashioned into a cocktail of your choosing. It also offers three-glass gin flights with the labels removed so you have to guess what's what.

GENTLEMEN BARISTAS

COFFEE

Map p452 (www.thegentlemenbaristas.com; 63 Union St; ⏰7am-5.30pm Mon-Fri, 8.30am-5pm Sat, to 4pm Sun; 📶; ⓊLondon Bridge or Borough)

TOP EXPERIENCE

VISIT SOUTHWARK CATHEDRAL

Southwark Cathedral, a mostly Victorian construction but with a history dating back many centuries, was the nearest church to what was once the only entry point into the city, London Bridge.

The Gothic arched nave is impressive, and remnants of an older roof structure are near the font on the western side of the church; the 15th-century **medieval roof bosses** on display are just a couple from the 150 carved and painted shields that once hung from the ceiling. In the north aisle of the nave is the **tomb of John Gower**, poet to Richard II and Henry IV. Pass the elegantly inlaid 16th-century **Nonsuch Chest**, made by German immigrants, in the Choir Aisle to admire the 16th-century saint-filled **High Altar Screen**. The earliest surviving section of the cathedral is the **retro-choir** (behind the high altar) at the eastern end, with four chapels.

Through the peaceful churchyard just across the fence from ever-busy Borough Market, you'll find the **herb garden**, planted with medicinal shrubs that would have been used in the medieval hospital once attached to the cathedral. In the nave's south aisle, the green alabaster **Shakespeare Memorial** carved in 1912 honours the famous playwright, who lived in Southwark.

DON'T MISS

- High Altar Screen
- Retro-choir
- Shakespeare Memorial

PRACTICALITIES

- Map p452, F3
- ☎020-7367 6700
- www.cathedral.southwark.anglican.org
- Montague Cl
- ⏰9am-5pm Mon-Fri, 9.30am-3.45pm & 5-6pm Sat, 12.30-3pm & 4-6pm Sun
- ⓊLondon Bridge

This slightly pretentious cafe makes great coffee, decent pastries and a small range of sandwiches. It attracts arty and media types who fill the tables in the exposed-brick rooms across two floors.

OMEARA CANTINA BAR

Map p452 (020-3179 2900; www.omearalondon.com; 6 O'Meara St; 5pm-midnight Mon-Wed, to 2am Thu, to 3am Fri & Sat, 1-11pm Sun; London Bridge) Down a little-used Southwark side street, Omeara is an intimate bar and live-music venue that keeps the party going inside the distressed-style interior of this railway arch with beats and a tequila- and mezcal-fuelled cocktail list until the wee hours. It's connected to Flat Iron Square (p167), so you can order bites from Lupins to snack on here.

MARKET PORTER PUB

Map p452 (020-7407 2495; www.themarketporter.co.uk; 9 Stoney St; 6-8.30am & 11am-11pm Mon-Fri, from noon Sat, to 10.30pm Sun; London Bridge) Market Porter is one of London's last remaining early-morning pubs that caters to Borough Market workers. Inside, this traditional Victorian stalwart has all the authentic wooden trimmings, but most drinkers hang out on pedestrianised Stoney St to people-watch. The upstairs dining room serves superior Sunday roasts.

CALL ME MR LUCKY BAR

Map p452 (020-7078 9634; http://callmemrlucky.com; 11 Southwark St; 5pm-midnight Mon-Wed, to 1am Thu-Sat; London Bridge) Every Breakfast Club restaurant in town has a speakeasy, and once you figure out the password for the London Bridge branch, you'll be shuffled behind the secret door and downstairs into the cavernous paper-lantern-lit Mexican-themed bar. The house specials list is unsurprisingly tequila-heavy, or you can try your luck on the 'wheel of fortune'.

MONMOUTH COFFEE COMPANY COFFEE

Map p452 (020-7232 3010; www.monmouthcoffee.co.uk; 2 Park St; 7.30am-6pm Mon-Sat; London Bridge) One of the city's most beloved coffee spots, Monmouth is a victim of its own success. The brews are top-notch (whether filter, which changes daily, or espresso-based), but the queues can be painful, and it's difficult to get a seat in the open-sided warehouse-style cafe. Fortunately, Monmouth is served at coffee shops around the city, so you can look for it elsewhere.

Bankside & Southwark

★LYANESS COCKTAIL BAR

Map p452 (020-3747 1063; https://lyaness.com; Sea Containers, 20 Upper Ground; 4pm-1am Mon-Wed, noon-2am Thu-Sat, to 12.30am Sun; ; Southwark) Six months after Dandelyan was named the best bar in the world, renowned mixologist Ryan Chetiyawardana closed it down. Reincarnated in that space with much the same atmosphere and modus operandi is Lyaness. The bar prides itself on unusual ingredients; look out for vegan honey, whey liqueur and onyx, a completely new type of alcohol.

★SEABIRD BAR

Map p452 (020-7903 3050; https://seabirdlondon.com; Hoxton Southwark, 40 Blackfriars Rd; noon-midnight Mon-Thu, to 1am Fri, 11am-1am Sat, to midnight Sun; Southwark) South Bank's latest rooftop bar might also be its best. Atop the new Hoxton Southwark (p423) hotel, sleek Seabird has palm-filled indoor and outdoor spaces where you can spy St Paul's from the comfort of your wicker seat. If you're hungry, seafood is the speciality, and the restaurant claims London's longest oyster list.

12TH KNOT BAR

Map p452 (020-3747 1063; www.facebook.com/12thknot; Sea Containers, 20 Upper Ground; 5pm-1am Tue & Wed, to 2am Thu-Sat; ; Southwark) On the 12th floor of luxe Sea Containers hotel, 12th Knot is a showstopper, with knockout views of the city and a table-width outdoor roof terrace to boot. The travel-themed cocktail menu picks up oddball ingredients along the way: champagne acid, Islay whisky mist and candied bacon. The dress code is smart casual, and it's best to book ahead.

ANCHOR BANKSIDE PUB

Map p452 (020-7407 1577; www.facebook.com/TheAnchorBankside; 34 Park St; 11am-11pm Mon-Wed, to 11.30pm Thu-Sat, noon-10.30pm Sun; London Bridge) Part of the Greene King pub chain, this 17th-century waterfront boozer looks charming and has a prime Thames-side location, but the food and beverage selection is disappointingly average. If you can't resist the pull of the

LONDON'S LOW LINE

Since the Victorian era, this part of South London has been criss-crossed by elevated railways, but over time many of the viaducts were rendered inaccessible by new construction and forgotten. But now, in an effort to match the enthusiasm of New York City's High Line, London developers have created the Low Line, a network of shops, restaurants, bars and cultural spaces in the once abandoned arches.

There's some on-the-ground signage and an online map (www.visitbankside.com), but the Low Line is still a work in progress. The route isn't as obvious as its NYC counterpart, but you can see what's happening in Flat Iron Square (p167), Borough Market (p163) and the Old Union Yard Arches, where Bala Baya (p169) is located.

terrace, know that you're in good company: 18th-century dictionary writer Samuel Johnson, whose brewer friend owned the joint, drank here, as did diarist Samuel Pepys before that.

Waterloo

★KINGS ARMS — PUB

Map p452 (020-7207 0784; www.thekingsarmslondon.co.uk; 25 Roupell St; 11am-11pm Mon-Sat, noon-10.30pm Sun; Waterloo) Set on old-school Roupell St (p167), this charming backstreet neighbourhood boozer serves up a rotating selection of traditional ales and bottled beers. The after-work crowd often makes a pit stop here before heading to Waterloo station, spilling out onto the street at peak hours. The farmhouse-style room at the back of the pub serves decent Thai food.

VAULTY TOWERS — BAR

Map p452 (020-7928 9042; www.vaultytowers.london; 34 Lower Marsh; noon-11pm Sun-Wed, to 1am Thu-Sat; Waterloo) This wacky bar is a mess of eccentric theatre props courtesy of its partner, nearby arts space Vaults (p175). You can't miss it on the street; it's covered with street-art-style characters that might have escaped from the spray-painted Leake Street Tunnel (p165). The bar is cashless, so bring your card.

UNDERSTUDY — BAR

Map p452 (020-7452 3551; www.nationaltheatre.org.uk; National Theatre, Upper Ground; noon-midnight Mon-Wed, to 1am Thu-Sat, to 10pm Sun; Waterloo) This riverside bar at the National Theatre (p174) is no imitator, and it really comes into the limelight when scores of tables are set out on the huge waterfront terrace, perfect for people-watching as the afternoon turns into evening. The taps are usually heavily stocked with Meantime from the brewery down the Thames in Greenwich.

SCOOTERCAFFE — CAFE

Map p452 (www.facebook.com/scootercaffe; 132 Lower Marsh; 8.30am-11pm Mon-Thu, to midnight Fri, 10am-midnight Sat, to 11pm Sun; Waterloo) Once a Vespa repair shop, this shabby-chic cafe is an adorable jumble of mismatched furniture, vintage prints and of course a couple of in-situ scooters. The cafe roasts its own beans, which are brewed on an antique 1957 espresso machine. After dark, caffeine is swapped for cocktails.

FOUR CORNERS — CAFE

Map p452 (020-8617 9591; www.four-corners-cafe.com; 12 Lower Marsh; 7.30am-6.30pm Mon-Fri, 9am-5pm Sat; Waterloo) With excellent coffee from Ozone Roasters and an unusually large selection of teas, this cafe attracts a loyal following. Four Corners is travel-themed, from the map-lined coffee counter to the old guidebook collection. You can even trade your old guidebooks for free coffee if they don't have that edition already.

☆ ENTERTAINMENT

Across the river and away from the naysayers in the buttoned-down City of London, playful South Bank has been a destination for entertainment since the Middle Ages. This area has a dense concentration of theatres, including the reconstructed Shakespeare's Globe, as well as Britain's largest cinema screen. The many venues inside Southbank Centre (p165) host performing arts and live music.

★ **SHAKESPEARE'S GLOBE** THEATRE

Map p452 (020-7401 9919; www.shakespearesglobe.com; 21 New Globe Walk; box office 10am-6pm; Blackfriars, London Bridge) One of the most famous playhouses in the world, Shakespeare's Globe will knock your theatrical socks off. This dutifully authentic reconstruction transports theatregoers back to Elizabethan times, with hard wooden seats and a central floor space open to the elements (cushions and ponchos are on sale). Groundling tickets are just £5 for every performance, but you're required to stand through it all.

The Globe's season runs from April to October and includes works by Shakespeare and his contemporaries, such as Christopher Marlowe. Also on the Globe's grounds is the Sam Wanamaker Playhouse, an indoor candlelit Jacobean-style theatre similar to what Shakespeare would have used in winter, which has year-round performances.

NATIONAL THEATRE THEATRE

Map p452 (020-7452 3000; www.nationaltheatre.org.uk; Upper Ground; Waterloo) The nation's flagship theatre delivers up to 25 shows every year across its three venues inside this brutalist block. Even if you're not here for a show, you can explore the foyers, which contain a bookshop, restaurants, bars and exhibition spaces. Get behind the scenes on a tour, including going backstage, a deep-dive into the building's architecture and an experience with the costume team.

ROYAL FESTIVAL HALL CONCERT VENUE

Map p452 (020-3879 9555; www.southbankcentre.co.uk/venues/royal-festival-hall; Southbank Centre, Belvedere Rd; ; Waterloo) The 2700-capacity Royal Festival Hall is one of the best places in London to hear modern and classical music, poetry and spoken-word performances. The hall has four resident orchestras, including the **London Philharmonic Orchestra** and the **London Sinfonietta**.

QUEEN ELIZABETH HALL LIVE PERFORMANCE

Map p452 (020-3879 9555; www.southbankcentre.co.uk/venues/queen-elizabeth-hall; Southbank Centre, Belvedere Rd; Waterloo) Queen Elizabeth Hall has a full programme of gigs, chamber orchestras, dance performances and opera throughout the year, on a smaller scale than the nearby Royal Festival Hall that's also part of Southbank Centre (p165). The space reopened in 2018 after a three-year refurb. In summer, don't miss the plant-strewn cafe-bar on the **roof** (noon-9pm Apr–mid-Jun & Sep-Oct, 10am-10.30pm mid-Jun–Aug).

BRIDGE THEATRE THEATRE

Map p452 (0333 320 0051; https://bridgetheatre.co.uk; 3 Potters Fields Park; London Bridge) London's first new major theatre in 80 years, Bridge Theatre seats 900 in a cool, modern space and focuses on new productions, with the occasional classic thrown in.

OLD VIC THEATRE

Map p452 (0344 871 7628; www.oldvictheatre.com; The Cut; Waterloo) This 1000-seater nonprofit theatre celebrated its 200th season in 2018 and continues to bring eclectic programming occasionally bolstered by big-name actors, such as Daniel Radcliffe.

YOUNG VIC THEATRE

Map p452 (020-7922 2922; www.youngvic.org; 66 The Cut; box office 10am-6pm Mon-Sat; Southwark) This groundbreaking theatre is as much about showcasing and discovering new talent as it is about people discovering theatre. The Young Vic features actors, directors and plays from across the world, many tackling contemporary political and cultural issues, such as the death penalty, racism or corruption, and often blending dance and music with acting.

BFI SOUTHBANK CINEMA

Map p452 (020-7928 3232; https://whatson.bfi.org.uk; Belvedere Rd; 9.45am-11pm; Waterloo) Tucked almost out of sight under the arches of Waterloo Bridge, the British Film Institute contains four cinemas that screen thousands of films each year (many arthouse), a gallery devoted to the moving image, and a mediatheque where you can watch movie and TV highlights from the BFI National Archive.

The BFI is the major venue for the **BFI London Film Festival**, which screens some 300 films from around the world each October.

BFI IMAX CINEMA

Map p452 (www.bfi.org.uk/bfi-imax; 1 Charlie Chaplin Walk; Waterloo) Oddly situated in a roundabout, the BFI IMAX has the largest cinema screen in the UK, at 20m high and 26m wide. It shows 2D and 3D blockbuster films as well as documentaries about travel, space and wildlife.

VAULTS
LIVE PERFORMANCE

Map p452 (☎020-7401 9603; www.thevaults.london; Leake St; Ⓤ Waterloo) Set in a series of dank railway arches under Waterloo station, Vaults puts on unexpected immersive supper clubs and theatre performances, and is a hub for alt art. The leftover props end up in the nearby Vaulty Towers (p173) bar. It's also home to the creative **Vault Festival**, with a lengthy program of boundary-pushing comedy, cabaret and theatre.

UNICORN THEATRE
THEATRE

Map p452 (☎020-7645 0560; www.unicorntheatre.com; 147 Tooley St; ⏲box office 9.30am-6pm Mon-Sat; 👪; Ⓤ London Bridge) Putting on about 20 different shows a year, the Unicorn Theatre offers quality performances for children aged from six months to 18 years. Productions are wide-ranging and perfectly tailored to the target audience.

SHOPPING

South Bank isn't a big shopping destination, but you can pick up quirky souvenirs from the gift shops at Tate Modern (p160), the National Theatre and Southbank Centre (p165). A handful of small indie shops can be found along Bermondsey St and below Oxo Tower (Map p452; www.oxotower.co.uk; Bargehouse St; ⏲11am-6pm Tue-Sun; Ⓤ Waterloo or Blackfriars)**.**

SUCK UK
GIFTS & SOUVENIRS

Map p452 (☎020-7928 0855; www.suck.uk.com; ground fl, Oxo Tower Wharf; ⏲10am-7pm Mon-Sat, to 5.30pm Sun; Ⓤ Waterloo) Suck UK's artsy, quirky gifts are so funny that you'll want to keep them for yourself. London's weather will likely call for an umbrella that changes colour when wet, or you can pick up a few items for home, perhaps a cat scratcher that looks like a DJ turntable or a doormat that says 'come in' but when turned upside down reads 'go away'.

LOVELY & BRITISH
GIFTS & SOUVENIRS

Map p452 (☎020-7378 6570; 132a Bermondsey St; ⏲10am-6pm Mon-Fri, to 7pm Sat, 11am-5pm Sun; Ⓤ London Bridge) This gorgeous Bermondsey boutique prides itself on stocking prints, jewellery and London-themed pieces of home decor created by British designers. It's an eclectic mix of items, with reasonable prices.

UTOBEER
DRINK

Map p452 (Unit 24, Borough Market; ⏲11am-5pm Mon, to 5.30pm Tue, to 6pm Wed & Thu, 10am-6pm Fri, 9am-5pm Sat; Ⓤ London Bridge) This beer shop inside Borough Market (p163) stocks hundreds of international bottled beers, with a large selection of American and European brews that are hard to source elsewhere in the city.

GABRIEL'S WHARF
FASHION & ACCESSORIES

Map p452 (www.facebook.com/gabrielswharf; btwn Queen's Walk & Upper Ground; Ⓤ Waterloo or Southwark) This small enclave slightly set back from the river is home to independent boutiques selling ceramics, art, clothes and jewellery, as well as a couple of restaurants and cafes. Opening hours vary by shop.

SOUTHBANK CENTRE BOOK MARKET
BOOKS

Map p452 (Queen's Walk; ⏲11am-7pm, shorter hours in winter; Ⓤ Waterloo) Under Waterloo Bridge, the outdoor Southbank Centre Book Market sells secondhand books of all sorts, as well as maps and prints, no matter the weather.

SPORTS & ACTIVITIES

THAMES ROCKETS
BOATING

Map p452 (☎020-7928 8933; www.thamesrockets.com; Boarding Gate 1, London Eye Millennium Pier; adult/child from £44.95/29.95; ⏲10am-6pm; 👪; Ⓤ Waterloo or Westminster) Thames Rockets runs adrenalin-pumping speedboat experiences, reaching 30 knots along the high-speed section of the Thames. The 50-minute Ultimate London Adventure and Captain Kidd's Canary Wharf Voyage are suitable for families; for something more grown-up, try Thames Lates in summer (which include a cocktail) or Break the Barrier for those who love speed.

Kensington & Hyde Park

KNIGHTSBRIDGE & SOUTH KENSINGTON | HYDE PARK & KENSINGTON GARDENS | CHELSEA & BELGRAVIA | VICTORIA & PIMLICO

Neighbourhood Top Five

❶ **Victoria & Albert Museum** (p178) Thumbing through an encyclopaedic A–Z of decorative and design works from across the globe while admiring the astonishing architecture and making hordes of unexpected discoveries.

❷ **Natural History Museum** (p182) Becoming hypnotised by the awe-inspiring stonework and inexhaustible collection of this world-leading museum, while putting aside time to delve into its bucolic Wildlife Garden.

❸ **Hyde Park** (p184) Enjoying a picnic in London's green lung and exploring its many sights and infinitely verdant scenery.

❹ **Science Museum** (p186) Nurturing a wide-eyed fascination for the complexities of the world and the cosmos in this electrifying museum.

❺ **Harrods** (p199) Shopping – or just window-shopping!

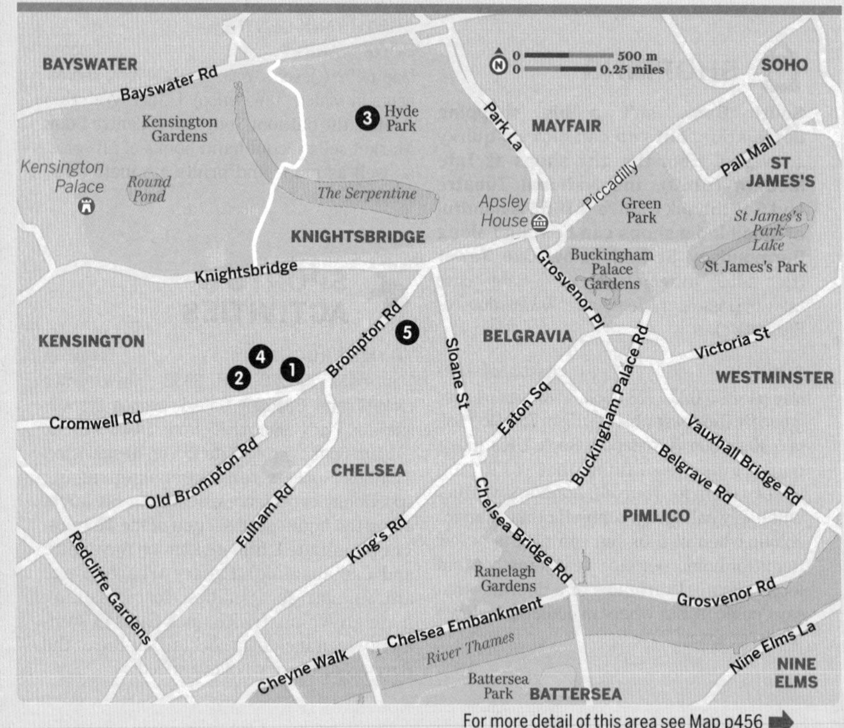

For more detail of this area see Map p456 ➡

Explore Kensington & Hyde Park

Educate yourself or catch up on all you've forgotten since school at South Kensington's magnificent museums of the arts and sciences. You'll need several days to do them all justice. Although museums don't open till 10am, queuing early means elbow room when the doors open.

Shoppers make a beeline for Knightsbridge, Harrods and Harvey Nichols, but to sidestep jostling crowds and enjoy sedate browsing visit tranquil shopping enclaves such as John Sandoe Books and Peter Harrington.

For a sight-packed day visit Hyde Park and conjoined Kensington Gardens – crucial for seeing why Londoners love their green spaces. Explore the opulence of Kensington Palace before investigating the park: the Albert Memorial, the Serpentine Sackler Galleries, the Diana, Princess of Wales Memorial Fountain, Speakers' Corner and all the bountiful greenery in between.

Super restaurants are never far away: Kensington, Knightsbridge and Chelsea take their dining seriously, so your best experiences could well be gastronomic, whether you're grazing, snacking or plain feasting.

Local Life

Hang-outs Rub shoulders with discerning, affable drinkers at the Anglesea Arms (p197) or Queen's Arms (p198), or snap your fingers with local jazz hounds at the swinging 606 Club (p198) and Pheasantry (p198).

Museums Late-night Fridays at the Victoria & Albert (p178) equals fewer crowds (especially children), meaning locals can get a look-in.

Parks On sunny days, Londoners dust off their shades, get outdoors to green expanses like Hyde Park (p184) and lie supine reading chunky novels.

Getting There & Away

Underground Kensington and Hyde Park link to the rest of London via South Kensington, Sloane Sq, Victoria, Knightsbridge and Hyde Park Corner stations. The main lines are Circle, District, Piccadilly and Victoria.

Bus Handy routes include 52 from Victoria to High St Kensington; 360 from South Kensington to Sloane Sq and Pimlico; and 11 from Fulham Broadway to the King's Rd, Sloane Sq and Victoria. Heritage Routemaster 9 runs from Kensington High St, via the Royal Albert Hall, Knightsbridge and Hyde Park Corner, through Piccadilly to Trafalgar Sq.

Bicycle Santander Cycles (p415) are handy for visiting and exploring the neighbourhood.

Lonely Planet's Top Tip

Catch the **Queen's Life Guard** (Household Cavalry) departing for Horse Guards Parade at 10.28am (9.28am Sundays) from Hyde Park Barracks for the daily Changing of the Guard, performing a ritual that dates to 1660. They troop via Hyde Park Corner and under Wellington Arch (p189), Constitution Hill and the Mall. It's not as busy as the Changing of the Guard at Buckingham Palace, and you can get closer to the action.

Best Eating

- Five Fields (p196)
- Dinner by Heston Blumenthal (p193)
- A Wong (p197)
- Launceston Place (p193)
- Rabbit (p196)

For reviews, see p192.

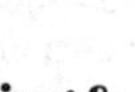

Best Drinking & Nightlife

- Tomtom Coffee House (p198)
- K Bar (p197)
- Coffee Bar (p197)
- Queen's Arms (p198)
- Anglesea Arms (p197)

For reviews, see p197.

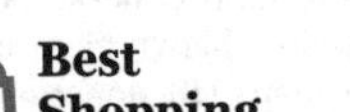

Best Shopping

- Harrods (p199)
- Conran Shop (p200)
- John Sandoe Books (p199)
- Peter Harrington (p199)
- Pylones (p199)

For reviews, see p199.

STEVE ALLEN/SHUTTERSTOCK ©

TOP EXPERIENCE

BE ASTONISHED AT THE V&A

The Victoria & Albert Museum was part of Prince Albert's legacy to the nation in the aftermath of the successful Great Exhibition of 1851. Its original aims – which still hold today – were the 'improvement of public taste in design' and 'applications of fine art to objects of utility'. In this endeavour, the museum continues to wow, astonish and inform.

Collection

Through 146 galleries, the museum houses the world's greatest collection of decorative arts, from ancient Chinese ceramics to modernist architectural drawings, Korean bronzes and Japanese swords, cartoons by Raphael, gowns from the Elizabethan era, ancient jewellery, a Sony Walkman – and much, much more.

Entrance

Entering the main Cromwell Rd entrance you'll arrive at the information desk, loomed over by the stunning blue-and-yellow blown-glass **chandelier** by Dale Chihuly. Museum maps (£1 donation requested) are available. If the Cromwell Rd entrance is too busy, take the stunning Exhibition Rd Courtyard entrance or enter from the tunnel in the basement, if arriving by Tube.

DON'T MISS

- Jewellery Gallery
- Photography Centre
- Raphael Cartoons
- Cast Courts
- Ardabil Carpet

PRACTICALITIES

- V&A
- Map p456, C4
- 020-7942 2000
- www.vam.ac.uk
- Cromwell Rd, SW7
- admission free
- 10am-5.45pm Sat-Thu, to 10pm Fri
- South Kensington

Level 0

The street level is mostly devoted to art and design from India, China, Japan, Korea and Southeast Asia, as well as European art. One of the museum's highlights is the **Cast Courts** in rooms 46a and 46b, containing staggering plaster casts collected in the Victorian era, such as Michelangelo's *David,* acquired in 1858.

More European excellence is in room 48a: the **Raphael Cartoons**, masterpieces in a suitably grand space.

The **China Gallery** (rooms 44 and 47e) displays lovely pieces, including a beautifully lithe wooden statue of Guanyin (a Mahayana bodhisattva) seated in a regal *lalitasana* pose dating to *around* 1200 CE (from Shanxi province); also take a gander at the beautiful art deco **woman's jacket** (made of silk with sequin edging), a very stylish pink evening item (1925–35). Within the subdued lighting of the **Japan Gallery** (room 45) stands a fearsome suit of armour in the Domaru style. More than 400 objects are within the **Islamic Middle East Gallery** (room 42), including ceramics, textiles, carpets, glass and woodwork from the 8th century up to the years before WWI. The exhibition's highlight is the gorgeous mid-16th-century **Ardabil Carpet**.

Level 1 & 3

The **British Galleries**, featuring every aspect of British design from 1500 to 1900, are divided between Levels 1 (1500–1760) and 3 (1760–1900). **The Great Bed of Ware** (room 57a) is a highlight, so famous it was even mentioned by Shakespeare. Level 3 also boasts the **Architecture Gallery** (rooms 127 to 128a), which vividly describes architectural styles via models and videos, and the spectacular, brightly illuminated **Contemporary Glass Gallery** (room 129).

Level 2

The **Jewellery Gallery** (room 91) is outstanding; the mezzanine level glitters with jewel-encrusted swords, watches and gold boxes. Marvel at **Queen Victoria's sapphire and diamond coronet** designed by Prince Albert. The **Photography Centre** (rooms 100 and 101) is a wonderful stroll through the history of photography from its 1830s' origins. Celebrating design classics is **Design since 1945** (room 76), which includes a 1985 Sony credit-card radio, a 1992 Nike Air Max shoe and the now ubiquitous selfie stick. Tucked away but well worth seeking out are the **Theatre & Performance** galleries (rooms 103 to 106), chronicling the British stage with costumes from shows such as *The Lion King* and a rare First Folio of Shakespeare's plays.

Level -1

Europe 1600–1815 displays pieces of 17th- and 18th-century European art and design; a highlight is the Sérilly Cabinet (1778). The Sainsbury Gallery exhibition space is also here.

MADEJSKI GARDEN & REFRESHMENT ROOMS

Cross the landscaped John Madejski Garden (a lovely shaded inner courtyard) to reach the original **Refreshment Rooms** (Morris, Gamble and Poynter Rooms; also called V&A Cafe). The rooms form the world's first museum restaurant; the Morris Room does a splendid afternoon tea for £30 per person. Otherwise, sample food that includes sandwiches, cakes and salads, plus beer and wine.

Temporary exhibitions are compelling and fun (admission fees apply; they often sell out, so book well in advance). There are also talks, workshops, events and one of the best museum shops (p200) around.

CERAMICS & FURNITURE

Among the pieces in the **Ceramics Gallery** (rooms 136 to 146) – the world's largest – are standout items from the Middle East and Asia. The **Dr Susan Weber Gallery** (rooms 133 to 135) celebrates furniture design over the past six centuries.

Victoria & Albert Museum

HALF-DAY HIGHLIGHTS TOUR

The art- and design-packed V&A is vast: we have devised an easy-to-follow tour of the museum highlights to help cover some signature pieces while also allowing you to appreciate some of the grandeur of the museum architecture.

Enter the V&A by the main entrance off Cromwell Rd and immediately turn left to explore the Islamic Middle East Gallery and to discover the sumptuous silk-and-wool ❶ **Ardabil Carpet**. Among the pieces from South Asia in the adjacent gallery is the terrifying automated ❷ **Tipu's Tiger**. Continue to the outstanding ❸ **Fashion Gallery** with its displays of clothing styles through the ages. The magnificent gallery opposite houses the ❹ **Raphael Cartoons**, large paintings by Raphael used to weave tapestries for the Vatican. Take the stairs to Level 1 and the Britain 1500–1760 Gallery;

Raphael Cartoons
These seven drawings by Raphael, depicting the acts of St Peter and St Paul, were the full-scale preparatory works for seven tapestries that were woven for the Sistine Chapel in the Vatican.

TRISTAN FEWINGS / STRINGER / GETTY IMAGES ©

Fashion Gallery
With clothing from the 18th century to the present day, this circular and chronologically arranged gallery showcases evening wear, undergarments and iconic fashion milestones, such as 1960s dresses designed by Mary Quant.

Great Bed of Ware
Created during the reign of Queen Elizabeth I, its headboard and bedposts are etched with ancient graffiti; the 16th-century oak Great Bed of Ware is famously name-dropped in Shakespeare's *Twelfth Night*.

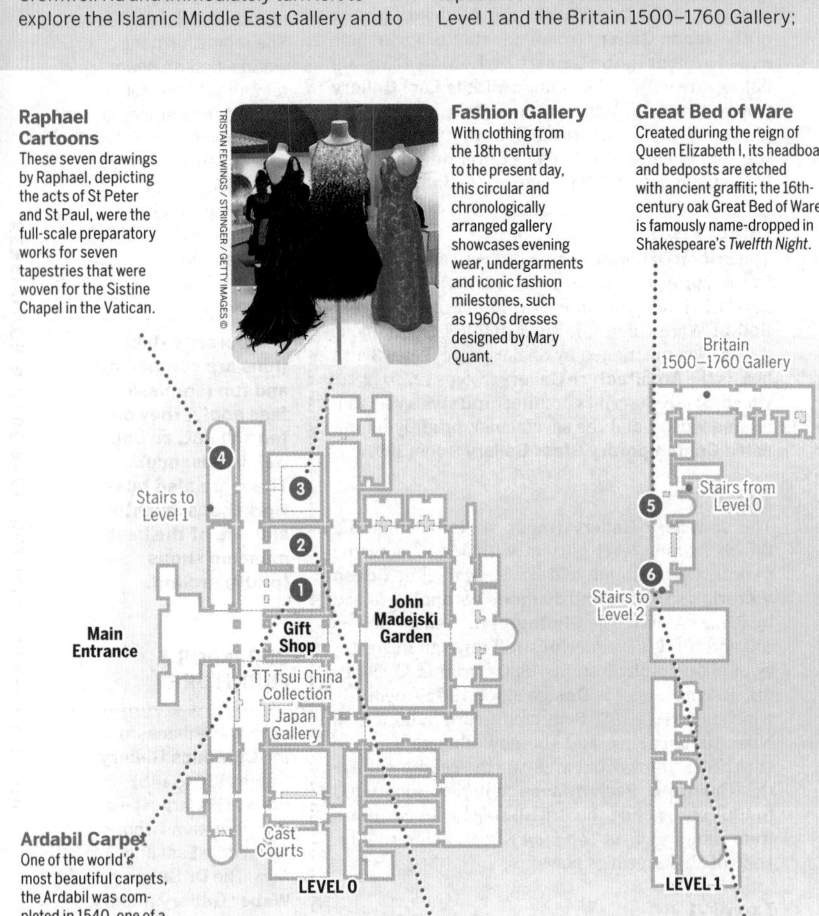

Ardabil Carpet
One of the world's most beautiful carpets, the Ardabil was completed in 1540, one of a pair commissioned by Shah Tahmasp, ruler of Iran. The piece is most astonishing for the artistry of the detailing and the subtlety of design.

Tipu's Tiger
This disquieting 18th-century wood-and-metal mechanical automaton depicts a European being savaged by a tiger. When a handle is turned, an organ hidden within the feline mimics the cries of the dying man, whose arm also rises.

Henry VIII's Writing Box
This exquisitely ornate walnut and oak 16th-century writing box has been added to over the centuries, but the original decorative motifs are superb, including Henry's coat of arms, flanked by Venus (holding Cupid) and Mars.

turn left in the gallery to find the 5 **Great Bed of Ware**, beyond which rests the exquisitely crafted artistry of 6 **Henry VIII's Writing Box**. Head up the stairs into the Ironwork Gallery on Level 2 for the 7 **Hereford Screen**. Continue through the Ironwork and Sculpture Galleries and through the Leighton Corridor to the glittering 8 **Jewellery Gallery**. Exit through the Stained Glass Gallery, at the end of which you'll find stairs back down to Level 1.

LAPAS77 / SHUTTERSTOCK ©

TRISTAN FEWINGS / STRINGER / GETTY IMAGES ©

TOP TIPS

➡ Museum attendants are at hand to help or join one of the daily free gallery tours.

➡ Photography is actively encouraged, but for some temporary exhibitions restrictions can apply.

➡ Avoid daytime crowds: visit the V&A in the evening, till 10pm on Fridays.

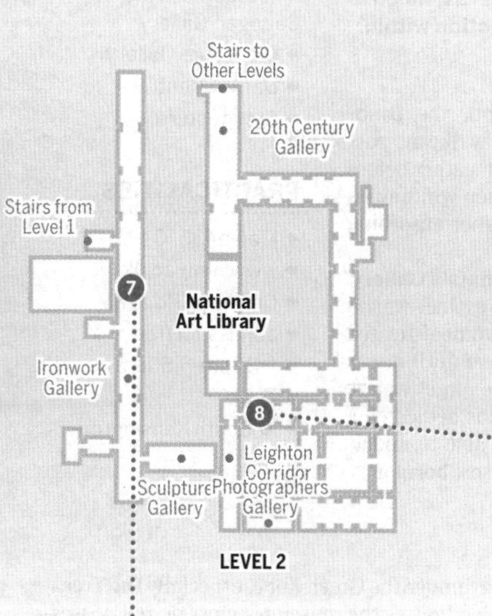

Jewellery Gallery
The beautifully illuminated Jewellery Gallery has a stunning collection of items from ancient Greece to the modern day, including a dazzling gold Celtic breastplate, animals fashioned by Fabergé and Queen Victoria's sapphire and diamond coronet.

GAID KORNSILAPA / SHUTTERSTOCK ©

Hereford Screen
Designed by George Gilbert Scott, this awe-inspiring choir screen is a labour of love, originally fashioned for Hereford Cathedral. It's an almighty conception of wood, iron, copper, brass and hardstone, and there were few parts of the V&A that could support its great mass.

GORDON BELL/SHUTTERSTOCK ©

TOP EXPERIENCE
DISCOVER THE NATURAL HISTORY MUSEUM

A sublime house of worship to science, this colossal building is infused with the irrepressible Victorian spirit of collecting, cataloguing and interpreting the natural world. The museum building is as much a reason to visit as the world-famous collection within.

Blue Zone

Undoubtedly the museum's star attraction, the **Dinosaurs Gallery** takes you on an impressive walkway, past a dromaeosaurus (a small and agile meat eater) before reaching a roaring animatronic T-rex and then winding its way through skeletons, fossils, casts and other absorbing dinosaur displays.

Another highlight of this zone is the **Mammals Gallery**, with extensive displays on both living and extinct warm-blooded animals, including the giant, wombat-related diprotodon, the largest marsupial ever to live until it was wiped out around 25,000 years ago. Lest we forget we are part of the animal kingdom, the museum has dedicated a gallery to **Human Biology**, where you'll be able to understand more about what makes us tick (senses, hormones, our brain...).

DON'T MISS

- Hintze Hall
- Treasures in the Cadogan Gallery
- Dinosaurs Gallery
- Darwin Centre
- Architecture

PRACTICALITIES

- Map p456, C4
- www.nhm.ac.uk
- Cromwell Rd, SW7
- admission free
- 10am-5.50pm
-
- U South Kensington

Green Zone

While children love the Blue Zone, adults may prefer the Green Zone, especially the Treasures in the **Cadogan Gallery** (1st floor), which houses the museum's most prized possessions, each with a unique history. Exhibits include a chunk of moon rock, an emperor penguin egg collected by Captain Scott's expedition and a first edition of Charles Darwin's *On the Origin of Species*. Equally rare and exceptional are the gems and rocks held in the **Vault**, including a Martian meteorite and the largest emerald ever found. Pause to marvel at the trunk section of a 1300-year-old **giant sequoia tree** (2nd floor): its size is mind-boggling.

Back on the ground floor, the superb **Creepy Crawlies Gallery** delves into insect life and whether they're our friends or foes (turns out they're both).

Red Zone

This zone explores the ever-changing nature of our planet and the forces shaping it. The earthquake simulator (in the **Volcanoes and Earthquakes Gallery**), which recreates the 1995 Kobe earthquake in a grocery store (of which you can see footage), is a favourite, as is the **From the Beginning Gallery**, which retraces Earth's history.

In **Earth's Treasury** find out more about our planet's mineral riches and their everyday uses: from jewellery to construction and electronics. Visitors can trace the evolution of our species in the **Human Evolution Gallery**, including an engrossing model of the face of Britain's oldest, almost complete *Homo Sapiens* skeleton: Cheddar Man, who lived around 10,000 years ago.

Access to most of the Red Zone galleries is via **Earth Hall** and an escalator that disappears into a huge metal sculpture of the Earth. **Sophie**, at the base, is the world's most complete stegosaurus.

Orange Zone

The **Darwin Centre** is the beating heart of the museum. The top two floors of the amazing 'cocoon' building are dedicated to explaining the museum's research – windows even allow you to see the researchers at work. To find out more, pop into the **Attenborough studio** for one of the weekly talks with museum scientists. The studio also shows films throughout the day.

Hintze Hall

When entering the museum's grand main entrance, this impressive central hall resembles a cathedral nave – fittingly, as it was built in a time when natural sciences were challenging Christian orthodoxy. Naturalist, first superintendent of the museum, and coiner of the word 'dinosaur' Richard Owen celebrated the building as a 'cathedral to nature'.

After 81 years in the Mammals Hall, the blue whale skeleton – Hope – was relocated to Hintze Hall, with the famous cast of a diplodocus skeleton (nicknamed Dippy) making way for the colossal marine mammal. The transfer itself was a mammoth and painstaking engineering project: disassembling and preparing 4.5-tonnes of bones for reconstruction in a dramatic diving posture that greets museum visitors.

TAKE A BREAK

The museum has several decent cafes for refuelling.

For a pint and tasty pub grub in a classic London mews, head to Queen's Arms (p198).

The museum is transforming its outdoor spaces, creating a piazza in the eastern grounds and enlarging the Wildlife Garden, a slice of English countryside in SW7 encompassing a range of British lowland habitats, including a meadow with farm gates, a bee tree where a colony of honey bees fills the air, and a pond (don't be surprised if you spot the occasional real sheep).

EXHIBITIONS

The museum hosts regular exhibitions (admission fees apply), some on a recurrent basis. A major fixture is autumn's **Wildlife Photographer of the Year**, with show-stopping images. See the website for details of other exhibitions.

TOP EXPERIENCE

CHILL OUT AT HYDE PARK

One of London's largest royal parks spreads itself over 142 hectares of neat gardens, wild expanses of overgrown grass and glorious trees. As well as being a fantastic green space in the middle of the city, it's home to a handful of fascinating sights and hosts Winter Wonderland from November to January.

Green Spaces

The eastern half of the park is covered with expansive lawns, which become one vast picnic-and-frolic area on sunny days. The western half is more untamed, with plenty of trees and areas of wild grass. If you're after somewhere more colourful (and some shade), head to the **Rose Garden** (Ⓤ Hyde Park Corner or Knightsbridge), a beautifully landscaped area with flowers year-round. A little further west, you'll find the **Holocaust Memorial Garden** (Ⓤ Hyde Park Corner, Knightsbridge), a simple stone marker in a grove of trees.

Speakers' Corner

Frequented by Karl Marx, Vladimir Lenin, George Orwell and William Morris, **Speakers' Corner** (Park Lane, W2; Ⓤ Marble Arch) in the northeastern corner of Hyde Park is traditionally the spot for oratorical flourishes and soapbox ranting. If you've got something to get off your chest, do so on Sunday, although you'll mainly have fringe dwellers, religious fanatics and hecklers for company.

It's the only place in Britain where demonstrators can assemble without police permission, a concession granted in 1872 after serious riots 17 years before when 150,000 people gathered to demonstrate against the Sunday Trading Bill before Parliament, only to be unexpectedly ambushed by police concealed within Marble Arch. Some historians also link Speakers' Corner with the nearby Tyburn gallows, where condemned criminals might speak to the crowd before being hanged.

DON'T MISS

- Serpentine Galleries
- Speakers' Corner
- Diana, Princess of Wales Memorial Fountain
- Rose Garden

PRACTICALITIES

- Map p456, D2
- www.royalparks.org.uk/parks/hyde-park
- 5am-midnight
- Ⓤ Marble Arch, Hyde Park Corner, Knightsbridge or Queensway

Diana, Princess of Wales Memorial Fountain

This **memorial fountain** (off West Carriage Dr, W2; ⏲10am-8pm Apr-Aug, to 7pm Sep, to 6pm Mar & Oct, to 4pm Nov-Feb; Ⓤ Knightsbridge, or Lancaster Gate) is dedicated to the late Princess of Wales. Envisaged by the designer Kathryn Gustafson as a 'moat without a castle' and draped 'like a necklace' around the southwestern edge of Hyde Park near the Serpentine Bridge, the circular double stream is composed of 545 pieces of Cornish granite, its waters drawn from a chalk aquifer more than 100m below ground. Unusually, visitors are actively encouraged to splash about, to the delight of children.

The Serpentine SolarShuttle Boat (p201) ferries passengers from the Serpentine Boathouse to the fountain on weekends from March to September (every day from mid-July to late August).

The Serpentine

Hyde Park is separated from Kensington Gardens by the L-shaped Serpentine, a small lake once fed by waters from the River Westbourne.

You can have a swim too – between May and September – at the Serpentine Lido (p201), where a swimming area within the lake is ring-fenced. There is also a paddling pool for children.

If you'd rather stay dry, rent a paddle boat from the Serpentine Boathouse (p201).

The Serpentine Galleries

Constituting some of the most important contemporary-art spaces in town, these two galleries are a major draw. South of the Serpentine lake is the original **Serpentine Gallery** (☎020-7402 6075; www.serpentinegalleries.org; Kensington Gardens, W2; ⏲10am-6pm Tue-Sun; 📶; Ⓤ Lancaster Gate or Knightsbridge) FREE, in which Damien Hirst, Andreas Gursky, Louise Bourgeois, Gabriel Orozco, Tomoko Takahashi and Jeff Koons have all exhibited, set in a 1930s former tea pavilion in Kensington Gardens.

Sister establishment the **Serpentine Sackler Gallery** (West Carriage Dr, W2; ⏲10am-6pm Tue-Sun; Ⓤ Lancaster Gate or Knightsbridge) FREE can be found within the **Magazine**, a former gunpowder depot, across the Serpentine Bridge. Built in 1805, it was augmented with a daring, undulating extension designed by Pritzker Prize–winning architect Zaha Hadid.

The galleries run a full program of exhibitions, readings and talks. A leading architect who has never previously built in the UK is annually commissioned to build a new 'Summer Pavilion' nearby, open from June to October.

TAKE A BREAK

In clement weather, packing a picnic and finding a patch of grass in the park should be your first choice. There are plenty of places around the park's periphery to stock up on supplies, not least the food hall in Harrods (p199).

Found the perfect spot? Hire a deckchair (one/four hours £1.80/4.80, all day £9). They are available throughout the park from March to October, weather permitting.

HISTORY

Henry VIII expropriated the park from the church in 1536. It then became a hunting ground for kings and aristocrats, and later a place for duels, executions and horse racing. The park was the site of the Great Exhibition in 1851, and during WWII became a vast potato bed. These days it's an occasional concert and music-festival venue.

TOP EXPERIENCE
EXPERIMENT AT THE SCIENCE MUSEUM

With seven floors of interactive, educational and eye-opening exhibits, this spellbinding collection mesmerises adults and children in equal measure.

Level Zero

The most popular galleries are on the ground floor (Level Zero), starting with **Exploring Space**, which features actual rockets and satellites and a full-size replica of 'Eagle', the lander that took Neil Armstrong and Buzz Aldrin to the moon in 1969.

Next is the **Making the Modern World Gallery**, an array of locomotives, planes, cars, engines and other revolutionary inventions (penicillin, cameras etc). You can also examine a Nazi V-2 Rocket, with a panel removed exposing its internal workings. Children under eight can head for the interactive, multi-sensory, fun-yet-educational **Pattern Pod** to explore patterns in the world.

Also on the ground floor is the fantastic **shop**, stuffed with lava lamps, alien babies, squidgy balls, bouncy globes, boomerangs and other delights for the legions of small, excited fingers.

Level 2

The superb **Information Age Gallery** showcases how information and communication technologies – from the telegraph to smartphones – have transformed our lives since the 19th century. Standout displays include wireless transmissions sent by a sinking *Titanic*, the first BBC radio broadcast and a Soviet BESM-6 supercomputer. The **Clockmaker's Museum** is an astonishing collection of timepieces, while the £24 million **Medicine Galleries** opened in 2019, illustrating the medical world via objects from the museum's collections and those of Sir Henry Wellcome, pharmacist, entrepreneur, philanthropist and collector. **Mathematics: The Winton Gallery**, designed by Zaha Hadid Architects, is a riveting exploration of maths in the real world, while the **Atmosphere Gallery** explains the science of the world's climate over billions of years and tackles the burning issue of contemporary climate change.

Level 3

The **Flight Gallery** (free tours 1pm most days) is a favourite place for children, with its gliders, hot-air balloons and aircraft, including the De Havilland Gipsy Moth Aeroplane 'Jason I' that Amy Johnson flew to Australia in 1930. This floor also features a **Red Arrows 3D** flight-simulation theatre (£5) and **Fly 360°** flight-simulator capsules (£12 per capsule). A further simulator, **Typhoon Force** (£4), replicates a low-level mission aboard a Typhoon fighter jet. **Space Descent** (£7) is a virtual-reality experience with (a digital) Tim Peake, the British astronaut. Interactive **Wonderlab: The Equinor Gallery** (adult/child £10/8) delves into scientific phenomena in a fun and educational way, with daily shows.

Basement & Garden

If you've got kids under the age of five, pop down to the basement (Level -1) and the Garden, where there's a fun-filled play zone, including a water-play area, besieged by tots in orange waterproof smocks.

DON'T MISS

- Exploring Space Gallery
- Information Age Gallery
- Making the Modern World Gallery
- Medicine Galleries
- Flight Gallery

PRACTICALITIES

- Map p456, C4
- ☎020-7942 4000, 0333 241 4000
- www.sciencemuseum.org.uk
- Exhibition Rd, SW7
- admission free
- ⌚10am-6pm, last entry 5.15pm
-
- U South Kensington

SIGHTS

Knightsbridge & South Kensington

NATURAL HISTORY MUSEUM MUSEUM
See p182.

VICTORIA & ALBERT MUSEUM MUSEUM
See p178.

SCIENCE MUSEUM MUSEUM
See p186.

BROMPTON ORATORY CHURCH
Map p456 (020-7808 0900; www.bromptonoratory.co.uk; 215 Brompton Rd, SW7; 6.30am-8pm Sun-Fri, to 7.45pm Sat; U South Kensington) The Church of the Immaculate Heart of Mary, also known as the London Oratory and the Oratory of St Philip Neri, is a Roman Catholic church that in London is second in size only to the incomplete Westminster Cathedral. Built in Italian baroque style in 1884, the interior is swathed in marble and statuary; much of the decorative work predates the church and was imported from Italian churches. The church was employed by the KGB during the Cold War as a dead-letter box.

ROYAL COLLEGE OF MUSIC MUSEUM MUSEUM
Map p456 (020-7591 4346; www.rcm.ac.uk/museum; Prince Consort Rd, SW7; U South Kensington) FREE This illustrious museum is closed for rebuilding and redevelopment until July 2021. Till then, a part of the museum collection can be explored digitally online via the website.

Hyde Park & Kensington Gardens

HYDE PARK PARK
See p184.

ROYAL ALBERT HALL HISTORIC BUILDING
Map p456 (0845 401 5034, box office 020-7589 8212; www.royalalberthall.com; Kensington Gore, SW7; tours adult/child from £14.25/7.25; tours from 10am; U South Kensington) Built in 1871, thanks in part to the proceeds of the 1851 Great Exhibition organised by Prince Albert (Queen Victoria's husband), this huge, domed,

TOP EXPERIENCE
EXPLORE LIFE AT KENSINGTON PALACE

Built in 1605, Kensington Palace became the favourite royal residence under William and Mary of Orange in 1689, and remained so until George III became king and relocated to Buckingham Palace. Today, it remains a residence for high-ranking royals, including the Duke and Duchess of Cambridge (Prince William and Kate).

Much of the palace is open to the public, however, including the King's and Queen's State Apartments. The **King's State Apartments** are the most lavish, starting with the **King's Staircase**, a dizzying feast of trompe l'oeil. The **Cupola Room**, once the venue of choice for music and dance, is arranged with gilded statues and a painted ceiling. The **Drawing Room** lies beyond.

Visitors can also access **the apartments** where Victoria (1819–1901) was born and lived until she became Queen. An informative account of her life is given in the exhibition Victoria: A Royal Childhood.

See the website for lists of exhibitions at the palace and activities, including absorbing family trails.

The **sunken garden** is ablaze with flowers in spring and summer. This area is also home to the popular Luna Cinema, with screenings of iconic movies in summer and at Christmas.

DON'T MISS

- Cupola Room
- King's Staircase
- Victoria's apartments
- Sunken garden

PRACTICALITIES

- Map p456; www.hrp.org.uk/kensington-palace
- Kensington Gardens, W8
- adult/child £21.50/10.70, cheaper weekdays after 2pm
- 10am-6pm, to 4pm Nov-Feb
- U High St Kensington

HYDE PARK'S SECRET PET CEMETERY

An oddity by Victoria Gate on the north side of Hyde Park, this small boneyard for over one thousand dogs, cats and other pets was founded in 1881, before interring its last furry occupant in 1903. With its midget headstones commemorating legions of affectionately named moggies and mongrels, the cemetery can only be visited on the Hidden Stories of Hyde Park tours (£10) arranged by Royal Parks (www.royalparks.org.uk) on the second Friday of the month; check the website for details.

red-brick amphitheatre, adorned with a frieze of Minton tiles, is Britain's most famous concert venue and home to the BBC's Promenade Concerts (the Proms) every summer.

The hall was never intended to be a concert venue but instead a 'Hall of Arts and Sciences', so it spent the first 133 years of its existence tormenting everyone with shocking acoustics. The 85 huge mushroom-like fibreglass acoustic reflectors first dangled from the ceiling in 1969, and a further massive refurbishment was completed in 2004.

To find out about the hall's intriguing history and royal connections, and to gaze out from the Gallery, book an informative one-hour front-of-house **tour** (Map p456; ☎020-7589 8212; adult/child £14.25/7.25; ⏲hourly 9.30am-4.30pm Apr-Oct, 10am-4pm Nov-Mar), operating most days.

There's a whole range of other tours, including a secret-history tour, an afternoon-tea tour, an architectural tour, a behind-the-scenes tour and tours with dining provided; booking tours online is slightly cheaper than over the phone. The behind-the-scenes tour is rather infrequent, taking place just 20 times a year.

★ALBERT MEMORIAL — MONUMENT

Map p456 (☎tours 0300 061 2270; Kensington Gardens, W2; tours £10; ⏲tours 2pm 1st Fri every other month, Apr-Oct; ⓤKnightsbridge or Gloucester Rd) This splendid Victorian confection on the southern edge of Kensington Gardens is as ostentatious as its subject wasn't. Queen Victoria's humble German husband Albert (1819–61) explicitly insisted he did not want a monument. Ignoring the good prince's wishes, the Lord Mayor instructed George Gilbert Scott to build the 53m-high, gaudy Gothic memorial – the 4.25m-tall gilded statue of the prince, surrounded by 187 figures representing the continents (Asia, Europe, Africa and America), the arts, industry and science, went up in 1876.

An eye-opening blend of mosaic, gold leaf, marble and Victorian bombast, the renovated monument is topped with a crucifix. The statue was painted black for 80 years, originally – some say – to disguise it from WWI Zeppelins (nonetheless, the memorial was selected by German bombers during WWII as a landmark). To step beyond the railings for a close-up of the staggering 64m-long *Frieze of Parnassus* along the base – carved in situ – join one of the 90-minute tours.

KENSINGTON GARDENS — PARK

Map p456 (☎0300 061 2000; www.royalparks.org.uk/parks/kensington-gardens; ⏲6am-dusk; ⓤQueensway or Lancaster Gate) A delightful collection of manicured lawns, tree-shaded avenues and basins immediately west of Hyde Park, the picturesque expanse of Kensington Gardens is technically part of Kensington Palace (p187), located in the far west of the gardens. The large **Round Pond** in front of the palace is enjoyable to amble around, and also worth a look are the lovely fountains in the **Italian Gardens** (Map p456; ⏲6am-dusk; ⓤLancaster Gate), believed to be a gift from Prince Albert to Queen Victoria; they are now the venue of a cafe.

The **Diana, Princess of Wales Memorial Playground** (Map p456; ⏲10am-7.45pm May-Aug, to 6.45pm Apr & Sep, to 5.45pm Mar & Oct, to 4.45pm Feb, to 3.45pm Nov-Jan; 👪; ⓤQueensway), in the northwest corner of the gardens, has some pretty ambitious attractions for children. Next to the playground stands the delightful **Elfin Oak**, a 900-year-old tree stump carved with elves, gnomes, witches and small creatures. To the east, George Frampton's celebrated **Peter Pan statue** (ⓤLancaster Gate) is close to the lake, while the opulent and elaborate Albert Memorial pokes into the sky south of Kensington Gardens, facing the Royal Albert Hall.

WELLINGTON ARCH MUSEUM

Map p456 (www.english-heritage.org.uk/visit/places/wellington-arch; Hyde Park Corner, W1; adult/child/family £5.70/3.40/14.80, with Apsley House £13.60/8.20; ⏲10am-6pm Apr-Sep, to 4pm Nov-Mar; Ⓤ Hyde Park Corner) Dominating the green space throttled by the Hyde Park Corner roundabout, this imposing neoclassical 1826 Corinthian arch originally faced the Hyde Park Screen, but was shunted here in 1882 for road widening. Once a police station, the arch today has four floors of galleries and temporary exhibition space as well as a permanent display about the history of the arch, and a gift shop. The open-air balconies (accessible by lift) afford unforgettable views of Hyde Park, Buckingham Palace and the Mall.

Originally crowned by a disproportionately large equestrian statue of the Duke of Wellington (which now stands in Aldershot in Hampshire), it was replaced by the current four-horse *Peace Descending on the Quadriga of War*, Europe's largest bronze sculpture, in 1912. Play your cards right and catch the Household Cavalry (which form the Queen's Life Guard) passing beneath the arch en route to the Changing of the Guard at around 10.45am and returning at 11.45am from Monday to Saturday and on Sundays at 9.45am and 10.45am (arriving five or so minutes early is a good idea).

Chelsea & Belgravia

★MICHELIN HOUSE HISTORIC BUILDING

Map p456 (81 Fulham Rd, SW3; Ⓤ South Kensington) Built for Michelin between 1905 and 1911 by François Espinasse, and completely restored in 1985, the building blurs the stylish line between art nouveau and art deco, both announcing the dawn of the machine age while giving a nod to natural forms. The iconic roly-poly Michelin Man (Bibendum) appears in the exquisite modern stained glass (the originals were removed at the outbreak of WWII and stored in the Michelin factory in Stoke-on-Trent, but subsequently vanished), while the lobby is decorated with tiles illustrating early-20th-century cars.

★NATIONAL ARMY MUSEUM MUSEUM

Map p456 (☎020-7730 0717; www.nam.ac.uk; Royal Hospital Rd, SW3; ⏲10am-5.30pm, to

TOP EXPERIENCE

REVISIT WATERLOO AT APSLEY HOUSE

This stunning house, containing exhibits about the Duke of Wellington, who defeated Napoleon Bonaparte at Waterloo, was once the first building to appear when entering London from the west and was therefore known as 'No 1 London'. Still one of London's finest, Apsley House was designed by Robert Adam for Baron Apsley in the late 18th century, but later sold to the first Duke of Wellington, who lived here until he died in 1852.

In 1947 the house was given to the nation; 10 of its rooms are open to the public. Wellington memorabilia, including his **death mask**, fills the basement gallery, while there's an astonishing **collection of china and silver**, including a dazzling **Egyptian service**, a divorce gift from Napoleon to Josephine, which she declined.

The stairwell is dominated by Antonio Canova's staggering 3.4m-high **statue** of a fig-leafed Napoleon with titanic shoulders, adjudged by the subject as 'too athletic'. The 1st-floor **Waterloo Gallery** runs the length of the building's west flank and contains 70 paintings, including works by Velázquez, Rubens, Van Dyck, Bruegel, Murillo and Goya. A highlight is the elaborate Portuguese silver service, presented to Wellington in honour of his triumph over 'Le Petit Caporal'.

DON'T MISS

- Egyptian service
- Canova's statue of Napoleon
- Waterloo Gallery paintings

PRACTICALITIES

- Map p456
- ☎020-7499 5676; www.english-heritage.org.uk/visit/places/apsley-house
- 149 Piccadilly, Hyde Park Corner, W1
- adult/child £10.50/6.30
- ⏲11am-5pm Wed-Sun Apr-Oct, 10am-4pm Sat & Sun Nov-Mar
- Ⓤ Hyde Park Corner

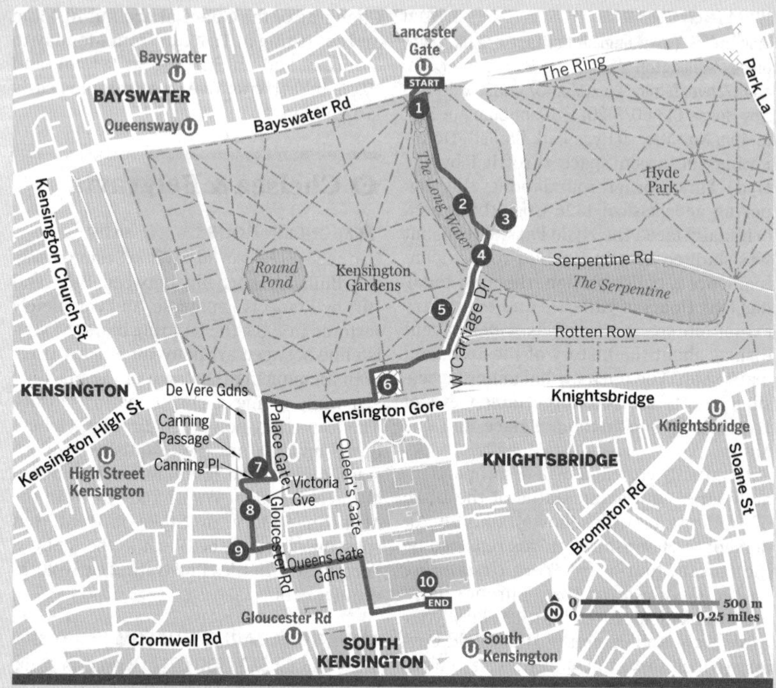

Neighbourhood Walk
Gardens & Mews

START LANCASTER GATE TUBE STATION
END NATURAL HISTORY MUSEUM
LENGTH 2.2 MILES; 1½ HOURS

From Lancaster Gate station head to the park. Bear left at the **1 Italian Gardens** (p188) – thought to be a gift from Prince Albert to Queen Victoria – and follow the path along Long Water until you reach **2 The Arch** (Map p456, C2; Hyde Park, W2; ⓤLancaster Gate), an imposing travertine statue by Henry Moore with fantastic views of Kensington Palace. As you reach the road, glance left at the **3 Serpentine Sackler Gallery** (p185), a former gun depot with a modern extension designed by prize-winning architect Zaha Hadid.

Cross the **4 bridge** over the Serpentine – the lake separates Hyde Park from Kensington Gardens – and enjoy the views. Turn right into Kensington Gardens, walk past the **5 Serpentine Gallery** (p185), a famous contemporary-art gallery, and make your way south to the **6 Albert Memorial** (p188), a Victorian Gothic confection. Continue west through the park, then exit onto Palace Gate and turn right onto Canning Place; take a moment to savour splendid **7 De Vere Gardens** and its lengthy line of grand houses.

Turn left onto Canning Passage, then left again onto Victoria Grove. The boutiques and wisteria-clad houses on this little square could be straight out of a Cotswold village. Bear right along **8 Launceston Place**, walking past ivy-covered walls and exquisite houses: this is among the most coveted real estate in London. Take a small detour down **9 Kynance Mews** on the right (there is a public right of way until about halfway down the mews) to see the storybook cottages. Then retrace your steps to explore the other section of Kynance Mews – with arches at either end – that leads to Gloucester Rd.

Walk south down Gloucester Rd, taking a left along Queen's Gate Gardens, then a right at Queen's Gate: the **10 Natural History Museum** (p182) is just ahead of you.

8pm 1st Wed of month; ⓤSloane Sq) FREE This inventively redesigned museum vibrantly relates the history of the British Army, from the perspective of its servicemen and servicewomen. Reopening a few years ago with a big bang, the museum has five state-of-the-art galleries, including the **Soldier Gallery**, the **Army Gallery**, the **Society Gallery** (exploring society's relationship with the army), the **Battle Gallery** (the army at war) and the **Insight Gallery** (on the impact of the British Army through the world). Free talks, workshops and tours are also hosted; see the website for details.

On the ground floor's lower level, **Play Base** (£5.75) offers a fun and immersive experience for under-nines (including an assault course and the chance to clamber aboard a command liaison vehicle), with six one-hour sessions starting from 9.40am to 4.20pm. There's a cafe (10am to 5pm) too, for museum-weary legs, caffeine shots and snacks.

SAATCHI GALLERY — GALLERY

Map p456 (www.saatchigallery.com; Duke of York's HQ, King's Rd, SW3; ⏲10am-6pm; ⓤSloane Sq) FREE This grandly housed gallery in the Duke of York's Headquarters hosts temporary exhibitions of experimental and thought-provoking work across a variety of media, much of it international in nature. The white and sanded bare-floorboard galleries are magnificently presented, while a cool shop chips in on the 1st floor. Check the (weirdly dated) website for details of current and forthcoming exhibitions. Exhibitions have also included non-contemporary and historic material, such as 2020's Tutankhamun: Treasures of the Golden Pharaoh.

KING'S ROAD — STREET

Map p456 (ⓤSloane Sq) At the countercultural forefront of London fashion during the technicolour 60s and anarchic 70s (Ian Fleming's fictional spy James Bond had a flat in a square off the road), the King's Rd today is more a stamping ground for the leisure-class shopping set. The last green-Mohawked punks – once tourist sights in themselves – shuffled off sometime in the 1990s. Today it's all Muji, Calvin Klein, Foxtons and a sprinkling of specialist shops; even pet canines are slim and snappily dressed.

In the 17th century, Charles II fashioned a love nest here for himself and his mistress Nell Gwyn, an orange-seller turned actress at the Drury Lane Theatre. Heading back to Hampton Court Palace at eventide, Charles would employ a farmer's track that inevitably came to be known as the King's Rd.

CHELSEA PHYSIC GARDEN — GARDENS

Map p456 (☎020-7352 5646; www.chelseaphysicgarden.co.uk; 66 Royal Hospital Rd, SW3; adult/child under 15yr/family £9.50/8.50/37; 11am-6pm Mon-Fri & Sun, to 4pm Nov-Feb; ⓤSloane Sq) You may bump into a wandering duck or two as you enter this walled pocket of botanical enchantment, established by the Apothecaries' Society in 1673 for students working on medicinal plants and healing. One of Europe's oldest of its kind, the small grounds are a compendium of botany, from carnivorous pitcher plants to rich yellow flag irises, a cork oak from Portugal, the largest outdoor fruiting olive tree in the British Isles, rare trees and shrubs.

ROYAL HOSPITAL CHELSEA — MUSEUM

Map p456 (☎020-7881 5493 for tours; www.chelsea-pensioners.co.uk; Royal Hospital Rd, SW3; ⏲grounds 10am-5pm, Great Hall 10am-noon & 2-4pm, museum 10am-4pm Mon-Fri; ⓤSloane Sq) FREE Designed by Christopher Wren, this superb structure was built in 1692 to provide shelter for ex-servicemen. Since the reign of Charles II, it has housed hundreds of war veterans, known as Chelsea Pensioners. They're fondly regarded as national treasures, and cut striking figures in the dark-blue greatcoats (in winter) or scarlet frock coats (in summer) that they wear on ceremonial occasions.

The **museum** contains a huge collection of war medals bequeathed by former residents and plenty of information about the institution's history and its residents. Visitors can also peek at the hospital's Great Hall refectory, Octagon Porch, chapel and courtyards. Chelsea Pensioner–led tours are also available (£13.50).

The ashes of former Prime Minister Margaret Thatcher are buried here, in the old **cemetery**. The extensive grounds are home to the Chelsea Flower Show, the annual jamboree of the gardening world, held in May.

CARLYLE'S HOUSE HISTORIC BUILDING

Map p456 (☎020-7352 7087; www.nationaltrust.org.uk/carlyles-house; 24 Cheyne Row, SW3; adult/child/family £8/4/20; ⏰11am-4.30pm Wed-Sun Mar-Oct; Ⓤ Sloane Sq) From 1834 until his death in 1881, the eminent Victorian essayist and historian Thomas Carlyle dwelt in this three-storey terrace house, bought by his parents when it was surrounded by open fields in what was then a deeply unfashionable part of town. The lovely Queen Anne property – built in 1708 – is magnificently preserved as it looked in 1895, when it became London's first literary shrine. It's not big but has been left much as it was when Carlyle was living here and Chopin, Tennyson and Dickens came to call.

CHELSEA OLD CHURCH CHURCH

Map p456 (☎020-7795 1019; www.chelseaoldchurch.org.uk; cnr Old Church St & Embankment, SW3; ⏰2-4pm Tue-Thu; Ⓤ South Kensington, Sloane Sq) This beautiful and original church stands behind a bronze monument to Thomas More (1477–1535), who had a close association with it. Original features of the largely rebuilt church (it was badly bombed in 1941) comprise more than 100 monuments dating from 1433 to 1957, including Thomas More (1532) and Henry James (1916). Don't miss the chained books at the western end of the southern aisle, the only ones of their kind in a London church.

The central tome is a 'Vinegar Bible' from 1717 (so-named after an erratum in Luke, chapter 20), alongside a Book of Common Prayer from 1723 and a 1683 copy of *Homilies*. Also look out for fragments of 17th-century Flemish stained glass, of exceptional clarity and artistry.

CHELSEA FLOWER SHOW

Held at the lovely Royal Hospital Chelsea, this horticultural **event** (☎020-3176 5800; www.rhs.org.uk/chelsea; Royal Hospital Chelsea, Royal Hospital Rd, SW3; £39.75-92.75; ⏰May; Ⓤ Sloane Sq) is arguably the world's most renowned flower show, attracting green fingers from all four corners of the globe. Tickets must be ordered in advance (none are on sale at the gate).

EATING

Quality and cashola being such easy bedfellows, you'll find some of London's finest establishments in the smart hotels and ritzy mews of Chelsea, Belgravia and Knightsbridge, but choice flourishes in all budget ranges. Chic and cosmopolitan South Kensington has always been reliable for pan-European options.

Knightsbridge & South Kensington

COMPTOIR LIBANAIS LEBANESE £

Map p456 (☎020-7225 5006; www.comptoirlibanais.com; 1-5 Exhibition Rd, SW7; mains from £9.95; ⏰8.30am-midnight Mon-Sat, to 10.30pm Sun; 🛜✍; Ⓤ South Kensington) If your battery is flat after touring the South Kensington museums, this colourful, good-looking and brisk restaurant just round the corner from the Tube station is a moreish stop for Lebanese mezze, wraps, tagines (slow-cooked casseroles), *mana'esh* (flatbreads), lamb and halloumi burgers, salads and fine breakfasts. When the sun's shining, the outside tables quickly fill with munchers and people-watchers. No reservations – just turn up (elbows sharpened).

The 'Feast' menu: with mezze to share, a main and a shared dessert is £26.95 per person, minimum two people.

★**V&A CAFE** CAFE £

Map p456 (☎020-7581 2159; www.vam.ac.uk/info/va-cafe; Victoria & Albert Museum, Cromwell Rd, SW7; mains £7.45-13.50; ⏰10am-5.10pm Sat-Thu, to 9.15pm Fri; 🛜; Ⓤ South Kensington) There is plenty of hot and cold food to choose from at the V&A Cafe, and the setting is quite astonishingly beautiful: the extraordinarily decorated Morris, Gamble and Poynter Rooms (1868) show Victorian Classical Revival style at its very best – these were the first museum cafes in the world. Plus there's often a piano accompaniment to your tea and cake.

CAMBIO DE TERCIO SPANISH ££

Map p456 (☎020-7244 8970; www.cambiodetercio.co.uk; 163 Old Brompton Rd, SW5; 2-/3-course meal from £19/23.50, tapas from £6.50, mains from £26; ⏰noon-2.30pm & 6.30-11pm; Ⓤ Gloucester Rd) A Spanish dining fixture in South Kensington for over 25 years, this award-winning restaurant is notable for its fine tapas as well as affordable and enjoyable lunchtime set menus. With mangetout, prawns, artichokes and free-range chicken, the lunchtime paella at £19 per person (minimum two) is excellent, while the Spanish wine selection is something to behold.

Finish off with hot chocolate and churros.

ZUMA JAPANESE **£££**

Map p456 (☎020-7584 1010; www.zumarestaurant.com; 5 Raphael St, SW7; mains £12-54; ⏰restaurant noon-3.30pm & 6-11pm Mon-Sat, to 10.30pm Sun, bar noon-11.45pm Mon-Sat, to 11.30pm Sun; 📶; ⓊKnightsbridge) Zuma oozes style – a modern-day take on the traditional Japanese *izakaya* ('a place to stay and drink sake'), where drinking and eating harmonise. The *robata* (chargrilled) dishes are the stars of the show; wash them down with one of 40 types of sake on offer. Booking is advised, although there are walk-in spaces at the *robata* and sushi counters.

★DINNER BY HESTON BLUMENTHAL MODERN BRITISH **£££**

Map p456 (☎020-7201 3833; www.dinnerbyheston.com; Mandarin Oriental Hyde Park, 66 Knightsbridge, SW1; 3-course set lunch £48, mains £44-52; ⏰noon-2.15pm & 6-9.30pm Sun-Wed, noon-2.30pm & 6-10pm Thu-Sat; 📶; ⓊKnightsbridge) With two Michelin stars, sumptuously presented Dinner is a gastronomic tour de force, taking diners on a journey through British culinary history (with inventive modern inflections). Dishes carry historical dates to convey context, while the restaurant interior is a design triumph, from the glass-walled kitchen and its overhead clock mechanism to the large windows looking onto the park. Book ahead.

Also at hand is a 16th-century Tudor-style private room that seats 12 guests, who dine at an extravagant sapele and rosewood oval table.

Hyde Park & Kensington Gardens

222 VEGAN **£**

Map p472 (☎020-7381 2322; www.222vegan.com; 222 North End Rd, W14; buffet £11.50, mains £10.50-12; ⏰noon-3.30pm & 5.30-10.30pm; 📶✍; ⓊWest Brompton or West Kensington) Popular for its all-you-can-eat lunchtime buffet and evening à la carte menu, which draws the West London vegan crowds, this North End Rd restaurant has a delicious choice of heart-and-soul-warming dishes such as pumpkin-and-pine nut risotto, spaghetti *polpette* (with quinoa and spinach 'meatballs'), seitan stroganoff or the asparagus-and-petit-pois burger, with blueberry-and-vanilla vegan cheesecake for pudding. Reserve ahead.

FINE BUT AFFORDABLE DINING

Chelsea and Kensington have some of the finest – and most expensive – restaurants in London. One way of enjoying them without breaking the bank is to go for the set lunch menus, which offer great value (two to three courses for less than £30).

KENSINGTON PALACE PAVILION BRITISH **££**

Map p456 (☎020-3166 6114; www.kensingtonpalacepavilion.co.uk; Kensington Gardens, W8; afternoon tea £34; ⏰10am-6pm; ✍; ⓊHigh St Kensington) Temporarily replacing the Orangery restaurant while it undergoes restoration until 2021, what the Kensington Palace Pavilion lacks in history it makes up for with the same excellent menu of breakfasts, light lunches and the standout afternoon tea. The sandwiches, scones and cakes stacked high on their elegant tiers are just the thing for refuelling after a visit to Kensington Palace (p187) itself.

To really stick your pinky finger out, go for the Royal Afternoon Tea (£88), while the children's afternoon tea (£16) is also available for young tea-quaffers.

★LAUNCESTON PLACE MODERN BRITISH **£££**

Map p456 (☎020-7937 6912; www.launcestonplace-restaurant.co.uk; 1a Launceston Pl, W8; mains £22-34, 2-/3-course set lunch £25/29, 2-/3-course set dinner £55-65; ⏰noon-2.30pm Tue-Sat, to 3.30pm Sun, 6-10pm Mon-Sat, 6.30-9pm Sun; 📶; ⓊGloucester Rd or High St Kensington) This exceptionally handsome, super-chic Michelin-starred restaurant is almost anonymous on a picture-postcard Kensington street of Edwardian houses. Prepared by London chef Ben Murphy, dishes occupy the acme of gastronomic pleasures and are

SEBASTIAN CONDREA/GETTY IMAGES ©

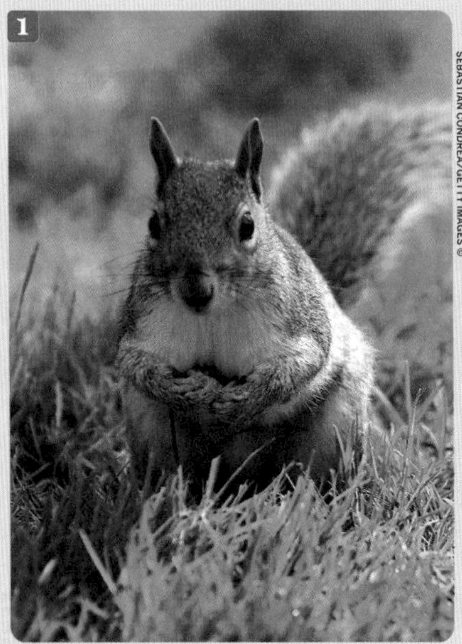

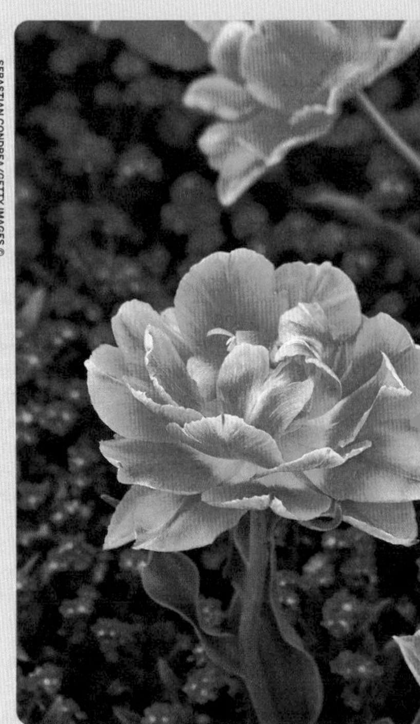

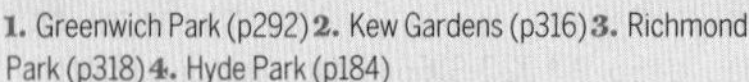

1. Greenwich Park (p292) 2. Kew Gardens (p316) 3. Richmond Park (p318) 4. Hyde Park (p184)

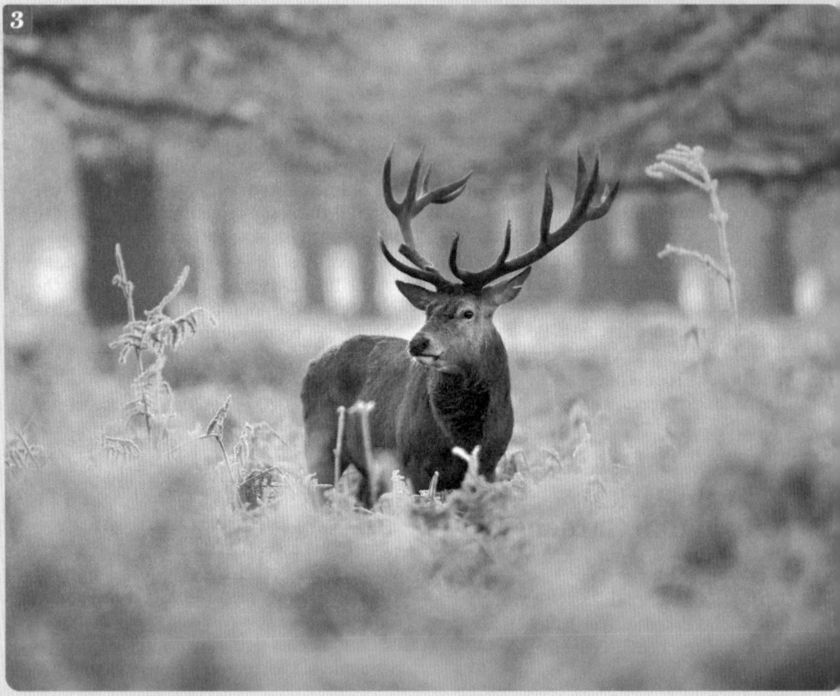

Parks & Gardens

Glance at a colour map of town and be struck by how much is olive green. London has some of the world's most superb urban parkland, most of it well tended, accessible and a delight in any season.

Hyde Park

Perhaps London's most famous and easily accessed expanse of urban greenery, Hyde Park is astonishing for the variety of its landscapes and trees. The lovely Serpentine separates it from that other grand London park, Kensington Gardens.

Greenwich Park

Delightfully hilly, elegantly landscaped and bisected by the meridian line, Greenwich Park offers sweeping perspectives from its highest point. London's oldest enclosed royal park, it is home to herds of deer and some of Greenwich's top highlights.

Victoria Park

Named after its eponymous royal benefactor, Victoria Park is one of East London's most pleasant and popular parks, enjoying an expensive regeneration several years back. In summer it becomes a venue for live music and festivals.

Richmond Park

An epic expanse of greenery in the southwest, royal Richmond Park is home to herds of deer, sublime views and a fantastic collection of trees, ponds, woodland and grass. Shake off the urban fumes and immerse yourself in its wild expanses.

Kew Gardens

To fall for Kew Gardens, all you need is an eye for fine architecture, a fondness for exploration and natural curiosity. Kids will adore the treetop walkway, fantastic play zones and the super new Children's Garden.

accompanied by an award-winning wine list. The adventurous will aim for the eight-course tasting menu (£85; vegetarian and vegan versions available).

Chelsea & Belgravia

WULF & LAMB VEGAN £

Map p456 (020-3948 5999; www.wulfandlamb.com; 243 Pavilion Rd, SW1; mains from £11.95; 8am-10pm Mon-Sat, 9am-9pm Sun; ; Sloane Sq) Picture-perfect Pavilion Rd, a side street tucked off Sloane Sq, has been redeveloped in recent years to create a village-like collection of independent, artisan retailers. Standing out amid the cheesemonger, butcher, coffee shop and many others is Wulf & Lamb, a vegan restaurant that offers an elegant setting for its animal-friendly menu. The restaurant is cashless.

Everything from the cakes to the wine is vegan, but you can't go wrong with the signature Wulf burger (a seitan patty in a toasted brioche bun) with a side of chargrilled broccoli, topped with shiitake sprinkles.

Head upstairs to the light, coolly designed dining space to enjoy your food, or in good weather, head downstairs to the patio garden.

★RABBIT MODERN BRITISH ££

Map p456 (020-3750 0172; www.rabbit-restaurant.com; 172 King's Rd, SW3; mains £6-20; noon-midnight Tue-Sat, to 5pm Sun, 6-11pm Mon; ; Sloane Sq) Three brothers grew up on a farm. One became a farmer, another a butcher, while the third worked in hospitality. So they pooled their skills and came up with Rabbit, a breath of fresh air in upmarket Chelsea. The restaurant rocks the agri-chic look, and the creative, seasonal and oft-changing Modern British menu is fabulous.

Whet your appetite with one of the 'mouthfuls' (eg mini-eclairs with mushroom and Marmite), literally bite-size pieces of deliciousness – one won't be enough. Then mix and match from the small-plates selection (plenty of vegetarian and vegan options) – two or three per person is about right. The drinks list is just as good, with a great selection of wines from the family vineyard in Sussex, and local beers and ciders. Note the kitchen closes at 10.30pm.

MEDLAR MODERN EUROPEAN £££

Map p456 (020-7349 1900; www.medlarrestaurant.co.uk; 438 King's Rd, SW10; set lunch/dinner £35/55; noon-3pm & 6.30-10.30pm Mon-Fri, 6-10.30pm Sat, 6-9.30pm Sun; ; Fulham Broadway or Sloane Sq) With its uncontrived yet crisply modern and cool green-on-grey design, Medlar is a King's Rd sensation. With no à la carte menu and scant pretentiousness, the prix fixe modern European cuisine is delightfully assured: the menu changes with the season but tries hard to promote British ingredients as well as underrated meats such as pigeon and guinea fowl, all beautifully presented.

★FIVE FIELDS MODERN BRITISH £££

Map p456 (020-7838 1082; www.fivefieldsrestaurant.com; 8-9 Blacklands Tce, SW3; 3-course set meal £85, tasting menu £75-95; noon-2pm Thu-Sat, 6.30-10pm Tue-Sat; ; Sloane Sq) The inventive British prix fixe cuisine, consummate service and enticingly light and inviting decor are hard to resist at this triumphant Michelin-starred Chelsea restaurant, but you'll need to plan early and book way up front. No children under 12.

★GORDON RAMSAY FRENCH £££

Map p456 (020-7352 4441; www.gordonramsayrestaurants.com/restaurant-gordon-ramsay; 68 Royal Hospital Rd, SW3; 3-course lunch/dinner £70/130; noon-2.15pm & 6.30-9.45pm Mon-Fri; ; Sloane Sq) One of Britain's finest restaurants and London's longest-running with three Michelin stars (held since 2001), this is hallowed turf for those who worship at the altar of the stove. The blowout Menu Prestige (£160) is seven courses of perfection, also available in vegetarian form (£160); a three-course vegetarian menu (£130) is also at hand. Smart dress code (enquire); reserve early.

For unstoppable enthusiasts, masterclasses with Chef de Cuisine Matt Abé are also available.

Victoria & Pimlico

★MARKET HALL VICTORIA INTERNATIONAL £

Map p456 (www.markethalls.co.uk/market/victoria; 191 Victoria St, SW1; mains from £5; 7am-11pm Mon-Fri, 9am-11pm Sat, to 10pm Sun, roof terrace from noon; ; Victoria) Garrulous, buzzing, young and fun, this market hall ranges over three floors with a total of

11 top-name open kitchens and three bars (including a rooftop one). Find Chinese *baozi* (Baoziinn), kebabs (Fanny's Kebabs), fish and chips (Kerbisher & Malt), a Jewish deli (Monty's Deli) and all manner of other goodies, including vegan (Cookdaily) and much more. Enjoy!

Tables are mainly arrayed for communal dining, so tuck your elbows in. Find Market Hall Victoria right opposite the exit from London Victoria train station, beyond the bus ranks.

★PIMLICO FRESH — CAFE £

Map p456 (☎020-7932 0030; 86 Wilton Rd, SW1; mains from £3.50; ⏰7.30am-7.30pm Mon-Fri, 9am-6pm Sat & Sun; ⓊVictoria) This chirpy two-room cafe will see you right, whether you need breakfast (French toast, bowls of porridge laced with honey, banana, maple syrup or yoghurt; £3.50), lunch (home-made quiches and soups, 'things' on toast) or just a good old latte and cake.

KAZAN — TURKISH ££

Map p456 (☎020-7233 7100; www.kazan-restaurant.com; 93-94 Wilton Rd, SW1; mains £6.50-22.50, set menus £15-35; ⏰noon-10.15pm Mon-Sat, to 9.15pm Sun; ⓊVictoria) Aromatic Kazan gets repeated thumbs up for its set Turkish mezze, shish kebabs and *kulbasti* (rosemary-rubbed grilled fillet of lamb). Flavours are rich and faultless, service is attentive and the Ottoman ambience alluring, but not over the top. Seafood and vegetarian options available; served before 6.30pm. The pre-theatre menu (£15) includes a mezze taster and a main. Booking ahead is recommended.

★A WONG — CHINESE ££

Map p456 (☎020-7828 8931; www.awong.co.uk; 70 Wilton Rd, SW1; dim sum from £2.50 each, mains £11-35, 'Taste of China' menu £100; ⏰noon-2.30pm & 5.30-10pm Tue-Sat; ⓊVictoria) With its relaxed, appealing vibe and busy open kitchen, Michelin-starred A Wong excels at lunchtime dim sum but also casts its net wide to haul in some very tasty sensations from across China: Shanghai *xiaolongbao* dumplings, Shaanxi *roujiamo* (pulled-lamb burger in a bun), Chengdu *doufuhua* (Chengdu 'street tofu'), spicy Sichuan aubergines, Peking duck and more, deliciously reinterpreted.

DRINKING & NIGHTLIFE

Kensington, Chelsea and Belgravia do not have London's oldest and most time-seasoned watering holes, but several very charming, characterful and distinctive pubs provide a congenial environment for a pint.

★K BAR — COCKTAIL BAR

Map p456 (☎020-7589 6300; www.townhousekensington.com/k-bar; Town House, 109-113 Queen's Gate, SW7; cocktails £10; ⏰4pm-midnight Mon-Thu, to 1am Fri, noon-1am Sat, to 11pm Sun; 📶; ⓊSouth Kensington) In a part of town traditionally bereft of choice, the K Bar is a reassuring presence. A hotel bar maybe, but don't let that stop you – the place exudes panache with its leather-panelled and green-marble counter bar, smoothly glinting brass, oak walls and chandeliers, drawing a cashed-up crowd who enjoy themselves. Cocktails are prepared with as much class as the ambience.

★ANGLESEA ARMS — PUB

Map p456 (☎020-7373 7960; www.angleseaarms.com; 15 Selwood Tce, SW7; ⏰11am-11pm Mon-Sat, to 10.30pm Sun; ⓊSouth Kensington) Seasoned with age and decades of ale-quaffing patrons (including Charles Dickens, who lived on the same road, and DH Lawrence), this old-school pub boasts considerable character and a strong showing of beers and gins (over two dozen), while the terrace out front swarms with punters in warmer months. Arch-criminal Bruce Reynolds masterminded the 1963 Great Train Robbery over drinks here.

The panelled dining room at the back offers an elegant setting for roasted monkfish-on-the-bone, venison haunch, vegan burgers and other top-quality pub food (mains £13 to £20) from noon. There's a crowd-pulling Sunday roast (from £16), too, and friendly, helpful staff add to the excellent experience.

COFFEE BAR — CAFE

Map p456 (www.harrods.com; Harrods, 87-135 Brompton Rd, SW1; ⏰10am-9pm Mon-Sat, 11.30am-6pm Sun; 📶; ⓊKnightsbridge) When your legs are turning to lead traipsing around Harrods, gravitate towards the shop's curvilinear deco-style bar in the Roastery and Bake Hall for some decidedly smooth coffee at the heart of the shopping action. Come evening, it's all coffee negronis and chilled espresso martinis. Sittings are limited to 45 minutes.

★**TOMTOM COFFEE HOUSE** CAFE
Map p456 (020-7730 1771; www.tomtomcoffee.co.uk; 114 Ebury St, SW1; mains from £7; 8am-6pm Mon-Fri, 9am-6pm Sat & Sun; ; Victoria) Tomtom has built its solid reputation on amazing coffee: not only are the drinks fabulously presented, but the selection is dizzying: from the usual espresso-based suspects to filter, and a full choice of beans. Take away or enjoy in the small interior or the tiny terrace outside if the weather's good.

QUEEN'S ARMS PUB
Map p456 (www.thequeensarmskensington.co.uk; 30 Queen's Gate Mews, SW7; noon-11pm; Gloucester Rd) Just around the corner from the Royal Albert Hall is this blue-grey-painted godsend. Located in an adorable cobbled-mews setting off bustling Queen's Gate, the pub beckons with a cosy interior, welcoming staff and a right royal selection of ales – including selections from small, local cask brewers – and ciders on tap. In warm weather, drinkers stand outside in the mews (only permitted on one side).

DRAYTON ARMS PUB
Map p456 (020-7835 2301; www.thedraytonarmssw5.co.uk; 153 Old Brompton Rd, SW5; 11am-11pm Mon, to 11.30pm Tue & Wed, to 1am Thu & Fri, 10am-midnight Sat, 10am-11pm Sun; Gloucester Rd) This vast Victorian corner boozer is delightful inside and out, with some bijou art-nouveau features, contemporary art on the walls, a fabulous coffered ceiling and a heated beer garden. The crowd is hip and down-to-earth, and the beer and wine selection great. The pub has a studio theatre (tickets from £5), with nightly productions at 7.30pm and matinees at weekends.

ENTERTAINMENT

This isn't the neighbourhood for cutting-edge clubs, but if jazz floats your boat, a couple of standout venues should top your London list.

★**606 CLUB** BLUES, JAZZ
(020-7352 5953; www.606club.co.uk; 90 Lots Rd, SW10; from £10; doors open 7pm Sun-Thu, 8pm Fri & Sat, plus 12.30pm Sun; Imperial Wharf) Named after its old address on the King's Rd, which cast a spell over London's jazz lovers back in the 80s, this choice, tucked-away basement jazz club and restaurant gives centre stage nightly to contemporary British-based jazz musicians. The club can only serve alcohol to nonmembers who are dining, and it is highly advisable to book to get a table.

There is no entry charge, but a 'music charge' (£10 Sunday lunch, £12 Monday to Thursday, £14 Friday and Saturday, £12 Sunday evening) will be added to your food/drink bill at the end. It's open for occasional Sunday lunches.

★**ROYAL ALBERT HALL** CONCERT VENUE
Map p456 (0845 401 5034; 020-7589 8212; www.royalalberthall.com; Kensington Gore, SW7; South Kensington) This splendid Victorian concert hall hosts classical music, rock and other performances, but is famously the venue for the BBC-sponsored Proms. Booking is possible, but from mid-July to mid-September Promenaders queue for £5 standing tickets that go on sale one hour before curtain-up. Otherwise, the box office and prepaid-ticket collection counter are through door 12 (south side of the hall).

★**PHEASANTRY** LIVE MUSIC
Map p456 (020-7439 4962; www.pizzaexpresslive.com/venues/chelsea-the-pheasantry; 152 King's Rd, SW3; from £10; 11.30am-11pm; Sloane Sq or South Kensington) Currently run by PizzaExpress, the Pheasantry on King's Rd is a 19th-century building that has been a ballet academy, a boho bar and a nightclub (where Lou Reed once sang). These days it ranges over three floors, with a lovely garden at the front for alfresco dining, but the crowd-puller is the nightly live cabaret and jazz in the basement.

Shows are generally at 8pm or 8.30pm; book online.

CADOGAN HALL CONCERT VENUE
Map p456 (020-7730 4500; www.cadoganhall.com; 5 Sloane Tce, SW1; tickets from £10; Sloane Sq) Home of the Royal Philharmonic Orchestra, 950-seat Cadogan Hall is a major venue for classical music, opera and

choral music, as well as dance, rock, jazz and family concerts.

ROYAL COURT THEATRE THEATRE

Map p456 (☎020-7565 5000; www.royalcourttheatre.com; Sloane Sq, SW1; tickets £12-38; Ⓤ Sloane Sq) Equally renowned for staging innovative new plays and old classics, the Royal Court is among London's most-progressive theatres and has continued to foster major writing talent across the UK for over 60 years. There are two auditoriums: the main Jerwood Theatre Downstairs and the much-smaller studio Jerwood Theatre Upstairs. Tickets for Monday performances are £12.

A limited number of restricted-view standing places go on sale one hour before each Jerwood Theatre Downstairs performance for just 10p each. Contact the theatre to check on availability. If you'd like to tread the floorboards, get in touch with the theatre for details of their occasional backstage tours.

SHOPPING

Awash with new money (much from abroad) and frequented by models, celebrities and Russian oligarchs, this well-heeled part of town is all about high fashion, glam shops, groomed shoppers and iconic top-end department stores. Even the charity shops along the chic King's Rd resemble fashion boutiques. It's not all top-end clothing, however, and you'll find some classic bookstores and specialist shops too.

★HARRODS DEPARTMENT STORE

Map p456 (☎020-7730 1234; www.harrods.com; 87-135 Brompton Rd, SW1; ⏲10am-9pm Mon-Sat, 11.30am-6pm Sun; Ⓤ Knightsbridge) Garish and stylish in equal measure, perennially crowded Harrods is an obligatory stop for visitors, from the cash-strapped to the big spenders. The stock is astonishing, as are many of the price tags. Many visitors don't make it past the ground floor where designer bags, myriad scents from the perfume hall and the mouth-watering counters of the food hall provide plenty of entertainment.

The food hall actually makes for an excellent and surprisingly affordable option for a picnic in nearby Hyde Park, while for full-on kitsch the 'Egyptian Elevator' resembles something out of an Indiana Jones epic. Shop sales start at noon on Sundays.

★JOHN SANDOE BOOKS BOOKS

Map p456 (☎020-7589 9473; www.johnsandoe.com; 10 Blacklands Tce, SW3; ⏲9.30am-6.30pm Mon-Sat, 11am-5pm Sun; Ⓤ Sloane Sq) Steeped in literary charm and a perfect antidote to impersonal book superstores, this three-storey bookshop in an 18th-century premises inhabits its own universe. A treasure trove of literary gems and hidden surprises, it's been in business for over six decades. Loyal customers swear by it, and knowledgeable booksellers spill forth with well-read pointers and helpful advice.

★PYLONES GIFTS & SOUVENIRS

Map p456 (☎020-7828 0004; www.pylones.com; SU 20, Victoria Place Shopping Centre, 115 Buckingham Palace Rd, SW1; ⏲8am-8pm Mon-Fri, 9am-7pm Sat, 10.30am-6.30pm Sun; Ⓤ Victoria) A burst of colour and Gallic creative exuberance, Pylones is always such a breath of fresh air, despite the location in a mall up the escalators at the back of Victoria station. It's hard to browse without purchasing something, whether it's a gaily coloured toaster, a vibrant and fun pencil case, a cheeping magnetic bird-shaped paperclip holder, foldaway hairbrush or wind-up toy.

PETER HARRINGTON BOOKS

Map p456 (☎020-7591 0220; www.peterharrington.co.uk; 100 Fulham Rd, SW3; ⏲10am-6pm Mon-Sat; Ⓤ South Kensington) Over three floors, Peter Harrington has a huge collection of first editions, signed modern art prints (Andy Warhol, Pablo Picasso, Bridget Riley, Elisabeth Frink, MC Escher, Damien Hirst among others) and more. Seize a signed first Bloomsbury paperback printing of JK Rowling's *Harry Potter and the Philosopher's Stone* (£20,000) or a more affordable first British impression of Roald Dahl's *The Magic Finger* (£300).

PICKETT GIFTS & SOUVENIRS

Map p456 (☎020-7823 5638; www.pickett.co.uk; cnr Sloane St & Sloane Tce, SW1; ⏲9.30am-7pm Mon, Tue, Thu & Fri, 10am-7pm Wed, 11.30am-6pm Sat; Ⓤ Sloane Sq) Walking into Pickett as an adult is a bit like walking into a sweet shop as a child: the exquisite leather goods are all so colourful and beautiful that you don't really know where to start. Choice items include the perfectly finished handbags, the exquisite roll-up backgammon sets and the men's grooming sets. All leather goods are made in Britain.

There are actually two shops next door to each other: one for men, one for women. Women's clutch bags start at around £345; men's bags range between £295 and £1000-plus. Everything bought here is delightfully gift wrapped, too.

HARVEY NICHOLS DEPARTMENT STORE

Map p456 (020-7235 5000; www.harveynichols.com; 109-125 Knightsbridge, SW1; 10am-8pm Mon-Sat, 11.30am-6pm Sun; Knightsbridge) At London's temple of high fashion, you'll find Chloé and Balenciaga bags, the city's best denim range, a massive make-up hall with exclusive lines and great jewellery. The food hall and in-house restaurant, Fifth Floor Cafe, are, you guessed it, on the 5th floor. From 11.30am to noon, it's browsing time only (big stores can't sell products until noon on Sundays).

JO LOVES COSMETICS

Map p456 (020-7730 8611; www.joloves.com; 42 Elizabeth St, SW1; 10am-6pm Mon-Wed, Fri & Sat, to 7pm Thu, noon-5pm Sun; Victoria) Famed British scent-maker Jo Malone opened this shop in 2013, here on a street where she once had a job as a young florist. It features the entrepreneur's signature candles, fragrances and bath products in a range of delicate scents – Pomelo is the most popular. All products come exquisitely wrapped in white boxes with red bows.

★CONRAN SHOP DESIGN

Map p456 (020-7589 7401; www.conranshop.co.uk; Michelin House, 81 Fulham Rd, SW3; 10am-6pm Mon, Tue & Fri, to 7pm Wed & Thu, to 6.30pm Sat, noon-6pm Sun; South Kensington) The original design store (going strong since 1987), the Conran Shop is a treasure trove of beautiful things – from radios to sunglasses, kitchenware to children's toys and books, bathroom accessories to greeting cards. Browsing bliss. Spare some time to peruse the magnificent art-nouveau/deco Michelin House (p189) the shop is housed in.

CHURCH'S SHOES

Map p456 (020-7589 9136; www.churchfootwear.com; 143 Brompton Rd, SW3; 10am-6.30pm Mon-Sat, noon-6pm Sun; Knightsbridge) Dating to 1873, Church's is a byword for elegant craftsmanship, manufacturing shoes that ooze quality and may even last you a lifetime (if pampered). The now Prada-owned company has pushed the fashion boat out so all styles now get a say, from classic to cutting edge: Oxfords, brogues, loafers, sneakers, sandals and more.

V&A SHOP ARTS & CRAFTS

Map p456 (www.vam.ac.uk/info/shopping-at-the-va; Victoria & Albert Museum, Cromwell Rd, SW7; 10am-5.30pm Sat-Thu, to 9.30pm Fri; South Kensington) Before checking out of the V&A, stop by the ground-floor shop facing the Cromwell Rd entrance and rummage through a stirring and very sharp display of (impulse purchase) gifts, books, fabrics and prints, all design-oriented and inspired by exhibitions and iconic pieces at the museum, as well as a delightful range of jewellery from independent jewellery-makers.

There are other shops within the museum, including an excellent bookshop.

PENHALIGON'S FASHION & ACCESSORIES

Map p456 (020-7823 9733; www.penhaligons.com; 25 King's Rd, SW3; 10am-7pm Mon-Sat, 11.30am-6pm Sun; Sloane Sq) Stepping through the door of this cute branch of the famous perfumery – dating to 1870 – is like walking into a floral spray of hyacinths, roses and peonies. The beautifully presented, very fancy bottled perfumes make exquisite gifts. There is another outlet on the ground floor in Harrods.

PETER JONES DEPARTMENT STORE

Map p456 (020-7730 3434; www.johnlewis.com/our-shops/peter-jones; Sloane Sq, SW1; 9.30am-8pm Mon-Fri, to 7pm Sat, noon-6pm Sun; Sloane Sq) An upmarket department store housed in a Grade II-listed 1930s building that occupies an entire block, Peter Jones' fortes are china, furnishings and gifts, though it stocks accessories and cosmetics too.

SPORTS & ACTIVITIES

WINTER WONDERLAND AMUSEMENT PARK

Map p456 (www.hydeparkwinterwonderland.com; Hyde Park, W1; 10am-10pm mid-Nov–early Jan; Hyde Park Corner) From mid-November to early January, this seasonal attraction in Hyde Park is full of winter festivities, shows, ice-skating, circus acts and more.

PURE GYM GYM

Map p456 (www.puregym.com; South Kensington Estate, 63-81 Pelham St, SW7; Ⓤ South Kensington) Pure Gym has over 60 gyms around the city.

WILL TO WIN (HYDE PARK TENNIS & SPORTS CENTRE) TENNIS

Map p456 (☎020-7262 3474; www.willtowin.co.uk/hyde-park-centreinfo; South Carriage Dr, Hyde Park, W2; tennis per hour adult £16-17, child 11.50-16; ⏲7am-9pm; Ⓤ Knightsbridge) Has six outdoor, floodlit hard tennis courts, a bowling green (from £8 per person per hour), a nine-hole putting course (£6) and an outdoor gym, as well as a cafe. Peak hours (after 5pm) are priciest for tennis.

SERPENTINE SOLARSHUTTLE BOAT BOATING

Map p456 (☎020-7262 1989; www.solarshuttle.co.uk; adult/child £5/3) Ferries passengers from the Serpentine Boathouse to the Diana, Princess of Wales Memorial Fountain (p185) at weekends from March to September (every day from mid-July to late August).

SERPENTINE BOATHOUSE BOATING

Map p456 (☎020-7724 4069; adult/child per 30min £8.50/6, per hour £10.50/7.50; ⏲10.30am-6pm late Mar-Oct; Ⓤ Hyde Park Corner, Knightsbridge) Rent a paddle boat from the Serpentine Boathouse.

SERPENTINE LIDO SWIMMING

Map p456 (☎020-7706 3422; Hyde Park, W2; adult/child £4.80/1.80, after 4pm, £4.10/1.10 family of 4 £12, after 4pm £9; ⏲10am-6pm Jun-early Sep; Ⓤ Hyde Park Corner or Knightsbridge) Perhaps the ultimate London pool is inside the Serpentine lake and is open during the summer months. Sun loungers are available for £3.50 for a whole day.

Clerkenwell, Shoreditch & Spitalfields

CLERKENWELL | OLD STREET | SPITALFIELDS | SHOREDITCH & HOXTON | HOXTON | SHOREDITCH | HOXTON

Neighbourhood Top Five

❶ **Shoreditch nightlife** (p214) Donning your craziest outfit, grooming your beard and heading to Shoreditch for cocktails and carousing in clubs like Fabric.

❷ **Super Market Sunday** (p221) Crawling the markets with the multicultural masses on a sunny Sunday in Spitalfields.

❸ **Vintage shopping** (p220) Finding that unique vinyl, 1960s dress or art-deco poster in one of Brick Lane's vintage shops, like Atika.

❹ **Museum of the Home** (p204) Stepping back through the living rooms of time at this wonderfully evocative domestic-interiors museum.

❺ **Brick Lane** (p220) Strolling through this unique neighbourhood, which bears witness to London's long migration history.

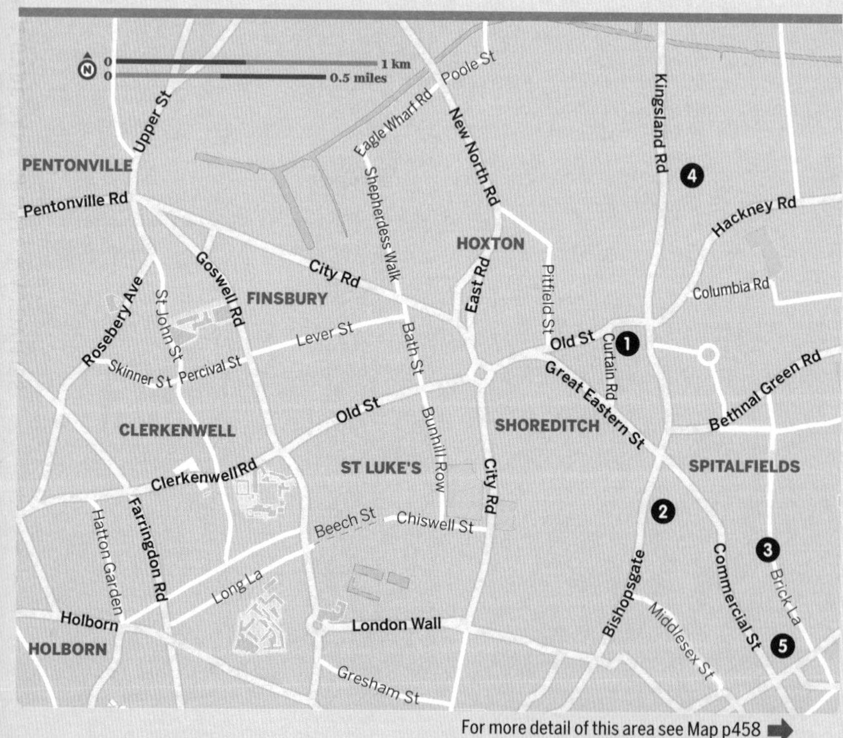

For more detail of this area see Map p458

Explore Clerkenwell, Shoreditch & Spitalfields

Swing by during the day to explore the area's boutiques, vintage shops, markets and cafes. But make sure you come back after dark for a meal at one of the many excellent eateries, followed by an evening flitting between kooky cocktail bars and subterranean nightspots.

Shoreditch can get pretty wild on Friday and Saturday nights, and many places stay open until dawn. Spitalfields is great fun too, although slightly more subdued. Clerkenwell by comparison is positively sedate.

Sunday is a great day to join the crowds shrugging off their hangovers with a stroll through Spitalfields' many markets, but note that Clerkenwell is eerily quiet.

Local Life

Nights out with a difference Mingle with London's hiperati at DreamBags JaguarShoes (p216); catch a jazz act with a prohibition-era concoction at Nightjar (p214); or belt out hip-hop karaoke jams at the Queen of Hoxton (p215), followed by alfresco drinks on the rooftop.

Coffee crawl The area has so many excellent cafes that a mild caffeine tremor is de rigueur. Sink a silky flat white or a shotgun espresso at Shoreditch Grind (p216) or Ozone Coffee Roasters (p209).

The pho mile Find your favourite Vietnamese restaurant on the Kingsland Rd/Old St strip or head to one of ours (p212).

Getting There & Away

Underground Farringdon and Barbican stations on the Circle, Hammersmith & City and Metropolitan lines are stopping-off points for Clerkenwell. These lines and the Central Line also head through Liverpool St, the closest Tube stop to Spitalfields. Old St, on the Bank branch of the Northern Line, is the best stop for the western edge of Hoxton and Shoreditch.

Overground Shoreditch High St and Hoxton are the closest stations to Spitalfields and the eastern parts of Shoreditch and Hoxton.

Bus Clerkenwell and Old St are connected with Oxford St by the 55 and with Waterloo by the 243. The 38 runs up Rosebery Ave and edges past Exmouth Market on its way from Victoria to Islington. The 8 and 242 zip through the city and up Shoreditch High St.

Lonely Planet's Top Tip

Fancy a late one? Fabric (p214), **XOYO** (p216), Cargo (p217) and the Horse & Groom (p217) all stay open until at least 3am on weekends. Brick Lane Beigel Bake (p212) will serve you munchies throughout the night, while the Fox & Anchor (p214) throws back its doors at 7am (8.30am on weekends) for breakfast with a pint.

Best Eating

- Clove Club (p210)
- Hawksmoor (p213)
- Smoking Goat (p209)
- Gate (p208)

For reviews, see p208.

Best Drinking & Nightlife

- Nightjar (p214)
- Cocktail Trading Co (p217)
- Fox & Anchor (p214)
- Discount Suit Company (p217)
- Zetter Townhouse Cocktail Lounge (p213)

For reviews, see p213.

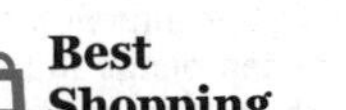

Best Shopping

- Sunday UpMarket (p218)
- Old Spitalfields Market (p219)
- Aida (p219)
- Libreria (p219)
- Rough Trade East (p219)

For reviews, see p218.

SIGHTS

Clerkenwell, Shoreditch and Spitalfields make up for in atmosphere and history what they lack in 'big ticket sights'. Here you'll come across some of London's oldest buildings, and poignant reminders of the capital's long history of migration. Far from simply being a historical repository, however, the area is the heart of London's creative industry, and it very much feels like it is actively shaping the next chapter in London's history.

Clerkenwell

ST JOHN'S GATE — HISTORIC BUILDING

Map p458 (www.museumstjohn.org.uk; St John's Lane, EC1; ⌚10am-5pm, closed Sun Oct-Jun; Ⓤ Farringdon) FREE This remarkable Tudor gate dates from 1504. During the 12th century, the Knights Hospitaller (a Christian and military order with a focus on providing care to the sick) established a priory here. Inside is a small museum that covers the history of the order (including rare examples of the knights' armour), as well as its 19th-century revival in Britain as the Christian Order of St John and the foundation of St John Ambulance.

The gate was erected as a grand entrance to the priory and survived despite most of the buildings being destroyed when Henry VIII dissolved monasteries throughout England between 1536 and 1540. It enjoyed a varied afterlife, not least as a Latin-speaking coffee house, which was run without much success by William Hogarth's father during Queen Anne's reign. Restored in the 19th century, it also housed the Old Jerusalem Tavern, where writers and artists, including Charles Dickens, met.

Try to time your visit to catch one of the comprehensive 80-minute **guided tours** (11am and 2.30pm Tuesdays, Fridays and Saturdays) of the gate and the priory church. You'll also be shown upstairs to the sumptuous 1902 chapter hall and council chamber (dating to 1504), which are still used by the order to this day. Donations are always welcome.

ST JOHN'S PRIORY CHURCH — CHURCH

Map p458 (www.museumstjohn.org.uk; St John's Sq, EC1; ⌚tours 11am & 2.30pm Tue, Fri &

TOP EXPERIENCE

LOOK INSIDE THE MUSEUM OF THE HOME

If you like nosing around other people's homes, you'll love this museum devoted entirely to middle-class domestic interiors – though note it's closed until 2021 for redevelopment.

Built in 1714 as a home for poor pensioners, these beautiful ivy-clad almshouses have been converted into a series of living rooms, dating from 1630 to the Victorian era. An extension completed in 1998 contains several 20th-century rooms (a flat from the 1930s, a 1960s suburban lounge and an all-too-familiar 1990s loft-style apartment) as well as a gallery for temporary exhibits, a shop and a cafe.

The rear **garden** is also organised by era, mirroring the museum's exploration of domesticity through the centuries. There's also a very impressive walled **herb garden**, featuring 170 different plants. The lawns at the front are a popular spot for lazing about.

One of the almshouses has been completely restored and furnished to show the living conditions of the original pensioners in the 18th and 19th centuries. It's the absolute attention to detail that impresses, right down to the vintage newspaper left open on the breakfast table.

DON'T MISS

- Period rooms
- Period and herb gardens
- Almshouse interiors

PRACTICALITIES

- Map p458, G2
- ☎020-7739 9893
- www.museumofthehome.org.uk
- 136 Kingsland Rd, E2
- admission free
- ⌚10am-5pm Tue-Sun
- Ⓤ Hoxton

Sat; Ⓤ Farringdon) The Priory Church is one of London's oldest churches. This whole area was originally part of the medieval St John's Priory and is now associated with the revived Order of St John. The walled garden, planted with medicinal herbs and flowers, was built as a memorial to St John's workers who died during the world wars. Sadly the church can only be visited as part of a guided tour of St John's Gate.

If the somewhat boxy street-level church doesn't seem like it ever belonged to a medieval priory, that's because it didn't. The real treasure lies beneath, where the nave of the original church has been preserved as a darkened crypt. Built in the 1380s in the Norman Romanesque style, it's one of the oldest buildings in London. Inside there's a sturdy alabaster effigy of a Castilian knight (1575) and a battered monument portraying the last prior, Sir William Weston, as a decaying body in a shroud (a memento mori designed to remind viewers of their own mortality).

The nave once abutted a large circular chancel that was demolished following the dissolution of the priory. Outside, the outline of the original church has been traced onto the square.

CHARTERHOUSE HISTORIC BUILDING

Map p458 (☎020-7253 9503; www.thecharterhouse.org; Charterhouse Sq, EC1; ⏰11am-5.20pm Tue-Sun; Ⓤ Barbican) FREE From a monastery, to a Tudor mansion, to the charitable foundation that's operated here since 1611, Charterhouse has played a discreet but important part in London's story. Visitors have free access to the small museum, the chapel and the main court, but must join a one-hour tour to see more (£15 and well worth it). These run two to three times daily and take in the most historic rooms and courts, and the cloister.

Although Charterhouse was founded in 1371 as a Carthusian monastery (the name derives from Chartreuse in France, where the order is based), the site's history began in 1348 when what is now Charterhouse Sq was used as a plague burial ground during the great epidemic of the Black Death. Some of the bodies were recently excavated during the Crossrail works (a new underground train line) and one skeleton is exhibited in the museum.

In 1537 the monastery was dissolved and the property transferred to King Henry VIII. The prior and 15 of the monks were executed. They were the first of England's Catholic martyrs of the Reformation and three of them were subsequently canonised.

The king sold the property in 1545 to Sir Edward North, who converted it into his London mansion, knocking down the original church and much of the cloister in the process. In 1611 it was purchased by Thomas Sutton, known at the time as the 'richest commoner in England'. In his will, Sutton directed that it should become a school for boys and an almshouse for 'destitute gentlemen'. Around 40 pensioners (known as 'brothers') still live here today; women were admitted for the first time in 2017. Charterhouse School moved to Surrey in 1872 and is still going strong.

ST ETHELDREDA'S CHURCH

Map p458 (☎020-7405 1061; www.stetheldreda.com; 14 Ely Pl, EC1; ⏰8am-5pm Mon-Sat, to 12.30pm Sun; Ⓤ Chancery Lane) FREE More than just a gorgeous oasis of peace, this stunner of a church is also the oldest Roman Catholic church in the UK, dating from the reign of Edward I. The town chapel of the Bishops of Ely dates from the mid-13th century to 1570 and is named after the 7th-century East Anglian princess and Fenland saint Etheldreda. The church was saved during the Great Fire of London by an abrupt change in the wind.

The church was hit in WWII by a Luftwaffe bomb that came through the roof during the Blitz and put paid to its surviving stained glass; the beautiful great east window was replaced in 1952.

MARX MEMORIAL LIBRARY LIBRARY

Map p458 (☎020-7253 1485; www.marx-memorial-library.org; 37a Clerkenwell Green,

SIGHTS FOR FREE

Sightseeing is cheap in this neighbourhood: the Museum of the Home is free, as are Charterhouse, St John's Gate, churches and, of course, wandering about – which is exactly what you should be doing on Sundays, when the buzz from Spitalfields Market is infectious.

Eschew the tours offered at the Museum of the Home, Charterhouse and St John's Gate, and enjoy the free general admission to these sights.

EC1; tours £5; ⊙tours 11am Tue & Thu; Ⓤ Farringdon) Built in 1738 to house a Welsh charity school, this unassuming building is an interesting reminder of Clerkenwell's radical history. From here in 1902 and 1903, during his European exile, Lenin edited 17 editions of the Russian-language Bolshevik newspaper *Iskra* (Spark). In 1933, 50 years after the death of Karl Marx and around the time of the Nazi book burnings, it was decided that the building would be converted into a library to honour the founder of communism.

Copies of *Iskra* have been preserved in the library, along with other socialist literature, Spanish Civil War banners and relics from various industrial disputes. Tours visit the room where Lenin worked and the building's 15th-century cellar.

If you think it's odd that Clerkenwell should have a memorial to Marx, you might be surprised to learn that from 1942 to 1951 a bust of Lenin stood in Holford Sq in neighbouring Finsbury, gazing towards his former residence. After being repeatedly vandalised it was moved to Islington Town Hall, where it remained on display until 1996, when it was consigned to a museum.

⊙ Old Street

BUNHILL FIELDS CEMETERY

Map p458 (entrances on Bunhill Row & City Rd, EC1; ⊙8am-dusk Mon-Fri, from 9.30am Sat & Sun; Ⓤ Old St) This cemetery just outside the city walls has been a burial ground for more than 1000 years. 'Bunhill' probably derives from the area's macabre historical name – 'Bone Hill'. Famous burials include literary giants Daniel Defoe, John Bunyan and William Blake. It's a lovely place for a stroll, and a rare green space in this built-up area.

WESLEY'S CHAPEL CHURCH

Map p458 (☎020-7253 2262; www.wesleyschapel.org.uk; 49 City Rd, EC1; ⊙10am-4pm Mon-Sat; Ⓤ Old St) Built in 1778, this warm and welcoming church was the place of work and worship for John Wesley, the founder of the Methodist Church. You can learn more about him in the **Museum of Methodism** downstairs, and visit his house (at the front) and his grave (behind the church).

TOP EXPERIENCE

VISIT ARTIST DENNIS SEVERS' HOUSE

This quirky hotchpotch of a cluttered house (built c 1724) is named after the late American eccentric who restored and turned it into what he called a 'still-life drama'. Severs was an artist who lived in the house (in a similar way to the original inhabitants) until his death in 1999.

Visitors today find they've entered the home of a family of Huguenot silk weavers, who were common to the Spitalfields area in the 18th century. However, while you see the Georgian interiors, with meals and drinks half-abandoned and rumpled sheets, and while you smell cooking and hear creaking floorboards, your 'hosts' always remain tantalisingly just out of reach.

From the cellar to the bedrooms, the interiors demonstrate both the original function and design of the rooms as well as the highs and lows of the area's history. The family's fortunes fade as you progress upstairs, ending in a state of near-destitution on the upper level.

The 'plot' isn't exactly obvious, but no matter, the house is wonderfully evocative and makes for a unique experience.

Night-time sessions are illuminated solely by candlelight and kerosene lamps and are particularly atmospheric; book online in advance. Visits take around 45 minutes.

DON'T MISS

- Silent Night tours
- The house cat
- Hogarth tableau

PRACTICALITIES

- Map p458, G6
- ☎020-7247 4013
- www.dennissevershouse.co.uk
- 18 Folgate St, E1
- day/night £10/15
- ⊙noon-2pm & 5-9pm Mon, 5-9pm Wed & Fri, noon-4pm Sun
- Ⓤ Liverpool St

Shoreditch & Hoxton

Hoxditch? Shoho? Often (confusingly) used interchangeably by Londoners, Hoxton and Shoreditch signify the area stretching north and east from the roundabout at Old St Tube station. The name Shoreditch relates to a settlement that grew up immediately north of the old city, around the junction of two important Roman thoroughfares: Kingsland Rd and Old St. Shoreditch was the name of the parish, within which was the village of Hoxton. These days Hoxton is generally known as the area to the north of Old St, up to Kingsland Rd, with Shoreditch being the roads to the south, stretching to the east as far as Brick Lane. But switch them around, or get them confused, and no one will bat an eyelid.

POSTAL MUSEUM & MAIL RAIL MUSEUM
(☎0300 0300 700; www.postalmuseum.org; 15-20 Phoenix Pl, WC1; adult/child £17/10; ⏰10am-5pm; 👪; Ⓤ Farringdon) Here's an underground experience you won't find on the Tube map. Built in 1927 to beat traffic congestion, the Post Office Railway was a subterranean train line used to move four million pieces of mail beneath the city streets every day until it was shuttered in 2003. Revamped and opened to the public for the first time in 2017, Mail Rail now delivers delighted visitors around the once little-known tracks below the largest sorting office, in trains based on the original designs.

Mail Rail is the headline attraction, but it's worth popping across the street to the surprisingly fascinating Postal Museum, which traces the history of Britain's postal system and how complicated it was to set up.

Claustrophobes beware: Mail Rail was originally made to carry post and not people, so while the carriages are wide enough for a single person, staff are sometimes intent on squeezing two people into one seat.

ST MARY'S SECRET GARDEN GARDENS
Map p458 (☎020-7739 2965; www.stmaryssecretgarden.org.uk; 50 Pearson St, E2; ⏰9am-5pm Mon-Fri, 10am-1pm Sat; Ⓤ Hoxton) FREE A little pocket of charming – not to mention unlikely – wilderness in the middle of a Hackney housing estate, St Mary's Secret Garden really does feel like a secret. Run and maintained by the surrounding community, the garden offers hands-on experiences in horticulture and ecotherapy, but you're free to simply visit for some peace and quiet. Its various mini areas include a wildflower meadow, a herb garden, a pond and several beehives.

Spitalfields

Crowded around its famous market and grand parish church, Spitalfields has long been one of the capital's most multicultural areas. Waves of Huguenot (French Protestant), Jewish, Irish and, more recently, Indian and Bangladeshi immigrants have made Spitalfields home.

A walk along Brick Lane is the best way to experience the sights, sounds and smells of Bangladeshi London, but to get a sense of what Georgian Spitalfields was like, branch off to Princelet, Fournier, Elder and Wilkes Sts. Having fled persecution in France, the Huguenots set up shop here from the late 17th century, practising their trade of silk weaving. The attics of these grand town houses were once filled with clattering looms and the area became famous for the quality of its silk, even providing the material for Queen Victoria's coronation gown.

CHRIST CHURCH SPITALFIELDS CHURCH
Map p458 (☎020-7377 2440; www.ccspitalfields.org; Commercial St, E1; ⏰10am-4pm Mon-Fri, from 1pm Sun; Ⓤ Liverpool St) This imposing English baroque structure, with a tall spire sitting on a portico of four great Tuscan columns, was designed by Nicholas Hawksmoor and completed in 1729. The heaviness of the exterior gives way to a brilliantly white and lofty interior, with Corinthian columns and large brass chandeliers.

OLD TRUMAN BREWERY HISTORIC BUILDING
Map p458 (☎020-7770 6000; www.trumanbrewery.com; Brick Lane, E1; Ⓤ Shoreditch High St) Founded here in the 17th century, Truman's Black Eagle Brewery was, by the 1850s, the largest brewery in the world. Spread over a series of brick buildings and yards straddling both sides of Brick Lane, the complex is now completely given over to edgy markets, pop-up fashion stores, vintage clothes shops, cafes and bars – it's at

its busy best when market stalls are set up on Sundays. Beer may not be brewed here any more, but it certainly is consumed.

After decades of decline, Truman's Brewery finally shut up shop in 1989 – temporarily as it turned out, with the brand subsequently resurrected in 2010 in new premises a bit further northeast in the neighbourhood of Hackney Wick.

Several of the brewery buildings are heritage listed, including the Director's House at 91 Brick Lane (built in the 1740s), the old Vat House directly opposite (c 1800) and the Engineer's House at 150 Brick Lane (dating from the 1830s).

EATING

In addition to a wealth of fantastic cafes and restaurants, this area has popular food markets with stalls devoted to a wide variety of cuisines. Check out Exmouth Market and Whitecross St Market for weekday lunches, and Brick Lane and the surrounding streets on Sundays. Hoxton's Kingsland Rd and Old St are well known for their reasonably priced Vietnamese eateries.

Clerkenwell

★BREDDOS TACOS — MEXICAN £

Map p458 (020-3535 8301; www.breddostacos.com; 82 Goswell Rd, EC1; tacos from £5, mains £7.50-17; noon-3pm & 5-11pm Mon-Fri, noon-11.30pm Sat; ; Old St, Farringdon) Started in an East London car park in 2011, Breddos found its first permanent home in Clerkenwell, dishing out some of London's best Mexican grub. Grab some friends and order each of the eight or so tacos, served in pairs, on the menu: fillings vary, but past favourites include confit pork belly, and veggie-friendly mole, *queso fresco* and egg.

PANZO — PIZZERIA £

Map p458 (www.panzopizza.com; 50 Exmouth Market, EC1; pizza £8-9; noon-10.30pm Tue-Thur, to 11.30pm Fri & Sat, to 9.30pm Sun & Mon; ; Farringdon) Never has pizza looked more mouth-watering than at Panzo's: oblong-shaped, loaded with toppings and enjoyed in a dining room bathed in the pink hues of copper-topped tables. It could hardly be more tempting. The pizza dough is made from a mix of rice, soy and wheat flours, and double-baked – unusual, but delicious.

POLPO — VENETIAN ££

Map p458 (020-7250 0034; www.polpo.co.uk; 3 Cowcross St, EC1; dishes £3-11; noon-11pm Mon-Sat; ; Farringdon) London's take on a Venetian *bacàri* (small bar), Polpo dishes out sharing plates of pasta, meat and *pizzette* (petite pizzas), with excellent options for vegetarians. The succulent meatballs keep Londoners coming back; despite the name, the octopus is best avoided. Portions are larger than *cicchetti* (bar snacks) found in Venice but smaller than a regular main, the perfect excuse to graze freely.

Polpo's tentacles extend across London, with four additional branches dotted around the city.

THE GATE — VEGETARIAN ££

Map p458 (020-7833 0401; www.thegaterestaurants.com; 370 St John St, EC1; mains £14-16; noon-10pm Mon-Sat, to 9.30pm Sun; ; Angel) The Gate can probably take a lot of credit for elevating vegetarian cuisine from uninspiring side dishes to starring in its own culinary right. Blending influences from Asia, the Middle East and Jewish traditions, the food is a riot of flavours. The elegant dining room is in tune with the locale: white walls and dark wooden tables and chairs.

★ST JOHN — BRITISH ££

Map p458 (020-7251 0848; www.stjohnrestaurant.com; 26 St John St, EC1; mains £17-26.50; noon-3pm & 6-11pm Mon-Fri, 6-11pm Sat, 12.30-4pm Sun; Farringdon) Around the corner from London's last remaining meat market, St John is the standard-bearer for nose-to-tail cuisine. With whitewashed brick walls, high ceilings and simple wooden furniture, it's surely one of the most humble Michelin-starred restaurants anywhere. The menu changes daily but is likely to include the signature roast bone marrow and parsley salad.

MORITO — TAPAS ££

Map p458 (020-7278 7007; www.morito.co.uk; 32 Exmouth Market, EC1; dishes £7-10; 8am-4pm & 5-11pm Mon-Fri, 9am-noon & 5-11pm Sat, 9am-4pm Sun; ; Farringdon) This diminutive eatery is a wonderfully authentic take on a Spanish tapas bar and has excellent eats. Seats are at the bar, along the window, or on one of the small tables inside or out. It's relaxed, convivial and often completely crammed; reservations are taken for lunch, but dinner is first come, first served, with couples generally going to the bar.

CARAVAN INTERNATIONAL ££

Map p458 (020-7833 8115; www.caravanrestaurants.co.uk; 11-13 Exmouth Market, EC1; mains £18.50-20, brunch £12-15; 8am-10.30pm Mon-Fri, from 9am Sat, to 4pm Sun; ; Farringdon) Perfect for a sunny day when its sides are opened onto bustling Exmouth Market, this place is a relaxed affair, offering all-day dining and drinking. The menu has a huge variety of dishes, drawing on flavours from all over the world. The coffee, roasted in the basement, is fantastic.

MODERN PANTRY FUSION ££

Map p458 (020-7553 9210; www.themodernpantry.co.uk; 47-48 St John's Sq, EC1; mains £17-22, breakfast £5-12; 8am-10pm Mon-Fri, 9am-10.30pm Sat, 10am-10pm Sun; ; Farringdon) This three-floor Georgian town house in the heart of Clerkenwell has a cracking all-day menu that is almost as pleasurable to read as it is to eat from. Ingredients are sublimely combined into unusual dishes such as miso-marinated onglet steak or Aleppo chilli- and garlic-marinated pork chop. The breakfasts are great too, though portions can be on the small side.

EAGLE GASTROPUB ££

Map p458 (020-7837 1353; www.theeaglefarringdon.co.uk; 159 Farringdon Rd, EC1; mains £11-21; 12.30-3pm & 6.30-10.30pm Mon-Fri, 12.30-3.30pm Sat & Sun; Farringdon) London's first gastropub may have seen its original owners move on, but it's still a great place for a bite and a pint, especially at lunchtimes when it's relatively quiet. The menu fuses British and Mediterranean elements, and the atmosphere is lively. Watch the chefs work their magic right behind the bar, above which is chalked the menu.

DANS LE NOIR EUROPEAN £££

Map p458 (020-7253 1100; www.london.danslenoir.com; 30-31 Clerkenwell Green, EC1; 2-/3-course menu £48/55; 6pm-midnight Tue-Fri, from noon Sat, from 1pm Sun, to 10pm Mon; ; Farringdon) The dining room is set up as normal at Dans Le Noir, but there's one huge difference: you can't see it. Pick your menu in the still-lit lobby (red for meat, blue for fish or green for vegetarian or vegan), and then one of the super-friendly visually impaired servers will lead you conga-line-style to your table in the pitch black.

Old Street

LOOK MUM NO HANDS! CAFE £

Map p458 (020-7253 1025; www.lookmumnohands.com; 49 Old St, EC1; dishes £5-13; 7.30am-10pm Mon-Fri, from 8.30am Sat, from 9am Sun; ; Barbican) Cyclists and non-cyclists alike adore this cafe-workshop, set in a light-filled space looking out onto Old St. Toasties and burgers are the savoury staples; cakes and startlingly impressive coffee complete the offering. There are a few outdoor tables, and staff can loan you a lock if you need to park your wheels.

Shoreditch

OZONE COFFEE ROASTERS CAFE £

Map p458 (020-7490 1039; www.ozonecoffee.co.uk; 11 Leonard St, EC2; mains £8-15; 7am-10pm Mon-Fri, 8.30am-5.30pm Sat & Sun; ; Old St) During the day this Kiwi-run cafe is full of artsy types hunched over their computers and new-media mavens appropriating booth seats for impromptu meetings. Coffee is Ozone's raison d'être (each preparation – latte, espresso, filter, press etc – is allocated a specific blend or coffee bean); but you could instead opt for a New Zealand wine to accompany your risotto or fish of the day.

★**SMOKING GOAT** THAI ££

Map p458 (www.smokinggoatbar.com; 64 Shoreditch High St, E1; dishes £4-29; noon-3pm & 5.30-11pm Mon-Thur, to 1am Fri & Sat, to 11pm Sun; Shoreditch High St) Trotting in on one of London's fleeting flavours of the week, Smoking Goat's modern Thai menu is top notch. The industrial-chic look of exposed brick, huge factory windows and original parquet floors surround the open kitchen. It's a tough place for the spice-shy; cool down with a cold one from the exquisite cocktail list. Don't miss the smoked five-spice chicken.

ANDINA PERUVIAN ££

Map p458 (☎020-7920 6499; www.andinalondon.com; 1 Redchurch St, E2; dishes £7-16; ⏰11am-11pm Mon-Fri, from 10am Sat & Sun; 📶; ⓤShoreditch High St) Cheerful Andina sits on the corner of trendy Redchurch St and serves high-quality Peruvian street food. The lively restaurant, set over two floors, is a great place to try *bistec rio negro* (marinated beef with plantain), piquant ceviches, tamales and succulent street-food bites. Unsurprisingly, it knocks out a mean pisco sour.

PRINCESS OF SHOREDITCH MODERN BRITISH ££

Map p458 (☎020-7729 9270; www.theprincessofshoreditch.com; 76-78 Paul St, EC2; mains £13-16; ⏰noon-3pm & 5-10pm Wed-Sat, noon-7pm Sun; 📶; ⓤOld St) The handsome pub downstairs is a buzzy place for a drink, but swirl up the tight spiral staircase and an entirely different Princess presents itself. Polished stemware glistens on wooden Edwardian tables, while the waitstaff buzz around delivering plates of inventive contemporary fare crafted from top-notch British ingredients.

ALBION BRITISH ££

Map p458 (☎020-7729 1051; https://boundary.london/albion; 2-4 Boundary St, E2; mains £8-20; ⏰8am-11pm; 📶👶; ⓤShoreditch High St) Those pining for dear Old Blighty's cuisine, *sans* grease and stodge, should earmark a visit to this self-consciously retro 'caff' for top-quality bangers and mash, game-meat pies, Welsh rarebit, full English breakfasts and, of course, fish and chips.

★CLOVE CLUB GASTRONOMY £££

Map p458 (☎020-7729 6496; www.thecloveclub.com; Shoreditch Town Hall, 380 Old St, EC1; lunch £65, dinner £95-145; ⏰noon-1.45pm Tue-Sat, 6-10.30pm Mon-Sat; ✍; ⓤOld St) From humble origins as a supper club in a London flat, the Clove Club has transformed into this impressive Michelin-starred restaurant, named one of the world's best in 2017. The menu is a mystery until dishes arrive at the table; expect intricately arranged plates with impeccably sourced ingredients from around the British Isles. Your wallet might feel empty, but you sure won't.

Neighbourhood Walk
East End Then & Now

START LIVERPOOL ST STATION
END OLD ST STATION
LENGTH 1.8 MILES; 1½ HOURS

This route leads straight through the heart of historic, multicultural Spitalfields and on to hipper-than-thou Shoreditch. You'll find it at its liveliest on a Sunday, when the various markets are effervescing – but be prepared for a much slower stroll. During the rest of the week, there are still plenty of diverting shops and bars to break your stride.

Leaving the Tube station, cross busy Bishopsgate, turn left and then right when you come to **1 Middlesex Street**. This used to be known as Petticoat Lane, after the lacy women's undergarments that were sold here, but that proved too saucy for the authorities and the name was changed in 1830 – to Middlesex! The East End locals weren't nearly so prudish, and the ragtag Sunday market that's been based here for more than 400 years is still known by its former name.

Veer left into Widegate St and continue into narrow **2 Artillery Passage**, one of Spitalfields' most atmospheric lanes, lined with historic shopfronts and drinking dens. From here, a left then a right will bring you onto Gun St and, at its far end, **3 Old Spitalfields Market** (p219).

Enter the market and turn right into the covered lane lined with fancy gift shops and eateries – a far cry from the fruit-and-veggie stands that the market was famous for until 1991 when 'New Spitalfields' opened in Leyton. Continue on through the artisan craft and fashion stalls of the market proper and then step out onto Commercial St.

Just over the road is the **4 Ten Bells** (p218) pub – famous as one of Jack the Ripper's possible pick-up joints – and the hulking presence of **5 Christ Church** (p207). Running between the two, Fournier St is one of Spitalfields' most intact Georgian streetscapes. As you wander along, note the oddball, Harry Potterish numbering (11½ Fournier St) and keep an eye out for famous artsy residents Tracey

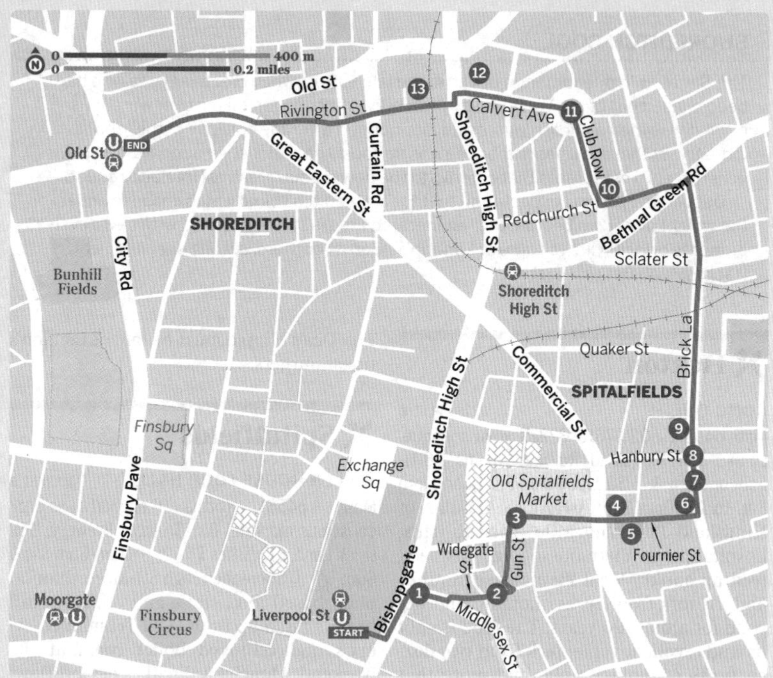

Emin and Gilbert & George. The last building on the left of Fournier St is ❻ **Brick Lane Great Mosque**.

Turn left onto buzzing and colourful ❼ **Brick Lane**. Today this narrow but famous thoroughfare is the centrepiece of a thriving Bengali community in an area nicknamed Banglatown. Expect to be cajoled by eager touts as you pass the long procession of curry houses. For the most part the standard is pretty average, despite extravagant claims to the contrary.

Stop at the corner of ❽ **Hanbury Street** to admire the graffiti and then continue on to ❾ **Old Truman Brewery** (p207). North of here Brick Lane is a very different place, stuffed with eclectic clothing shops, old-time Jewish bagel bakeries, and a surfeit of cafes and bars.

Further up, at the traffic lights cross Bethnal Green Rd, turn left and then veer right onto Redchurch St, where there are more interesting independent shops to peruse. As you turn right into Club Row, keep an eye out for an elaborate black-and-red piece of street sculpture called ❿ **Portal**, dedicated to the artist CityZenKane's late son.

Leafy Club Row terminates in ⓫ **Arnold Circus**, a circular intersection topped with a wooded mound and a bandstand. Until 1891 this was the very heart of London's worst slum, the Old Nichol rookery. Nearly 6000 people lost their homes when the slum was cleared, with most having no choice but to rent similarly impoverished rooms further east. The rubble from the 730 demolished houses lies under the bandstand.

Take the third road on the left (Calvert Ave) and walk past ⓬ **St Leonard's Church** (built in the Palladian style in around 1740) to Shoreditch High St. Turn left and cross over to Rivington St.

Just past the railway bridge, look out for a wrought-iron gate on the right leading into ⓭ **Cargo** (p217). Just inside the gate, protected under perspex, there's a piece by famous graffiti artist Banksy picturing a security guard holding a poodle on a leash. Banksy's just one of many accomplished street artists to have left their mark on Shoreditch's streets – you'll spot plenty more as you continue along Rivington St.

At the end of Rivington, turn right onto Great Eastern St and then veer left onto traffic-clogged Old St. Believed to have had its origins as a Roman road, it remains a major route. Soon the distinctive arcs straddling the Old St Tube station will come into view.

SHOREDITCH COOL

The Shoreditch phenomenon began in the late 1990s, when creative types who had been chased out of the West End by prohibitive rents began taking over warehouses in what was then an urban wasteland, abandoned after the collapse of the fabrics industry. Within a few years the area was seriously cool, boasting oddball bars, clubs, galleries and restaurants that catered to the new media/creative/freelance squad.

Despite the general expectation that the Shoreditch scene would collapse under the weight of its own beards, the regenerated area is still flourishing, with new developments bringing life to some of London's poorest corners, spilling over into nearby Hackney and Bethnal Green.

Hoxton

SÔNG QUÊ VIETNAMESE £

Map p458 (020-7613 3222; www.songque.co.uk; 134 Kingsland Rd, E2; mains £8-11; noon-3pm & 5.30-11pm Mon-Fri, noon-11pm Sat, to 10.30pm Sun; Hoxton) A pillar of Kingsland Rd's 'Pho Mile', this no-frills, hospital-green Vietnamese joint has been feeding hungry local Vietnamese families and visitors from across London and beyond for almost 20 years. The food is spot on and excellent value; pick from two dozen types of fantastic pho and more that line the sticky menu pages.

GREEN PAPAYA VIETNAMESE, CHINESE £

Map p458 (020-7729 3657; www.green-papaya.com; 97 Kingsland Rd, E2; mains £7-10; noon-11pm Tue-Sat, to 10.30pm Sun; Hoxton) Green Papaya has stiff competition along Hoxton's 'Pho Mile', but if you can't decide where to stop, this spot offers the best of two worlds: both belly-warming Vietnamese and Xi'anese options line the menu. The crispy squid is a neighbourhood favourite, and the temptation to ditch the pho for hand-rolled Xi'anese noodles is strong – don't resist.

MEATMISSION BURGERS £

Map p458 (020-7739 8212; www.meatliquor.com/restaurant/meatmission; 15 Hoxton Market, N1; burgers £6-10; noon-midnight Mon-Sat, to 11pm Sun; Old St) Worship at this temple to the burger gods, somewhat sacrilegiously set in the former Hoxton Market Christian Mission and complete with stained-glass windows and a war memorial. Food is served on giant silver baking sheets below the watchful Masonic Eye of Providence painted on the ceiling. The Dead Hippie must be one of London's finest burgers.

Spitalfields

BOILER HOUSE FOOD HALL MARKET £

Map p458 (https://theboilerhouse.org/conscious-market; Old Truman Brewery, 152 Brick Lane, E1; dishes £5-12; 11am-6pm Sat & Sun; Shoreditch High St) More than 50 plant-based food stalls and ethical retail brands pitch up in the Old Truman Brewery's high-ceilinged boiler room at the weekend. Munch on the likes of cauliflower 'wings', vegan hot dogs, barbecue seitan brisket sandwiches, and 'tofish' and chips.

BEIGEL BAKE BAKERY £

Map p458 (071 729 0616; 159 Brick Lane, E1; filled bagels £1-5; 24hr; Shoreditch High St) This relic of the Jewish East End still does a brisk trade serving dirt-cheap homemade bagels (stuffed with smoked salmon and cream cheese, salt beef and pickles, or a handful of other fillings) to hungry shoppers and late-night boozers. There's a queue no matter the time of day or night, but the curt staff keep things moving.

GUNPOWDER INDIAN £

Map p458 (020-7426 0542; www.gunpowderlondon.com; 11 White's Row, E1; plates £5-15; noon-3pm & 5.30-10.30pm Mon-Sat; Liverpool St or Aldgate East) As you walk into this tiny Indian place, it's the aroma that hits you: the delicious tang of spices and incense. The punchy food is inspired by family recipes and home cooking: plates are small and designed for sharing. The flavours of each dish are divine, though not always suitable for the heat-fearing.

SOM SAA THAI ££

Map p458 (020-7324 7790; www.somsaa.com; 43a Commercial St, E1; dishes £8-19; 6-10.30pm Mon, noon-2.30pm & 6-10.30pm Tue-Sat; Aldgate East) So beloved is Som Saa that it successfully crowdfunded £700,000 to open its first permanent restaurant in this old fabric warehouse. The menu has expanded since its pop-up days but still has a laser-like focus on deliciously authentic curries, grilled meats, salads and stir-fries. Do as the other tables do and order the crowd favourite *nahm dtok pla thort* (whole deep-fried seabass).

POPPIE'S FISH & CHIPS ££

Map p458 (020-7247 0892; www.poppiesfishandchips.co.uk; 6-8 Hanbury St, E1; mains £12-17; 11am-11pm Mon-Sat, to 10.30pm Sun; Liverpool St) This glorious recreation of a 1950s East End chippy comes complete with wait-staff in pinnies and hairnets, and Blitz memorabilia. As well as the usual fishy suspects, it does old-time London staples – jellied eels and mushy peas – plus kid-pleasing, sweet-tooth desserts (sticky toffee pudding or apple pie with ice cream), and there's a wine list.

GALVIN LA CHAPELLE FRENCH £££

Map p458 (020-7299 0400; www.galvinrestaurants.com; 35 Spital Sq, E1; mains £32-43, 2-/3-course lunch or early dinner £39/43; noon-2.30pm & 6-10.30pm Mon-Sat, to 9.30pm Sun; Liverpool St) For lashings of la-di-da with an extra serve of ooh la la, you can't beat the incredibly grand surrounds of this soaring Victorian hall, inhabited by bow-tied and waistcoated waitstaff and very well-heeled guests. The Michelin-starred menu rises to the challenge, delivering traditional French cuisine with lots of contemporary embellishments. Early diners can take advantage of a good-value set menu.

★HAWKSMOOR SPITALFIELDS BRITISH£££

Map p458 (020-7426 4850; www.thehawksmoor.com; 157a Commercial St, E1; mains £15-60; noon-3pm & 5-10.30pm Mon-Fri, noon-10.30pm Sat, noon-9pm Sun; Shoreditch High St) You could easily miss Hawksmoor, discreetly signed and clad in black brick, but dedicated carnivores will find it worth seeking out. The dark wood and velvet curtains make for a handsome setting in which to gorge yourself on the best of British beef. The Sunday roasts (£22) are legendary, but it's *the* place in London to order a steak.

WRIGHT BROTHERS SEAFOOD £££

Map p458 (020-7324 7730; https://thewrightbrothers.co.uk; 8a Lamb St, E1; mains £19-65; noon-10.30pm Mon-Sat, to 9pm Sun; Liverpool St) For the Wright Brothers, the oyster is their world: they operate the Duchy of Cornwall oyster farm on Prince Charles' estate. This chic dining bar serves up freshly shucked shellfish, delicately constructed fish dishes and exquisite cocktails, all on the edge of Spitalfields Market.

DRINKING & NIGHTLIFE

Shoreditch is the torchbearer of London's nightlife: there are dozens of bars, clubs and pubs, open virtually every night of the week (and until the small hours at weekends) and it can get pretty rowdy. Clerkenwell is more sedate, featuring lovely historic pubs and fine cocktail bars. Spitalfields sits somewhere in between the two extremes and tends to be defined by its City clientele on week nights and market-goers on Saturday and Sunday.

Clerkenwell

★ZETTER TOWNHOUSE COCKTAIL LOUNGE COCKTAIL BAR

Map p458 (020-7324 4545; www.thezettertownhouse.com/clerkenwell/bar; 49-50 St John's Sq, EC1; 7am-midnight Sun-Wed, to 1am Thu-Sat; Farringdon) Behind an unassuming door on St John's Sq, this ground-floor bar is decorated with plush armchairs, stuffed animal heads and a legion of lamps. The cocktail list takes its theme from the area's distilling history – recipes of yesteryear plus homemade tinctures and cordials are used to create interesting and unusual tipples.

JERUSALEM TAVERN PUB

Map p458 (020-7490 4281; www.stpetersbrewery.co.uk; 55 Britton St, EC1; noon-11pm Mon-Fri; Farringdon) Housed in a building from 1720, this tiny, atmospheric pub covered in wood panelling, delft tiles and scuffed paintwork is the only London dispensary of the fantastic beers from St Peter's Brewery in Suffolk. Be warned: seating's limited and it's hugely popular. Arrive early to nab the raised 'pulpit' seats, but you'll likely be relegated to the overflow area in the street.

YE OLDE MITRE PUB

Map p458 (www.yeoldemitreholborn.co.uk; 1 Ely Ct, EC1; ⏲11am-11pm Mon-Fri; 📶; Ⓤ Farringdon) A delightfully cosy historic pub with an extensive beer selection, tucked away in a backstreet off Hatton Garden, Ye Olde Mitre was originally built in 1546 for the servants of Ely Palace. There's no music, so rooms echo only with amiable chit-chat. Queen Elizabeth I danced around the cherry tree by the bar, or so they say.

★FABRIC CLUB

Map p458 (☎020-7336 8898; www.fabriclondon.com; 77a Charterhouse St, EC1; ⏲11pm-7am Fri, to 8am Sat, to 5.30am Sun; Ⓤ Farringdon) The monarch of London's after-hours scene, Fabric is a huge subterranean rave cave housed in a converted meat cold store. Each room has its own sound system, which you'll really feel in Room One – it has a 'bodysonic' vibrating dance floor that's attached to 450 bass shakers, which emit low-end frequencies so the music radiates into your muscles just by standing there.

Following a temporary closure in 2016 because of drug-related deaths in the club, Fabric operates a very strict door policy (you must be aged over 19 and have a formal ID) and a zero-tolerance policy towards drug use. Searches are thorough.

Annoyingly, there's a £15 minimum if you're paying for drinks by card. Bring cash.

CAFÉ KICK BAR

Map p458 (☎020-7837 8077; www.cafekick.co.uk; 43 Exmouth Market, EC1; ⏲11am-11pm Mon-Thur, to midnight Fri & Sat, noon-10.30pm Sun; Ⓤ Farringdon or Angel) A bare-boards bar with a Continental European feel, where the action centres on a handful of foosball tables. The bar is big on any and all kinds of sport, which you can watch on one of the many screens.

BOUNCE BAR

Map p458 (www.bouncepingpong.com/farringdon; 121 Holborn, EC1; from £6 per person; ⏲11pm Mon & Tue, to midnight Wed, to 1am Thu, noon-1am Fri & Sat, noon-11pm Sun; Ⓤ Chancery Lane) This 1950s-themed basement cocktail bar in Holborn is the self-declared home of ping-pong, reputedly located in the exact spot the sport was invented. At one end there are 17 table tennis tables – including one from the 2012 London Olympics – and at the other an Italian restaurant.

★FOX & ANCHOR PUB

Map p458 (☎020-7250 1300; www.foxanddanchor.com; 115 Charterhouse St, EC1; ⏲7am-11pm Mon-Fri, from 8.30am Sat, from 11am Sun; 📶; Ⓤ Barbican) Behind the Fox & Anchor's wonderful 1898 art-nouveau facade is a stunning traditional Victorian boozer, one of the last remaining market pubs in London that's permitted to serve alcohol before 11am. Fully celebrating its proximity to Smithfield Market, the grub is gloriously meaty. Only the most voracious of carnivores should opt for the City Boy Breakfast (£19.50).

VINOTECA WINE BAR

Map p458 (☎020-7253 8786; www.vinoteca.co.uk; 7 St John St, EC1; ⏲noon-11pm Mon-Sat; 📶; Ⓤ Farringdon) Simple yet elegant oak decor, an astonishingly comprehensive wine list and amiable service make this a popular choice with suited City workers and local creatives. All wines are also available by the bottle at the on-site shop, and the food is good too.

🍷 Old Street

★NIGHTJAR COCKTAIL BAR

Map p458 (☎020-7253 4101; https://barnightjar.com; 129 City Rd, EC1V; music cover £5-8; ⏲6pm-1am Sun-Wed, to 2am Thu, to 3am Fri & Sat; Ⓤ Old St) Behind a nondescript, gold-knobbed door just north of the Old Street roundabout is this bona fide speakeasy, pouring award-winning libations from a four-section menu that delineates the evolution of the cocktail. Leather banquettes, brick-walled booths and art deco liquor cabinets stocked with vintage spirits set the perfect scene for jazz and blues acts that take the stage nightly at 9.30pm.

With an extensive spirits list, you can bet on a concoction for all tastes – and if nothing on the menu appeals, expert mixologists will whip up whatever suits you.

The overproof, tiki-inspired 'barrel-aged zombie', featuring four types of rum, absinthe, brandy, fresh pineapple juice and a booze-soaked cake-slice garnish, will send you stumbling out the door in one round – but Asian street food, served until 11pm, should help soak it all up. Service is seated only, so dress smart and book in advance.

GIBSON COCKTAIL BAR

Map p458 (020-7608 2774; www.thegibsonbar.london; 44 Old St, EC1; 5pm-1am Mon-Thur, to 2am Fri & Sat, 1-10.30pm Sun; Old St) Hope you packed your explorer's hat, because the Gibson will take you on an adventure. The cocktail menu hops through the calendar month by month, and you decide what season to visit. Perhaps some hemp oil and cannabis jelly to forget February, or flambéed pineapple skin or smoky mezcal and popping candy to heat up your summer?

The vessels are as wacky and wonderful as the ingredients. The space is teensy, so book a table in advance.

Hoxton

GLORY GAY & LESBIAN

Map p458 (020-7684 0794; www.theglory.co; 281 Kingsland Rd, E2; 5pm-midnight Mon-Thur, to 2am Fri & Sat, 1-11pm Sun; Haggerston) A charming cast has taken over this cosy corner pub, transforming it into one of London's most legendary queer cabaret venues. Order a Twink in Pink or a Schlong Island Iced Tea from the cocktail list and brace yourself for whatever wackiness is on offer. All genders welcome.

HAPPINESS FORGETS COCKTAIL BAR

Map p458 (www.happinessforgets.com; 8-9 Hoxton Sq, N1; 5-11pm; ; Old St) This low-lit, basement bar with good-value cocktails is relaxed and intimate, overseen by dapper-looking staff in white shirts and colourful suspenders. Look for the Petit Pois Bistro on the street level and take the stairs heading down. It's worth reserving, and you won't want to leave.

BRIDGE BAR

Map p458 (020-3489 2216; 15 Kingsland Rd, E2; noon-2.30am; Hoxton) It doesn't look like much from the outside, but shuffle into this eastern Mediterranean-style cafe-bar and you'll find an Aladdin's cave. Upstairs is particularly over the top. Hold court with a strong drink (coffee or spirits) and a slice of baklava.

RED LION PUB

Map p458 (www.redlionhoxton.co.uk; 41 Hoxton St, N1; noon-11pm; ; Old St) Just far enough from Hoxton Sq to avoid being overrun by weekend blow-ins, the Red Lion has a local-pub vibe – but given this is Hoxton, the locals are anything but typical. It's spread over four floors, but the roof terrace is the major draw.

Shoreditch

MIKKELLER BAR LONDON CRAFT BEER

Map p458 (https://mikkeller.com; 2-4 Hackney Rd, E2; noon-10.30pm Mon-Thur, to 11.30pm Fri & Sat, to 10pm Sun; Shoreditch High St or Old St) Legendary Danish microbrewery Mikkeller is known for its collaborations, but its latest is next level. Mikkeller's founder met musician Rick Astley on a previous brewing project, and the two have joined forces again to open Mikkeller's first UK bar. The pub unsurprisingly opts for a Scandi-chic interior, and lyrics from Astley's songs are enshrined in golden plaques on the tables and bar.

QUEEN OF HOXTON BAR

Map p458 (020-7422 0958; www.queenofhoxton.com; 1 Curtain Rd, EC2; 4pm-midnight Mon-Wed, to 2am Thu-Sat; ; Liverpool St) This industrial-chic bar has a games room, basement and varied music nights (including oddballs such as hip-hop karaoke and ukulele jamming sessions), but the real drawcard is the vast rooftop bar, decked out with flowers, fairy lights and even a wigwam. It has fantastic views across the city.

BLACK ROCK BAR

Map p458 (020-7247 4580; www.blackrock.bar; 9 Christopher St, EC2; 5pm-midnight Mon-Wed, to 1am Thu, to 2am Fri & Sat; Moorgate or Liverpool St) Whisky might not grow on trees, but at Black Rock, it sure grows in them. The centrepiece of this tiny bar is a 5m-long, 185-year-old oak tree that's been split in half and carved out to hold two rivers of whisky, which age as they're stored in the wood and are poured straight into your glass from taps at the end of the trunk.

SHOREDITCH GRIND COFFEE

Map p458 (☎020-7490 7490; www.grind.co.uk; 213 Old St, EC1; ⊙7am-11pm Mon-Thu, to 1am Fri & Sat, 9am-7pm Sun; 🛜; ⓤOld St) Housed in a striking little round building, this hip cafe serves top coffee, cooked breakfasts (until a decadent 5pm and all day on weekends), and then rustic pizzas and cocktails after dusk. Sit at a window and watch the hipsters go by.

BALLIE BALLERSON BAR

Map p458 (☎020-3950 2424; www.ballieballerson.com; 97-113 Curtain Rd, EC2; admission from £6, cocktails from £9; ⊙6-11pm Tue & Wed, to midnight Thu, to 2am Fri, noon-2am Sat, 2.30-11pm Sun; ⓤShoreditch High St) As its name subtly indicates, Ballie Ballerson is themed on balls. And alcohol, which comes in the form of cocktails. But back to the balls: there are two giant pits, full of the things, over one million apparently (we'll take their word for it), and an additional VIP pit, with golden balls, so you know you're special if you end up in there.

XOYO CLUB

Map p458 (☎020-7608 2878; www.xoyo.co.uk; 32-37 Cowper St, EC2; ⊙9.30pm-late Fri & Sat; ⓤOld St) This no-frills Shoreditch basement venue throws together a pulsing and popular mix of gigs and club nights. It hosts a rotating selection of resident DJs and a varied line-up of indie, hip-hop, electro, drum and bass 'n' dubstep artists. Tickets are sometimes available at the door, but it's better to check gigs online and book ahead.

SHOREDITCH SKY TERRACE BAR

Map p458 (☎020-3310 5555; www.shoreditch.courthouse-hotel.com; 335-337 Old St, EC1; ⊙4pm-midnight May-Oct; 🛜; ⓤOld St) Set atop the Grade II–listed Courthouse Hotel in the centre of Shoreditch, this rooftop bar has fantastic views of London's skyline. During the week it's a great spot for a date – the atmosphere is lively but tables are spaced far enough apart to ensure privacy. Come the weekend it's more of a party venue, as DJs take the stage.

BAR KICK BAR

Map p458 (☎020-7739 8700; www.cafekick.co.uk/bar-kick; 127 Shoreditch High St, E1; ⊙11am-11pm Mon-Wed, to midnight Thu-Sat, to 10.30pm Sun; 🛜; ⓤShoreditch High St) With its lively vibe, Kick is a fab place to watch big football games. The flag-adorned ground floor features four foosball tables, downstairs has leather sofas and simple tables and chairs, and there are spots on the pavement too. There's a generous happy hour from 4pm to 7pm.

OLD STREET RECORDS BAR

Map p458 (☎020-3006 5911; www.oldstreerecords.com; 350-354 Old St, EC1; ⊙8am-1am Mon-Wed, to 2am Thu-Sat, to 5pm Sun; ⓤOld St) This spacious music bar in the heart of Shoreditch has become an institution in the area. It has live performances six nights a week, ranging across jazz, soul, funk and rock. House-made pizzas are top-notch, and happy hour runs from 5pm to 8pm.

OLD BLUE LAST PUB

Map p458 (www.theoldbluelast.com; 38 Great Eastern St, EC2; ⊙noon-midnight Sun-Thu, to 1am Fri & Sat; 🛜; ⓤOld St) Frequently crammed with a hip teenage-and-up crowd, this scuffed corner pub's edgy credentials are courtesy of *Vice* magazine, the bad-boy rag that owns the place. It hosts some of the best Shoreditch parties and lots of live music.

CALLOOH CALLAY COCKTAIL BAR

Map p458 (☎020-7739 4781; www.calloohcallaybar.com; 65 Rivington St, EC2; ⊙6pm-1am; ⓤOld St, Shoreditch High St) Given it's inspired by *Jabberwocky,* Lewis Carroll's nonsensical poem, this bar's eccentric decor is to be expected, and the top-notch cocktails have placed it on the 'World's 50 Best Bars' list four times over. *Through the Looking Glass* isn't just the name of Carroll's novel here; try it yourself and see what happens.

Get friendly with the staff or apply for (free) membership to get into the private upstairs club called **JubJub**, a speakeasy within the speakeasy.

DREAMBAGS JAGUARSHOES BAR

Map p458 (☎020-7683 0912; www.jaguarshoes.com; 32-36 Kingsland Rd, E2; ⊙noon-1am Mon-Sat, to midnight Sun; 🛜; ⓤHoxton) The bar is named after the pre-existing signs on the two shops whose space it now occupies, a nonchalance that typifies Shoreditch chic. The street-level interior is filled with Formica-topped tables and hung with art. Downstairs there's a larger space where DJs hit the decks at weekends.

BOOK CLUB BAR

Map p458 (www.wearetbc.com; 100-106 Leonard St; ⌚8.30am-midnight Mon-Wed, to 2am Thu, to 3am Fri, 10am-3am Sat, 10am-midnight Sun Ⓤ Old Street) A creative vibe animates this fantastic one-time Victorian warehouse. Book Club hosts DJs and oddball events (neon naked life drawing, speed dating, 'Bedtime Stories for the End of the World' and the 'Crap Film Club') to complement the drinking and enthusiastic ping-pong and pool playing. Food is served throughout the day and there's a scruffy basement bar below.

BREWDOG SHOREDITCH CRAFT BEER

Map p458 (☎020-7729 8476; www.brewdog.com/bars/uk/shoreditch; 51 Bethnal Green Rd, E1; ⌚noon-midnight Mon-Thu & Sun, to 2am Fri & Sat, to 2am & Sat; 📶; Ⓤ Shoreditch High St) This small bar is a craft-beer aficionado's paradise, with BrewDog's usuals on tap, including Punk IPA and Dead Pony Club, plus some of the brewery's experimental suds and guest beers from around the world. If one of those doesn't suit, bottled options are stacked in a nearby fridge. Grab a seat in the plush booths downstairs that are seemingly forgotten by the masses.

CARGO CLUB

Map p458 (www.cargo-london.com; 83 Rivington St, EC2; ⌚noon-1am Sun-Wed, to 3am Thu & Fri, to midnight Sat; Ⓤ Shoreditch High St) Cargo has seen better days but still packs in a crowd several nights weekly. Under its brick railway arches, you'll find a dance floor and bar, and there's also an outside terrace with two stencil works by Banksy. Drinks can be insanely overpriced, and the cover charge at peak times is steep – know what you're getting into or be too drunk to care.

HORSE & GROOM PUB

Map p458 (www.thehorseandgroom.net; 28 Curtain Rd, EC2; ⌚11.30am-11pm Mon-Wed, to 2am Thu, to 4am Fri, 6pm-4am Sat; Ⓤ Shoreditch High St) Nicknamed the 'disco pub', this relaxed venue has two intimate spaces with hedonistic nights of house, funk, soul and, of course, disco. The site's had a long history in entertainment – under the women's toilets, archaeologists have found the remains of the theatre where Shakespeare premiered *Romeo and Juliet* and *Henry V*.

🍷 Spitalfields

★DISCOUNT SUIT COMPANY COCKTAIL BAR

Map p458 (☎020-7247 8755; www.discountsuitcompany.co.uk; 29a Wentworth St, E1; ⌚5pm-midnight Mon-Thu, 2pm-1am Fri & Sat, 5-11pm Sun; Ⓤ Aldgate East) Tucked away like a hidden seam, Discount Suit Company is one of the city's finest speakeasies – though on weekends you'll see that this closet-sized space is no secret. Superb, reasonably priced concoctions (a rarity in this area) are created behind the bar, originally a storeroom for the suit company above. Superfriendly staff and mixologists who'll happily go off-piste seal the deal.

Look for the 'City Wear' shop signs at the corner of Wentworth St and Bell Lane.

MAYOR OF SCAREDY CAT TOWN BAR

Map p458 (www.themayorofscaredycattown.com; 12-16 Artillery Lane, E1; ⌚5pm-midnight Mon-Thu, from 3pm Fri, from noon Sat, noon-10.30pm Sun; Ⓤ Liverpool St) This wood and brick secret basement bar is a refreshingly tongue-in-cheek alternative to a downstairs cocktail-bar scene that can take itself too seriously. Enter through the Smeg fridge door in the wall of the Breakfast Club cafe. Give the password (ask to see the Mayor of Scaredy Cat Town) and staff will let you in. Cocktails £9 to £11.

★COCKTAIL TRADING CO COCKTAIL BAR

Map p458 (☎020-7427 6097; www.thecocktailtradingco.co.uk; 68 Bethnal Green Rd, E1; ⌚5-11.30pm Mon-Wed, to midnight Thu & Fri, 2pm-midnight Sat, 2-10.30pm Sun; Ⓤ Shoreditch High St) In an area famous for its edgy, don't-give-a-damn attitude, this exquisite cocktail bar stands out for its classiness and cocktail confidence. The drinks are truly unrivalled, from flavours to presentation – bottles presented in envelopes, ice cubes as big as Rubik's Cubes and so on. The decor is reminiscent of a colonial-era gentlemen's club, just warmer and more welcoming.

NUDE ESPRESSO COFFEE

Map p458 (www.nudeespresso.com; 26 Hanbury St, E1; ⌚8am-5pm Mon-Fri, from 9.30am Sat & Sun; Ⓤ Shoreditch High St) This simply styled, cosy coffee shop serves top-notch brews that are roasted across the street. Along with the usual options, Nude has rotating single-origin coffees as well as slow-brew and espresso-based blends. Pair your beans with a sweet treat or full brunch (served until 2.30pm on weekdays and 3pm on weekends) to refuel while Brick Lane shopping.

GOLDEN HEART PUB

Map p458 (110 Commercial St, E1; 11am-midnight Sun-Wed, to 2am Thu-Sat; Shoreditch High St) It's a distinctly bohemian crowd that mixes in the cosy, traditional interior of this brilliant Spitalfields pub, famous as the watering hole for the cream of London's art crowd. The highlight of a visit is a chat with Sandra, the landlord-celebrity who talks to all comers and keeps things fun.

TEN BELLS PUB

Map p458 (www.tenbells.com; 84 Commercial St, E1; noon-midnight Sun-Wed, to 1am Thu-Sat; ; Shoreditch High St) This landmark Victorian pub with large windows and beautiful tiles is perfectly positioned for a pint after exploring Spitalfields Market. The most famous of London's Jack the Ripper pubs, it was patronised by his last victim before her grisly end, and possibly by the serial killer himself. Gin menu, pork scratchings and pie of the day offered.

93 FEET EAST BAR

Map p458 (www.93feeteast.co.uk; 150 Brick Lane, E1; 6-11pm Thu, to 1am Fri & Sat, 3-10.30pm Sun; Shoreditch High St) Part of the Old Truman Brewery complex (p207), this venue has a courtyard, two big rooms and an outdoor terrace that gets packed with a cool crowd on sunny afternoons. There are DJs and plenty of live music on offer.

ENTERTAINMENT

SADLER'S WELLS DANCE

Map p458 (020-7863 8000; www.sadlerswells.com; Rosebery Ave, EC1; Angel) A glittering modern venue that was first established in 1683, Sadler's Wells is the most eclectic modern-dance and ballet venue in town, with experimental dance shows of all genres and from all corners of the globe. The Lilian Baylis Studio stages smaller productions.

RICH MIX ARTS CENTRE

Map p458 (020-7613 7498; www.richmix.org.uk; 35-47 Bethnal Green Rd, E1; 9am-11pm Mon-Fri, from 10am Sat & Sun; Shoreditch High St) Founded in 2006 in a converted garment factory, this nonprofit cultural centre has a three-screen cinema, a bar and a theatre. Films shown run the gamut from mainstream to obscure film festivals, and the programming for performing arts is hugely eclectic, with anything from spoken word to live music and comedy. It's open every day except Christmas Day.

CAFÉ 1001 LIVE MUSIC

Map p458 (020-7247 6166; www.cafe1001.co.uk; 91 Brick Lane, E1; 6am-midnight; ; Liverpool St) A popular and huge cafe with grills and cakes, lounge seating during the day and a mix of events across two stages in the evenings (DJs, live music, open mic nights, spoken word etc). It gets packed at weekends.

SHOPPING

This is a top area for discovering cool boutiques and market stalls that showcase up-and-coming designers, not to mention endless vintage stores. There are tonnes of shops on and around Brick Lane, especially in burgeoning Cheshire St, Hanbury St and the Old Truman Brewery. Clerkenwell is mostly known for its jewellery and the work of its artisan craftspeople.

★**SUNDAY UPMARKET** MARKET

Map p458 (020-7770 6028; www.sundayupmarket.co.uk; Old Truman Brewery, 91 Brick Lane, E1; 11am-5.30pm Sat, 10am-6pm Sun; Shoreditch High St) The Sunday Upmarket (also open on Saturday) sprawls among the beautiful brick buildings of the Old Truman Brewery (p207), on both sides of Brick Lane between Hanbury and Buxton Sts. Vintage fiends, fashionistas and foodies will be occupied for hours – it's a buzzing place to while away a weekend (though it does get incredibly crowded).

Traders serve drool-inducing eats in the glass-sided building on the corner of Brick Lane and Hanbury St, above a huge vintage market. Bric-a-brac and fashion accessories are on show in the Tea Rooms (p220) and the Backyard Market (p220), and the Boiler House Food Hall (p212) is the icing on the cake, if you haven't already gotten your fill.

INSPITALFIELDS GIFTS & SOUVENIRS

Map p458 (020-7247 2477; www.inspitalfields.co.uk; Old Spitalfields Market, 13 Lamb St, E1; 10am-7pm; Aldgate East or Liverpool St) Here's the place to pick up that T-rex skull centrepiece or avocado-print wrapping paper you never knew you needed. InSpitalfields is spellbinding, and every item is bound to make you chuckle or at least stop and stare in wonder. You'll also find a good selection of non-tacky London-themed souvenirs.

★AIDA FASHION & ACCESSORIES

Map p458 (020-7739 2011; www.aidashoreditch.co.uk; 133 Shoreditch High St, E1; 10.30am-7pm Mon-Sat, noon-6pm Sun; Shoreditch High St) Brick walls, minimalist wood and metal fixtures, and pops of green from potted plants make this concept shop a delight to peruse. Indie brands abound in the form of menswear, womenswear, shoes and accessories, plus home goods, books, fragrances and skincare. Browsing's all the better with a coffee, juice or latte from the shop's **cafe** – spring for the signature rose.

ROUGH TRADE EAST MUSIC

Map p458 (020-7392 7788; www.roughtrade.com; Old Truman Brewery, 91 Brick Lane, E1; 9am-9pm Mon-Thu, to 8pm Fri, 10am-8pm Sat, 11am-7pm Sun; Shoreditch High St) It's no longer directly associated with the legendary record label (home to the Smiths, the Libertines and the Strokes, among others), but this huge record shop is still tops for picking up indie, soul, electronica and alternative music. In addition to an impressive selection of CDs and vinyl, it also dispenses coffee and stages gigs and artist signings.

★OLD SPITALFIELDS MARKET MARKET

Map p458 (www.oldspitalfieldsmarket.com; Commercial St, E1; 10am-8pm Mon-Fri, to 6pm Sat, to 5pm Sun; Liverpool St, Shoreditch High St or Aldgate East) Traders have been hawking their wares here since 1638, and it's still one of London's best markets. Sundays are the biggest days, but Thursdays are good for antiques, and crates of vinyl take over every other Friday. The market upped its foodie credentials with the **Kitchens**, 10 food counters that are the perfect antidote to the mostly bland chain restaurants on the market's periphery.

Big names from East London's street-food scene have taken up residence: don't miss the bao from **Yum Bun**, pastrami sandwiches from **Monty's Deli** or *shengjianbao* (pan-fried soup dumplings) from **Dumpling Shack**.

BRICK LANE VINTAGE MARKET VINTAGE

Map p458 (020-7770 6028; www.vintage-market.co.uk; Old Truman Brewery, 85 Brick Lane, E1; 11am-6pm Mon-Sat, from 10am Sun; Shoreditch High St) This basement fashion emporium is a sprawling sea of vintage threads from the 1920s to the 1990s, plus a few tucked-away stands of vinyl. Stalls are hired out and run individually, so be sure to pay before moving on to the next one. Shopping can get elbow-to-elbow busy at the weekend.

PAM PAM SHOES

Map p458 (020-3601 7860; https://pampamlondon.com; 129 Bethnal Green Rd, E2; 11am-6.30pm Mon-Wed & Fri, to 7pm Thu, noon-5pm Sun; Shoreditch High St) Ladies get their kicks at this female-run trainer boutique, which was the first in the UK to offer a women's-only selection of premium sneakers. In addition to limited edition pairs and special releases (announced on their social channels @pampamlondon), you'll find clothing, accessories, jewellery, beauty products and small homewares handpicked from local and global indie designers.

★LIBRERIA BOOKS

Map p458 (https://libreria.io; 65 Hanbury St, E1; 10am-6pm Tue & Wed, to 8pm Thu-Sat, 11am-6pm Sun; Aldgate East) Mismatched vintage reading lamps spotlight the floor-to-ceiling canary-yellow shelves at this delightful indie bookshop, where titles are arranged according to themes like 'wanderlust', 'enchantment for the disenchanted', and 'mothers, madonnas and whores'. Cleverly placed mirrors add to the labyrinthine wonder of the space, which is punctuated with mid-century furniture that invites repose and quiet contemplation.

Libreria is so invested in the transcendence of the physical page that mobile phones are banned, save for the quick photo snap – and it's the kind of place you'll definitely want to post on Instagram. It doubles as a cultural venue, with plenty of readings, lectures, social events and workshops – there's a risograph printer in the basement for those who care to get inky. Check the website for details.

ATIKA FASHION & ACCESSORIES

Map p458 (☎020-7377 0730; www.atikalondon.co.uk; 55-59 Hanbury St, E1; ⏰11am-7pm Mon-Sat, noon-6pm Sun; Ⓤ Aldgate East) One of the capital's biggest vintage clothing stores, Atika has more than 20,000 hand-selected items for men and women covering the last four decades. The eclectic selection includes anything from mainstream brands such as Nike to mid-century Japanese kimonos and American workwear like Carhartt. Up-and-coming labels also compete for space.

BACKYARD MARKET MARKET

Map p458 (☎020-7770 6028; www.backyardmarket.co.uk; Old Truman Brewery, 146 Brick Lane, E1; ⏰11am-6pm Sat, 10am-5pm Sun; Ⓤ Shoreditch High St) Turn past the smoky food stalls and the cavernous Tea Rooms to find the hidden-in-plain-sight Backyard Market.

Stalls selling clothes, jewellery and unique prints snake around this large section of brick warehouse, part of the Old Truman Brewery complex (p207). It's generally less crowded and chaotic than Brick Lane's other weekend markets.

TATTY DEVINE JEWELLERY

Map p458 (☎020-7739 9191; www.tattydevine.com; 236 Brick Lane, E2; ⏰10am-6pm Mon-Fri, from 11am Sat, to 5pm Sun; Ⓤ Shoreditch High St) Harriet Vine and Rosie Wolfenden design the witty laser-cut acrylic jewellery on sale in this small space. Their original creations feature flora- and fauna-inspired jewellery, as well as pieces sporting Day of the Dead–style skulls, gin bottles and glittery lightning bolts. Name necklaces (made to order in 30 minutes) are a treat. All pieces are handmade in the UK.

Tatty Divine has another branch on Monmouth St in Covent Garden.

TEA ROOMS MARKET

Map p458 (☎020-7770 6028; www.bricklanetearooms.co.uk; Old Truman Brewery, 146 Brick Lane, E1; ⏰11am-6pm Sat, 10am-5pm Sun; Ⓤ Shoreditch High St) Whether you're after retro maps, air plants in science-class-beaker terrariums, vintage special-occasion glassware or taxidermied birdlife, this warren of stalls should see you right. **Long & Short Coffee Roastery** has a cosy cafe in the back if you need a pick-me-up after a long bout of Brick Lane browsing.

SUPER MARKET SUNDAY

Head to the East End on a Sunday and it can feel as though you can't move for markets. Starting at Columbia Road Flower Market (p225) in East London and working your way south via Brick Lane and its Sunday Upmarket (p218) to Old Spitalfields Market (p219) makes for a colourful consumerist crawl.

COLLECTIF FASHION & ACCESSORIES

Map p458 (☎020-7650 7777; www.collectif.co.uk; 58 Commercial St, E1; ⏰10am-6pm; Ⓤ Aldgate East) If you love the feminine silhouette of the 1940s and the pin-up look of the 1950s, you will swoon over Collectif's vintage-inspired dresses, shirts, coats and accessories, with racks upon racks of eye-popping polka dots and bright patterns.

BOXPARK SHOPPING CENTRE

Map p458 (www.boxpark.co.uk/shoreditch; 2-10 Bethnal Green Rd, E1; ⏰8am-11pm Mon-Sat, 10am-10pm Sun; 📶; Ⓤ Shoreditch High St) The world's first pop-up mall, Boxpark is a shopping and street-food enclave made from upcycled shipping containers. Fashion, design and gift shops populate the ground floor; head to the upper level for restaurants, bars and a terrace. Opening hours vary by trader; retail outlets are required to close up shop by 6pm on Sunday, but food and bar venues stay open later.

MR START CLOTHING

Map p458 (http://mr-start.com; 40 Rivington St, EC2; ⏰10.30am-6.30pm Mon-Wed & Fri, to 7pm Thu, 11am-6pm Sat, noon-5pm Sun; Ⓤ Old St) This supremely elegant and cool menswear boutique is brought to you by fashion designer Philip Start. It offers casualwear as well as tailoring, all made with gorgeous textiles – think cashmere, merino, silk and the finest cottons.

BRICK LANE MARKET MARKET

Map p458 (☎020-7364 1717; www.visitbricklane.org; Brick Lane, E1; ⏰10am-5pm Sun;

Ⓤ Shoreditch High St) Every Sunday, the stretch of Brick Lane between Buxton St and Bethnal Green Rd is closed to traffic so stallholders can set up shop. Stands of fried dumplings and fresh fruit smoothies rub shoulders with tables of vintage cameras, vegan skincare products, tatty household bric-a-brac and secondhand clothes. Guitar-wielding buskers, hula-hoopers and working street artists give the area an almost festival-like atmosphere.

LABOUR & WAIT HOMEWARES

Map p458 (www.labourandwait.co.uk; 85 Redchurch St, E2; ⏲11am-6.30pm, to 6pm Sat & Sun; Ⓤ Shoreditch High St) Dedicated to simple and functional, yet scrumptiously stylish, traditional British and European homewares, Labour & Wait specialises in items by independent manufacturers who make their products the old-fashioned way.

Browse shaving soaps, enamel coffee pots, luxurious lambswool blankets, elegant ostrich-feather dusters and even kitchen sinks.

ACTIVITIES

★SHOREDITCH STREET ART TOURS WALKING

Map p458 (☎07834 088533; www.shoreditchstreetarttours.co.uk; tours start at Goat Statue, Brushfield St, E1; tours adult/child under 16yr £15/10; ⏲usually 10am or 1.30pm Fri-Sun; Ⓤ Liverpool St) The walls of Brick Lane and Shoreditch are an ever-changing open-air gallery of street art, moonlighting as the canvas for legends such as Banksy and Eine as well as more obscure artists. Passionate guide Dave, bored of his job in the City, once spent his lunch breaks roaming these streets, but he now helps translate the stunning pieces to a rapt audience.

Tours must be booked online, but you pay (cash only) in person at the start.

East London & Docklands

WAPPING | WHITECHAPEL | BETHNAL GREEN | DALSTON | HACKNEY | BOW & MILE END | LIMEHOUSE | ISLE OF DOGS | ROYAL VICTORIA DOCKS | LOWER LEA VALLEY | DE BEAUVOIR TOWN

Neighbourhood Top Five

❶ **Columbia Road Flower Market** (p225) Stopping to smell the roses amid the bedlam and barrow-boy banter of London's most fragrant market.

❷ **Broadway Market** (p242) Strolling along Regent's Canal, feasting from a market stall, perusing the stores and then staking a place at one of the pubs.

❸ **Whitechapel Gallery** (p226) Musing over edgy exhibitions at a gallery with a reputation for championing fresh new talent.

❹ **Museum of London Docklands** (p230) Discovering the city's maritime past amid the ultramodern tower blocks of the Isle of Dogs.

❺ **Trinity Buoy Wharf** (p229) Scoping out London's only lighthouse and the city's smallest museum at this waterside arts enclave.

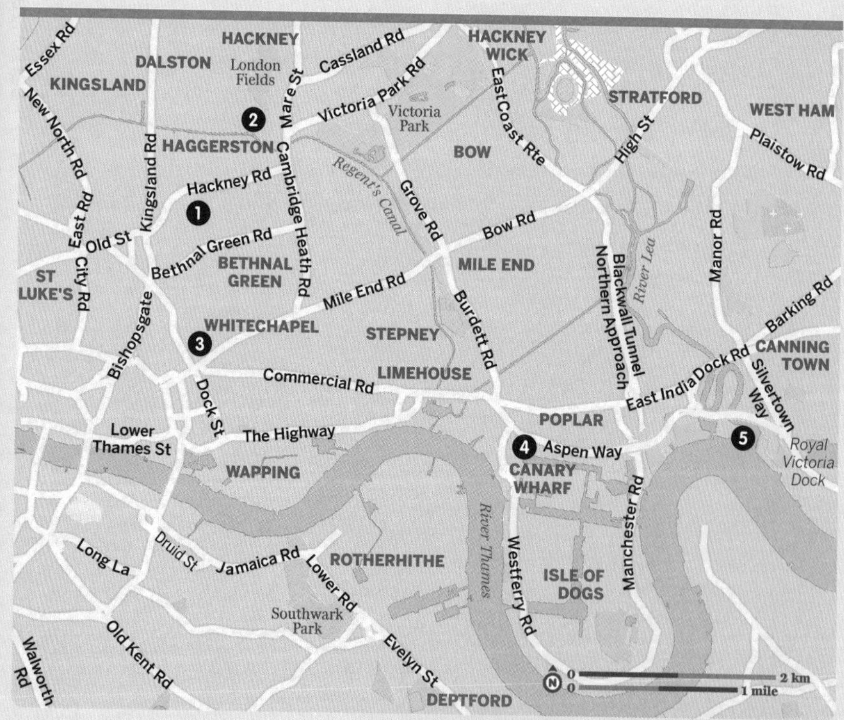

For more detail of this area see Map p462 and p464

Explore East London & Docklands

East London doesn't have what you might call blockbuster sights, and the main attractions are quite spread out. It includes the heart of the old East End (Whitechapel, Bethnal Green, Stepney, Mile End, Bow) and most of London's historic Docklands (Wapping, Limehouse, the Isle of Dogs, Royal Victoria Docks), along with gritty but hip Hackney and Dalston to the north, and Stratford further east.

Your best bet is to head to a sight that interests you and then spend some time exploring the surrounding neighbourhood before popping back on public transport to visit the next place. Time your visit to Bethnal Green for a Sunday so that you can experience the flower market. Save strolling around the cluster of sights at Queen Elizabeth Olympic Park for a sunny day.

Local Life

Picnics On sunny Saturdays, East Londoners of all stripes grab goodies from Broadway Market (p242) and head to London Fields (p227) for a picnic and a dip in the Lido.

Gallery With free admission and no permanent collection, there's always something new to check out at Whitechapel Gallery (p226).

One-stop shops Creatives camp out with laptops, socialise with friends, shop for records or flowers, and even indulge in a little self-care at multi-vendor Mare Street Market (p234).

Getting There & Away

Underground Three lines cut straight through the East End: the Central Line (stopping at Bethnal Green, Mile End and Stratford) and the conjoined District and Hammersmith & City Lines (Whitechapel, Mile End).

Overground Trains play a bigger part in the network here than they do in other parts of London, with three main lines and stops in Wapping, Whitechapel, Bethnal Green, London Fields, Dalston, Hackney, Hackney Wick and Stratford.

DLR Starting at Tower Gateway or Bank, the DLR provides a scenic link to Limehouse and the Isle of Dogs, as well as joining the dots with Stratford.

Bus The 277 bus (Highbury Corner to the Isle of Dogs) is handy for Victoria Park.

Lonely Planet's Top Tip

The most relaxed way to explore East London is along the water. Cyclists and pedestrians can drop down to Regent's Canal at the bottom of Broadway Market and follow the waterway to Limehouse. Branching east at Victoria Park, the Hertford Union Canal delivers you to Hackney Wick and Olympic Park. From Limehouse Basin you can also pick up the Thames Path and follow it to St Katharine Docks.

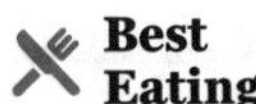

Best Eating

- Silo (p235)
- Berber & Q (p233)
- Barge East (p235)
- Temple of Seitan (p233)
- Bistrotheque (p231)

For reviews, see p230.

Best Drinking & Nightlife

- Netil360 (p238)
- High Water (p237)
- Satan's Whiskers (p237)
- Cat & Mutton (p240)
- Dove (p239)

For reviews, see p236.

Best Local History

- Museum of London Docklands (p230)
- Sutton House (p226)
- Ragged School Museum (p227)
- Hackney Museum (p227)
- House Mill (p230)

For reviews, see p226.

WORTH A DETOUR

CABLE STREET

Cutting a line between Wapping and Whitechapel, Cable St takes its name from the use of the length of the thoroughfare to twist hemp rope into ships' cables (similarly named, the shorter and narrower Twine Ct runs south from here). It's most famous for the Battle of Cable St (1936), in which the British fascist Oswald Mosley planned to march a bunch of his blackshirts into the area, supposedly as a celebration of the fourth anniversary of the British Union of Fascists. Although pockets of fascist supporters existed in the East End, the march was successfully repelled by local people – over 100,000 Jews, communists, dockers, trade unionists and other ordinary East Enders turned out in solidarity against them. At No 236 you'll find the old St George's Town Hall, its west wall completely covered in a large, vibrant mural commemorating the riots.

The church just behind this building is St George-in-the-East, built in 1729 by Nicholas Hawksmoor, and later damaged in the Blitz. The tower and exterior walls, enclosing a smaller modern core, are all that remains.

SIGHTS

Wapping

Once notorious for slave traders, drunk sailors and prostitutes, the towering early-19th-century warehouses of Wapping (pronounced 'whopping') still give an atmospheric picture of the area's previous existence.

Although there's nothing to actually mark it, down on the riverside below Wapping New Stairs (near the marine police station) was Execution Dock, where convicted pirates were hanged and their bodies chained in a gibbet at low tide, to be left until three tides had washed over their heads. Among the more famous people who died this way was Captain William Kidd, hanged here in 1701, and whose grisly tale you can read about in the nearby Captain Kidd pub (p236).

ST KATHARINE DOCKS HARBOUR

Map p462 (☎020-7264 5287; www.skdocks.co.uk; 50 St Katharine's Way, E1; Ⓤ Tower Hill) Sitting in the shadow of Tower Bridge, this once-booming part of London's Docklands was built in 1828 by engineer-extraordinaire Thomas Telford. To make way for it, 1250 'insanitary' houses were razed and 11,300 people made homeless. The dock was badly bombed during WWII and was finally abandoned altogether in 1968. Its current incarnation, as a marina for luxury yachts, surrounded by cafes, restaurants and twee shops, dates from the 1980s.

It's the perfect starting point for a stroll along the Thames Path to Wapping and Limehouse.

ST GEORGE-IN-THE-EAST CHURCH

Map p462 (☎020-7481 1345; www.stgeorgeintheeast.org; 16 Cannon St Rd, E1; Ⓤ DLR Shadwell) This church was erected by Nicholas Hawksmoor in 1729 and badly damaged in the Blitz. All that now remains is a shell enclosing a smaller modern core.

CABLE STREET MURAL PUBLIC ART

Map p462 (236 Cable St, E1; DLR Shadwell) Painted on the side of the former St George's Town Hall (now a library), this large mural commemorates the riots that took place here in October 1936, when the British fascist Oswald Mosley led a bunch of his blackshirt thugs into the area to intimidate the local Jewish population. They were repelled by local people – Jews and non-Jews alike.

Whitechapel

WHITECHAPEL ROAD STREET

Map p462 (E1; Ⓤ Whitechapel) The East End's main thoroughfare hums with a constant cacophony of Asian, African, European and Middle Eastern languages, its busy shops and market stalls selling everything from Indian snacks to Nigerian fabrics and Turkish jewellery, as the area's multitudinous ethnic groupings rub up against each other more or less comfortably. It's a bit chaotic, but heaving with life.

TRINITY GREEN ALMSHOUSES
HISTORIC BUILDING

Map p462 (Mile End Rd, E1; ⓤWhitechapel) These poorhouses were built for injured or retired sailors in 1695. The two rows of almshouses run at right angles away from the street, facing a village-type green and a chapel with a clock tower.

BLIND BEGGAR
HISTORIC BUILDING

Map p462 (337 Whitechapel Rd, E1; ⓤWhitechapel) William Booth, the founder of the Salvation Army, preached his first streetside sermon outside this pub in 1865. It's also famous as the place where notorious gangster Ronnie Kray shot and killed George Cornell in 1966 during a turf war over control of the East End's organised crime. Kray was jailed for life and died in 1995.

WILLIAM BOOTH STATUE
MONUMENT

Map p462 (Mile End Rd, E1; ⓤWhitechapel) A statue of the Salvation Army founder, erected near the place where he gave his first streetside sermon.

TOWER HOUSE
NOTABLE BUILDING

Map p462 (81 Fieldgate St, E1; ⓤWhitechapel) This enormous building, now redeveloped as an apartment block, was once a hostel and then a dosshouse. Past residents included Joseph Stalin and authors Jack London and George Orwell. The latter described it in detail in his *Down and Out in Paris and London* (1933).

EAST LONDON MOSQUE
MOSQUE

Map p462 (☎020-7650 3000; www.eastlondonmosque.org.uk; 46-92 Whitechapel Rd, E1; ⌚10am-11pm; ⓤWhitechapel) This large mosque is capped with a dome and one large and two smaller minarets, each topped with a crescent moon. The exterior is relatively unadorned except for some accents in blue tile. Unless you're coming to pray, visits should be pre-booked online.

⊙ Bethnal Green

★COLUMBIA ROAD FLOWER MARKET
MARKET

Map p462 (www.columbiaroad.info; Columbia Rd, E2; ⌚8am-3pm Sun; ⓤHoxton) A wonderful explosion of colour and life, this weekly market sells a beautiful array of flowers, pot plants, bulbs, seeds and everything you might need for the garden. It's a lot of fun and the best place to hear proper Cockney barrow-boy banter ('We got flowers cheap enough for ya muvver-in-law's grave' etc). It gets really packed, so go as early as you can, or later on when the vendors sell off cut flowers cheaply.

HACKNEY CITY FARM
FARM

Map p462 (www.hackneycityfarm.co.uk; 1a Goldsmiths Row, E2; ⌚10am-4.30pm Tue-Sun; ⓤHoxton) FREE If there's a less bucolic landscape than Hackney Rd, we can't imagine it. All the more reason to bring a slice of the country to kids who have only ever known eggs to have come from a supermarket. There are plenty of animals to pat and, after appropriate handwashing, a cafe serving homemade gelato.

⊙ Dalston

RIDLEY ROAD MARKET
MARKET

Map p462 (www.hackney.gov.uk/ridley-road-market; Ridley Rd, E8; ⌚9.30am-5pm Mon-Sat; ⓤDalston Kingsland) Massively popular with the ethnically diverse community it serves, this market is best for its exotic fruit and vegetables, whole fish and colourful fabrics. You'll also find the usual assortment of plastic tat, cheap clothing and joss sticks.

DALSTON EASTERN CURVE GARDEN
GARDENS

Map p462 (www.dalstongarden.org; 13 Dalston Lane, E8; ⌚11am-7pm Sun-Thu, to 10pm Fri & Sat; ⓤDalston Junction) FREE This garden is typical of the kind of grassroots regeneration happening around Dalston: a project led by the community, for the community – and a roaring success. There's a simple cafe and regular workshops and events, from gardening sessions to acoustic music. It's a nice green space in an otherwise urban precinct.

The site used to be a derelict railway line and old sleepers have been used to make a boardwalk and raised beds for the veggie patch. Sadly a question mark hangs over the garden's future as there are plans to redevelop the neighbouring shopping centre.

Hackney

SUTTON HOUSE HISTORIC BUILDING

Map p462 (NT; 020-8986 2264; www.nationaltrust.org.uk/sutton-house; 2-4 Homerton High St, E9; adult/child £8/4; noon-5pm Wed-Sun, daily Aug, closed Jan; Hackney Central) It would be quite possible to walk straight past this relatively inconspicuous brick house without noticing its great age. Originally known as Bryk Place, it was built in 1535 by Sir Ralph Sadleir, a prominent courtier of Henry VIII, when Hackney was still a village. Highlights include the Linenfold Parlour, where the Tudor oak panelling on the walls has been carved to resemble draped cloth; the panelled Great Chamber; the Victorian study; and the Georgian parlour.

Abandoned and taken over by squatters in the 1980s, Sutton House could have been lost to history. Enter the National Trust, which has set about conserving and preserving it – including some of the squatters' artwork upstairs. The house is also used by community groups for language classes and music therapy.

VIKTOR WYND MUSEUM OF CURIOSITIES, FINE ART & NATURAL HISTORY MUSEUM

Map p462 (020-7998 3617; www.thelasttuesdaysociety.org; 11 Mare St, E8; £8; noon-11pm Wed-Sat, to 10pm Sun; Bethnal Green) Museum? Art project? Cocktail bar? This is not a venue that's easily classifiable. Inspired by Victorian-era cabinets of curiosities, Wynd's wilfully eccentric collection includes stuffed birds, pickled genitals, two-headed lambs, shrunken heads, a key to the Garden of Eden, dodo bones, celebrity excrement and a gilded hippo skull that belonged to Pablo Escobar. A self-confessed 'incoherent vision of the world displayed through wonder'; make of it what you will. Or stop by for a cocktail at the bar upstairs (p240).

A subjective and thought-provoking collection, it's an admirable and frequently illuminating attempt to convey the wonder and horrors of the natural world. There are also exhibitions, lectures and taxidermy workshops. You must be over 21 to enter.

TOP EXPERIENCE
GET ARTY AT WHITECHAPEL GALLERY

A firm favourite of art students and the avant-garde cognoscenti, this ground-breaking gallery doesn't have a permanent collection but instead is devoted to hosting edgy exhibitions of contemporary art (only some of which are ticketed). It first opened the doors of its main art-nouveau building in 1901 and in 2009 it extended into the library next door, doubling its exhibition space to 10 galleries.

Founded by Victorian philanthropist Canon Samuel Barnett to bring art to the East End, the gallery made its name staging exhibitions by both established and emerging artists, including the first UK shows by Pablo Picasso (whose *Guernica* was exhibited here in 1939), Jackson Pollock, Mark Rothko, Frida Kahlo and Nan Goldin. British artists David Hockney and Gilbert & George also debuted here.

The gallery's ambitiously themed shows change every couple of months and there's often live music, poetry readings, talks and films on Thursday evenings. It also co-sponsors several awards, including the Max Mara Art Prize for UK-based female artists and the Jarman Awards for artists working with moving images.

DON'T MISS

- Rachel Whiteread's frieze of gilded leaves on the art-nouveau facade
- Bookshop

PRACTICALITIES

- Map p462, B5
- 020-7522 7888
- www.whitechapelgallery.org
- 77-82 Whitechapel High St, E1
- admission free
- 11am-6pm Tue, Wed & Fri-Sun, to 9pm Thu
- Aldgate East

ST AUGUSTINE'S TOWER CHURCH

Map p462 (020-8986 0029; www.hhbt.org.uk; Mare St, E8; Hackney Central) Set at the edge of the beautiful St John's Churchyard Gardens, this 13th-century tower is the oldest building in Hackney and the only remains of a church that was demolished in 1798. The tower's 135 steps can be climbed on occasional open days; see the website for details.

HACKNEY MUSEUM MUSEUM

Map p462 (020-8356 3500; www.hackney.gov.uk/museum; 1 Reading Lane, E8; 9.30am-5.30pm Tue, Wed, Fri & Sat, to 8pm Thu; Hackney Central) FREE Devoted to items relating to Hackneyites past and present, this interesting little museum is as diverse as the ethnically mixed community it serves. Most exhibits are everyday things used by everyday people, but more unusual items include a 1000-year-old Saxon log boat and a coin from the 'Hackney hoard'. This was one of 160 gold coins discovered in 2007 after being hidden by a Jewish family who moved to Hackney to escape the Nazis, only to die in the Blitz.

LONDON FIELDS PARK

Map p462 (Richmond Rd, E8; London Fields) A strip of green in an increasingly hip part of Hackney, London Fields is where locals hang out after a meander up Broadway Market (p242). The park also has two children's play areas, a decent pub and the London Fields Lido (p243).

Bow & Mile End

VICTORIA PARK PARK

Map p462 (www.towerhamlets.gov.uk/victoriapark; Grove Rd, E3; 7am-dusk; Hackney Wick) The 'Regent's Park of the East End', this 86-hectare leafy expanse of ornamental lakes, monuments, tennis courts, flower beds and lawns was opened in 1845. It was the first public park in the East End, given the go-ahead after a local MP presented Queen Victoria with a petition of 30,000 signatures. It quickly gained a reputation as the 'People's Park' when many rallies were held here.

On summer weekends it's busy with picnicking families, frolicking East Londoners, cyclists, joggers and skateboarding youths. Street food stalls, ice-cream vans and occasional music festivals also boost visitor numbers. Hertford Union Canal runs along the south perimeter and on to Hackney Wick.

MILE END PARK PARK

Map p462 (www.towerhamlets.gov.uk/mileendpark; Mile End) The 36-hectare Mile End Park is a long, narrow series of interconnected green spaces wedged between Burdett and Grove Rds and Regent's Canal. Landscaped to great effect during the millennium year, it incorporates a go-kart track, a skate park, an ecology area, a climbing wall and a sports stadium. The centrepiece, though, is architect Piers Gough's plant-covered Green Bridge linking the northern and southern sections of the park over busy Mile End Rd.

TOWER HAMLETS CEMETERY PARK CEMETERY

Map p462 (020-8983 1277; www.fothcp.org; Southern Grove, E3; Mile End) Opened in 1841 this 13-hectare cemetery was the last of the 'Magnificent Seven': suburban cemeteries (including Highgate and Abney Park) created by an act of Parliament in response to London's rapid population growth. Some 270,000 souls were laid to rest here until the cemetery was closed to burials in 1966 and turned into a park and local nature reserve in 2001. Today it's an eerily beautiful site, its crumbling Victorian monuments draped in ever-encroaching greenery.

RAGGED SCHOOL MUSEUM MUSEUM

Map p462 (020-8980 6405; www.raggedschoolmuseum.org.uk; 46-50 Copperfield Rd, E3; 10am-5pm Wed & Thu, 2-5pm 1st Sun of month; Mile End) FREE Both adults and children are inevitably charmed by this combination of mock Victorian schoolroom (with hard wooden benches and desks, slates, chalk, inkwells and abacuses), recreated East End kitchen and social-history museum. The school closed in 1908, but you can experience what it would have been like during its Sunday openings, when you can take part in a lesson. As a pupil you'll be taught reading, writing and 'rithmetic by a strict school ma'am in full Victorian regalia.

The museum celebrates the legacy of Dr Thomas Barnardo, who founded this school for destitute East End children in 1877. 'Ragged' refers to the pupils' usually torn, dirty and dishevelled clothes.

Sunday lessons take place at 2.15pm and 3.30pm (donations requested).

Limehouse

There isn't much to Limehouse, although it became the centre of London's Chinese community – its first Chinatown – after 300 sailors settled here in 1890. It gets a mention in Oscar Wilde's *The Picture of Dorian Gray* (1891), when the protagonist passes by this way in search of opium.

ST ANNE'S LIMEHOUSE CHURCH
Map p462 (020-7987 1502; www.stanneslimehouse.org; Commercial Rd, E14; services only; DLR Westferry) Nicholas Hawksmoor's earliest church (built 1714–27) still boasts the highest church clock in the city. In fact, the 60m-high tower was until recently a 'Trinity House mark' for navigation on the Thames, which is why it often flies the Royal Navy's white ensign.

Isle of Dogs

This odd protuberance on a loop in the Thames, made an island by various dock basins and canals, is completely dominated by the cluster of tower blocks at Canary Wharf, the centrepiece of which is One Canada Square. Londoners are divided on their opinion of this area – despite its perceived soullessness, its radical redevelopment is certainly impressive.

Etymologists are still out to lunch over the origin of the island's name. Some believe it relates to the royal kennels, which were located here during the reign of Henry VIII. Others maintain it's a corruption of the Flemish word *dijk* (dyke), recalling the Flemish engineers who shored up the area's muddy banks.

MUDCHUTE FARM
Map p464 (020-7515 5901; www.mudchute.org; Pier St, E14; 9am-5pm; ; DLR Mudchute) FREE Entering Mudchute Park from East Ferry Rd through the canopy of trees, you're greeted by the surprising sight of cows and sheep roaming in 13 grassy hectares of parkland. There are also pigs, goats, horses, llamas, alpacas, donkeys, ducks, turkeys, chickens…junior city slickers love this place! Looking back to the skyscrapers of Canary Wharf gives you a clear sense of the contrasts of this part of London. There's also a good cafe and a farm shop.

ONE CANADA SQUARE NOTABLE BUILDING
Map p464 (1 Canada Sq, E14; Canary Wharf) Cesar Pelli's pyramid-capped 235m-high skyscraper was built in 1991, and was the UK's tallest building when it opened – a title it held until 2010, when the Shard (p164) knocked it off its perch.

Royal Victoria Docks

EMIRATES AIR LINE CABLE CAR
Map p462 (www.emiratesairline.co.uk; 27 Western Gateway, E16; one way adult/child £4.50/2.30, with Oyster Card £3.50/1.70; 7am-9pm Mon-Thu, to 11pm Fri, 8am-11pm Sat, 9am-9pm Sun; Royal Victoria, North Greenwich) This cable car makes quick work of the journey from the Greenwich Peninsula to the Royal Docks. Although it's mostly patronised by tourists for the views over the river – and the views are good – it's also a listed part of the transport network, meaning you can pay with your Oyster Card and nab a discount while you're at it.

Capable of ferrying 2400 people per hour across the Thames in either direction. Sometimes closed in high wind.

BILLINGSGATE FISH MARKET MARKET
Map p464 (020-7987 1118; Trafalgar Way, E14; 4-8.30am Tue-Sat; DLR Blackwall) This wholesale fish market is open to the public, but you'll have to be up at the crack of dawn to see it in action. Formerly established in 1699 in the City between London Bridge and the Tower, the market moved to Poplar in 1982 and currently sells 25,000 tonnes of seafood annually.

Lower Lea Valley

From the mills of Cistercian monks in the 12th century to the Stratford railway hub of the 1880s (from which goods from the Thames were transported all over Britain), the tidal Lower Lea Valley had long been the source of what Londoners required to fuel their industries. However, before building work on the Queen Elizabeth Olympic Park began in 2008, this vast area of East London had become derelict, polluted and largely ignored.

TOP EXPERIENCE
SEE SCULPTURE AT TRINITY BUOY WHARF

As the site of London's only lighthouse, its smallest museum and the world's longest-running song, Trinity Buoy Wharf is an enclave of quirky superlatives, housing large-scale sculptures and immersive art installations.

The 1866 **lighthouse** was a training venue for prospective lighthouse keepers and a testing grounds for new technologies – scientist Michael Faraday even conducted experiments there. His legacy persists at **The Faraday Effect**, a museum housing a replica of his workshop.

Today, the lighthouse is more experiential than experimental. Composed of 234 Tibetan singing bowls, sound art display **Longplayer** is a haunting harmony devised to play for 1000 years. With a 31 December 2999 end date, the song may become history's longest.

The music doesn't stop there – **Lightship 95**, the apple red boat moored alongside the wharf, is a recording studio that's hosted the likes of Ed Sheeran, Lana Del Ray and George Ezra.

The wharf's historic structures juxtapose with modern, sustainable 'cargotecture': five shipping container buildings that house artists' studios and offices, plus the **Orchard Cafe**, adorned with a sculpture of a black cab sprouting a tree.

DON'T MISS...

- Longplayer
- The Faraday Effect
- Lightship 95
- Orchard Cafe

PRACTICALITIES

- Map p462, H6
- 020-7515 7153
- www.trinitybuoywharf.com
- 64 Orchard Pl, E14
- admission free
- 9am-5pm
- Canning Town

Creating world-class sporting facilities for the 2012 Olympic Games was at the forefront of this area's redevelopment, but this was well balanced with the aim of regenerating the area for generations to come. More than 30 new bridges were built to criss-cross the River Lea. Waterways in and around the park were upgraded, with waste cleared and contaminated soil cleaned on a massive scale.

★QUEEN ELIZABETH OLYMPIC PARK — PARK

Map p462 (www.queenelizabetholympicpark.co.uk; E20; Stratford) The glittering centrepiece of London's 2012 Olympic Games, this vast 227-hectare expanse includes the main Olympic venues as well as playgrounds, walking and cycling trails, gardens and a diverse mix of wetland, woodland, meadow and other wildlife habitats – an environmentally fertile legacy for the future. The main focal point is London Stadium (p230), now the home ground for West Ham United FC.

Other signature buildings include the London Aquatics Centre (p243), Lee Valley VeloPark (p243), ArcelorMittal Orbit and the Copper Box Arena (p241), a 7000-seat indoor venue for sports and concerts. There's also **Here East**, a vast 'digital campus' covering an area equivalent to 16 football fields. Development of the **East Bank**, a waterfront cultural and educational district, is in the works.

For a different perspective on the park, or if you're feeling lazy, take a tour through its waterways with Lee & Stort Boats (p243).

ARCELORMITTAL ORBIT — TOWER

Map p462 (0333 800 8099; www.arcelormittalorbit.com; 3 Thornton St, E20; adult/child £12.50/7.50, with slide £17.50/12.50; 11am-3pm Mon-Fri, 10am-7pm Sat & Sun; Stratford) Turner Prize–winner Anish Kapoor's 115m-high, twisted-steel sculpture towers strikingly over the southern end of Queen Elizabeth Olympic Park. In essence it's an artwork, but at the 80m mark it also offers an impressive panorama from a mirrored viewing platform, which is accessed by a lift from the base of the sculpture (the tallest in the UK). A dramatic tunnel slide running down the tower is the world's highest and longest, coiling 178m down to ground level.

Descend 4m (via a caged external staircase) from the platform for more vistas, interpretative screens and an outside section. From here, you can opt to skip down 455 steps to the ground (accompanied by soundscapes of London) or hop back in the lift. Alternatively, weave your way down on the superb tunnel slide (worth the extra £5, children must be over eight years old), which takes 40 seconds to get you back down. For further thrills, take a **free-fall abseil** off the tower (£85; book ahead; kids must be over 14).

HOUSE MILL
HISTORIC BUILDING

Map p462 (020-8980 4626; www.housemill.org.uk; Three Mill Lane, E3; adult/child £4/free; 11am-4pm Sun May-Oct, 1st Sun of month only Mar, Apr & Dec; Bromley-by-Bow) One of two remaining mills from a trio that once stood on this small island in the River Lea, House Mill (1776) operated as a sluice tidal mill, grinding grain for a nearby distillery until 1941. Tours, which run according to demand and last about 45 minutes, take visitors to all four floors of the mill and offer a fascinating look at traditional East End industry.

LONDON STADIUM
STADIUM

Map p462 (020-8522 6157; www.london-stadium.com; Queen Elizabeth Olympic Park, E20; tours adult/child £19/11; tours 10am-4.15pm Sun-Fri, to 4.45pm Sat; Pudding Mill Lane) Still known to most Londoners as the Olympic Stadium, this large sportsground is the main focal point of Queen Elizabeth Olympic Park (p229). It had a Games capacity of 80,000, which has been scaled back to 54,000 seats for its new role as the home ground for West Ham United FC. It's also used for athletics and other large sporting events and concerts. They offer match-day tours; when nothing's on, guided multimedia tours are available (book on the website before heading out).

EATING

East London's multiculturalism has ensured that its ethnic cuisine stretches far and wide, with some fantastic low-key eateries serving authentic and

TOP EXPERIENCE
EXPLORE THE DOCKLANDS MUSEUM

Housed in an 1802 warehouse, the Museum of Londn's Docklands combines artefacts and multimedia displays that chart the city's history through its river and docks. Begin on the 3rd floor in the introductory **No. 1 Warehouse** section and work your way down through the ages. The **Trade Expansion** gallery includes a reconstructed late-18th-century Legal Quay and an iron gibbet once used to display the bodies of executed pirates. The most illuminating and disturbing gallery is **London, Sugar & Slavery**, which examines the city's role in the transatlantic slave trade.

Highlights of the 2nd floor include **Sailortown**, a recreation of the cobbled streets, bars and lodging houses of a mid-19th-century dockside community. There are also fascinating displays about the docks during the world wars and their controversial transformation into London's second financial district during the 1980s.

There's lots for kids to enjoy, including the hands-on **Mudlarks** gallery, where children can tip the clipper, admire a block model of the docklands and try on old-fashioned diving helmets. The museum stages special exhibitions every few months, for which there is usually a charge.

DON'T MISS

- London, Sugar & Slavery
- Sailortown
- Docklands at War
- New Port New City

PRACTICALITIES

- Map p464, A1
- 020-7001 9844
- www.museumoflondon.org.uk/docklands
- West India Quay, E14
- admission free
- 10am-6pm
- DLR West India Quay

value-for-money fare. But the area's gentrification has introduced a slew of gastropubs and more upmarket restaurants, too. Excellent coffee shops have sprouted up all over the East End, though you can still find plenty of greasy-spoon caffs and places that serve a traditional pie with mash and liquor (parsley sauce). Places to head if you want to sniff out your own favourites include Columbia Rd, Broadway Market and the streets just to the north of Victoria Park.

Whitechapel

TAYYABS PUNJABI £

Map p462 (020-7247 6400; www.tayyabs.co.uk; 83-89 Fieldgate St, E1; mains £7-17; noon-11.30pm; ; Whitechapel) This buzzing (OK, crowded) Punjabi restaurant is in another league to its Brick Lane equivalents. *Seekh* kebabs (tandoor-cooked mince skewers), masala fish and other starters served on sizzling hot plates are delicious, as are accompaniments such as dhal, naan and raita. On the downside, it can be noisy, service can be haphazard and queues often snake out the door.

CAFÉ SPICE NAMASTÉ INDIAN ££

Map p462 (020-7488 9242; www.cafespice.co.uk; 16 Prescot St, E1; mains £7-27; noon-3pm & 6.15-10.30pm Mon-Fri, 6.30-10.30pm Sat; ; Tower Hill) TV chef Cyrus Todiwala has taken an old magistrates' court just a 10-minute walk from Tower Hill, decorated it in carnival colours and filled it with fragrant aromas. The Parsi and Goan menu is famous for its superlative *dhansaak* (lamb stew with rice and lentils), but the tandoori and vegetarian dishes are just as good.

Wapping

SMITH'S SEAFOOD £££

Map p462 (020-7488 3456; www.smithsrestaurants.com; 22 Wapping High St, E1; mains £18-50, 2-/3-course lunch £26.50/31.50, 3-course dinner £34.50; noon-4pm & 6-10.30pm Mon-Sat, noon-5.30pm Sun; Tower Hill) Thames views through floor-to-ceiling windows distract admirably from a slightly dated ambience, as do the wonderful dishes that progress from the kitchen. The menu is enormous and while seafood dominates, there are some meat and vegetarian dishes as well. Save room for the steamed pudding.

Bethnal Green

E PELLICCI CAFE £

Map p462 (020-7739 4873; www.epellicci.com; 332 Bethnal Green Rd, E2; dishes £2-14; 7am-4pm Mon-Sat; Bethnal Green) Opened in 1900, this diminutive Anglo-Italian caff captures the distilled essence of the old East End. Portions are generous and although the food's nothing special (fry-ups, pasta, sandwiches), the warm welcome and the banter from the gregarious staff and ragtag collection of local characters crammed around tightly packed tables make it well worth a visit.

GALLERY CAFE VEGETARIAN £

Map p462 (020-8980 2092; www.stmargaretshouse.org.uk; 21 Old Ford Rd, E2; mains £6-10; 8am-8pm; ; Bethnal Green) Set in the basement of a lovely Georgian building, this pretty cafe serves simple but delicious vegan and vegetarian fare to relaxed locals. Sadly the service can be just as relaxed. There's a cute courtyard at the front for sunny days. Check the website for sporadic evening events such as live music, comedy and film nights.

CORNER ROOM MODERN BRITISH ££

Map p462 (020-7871 0460; www.townhallhotel.com; Patriot Sq, E2; mains £14-26, 5-course dinner £39; noon-2.30pm & 6-9.45pm; Bethnal Green) Tucked away on the 1st floor of the Town Hall Hotel, this relaxed industrial-chic restaurant serves expertly crafted dishes with complex yet delicate flavours, highlighting the best of British seasonal produce, with a French touch.

BISTROTHEQUE MODERN BRITISH ££

Map p462 (020-8983 7900; www.bistrotheque.com; 23-27 Wadeson St, E2; mains £14-31, 3-course early dinner £25; 6-10.30pm Mon-Fri, 11am-4pm & 6-10.30pm Sat & Sun; Bethnal Green) This unmarked warehouse conversion ticks all the boxes of a contemporary upmarket London bistro (the name made more sense when there was a club-like cabaret space downstairs). The food and

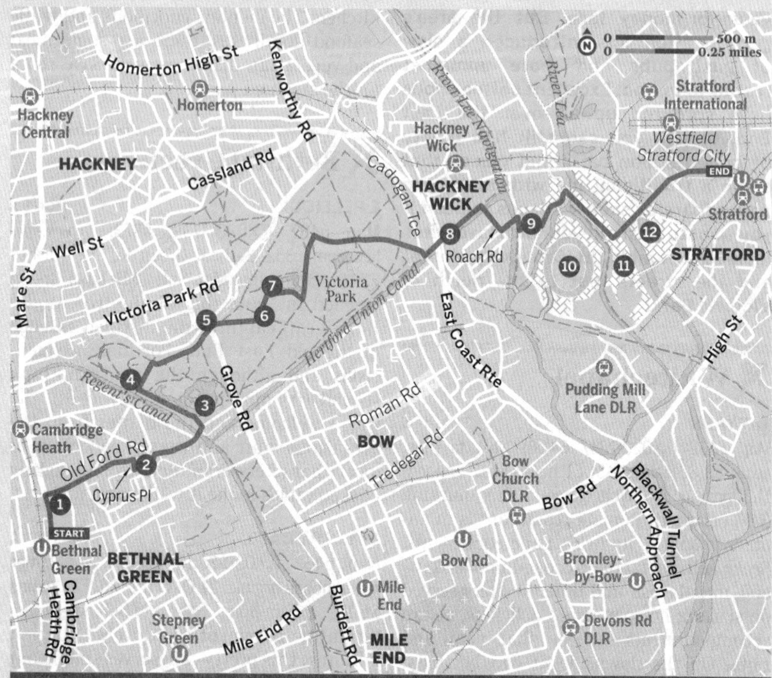

Neighbourhood Walk
East End Eras

START BETHNAL GREEN STATION
END STRATFORD STATION
LENGTH 3.6 MILES: 2½ HOURS

This route offers insight into the old and new of East London. Exit the Tube station towards the 1 **Museum of Childhood**; just past it, turn right onto Old Ford Rd and continue to Cyprus Pl and turn right. The area was heavily bombed during WWII and the many tower blocks were subsequently erected on the bomb sites. As you turn left onto beautifully preserved 2 **Cyprus Street** you'll get a taste of what Victorian Bethnal Green would have looked like. At the end of the street turn left then right, back onto Old Ford Rd. Just over Regent's Canal lies 3 **Victoria Park** (p227). Take the path on the left along the lake to the 4 **Dogs of Alciabiades** howling on plinths. Turn right here and then right again at the next gate. When you reach the wrought-iron gates, cross the road and enter the eastern section of the park near the 5 **Royal Inn** (p240). Veer right for a look at the neo-Gothic 6 **Burdett-Coutts Memorial**, a former public fountain that was a gift of Angela Burdett-Coutts, once the richest woman in England and a prominent philanthropist. From here, ramble past 7 **East Lake** to the park's eastern tip and exit via St Mark's Gate. Cross Cadogan Tce and join the much-graffitied 8 **canal path**. This area is Hackney Wick, home to a warren of warehouses and a community of artists. Cross the canal at the metal footbridge with the big hoop, continue onto Roach Rd and then turn left to cross the bridge and enter 9 **Queen Elizabeth Olympic Park** (p229). Keeping the main 10 **stadium** on your right, cross the River Lea and walk through the playground towards the tangled tentacles of the 11 **ArcelorMittal Orbit** (p229). Turn left, cross the bridge and examine the elegant curves of the 12 **London Aquatics Centre** (p243). From here you can either head straight on to Stratford Station or continue following the river north to explore the park's wetlands.

service are uniformly excellent. One of the best weekend brunch spots in Hackney.

BRAWN EUROPEAN ££

Map p462 (020-7729 5692; www.brawn.co; 49 Columbia Rd, E2; mains £14-22; 6-10.30pm Mon, from noon Tue-Thu, noon-11pm Fri & Sat; Hoxton) There's a French feel to this relaxed corner bistro, yet the menu wanders into Italian and Spanish territory as well. Dishes are seasonally driven and delicious, and there's an interesting selection of European wine on offer. Booking ahead is recommended.

LAXEIRO TAPAS ££

Map p462 (020-7729 1147; www.laxeiro.co.uk; 93 Columbia Rd, E2; tapas £7-17; 11am-3pm & 7-11pm Tue-Fri, 10am-4pm & 7-11pm Sat, 9am-4.30pm Sun; Hoxton) Regulars return to this stylish, family-run restaurant for the friendly service and authentic tapas – the barbecued pork shoulder is a sure-fire winner. The handful of more ambitious dishes includes large serves of paella to be shared. In summer there are tables outside on the picturesque street.

De Beauvoir Town

★BERBER & Q NORTH AFRICAN ££

Map p462 (020-7923 0829; www.berberandq.com; 338 Acton Mews, E8; mains £13-18; 6-11pm Tue-Fri, 11am-3pm & 6-11pm Sat & Sun; Haggerston) A mouth-watering barbecue smell greets you as you enter under the railway arches into this very cool Berber-style grill house. Lamb shawarma (kebab) is meltingly tender, while piquant treats include dukkah-crusted lamb nuggets, wood-roasted prawns with garlic confit, spiced beef *kofte*, and vegetarian-friendly shiitake-and-oyster mushroom kebab with porcini tahini.

Dalston

CHICK 'N' SOURS CHICKEN £

Map p462 (020-3620 8728; www.chicknsours.co.uk; 390 Kingsland Rd, E8; mains £9-11; 5.30-10pm Mon-Thu, noon-10.30pm Fri & Sat, noon-9pm Sun; Haggerston) It's a simple scenario but a goodie: fried free-range chicken and sours served in a hip little place with crazy tiling, patterned lino and a big red neon sign. Serves are substantial and come with a variety of sauces and on-trend extras such as pickled watermelon. Crispy Szechuan aubergine is a zingy way to start, washed down with a gin sour.

L'ATELIER CAFE £

Map p462 (020-7254 3238; www.facebook.com/LatelierDalston; 31 Stoke Newington Rd, N16; mains £4-9; 8am-4pm Mon & Tue, to 5pm Wed-Fri, 9am-5pm Sat & Sun; Dalston Kingsland) L'Atelier sports the kitsch/vintage decor that is standard in N16 – mismatched furniture, retro posters, fresh flowers at every table – with French music and the smell of espresso coffee for added ambience. It's a lovely spot to grab an all-day breakfast, salad or open sandwich and a cup of something.

MANGAL OCAKBASI TURKISH ££

Map p462 (020-7275 8981; www.mangal1.com; 10 Arcola St, E8; mains £8-15; noon-midnight Sun-Thu, to 1am Fri & Sat; Dalston Kingsland) Mangal is the quintessential Turkish *ocakbasi* (open-hooded charcoal grill, the mother of all barbecues): brightly lit, smoky and serving superb mezze, grilled vegetables, lamb chops, quail and a lip-smacking assortment of kebabs. Serves are massive. BYO alcohol. This is the original Mangal but some argue that Mangal 2, just around the corner on Stoke Newington Rd, has more atmosphere.

Hackney

★TEMPLE OF SEITAN VEGAN £

Map p462 (http://templeofseitan.co.uk; 5 Morning Lane, E9; mains £6-8; noon-9pm Mon-Sat, to 6pm Sun; Hackney Central) Vegans, hail seitan – devilishly good meat-free alternatives are cleverly composed into belt-busting fried Chick'n at this Hackney hole-in-the-wall. Pick from burgers, wraps, popcorn bites or sloppily sauced wings. The focus is on fake fowl, but there are a few beef-esque picks (go for BBQ bacon burger). Add the mac and cheese and a salted caramel milkshake for the perfect sin.

Seating is limited, save for a few window-side stools. There's a second, larger location in Camden at 103a Camley St, where you can gorge alfresco.

CANARY WHARF DEVELOPMENT

You'd probably never guess it while gazing up at the skyscrapers that dominate Canary Wharf, but from the 16th century until the mid-20th century, this area was the centre of the world's greatest port, making it the hub of the British Empire and its enormous global trade. At the docks here, cargo was landed from around the world, bringing jobs to a tight-knit working-class community. Even up to the start of WWII this community still thrived, but that all changed when the docks were badly firebombed during the Blitz.

After the war the docks were in no condition to cope with the postwar technological and political changes as the British Empire evaporated. At the same time enormous new bulk carriers and container ships demanded deep-water ports and new loading and unloading techniques. From the mid-1960s, dock closures followed one another as fast as they had opened, and the number of dock workers dropped from as many as 50,000 in 1960 to about 3000 by 1980.

The financial district that exists at Canary Wharf today was begun by the London Docklands Development Corporation, a body established by the Thatcher Government in the freewheeling 1980s to take pressure for office space off the City. This rather artificial enclave had a shaky start. The low-rise toytown buildings had trouble attracting tenants, the Docklands Light Railway – the main transport link – had teething troubles, and the landmark One Canary Wharf tower had to be rescued from bankruptcy twice. Now, however, the place swarms during the working week with dark-suited office workers en route to their desks in the sky.

CLIMPSON & SONS CAFE £

Map p462 (www.climpsonandsons.com; 67 Broadway Market, E8; dishes £4-8; ⏲7.30am-5pm, from 8.30am Sat, from 9am Sun; ⓊLondon Fields) Small and sparsely furnished, this deservedly popular cafe has assumed the name of the butcher that once stood here. The coffee is superb – it roasts its own just around the corner – and it also does a fine line in breakfasts, sandwiches, salads and pastries.

MARE STREET MARKET INTERNATIONAL £

Map p462 (☎020-3745 2470; http://marestreetmarket.com; 117 Mare St, E8; mains £5-14; ⏲8am-11pm Mon, to midnight Tue-Thu, to 1am Fri, 9am-1am Sat, 9am-11pm Sun; ⓊLondon Fields) The darlings of Hackney commune at this multi-use market, which sees creatives tapping away on laptops by day and hip young things sipping craft cocktails by night. An open kitchen area serves breakfast, Italian-inspired bites, sourdough pizzas and Sunday roasts; there's an adjacent dining room that doubles as an antiques showroom, offering table service and the same menu.

Several other vendors take up shop in the market – there's a deli, wine bar, bottle shop, florist, record store, barber and coffee shop, plus a pop-up space with short-term tenants like a vegan nail salon. Hours vary across outfitters; check the website for details.

RANDY'S WING BAR AMERICAN £

Map p462 (☎020-8555 5971; www.randyswingbar.co.uk; 28 East Bay Lane, E20; mains £7-10; ⏲noon-11pm Mon-Sat, to 8pm Sun; 👪; ⓊHackney Wick) What began life as a street-food cart has developed into a fully fledged restaurant, and happily the flavours have been unaffected by the presence of a roof. Unsurprisingly, chicken wings are the signature dish, with six varieties on offer, from Indian and Korean to good ole American. There are also three similarly multicultural burgers.

GREEN PAPAYA VIETNAMESE, CHINESE £

Map p462 (☎020-8985 5486; www.greenpapaya.com; 191 Mare St, E8; mains £8-14; ⏲noon-3pm & 5-11pm Tue-Fri, 1-10.30pm Sat & Sun; 🌶; ⓊLondon Fields) This neighbourhood restaurant differentiates itself from the great mass of East London Vietnamese joints by incorporating hand-pulled noodle and lamb dishes from Xi'an in central China. The Vietnamese side of the menu is particularly strong on seafood dishes.

LITTLE GEORGIA GEORGIAN £

Map p462 (☎020-7739 8154; https://littlegeorgia.co.uk; 87 Goldsmith's Row, E2; brunch dishes £6-9.50, mains £12-15; ⏲6.30-11pm Tue-Fri, from 11am Sat & Sun; Ⓤ Hoxton) A charming slice of the Caucasus in East London, this cosy eatery is a good introduction to the cuisine of Georgia. During the day it serves cooked breakfasts and a delicious range of salads and sandwiches.

BEST TURKISH KEBAB KEBAB £

(www.thebestturkishkebab.com; 125 Stoke Newington Rd, N16; lamb doner/burger £5.50/3.50; ⏲noon-2am; Ⓤ Rectory Rd) This friendly, family-run kebab shop has been serving up superlatively good doners for more than three decades and shows no signs of slowing down. As well as the usual chicken and lamb options, you can grab a king-size burger for just £3.50, and there are also vegetarian choices.

★BARGE EAST BRITISH ££

Map p462 (☎020-3026 2807; www.bargeeast.com; River Lee, Sweetwater Mooring, White Post Lane, E9; small plates £7-8.50, mains £14-19; ⏲5-11pm Mon-Thu, noon-11.30pm Fri, 10am-10.30pm Sat, 11am-10.30pm Sun; Ⓤ Hackney Wick) Moored along the River Lee in Hackney Wick is the *De Hoop*, a 100-tonne barge that sailed from Holland to offer seasonal fare and delicious drinks with waterside views. Small plates like nduja Scotch eggs with black garlic or large dishes of Szechuan aubergine with cashew cream wash down splendidly with cocktails like the Earl Grey–based East London iced tea.

The 114-year-old vessel is a great weekend pick, with a two-plate bottomless Bloody Mary brunch (£39) and fine Sunday roasts (two/three courses £23/29). There's plenty of alfresco seating on the bank, plus regular live music – check the website for dates.

FORMANS BRITISH ££

Map p462 (☎020-8525 2365; www.formans.co.uk/restaurant; Stour Rd, E3; brunch £6-10, mains £15-24; ⏲7-11pm Thu & Fri, 10am-3pm & 7-11pm Sat, noon-5pm Sun; 📶; Ⓤ Hackney Wick) Curing fish since 1905, riverside Formans boasts prime views over the River Lea and the Olympic Stadium. The menu includes a delectable choice of smoked salmon (including its signature 'London cure'), plenty of other seafood and a few nonfishy options. There's a great selection of British wines and spirits too.

LARDO ITALIAN ££

Map p462 (☎020-8985 2683; www.lardo.co.uk; 197-201 Richmond Rd, E8; mains £9-17; ⏲11am-10.30pm Mon-Sat, to 9.30pm Sun; Ⓤ Hackney Central) A simple, one-room affair that celebrates *lardo* – the cured back fat of rare-breed pigs scented with aromatic herbs. You'll find it on excellent pizzas and among the antipasti. A couple of pasta and main dishes round out the menu.

★SILO BRITISH £££

Map p462 (☎020-7993 8155; https://silolondon.com; Unit 7, Queen's Yard, E9; 6-course tasting menu £50, brunch dishes £7.50-11.50; ⏲6-10pm Tue-Fri, 11am-3pm & 6-10pm Sat, 11am-3pm Sun; Ⓤ Hackney Wick) 🌿 Brighton's Silo, the world's first zero-waste restaurant, has moved to Hackney Wick. Here, trailblazing chef Doug McMaster fashions lesser-loved ingredients and wonky produce into the likes of beetroot prune with egg-yolk fudge or Jerusalem artichoke in brown butter. The canalside space – where everything down to the lampshades is upcycled – is as gorgeous as the dishes on the ever-changing menu.

Naturally, Silo's sustainability philosophy carries over to liquid offerings – biodynamic, zero-sulphite wines are sourced from artisanal producers, and the restaurant even ferments their own booze-less brews from leftover ingredients. A cocktail flight pairing with dinner is available for £50.

On weekends, dishes like multigrain porridge with sourdough miso caramel or slow-roasted mushrooms with hemp crème fraiche are excellent value, making your brunch habit plenty sustainable, too.

Bow & Mile End

TOWPATH CAFE £

Map p462 (☎020-7254 7606; rear 42-44 De Beauvoir Cres, N1; mains £8-11; ⏲9am-5pm Tue & Wed, to 9.30pm Thu-Sun; Ⓤ Haggerston) Occupying four small units facing Regent's Canal towpath, this simple cafe is a super place to sit in the sun and watch the ducks and narrow boats glide by. The coffee and food are excellent, with delicious cookies and brownies on the counter and cooked dishes chalked up on the blackboard daily.

EMPRESS MODERN BRITISH ££

Map p462 (☎020-8533 5123; www.empresse9.co.uk; 130 Lauriston Rd, E9; mains £13-29; ⏲6-10.15pm Mon, noon-3pm & 6-10.15pm Tue-Sat, noon-9.30pm Sun; 🚌277) This upmarket pub conversion belts out delicious Modern British cuisine in very pleasant surroundings. On Mondays there's a £11 main-plus-drink supper deal and on weekends it serves an excellent brunch.

Isle of Dogs

THE GUN BRITISH ££

Map p464 (020-7515 5222; www.thegundocklands.com; 27 Coldharbour, E14; mains £14-27; 11.30am-midnight; ; Canary Wharf) Set at the end of a residential street that somehow survived the Blitz, this early-18th-century riverside pub has been seriously dolled up, but still manages to ooze history. It's claimed that Lord Nelson had secret assignations with Lady Emma Hamilton here (hence the names on the toilet doors). The menu's excellent, focusing on British meats, especially game.

PLATEAU FRENCH ££

Map p464 (020-7715 7100; www.plateau-restaurant.co.uk; L4 Canada Pl, E14; mains £18-32; 11.30am-10.30pm Mon-Sat; ; Canary Wharf) Occupying a squat glass box right in the centre of the Canary Wharf business district, Plateau's Eero Saarinen tulip chairs fill up with tower-block escapees at lunchtime, making the most of the excellent menu and park views. Options include tasty soups, roasted game meats and perfectly cooked fish dishes.

DRINKING & NIGHTLIFE

The locus of London cool continues in its relentless march east, from Soho in the 1960s to Shoreditch in the 1990s, and now to Dalston, Hackney and Hackney Wick. Dalston has the liveliest strip, but there are also great venues scattered around warehouses in the vicinity of Hackney's Mare St and along the canals in Hackney Wick. Head to Broadway Market, Columbia Rd or Whitechapel for rejuvenated historic pubs.

Wapping

PROSPECT OF WHITBY PUB

Map p462 (020-7481 1095; www.greeneking-pubs.co.uk; 57 Wapping Wall, E1; noon-11pm Mon-Thu, 11am-midnight Fri & Sat, noon-10.30pm Sun; ; Wapping) Once known as the Devil's Tavern due to its unsavoury clientele, the Prospect first opened its doors in 1520, although the only part of the original pub remaining is the flagstone floor. Famous patrons have included Charles Dickens and Samuel Pepys. There's a smallish terrace overlooking the Thames, a restaurant upstairs, open fires in winter and a pewter-topped bar.

TOWN OF RAMSGATE PUB

Map p462 (020-7481 8000; www.townoframsgate.pub; 62 Wapping High St, E1; noon-

COCKNEY RHYMING SLANG

Traditionally cockneys were people born within earshot of the Bow Bells – the church bells of St Mary-le-Bow (p149) on Cheapside. Since few people actually live in the City these days, this definition has broadened to take in those living further east. The term cockney is often used to describe anyone speaking what is also called Estuary English (in which 't' and 'h' are routinely dropped and glottal stops – what the two 't's sound like in 'bottle' – abound).

True cockney speech also uses something called rhyming slang, which may have developed among London's costermongers (street traders) and criminals as a code to avoid police attention. This code replaced common nouns and verbs with rhyming phrases. So 'going up the apples and pears' meant going up the stairs, the 'trouble and strife' was the wife, 'telling porky pies' was telling lies and 'would you Adam and Eve it?' was 'would you believe it?' Over time the second of the two words tended to be dropped so the rhyme vanished.

Few, if any, people still use pure cockney but a good many still understand it. You're more likely to come across it in residual phrases such as 'telling porkies' (lying), 'use your loaf' ('loaf of bread' for head), 'ooh, me plates' ('plates of meat' for feet) or 'me old china' ('china plate' for mate).

11pm Sun-Wed, to midnight Thu-Sat; 📶; ⓊWapping) This ancient pub was built in 1545 on the site of an older watering hole, the Hostel, which served ale during the Wars of the Roses. Its historic ambience is complemented by river views and healthy servings of food from its carvery.

CAPTAIN KIDD PUB

Map p462 (☎020-7480 5759; 108 Wapping High St, E1; ⏰noon-11pm; 📶; ⓊWapping) With its large windows, fine beer garden and displays recalling the hanging nearby of the eponymous pirate in 1701, this is a favourite riverside pub. Although it inhabits a 17th-century building, the pub itself only dates from the 1980s. It stocks a good range of Samuel Smith craft beer from Yorkshire.

Whitechapel

CULPEPER PUB

Map p458 (☎020-7247 5371; www.theculpeper.com; 40 Commercial St, E1; ⏰11am-midnight Mon-Thu, to 2am Fri & Sat, to 11pm Sun; ⓊAldgate East) Stripped back to bare bricks and smartened up with potted plants and industrial light fixtures, this corner pub serves an interesting selection of wine, beer and cocktails to a fashionable young crowd. The highlight is the rooftop greenhouse and terrace bar (summer only).

Bethnal Green

★SATAN'S WHISKERS COCKTAIL BAR

Map p462 (☎020-7739 8362; www.satanswhiskers.com; 343 Cambridge Heath Rd, E2; ⏰5pm-midnight; ⓊBethnal Green) Small neon red lettering is the only sign that you're about to enter a world-class cocktail bar. With an ever-changing drinks menu, snug booths, crazy taxidermy and a killer soundtrack, it's a memorable stop on an East London bar hop.

CARPENTER'S ARMS PUB

Map p462 (☎020-7739 6342; www.carpentersarmsfreehouse.com; 73 Cheshire St, E2; ⏰4-11.30pm Mon-Thu, noon-midnight Fri & Sat, noon-10.30pm Sun; 📶; ⓊShoreditch High St) Once owned by infamous gangsters the Kray brothers (who bought it for their old ma to run), this chic yet cosy pub has been beautifully restored and its many wooden surfaces positively gleam. A back room and small yard provide a little more space for the convivial drinkers. There's a huge range of draught and bottled beers and ciders.

ROYAL OAK PUB

Map p462 (☎020-7729 2220; www.royaloaklondon.com; 73 Columbia Rd, E2; ⏰6.30-10pm Mon-Fri, from noon Sat, noon-4pm & 5-9pm Sun; ⓊHoxton) This lovely wood-panelled pub really hits its stride on Sundays when London's famous flower market (p225) is just outside the door. There's a handsome central bar with a better-than-average wine list, plus a little garden at the back.

SAGER + WILDE WINE BAR

Map p462 (☎020-8127 7330; www.sagerandwilde.com; 193 Hackney Rd, E2; ⏰5pm-midnight Mon-Wed, to 1am Thu & Fri, noon-1am Sat, noon-midnight Sun; 📶; ⓊHoxton) A handsome addition to the East End drinking scene, this quietly stylish wine bar offers a modish bar-bites menu, an eye-catching glass-brick bar counter, and excellent wines by the bottle and glass. There are a few outdoor tables for street-side sipping.

BETHNAL GREEN WORKING MEN'S CLUB CLUB

Map p462 (☎020-7739 7170; www.workersplaytime.net; 42-44 Pollard Row, E2; ⏰pub 6pm-late Wed-Sat, club hours vary; ⓊBethnal Green) As it says on the tin, this is a true working men's club. Except that this one has opened its doors and let in all kinds of off-the-wall club nights, including trashy burlesque, LGBTIQ+ shindigs, retro nights, beach parties and bake-offs. Expect sticky carpets, a shimmery stage set and a space akin to a school-hall disco.

Dalston

★HIGH WATER COCKTAIL BAR

Map p462 (☎020-7241 1984; www.highwaterlondon.com; 23 Stoke Newington Rd, N16; ⏰4.30pm-2am Mon-Thu, 3.30pm-3am Fri & Sat, 3.30pm-2am Sun; ⓊDalston Kingsland) Table service is offered at this narrow, brick-walled bar – but if you like to indulge in conversations with complete strangers, we suggest grabbing a seat at the bar. That way you can interrogate the charming staff about what corners of their largely self-devised cocktail list will best cater to your taste, and then watch them concoct it.

DALSTON SUPERSTORE GAY & LESBIAN

Map p462 (020-7254 2273; www.dalstonsuperstore.com; 117 Kingsland High St, E8; 5pm-2am Mon, noon-2am Tue-Fri, noon-3am Sat, 10am-2am Sun; Dalston Kingsland) Bar, club or diner? Gay, lesbian or straight? Dalston Superstore is hard to pigeonhole, which we suspect is the point. This two-level industrial space is open all day but really comes into its own after dark when there are club nights in the basement.

LOADING BAR

(https://loading.bar; 97 Stoke Newington Rd, N16; 5pm-midnight Mon-Thu, to 2am Fri, 11am-2am Sat, 11am-11pm Sun; Dalston Kingsland) Split over two levels, Loading is a game-themed bar with themed cocktails. There are hundreds of board games to choose from on the ground floor and every console imaginable in the basement, as well as retro arcade games.

SHACKLEWELL ARMS PUB

Map p462 (020-7249 0810; www.shacklewellarms.com; 71 Shacklewell Lane, E8; 5pm-midnight Mon-Thu, 4pm-3am Fri & Sat, 4pm-midnight Sun; Dalston Kingsland) Dalston's premier indie-rock pub is as sticky-floored and grungy as you'd hope it would be. There's a popular pool table and a garden bar, but the main attraction is the band room, which stages live music most nights.

RUBY'S COCKTAIL BAR

Map p462 (www.rubysdalston.com; 76 Stoke Newington Rd, N16; 6.30pm-midnight Tue-Thu, to 2am Fri & Sat; Dalston Kingsland) Tucked away in a basement, this artfully dishevelled, candlelit cocktail bar delivers a speakeasy vibe, although you're more likely to hear hair metal being played than honky-tonk piano. On Fridays and Saturdays they open a much larger lounge next door and let loose some feel-good disco tunes. Plus there are £5 cocktail specials on (when else but) Ruby Tuesdays.

RIDLEY ROAD MARKET BAR BAR

Map p462 (www.ridleyroadmarketbar.com; 49 Ridley Rd, E8; 6pm-12.30am Tue, to 2am Wed, to 3am Thu-Sat, 5pm-11pm Sun; Dalston Junction) This ramshackle charmer of a bar has a retro tropical theme, a friendly atmosphere and affordable drinks – think cans of Red Stripe (£3) and frozen cocktails in plastic cups (£5). Pizza is available from Slice Girls, and the music is a mix of pop, jazz and soul. Card only.

FARR'S SCHOOL OF DANCING BAR

Map p462 (020-7923 4553; www.farrsschoolofdancing.com; 17-19 Dalston Lane, E8; 4-11pm Mon-Wed, to midnight Thu, to 1am Fri, noon-1am Sat, 6-11pm Sun; ; Dalston Junction) There was actually a dance school here in the 1930s, but rest assured, nobody's going to expect you to tackle a tango in this big, knowingly grungy boozer nowadays. You could, however, conceivably bust a move to '80s tunes as the evening progresses. Expect a big central bar, mismatched tables topped with candles and flowers, and a relaxed, good-time crowd.

DRAUGHTS CAFE, BAR

Map p462 (07930 936237; www.draughtslondon.com; 41 Kingsland High St, E8; 10am-11pm; Haggerston) London's first board-game themed cafe-bar – it has over 900 to choose from – offers a delightfully geeky way to while away an afternoon. Food, wine and ale are served all day, and staff are on hand to explain rules and advise which games are best suited to your group's wants. There's a £6 charge if you start playing a game.

DALSTON ROOF PARK BAR

Map p462 (020-7275 0825; www.dalstonroofpark.com; Print House, 18 Ashwin St, E8; 5-10pm Mon, to 11pm Tue-Fri, to midnight Sat, 3pm-midnight Sun; Dalston Junction) It's spaces like Dalston Roof Park that make you regret the fact that London isn't sunny year-round. Because when you sit in the colourful chairs on the bright-green AstroTurf looking over the Dalston skyline with a drink in your hand, it really is something.

Hackney

★NETIL360 BAR

Map p462 (www.netil360.com; 1 Westgate St, E8; noon-8.30pm Wed & Sun, to 10.30pm Thu-Sat Apr-Dec; ; London Fields) Perched atop Netil House, this uberhip rooftop cafe-bar offers incredible views over London, with brass telescopes enabling you to

A HERO RISES IN THE EAST

Daniel Mendoza (1764–1836), the father of 'scientific boxing' who billed himself as 'Mendoza the Jew', was the first bare-knuckle boxer to employ strategy and speed in the ring. Mendoza was born in Aldgate and left school at age 13, taking odd jobs as a porter, being taunted as an outsider and getting into scrapes. He was eventually discovered by 'gentleman boxer' Richard Humphreys, 20 years his senior, who took him under his wing and started him training. Mendoza developed a style of fighting in direct opposition to the norm of the day, where two fighters would stand face to face and slug it out until one collapsed.

Mendoza began a highly successful career in the ring, but eventually fell out with his mentor. His most infamous fight came during a grudge match in 1788 with Humphreys. Just as Mendoza was about to administer the coup de grâce, Humphreys' second grabbed Mendoza's arm, a moment caught in a contemporary print called *Foul Play*, on display in the closed-till-2023 National Portrait Gallery. Mendoza went on to fight Humphreys fairly two more times, emerging the victor and moral superior.

Mendoza was the first sportsman in Britain to achieve cult status – a veritable David Beckham of 18th-century London. He made (and lost) a fortune, wrote his memoirs and a how-to book called *The Art of Boxing*, mixed with the high and mighty (including royalty), and sold branded trinkets and images of himself. Most importantly he advanced the cause of Jews in a country that had only allowed them back the century before. People learned for the first time that a Jew could and would fight back – and win.

get better acquainted with workers in 'the Gherkin' building. In between drinks you can knock out a game of croquet on the Astroturf, or perhaps book a hot tub for you and your mates to stew in.

MARTELLO HALL BAR

Map p462 (020-3889 6173; www.martellohall.com; 137 Mare St, E8; 10am-11pm Mon-Wed, to 1am Thu, to 3am Fri & Sat, noon-midnight Sun; ; London Fields) If Dr Jekyll was a louche Hackney hipster, this is where he'd hang out – sipping on gin made by Nicola, the bar's own shiny copper still. A steampunky belt-driven fan whirs overhead, while liqueur bottles glitter like secret elixirs in the candlelight. At the rear, an open kitchen turns out house fried chicken, pizza and £25 weekend 'bottomless brunches'.

HOWLING HOPS BAR

Map p462 (020-3583 8262; www.howlinghops.co.uk; 9a Queen's Yard, White Post Lane, E9; noon-11pm Sun-Thu, to 1am Fri & Sat; Hackney Wick) You won't find cans, bottles or barrels in this pleasantly grungy brewery bar, just 10 gleaming tanks containing ales and lagers straight from the source. It shares the old Victorian warehouse with Colombian street-food eatery Maize Blaze, and there's also a counter serving excellent coffee.

★DOVE PUB

Map p462 (020-7275 7617; www.dovepubs.com; 24-28 Broadway Market, E8; noon-11pm Sun-Fri, from 11am Sat; ; London Fields) The Dove has a rambling series of wooden floorboard rooms and a wide range of Belgian Trappist, wheat and fruit-flavoured beers. Drinkers spill on to the street in warmer weather, or hunker down in the low-lit back room with board games when it's chilly. Pub meals with good vegetarian options are available, too.

CRATE BREWERY MICROBREWERY

Map p462 (020-8533 3331; www.cratebrewery.com; 7 Queen's Yard, White Post Lane, E9; noon-11pm Sun-Thu, to midnight Fri & Sat; ; Hackney Wick) No wonder the cool kids swarm to Hackney Wick: these Victorian warehouses make ideal craft breweries. Inside, pizza and various cask beers and ciders are dispensed under light fixtures fashioned from old bed springs. On Sundays, the canalside tables fill up quickly.

PEOPLE'S PARK TAVERN PUB

Map p462 (020-8533 0040; www.peoplesparktavern.pub; 360 Victoria Park Rd, E9; noon-midnight, 1pm-2am Fri & Sat; ;

(UHomerton) If you're wandering through Victoria Park and fancy either a refreshing beverage or a game of minigolf, here's where to head. There's a fabulous beer garden, right on the park, and it also has an in-house microbrewery. Comedy, live music and DJs are all part of a busy weekly entertainment roster.

★CAT & MUTTON PUB

Map p462 (020-7249 6555; www.catandmutton.com; 76 Broadway Market, E8; noon-11pm Mon, to midnight Tue-Thu, to 1am Fri, 10am-1am Sat, noon-11.30pm Sun; ULondon Fields) At this fabulous Georgian pub, Hackney locals sup pints under the watchful eyes of hunting trophies, B&W photos of old-time boxers and a large portrait of Karl Marx. If it's crammed downstairs, head up the spiral staircase to the comfy couches. Weekends get rowdy, with DJs spinning their best tunes until late.

LAST TUESDAY SOCIETY CLUB

Map p462 (020-7998 3617; www.thelasttuesdaysociety.org; Viktor Wynd Museum of Curiosities, Fine Art & Natural History, 11 Mare St, E8; noon-11pm Wed-Sat, to 8pm Sun; UBethnal Green) London's most curious cocktail bar and *Wunderkabinett* of taxidermy, tribal masks and ephemera from across the globe (p226), with experimental drinks starting with Absinthe Hour at 6pm weekdays. It's busy on weekends; call ahead if you want to book a table. It runs special events from masked balls (St Valentine's Day, Halloween) to 'Hallouminati' wine and cheese nights.

ROYAL INN ON THE PARK PUB

Map p462 (020-8985 3321; www.royalinnonthepark.com; 111 Lauriston Rd, E9; noon-11pm; ; 277) On the northern border of Victoria Park, this excellent establishment – once a poster pub for Transport for London – has 10 real ales and Belgian and Czech beers on tap, outside seating to the front and a large courtyard at the back.

NO 90 BAR

Map p462 (020-8986 0090; www.number90bar.co.uk; 90 Wallis Rd, E9; noon-11.30pm Tue-Thu & Sun, to 1am Fri-Sat; UHackney Wick) Occupying a cavernous brick warehouse right on the canal, No 90 serves craft beer, wine and cocktails to local artists and Sunday sippers. DJs play most nights and there's occasional live music.

KING EDWARD VII PUB

(020-8534 2313; www.kingeddies.co.uk; 47 Broadway, E15; 11am-midnight Mon-Sat, from noon Sun; UStratford) Built in the 19th century, this lovely old boozer has a series of handsome rooms set around a central bar. The front bar and saloon are the most convivial, and there's a little courtyard at the back. Thursday is open-mic night.

Limehouse

GRAPES PUB

Map p462 (020-7987 4396; http://thegrapes.co.uk; 76 Narrow St, E14; noon-11pm, to 10.30pm Sun; UDLR Limehouse) One of Limehouse's renowned historic pubs, the Grapes dates from 1583 and has insinuated its way into the writing of Pepys, Dickens, Wilde, Arthur Conan Doyle and Peter Ackroyd.

It really is tiny, especially the riverside terrace, which can only really comfortably fit about a half-dozen close friends, but its cosy wood-lined interior exudes plenty of old-world charm.

OLD SHIP GAY

Map p462 (020-7791 1301; www.oldship.net; 17 Barnes St, E14; noon-midnight Wed-Sun, to 11am Mon & Tue; UDLR Limehouse) In every respect this is your typical little East End corner pub – except, that is, for the drag-queen cabaret shows on weekends and Saucy Sophie's quiz on Wednesdays.

WHITE SWAN GAY

Map p462 (020-7780 9870; www.bjswhiteswan.com; 556 Commercial Rd, E14; 8pm-2am Tue-Thu, to 5am Fri & Sat, to 2am Sun; UDLR Limehouse) The White Swan is a fun East End kind of place, with a large dance floor, a basement club and a more relaxed pub area. Club classics and cheesy pop predominate, and there are regular drag shows and singalongs around the piano.

ENTERTAINMENT

WILTON'S — THEATRE

Map p462 (☎020-7702 2789; www.wiltons.org.uk; 1 Graces Alley, E1; ⓤTower Hill) A gloriously atmospheric example of a Victorian music hall, Wilton's hosts a variety of shows, from comedy and classical music to theatre and opera. The **Mahogany Bar** (5pm to 11pm Monday to Saturday) is a great way to get a taste of the place if you're not attending a performance.

VORTEX JAZZ CLUB — JAZZ

Map p462 (☎020-7254 4097; www.vortexjazz.co.uk; 11 Gillett Sq, N16; ⏱8pm-midnight; ⓤDalston Kingsland) With a fantastically varied menu of jazz, the Vortex hosts an outstanding line-up of musicians, singers and songwriters from the UK, the US, Europe, Africa and beyond. It's a small venue so make sure you book if there's an act you particularly fancy.

HACKNEY EMPIRE — THEATRE

Map p462 (☎020-8985 2424; www.hackneyempire.co.uk; 291 Mare St, E8; ⓤHackney Central) One of London's most beautiful theatres, this renovated Edwardian music hall (1901) offers an extremely diverse range of performances, from hard-edged political theatre to musicals, opera and comedy. It's one of the best places to catch a pantomime at Christmas.

GENESIS — CINEMA

Map p462 (☎020-7780 2000; www.genesiscinema.co.uk; 93-95 Mile End Rd, E1; ⓤStepney Green) Snuggle up under a blanket on a couch to watch a flick at this wonderful little five-screen cinema.

COPPER BOX ARENA — CONCERT VENUE

Map p462 (☎020-8221 4900; http://copperboxarena.org.uk; Copper St, E20; ⓤHackney Wick) The handball arena during the 2012 Olympic Games, this 7000-seat indoor venue is now used for for badminton, other sports and concerts.

CAFE OTO — LIVE MUSIC

Map p462 (www.cafeoto.co.uk; 18-22 Ashwin St, E8; ⏱9.30am-late; 📶; ⓤDalston Junction) Dedicating itself to promoting experimental and alternative musicians, this is Dalston's premier venue for music nerds to stroke their proverbial beards while listening to electronic bleeps, Japanese psychedelica or avant-folk.

Set in a converted print warehouse, it's one of London's most idiosyncratic live-music venues. When there are no gigs on, it's open as a cafe-bar.

AN EAST LONDON PLAYLIST

- *Mile End* – Pulp (1995)
- *Dagenham Dave* – Morrissey (1995)
- *Dalston* – Razorlight (2004)
- *Ill Manors* – Plan B (2012)
- *River Lea* – Adele (2015)

DALSTON JAZZ BAR — JAZZ

Map p462 (☎020-7254 9728; www.dalstonjazzbartheclub.co.uk; 4 Bradbury St, N16; ⏱3pm-1am Thu-Sat; ⓤDalston Kingsland) Hidden just off the chaos of Kingsland High St, Dalston Jazz Bar also operates as a neighbourhood cocktail bar and eatery. The jazz part of the equation only kicks in late at night, late in the week, with live musicians and 'jazz DJs' from Thursday to Saturday.

ARCOLA THEATRE — THEATRE

Map p462 (☎020-7503 1646; www.arcolatheatre.com; 24 Ashwin St, E8; ⓤDalston Junction) Dalston's a fair schlep from the West End, but drama buffs still flock to this innovative theatre for its adventurous and eclectic productions.

A unique annual feature is **Grimeborn**, an opera festival focusing on lesser-known or new works – it's Dalston's answer to East Sussex's world-famous **Glyndebourne** (☎01273-812321; www.glyndebourne.com) opera festival, taking place around the same time (August).

RIO CINEMA — CINEMA

Map p462 (☎020-7241 9410; www.riocinema.org.uk; 107 Kingsland High St, E8; ⓤDalston Kingsland) The Rio is Dalston's neighbourhood art-house, classic and new-release cinema, and a venue for non-mainstream festivals such as the East End Film Festival, the London Turkish Film Festival and the Fringe! Queer Film & Arts Fest. It also holds regular Q&A sessions with film directors.

SHOPPING

There are some wonderfully quirky little stores lining Columbia Rd and Broadway Market, although some only open on the weekends. If you're after something a little more mainstream, the vast Westfield Stratford City can't fail to satisfy. There's also a shopping mall beneath the Canary Wharf skyscrapers, with similar shops, bars and restaurants. Bargain hunters in the know stake out the outlet stores along Hackney's Morning Lane and Chatham Place.

★BROADWAY MARKET — MARKET

Map p462 (www.broadwaymarket.co.uk; Broadway Market, E8; 9am-5pm Sat; 394) There's been a market down here since the late 19th century, but the focus these days is artisanal food, handmade gifts and unique clothing.

Cafes along both sides of the street (open seven days a week) do a roaring trade with coffee-drinking shoppers. Stock up on edible treats then head to London Fields (p227) for a picnic.

BEYOND RETRO — VINTAGE

Map p462 (020-7729 9001; www.beyondretro.com; 92-100 Stoke Newington Rd, N16; 10.30am-7pm Mon, Tue & Sat, to 8pm Wed-Fri, 11.30am-6pm Sun; Dalston Kingsland) A riot of colour, frill, feathers and flares, this vast store has every imaginable type of vintage clothing for sale, from hats to shoes.

There's another branch in **Bethnal Green** (Map p462; 020-7729 9001; www.beyondretro.com; 110-112 Cheshire St, E2; 11am-7pm Mon-Sat, 11.30am-6pm Sun; Shoreditch High St).

★ARTWORDS — BOOKS

Map p462 (020-7923 7507; www.artwords.co.uk; 20-22 Broadway Market, E8; 9am-8pm Mon-Fri, 10am-6pm Sat & Sun; 394) Imbibe beauty from the page at this atmospheric bookseller specialising in visual arts publications from the UK, Europe, North America and Australia. In the stacks you'll find contemporary fine-art titles, plus plenty of photography, design, media, film and creative philosophy picks. There's a great selection of indie mags, too – tote 'em all home in one of their typography-heavy canvas bags.

TRAID — CLOTHING

Map p462 (020-7923 1396; www.traid.org.uk; 106-108 Kingsland High St, E8; 11am-7pm Mon-Sat, noon-6pm Sun; Dalston Kingsland) Banish every preconception you have about charity shops, for Traid is nothing like the ones you've seen before: big and bright, with not a whiff of mothball. The offerings aren't necessarily vintage but rather quality, contemporary secondhand clothes for a fraction of the usual prices. It also sells its own creations made from offcuts.

BURBERRY OUTLET STORE — CLOTHING

Map p462 (www.burberry.com; 29-31 Chatham Pl, E9; 10am-7pm Mon-Sat, 11.30am-6pm Sun; Hackney Central) This backstreet outlet shop has excess international stock from the luxury British brand's current and last-season collections. Prices are around 30% lower than those in department stores; it's a detour worth the money.

WESTFIELD STRATFORD CITY — MALL

(http://uk.westfield.com; Westfield Ave, E20; 10am-9pm Mon-Fri, from 9am Sat, noon-6pm Sun; ; Stratford) Right by Queen Elizabeth Olympic Park, this is Britain's third-largest mall – a behemoth containing more than 250 shops, 70 places to eat and drink, a 17-screen cinema, a bowling alley, a casino and a Premier Inn hotel.

SPORTS & ACTIVITIES

SECRET ADVENTURES — TOURS

Map p462 (https://secretadventures.org; 1e Mentmore Terr, E8; tours from £20; 10am-6pm; London Fields) Specialising in escapes around the East End, London and beyond, this Hackney-based outfitter organises experiences like night-time kayaking to Crate Brewery (p239), historic wooden boat cruises to Tower Bridge, canoe trips around Olympic Park (p229) and even escapes as far afield as Scotland.

If land-based adventures are more your speed, try one of their adventure film screenings in an old chapel or barn, complete with campfire marshmallow roasts and hot toddies. Options vary throughout the year – check the website for details.

LONDON AQUATICS CENTRE SWIMMING

(☎020-8536 3150; www.londonaquaticscentre.org; Carpenters Rd, E20; adult/child from £5/3; ⏰6am-10.30pm; Ⓤ Stratford) The sweeping lines and wavelike movement of Zaha Hadid's award-winning Aquatics Centre make it the architectural highlight of Queen Elizabeth Olympic Park (p229). Bathed in natural light, the 50m competition pool beneath the huge undulating roof (which sits on just three supports) is an extraordinary place to swim. There's also a second 50m pool, a diving area, a gym, a crèche and a cafe.

LEE VALLEY VELOPARK CYCLING

Map p462 (☎0300 003 0613; www.visitleevalley.org.uk/velopark; Abercrombie Rd, E20; 1hr taster £50, pay-and-ride from £5, bike & helmet hire adult/child from £12/8; ⏰9am-10pm Mon-Fri, 8am-9pm Sat & Sun; 📶; Ⓤ Stratford International) The beautifully designed, cutting-edge velodrome at Queen Elizabeth Olympic Park (p229) is open to the public – either to wander through and watch the pros tear around the steep-sloped circuit, or to have a go yourself. Both the velodrome and the attached **BMX park** offer taster sessions. Mountain bikers and road cyclists can attack the tracks on a pay-and-ride basis.

ALFRED LE ROY CRUISE

Map p462 (www.alfredleroy.com; Queen's Yard, White Post Lane, E9; from £26; ⏰Sat & Sun; Ⓤ Hackney Wick) When it's not moored as a floating bar outside Crate Brewery (p239), this narrow boat heads out on booze cruises by Queen Elizabeth Olympic Park. On Saturdays it heads upriver to Springfield Park at noon, and downriver to Limehouse Basin at 3.30pm. Book online.

LONDON FIELDS LIDO SWIMMING

Map p462 (☎020-7254 9038; www.better.org.uk/leisure-centre/london/hackney/london-fields-lido; London Fields West Side, E8; adult/child £5/3; ⏰6.30am-9pm; Ⓤ London Fields) Built in the 1930s but abandoned by the 1980s, this heated 50m Olympic-size outdoor pool reopened in 2006 and gets packed with swimmers and sunbathers during summer. Swim tickets can be booked online, too.

LEE & STORT BOATS CRUISE

Map p462 (☎0845 116 2012; www.leeandstortboats.co.uk; Stratford waterfront pontoon, E20; adult/child £9/5; ⏰daily Apr-Sep, Sat & Sun Mar & Oct; Ⓤ Stratford) Lee & Stort offers 45-minute tours on the waterways through Queen Elizabeth Olympic Park (p229).

Check the display boards in the park for departure times, which are usually on the hour from noon onwards.

Hampstead & North London

KING'S CROSS & EUSTON | REGENT'S PARK | PRIMROSE HILL | CAMDEN TOWN | HAMPSTEAD | HIGHGATE | HIGHBURY | ISLINGTON | STOKE NEWINGTON | KENTISH TOWN

Neighbourhood Top Five

❶ **Hampstead Heath** (p255) Taking in the sweeping views of London from Parliament Hill, getting a culture fix at beautiful Kenwood House and/or slumping in a couch at the Garden Gate pub to recover.

❷ **Camden Market** (p254) Soaking up the sights, sounds, smells and frantic energy of this legendary market.

❸ **British Library** (p246) Discovering the treasures of the nation's 'collective memory' and marvelling at the sheer volume of knowledge stored within its walls.

❹ **Wellcome Collection** (p252) Enjoying a thought-provoking afternoon exploring questions of life, death and art at this intriguing gallery.

❺ **Tottenham Hotspur Stadium** (p259) Touring this state-of-the-art stadium, with its retractable pitch, which hosts both 'real' and American football games.

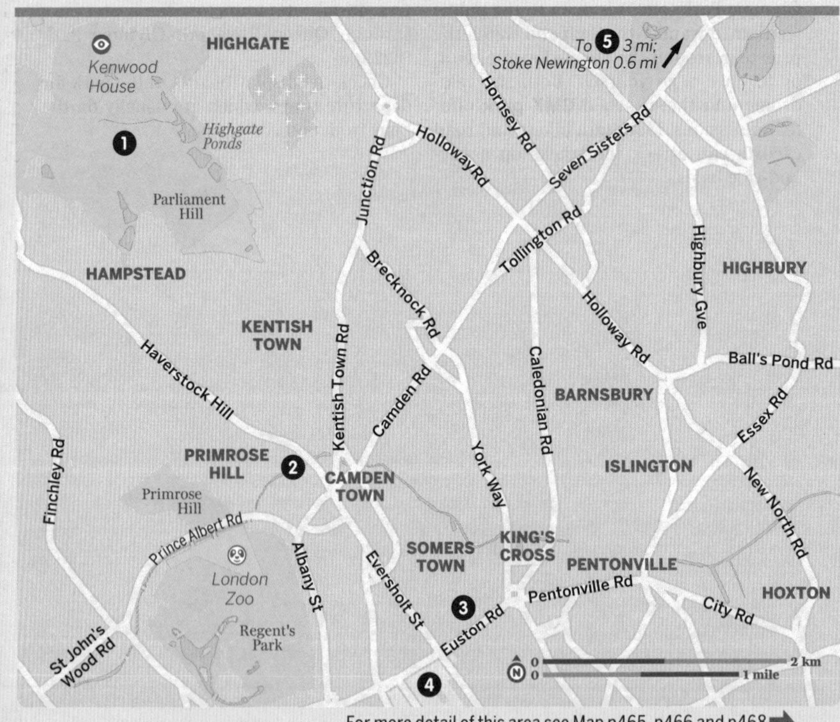

For more detail of this area see Map p465, p466 and p468

Explore Hampstead & North London

North London is a big place – you could spend a week exploring its parks, checking out the sights, lounging in gastropubs and sampling the nightlife. So if you're short on time, you'll have to pick and choose carefully.

Camden Market (p254) has an intoxicating energy, while Hampstead Heath (p255) offers glorious – and often hilly – walks and wonderful city views. Because these are residential areas, they tend to be quiet during the week and busy at weekends.

King's Cross, once an industrial wasteland and now a supercool new neighbourhood, is a great place to hang out – be it for an alfresco lunch, an ice cream or a drink – though with its central location and numerous offices, it's busier on weekdays. There are also two museums to explore, and on weekends you can tour the exquisite St Pancras building (p250).

Walk along Regent's Canal (p252) to link places such as King's Cross, Camden and Regent's Park (p252) – it's a route that's both practical and scenic.

Local Life

Live music North London is known for being the home of indie rock. Music fans flock to bars and theatres around Camden Town and Kentish Town to hear bands aiming for the big time.

Sunday pub lunches Hampstead is a good place to experience this British institution, although there are suitable venues all over North London.

Swimming Hampstead Heath ponds (p271) are open year-round, and a small group of hard-core aficionados swim every day, rain or shine.

Getting There & Away

Underground North London is served by the Northern, Piccadilly, Victoria, Jubilee and Bakerloo Lines. Additionally, the Circle, Hammersmith & City and Metropolitan Lines call into King's Cross St Pancras, Euston Sq and Baker St.

Overground The Overground crosses North London from east to west, with useful stops at Highbury & Islington, Caledonian Rd & Barnsbury, Camden Rd, Kentish Town West and Hampstead Heath.

Bus A good network of buses in North London connects neighbourhoods to one another and to the city centre. Buses are useful for getting to the zoo (routes 88 and 274) and the northern part of Hampstead Heath (210).

Lonely Planet's Top Tip

If the sun's shining, drop any plans you might have made and head straight to a park. North London has some of the capital's biggest and best green spaces. Pack a picnic and after lunch do what Londoners do: head for a pub!

Best Eating

- Trullo (p264)
- Sambal Shiok (p263)
- Ottolenghi (p264)
- Hook Camden Town (p261)
- Yipin China (p264)

For reviews, see p258.

Best Drinking & Nightlife

- Holly Bush (p267)
- Drink, Shop & Do (p265)
- Garden Gate (p267)
- Euston Tap (p265)
- Bull & Gate (p267)

For reviews, see p265.

Best Live Music

- Green Note (p268)
- Dublin Castle (p270)
- O2 Forum (p270)
- Jazz Cafe (p268)
- Blues Kitchen (p268)

For reviews, see p268.

PAWEL LIBERA/LIGHTROCKET VIA GETTY IMAGES © SCULPTURE: NEWTON BY EDUARDO PAOLOZZI

TOP EXPERIENCE

STROLL THROUGH THE BRITISH LIBRARY

Consisting of low-slung red-brick terraces, which consumed 10 million bricks and 180,000 tonnes of concrete, and fronted by a large piazza featuring an oversized statue of Sir Isaac Newton, Colin St John Wilson's building is a love-it-or-hate-it affair. Indeed, when it opened in 1998 after 15 years of construction, Prince Charles likened it to a 'secret-police headquarters'. Nonetheless, it is home to some of the greatest treasures of the written word and is the English-speaking world's collective memory.

The Collection

The British Library is the UK's principal copyright library, which means that it automatically receives a copy of everything published in Britain (as well as Ireland). Among its more than 170 million items are historic manuscripts, books, maps, journals, newspapers and sound recordings.

King's Library Tower

In the middle of the building is a six-storey, 17m-high glass-walled tower containing the wonderful King's Library, the 85,000-volume collection of King George III given to the nation by his son, George IV, in 1823. It is one of the 'foundation collections': items donated by or acquired from various luminaries, such as the collector and architect Sir Hans Sloane, which formed the basis of the library and the British Museum.

DON'T MISS

- Sir John Ritblat Treasures Gallery
- King's Library Tower
- Temporary exhibitions
- *Sitting on History* bench

PRACTICALITIES

- Map p466, A6
- 0330-333 1144
- www.bl.uk
- 96 Euston Rd, NW1
- admission free
- 9.30am-8pm Mon-Thu, to 6pm Fri, to 5pm Sat, 11am-5pm Sun
- (wi-fi)
- U King's Cross St Pancras

Sir John Ritblat Treasures Gallery

Housing the Treasures of the British Library, the library's most precious and high-profile documents, this darkened gallery is the highlight of any visit. The collection spans almost three millennia and contains manuscripts, religious texts, maps, music scores, autographs, diaries and more.

Rare texts from all the main religions include the **Codex Sinaiticus**, the first complete text of the New Testament, written in Greek in the 4th century; a **Gutenberg Bible** (1455), the first Western book printed using movable type; the Buddhist **Diamond Sutra**, the world's earliest printed book; and spectacularly illustrated Jain, Muslim and Judaic sacred texts such as the **Golden Haggadah**.

The gallery holds historical documents, too, including two of the four remaining copies of the **Magna Carta** (1215), the charter credited with setting out the basis of human rights in English law. Literature is also well represented, with **Shakespeare's First Folio** (1623) and manuscripts by some of Britain's best-known authors, such as Lewis Carroll, Jane Austen, George Eliot and Thomas Hardy. Music fans will love the Beatles' handwritten lyrics (including 'A Hard Day's Night' scribbled on the back of one of Julian Lennon's birthday cards), and original scores by Bach, Handel, Mozart and Beethoven.

Pick up one of the handsets on the wall to hear selections from the Sound Archive, including the first-ever recording, made by Thomas Edison in 1877.

Exhibitions

The library runs regular high-profile exhibitions in the PACCAR Exhibition Gallery, all connected to its records; admission charges vary. Smaller free exhibitions take place around the library and focus on particular authors, genres or themes (science fiction, the census, crime fiction etc).

Guided Tours

One-hour tours (adult/child £10/8) focus on the John Ritblat Gallery (11am Monday to Saturday, 11.30am on Sunday) and on the building itself (2pm Monday to Saturday, 3pm on Sunday). Available by arrangement are more specialised tours, such as ones of the conservation studios.

TAKE A BREAK

Origin Coffee Roasters (p266), by the British Library piazza, serves great coffee in lovely designer surroundings.

For cheap, quick and tasty food, head to Roti King (p258), which serves Malaysian *roti canai* (flatbread) with curry.

Art is strewn throughout the library. In the piazza there's Eduardo Paolozzi's statue of Sir Isaac Newton, and Antony Gormley's sculpture called *Planets*. Inside are portraits by Godfrey Kneller and David Hockney, RB Kitaj's tapestry *If Not, Not* and Bill Woodrow's bronze sculpture of a chained and open book that forms a bench called *Sitting on History*.

READER PASS

Hundreds of people come to work here every day. To access the library's 11 reading rooms, however, you'll need a Reader Pass. Passes are only issued if you can demonstrate a need to see specific collection items – usually for an academic or research purpose.

ANNA MOSKVINA/SHUTTERSTOCK ©

TOP EXPERIENCE

EXPLORE HABITATS IN ZSL LONDON ZOO

Established in 1828, London's zoo is the world's oldest. The emphasis nowadays is on conservation, education and breeding, with fewer species and more spacious conditions.

A main draw is **Land of the Lions**, a 2500-sq-metre enclosure that recreates the environment of Gir Forest National Park in India where the last Asiatic lions live in the wild. There are four lions in the enclosure, as well as Hanuman langur monkeys and band of dwarf mongooses.

In **Gorilla Kingdom** Alika (b 2014) and Gernot (b 2015) are endlessly entertaining to watch, and incredibly reminiscent of human toddlers. The two babies and four adults have a wide outdoor enclosure and an indoor space complete with swing ropes and climbing frames.

Another popular attraction is **Penguin Beach**, a key element of the zoo's Humboldt penguin breeding program.

Rainforest Life – with South American sloths, monkeys and birds – is one of several immersive exhibits where the animals wander freely among visitors. The building also has a darkened area called **Night Life**, which houses intriguing nocturnal animals such as slender lorises, Malagasy giant rats and blind cave fish. Walk through the **In with the Lemurs** enclosure and the curious and playful ring-tailed critters will come within touching distance.

On a rainy or cold day, visit indoor attractions such as **Butterfly Paradise**, **Reptile House** and a building called **B.U.G.S.**, which is full of – guess what? The architecturally significant canalside **Snowden Aviary** is being renovated to house leaping and swinging black-and-white colobus monkeys.

DON'T MISS

- Land of the Lions
- Night Life
- Penguin Beach
- Gorilla Kingdom
- In with the Lemurs

PRACTICALITIES

- Map p468, B4
- 0344-225 1826
- www.zsl.org/zsl-london-zoo
- Outer Circle, Regent's Park, NW1
- depending on date, adult £25-32.50, child £16-20.50
- 10am-6pm Apr-Aug, to 5pm mid-Feb–Mar, Sep & Oct, to 4pm Nov–mid-Feb
-
- 88, 274

TOP EXPERIENCE

ESCAPE TO ELEGANT KENWOOD HOUSE

This magnificent neoclassical mansion stands at the northern end of Hampstead Heath amid a glorious sweep of landscaped gardens.

The 17th-century house, expanded and remodelled by Scottish architect Robert Adam between 1764 and 1779, was extensively refurbished in 2013, with rooms repainted in Adam's original colours. The **Great Library**, with its powder-pink and sky-blue vaulted ceiling and vignette paintings, is magnificent. It's one of 15 rooms over two floors open to the public.

The former owner was Edward Cecil Guinness, 1st Earl of Iveagh, who donated the house and its wonderful collection of art to the nation in 1927. The **Iveagh Bequest** contains paintings by Rembrandt, Constable, Turner, Gainsborough, Reynolds, Hals, Vermeer and Van Dyck. Head up Adam's **Great Stairs** for the **Suffolk Collection**, consisting of Jacobean and Stuart portraits. Also here is a wonderful collection of miniature paintings, Georgian jewellery and a rather esoteric assortment of shoe buckles. If you've got the kids, the **Orangery** on the ground floor has games and family activities.

The gardens are another highlight, offering fine views and sculptures by Henry Moore (*Two Piece Reclining Figure*, 1964) and Barbara Hepworth (*Monolith Empyrean*, 1953). There's also the recently opened **Dairy** (1795), where 18th-century ladies took tea. It's open on the last Sunday of the month. The old servants' wing now houses the **Brew House**, a sit-down cafe and a snack bar.

Download an app and visit Kenwood House on your own or join a 50-minute guided tour (£8, free for National Trust members), which departs at 2pm daily except Tuesday and Thursday, when there are 15-minute spotlight tours at 11.30am, 12.30pm and 2pm.

DON'T MISS

- Rembrandt self-portrait
- The Great Library
- Landscaped gardens
- Suffolk Collection
- Dairy

PRACTICALITIES

- EH
- Map p465, B2
- ☎020-8348 1286
- www.english-heritage.org.uk/visit/places/kenwood
- Hampstead Lane, NW3
- admission free
- 10am-4pm
- 210

SIGHTS

North London is a collection of small neighbourhoods, originally ancient villages that were slowly drawn into London's orbit as the metropolis expanded. It's a very green area, home to some of the largest and most beautiful park spaces in the city. Sights are pretty scattered in the northern half of the area, where you'll need some leg power to explore hilly Hampstead. King's Cross, however, is a lot more compact. A walk along Regent's Canal will link Regent's Park, Camden and King's Cross.

King's Cross & Euston

King's Cross used to be something of a blind spot on London's map, somewhere you only ever went *through* rather than *to*. The surrounding streets were the capital's red-light district, and when the British Library first opened here in 1998, drug addicts could regularly be found in the toilets. In fact, it was the area's reputation that poured cold water on plans to renovate the hotel at St Pancras station in the 1980s and 1990s.

But after St Pancras station was totally restored and reopened as the London terminal for Eurostar trains to Paris and Brussels in 2007, things began to change. Today King's Cross's transformation isn't far removed from the metamorphosis of Stratford after the 2012 Olympic Games. Not only do friends now gather and chat on the plaza in front of King's Cross station, but families also stroll through the former railyards behind the station, along broad avenues lined with trees. This one-time industrial wasteland has become home to dozens of hip new eateries, glitzy corporate headquarters and lots of green spaces.

BRITISH LIBRARY LIBRARY

See p246.

ST PANCRAS STATION & HOTEL HISTORIC BUILDING

Map p466 (020-7843 7688; https://stpancras.com; Euston Rd, NW1; King's Cross St Pancras) Looking at the jaw-dropping Gothic splendour of St Pancras (1868), it's hard to believe that the Midland Grand Hotel languished empty for decades and even faced demolition in the 1960s. Now home to a five-star hotel, 67 luxury apartments and the Eurostar terminal, the entire complex has regained its former glory. Tours (£24; 10.30am, noon, 2pm and 3.30pm Saturday and Sunday) take you on a fascinating journey through the building's history, from its inception as the southern terminus for the Midland Railway line.

Designed by George Gilbert Scott (who also built the Albert Memorial in Hyde Park and the Foreign and Commonwealth Office on Whitehall), the Midland Grand Hotel was the most luxurious hotel in London when it first opened in 1873. All of the materials (including the stone, iron and 60 million red bricks) were brought down from the Midlands as a showcase for the kind of products the railway link could provide. The whole thing cost an astonishing £438,000 – approximately £49 million in today's money.

You can get an idea of the original over-the-top decor in **George's Bar**, which was originally the hotel's reception. The adjoining dining room (now the fine-dining **Gilbert Scott Restaurant** run by acclaimed chef Marcus Wareing) showcases the more restrained style of a 1901 refurbishment. The building was incredibly modern for its time, with England's first hydraulic lift, London's first revolving door and a thick layer of concrete between the floors to act as a firebreak. Ironically this contributed to its undoing, as it made it extremely difficult to adapt the rooms to include such 'mod-cons' as en suite bathrooms and electricity.

The hotel closed in 1935 and was used for railway offices before being abandoned in 1985. It was only when plans to use St Pancras as the Eurostar terminal came up in the 1990s that local authorities decided to renovate the building and open a hotel. The Eurostar first arrived at **St Pancras International** in 2007 and the St Pancras Renaissance Hotel London (p357) opened its doors four years later.

Tours take you up the hotel's glorious grand staircase (the *real* star of the Spice Girls' 1995 *Wannabe* video) and along the exquisitely decorated corridors. They then head into the station proper, where sky-blue iron girders arc over what was, at the time, the largest unsupported space ever built. A modern addition to the concourse is **Meeting Place**, a giant statue of two lovers embracing, by sculptor Paul Day – be sure to examine the wonderful railway-themed frieze winding around its base. Also worth a look is the bronze **statue of poet laureate John Betjeman** (1906–84), an early supporter of Victorian architecture who was instrumental in saving the station. The fabulously ornate **Booking Office Bar & Restaurant** (Map p466; ☎020-7841 3566; www.stpancraslondon.com; St Pancras Renaissance Hotel London, Euston Rd, NW1; ⊙6.30am-1am Mon-Fri, 7am-1am Sat, to midnight Sun; ⓤKing's Cross St Pancras) nearby is housed in the station's original ticket office.

GRANARY SQUARE — SQUARE

Map p466 (www.kingscross.co.uk; Stable St, N1; ⓤKing's Cross St Pancras) Positioned on a sharp bend in the Regent's Canal north of King's Cross station, Granary Sq is at the heart of a major redevelopment of a 27-hectare expanse, once full of abandoned freight warehouses and an enormous granary. The square's most striking feature is the fountain made of 1080 individually lit water jets, which pulse and dance in sequence. On hot spring and summer days, it becomes a busy urban beach.

The vast brick 1852 warehouse designed by Lewis Cubitt and fronting the square is now home to some excellent eating spots as well as the main campus of **Central St Martins University of the Arts London** (www.arts.ac.uk/colleges/central-saint-martins). Also worth noting is the wavy glass frontage of the canalside **Kings Place** building to the east. Completed in 2008, it's home to a concert hall, restaurants, commercial galleries, and the offices of the *Guardian* and *Observer* newspapers. The excellent gallery House of Illustration is at No 2.

GASHOLDER PARK — PARK

Map p466 (www.kingscross.co.uk/gasholder-park; ⓤKing's Cross St Pancras) Part of the impressive redevelopment of the King's Cross area, this urban green space on Regent's Canal is a masterpiece of regeneration. The cast-iron structure was the frame of Gasholder No 8, the largest gas-storage cylinder in the area (originally located across the canal). Carefully renovated, and with the addition of a central lawn, beautiful benches and a mirrored canopy, it has metamorphosed into a gorgeous pocket-sized park.

KING'S CROSS STATION — HISTORIC BUILDING

Map p466 (www.kingscross.co.uk/kings-cross-station; Euston Road; ⓤKing's Cross St Pancras) With its clean lines and the simple arches of its twin train sheds, you might be forgiven for thinking that King's Cross is a more modern building than its show-off neighbour St Pancras, but in fact it opened its doors more than a decade earlier in 1852. Designed by Lewis Cubitt and built in the classic muddy-yellow London stock brick, it stands apart from the prevailing Victorian sensibility of more is more.

A major refurbishment was completed in 2012, with the opening of a new departures terminal under an exceedingly beautiful, curving, canopy-like roof formed from a lattice-like web of steel. Shabby extensions have been removed from the front of the building, showcasing the facade and opening up an expansive plaza crowned with a **Henry Moore sculpture** entitled *Large Spindle Piece* (1974).

Of course, for many people – especially the young – King's Cross station means just one thing: the departure point for Hogwarts School of Witchcraft and Wizardry. You'll need to be embarking on an actual train journey to visit the platforms, so the kind people at Network Rail have moved the magical portal leading to **Platform 9¾** to a more convenient location in the departures terminal. A sign has been permanently erected, along with a luggage trolley half disappearing into the wall and carrying a trunk and an owl cage. You can have your picture taken by wizards from the (inevitable) Harry Potter Shop (p271) next door.

HOUSE OF ILLUSTRATION — GALLERY

Map p466 (☎020-3696 2020; www.houseofillustration.org.uk; 2 Granary Sq, N1; adult/child £8/4; ⊙10am-6pm Tue-Sun; ⓤKing's Cross St Pancras) This charity-run gallery founded by the legendary Sir Quentin Blake (famed as the illustrator of Roald Dahl's books) is the UK's sole public gallery purely dedicated to illustration and graphics. It stages ever-changing exhibitions – everything from cartoons and book illustrations to advertisements and scientific drawings.

LONDON CANAL MUSEUM — MUSEUM

Map p466 (☎020-7713 0836; www.canalmuseum.org.uk; 12-13 New Wharf Rd, N1; adult/child £5/2.50; ⊙10am-4.30pm Tue-Sun & Mon bank holidays; ⓤKing's Cross St Pancras) This little museum on the Regent's Canal (p252) traces the history and everyday life of families living and working on London's impressively long and historic canal system. The exhibits in the stables upstairs are dedicated to the history of canal transport, including more recent developments such as the clean-up of the Lea River for the 2012 Olympic Games. The museum is housed in a warehouse dating from 1857, where ice was once stored in two deep wells.

The ice trade was huge in refrigerationless Victorian London, with 35,000 tonnes imported from Norway in 1899 alone, arriving in the city at Regent's Canal Dock before being transported along the canal. You can access the wharf at the back of the museum where narrow boats are moored. Pick up a copy of the museum's *The East End Canal Tales* by Carolyn Clark to sail through the canal and its industries' fascinating history, meeting a colourful cast of characters who lived and worked on them along the way. Bon voyage!

Regent's Park

ZSL LONDON ZOO ZOO

See p248.

★**REGENT'S CANAL** CANAL

Map p468 (https://canalrivertrust.org.uk/enjoy-the-waterways/canal-and-river-network/regents-canal) To escape the crowded streets and enjoy a picturesque, waterside side stretch of North London, take to the canals that once played such a vital role in the transport of goods across the capital. The towpath of the Regent's Canal also makes an excellent shortcut across North London, either on foot or by bike. In full, the ribbon of water runs 8.5 miles from Little Venice (where it connects with the Grand Union Canal) to the Limehouse Basin and the Thames.

REGENT'S PARK PARK

Map p468 (www.royalparks.org.uk/parks/the-regents-park; 5am-dusk; Regent's Park or Baker St) The largest and most elaborate of central London's many Royal Parks, Regent's Park is one of the capital's loveliest green spaces. Among its many attractions are London Zoo (p248), Regent's Canal, an ornamental lake, and sports pitches where locals meet to play football, rugby and volleyball. **Queen Mary's Gardens**, towards the south of the park, are particularly pretty, especially in June when the roses are in bloom. Performances take place here in an open-air theatre (p269) during summer.

ABBEY ROAD STUDIOS HISTORIC BUILDING

(020-7266 7000; www.abbeyroad.com; 3 Abbey Rd, NW8; St John's Wood) Beatles

The Wellcome Collection explores the complex links between medicine, science, life and art. The building is light and modern, with varied and interactive displays over three floors ranging from interviews with researchers, doctors and patients, to historical and contemporary art depicting medicine and models of human organs.

The heart of the permanent collection is Sir Henry Wellcome's eccentric array of objects from around the world in the **Medicine Man** gallery. Wellcome (1853–1936), a pharmacist, entrepreneur and collector, was fascinated by medicine and amassed from different civilisations more than one million objects associated with life, birth, death and sickness, including everything from penis votives (impotence?) and shrunken heads to a guillotine blade and Napoleon's toothbrush.

The new **Being Human** gallery has interactive displays and provocative artworks focusing on what it means to be human in the 21st century, and explores the hopes and fears provoked by new forms of medical knowledge.

The museum also runs outstanding (and free) temporary exhibitions on topics exploring the frontiers of modern medicine. Don't miss the fabulous **Reading Room** with its own special art collection.

DON'T MISS

- Medicine Man gallery, featuring objects from Henry Wellcome's own collection
- Temporary exhibitions
- Reading Room and its art collection

PRACTICALITIES

- Map p468, F6
- 020-7611 2222
- www.wellcomecollection.org
- 183 Euston Rd, NW1
- admission free
- 10am-6pm Tue, Wed & Fri-Sun, to 9pm Thu
- Euston Sq or Euston

WALKING ALONG REGENT'S CANAL

The canals that were once a trade lifeline for the capital are now a favourite escape for Londoners, providing a quiet walk away from traffic and crowds. For visitors, an added advantage of the Regent's Canal towpath is that it provides an easy (and delightful) shortcut across North London.

You can make do with walking from Little Venice to Camden Town in less than an hour, passing Regent's Park and ZSL London Zoo (p248) as well as beautiful villas designed by architect John Nash and redevelopments of old industrial buildings. Allow 25 to 30 minutes between Little Venice and Regent's Park, and 15 to 20 minutes between Regent's Park and Camden Town. There are plenty of well-signed exits along the way.

If you decide to continue on, it's worth stopping at the London Canal Museum (p251) in King's Cross to learn more about the canal's history. Shortly afterwards you'll hit the 878m-long Islington Tunnel and have to take to the roads for a spell. After joining the path again near Colebrooke Row, you can follow the water all the way to the Thames at Limehouse Basin, or divert on to the Hertford Union Canal at Victoria Park (p227) and head to Queen Elizabeth Olympic Park (p229).

aficionados can't possibly visit London without making a pilgrimage to this famous recording studio in St John's Wood. The studios themselves are off-limits, so you'll have to content yourself with examining the decades of fan graffiti on the fence outside. Stop-start local traffic is long accustomed to groups of tourists lining up on the zebra crossing to re-enact the cover of the fab four's 1969 masterpiece *Abbey Road*. In 2010 the crossing was rewarded with Grade II heritage status.

LORD'S STADIUM

(☎020-7616 8500; https://apps.lords.org/lords/tours-and-museum; St John's Wood Rd, NW8; tours adult/child £25/16; ⏲4-6 tours daily year-round; 📶; Ⓤ St John's Wood) The 'home of cricket' is a must for any devotee of this particularly English game. Book early for the Test matches (p269) here, but cricket buffs should also take the absorbing and anecdote-filled 100-minute tour of the ground and facilities (online booking required). Tours take in the famous Long Room, where members watch the games surrounded by portraits of cricket's great and good, and a museum featuring evocative memorabilia that will appeal to fans both old and new.

The famous little urn containing the Ashes, the prize of the most fiercely contested competition in cricket, resides here permanently. There are no tours on major match days. Tour hours vary through the year (consult the website) but usually depart hourly from 10am to 3pm April to October and at 10am, 11am, noon and 2pm the rest of the year.

LONDON CENTRAL MOSQUE MOSQUE

Map p468 (☎020-7725 2213, 020-7725 2152; www.iccuk.org; 146 Park Rd, NW8; Ⓤ St John's Wood) Completed in 1977 this striking large white mosque is topped with a glistening golden dome and a minaret, and can hold more than 5000 worshippers. Provided you take your shoes off and dress modestly (females must cover their hair), you're welcome to go inside but, as is the way with mosques, the interior is very simple.

⊙ Primrose Hill

Wedged between well-heeled Regent's Park and somewhat grungy Camden, the minuscule neighbourhood of Primrose Hill is high on the property wish list of many Londoners – but utterly unaffordable for most. With its independent boutiques, good restaurants and appealing pubs, it has a rare village feel.

PRIMROSE HILL PARK

Map p468 (Ⓤ Chalk Farm) On summer weekends, Primrose Hill park is absolutely packed with locals enjoying a picnic and the extraordinary views over the city skyline. Come weekdays, however, and there are mostly just dog walkers and nannies. It's a lovely place to enjoy a quiet stroll or an alfresco lunch.

⊙ Camden Town

JEWISH MUSEUM LONDON MUSEUM

Map p468 (☎020-7284 7384; www.jewishmuseum.org.uk; 129-131 Albert St, Raymond Burton House, NW1; adult/child/family £7.50/3.50/18; ⊙10am-5pm Sat-Thu, to 2pm Fri; Ⓤ Camden Town) This interesting museum has permanent and informative displays over four floors looking at Judaism, its beliefs and rituals; the history of Jewish people in Britain from Norman times; and the Holocaust. One of its more important artefacts is a *mikveh* (sunken ritual bath), dating from the mid-12th century, just decades before the Jews were expelled from England for nearly 400 years. It was recovered from Milk St in the City of London in 2001.

Don't miss the recreation of a Jewish East End street, with tailoring and cabinet-making workshops in the history section. There's also a gallery for temporary exhibitions on the 3rd floor. Oddly the cafe on the ground floor is not kosher.

VAGINA MUSEUM MUSEUM

Map p468 (☎020-3715 8943; www.vaginamuseum.co.uk; Units 17 & 18, Chalk Farm Rd, Stables Market, NW1; ⊙10am-6pm Mon-Sat, 11am-6pm Sun) FREE Eager beavers won't want to beat around the bush and delay entry to this unique exhibition – the only one of its kind in the world (though we're told there's a museum devoted to that *other* bodypart in Reykjavik). You'll find nothing lascivious here – it's all about education and quite earnest in its presentation of this 'taboo subject'. As a poster states: '50% of the world's population has one [and] most came into the world through one'. Food for thought.

⊙ Hampstead

The most affluent and leafiest part of North London, Hampstead has long been associated with intellectuals and artists, although these days it's mainly bankers and foreign oligarchs who can afford to buy property here.

KENWOOD HOUSE HISTORIC BUILDING

See p249.

FENTON HOUSE HISTORIC BUILDING

Map p465 (NT; ☎020-7435 3471; www.nationaltrust.org.uk/fenton-house; Hampstead Grove, NW3; adult/child/family £9/4.50/23.75, with 2 Willow Road adult/child £14.50/7.25; ⊙11am-5pm

TOP EXPERIENCE

GRAB A BARGAIN AT CAMDEN MARKET

Although – or perhaps because – it stopped being cutting-edge several thousand cheap leather jackets ago, Camden Market attracts millions of visitors each year and is one of London's most popular attractions. What started out as a collection of attractive craft stalls beside Camden Lock on the Regent's Canal now extends most of the way from Camden Town Tube station to Chalk Farm Tube station.

There are two main market areas – **Camden Lock Market** (p270) on Regent's Canal and **Stables Market** (p270) further west – although they seem to blend together with the crowds snaking along and the 'normal' shops lining the streets. You'll find a bit of everything: clothes (of variable quality) in profusion, bags, jewellery, arts and crafts, candles, incense and myriad decorative titbits. Some side streets such as **Inverness Street** south of the canal are lined with stalls selling cheap T-shirts, hats and plastic bangles.

There are dozens of food stalls in the **West Yard** (p262) of Camden Lock Market, offering every possible cuisine under the sun. You can eat at the big communal tables or by the canal.

DON'T MISS

- Stables Market
- Camden Lock Market
- Amy Winehouse Statue
- Lunch at West Yard food stalls

PRACTICALITIES

- Map p468, D3
- www.camdenmarket.com
- Camden High St, NW1
- ⊙10am-late
- Ⓤ Camden Town or Chalk Farm

TOP EXPERIENCE
RAMBLE ON HAMPSTEAD HEATH

Sprawling Hampstead Heath, with its rolling woodlands and meadows, feels a million miles away – despite being about 3.5 miles from Trafalgar Sq. It covers 320 hectares, most of it woods, hills and meadows, and is home to about 180 bird species, 25 species of butterflies, grass snakes, bats and a rich array of flora.

It's a wonderful place for a ramble, especially to the top of **Parliament Hill**, which offers expansive views across flat-as-a-pancake London and is one of the most popular places in London to fly a kite. Alternatively head up the hill to **Kenwood House** (p249), a grand 18th-century house with lovely landscaped gardens, or lose yourself in the **West Heath**. Signage is limited, but getting a little lost is part of the experience.

If walking is too pedestrian for you, the bathing ponds are another major attraction. There are separate ones for men and women, and a less secluded **mixed pond** (p271).

Once you've had your fill of fresh air and/or culture, do as Londoners do and head to one of the wonderful pubs around the heath for a restorative pint.

DON'T MISS

- Views from Parliament Hill
- Swimming in one of the heath ponds
- Kenwood House

PRACTICALITIES

- Map p465, B3
- www.cityoflondon.gov.uk/things-to-do/green-spaces/hampstead-heath
- Ⓤ Hampstead Heath or Gospel Oak

Wed-Sun mid-Mar–Oct; Ⓤ Hampstead) One of the oldest houses in Hampstead, this merchant's residence built in 1686 has fine collections of porcelain and keyboard instruments, including an early-17th-century harpsichord once played by Handel and still played at 2.30pm on Wednesday. The interior is very evocative thanks to original Georgian furniture and period art such as 17th-century needlework pictures. There's a charming walled garden with roses and a 300-year-old orchard behind the manse.

On fine days climb to the top floor to enjoy panoramic views of London from the balcony.

2 WILLOW ROAD — NOTABLE BUILDING

Map p465 (NT; ☎020-7435 6166; www.nationaltrust.org.uk/2-willow-road; 2 Willow Rd, NW3; adult/child £8.50/4.25, with Fenton House £14.50/7.25; ⊙11am-5pm Wed-Sun Mar-Oct; Ⓤ Hampstead Heath) Fans of modern architecture will want to have a look at this Modernist structure, the central house in a block of three designed by the 'structural rationalist' Ernő Goldfinger in 1939. Many people think it looks uncannily like the sort of mundane 1950s architecture you see everywhere. It may do now, but 2 Willow Rd was a forerunner; the others were just imitations – and mostly bad ones at that.

The interior, with its cleverly designed storage space and collection of artworks by Henry Moore, Max Ernst and Bridget Riley, is certainly interesting and accessible to all. A visit is by one-hour guided tour only (11am, noon, 1pm and 2pm) until 3pm, after which unguided visits are allowed.

KEATS HOUSE — MUSEUM

Map p465 (☎020-7332 3868; www.cityoflondon.gov.uk/keats; 10 Keats Grove, NW3; adult/child £7.50/free; ⊙11am-5pm Wed-Sun; Ⓤ Hampstead Heath) This elegant Regency house, once a duplex called Wentworth Place, was home to the golden boy of the Romantic poets, John Keats, from 1818 to 1820. It was here that Keats met his fiancée Fanny Brawne, literally the girl next door. And it was here that he wrote many of his most celebrated poems, including 'Ode to a Nightingale'. The house is sparsely but evocatively furnished, and the museum does a great job of recounting Keats' short and intense life.

A 10-minute biographical film is shown downstairs and there are listening stations in many of the nine rooms on ground and 1st floors where you can listen to some of Keats' poems and excerpts from letters written by both him and Fanny Brawne. Don't miss Mrs Brawne's kitchen and wine cellar in the basement.

FREUD MUSEUM MUSEUM

(☎none; www.freud.org.uk; 20 Maresfield Gardens, NW3; adult/child £10/free; ⊙noon-5pm Wed-Sun; Ⓤ Finchley Rd) After fleeing Nazi-occupied Vienna in 1938, Sigmund Freud lived the last year of his life in this house. The house, on a quiet, tree-lined residential street, contains the psychiatrist's study and library, with his famous couch and its carpet covering, books and collection of small Egyptian figures and other antiquities, which he'd brought with him from Austria. One room upstairs is dedicated to his daughter, Anna, an eminent child psychoanalyst, who lived in the house until her death in 1982.

Highgate

HIGHGATE WOOD PARK

Map p465 (www.cityoflondon.gov.uk/things-to-do/green-spaces/highgate-wood; Archway Rd, N10; ⊙7.30am-sunset; Ⓤ Highgate) With more than 28 hectares of ancient woodland, this park is a wonderful spot for a walk any time of the year. It's also teeming with life: 70 different bird species have been recorded here, along with seven types of bat and a wealth of insect life and flora. There's a huge clearing in the centre for sports, and it also has a popular playground and a cafe.

Highbury

ARSENAL EMIRATES STADIUM STADIUM

Map p466 (☎020-7619 5003; www.arsenal.com/tours; Hornsey Rd, N7; self-guided tours adult/child £25/16, guided tours £40/20; ⊙10am-5pm Mon-Fri, 9.30am-6pm Sat, 10am-4pm Sun; Ⓤ Holloway Rd) When Arsenal FC moved to this stadium in 2006, fans claimed it would never be the same again. It's true that the 60,200-seat stadium lacks some of the bonhomie of the old art deco Highbury ground, but it's still a sell-out at every game. Match tickets are tricky to come by, even if you have a first-born to sacrifice, but fans can still get inside on a stadium tour.

Self-guided audio tours (available in 10 languages) are very entertaining, or you can shell out for a guided tour with one of three former Arsenal players. Both options take you everywhere, from the back entrance used by the players to the entertainment suites like the Directors' Box where

TOP EXPERIENCE

GO GOTHIC IN HIGHGATE CEMETERY

A Gothic wonderland of shrouded urns, obelisks, sleeping angels and overgrown graves, Highgate is a Victorian Valhalla spread over 20 wild hectares. On the eastern side you can pay your respects Karl Marx and Mary Ann Evans (better known as novelist George Eliot). The real highlight, however, is the overgrown West Cemetery, where a maze of winding paths leads to the Circle of Lebanon – rings of tombs flanking a circular path and topped with a majestic cedar of Lebanon.

Admission to the **West Cemetery** is by guided tour only; bookings are essential for weekday tours. Guides will explain the various symbols and point out the tombs of the eminent dead. Tours of the **East Cemetery** (adult/child £8/4) take place at 2pm on certain Saturdays.

Highgate remains a working cemetery. The most recent well-known interment was that of singer George Michael in 2016 who is buried in the private section closed to the public. Also of note here is Russian dissident and naturalised Briton Alexander Litvinenko, who died in 2006, poisoned with the radioactive isotope Polonium 210 allegedly by Russian agents.

DON'T MISS

- Karl Marx's grave
- Tour of the West Cemetery
- Circle of Lebanon

PRACTICALITIES

- Map p465, D2
- ☎020-8340 1834
- www.highgatecemetery.org
- Swain's Lane, N6
- adult/child £4/free
- ⊙10am-5pm Mar-Oct, to 4pm Nov-Feb
- Ⓤ Archway

WORTH A DETOUR

WILLIAM MORRIS GALLERY

Fans of Victoriana and the Arts and Crafts movement should make their way to this sensational little **gallery** (020-8496 4390; www.wmgallery.org.uk; Lloyd Park, Forest Rd, E17; 10am-5pm Tue-Sun; Walthamstow Central) FREE in Walthamstow in northeast London. It is the former family home of designer William Morris (1834–96), founder of iconic interior design company Morris & Co and famous far and wide for his patterned wallpaper.

Housed in a beautiful Georgian mansion, the exhibition gives pride of place to Morris' wide-ranging artistic endeavours, with a fantastic workshop explaining his production processes, and a wonderfully evocative recreation of his shop. But it depicts a much more complete portrait of the artist by also covering his writing (for which he was more famous in his lifetime) and activism. Morris was appalled by the consequences of industrialisation on manufacturing processes and quality, on people's living conditions and on the environment, and he became a socialist in the 1880s, campaigning tirelessly against capitalism.

The strength of the gallery is its beauty and interactive quality, which children will love. Kids will also love the lovely park at the back, complete with play area. The 1st floor hosts temporary exhibitions. The gallery's **shop** sells beautiful, Morris-inspired design objects and the **Tea Room** in the glasshouse is the perfect place for a break or a light lunch.

To get here from Walthamstow Central Tube station, turn right (east) on Selborne Rd and then take the first left onto Hoe St. Continue north on this road for 600m and then turn left into Gaywood Rd. The gallery is across the road at the end of the street.

corporate bigwigs watch the game. You'll get to walk to the pitch through 'the tunnel', sit on the team's pitch-side benches in the home dugout, even check out the home and away feng-shui-approved changing rooms, which are complete with spa facilities and physiotherapy suite.

Tours include entry to a small but complete museum that focuses on the history of the club and its 100 million fans worldwide. Visits start and end in the stadium's enormous shop overflowing with Arsenal merchandise.

Islington

Boutique- and eatery-lined Upper St, Islington, is generally portrayed in the press as a hotbed of 'champagne socialism' (a British term referring to certain upper-middle-class so-called socialists whose lifestyles contradict their political convictions), due in part to its association with New Labour in the 1990s when the Blairs lived here. The area's gentrification is reflected in design stores, excellent eateries and a thriving theatre scene, but there are still enough raucous pubs and live-music venues to add some edge.

Less than 200 years ago, Islington was still a quiet village surrounded by farmland, set on the banks of the pleasantly languid New River (now culverted over). Before 1855, Upper St was a veritable livestock highway, with an annual traffic flow that included 50,000 cattle and half a million sheep. By the end of that century, Islington had completely lost its rural feel.

Islington's literary associations are legion. George Orwell was living at 27 Canonbury Sq when he published *Animal Farm* in 1945. The playwright Joe Orton (1933–67) had been living at 25 Noel Rd for seven years when his lover, Kenneth Halliwell, bludgeoned him to death and then committed suicide.

ESTORICK COLLECTION OF MODERN ITALIAN ART GALLERY

Map p466 (www.estorickcollection.com; 39a Canonbury Sq, enter from Canonbury Rd, N1; adult/child £7.50/free; 11am-6pm Wed-Sat, noon-5pm Sun, to 9pm 1st Thu of month; Highbury & Islington) Housed in a listed Georgian town house, the rather esoteric Estorick is the only gallery in Britain devoted to Italian art, with a strong emphasis on *futurismo* (futurism), an early-20th-century artistic movement centred in Italy that responded to the pace of technological development.

WORTH A DETOUR

ALEXANDRA PALACE & PARK

Built in 1873 as North London's answer to Crystal Palace, which was relocated to South London from Hyde Park in 1852, **Alexandra Palace** (020-8365 2121; www.alexandrapalace.com; Alexandra Palace Way, N22; 9am-5pm, varies depending on events; Alexandra Palace, Wood Green) suffered the ignoble fate of burning to the ground only 16 days after opening. But encouraged by attendance figures, investors decided to rebuild, and it reopened just two years later. During WWI it housed German prisoners of war, and in 1936 it was the scene of the world's first TV transmission – a variety show called *Here's Looking at You*. The palace burned down again in 1980 but was rebuilt for the third time and reopened in 1988. The East Court theatre (1875) with its Victorian stage machinery reopened in 2018 after 80 years of neglect.

Today the Great Hall and adjoining Palm Court at 'Ally Pally' are used as a multipurpose conference and exhibition centre, with additional facilities including an indoor ice-skating rink open year-round, a pub restaurant with panoramic terrace, and a popular playground and boating lake. It hosts occasional club nights and concerts, too.

The park in which it stands sprawls over some 196 acres. Locals come to enjoy the sweeping views of London and a farmers' market (open 10am to 3pm on Sunday).

The fireworks held here on Bonfire Night are some of the most spectacular in town, lighting up the city skyline. From the Wood Green Underground station, catch bus W3 direct to the palace.

The collection of paintings, drawings, etchings and sculpture was amassed by American writer and art dealer Eric Estorick and his wife, Salome Dessau. The permanent collection includes works by greats such as Giacomo Balla, Umberto Boccioni, Gino Severini, Amedeo Modigliani and Carlo Carrà.

CANONBURY SQUARE SQUARE

Map p466 (Canonbury Rd, N1; 8am-dusk; Highbury & Islington) A short walk from bustling Upper St, this pretty, park-like square was once home to authors Evelyn Waugh and George Orwell. The latter moved here with his family after his flat in St John's Wood was destroyed during the Blitz. His house at number 27b is marked by a historical plaque, while Waugh's residence at number 17a is unmarked. It's worth pausing in the leafy centre to soak up the atmosphere and peruse the dedications on the benches.

A short distance to the east, on Canonbury Pl opposite No 29, is privately owned **Canonbury Tower**, a relic of the area's original manor house. Dating from 1509, the house was known to have hosted famous figures such as Sir Francis Bacon and Queen Elizabeth I. It is unmarked and not open to the public.

EATING

North London is full of eating gems, including historic pubs, smart cafes, market stalls and ethnically diverse restaurants. It's particularly good for vegetarians, with some excellent exclusively vegetarian and vegan establishments, and plenty of others offering a good meat-free selection.

King's Cross & Euston

★ROTI KING MALAYSIAN £

Map p468 (020-7387 2518; https://rotiking.has.restaurant; 40 Doric Way, NW1; mains £5-7.50; noon-3pm & 5-10.30pm Mon-Fri, noon-10.30pm Sat; ; Euston) The neon sign pointing you in the direction of this pocket-sized basement restaurant doesn't look too promising but the queues do. It's all about *roti canai* (£5 to £6.50), a flaky flatbread typical of Malaysia, served with fragrant bowls of curry or stuffed with tasty fillings. At last, a genuine budget option that isn't a sandwich or a salad.

★BAR PEPITO TAPAS £

Map p466 (020-7841 7331; https://camino.uk.com/restaurant/bar-pepito; 3 Varnishers Yard, The Regent Quarter, N1; tapas £2.50-15; 5pm-midnight Mon-Fri, 6pm-midnight Sat; King's

Cross St Pancras) This tiny, intimate Andalusian bodega specialises in sherry and tapas. Novices fear not: the staff are on hand to advise. They're also experts at food pairings (top-notch ham and cheese selections). To go the whole hog, try a tasting flight of selected sherries with snacks to match.

EKACHAI SOUTHEAST ASIAN £

Map p466 (020-7278 9385; www.ekachai.co.uk/locations/kings-cross; 66 York Way, N1; mains £8.95-10.25; noon-10pm; ; King's Cross St Pancras) You probably wouldn't write home to grandma in Bangkok (or Singapore for that matter) about Ekachai, but if you're in the King's Cross area and need a rice or noodle fix, this pan-Southeast Asia eatery is your best budget option. From Indonesian *nasi goreng* and Thai green curries to Malaysian laksa or Hong Kong beef noodle soup, the world is your oyster.

TERRACE CAFE & RESTAURANT MODERN BRITISH £

Map p466 (0330-333 1144; www.bl.uk/visit/eat-drink-shop; 1st fl, British Library, 96 Euston Rd, NW1; mains £5-10; 9.30am-5pm Mon-Fri, to 4pm Sat & Sun; ; King's Cross St Pancras) A self-service cafeteria with a more expensive serviced-restaurant section (mains £11.95 to £18.95) side by side offer a range of hot and cold mains – pick from the well-assorted salad bar, or the pie, pasta or curry of the day. The seating area has great views of the towering King's Library, and there's a fabulous terrace to be enjoyed in the warmer months.

ADDIS ETHIOPIAN £

Map p466 (020-7278 0679; www.addisrestaurant.co.uk; 40-42 Caledonian Rd, N1; mains £10-16; 5-11pm Mon-Fri, noon-11pm Sat & Sun; ; King's Cross St Pancras) Cheery Addis serves pungent Ethiopian dishes such as *ayeb be gomen* (cottage cheese with spinach and spices), *ful musalah* (crushed fava beans topped with feta cheese and falafel and sautéed in ghee) and more exotic *dulet* (lamb and lamb offal cooked with spices), all of which are eaten on a platter-sized piece of soft but slightly elastic *injera* bread.

There's live Ethiopian music on Sunday from 6.30pm. .

DIWANA BHEL POORI HOUSE INDIAN £

Map p468 (020-7387 5556; www.diwanabph.com; 121-123 Drummond St, NW1; mains £6.50-11.25; noon-11.30pm Mon-Sat, to 10.30pm Sun; ; Euston) One of the best Indian vegetarian restaurants in London, Diwana specialises in Bombay-style *bhel puri* (a tangy, soft and crunchy 'party mix' dish; £3.95) and dosas (filled crispy pancakes made from rice flour; £7.95). Solo diners should consider a thali

WORTH A DETOUR

TOTTENHAM HOTSPUR STADIUM

This state-of-the-art 62,300-seat **stadium** (020-3929 1882; www.tottenhamhotspur.com/the-stadium; 748 High Rd, N17; adult/child £30/15; 10am-6pm Mon-Sat, 10.30am-4.30pm Sun; ; White Hart Lane, Seven Sisters then bus 149 or 259) in Tottenham, with a retractable pitch that hosts both 'real' and American football games, opened in April 2019 replacing the White Hart Lane ground (in place since 1899) and costing upwards of £850 million to build. Even if you're not a Spurs supporter or even a fan of either game, you may want to visit what could be called the Eighth Wonder of the World.

Tottenham Experience guided tours lasting 90 minutes depart every half-hour and are led by young and very enthusiastic supporters who bring life to the back story of both stadium and club. It starts in the very well stocked shop (of course) and leads to the West Atrium on level 9, with its time capsule (to be opened in 2068) and 69m LED screen. Then it's up to the Stratus West lounge for stunning views of the pitch, stands and four mammoth TV screens. The exclusive Loge on level 4 where VIPs watch the matches is next and then comes the famous tunnel with the exhortation 'Come on You Spurs' leading to the home dugout. You'll also get to see the various changing rooms, with the home one especially luxurious and the NFL locker room containing giant-sized fixtures and fittings. The tour also includes visits to the press box and conference rooms. New features will include a high-tech museum of club artefacts and history, and an adrenalin-raising Skywalk some 50m above the South Stand and just below the club's celebrated statue of its mascot, the Cockerel.

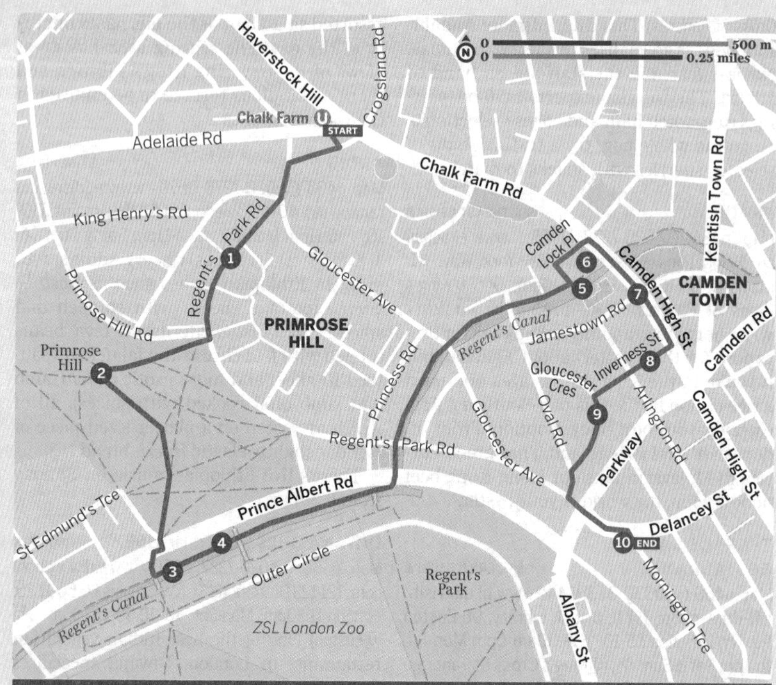

Neighbourhood Walk
A Northern Point of View

START CHALK FARM TUBE STATION
END EDINBORO CASTLE PUB
LENGTH 2.5 MILES; TWO HOURS

This walk takes in North London's most interesting areas, including celebrity-infested Primrose Hill and chaotic Camden Town, home to loud guitar bands and the last of London's cartoon punks. When you come out of Chalk Farm station, cross the road and walk up – it's hilly. Turn left on the railway bridge and continue up the southern, boutique-lined stretch of 1 **Regent's Park Road**. This is affluent neighbourhood is home to celebrities, so look out for famous faces.

When you reach 2 **Primrose Hill** (p253), walk to the top of the park for breathtaking views of central London's skyline. On sunny days the park is full sunbathers, picnickers and footballers.

Walk downhill through the park, bearing right towards Primrose Hill Lodge. Cross the road and join the towpath along 3 **Regent's Canal**, turning left. You'll walk past the large Snowden Aviary at 4 **London Zoo** (p248), quaint narrow boats, superb mansions and converted industrial buildings.

Continue on to 5 **Camden Lock**, turn left and head into the 6 **Camden Lock Market** (p270). With its original fashion, ethnic art and dozens of food stalls, it's a fun, buzzing place, particularly at weekends. Exit onto 7 **Camden High Street**, taking note of the giant Doc Martens boots, angels and dragons projecting from the upper levels of the shops. Turn right onto 8 **Inverness Street**, which hosts its own little market of T-shirts and baseball caps and is lined with bars.

At 9 **Gloucester Crescent** turn left and walk past the glorious Georgian town houses. Eventually, turn left onto Oval Rd, cross Parkway onto Delancey St and make a beeline for the 10 **Edinboro Castle** (p266) pub, where this walk ends with a well-deserved drink! Camden Town Tube station is a five-minute walk away.

(a complete meal consisting of lots of small dishes; £6.95 to £11.25). The all-you-can-eat lunchtime buffet (£7.50) is legendary.

REAL FOOD MARKET MARKET £

Map p466 (www.realfoodfestival.co.uk/real-food-markets/kings-cross-market; King's Cross Sq, N1; dishes £4-12; noon-7pm Wed-Fri; ; King's Cross St Pancras) This vibrant market in front of King's Cross station brings together two dozen gourmet food stalls three times a week. You can get anything from lovely cheeses, cured meats, smoked haddock and artisan bread to takeaway items such as wraps, curries and delicious cakes.

★RUBY VIOLET ICE CREAM £

Map p466 (020-7609 0444; www.rubyviolet.co.uk; Midlands Goods Shed, 3 Wharf Rd, N1; 1 scoop £3; 11am-7pm Mon & Tue, to 10pm Wed-Sun; ; King's Cross St Pancras) Ruby Violet takes ice cream to the next level: flavours are wonderfully original (masala chai, raspberry and sweet potato) and toppings and hot sauces are shop-made. Plus, there's Pudding Club on Friday and Saturday nights, when you can dive into a mini-baked Alaska or hot chocolate fondant. Eat in or sit by the fountain on Granary Sq (p251).

CARAVAN INTERNATIONAL ££

Map p466 (020-7101 7661; www.caravanrestaurants.co.uk; 1 Granary Sq, N1; small plates £7.50-9, mains £17.50-19; 8am-10.30pm Mon-Fri, 10am-10.30pm Sat, to 4pm Sun; ; King's Cross St Pancras) Housed in the lofty Granary Building, the King's Cross redevelopment's first tenant (2012) is a vast industrial-chic destination for tasty fusion bites from around the world. You can opt for several small plates to share tapas-style, or stick to main-sized dishes. The outdoor seating area on Granary Sq is especially popular on warm days, and cocktails are popular regardless of the weather.

Primrose Hill

QUEEN'S GASTROPUB ££

Map p468 (020-7586 0408; www.thequeensprimrosehill.co.uk; 49 Regent's Park Rd, NW1; mains £12-22; noon-10pm Mon-Sat, to 9pm Sun; ; Chalk Farm) This gorgeous pub in well-heeled Primrose Hill serves up excellent British seasonal food that takes no risks: fish and chips, pies and burgers. But the vegetarian selection is good, there's a creditable wine and beer selection and, more importantly, plenty of people-watching to do while eating and drinking – Jude Law has been known to come here for a tipple.

Camden Town

★HOOK CAMDEN TOWN FISH & CHIPS £

Map p468 (020-7482 0475; www.hookrestaurants.com; 63-65 Parkway, NW1; mains £11-17; noon-3pm & 5.30-9pm Mon, to 10pm Tue-Thu, to 10.30pm Fri & Sat, to 9pm Sun; ; Camden Town) In addition to working entirely with sustainable small fisheries and local suppliers, Hook makes all its sauces on-site and wraps its fish in recycled materials, supplying diners with extraordinarily fine-tasting morsels. Totally fresh, the fish arrives in panko breadcrumbs or tempura batter, with seaweed salted chips. Wash it down with craft beer, wines and cocktails. There's also a great kids' menu.

WEST YARD MARKET MARKET £

Map p466 (www.camdenmarket.com/food-drink; Camden Lock Market, Camden Lock Pl, NW1; mains £7-12; noon-5pm; ; Camden Town) There are dozens of food stalls in the West Yard of Camden Lock Market, offering every imaginable cuisine – from French and Argentinian to Japanese and Caribbean. Quality is generally pretty good and it's affordable. You can eat at the big communal tables or by the canal.

★CHIN CHIN LABS ICE CREAM £

Map p466 (07885 604284; www.chinchinlabs.com; 49-50 Camden Lock Pl, NW1; ice cream from £4.95; noon-7pm; Camden Town) This is food chemistry at its absolute best. Chefs prepare the ice-cream mixture and freeze it on the spot by adding liquid nitrogen. Flavours change regularly and match the seasons (tonka bean, Valrhona chocolate, burnt-butter caramel or pandan leaf, for instance). The dozen toppings and sauces are equally creative. Try the ice-cream sandwich (£5.65): ice cream wedged inside gorgeous brownies or cookies.

It's directly opposite Shaka Zulu inside Camden Lock Market.

NAMAASTE KITCHEN INDIAN ££

Map p468 (☎020-7485 5977; www.namaastekitchen.co.uk; 64 Parkway, NW1; mains £9.95-22.95; ⏰noon-11.30pm Mon-Sat, to 11pm Sun; 🌱; Ⓤ Camden Town) Although everything is of a high standard, if there's one thing you should try at Namaaste, it's the kebab platter: the meat and fish coming off the kitchen grill are beautifully tender and incredibly flavoursome. The bread basket is another hit, with specialities such as spiced *missi roti* (flatbread of wholewheat and gram flour and spices).

YORK & ALBANY MODERN BRITISH ££

Map p468 (☎020-7592 1227; www.gordonramsayrestaurants.com/york-and-albany; 127-129 Parkway, NW1; mains £15.50-28, 2-/3-course lunch £19/23; ⏰7am-midnight Mon-Sat, to 11pm Sun; 🌱; Ⓤ Camden Town) Part of chef Gordon Ramsay's culinary empire, this lively hotel brasserie serves British classics in its light-filled dining room from breakfast (£11 to £15) and lunch to tea and dinner seven days a week. It also churns out great wood-fired pizzas next door at Ramsay's Street Pizza and offers some sort of meal/drink deal most week nights (eg 'Bottomless Pizza' for £15).

POPPIE'S FISH & CHIPS ££

Map p468 (☎020-7267 0440; https://poppiesfishandchips.co.uk; 30 Hawley Cres, NW1; mains £6.90-21.95; ⏰11am-11pm Sun-Thu, to midnight Sat & Sun; Ⓤ Camden Town) The largest of the three branches of this high-viz chippie serves reliable fish (choose from a half dozen types) and chips to up to 110 diners over two levels just opposite the major magnet that is Camden Market. Great decor, too, with reclaimed (or repurposed) 1940s fixtures and fittings throughout.

SHAKA ZULU SOUTH AFRICAN ££

Map p468 (☎020-3376 9911; www.shaka-zulu.com; Camden Lock Market, Chalk Farm Rd, NW1; mains £14.50-26; ⏰noon-3pm & 5pm-midnight Sun-Thu, noon-2am Fri & Sat; Ⓤ Camden Town) This huge South African restaurant dominates two floors in Camden Lock Market. The food is heavily themed (obviously) on South African cuisine, and if you're feeling adventurous you can try some game meat, with dishes including zebra, buffalo and wild boar. The extensive cocktail list is also worth a browse, and you have a vast range of South African wines to choose from.

Hampstead

STAG GASTROPUB £

Map p465 (☎020-7722 2646; www.thestagnw3.com; 67 Fleet Rd, NW3; mains £9-17.50; ⏰noon-11pm Mon-Thu, to midnight Fri & Sat, to 10.30pm Sun; Ⓤ Hampstead Heath) Although the Stag in Belsize Park is a fantastic pub for craft beer, it's known in North London for its outstanding food: the Sunday roast and beef-and-ale pie in particular. The summer barbecue in the garden is another delight. The only drawbacks are that service can be slow and the welcome less than effusive.

WOODLANDS INDIAN £

Map p465 (☎020-7794 3080; www.woodlandsrestaurant.co.uk; 102 Heath St, NW3; dishes £5-13, thali £19; ⏰6-10.45pm Tue-Thu, noon-3pm & 6-11pm Fri-Sun; 🌱; Ⓤ Hampstead) Don't expect cutting-edge decor or faultless service, but this South Indian restaurant is a great bet for an affordable vegetarian meal in Hampstead. It caters superbly to vegan, gluten-free and dairy-free diners as well. Try one of the four dosas (£9) on the menu.

GINGER & WHITE CAFE £

Map p465 (☎020-7431 9098; www.gingerandwhite.com; 4a-5a Perrin's Ct, NW3; mains £7.75-10.25; ⏰7.30am-5.30pm Mon-Fri, 8.30am-5.30pm Sat & Sun; 📶🌱👪; Ⓤ Hampstead) This lovely cafe on a quiet alleyway is a long-standing Hampstead favourite for its excellent coffee, simple but delicious food and light, airy set-up. Depending on the time of day, the clientele will consist of young mothers, professionals using the window seats as office space, or devoted locals enjoying all-day breakfast and on a first-name basis with staff.

LA CAGE IMAGINAIRE FRENCH ££

Map p465 (☎020-7794 6674; www.la-cage-imaginaire.co.uk; 16 Flask Walk, NW3; 2-/3-course set lunch £15.95/19.95, dinner £22.95/25.95; ⏰noon-11pm; Ⓤ Hampstead) This delightful and very *chouette* (cute) French restaurant is an excellent budget option in pricey Hampstead, with such Gallic comfort food as onion soup and frogs' legs for starters followed by *coq au vin* or beef *bourguignon* and apple and prune Tatin for dessert. Warm welcome, charming service.

WELLS TAVERN GASTROPUB ££

Map p465 (☎020-7794 3785; www.thewellshampstead.co.uk; 30 Well Walk, NW3; mains £12.50-

19.50; ⏲noon-3pm & 6-10pm Mon-Fri, noon-4pm & 7-10pm Sat & Sun; 📶; ⓊHampstead) This popular gastropub has a surprisingly modern interior, given its traditional exterior. The menu is proper posh English pub grub – Cumberland sausages, mash and onion gravy, and full roasts with all the trimmings. At weekends you'll need to fight to get a table if you haven't booked ahead. The outdoor tables are prime spots for contemplation.

GAUCHO ARGENTINE £££

Map p465 (☎020-7431 8222; www.gauchorestaurants.com/restaurants/hampstead; 64 Heath St, NW3; mains £16.50-49.50, 2-/3-course lunch £22/28; ⏲noon-11pm Sun-Wed, to midnight Thu-Sat; ⓊHampstead) Carnivores rejoice; this is one of the finest places in London for a steak (though all toppings and sauces are extra). There are a half-dozen branches of this Argentinian grill across the capital, but this one has the advantage of being less busy than its counterparts – it is huge – and it serves a special *asado* (barbecue) menu, complete with alfresco seating.

Islington

SAMBAL SHIOK MALAYSIAN £

Map p466 (☎020-7619 9888; www.sambalshiok.co.uk; 71 Holloway Rd, N7; mains £6.90-13.80; ⏲5.30-10pm Tue-Fri, 11.30am-3.15pm & 5.30-10pm Sat; ⓊHolloway Rd) Sambal Shiok calls itself a laksa bar – and indeed it makes the tastiest laksa this side of Kuala Lumpur. A fragrant coconut noodle dish, laksa is best when ingredients are freshly ground, which they are here at this tiny restaurant on Holloway Rd, about a 15-minute walk from the Underground station. Be prepared to wait in line if you don't have a booking.

OI VITA PIZZERIA £

(☎020-3302 8700; https://oivita.london; 67 Newington Green Rd, N1; pizza £7.45-15.95; ⏲5-10.30pm Mon-Thu, to 11pm Fri, noon-11pm Sat, to 10.30pm Sun; ⓊCanonbury) This lovely little pizzeria is run by two Italian guys – Nicola chefs and Matteo serves – who import most ingredients from their homeland. The pizzas are cooked in a massive wood-fired stone oven, and the signature dessert is deep-fried dough balls topped with Nutella and white-chocolate sauce (£5.45).

NORTH LONDON'S BEST VEGETARIAN RESTAURANTS

North London is the place to go for creative, filling and absolutely delicious vegetarian cuisine to suit all tastes. Here are some of the best. Note: unlike the first two, Addis and Good Egg are not strictly vegetarian, but both Ethiopian and Israeli cuisine has a rich vegetarian tradition, which is well represented with eight mains on each restaurant's menu.

Woodlands (p262)

Rasa N16 (p265)

Addis (p259)

Good Egg (p265)

LE MERCURY FRENCH £

Map p466 (☎020-7354 4088; www.lemercury.co.uk; 140a Upper St, N1; mains £11-95-13.95; ⏲noon-midnight Mon-Thu, to 12.30am Fri & Sat, to 11.30pm Sun; ⓊHighbury & Islington or Angel) An excellent and very central budget French eatery, Le Mercury seems to have everything you could need in its winning formula: romantic atmosphere, with candlelit, petite tables and plants everywhere, combined with superb French food at unbeatable prices. Londoners have long known about this place, so reservations are advised.

PIEBURY CORNER BRITISH £

Map p466 (☎020-7688 2987; https://pieburycorner.com; 3 Caledonian Rd, N1; pies £3-6; ⏲11am-11pm Mon-Fri, noon-11pm Sat, to 6pm Sun; ⓊKing's Cross St Pancras) If you're wondering what all the fuss is about English pies, there's no better place to sample some than this simple little eatery. Choose from the usual steak and kidney and chicken and mushroom to the rarer ox cheek, venison and mushroom. Add the almost mandatory creamy mash and crushed minty peas for £5 and the picture is complete.

CHILANGO MEXICAN £

Map p466 (☎020-7704 2123; www.chilango.co.uk; 27 Upper St, N1; burritos & tacos £6.95-8.95; ⏲11am-10pm Mon-Wed, to 11pm Thu-Sat, noon-10pm Sun; 🌶; ⓊAngel) The good value and tastiness of Chilango's Mexican fare is no secret among Islingtonians on a budget. Burritos come bursting to the seams with your choice of meat (chicken, prawns, pork or beef), beans, salad, rice and sauces. Vegetarians are well catered for too. Eat in the bright, colourful interior on two levels or take it away.

★OTTOLENGHI — MEDITERRANEAN ££

Map p466 (020-7288 1454; www.ottolenghi.co.uk; 287 Upper St, N1; breakfast £5.90-12.50, mains lunch/dinner from £16.50/10; 8am-10.30pm Mon-Sat, 9am-7pm Sun; ; Highbury & Islington) Mountains of meringues tempt you through the door of this deli-restaurant, where a sumptuous array of baked goods and fresh salads greets you. Meals are as light and bright as the brilliantly white interior design, with a strong influence from the eastern Mediterranean. Mains at lunch are full platters and include two salads.

★DUKE OF CAMBRIDGE — GASTROPUB ££

Map p466 (020-7359 3066; www.dukeorganic.co.uk; 30 St Peter's St, N1; mains £15-23.50; noon-3pm & 5.30-9.30pm Mon-Wed, to 10pm Thu & Fri, noon-10pm Sat, to 9.30pm Sun; ; Angel) The UK's first certified organic pub is a great place to avoid the crowds, as it's tucked some way down a side street in Islington where casual passers-by rarely tread. It has a fantastic selection of beers and ales on tap, a great (biodynamic) wine list and an interesting organic menu with a Mediterranean slant. Lovely back skylight.

★TRULLO — ITALIAN ££

Map p466 (020-7226 2733; www.trullorestaurant.com; 300-302 St Paul's Rd, N1; mains £16.50-24; 12.30-2.45pm & 6-10.15pm Mon-Sat, to 9.15pm Sun; Highbury & Islington) Trullo's daily homemade pasta is delicious (pappardelle, fettuccine), but the main attraction here is the charcoal grill, which churns out the likes of succulent Italian-style pork chops, lamb rump and fish. The all-Italian wine list is brief but well chosen. Service is excellent, although dinner time can get packed. Book well in advance.

OLDROYD — MEDITERRANEAN ££

Map p466 (020-8617 9010; www.oldroydlondon.com; 344 Upper St, N1; mains £14-21; 12.30-2.45pm & 6-10pm Mon-Thu, 12.30-10pm Sat, to 9pm Sun) This tiny eatery on Upper St in Islington serves up some of the biggest-flavoured Mediterranean dishes in town. The choices are as limited as the seats, with usually just four mains: a meat, a fish and two vegetarian ones (though there are a half-dozen starters as well). Seating is on two levels. Weekday lunch is a snip at £10.

SMOKEHOUSE — BARBECUE ££

Map p466 (020-7354 1144; www.smokehouseislington.co.uk; 63-69 Canonbury Rd, N1; mains £15-20; 6-10pm Mon-Thu, to 10.30pm Fri, noon-4pm & 6-10.30pm Sat, noon-9pm Sun; ; Highbury & Islington) In this lovely, light-filled pub, elegantly turned out in dark wood and whitewashed walls, you'll find a meaty menu of international dishes, all imbued with a smoky flavour; everything is grilled, roasted or smoked on the premises – from the poussin to the crab bisque. Ingredients are carefully sourced and skilfully combined, and there is a particularly extensive beer list.

IBERIA — GEORGIAN ££

Map p466 (020-7700 7750; www.iberiarestaurant.co.uk; 294-296 Caledonian Rd, N1; mains £8.70-16.50; 6-11pm Tue-Fri, 1-11pm Sat, 1-9pm Sun; Caledonian Rd & Barnsbury) On a strip of so-so ethnic eateries, Iberia stands out for its pleasant surrounds, friendly service and excellent and very traditional Georgian fare. If you're not familiar with the cuisine, expect a meaty morph of Russian and Middle Eastern flavours. Go for the staple *khachapuri* (£7.90), a filling flatbread stuffed with Georgian cheese; and the scrumptious *khinkali* (14.60), pork and beef dumplings.

KIPFERL — AUSTRIAN ££

Map p466 (020-7704 1555; www.kipferl.co.uk; 20 Camden Passage, N1; mains £10.50-19.50; 11am-10pm Tue-Thu, 9am-11pm Fri & Sat, to 9pm Sun; Angel) Part cafe, part restaurant and totally Austrian, Kipferl serves classic comfort food such as Wiener schnitzel (£15.50), *Käsespatzle* (egg noodles with cheese; £14.50) and spinach dumplings (£13.50). Otherwise just sidle in and choose a coffee from the 'colour palette' menu that is typical of Viennese cafes, and pick from the mouth-watering selection of cakes (Sachertorte, *Apfelstrudel* etc).

YIPIN CHINA — CHINESE ££

Map p466 (020-7354 3388; https://yipinchina.co.uk; 72 Liverpool Rd, N1; mains £8-22; noon-11pm; ; Angel) As authentic a Chinese restaurant as you'll find in London (it's usually full of Chinese diners – a good sign), Yipin specialises in the spicy and fragrant cuisine of Hunan, and there are plenty of fiery Sichuanese and familiar

Cantonese dishes to choose from, too. The lengthy picture menu makes the choosing (slightly) easier.

PRAWN ON THE LAWN SEAFOOD £££

Map p466 (020-3302 8668; http://prawnonthelawn.com; 292-294 St Paul's Rd, N1; small plates £7.50-10, platters £22-39; noon-10pm Tue-Sat, to 4pm Sun; Highbury & Islington) This B&W-tiled establishment both sells the freshest of fish and shellfish as a fishmonger's and serves it as a restaurant. Consult the ever-changing blackboard for the likes of Padstow crab salad, Sichuan prawns, taramasalata, and seafood stew not unlike Italian *brodetto*. Watch the briny critters be transported from their mountains of ice into the fire of the open kitchen.

Stoke Newington

GOOD EGG JEWISH £

(020-7682 2120; http://thegoodeggn16.com; 93 Stoke Newington Church St, N16; mains £9.50-15.50; 9am-5pm Mon, to 11pm Tue-Fri, 10am-11pm Sat & Sun; ; 73) Working the culinary trend of the moment – Levantine food meets modern European cuisine – the Good Egg, with its long opening hours, is many things to many people: a family-friendly cafe, a trendy restaurant to share dishes and the best place in Stoke Newington for brunch (£6.50 to £13.50). The trick is that it consistently delivers. Expect queues, especially at the weekend.

RASA N16 INDIAN £

(020-7249 0344; http://rasarestaurants.com/rasa-n16; 55 Stoke Newington Church St, N16; mains £5.50-7.95; 6-10.45pm Mon-Thu, to 11.30pm Fri, noon-3pm & 6-11.30pm Sat, noon-2.45pm & 6-10.45pm Sun; ; 73) This shocking-pink South Indian vegetarian eatery is Stoke Newington's best-known – and most visible – restaurant. Friendly service, a calm atmosphere, reasonable prices and outstanding food from the Indian state of Kerala are its distinctive features. The multicourse Keralan Feast (vegetarian/vegan £19.99/22.50) is for the truly ravenous.

DRINKING & NIGHTLIFE

Camden Town is one of North London's favoured drinking areas, with more bars and pubs pumping out music than you could ever manage to crawl between. The hills of Hampstead are a real treat for old-time-pub aficionados, while Islington is known for its theatre pubs and tucked-away wine and cocktail bars. As for King's Cross, there are new places opening all the time, many in converted Victorian buildings north of the station.

King's Cross & Euston

EUSTON TAP BAR

Map p468 (020-3137 8837; www.eustontap.com; 190 Euston Rd, NW1; noon-11.30pm Mon-Thu, to midnight Fri & Sat, to 10pm Sun; Euston) This specialist drinking spot inhabits a monumental stone structure on the approach to Euston station. Craft-beer devotees can choose between 15 cask ales, 28 keg beers and 150 brews by the bottle. Grab a seat on the pavement, take the tight spiral staircase upstairs or buy a bottle to take away.

CAMINO BAR

Map p466 (020-7841 7330; https://camino.uk.com/restaurant/kings-cross; 3 Varnishers Yard, The Regent Quarter, N1; noon-midnight Mon-Thu, to 1am Fri & Sat, to 11pm Sun; ; King's Cross St Pancras) This festive boozer is popular with London's Spanish community and therefore feels quite authentic. Drinks, too, are representative of what you'd find in Spain: cava, Estrella on tap and a long all-Spanish wine list. DJs hit the turntables from Thursday to Saturday. In summer the courtyard gets absolutely rammed with merrymakers.

ORIGIN COFFEE ROASTERS CAFE

Map p466 (020-7387 8684; www.origincoffee.co.uk; 96 Euston Rd, British Library, NW1; 7.30am-6pm Mon-Thu, to 5.30pm Fri, 9am-4pm Sat, 10am-4pm Sun; King's Cross St Pancras) This little cafe just before the entrance to the British Library piazza scores highly on design but even more on its coffee. One of just three London outlets from specialist coffee roaster Origin, whose raison d'être is provenance and processing, it offers regularly changing feature coffees and a selection of espresso-based concoctions and filter options.

★BIG CHILL BAR

Map p466 (☎020-7427 2540; https://bigchillbar.com; 257-259 Pentonville Rd, N1; ⊙11am-midnight Sun-Wed, to 1am Thu, to 3am Fri & Sat; 📶; ⓤKing's Cross St Pancras) Come the weekend, the only remotely chilled-out space in this large, buzzy bar is its first-rate and generously proportioned rooftop terrace. Count on a varied playlist of live music and DJs. The sound system is fantastic and entry is free apart from the last Saturday of the month.

EGG LDN CLUB

Map p466 (☎020-7871 7111; www.egglondon.co.uk; 200 York Way, N7; ⊙10.30pm-5am Tue-Thu, to 6am Fri, to 7am Sat; ⓤCaledonian Rd & Bansbury or King's Cross St Pancras) Egg has a superb layout with two vast exposed-concrete rooms, a wooden loft space, a garden and a roof terrace in an old Victorian warehouse. It specialises in house and techno and attracts some heavyweight DJs, particularly on Saturday nights. On Friday and Saturday, it runs a free shuttle bus from 11pm, leaving from 68 York Way, outside King's Cross station.

Camden Town

★EDINBORO CASTLE PUB

Map p468 (☎020-7255 9651; www.edinborocastlepub.co.uk; 57 Mornington Tce, NW1; ⊙noon-11pm Mon-Sat, to 10.30pm Sun; 📶; ⓤCamden Town) Large and relaxed, the Edinboro offers a fun atmosphere, a fine bar and a full menu. The highlight, however, is the huge beer garden, complete with warm-weather barbecues and decorated with coloured lights on long summer evenings. Patio heaters appear in winter.

LOCK TAVERN PUB

Map p468 (☎020-7482 7163; www.lock-tavern.com; 35 Chalk Farm Rd, NW1; ⊙noon-midnight Sun-Thu, to 1am Fri & Sat; ⓤChalk Farm) A Camden institution, the black-clad Lock Tavern rocks: it's cosy inside, and it has a rear beer garden and a great roof terrace from where you can watch the market throngs. Beer is plentiful here and it proffers a prolific roll call of guest bands and well-known DJs at weekends to rev things up. Dancing is encouraged. Entry is always free.

TAPPING THE ADMIRAL PUB

Map p468 (☎020-7267 6118; www.tappingtheadmiral.co.uk; 77 Castle Rd, NW1; ⊙noon-11pm Sun-Tue, to midnight Wed-Sat, to 10.30pm Sun; 📶; ⓤCamden Town or Kentish Town West) Enjoy a fine selection of real ale in this cosy, eclectic, nautical-themed award-winning boozer. Regulars keep the bar propped up and the dimly lit location's atmosphere is enhanced by a friendly pub cat. Ask the bar staff to explain the pub's name. Hint: the admiral in question lords over Trafalgar Sq.

BREWDOG CAMDEN CRAFT BEER

Map p468 (☎020-7284 4626; www.brewdog.com/uk/bars/uk/brewdog-camden; 113 Bayham St, NW1; ⊙noon-11.30pm Mon-Thu, to midnight Fri & Sat, to 10.30pm Sun; 📶; ⓤCamden Town) The hair of this particular dog is craft beer, with around 20 different brews on tap. BrewDog's own brewery is up in Scotland, but more than half of the bar's stock is comprised of guest beers sourced from boutique breweries the world over. Mop it all up with a burger or chicken wings (£9.50 to £11).

Kentish Town

BULL & GATE PUB

Map p465 (☎020-3437 0905; www.bullandgatenw5.co.uk; 389 Kentish Town Rd, NW5; ⊙11am-11pm Mon-Wed, to midnight Thu & Fri, 10am-midnight Sat, noon-10.30pm Sun; 📶; ⓤKentish Town) Once one of the best places to see unsigned but promising talent, the legendary Bull & Gate's old-school music venue has metamorphosed into an elegant gastropub-cum-piano bar. The upstairs Boulogne Bar has been lavishly decorated in the spirit of an old gentleman's club – expect excellent cocktails and a posh (for Kentish Town) clientele.

Hampstead

★HOLLY BUSH PUB

Map p465 (☎020-7435 2892; www.hollybushhampstead.co.uk; 22 Holly Mount, NW3; ⊙noon-11pm Mon-Sat, to 10.30pm Sun; 📶; ⓤHampstead) This beautiful Grade II-listed Georgian pub boasts a splendid antique interior, with open fires in winter. It has a knack for making you stay longer than you planned. Set above Heath St, in a secluded hilltop location, it's reached via the Holly Bush Steps.

SPANIARD'S INN PUB

Map p465 (020-8731 8406; www.thespaniardshampstead.co.uk; Spaniards Rd, NW3; noon-11pm Mon-Sat, to 10.30pm Sun; ; 210) Dating from 1585, this historic tavern has more character than a West End musical. It was supposedly highwayman Dick Turpin's hang-out between robberies, but it's also been a watering hole for more savoury characters like Romantic poets Keats and Byron and artist Sir Joshua Reynolds. It even gets a mention in *The Pickwick Papers* by Charles Dickens and Bram Stoker's *Dracula*.

There's a big, blissful garden that gets crammed at weekends.

GARDEN GATE PUB

Map p465 (020-7435 4938; www.thegardengatehampstead.co.uk; 14 South End Rd, NW3; noon-11pm Mon-Thu, to midnight Fri, 10am-midnight Sat, noon-10.30pm Sun; ; Hampstead Heath) At the bottom of Hampstead Heath hides this gem housed in a 19th-century cottage with a gorgeous beer garden. The interior is wonderfully cosy, with dark-wood tables, upholstered chairs and an assortment of distressed sofas. It serves Pimms and lemonade in summer and mulled wine in winter, both ideal after a long walk. The food (mains £11 to £20) is good too.

Highgate

★FLASK PUB

Map p465 (020-8348 7346; www.theflaskhighgate.com; 77 Highgate West Hill, N6; 11.30am-11pm Mon-Fri, noon-11pm Sat, to 10.30pm Sun; ; Highgate) Charming nooks and crannies, an old circular bar and an enticing beer garden make this 1663 pub the perfect place for a pint while walking between Hampstead Heath and Highgate Cemetery. In winter ,huddle before the open fires and enjoy the Sunday roast (mains £15 to £18.50). It really is just like a country pub in the city.

Islington

69 COLEBROOKE ROW COCKTAIL BAR

Map p466 (07540 528 593; www.69colebrookerow.com; 69 Colebrooke Row, N1; 5pm-midnight Sun-Wed, to 1am Thu, to 2am Fri & Sat; Angel) Also known as 'the bar with no name', this tiny establishment may be nothing much to look at, but it has a stellar reputation for its cocktails (£11). The seasonal drinks menu is steeped in ambitious flavours and blends, with classic drinks for more conservative palates. Hard to find a seat at the best of times, so make sure you book ahead.

Also runs two-hour cocktail masterclasses (£50) from 2pm at the weekend.

CASTLE PUB

Map p466 (020-7713 1858; www.thecastleislington.co.uk; 54 Pentonville Rd, N1; 11am-11pm Mon-Thu, to midnight Fri & Sat, to 10.30pm Sun; ; Angel) A gorgeous, boutique pub – if there is such a thing – with a winning formula of snazzy decor (wooden floors, designer wallpaper, soft furnishings and large maps on the walls), good gastropub food (mains £12.50 to £16.50), a rotating selection of craft beers and, to top it all off, a wonderful roof terrace.

CRAFT BEER CO CRAFT BEER

Map p466 (020-7278 0318; www.thecraftbeerco.com/islington; 55 White Lion St, N1; 4-11pm Mon-Wed, to midnight Thu, noon-1am Fri & Sat, to 10.30pm Sun; ; Angel) One of eight Craft Beer Co locations in London, this lovely pub is riding the wave of the craft-beer craze, pushing the envelope by giving its drinkers a daily beer menu with two dozen brews from around the world, offered from kegs and casks and lots more in bottles and cans.

Naturally, it has a burger menu (£9 to £12.25) to turn a couple of pints into a night.

BULL PUB

Map p466 (020-7354 9174; www.thebullislington.co.uk; 100 Upper St, N1; noon-11pm Sun-Tue, to midnight Wed & Thu, to 1am Fri & Sat; ; Angel) One of Islington's liveliest pubs (with DJs on weekend nights and sports events on TV), the Bull serves a large range of draught lager, real ales, fruit beers, ciders and wheat beer, plus a good selection of wine. The mezzanine is generally a little quieter than downstairs, although on weekend nights you'll often struggle to find a seat.

Stoke Newington

AULD SHILLELAGH PUB

(020-7249 5951; www.theauldshillelagh.com; 105 Stoke Newington Church St, N16; 11am-midnight Sun-Thu, to 1am Fri & Sat; 73) We're going out on a limb and calling this London's best Irish pub. The staff are sharp, the Guinness is good, and the live entertainment is frequent and varied (from trad bands to rappers, sometimes even both at once). It's a great spot to watch the rugby or football, and there's a beer garden out the back.

ENTERTAINMENT

North London is the home of indie rock, and many a famous band started out playing in the area's grungy bars. Indeed, Camden High St has become a rock music Walk of Fame, with the first of a planned 400 granite plaques unveiled to the Who. You can be sure to find live music of some kind every night of the week. A number of venues are multipurpose, with gigs in the first part of the evening (generally around 7pm or 8pm), followed by club nights beginning around midnight.

★GREEN NOTE — LIVE MUSIC

Map p468 (☎020-7485 9899; www.greennote.co.uk; 106 Parkway, NW1; ⏲7-11pm Sun-Thu, to midnight Fri & Sat; ⓊCamden Town) Camden may be the home of punk, but it also has the Green Note: one of the best places in London to see live folk and world music, with gigs every night of the week. The setting is intimate: a tiny bare-brick room with mics set up in a corner, backdropped by red curtains. Most tickets are under £10 (£12 at the door).

Acts include many British and Irish folk, bluegrass and traditional bands, as well as really eclectic musicians from around the world. Beer, wine and vegetarian snacks and tapas are available.

JAZZ CAFE — LIVE MUSIC

Map p468 (☎020-7485 6834; www.thejazzcafelondon.com; 5 Parkway, NW1; ⏲7-11pm Sun-Thu, to 3am Fri & Sat; ⓊCamden Town) The name would have you think jazz is the main staple, but it's only a small slice of what's on offer here. The intimate club-like space also serves up funk, hip-hop, R&B, soul and rare groove, with big-name acts regularly playing nightly at 7pm. Friday (world music) and Saturday (soul, disco and house) club nights start at 10.30pm.

★KING'S HEAD THEATRE — THEATRE

Map p466 (☎020-7226 4443; www.kingsheadtheatre.com; 115 Upper St, N1; ⓊAngel) This stalwart pub theatre hosts new plays and musicals, along with revivals of classics. Classical music and opera are part of the mix, too. It's always been one of our favourite places for off-West End theatre.

ALMEIDA — THEATRE

Map p466 (☎020-7359 4404; www.almeida.co.uk; Almeida St, N1; tickets £10-42.50; ⓊHighbury & Islington) Housed in a Grade II–listed Victorian building, this plush 325-seat theatre can be relied on for imaginative programming. Its emphasis is on new, up-and-coming talent. For theatregoers aged 25 and under, £5 tickets (two per person) are available for select performances.

BLUES KITCHEN — LIVE MUSIC

Map p468 (☎020-7387 5277; www.thebblueskitchen.com; 111-113 Camden High St, NW1; ⏲noon-midnight Mon & Tue, to 1am Wed & Thu, to 2am Fri, 10am-3am Sat, to 1am Sun; ⓊCamden Town) The Blues Kitchen's recipe for success is simple: select brilliant blues bands, host them in a fabulous bar, make it (mostly) free, and offer some excellent food and drink. Which means that the crowds keep on comin'. There's live music every night (usually from 9.45pm) – anything from folk and soul to rock 'n' roll – and blues jams from 8.30pm on Sundays.

★BOOGALOO — CABARET

Map p465 (☎020-8340 2928; www.theboogaloo.co.uk; 312 Archway Rd, N6; ⏲5pm-midnight Mon-Wed, 12.30pm-1am Thu, to 2am Fri, 10.30am-2am Sat, to midnight Sun; 📶; ⓊHighgate) 'London's Number 1 Jukebox' is how Boogaloo flaunts itself: its celebrity-musician-selected jukebox playlists feature the favourite 10 songs of the likes of Nick Cave, Sinead O'Connor and Kate Moss, to name but a few. There's plenty to boogie to (and dance classes to perfect your moves), as well as live music, pub quizzes and comedy nights.

FEST CAMDEN — LIVE MUSIC

Map p468 (☎020-7428 4922; www.festcamden.com; Chalk Farm Rd, NW1; ⏲noon-11pm Sun-Wed, to 2.30am Thu-Sat; ⓊChalk Farm) Tucked away in what used to be the horse hospital in Camden Stables Market, this space now hosts a diverse range of events, from cinema nights to club nights and from cabaret to comedy.

★SCALA LIVE MUSIC

Map p466 (☎020-7833 2022; www.scala.co.uk; 275 Pentonville Rd, N1; cover £10-35; ⓤKing's Cross St Pancras) Opened in 1920 as a cutting-edge golden-age cinema, Scala slipped into porn-movie hell in the 1970s, only to be reborn as a club and live-music venue in the early 2000s. It's one of the top places in London to catch an intimate gig and is a great dance space, too, hosting a diverse range of club nights.

★CECIL SHARP HOUSE TRADITIONAL MUSIC

Map p468 (☎020-7485 2206; www.cecilsharphouse.org; 2 Regent's Park Rd, NW1; ⏲9am-11pm; ⓤCamden Town) Home to the English Folk Dance and Song Society, this institute keeps all manner of folk traditions alive. Performances and classes range from traditional British music and ceilidh dances to bell-jingling Morris dancing and clog-stamping, all held in its mural-covered Kennedy Hall. The dance classes are oodles of fun and there's a real community vibe; no experience necessary.

ANGEL COMEDY COMEDY

Map p466 (www.angelcomedy.co.uk; 2 Camden Passage, N1; ⏲shows generally 8pm Sun-Thu, 7pm & 9.15pm Fri & Sat; ⓤAngel) There's free comedy every night at this great little club upstairs at the Camden Head pub. Monday is improv night, and on other evenings you might get anything from a new act to a famous name road-testing new material; check the website for listings. Donations are gratefully received.

ELECTRIC BALLROOM LIVE MUSIC

Map p468 (☎020-7485 9007; www.electricballroom.co.uk; 184 Camden High St, NW1; cover £5-15; ⓤCamden Town) One of Camden's historic venues, the Electric Ballroom has been entertaining North Londoners since 1938. Many great bands and musicians have played here, from Blur to Paul McCartney, The Clash and U2. There are constantly changing club nights on Fridays, while on Saturdays it hosts Electric Luv, a crowd-pleaser in two rooms with commercial, charts, club classics and R&B.

LORD'S SPECTATOR SPORT

(☎020-7616 8500; www.lords.org; St John's Wood Rd, NW8; 📶; ⓤSt John's Wood) For cricket devotees a trip to Lord's (p253) is often as much a pilgrimage as anything else. As well as being home to Marylebone Cricket Club, the ground hosts Test matches, one-day internationals and domestic cricket finals. International matches are usually booked months in advance, but tickets for county cricket fixtures are reasonably easy to come by.

REGENT'S PARK OPEN AIR THEATRE THEATRE

Map p468 (☎0333 400 3562; www.openairtheatre.org; Queen Mary's Gardens, Regent's Park, NW1; ⏲May-Sep; 👪; ⓤBaker St) A popular and very atmospheric summertime fixture in London, this 1250-seat outdoor auditorium plays host to four productions a year: famous plays, new works, musicals and usually one production aimed at families.

ROUNDHOUSE CONCERT VENUE

Map p468 (☎0300 678 9222; www.roundhouse.org.uk; Chalk Farm Rd, NW1; ⓤChalk Farm) Built as a railway repair shed in 1847, this unusual Grade II–listed round building became an arts centre in the 1960s and hosted legendary bands before falling into near-dereliction in 1983. Its 21st-century resurrection as a creative hub has been a great success and it now hosts everything from big-name concerts to dance, circuses, stand-up comedy, poetry slams and improvisation.

UNION CHAPEL CONCERT VENUE

Map p466 (☎020-7226 1686, 020-7359 4019; www.unionchapel.org.uk; 19 Compton Tce, N1; ⓤHighbury & Islington) One of London's most atmospheric and individual music venues, the Union Chapel is an 1877 design by James Cubitt that still holds services as well as concerts and the monthly Live at the Chapel (£20) comedy club at 6.30pm on Saturday. It also runs Daylight Music, free gigs (£5 donation suggested) that regularly take place on Saturdays from noon to 2pm.

DUBLIN CASTLE LIVE MUSIC

Map p468 (☎07949 575 149; www.thedublincastle.com; 94 Parkway, NW1; ⏲1pm-midnight Mon-Wed, noon-2am Thu-Sun; ⓤCamden Town) Live punk or alternative bands play most nights from 7.15pm in this comfortingly grungy pub's back room (cover charges are usually £5 to £8). DJs take over after the bands on Friday, Saturday and Sunday nights.

HAMPSTEAD THEATRE THEATRE

(☎020-7722 9301; www.hampsteadtheatre.com; Eton Ave, NW3; ⓤSwiss Cottage) The Hampstead is famed for staging new writing and taking on emerging directors. It was an early champion of Harold Pinter, which shows it knows a good thing when it sees one.

O2 FORUM CONCERT VENUE

Map p465 (020-3362 4110; https://academymusicgroup.com/o2forumkentishtown; 9-17 Highgate Rd, NW5; tickets from £24; Kentish Town) You can find your way to the O2 Forum – once the famous Town & Country Club – by the ticket touts that line the way from Kentish Town Tube station. This art deco former cinema (built 1934) is spacious yet intimate enough for bands and comedians starting to break through (or big names a little past their prime).

SHOPPING

Shopping in Camden Town is all about market stalls, Doc Martens boots and secondhand clothes. Islington is great for antiques, quality vintage clothes and design objects.

★STABLES MARKET MARKET

Map p468 (www.camdenmarket.com; Chalk Farm Rd, NW1; 10am-late; Chalk Farm) Connected to the Camden Lock Market, the Stables overflows with antiques, Asian artefacts, rugs, retro furniture and street clothing. As the name suggests, this is where up to 800 horses (who worked hauling barges on Regent's Canal) were housed. One potential draw here beyond shopping is the bronze statue of Amy Winehouse (1983–2011), the late and much missed singer-songwriter who lived in the neighbourhood.

★ANNIE'S VINTAGE COSTUME & TEXTILES VINTAGE

Map p466 (07968 037993; www.anniesvintageclothing.co.uk; 12 Camden Passage, N1; 10am-6pm; Angel) One of London's most enchanting vintage shops, this high-end boutique has costumes to make you look like Greta Garbo. Many a famous designer has come here for inspiration, so you might also get to do some celebrity-spotting.

★CAMDEN LOCK MARKET MARKET

Map p468 (www.camdenmarket.com; Camden Lock Pl, NW1; 10am-late; Camden Town) Right next to the canal lock, this section of Camden Market is the place to go for diverse food stalls in the West Yard (p262), as well as for several nice bars with views of the canal. There are also shops selling crafts, ceramics and clothes.

★CAMDEN PASSAGE MARKET ANTIQUES

Map p466 (www.camdenpassageislington.co.uk; Camden Passage, N1; 9am-6pm Wed & Sat; Angel) Not to be confused with Camden Market (p254), Camden Passage is a pretty cobbled lane in Islington lined with antique stores, vintage-clothing boutiques and cafes. Scattered along the lane are three not-so-separate market areas. The main market days are Wednesday and Saturday, though some open on Thursday, Friday and Sunday as well, and the shops are open all week.

MARY'S LIVING & GIVING SHOP CLOTHING

Map p466 (020-7226 8840; www.savethechildren.org.uk/shop/marys-living-and-giving-shops/islington; 138 Upper St, N1; 10am-6pm Mon-Sat, noon-4pm Sun) This is not your average Save the Children charity shop: the boutique is done up beautifully and the quality of the clothes on offer is top-notch. Allow £60 to £80 for designer dresses and jackets, £7 to £10 for high-street-brand tops.

EXCLUSIVO FASHION & ACCESSORIES

Map p465 (020-7431 8618; 2 Flask Walk, NW3; 12.30-6pm; Hampstead) If you've ever dreamed of owning a pair of Manolo Blahniks, Stella McCartney sneakers or a Pucci dress, but have always baulked at the prices, Exclusivo might just be your chance. This tiny shop specialises in top-quality secondhand designer garments and accessories, and while prices remain high, they'll be a fraction of the original price tag.

SAMPLER WINE

Map p466 (020-7226 9500; www.thesampler.co.uk; 266 Upper St, N1; 11.30am-9pm Mon-Sat, to 7pm Sun; Highbury & Islington) One of London's leading wine shops, this brilliant place allows you to sample up to 80 different wines before buying. Just load up a smart card and use it to sample from the machines – from as little as 50p for a sample and up to £50 for a premium vintage champagne. Wines are organised by grape variety. Staff are friendly and knowledgeable.

This is London's leading champagne retailer and also sells beer and spirits.

GILL WING GIFTS GIFTS & SOUVENIRS

Map p466 (020-7359 7697; www.gillwinggifts.com; 194-195 Upper St, N1; 9am-6pm, from 10am Sun; Highbury & Islington) This operation inhabits multiple stores on Upper St, including Gill Wing Cookshop with kitchenware at 190 and Gill Wing Jewellery at 182, but our favourite is this flagship gift shop. It's basically impossible to walk past without stopping to admire the colourful window full of glasses, cards, children's toys and other eclectic titbits.

HOUSMANS BOOKS

Map p466 (020-7837 4473; www.housmans.com; 5 Caledonian Rd, N1; 10am-6.30pm Mon-Sat, noon-6pm Sun; King's Cross St Pancras) If you're searching for hard-to-find tomes on a progressive, radical, pacifist, feminist, socialist, communist or LGBTIQ+ theme, this long-standing, not-for-profit bookshop is your best bet.

HARRY POTTER SHOP AT PLATFORM 9¾ GIFTS & SOUVENIRS

Map p466 (020-3427 4200; www.harrypotterplatform934.com; King's Cross Station, N1; 8am-10pm Mon-Sat, 9am-10pm Sun; King's Cross St Pancras) Pottermania refuses to die down and Diagon Alley remains impossible to find, but if you have junior witches and wizards seeking a wand of their own, take the family directly to King's Cross station. This little wood-panelled store also stocks jumpers sporting the colours of Hogwarts' four houses (Gryffindor having pride of place) and assorted merchandise, including, of course, the books.

TWENTYTWENTYONE GIFTS & SOUVENIRS

Map p466 (020-7288 1996; www.twentytwentyone.com; 274-275 Upper St, N1; 10am-6pm Mon-Sat, 11am-5pm Sun; Highbury & Islington) Crammed with exceedingly cool, mainly northern-European-designed objects, this is a great spot for quirky gifts or high-quality homewares. A £465 toilet-brush holder by Alex Mowat, anyone?

SPORTS & ACTIVITIES

★HAMPSTEAD HEATH PONDS SWIMMING

Map p465 (www.cityoflondon.gov.uk/things-to-do/green-spaces/hampstead-heath/activities-at-hampstead-heath; Hampstead Heath, NW5; adult/child £4/1; from 7am, closing times vary with season; Hampstead Heath) Set amid the gorgeous heath, Hampstead's three bathing ponds (men's, women's and mixed) offer a cooling dip in murky brown water. Despite what you might think from its appearance, the water is tested daily and meets stringent quality guidelines.

The men's and women's ponds are open year-round and are supervised by a lifeguard. Opening times vary with the seasons; the ponds are generally open from 7am, and close at 2.30pm in winter and 8.45pm in the height of summer. The men's pond is popular with gay men and the surrounding lawns are a prime sunbathing and posing spot whenever the sun's out. There's also a nude sunbathing area within the changing-room enclosure. The women's pond is the most tucked away and has a particularly rural feel. The mixed pond closes in winter; it's the least secluded of the three and can sometimes get crowded in summer.

Notting Hill & West London

NOTTING HILL & WESTBOURNE GROVE | EARL'S COURT & WEST BROMPTON | MAIDA VALE | SHEPHERD'S BUSH | HAMMERSMITH | HOLLAND PARK

Neighbourhood Top Five

❶ **Portobello Road Market** (p276) Spending a Saturday afternoon browsing eclectic stalls selling street food, antiques, books, vintage fashion and vinyl, among other things, and putting your feet up in a local cafe.

❷ **Design Museum** (p275) Getting your camera out at this fabulous museum dedicated to the centrality of design in everyday life.

❸ **Boat Trip** (p276) Boarding a boat for the leisurely trip between Little Venice and Camden, along Regent's Canal.

❹ **Windsor Castle** (p282) Raising a pint in the garden or snug interior of this classic tavern on Campden Hill Rd.

❺ **Electric Cinema** (p284) Cosying up in a front-row double bed with a glass of vino at one of the UK's oldest cinemas.

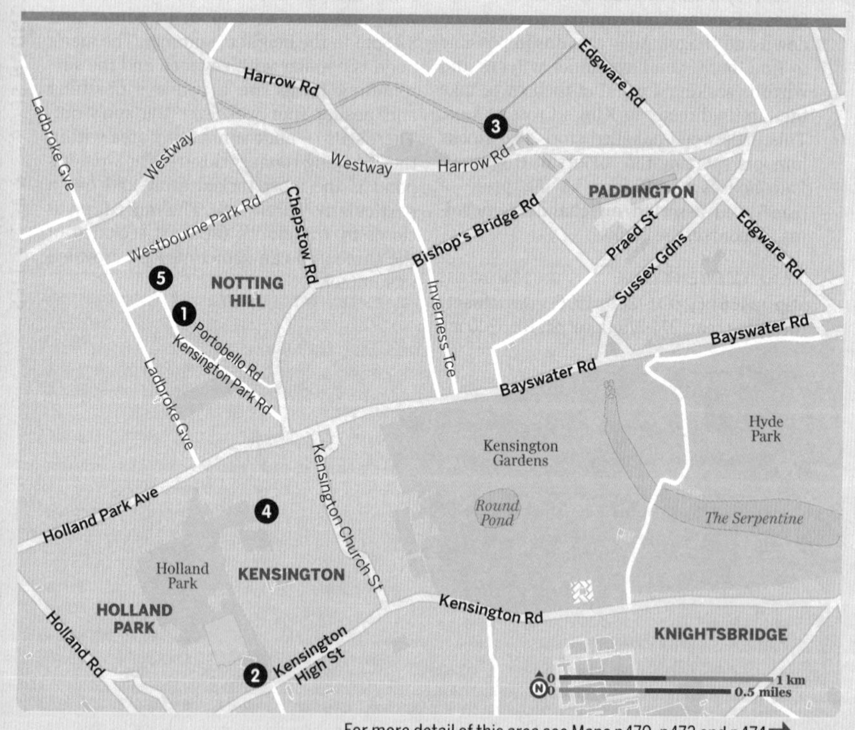

For more detail of this area see Maps p470, p472 and p474

Explore Notting Hill & West London

Most people come to West London for three reasons: for Portobello Road Market, for outstanding dining, or because they're sleeping in one of the area's choice accommodation options.

West London is light on sights, but you should allow half a day for the Design Museum and Portobello Road Market, and another half-day to walk along the Grand Union Canal towards Little Venice, maybe with a pint at one of the waterside pubs en route.

Some excellent restaurant and entertainment options will save those staying in the area from legging it into the West End (although it's close enough to do so if you want). For eating, Notting Hill has a great concentration of good names, but cast your net further and land superb pickings in Hammersmith and Shepherd's Bush.

For nightlife, Notting Hill and Shepherd's Bush are the most vibrant, while Kensington is home to one of the capital's most interesting rooftop clubs. Other areas will be pretty quiet once the pubs have rung the 11pm bell.

Local Life

Fruit and vegetable markets Although also popular with tourists, Portobello Road Market (p276) is where many Notting Hill residents shop for their daily fruit and veg. Shepherd's Bush Market (p287) is a deeply local mainstay.

Waterside strolling Little Venice (p276) sees local families going for a walk along the canal's tow paths at weekends.

London staples Cockney's Pie and Mash (p280) caters to local working-class palates with pie, mash and liquor (parsley sauce).

Getting There & Away

Underground The west–east Central Line stops at Queensway (Bayswater), Notting Hill Gate and Shepherd's Bush. For Paddington, Westbourne Grove and the western end of Shepherd's Bush, there's the painfully slow Hammersmith & City Line. Earl's Court and Hammersmith are on the zippy Piccadilly Line.

Bicycle Santander Cycles (p415) are useful to get from one neighbourhood to another, with docking stations across West London.

Lonely Planet's Top Tip

To make the best of your time at Portobello Road Market, do a one-way circuit (p279) between Notting Hill Gate and Ladbroke Grove Tube stations. The flow tends to go from Notting Hill to Ladbroke Grove, but either way works fine.

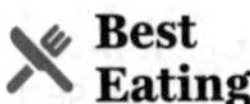

Best Eating

- Dishoom (p280)
- Flat Three (p281)
- Gate (p281)

For reviews, see p278.

Best Drinking & Nightlife

- Troubadour (p283)
- Windsor Castle (p282)
- Paradise by Way of Kensal Green (p283)
- Scarsdale Tavern (p283)
- Dove (p284)

For reviews, see p282.

Best Entertainment

- Bush Theatre (p284)
- Electric Cinema (p284)
- Riverside Studios (p285)
- Opera Holland Park (p284)
- Puppet Theatre Barge (p284)

For reviews, see p284.

SIGHTS

A large and fairly spread out neighbourhood – well linked by public transport – West London has several interesting house museums as well as the triumphant Design Museum. Portobello Road Market is the main draw to Notting Hill for most visitors.

Notting Hill & Westbourne Grove

★MUSEUM OF BRANDS — MUSEUM

Map p470 (020-7243 9611; www.museumofbrands.com; 111-117 Lancaster Rd, W11; adult/child/family £9/5/24; 10am-6pm Mon-Sat, 11am-5pm Sun; Ladbroke Grove) This ambitious shrine to nostalgia is the brainchild of consumer historian and enthusiast Robert Opie, who has amassed advertising memorabilia and packaging since his teenage years. Arranged as a winding time tunnel leading from Victorian times up to the here and now, you'll pass by Monopoly sets, the first appearances of Mickey Mouse and Disney, a primitive version of Cluedo, Teazie-Weazie powder shampoo, radios and TVs, plus ephemera celebrating pop-culture sensations such as the Fab Four, Mork and Mindy, Star Wars, Star Trek, Buzz Lightyear, Pokemon, the Simpsons et al.

An annual adult ticket is £17. The museum also has a cafe at the rear and an excellent shop. See the website for details on exhibitions, talks and masterclasses at the museum.

Kensington High Street

HOLLAND PARK — PARK

Map p472 (Ilchester Pl, W8; 7.30am-dusk; ; High St Kensington or Holland Park) This handsome park divides into dense woodland in the north, spacious and inviting lawns by **Holland House**, sports fields in the south, and some lovely gardens, including the restful **Kyoto Garden**. The park's splendid peacocks are a gorgeous sight and a playground keeps kids occupied. Holland House – largely bombed to smithereens by the Luftwaffe in 1940 – is the venue of Opera Holland Park (p284) in summer.

LEIGHTON HOUSE — HOUSE

Map p472 (Mon-Fri 020-7602 3316, Sat & Sun 020-7471 9160; www.leightonhouse.co.uk; 12 Holland Park Rd, W14; adult/child under 12yr £9/free; 10am-5.30pm Wed-Mon; High St Kensington) Sitting on a quiet street just west of Holland Park and designed in 1866 by George Aitchison, Leighton House was home to the eponymous Frederic, Lord Leighton (1830–96), a painter belonging to the Aesthetic movement. The ground floor is served up in an Orientalist style, its exquisite **Arab Hall** added in 1879 and densely covered with blue and green tiles from Damascus in Syria and Iznik in Turkey.

A fountain tinkles away in the centre beneath the golden dome; even the wooden latticework of the windows and gallery was brought from Damascus. A fireplace upstairs inlaid with Chinese tiles, a stuffed peacock at the foot of the stairs and peacock quills in the fireplace amplify the Byzantine mood. The house also contains notable Pre-Raphaelite paintings by Burne-Jones, Watts, Millais and Lord Leighton himself. Check the website for details of public evening events, including music, talks and workshops.

Leighton House was undergoing restoration in 2020 and only opening on Saturday and Sunday from 10am to 5.30pm until spring 2021, before closing entirely and reopening, with normal opening hours, in autumn 2021.

18 STAFFORD TERRACE — HOUSE

Map p472 (Mon-Fri 020-7602 3316, Sat & Sun 020-7938 1295; www.rbkc.gov.uk/subsites/museums/18staffordterrace1.aspx; 18 Stafford Tce, W8; adult/child £9/free, tours £12/free; guided tours 11am, self-guided tours 2-5.30pm Wed, Sat & Sun mid-Sep–mid-Jun; High St Kensington) Formerly known as Linley Sambourne House, 18 Stafford Terrace, tucked away behind Kensington High St, was the home of *Punch* cartoonist and amateur photographer Linley Sambourne and his wife Marion from 1875 to 1914. What you see is pretty much the typical home of a comfortable middle-class Victorian family, with dark wood, Turkish carpets and sumptuous stained glass throughout. You can visit some nine rooms by 75-minute guided morning tours (costumed on Saturdays; adult/child £20/free) or by self-guided visits in the afternoons.

Evening costume tours (held only on select nights in October and November;

adult/child £20/free), with actors performing characters from the house, heighten the atmosphere.

ST MARY ABBOTS CHURCH

Map p472 (☎020-7937 5136; www.smaw8.org; Kensington Church St, W8; ⓤHigh St Kensington) Designed by Sir George Gilbert Scott and sporting the tallest church spire in London, graceful St Mary Abbots is a haven of peace and calm. St Mary Abbots was seriously damaged by Luftwaffe fire-bombs in 1944, though the main structure survived (apocryphally, an air-raid warden played the organ to keep its pipes clear of water as firefighters doused the flames). The church, with its huge and inviting interior, is undergoing an ambitious plan of restoration.

Earl's Court & West Brompton

BROMPTON CEMETERY CEMETERY

Map p472 (☎020-7352 1201; www.royalparks.org.uk/parks/brompton-cemetery; Old Brompton Rd, SW5; tour £6; ⊙7am-dusk; ⓤWest Brompton or Fulham Broadway) The UK's sole cemetery owned by the Crown, this atmospheric 19th-century, 16-hectare boneyard's most famous denizen may be suffragette Emmeline Pankhurst, but it's also fascinating as the possible inspiration for many of Beatrix Potter's characters. A local resident in her youth, Potter may have noted some of the names on headstones: there's a George Nutkins, Mr McGregor, Jeremiah Fisher, Tommy Brock – even a Peter Rabbet! The chapel and colonnades at one end are modelled on St Peter's in Rome.

Two-hour **tours** (suggested donation £8; cash only) depart at 2pm from the chapel every Sunday from May to August (and two Sundays a month in September, October, November, March and April). There is no need to reserve, just turn up. At the time of writing, visits to the catacombs were to become a more regular option, due to their popularity (see www.brompton-cemetery.org.uk for details). The catacombs can also be visited during the annual summer open day. See the website for a map and list of notable individuals buried within the cemetery grounds. A visitor centre in the North Lodge East (by the cemetery entrance off Old Brompton Rd) is open between 10am and 4pm on Friday, Saturday and Sunday.

TOP EXPERIENCE

SEE THE FUTURE AT THE DESIGN MUSEUM

Relocated from its former Thames location to an eye-popping £83m home by Holland Park, this stunning museum is dedicated to the centrality and influence of design in everyday life. With a revolving program of special exhibitions, the museum is a must-see for those with an eye for modern and contemporary aesthetics. Splendidly housed in the refitted former Commonwealth Institute (which opened in 1962), the lavish interior – all smooth Douglas fir and marble – is itself a design triumph.

Most exhibitions are ticketed (from £14.50), as are talks in the auditorium (from £5), but the extensive 2nd-floor **Designer Maker User** gallery is free. Exploring the iconography of design classics, the gallery contains almost 1000 objects that trace the history of modern design, from 1980s Apple computers to water bottles, typewriters, prosthetic limbs and a huge advert for the timeless VW Beetle. You can also watch a 3-D printer in action.

Encounter the museum's **Designers in Residence** on the 2nd floor when the room is open (otherwise you can see them working through the glass). Also note the original stained glass in the shop on the ground floor, where you can also find a cafe (a restaurant is on the 2nd floor).

DON'T MISS

- Designer Maker User gallery
- Designers in Residence
- The stained glass in the shop
- The museum's architecture

PRACTICALITIES

- Map p472, E2
- ☎020-3862 5900
- www.designmuseum.org
- 224-238 Kensington High St, W8
- admission free
- ⊙10am-6pm, to 8pm or 9pm 1st Fri of month
- Wi-Fi
- ⓤHigh St Kensington

STAMFORD BRIDGE STADIUM

Map p472 (☎0371 811 1955; www.chelseafc.com; Stamford Bridge, Fulham Rd, SW6; tours adult/child £24/15; ⏱museum 9.30am-6.30pm Jul & Aug, to 5.30pm Apr-Jun, to 5pm Sep-Mar; tours 10am-5pm Jul & Aug, to 4pm Apr-Jun, to 3pm Sep-Mar; ⓤFulham Broadway) Chelsea (aka the Blues) is one of London's wealthiest football clubs, and Stamford Bridge is hallowed turf for fans after a souvenir kit or a tour of the stadium. There's a variety of tours available, but all include entry to the Chelsea FC Museum. Admission to the museum alone (without the tour) is £12 for adults and £10 for children.

Maida Vale

LITTLE VENICE CANAL

Map p470 (ⓤWarwick Ave) It was Lord Byron who dreamed up this evocative phrase to describe the junction between Regent's Canal (p252) and the Grand Union Canal, a confluence overseen by beautiful mansions and navigated by colourful narrow boats. The canals date to the early 19th century when the government was trying to develop new transport links across the country.

GRAND UNION CANAL CANAL

Map p470 (ⓤWarwick Ave) Dating from the early 19th century, the Grand Union Canal actually finishes up in Birmingham (you can journey much of its length by bicycle); horse-drawn barges were ideal for carrying coal and other bulk commodities such as grain or ice (the latter was imported from Norway by ship to Limehouse and then conveyed along the canal). Little Venice is an important mooring point for narrow boats (many of them permanent homes), which keeps the boating spirit bubbling away.

Shepherd's Bush

KENSAL GREEN CEMETERY CEMETERY

(☎020-8969 0152; www.kensalgreencemetery.com; Harrow Rd, W10; tours £7; ⏱9am-5pm Mon-Sat, 10am-5pm Sun, to 6pm Sun in summer; ⓤKensal Green) For many years the most fashionable necropolis in England (you wouldn't be seen dead anywhere else), Kensal Green Cemetery accepted its first occupants in 1833. This Gothic boneyard is the final resting place of many illustrious names, including Charles Babbage,

Buzzing Portobello Road Market is an iconic London attraction with an eclectic mix of street food, fruit and veg, antiques, curios, collectables, vibrant fashion and trinkets. The shops along Portobello Rd open daily and the fruit-and-veg stalls (from Elgin Cres to Talbot Rd) only close on Sunday. The busiest day by far is Saturday, when antique dealers set up shop (from Chepstow Villas to Elgin Cres), but it's all elbows. This is also when the fashion market (beneath Westway, from Portobello Rd to Ladbroke Grove) is in full swing – although you can also browse for fashion on Friday and Sunday.

Among the vintage and 'firsthand' fashion stalls of Westway, you'll also find accessories, shoes, jewellery and CDs. More niche, **Portobello Green Arcade** (p286) is home to some cutting-edge clothing and jewellery outlets. Across the way, **Acklam Village Market** (p280) is a popular weekend street-food market with snacks from across the globe and terrific live music.

Towards the north end of Portobello Rd, Golborne Rd is famous for vintage furniture, clothes shops, delis, a Portuguese patisserie and an assortment of hip cafes.

Not all vendors at Portobello Road Market accept credit cards, so bring cash.

DON'T MISS

- Fashion market
- Designers at Portobello Green Arcade
- Fruit-and-veg stalls
- Antiques market

PRACTICALITIES

- Map p470, B4
- www.portobellomarket.org
- Portobello Rd, W10
- ⏱9am-6pm Mon-Wed, to 7pm Fri & Sat, to 1pm Thu
- ⓤNotting Hill Gate or Ladbroke Grove

NOTTING HILL CARNIVAL

Every year, for three days that include the last weekend of August, Notting Hill echoes to the beats of calypso, ska, reggae and soca during Notting Hill Carnival. Launched in 1964 by the local Afro-Caribbean community, which was keen to celebrate its culture and traditions, it has grown to become Europe's largest street festival (over two million visitors in total) and a highlight of the annual calendar in London.

The carnival includes events showcasing the five main 'arts': the 'mas' (derived from masquerade), which is the main costume parade; pan (steel bands); calypso music; static sound systems (anything goes, from reggae, dub and funk to drum 'n' bass); and the mobile sound systems. The 'mas' is generally held on the Monday and is the culmination of the carnival's celebrations. See www.nhcarnival.org for a breakdown of music and events. Processions finish around 9pm, although parties in bars, restaurants and seemingly every house in the neighbourhood go on late into the night.

Another undisputed highlight of the carnival is the food: there are dozens of Caribbean food stands and celebrity chefs such as Levi Roots often make an appearance.

Isambard Kingdom Brunel, Wilkie Collins, Anthony Trollope, William Makepeace Thackeray, Baden Powell and the almost comically named Dr Albert Isaiah Coffin. The cemetery remains in high demand among the deceased: a prime lot today costs £22,000 (plus burial fees).

Supposedly based on the Cimetière du Père-Lachaise in Paris, the 29-hectare cemetery is distinguished by its Greek Revival architecture, arched entrances and the outrageously ornate tombs that bear testament to 19th-century delusions of grandeur. Two-hour **tours** (£7) of the cemetery are offered on Sundays at 2pm (from March to October; first and third Sundays per month other times) by the Friends of Kensal Green Cemetery (www.kensalgreen.co.uk). Some of these tours also visit the catacombs beneath the Anglican Chapel (although at the time of writing, they were still closed for the restoration of the chapel). The cemetery is laid out alongside the Grand Union Canal, which makes for splendid walks alongside the water, especially if the sun obliges.

⊙ Hammersmith

FULHAM PALACE HISTORIC BUILDING

(www.fulhampalace.org; Bishop's Ave, SW6; ⊙museum & palace 10.30am-5pm, to 4pm winter, gardens dawn-dusk daily; Ⓤ Putney Bridge) **FREE** Within glorious stumbling distance of the Thames, this summer home of the bishops of London from 704 to 1975 is a lovely blend of architectural styles immersed in beautiful gardens. Until 1924, when it was filled with rubble, the longest moat in England enclosed the palace. The oldest surviving chunk is the little red-brick Tudor gateway, while the main building dates from the mid-17th century and was remodelled in the 19th century.

The lovely courtyard draws watercolourists on sunny days, and the genteel, recently refurbished **Drawing Room Café** (www.fulhampalace.org/visit/cafe; mains from £5, afternoon tea from £5; ⊙9.30am-5pm Apr-Oct, to 4pm Nov-Mar) at the rear, looking out onto the gorgeous lawn, is a superlative spot for some carrot cake and a coffee. It also has a pretty **walled garden** (10.15am to 4.15pm summer, to 3.45pm winter) and, detached from the main house, a **chapel** designed by William Butterfield in 1866.

Set in the rooms around the Tudor courtyard, the new **museum** at the palace is free. The collection explores the palace's history and the lives of some of the notable Bishops of London who resided here. Children can pick up a free family trail here to help them explore.

Guided history tours (£6, children free, 1½ hours, four to five tours per month) usually take in the Great Hall, the Victorian chapel, Bishop Sherlock's Room and Bishop Howley's dining room. There are also **garden walks** (£6, 1¼ hours); check the website for dates and times. The lawn is also a venue for **Luna Cinema**, the popular summer outdoor-cinema club that shows films at famous spots around town and the UK; outdoor theatre and summer jazz evenings are also staged.

The surrounding land, once totalling almost 15 hectares but now reduced to just over 5 hectares, forms **Bishop's Park**, a beautiful park with a lovely promenade along the river and the usual assortment of playgrounds, fountains and cafe.

WILLIAM MORRIS SOCIETY MUSEUM

Map p472 (020-8741 3735; www.williammorrissociety.org; 26 Upper Mall, W6; 2-5pm Thu & Sat; Ravenscourt Park) FREE Tucked away in the coach house and basement of Kelmscott House (William Morris' former home), this small riverside museum stages temporary exhibitions on all things William Morris. It has a downstairs shop (with a fireplace designed by Morris) and a still-working printing press (demonstrations given on Saturdays). You can download an intriguing and informative local Arts and Crafts riverside walk that the society has devised, perfect for a sunny Hammersmith day.

Short films on Morris and the house are run and you can also access a small part of the garden, although the rest of the house and the main garden are out of bounds for most of the year. Talks on William Morris are occasionally given in the coach house and exhibitions are also held; see the website for details and tickets.

EATING

West London has some excellent dining choices, generally – though not exclusively – at the more affordable end of the budget spectrum. You'll find everything from international street food (Acklam Village Market), pie and mash, fish and chips, and Japanese fast food to Danish treats, smart Greek and vegetarian and vegan-friendly offerings, plus top-end Michelin-starred gourmet cuisine.

Notting Hill & Westbourne Grove

FISH HOUSE FISH & CHIPS £

Map p470 (020-7229 2626; www.deepbluerestaurants.com; 29 Pembridge Rd, W11; mains £6.50-9; 11.30am-10pm; ; Notting Hill Gate) A worthy refuelling stop during a Portobello Market foray, this well-placed white-tile chippie does a brisk trade in fresh fish, wrapped in light and crispy batter and paired with tasty chips. There's sit-down dining upstairs on two further floors, or you can take a seat by the window in the front. All fish is caught in sustainable waters.

HONEST BURGERS BURGERS £

Map p470 (020-7229 4978; www.honestburgers.co.uk; 189 Portobello Rd, W11; mains from £9; 11am-11pm Mon-Sat, to 10pm Sun; ; Ladbroke Grove) When the burger munchies strike, this Portobello branch of the winning, no-nonsense Brixton chain can sit you down for a helping of its juicy trademark dish, with a serving of its irresistible rosemary salted chips. Vegetarians can find tasty solace devouring the courgette and sweetcorn fritter with chips or meat-free burger thrown together with vegan smoked Gouda, vegan mayo and chips.

ARANCINA ITALIAN £

Map p470 (020-7221 7776; www.arancina.co.uk; 19 Pembridge Rd, W11; mains £3.30-23; 8am-11pm Mon-Sat, 9am-11pm Sun; Notting Hill Gate) With a perennial scrum around it thanks to its whiff of freshly baked pizza, Arancina sells Sicilian snacks and has half an orange Fiat Cinquecento (500; the original '60s version) in the window. Try the *arancine* (fried balls of rice with fillings; £3.30) or a slice of perfect pizza (£4.20), a craft beer (£4.50) or a glass of red (£5.20).

For those wondering where the other half of the Fiat Cinquecento is – it's in the other branch of Arancina in Boxpark Croydon. The car conveyed the two brothers for five days from Italy to the UK, where they set up Arancina, back in the 1990s.

LOWRY & BAKER CAFE £

Map p470 (020-8960 8534; 339 Portobello Rd, W10; mains from £7.50; 8am-4pm Mon-Sat, from 10am Sun; ; Ladbroke Grove or Westbourne Park) With its colourfully mixed-up cups, saucers and cutlery, and snug interior, this appealing cafe has a jumble-sale charm. It offers fine Monmouth coffee and tasty platters, and it's a great spot for breakfast (homemade granola, toasted brioche etc) or brunch (such as avocado on toast with poached eggs), or just for putting your feet up after schlepping around Portobello Road Market.

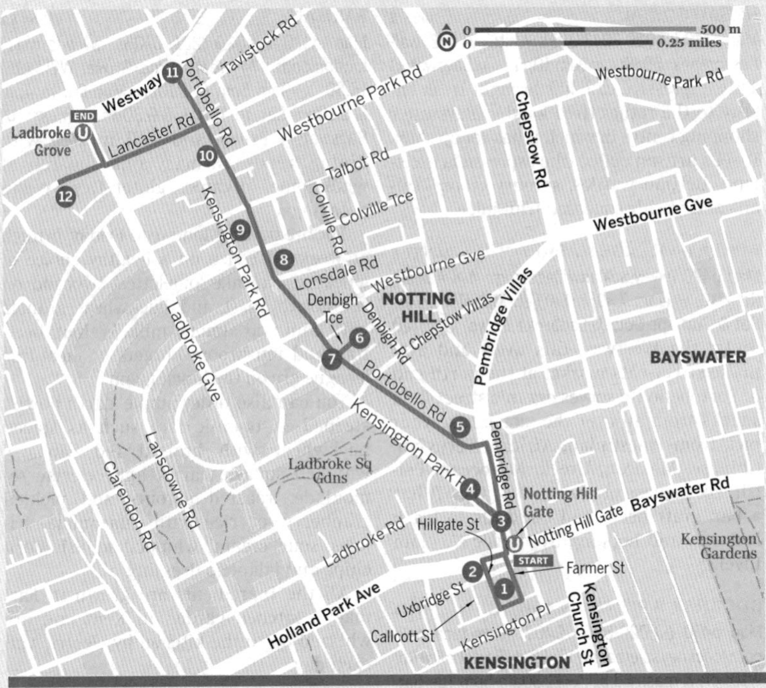

Neighbourhood Walk **Notting Hill**

START NOTTING HILL GATE TUBE STATION
END LADBROKE GROVE TUBE STATION
LENGTH 1.5 MILES; TWO HOURS

Notting Hill is best visited for Portobello Road Market. From Notting Hill Gate station, leave the south side exit and turn left down Farmer St into 1 **Hillgate Village**, with its picture-postcard painted houses. Callcott St is particularly photogenic. Loop around and leave Hillgate St by the iconic 2 **Coronet cinema** featured in the rom-com *Notting Hill*. Turn right and cross at the lights to the junction with Pembridge Rd; the tollgate – the 'gate' of Notting Hill Gate – once stood here.

Along Pembridge Rd, at the junction with Kensington Park Rd, was once the main entrance to the huge 19th-century 3 **Hippodrome**. The Hippodrome vanished in the 1840s, although its layout survives in the road contours to the west. Note the pea-green Victorian 4 **Cabmen's Shelter** here on Kensington Park Rd, now serving as a cafe. Bend into Portobello Rd and spot the blue plaque high at 5 **No 22**, commemorating George Orwell, who lived here. Keep walking along Portobello Rd and pop into charming 6 **Denbigh Terrace**, with its pastel-coloured houses. Note the steeple of sand-coloured 7 **St Peter's Church** on the far side of Portobello Rd.

Continue along Portobello Rd and note the 8 **shop** named 'Notting Hill' at No 142 on your right: the bookshop of William Thacker (Hugh Grant) in the eponymous film (now a clothes and souvenir shop). Then pop into the historic 9 **Electric Cinema** (p284) to admire the classic interior. Further down, the blue front door at 10 **280 Westbourne Park Road**, William Thacker's flat in the film *Notting Hill*, still attracts devotees.

At 11 **Portobello Green Arcade** (p286), browse designer clothes shops and quirky boutiques. Backtrack down Portobello Rd and turn west into Lancaster Rd to visit the enticing 12 **Museum of Brands** (p274). Ladbroke Grove station is a short walk north.

URBAN SOCIAL

CAFE £

Map p470 (020-7243 9031; Whiteleys, W2; waffles/crepes £5/8; 9am-10pm; Bayswater) This impressive cafe has brought fresh energy to the rather tired-looking Bayswater shopping centre in which it has set up shop. It sells artisan coffee (the espresso is excellent), Belgian waffles, savoury crepes, salads and freshly squeezed fruit juice.

ACKLAM VILLAGE MARKET

MARKET £

Map p470 (www.acklamvillage.com; 4-8 Acklam Rd, W10; 11am-7.30pm Sat Feb, Mar, Nov & Dec, Sat & Sun Apr-Oct; Ladbroke Grove) Stuffed under the Westway, this lively and aromatic street-eats market at the north end of Portobello Rd serves organic street-food snacks from all over the globe: take your pick from Palestinian, African, Peruvian, Chinese, Mexican, Greek, Moroccan, Polish, Portuguese or plain old British. It has a bar, craft beers and cocktails to wash it down, and hopping live music (Acklam Live).

COCKNEY'S PIE AND MASH

PIES £

Map p470 (020-8960 9409; www.facebook.com/cockneyspiemashW10; 314 Portobello Rd, W10; pie & mash £3.50; 11.30am-5pm Tue-Sat; Ladbroke Grove or Westbourne Park) For fine helpings of London's classic working-class staples: pie, mash and liquor (parsley sauce) in a standard-issue, no-nonsense white-tile-wall space.

★MAZI

GREEK ££

Map p470 (020-7229 3794; www.mazi.co.uk; 12-14 Hillgate St, W8; mains £10-24, set lunch 2/3 courses £14.95/19.95; noon-3pm Tue-Sun, 6.30-10.30pm Mon-Sat, 6.30-10pm Sun; ; Notting Hill Gate) Tucked away on pretty Hillgate St, Mazi offers a modern take on Greek cuisine, with a lively, seasonally updated menu that encourages sharing (*mazi* means 'together'). The interior is bright and neat, and there's a small back garden (open April to October) and an all-Greek wine list (plus £10 cocktails). It's small and popular, so reservations are important.

The shredded lamb shoulder fricassee with *avgolemono* (egg and lemon) sauce or the grilled octopus with herb potato salad and olive tapenade is an excellent selection.

FARMACY

VEGAN ££

Map p470 (020-7221 0705; www.farmacylondon.com; 74 Westbourne Grove, W2; £15-16.50; 9am-5pm & 6-10pm Mon-Fri, to 4pm & 6-10pm Sat, to 4pm & 6-9.30pm Sun; ; Bayswater) Pricey and well in step with dining trends, Farmacy aims squarely at wholesome, organic, gluten-free, vegan detoxing.

For breakfast (Monday to Friday, brunch at weekends), size up a healthy choice of chickpea pancake 'omelettes', avocado on sourdough toast and buckwheat granola with fruit and almond milk. Walnut, beetroot and mushroom burgers or meat-free lasagne are on the lunch menu.

You can also order ample 'earth bowls', steeped in organic fare such as spiced buckwheat with braised red cabbage, whipped squash, carrot and celeriac remoulade, roasted sprouts and pickled cranberry, or rice with guacamole, frijoles, sour 'cream', whipped squash, corn chips and jalapeño dressing.

All the Ingredients are grown in Farmacy's kitchen garden in Kent and are whizzed up to the kitchen by electric van each day.

Kensington High Street

★DISHOOM

INDIAN ££

Map p472 (020-7420 9325; www.dishoom.com/kensington; 4 Derry St, W8; 8am-11pm Mon-Fri, 9am-11pm Sat & Sun; ; High St Kensington) Dishy Dishoom is not only a delightful art deco–style treat and a delicious picture to behold, but also serves some of the finest Indian food in London. Staff at this new Kensington branch of the famous restaurant are also first rate, though you may have to wait in the evening (no reservations for groups of less than six after 6pm).

DIRTY BONES

AMERICAN ££

Map p472 (020-3019 9061; www.dirty-bones.com; 20 Kensington Church St, W8; mains £9-18; 5pm-midnight Mon-Thu, to 1am Fri, 11am-1am Sat, 11am-11pm Sun; High St Kensington) Situated in a low-lit basement, Dirty Bones divides into a throwback cocktail bar – decorated with a pinball machine and other retro devices – a lounge and a restaurant. The menu is predominantly gung-ho, meaty

US comfort food (tempered with vegan choices) such as hot dogs, 'flat iron' steaks, ribs and crispy fried chicken, with an occasional maverick inclusion (cheeseburger *gyoza* dumplings).

Decent cocktails are another plus, while live bands kick off every Thursday (from 8pm), with DJs taking up the slack on Friday and Saturday (from 9pm).

Holland Park

★FLAT THREE INTERNATIONAL ££

Map p472 (020-7792 8987; www.flatthree.london; 120-122 Holland Park Ave, W11; £18-36, 5-course menu; noon-2.30pm Fri & Sat, 6-9.30pm Tue-Sat; ; UHolland Park) With pronounced Japanese, Korean and Scandinavian inflections, this lovely downstairs Holland Park restaurant is full of surprises and creative discoveries.

Juliana and her team have crafted something delectable in the kitchen, matched by a natural, simple and appealing dining space. Vegans will find themselves well looked after, too. The five-course menu is excellent, while superb cocktails add the final touch.

Expect to discover dishes such as *mochi* flatbread, plaice roe and fermented butter, salt-marsh-lamb rump and smoked cashew, Korean rice porridge, jelly ear and oyster mushrooms.

Shepherd's Bush

POTLI INDIAN £

Map p472 (020-8741 4328; www.potli.co.uk; 319-321 King St, W6; weekday 1-/2-course set lunch £7.95/10.95, weekend 3-course set lunch £14.95, mains £8-15; noon-2.30pm & 6-10.15pm Mon-Thu, to 3pm & 5.30-10.30pm Fri & Sat, noon-10pm Sun; ; UStamford Brook or Ravenscourt Park) With its scattered pieces from Mumbai's Thieves Market, Indian-market-kitchen/bazaar cuisine, homemade pickles and spice mixes, plus an accent on genuine flavour, tantalising Potli deftly captures the aromas of its culinary home. Downstairs there's an open kitchen, and service is friendly. But it's the alluring menu – where flavours are teased into a rich and authentic Indian culinary experience – that's the real crowd-pleaser.

MR FALAFEL MIDDLE EASTERN £

Map p472 (07307 635548; www.mrfalafel.co.uk; Units T4–T5, New Shepherd's Bush Market, W12; falafels from £4.75; 11am to 6pm Mon-Sat; ; UShepherd's Bush Market) This simple and popular cafe is the place for Palestinian falafel wraps, done to a turn. There's a whole host of choice wrap fillings to go with your falafels: avocado, halloumi, *makdoos* (pickled aubergines), *ful medames* (mashed beans flavoured with cumin, garlic and lemon juice), olives, feta cheese and spicy potatoes, or just the classic wrap with falafel, hummus and fried aubergines.

PRINCESS VICTORIA GASTROPUB ££

Map p472 (020-8749 4466; www.princessvictoria.co.uk; 217 Uxbridge Rd, W12; mains £12-22.50; 11am-11pm Mon-Thu, to midnight Fri & Sat, to 10.30pm Sun; ; 207, 607, UShepherd's Bush Market) Grandly restored, the roomy interior of this imposing former Victorian gin palace soaks up pretty much any hubbub thrown at it, with ample elbow space and a setting of gorgeous skylights and period details. The menu is a gastronomic event, wine-lovers are well supplied and the walled herb garden at the rear is a choice setting for one of the gin-infused cocktails.

Troubadours can take part in open-mic night on Tuesdays, from 8pm, with a free tipple thrown in. If you overdo things on the gin, one of the pub's five new and rather smart bedrooms upstairs can help see you through the night.

Hammersmith & Chiswick

GATE VEGETARIAN ££

Map p472 (020-7833 0401; www.thegaterestaurants.com; 51 Queen Caroline St, W6; mains £14-17; noon-2.30pm Mon-Fri, to 3pm Sat & Sun, 6-10.30pm daily; ; UHammersmith) With four restaurants in town, this cool-looking eatery defies its negative feng shui location (behind the Hammersmith Apollo, off Hammersmith flyover) and capitalises on a varied and inviting menu (shiitake ginger *gyoza*, wild mushroom risotto cake, beetroot cheeseburger, red thai curry with tofu), great weekend brunches, welcoming staff and relaxed atmosphere to make the trek here worthwhile. Bookings crucial.

RIVER CAFE ITALIAN £££

Map p472 (☎020-7386 4200; www.rivercafe.co.uk; Rainville Rd, Thames Wharf, W6; mains from £38; ⊙12.30-2.30pm & 6.30-9pm Mon-Sat, noon-3pm Sun; 📶; ⓤHammersmith) The Thames-side name that spawned the world-famous eponymous cookery books offers simple, precise (and pricey) cooking that showcases seasonal ingredients sourced with fanatical expertise; the menus change daily. Booking is essential, as it's Michelin-starred and a favourite of cashed-up London gastronomes. Its popularity, however, means you need to fit into two-hour slots and service can seem rushed.

DRINKING & NIGHTLIFE

West London has everything from historic riverside inns to classic Kensington pubs, microbrewery bars crammed with choice, tucked-away boozers, trendy cocktail bars and pubs perched by the canal. It's worth coming here for a pub crawl alone.

Notting Hill & Westbourne Grove

★**WINDSOR CASTLE** PUB

Map p472 (☎020-7243 8797; www.thewindsorcastlekensington.co.uk; 114 Campden Hill Rd, W11; ⊙noon-11pm Mon-Sat, to 10.30pm Sun; 📶; ⓤNotting Hill Gate) This classic tavern on the brow of Campden Hill Rd has history, nooks and charm on tap. Alongside a decent beer selection and a solid gastropub-style menu, it has a historic compartmentalised interior, a roaring fire (in winter), a delightful beer garden (in summer) and affable regulars (all seasons). In the old days, Windsor Castle was visible from the pub, hence the name.

PERGOLA OLYMPIA BAR

Map p472 (☎07940 501 343; www.pergolalondon.com/pergola-olympia; Level 5 Rooftop, Olympia Car Park, Olympia Way, W14; ⊙5-11pm Wed-Fri, noon-11pm Sat) On the roof of Olympia London car park and part of Olympia's costly regeneration, the vast expanse of (cashless) Pergola goes for a rustic-chic look of hanging baskets, hanging ivy tresses and brickwork with long views through a wall of windows. Comfort food eats are cooked up by three restaurants: Mamalan (Chinese *baozi*), Wildcard (burgers, chicken) and Salt Shed (steaks and chips).

NOTTING HILL ARTS CLUB CLUB

Map p470 (www.nottinghillartsclub.com; 21 Notting Hill Gate, W11; from £4; ⊙hours vary; 📶; ⓤNotting Hill Gate) London wouldn't be what it is without places like NHAC, which mixes underground and retro-music club nights with the odd big pop name. The small basement venue attracts a musically curious crowd, with live performances (usually 7pm to 10pm) and club nights (10pm to 2am) on Fridays and Saturdays and some week nights. Club nights run till 2am.

UNION TAVERN PUB

Map p470 (☎020-7286 1886; www.uniontavern.co.uk; 45 Woodfield Rd, W9; ⊙noon-11pm Mon-Thu, to midnight Fri & Sat, to 10.30pm Sun; 📶; ⓤWestbourne Park) With just the right mix of shiny gastropub, rough-and-ready local appeal, good Grand Union Canal location (with waterside terrace) and a really strong selection of London craft beers, this Fuller's pub is a super choice for a pint or two on your way to or from Portobello Road Market.

PORTOBELLO STAR COCKTAIL BAR

Map p470 (☎020-7229 8220; www.portobellostarbar.co.uk; 171 Portobello Rd, W11; cocktails from £6; ⊙4-11.30pm Mon-Wed, noon-11.30pm Thu, 11am-12.30am Fri, 10am-12.30am Sat, 11am-11.30pm Sun; 📶; ⓤLadbroke Grove) Gin and alluring cocktails are on the menu at this former pub, refreshed into a nifty, narrow cocktail bar.

There's live music every Thursday from 7.30pm, while DJs are in charge on Friday and Saturday evenings. The Portobello Star also runs Ginstitute (p287), just up the road.

Kensington High Street

SCARSDALE TAVERN PUB

Map p472 (☎020-7937 1811; www.scarsdaletavern.co.uk; 23a Edwardes Sq, W8; ⊙noon-11pm Mon-Sat, to 10.30pm Sun; 📶; ⓤHigh St Kensington) This Fuller's pub, quietly located along Edwardes Sq, is a lovely place for a pint of ale or some satisfying food. Out the front in warmer weather, there's a constant bevy of garrulous drinkers, who never want to go home.

Earl's Court & West Brompton

★TROUBADOUR BAR

Map p472 (020-7341 6333; www.troubadourlondon.com; 263-267 Old Brompton Rd, SW5; cafe 9am-midnight, club 8pm-12.30am or 2am Mon-Sat, to 11.30pm Sun; ; Earl's Court) On a comparable spiritual plane to Paris' Shakespeare and Company bookshop, this eccentric, time-warped and convivial boho bar-cafe has been serenading drinkers since 1954. Adele, Ed Sheeran, Joni Mitchell, Jimi Hendrix and Bob Dylan have performed here, and there's still live music (largely jazz and folk) most nights downstairs. A wide-ranging wine list, Sunday roasts and a pleasant rear garden complete the picture.

ATLAS PUB

Map p472 (020-7385 9129; www.theatlaspub.co.uk; 16 Seagrave Rd, SW6; noon-11pm Mon-Sat, to 10.30pm Sun; ; West Brompton) A garrulous hubbub frequently spilling from its ivy-clad and port-coloured facade, this Victorian-era pub tempts locals, visitors, foodies and drinkers alike with a delicious wood-panelled interior, a winning Mediterranean menu, a lovely side courtyard, and a fine range of draught and bottled beers, wines and gins.

Maida Vale

WATERWAY BAR

Map p470 (020-7266 3557; www.thewaterway.co.uk; 54 Formosa St, W9; 10.30am-11pm Mon-Fri, 10am-11pm Sat, to 10.30pm Sun; ; Warwick Ave) Don't come here for the selection of beer or ales or the expensive nosh; this place, hard by the Grand Union Canal in Little Venice, is all about location, and it's hard to imagine a better place to while away a weekend afternoon. Children are welcome until 9.30pm.

Shepherd's Bush

PARADISE BY WAY OF KENSAL GREEN BAR

(020-8969 0098; www.theparadise.co.uk; 19 Kilburn Lane, W10; club nights before/after 11pm £7/10; 4pm-midnight Mon-Wed, to 1am Thu, to 1.30am Fri, noon-1.30am Sat, to 11.30pm Sun; ; Kensal Green) With its statues, religious paintings, gaunt oil portraits, panelling and dense drapes, the wildly eclectic, eccentric, boho and Gothic Kensal Green bar-club is a top choice for offbeat charm and downright panache.

The menu is superb, and the weekly club nights Paradise Presents (hip-hop and R&B) on Fridays and Blondie 2 Biggie (hip-hop, pop and disco) on Saturdays are truly massive.

BREWDOG CRAFT BEER

Map p472 (020-8749 8094; www.brewdog.com; 15 Goldhawk Rd, W12; noon-midnight Mon & Fri, to 11pm Tue & Thu, 11am-midnight Sat, to 10.30pm Sun; ; Shepherd's Bush or Goldhawk Rd) Craft-beer specialist BrewDog has over 40 beers on tap – from its brewery in Scotland as well as guest beers from far and wide.

These include the heady punch of BrewDog vs Fierce: Very Big Moose (12%); designated drivers can stick to the alcohol-free Punk AF (0.5%); others can aim down the middle with a Dead Pony Club (3.8%).

The selection of bottled beers and ciders is broad; bites are of the burger and chicken wings variety.

LIBRARY BAR BAR

Map p472 (www.bushtheatre.co.uk; 7 Uxbridge Rd; 10am-11pm Mon-Sat; ; Shepherd's Bush Market) Tread the bare wood floorboards of this roomy bar/cafe in this erstwhile library, and grab a paperback play or two from the dense collection stuffed onto shelves.

It's a great place for brekkie, to sink a cocktail or craft beer, or hang out for some pre-theatre snacking. The garden terrace is inviting, especially when the sun is beaming.

Hammersmith

DOVE
PUB

Map p472 (020-8748 9474; www.dovehammersmith.co.uk; 19 Upper Mall, W6; 11am-11pm Mon-Sat, noon-10.30pm Sun; ; Hammersmith or Ravenscourt Park) Severely inundated by the epic floodwaters of 1928, this gem of a 17th-century Fuller's pub revels in historic charm and superb Thames views. Scottish poet James Thompson was reputedly inspired to write the lyrics of 'Rule Britannia' here in the 18th century. It was Graham Greene's local, Hemingway and Dylan Thomas drank here too, and William Morris lived nearby.

To your right as you walk in is what was once listed as the world's smallest bar. If the sun comes out, fight for a spot on the lovely terrace (forget it on Boat Race day). In winter, warm your toes by the open fire.

ENTERTAINMENT

Theatre, live music, opera, comedy, classic deco cinemas screening arthouse and independent films: they're all covered in West London.

★BUSH THEATRE
THEATRE

Map p472 (020-8743 5050; www.bushtheatre.co.uk; 7 Uxbridge Rd, W12; 10am-11pm Mon-Sat; Shepherd's Bush) Located in the former Passmore Edwards Public Library building, this West London theatre is renowned for encouraging new writing. Its success since 1972 is down to strong plays from the likes of Jonathan Harvey, Conor McPherson, Stephen Poliakoff, Caroline Horton and Tanya Ronder. The Holloway Theatre is the main space; the Studio is the smaller, 70-seat venue. There's an excellent cafe and bar (p283).

Holloway Theatre tickets cost £20 and Studio tickets are £10, though a limited number of unreserved £10 tickets are available on the morning of each performance for the Holloway Theatre.

ELECTRIC CINEMA
CINEMA

Map p470 (020-7908 9696; www.electriccinema.co.uk; 191 Portobello Rd, W11; tickets £17.50-45; Ladbroke Grove) Having notched up its centenary in 2011, the Electric is one of the UK's oldest cinemas, now updated. Avail yourself of the luxurious leather armchairs, sofas, footstools and tables for food and drink in the auditorium, or select one of the six front-row double beds! Tickets are cheapest on Mondays, while children's tickets are £10.

★PUPPET THEATRE BARGE
PUPPET THEATRE

Map p470 (020-7249 6876; www.puppetbarge.com; opposite 35 Blomfield Rd, W9; adult/child £13/9; Oct–mid-Jul; Warwick Ave) This utterly charming marionette (aka puppet) theatre can be found in a converted barge moored in Little Venice – an area as pretty as it sounds. The theatre has been here for almost 40 years and holds regular performances during weekends and school holidays. Ducking into its interior to see a show is an intimate, magical experience.

From mid-July to October it moves home and can be found on the River Thames in delightful Richmond, southwest London.

ELECTRIC CINEMA WHITE CITY
CINEMA

(020-7908 9696; www.electriccinema.co.uk; 2 Television Centre, 101 Wood Lane, W12; tickets adult/child £20/10; Wood Lane or White City) Located in the former home of the BBC, this very dishy deco-style cinema offers mohair armchairs, chair-side tables with lamps, and footstools. Descend the spiral stairs from the elegant Allis bar/restaurant to the swish lobby where caramel, chocolate and cream hues converge and a further bar and three studios await. Comfy armchairs in each studio are £20.

Children are half-price and tickets are cheapest on Mondays.

EVENTIM APOLLO
LIVE PERFORMANCE

Map p472 (0844 249 1000 ticket hotline, 020-8563 3800; www.eventimapollo.com; 45 Queen Caroline St, W6; £10-65; ; Hammersmith) Hosting such musical titans as Sting, Kate Bush and Paul Weller, as well as comedians, celebrity scientists such as Professor Brian Cox and travelling roadshows, this 3655-seat 1930s venue (formerly the Hammersmith Apollo) is one of London's leading performance and live-music venues.

OPERA HOLLAND PARK
OPERA

Map p472 (information 020-3846 6222, tickets 0300 999 1000; www.operahollandpark.com; Holland Park, W8; tickets £20-80; High St Kensington or Holland Park) Sit under the 1000-seat canopy, temporarily erected every summer for a nine-week season in the middle of Holland Park (p274), for a mix of crowd-pleasers and more-obscure works. Four or five operas are generally performed each year. There is no dress code, and performances finish by 10.30pm.

O2 SHEPHERD'S BUSH EMPIRE CONCERT VENUE

Map p472 (020-8354 3300; www.academymusicgroup.com/o2shepherdsbushempire; Shepherd's Bush Green, W12; tickets £15-40; ; Shepherd's Bush) This famous midsized venue (standing capacity is 2000) attracts all manner of top acts and back-catalogue giants. Built as a music hall in 1903, the floor doesn't slope, so the view from the back is no good if you're not so tall (it's worth paying for the balcony, or arrive early and get up front).

RIVERSIDE STUDIOS PERFORMING ARTS

Map p472 (020-8237 1000; www.riversidestudios.co.uk; 101 Queen Caroline St, W6; Hammersmith) Reopened after a five-year refit, the new Riverside has two theatres, two cinema screens, a state-of-the-art TV studio, brasserie, cafe and bar. The Riverside hosts an eclectic mix of performing arts, from circus to theatre and comedy, plus art-house cinema. The wholesale redevelopment has made the complex more accessible to the public and also incorporates a new riverside walkway.

LYRIC HAMMERSMITH THEATRE

Map p472 (020-8741 6850; www.lyric.co.uk; King St, Lyric Sq, W6; tickets £15-40; Hammersmith) Extended with a new wing several years back and refurbishing its Frank Matcham-designed Victorian auditorium in 2018, the Lyric turns classics on their heads, staging a stimulating choice of productions from the highbrow to more-accessible theatre.

SHOPPING

Save most of your shopping energy for the bonanza of independent vintage vinyl, vintage togs and niche interest shops around Portobello Rd and its famous market. Kensington Church St is excellent for antiques as well as top-grade charity shops. For vast mall shopping with everything under one roof, head to Westfield.

PORTOBELLO ROAD MARKET MARKET

See p276.

★JAPAN HOUSE DESIGN

Map p472 (020-3972 7100; www.japanhouselondon.uk; 101-111 Kensington High St, W8; 10am-8pm Mon-Sat, noon-6pm Sun; High St Kensington) A cultural outpost of Japan in London, Japan House presents and celebrates Japanese art, design, culture, technology, craftsmanship and gastronomy in a particularly handsome space on Kensington High St. The shop on the ground floor teems with beautifully conceived Japanese utensils and kitchen items, while downstairs is a very cool gallery space, featuring Japanese art exhibitions, art films and creative installations.

CHINESE TEA COMPANY TEA

Map p470 (020-8960 0096; www.the-chinese-tea-company.com; 14 Portobello Green Arcade, 281 Portobello Rd, W10; 11am-6pm Mon-Sat; Ladbroke Grove) Owner Juyan – from Zhejiang in southeastern China – offers pointers in the world of Chinese tea at this bijou specialist shop in Portobello Green Arcade. Whatever your choice of Chinese tea *(chá)* – Pu'er, Tie Guanyin, Jasmine, Mogan Shan red tea or Lion's Peak Long Jing – you'll find it here, as well private tea tastings (£25 to £30).

If you get carried away, join one of its tea tours to China.

ROYAL TRINITY HOSPICE CLOTHING

Map p472 (020-7361 1530; www.royaltrinityhospice.london/kensington; 31 Kensington Church St, W8; 10am-6pm Mon-Sat, 11am-5pm Sun; High St Kensington) For designer labels and top-end items in men's clothing and accessories, it's well worth a browse through this well-supplied charity shop on Kensington Church St. Stock turnover is pretty high, so fresh items are always coming in.

LUTYENS & RUBINSTEIN BOOKS

Map p470 (020-7229 1010; www.lutyensrubinstein.co.uk; 21 Kensington Park Rd, W11; 10am-6pm Mon & Sat, to 6.30pm Tue-Fri, 11am-5pm Sun; Ladbroke Grove) Lutyens & Rubinstein is a tremendous, discerning and compact (ground floor, slender mezzanine and basement) bookshop. It's a squeeze, but its small size pays dividends. Established by a pair of literary agents, the focus is on 'excellence in writing', as determined by customers and readers, so every book comes recommended. Don't expect huge piles of bestsellers, stuffed dump-bins or buy-one-get-one-frees.

FOUND AND VISION VINTAGE

Map p470 (☎020-8964 5656; www.foundandvision.com; 318 Portobello Rd, W10; ⊙10.30am-6pm Mon-Sat; ⓤLadbroke Grove) A glorious selection makes this funky Portobello Rd stop – its name a play on Bowie's synth-led classic from 1977 album *Low* – a paradise for hunters of vintage clothing, with an abundance of killer 1970s lounge suits, Adolfo knit dresses, Vivienne Westwood blouses, Missoni sweaters, Versace tops and much more.

DAUNT BOOKS BOOKS

Map p472 (☎020-7727 7022; www.dauntbooks.co.uk; 112-114 Holland Park Ave, W11; ⊙9am-7.30pm Mon-Sat, 11am-6pm Sun; ⓤHolland Park) With its light wood floor and engaging staff, Daunt Books is a major fixture in the London book-selling world. The flagship Daunt Books branch may be on Marylebone High St, but this branch oozes quality. Travel is a forte, while tots will adore the ample kids' section at the rear. Children's story time is every Wednesday at 11am.

NOTTING HILL BOOKSHOP BOOKS

Map p470 (☎020-7229 5260; www.thenottinghillbookshop.co.uk; 13 Blenheim Cres, W11; ⊙9am-7pm Mon-Sat, 10am-6pm Sun; ⓤLadbroke Grove) This fine, rather small, general bookshop – the inspiration behind the bookshop in Hugh Grant and Julia Roberts' monster rom-com *Notting Hill* – still sees a regular stream of pilgrims (of all ages) who pose outside for snaps. An understandable and very browsable accent on travel books endures, but fiction provides equilibrium and there's a strong children's section at the rear.

PORTOBELLO GREEN ARCADE CLOTHING

Map p470 (281 Portobello Rd, W10; ⊙9am-6pm Mon-Sat, 11am-6pm Sun; ⓤLadbroke Grove) Portobello Green Arcade is home to a community of cutting-edge clothing and jewellery designers as well as vintage vinyl merchants and small, independent niche shops, such as **Adam** (☎020-8960 6944; www.adamoflondon.com; 11 Portobello Green Arcade; ⊙10am-5.30pm Tue-Sat, noon-5pm Sun) and the Chinese Tea Company (p285).

CERAMICA BLUE HOMEWARES

Map p470 (☎020-7727 0288; www.ceramicablue.co.uk; 10 Blenheim Cres, W11; ⊙10am-6.30pm Mon-Sat, 11am-5pm Sun; ⓤLadbroke Grove) A lovely spot for colourful, eclectic and handsome crockery, imported from more than a dozen countries. There are Japanese eggshell-glaze teacups, serving plates with tribal South African designs, candelabras from Italy, gorgeous tablecloths from Provence, hand-decorated glass from Turkey, hand-painted terracotta from Spain, coloured glass plates from Germany, Chinese plates made from bamboo sawdust, fun tea towels and much more.

WESTFIELD MALL

Map p472 (☎020-3371 2300; http://uk.westfield.com/london; Ariel Way, W12; ⊙10am-10pm Mon-Sat, noon-6pm Sun; ⓤWood Lane) With a humongous cousin in Stratford (and one pencilled in for Croydon), this full-on retail mecca was London's first mall and is now, after an extension opened in 2018, Europe's largest shopping centre. As well as having 450-odd shops, Westfield has a raft of eateries (chains only), bars, a cinema, a kids' activity centre and regular events, from fashion shows to book signings.

ROUGH TRADE WEST MUSIC

Map p470 (☎020-7229 8541; www.roughtrade.com; 130 Talbot Rd, W11; ⊙10am-6.30pm Mon-Sat, 11am-5pm Sun; ⓤLadbroke Grove) Once home to the eponymous post-punk label, this compact shop offers vintage and alternative vinyl and puts on the occasional gig too. Head downstairs for a selection of secondhand music biographies and other books.

MUSIC & VIDEO EXCHANGE MUSIC

Map p470 (☎020-7243 8573; www.mgeshops.com; 38 Notting Hill Gate, W11; ⊙10am-8pm; ⓤNotting Hill Gate) A nirvana for vinyl junkies, the erstwhile Record & Tape Exchange has been around since three years before Jimi Hendrix died (a short walk away in Landsdowne Cres). If you're after a 2005 gate-fold Goldfrapp *Supernature* or a 1968 pressing of *Electric Ladyland*, staff can point you in the right direction; otherwise just do what everyone is doing, browsing through the record, CD and DVD stacks.

There's a big inflow and outflow of stock, with prices depreciating the longer an item sits in the shop. Find rock and pop on the ground floor, classical and easy listening downstairs, and soul, funk and reggae upstairs. There's always something decent playing on each floor.

RETRO WOMAN CLOTHING EXCHANGE VINTAGE

Map p470 (☎020-7565 5572; www.mgeshops.com; 20 Pembridge Rd, W11; ⏰10am-8pm; Ⓤ Notting Hill Gate) More secondhand than vintage, but very popular, Retro Woman has racks upon racks of hand-me-down fashion and big-name designer goodies, including a galaxy of shoes and self-confessed 'nylon monstrosities' from the '70s. There are always fresh items coming in through the door and togs get reduced in price over time. A Retro Man Clothing Exchange is along the road at number 34.

SHEPHERD'S BUSH MARKET MARKET

Map p472 (www.myshepherdsbushmarket.com; ⏰10am-6pm Mon-Sat; Ⓤ Shepherd's Bush or Goldhawk Rd) Running since 1914, this fruit-and-veg market stretches underneath the Hammersmith & City and Circle Lines between Goldhawk Rd and Shepherd's Bush Tube stations. Popular with local African and Afro-Caribbean communities, it's stockpiled with mangoes, passion fruit, okra, plantains, sweet potatoes and other exotic fare.

HONEST JON'S MUSIC

Map p470 (☎020-8969 9822; www.honestjons.com; 278 Portobello Rd, W10; ⏰10am-6pm Mon-Sat, 11am-5pm Sun; Ⓤ Ladbroke Grove) Flogging old-school reggae, jazz, funk, soul, dance, jazz and blues vinyl to Notting Hill's musical purists since 1974, with a large volume of CDs. Check the extensive listings, including the rarest of the rare, on the website.

BISCUITEERS FOOD

Map p470 (☎020-7727 8096; www.biscuiteers.com; 194 Kensington Park Rd, W11; ⏰10am-6pm Mon-Sat, 11am-5pm Sun; Ⓤ Notting Hill Gate) Achieving an almost surreal level of quaintness, Biscuiteers is a Notting Hill cafe specialising in hand-iced treats, ranging from biscuits to cupcakes to chocolates. You can try your own hand at the art of icing decoration by joining one of the on-site classes.

RELLIK VINTAGE

Map p470 (☎020-8962 0089; www.rellik london.co.uk; 8 Golborne Rd, W10; ⏰10am-6pm Tue-Sat; Ⓤ Westbourne Park) Incongruously located opposite one of London's most notorious tower blocks – the grimly iconic concrete Trellick Tower – Rellik is a fashionista-favourite retro store. It stocks mainly vintage women's clothes and accessories from the 1950s to the 1990s, and rummaging among the frippery, it's not unusual to find an Yves Saint Laurent coat, a Chloé suit or an Ossie Clark dress.

SPORTS & ACTIVITIES

★KIDZANIA AMUSEMENT PARK

(www.kidzania.co.uk; Westfield, Ariel Way, W12; child/adult from £20/16, child annual pass £129; ⏰hr vary; 📶👪; Ⓤ Shepherd's Bush, White City) Self-billed as 'an indoor city run by kids', Kidzania is a hoot and a half and teaches children important life skills to boot. Kids aged four to 14 can turn their little hands to all manner of grown-up tasks, such as being surgeons, police officers, pilots, fire-fighters and much more. Children under seven need to be accompanied by a grown-up.

★LONDON WATERBUS COMPANY CRUISE

Map p470 (☎07917 265114; www.londonwaterbus.com; Browning's Pool, Warwick Cres, W2; tours adult/child one way £12/9; ⏰hourly 10am-5pm Apr-Oct, weekends only & less frequent departures other months; Ⓤ Warwick Ave or Camden Town) These enclosed barges take enjoyable 50-minute trips on Regent's Canal between Little Venice and Camden Lock, passing by Regent's Park and stopping at London Zoo. Fewer departures go outside high season; check the website for schedules. One-way tickets (adult/child £32/25 from Little Venice or £30/22 from Camden Lock) include zoo entry and allow passengers to disembark within the zoo grounds. Buy tickets on board.

GINSTITUTE DISTILLERY

Map p470 (☎020-3034 2234; www.theginstitute.com; 186 Portobello Rd, W11; adult £120; ⏰sessions 7pm Mon-Thu, noon, 2pm, 5pm & 7pm Fri, 11am, 1pm, 3pm, 5pm & 7pm Sat, 1pm & 4pm Sun; 🐾; Ⓤ Notting Hill Gate) Ginstitute offers a thoroughly interactive three-hour gin experience, where you'll learn about the history of the beverage in Britain – which is as fascinating as it is depressing – and how it's made. The booking includes a cocktail reception, a gin lecture, a 70cl bottle of

Portobello Road No 171 gin, plus a 70cl bottle of your personally devised gin blend.

Also on the menu is a £60 masterclass (8.30pm on Thursday, Friday and Saturday) that teaches you how to concoct the perfect gin cocktail (five of them). A £90 ticket includes a five-course menu with cocktails, wines and spirits.

ROBERSON WINE WINERY

Map p472 (☎020-7381 7871; www.londoncru.co.uk; 21-27 Seagrave Rd, SW6; tours £15; ⏲9am-5pm Mon-Fri; ⓤWest Brompton) One of London's handful of wineries, Roberson Wine is tucked away off a nondescript Fulham street. The enterprise solely uses grapes from English vineyards and uses state-of-the-art fermentation tanks to turn them into wines, which you can sample in several top London restaurants or buy onsite during business hours. Tours are by appointment.

QUEENS ICE & BOWL SKATING

Map p470 (☎020-7229 0172; www.queensiceandbowl.co.uk; 17 Queensway, W2; adult/child £12/11, skate hire £2.50; ⏲10am-6.45pm & 8-10.45pm; ⓤQueensway) London may have a generous crop of winter outdoor ice rinks, but Queen's Ice Rink in Queensway is open all year. A great hit with novices and ice-skaters of all ages, the rink has been sending generations of youngsters and adults, arms whirling, around its ice for decades. There's a fun ten-pin bowling alley (10am to 11pm, £10.50/8.50 per adult/child per game; book online for cheaper rates) right alongside.

Each skating session is two hours long; prices are slightly cheaper off-peak (Monday to Friday 10am to 5pm, other than school holidays). Ice-skating classes are also available. Also on the menu are ice karting and beer pong.

PORCHESTER SPA SPA

Map p470 (☎020-7313 3858; www.porchesterspatreatments.co.uk; Porchester Centre, Queensway, W2; £28.90; ⏲10am-10pm; ⓤBayswater or Royal Oak) Housed in a gorgeous, art deco building, the Porchester is a no-frills spa run by Westminster Council. With a 30m swimming pool, a large Finnish-log sauna, two steam rooms, three Turkish hot rooms and a massive plunge pool, there are plenty of affordable treatments on offer, including massages.

It's women only on Tuesdays, Thursdays and Fridays all day and between 10am and 4pm on Sundays; and men only on Mondays, Wednesdays and Saturdays. Couples are welcome from 4pm to 8pm on Sundays.

Greenwich

Neighbourhood Top Five

❶ **Painted Hall** (p293) Enduring a crick in the neck to appreciate the amazing baroque ceiling paintings in the recently restored 'Sistine Chapel of the UK'.

❷ **National Maritime Museum** (p294) Tracking down Nelson's Trafalgar uniform and getting educated on Britain's lengthy seafaring history.

❸ **Royal Observatory** (p291) Standing astride two hemispheres, solving the mystery of longitude and exploring the cosmos.

❹ **Greenwich Park** (p292) Huffing and puffing up to the iconic view of Canary Wharf from the top of the hill before exploring 74 hectares of London's first enclosed royal park.

❺ **Deptford** (p296) Going off-piste in this changing neighbourhood full of markets, breweries, craft-beer bars and other hip hang-outs.

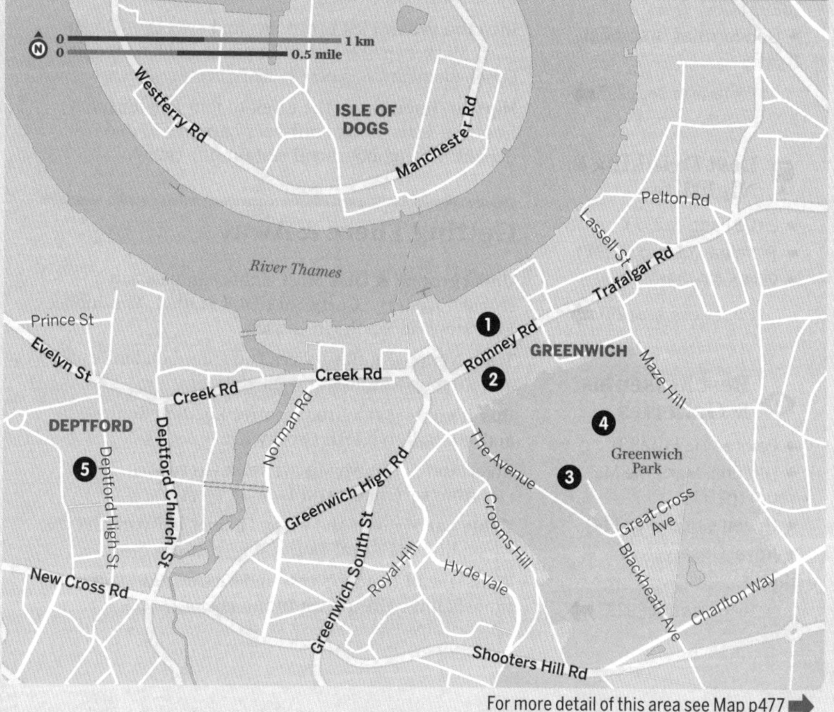

For more detail of this area see Map p477

Lonely Planet's Top Tip

Maritime Greenwich is all about the river, so make your arrival on, under or over the water. Thames Clippers services dock at Greenwich Pier, while the Emirates Air Line cable car (p228) soars 90m high before landing in North Greenwich. A historic foot tunnel, opened in 1902, dives below the surface. See if you can find the view of Greenwich that Venetian artist Canaletto portrayed in *Greenwich Hospital from the North Bank of the Thames* (1752), now in the National Maritime Museum's collection.

Best Eating

- Marcella (p297)
- Greenwich Market (p297)
- Goddards at Greenwich (p297)

For reviews, see p297.

Best Drinking & Nightlife

- Little Faith (p297)
- Trafalgar Tavern (p298)
- Villages (p298)

For reviews, see p297.

Best Museums & Galleries

- Painted Hall (p293)
- National Maritime Museum (p294)
- Queen's House (p294)
- Royal Observatory (p291)

For reviews, see p293.

Explore Greenwich

If Greenwich's grand sights belonged to a British town beyond the capital, they would elevate it to one of the top destinations in the UK. That they belong to a district of London alone naturally makes this quaint Unesco-listed area a must-see neighbourhood.

Most visitors dedicate only a day to Greenwich (pronounced '*gren*-itch'), but it's a lot of culture and history to pack into a single session, with the Royal Observatory, Queen's House, National Maritime Museum and Old Royal Naval College demanding several hours each. The recently reopened Painted Hall, covered in huge murals, is unmissable. Fortunately, all of Greenwich's big-hitting sights are within an easily walkable area.

For a more local look at this part of London, venture to edgy Deptford or high-rise-ridden North Greenwich, both rapidly developing in very different ways.

Local Life

Waterfront walks Head underwater through the Greenwich Foot Tunnel (p295) before strolling the picturesque river, popping into Thames-side pubs such as Trafalgar Tavern (p298), or following in Olympians' footsteps past art installations in redeveloped North Greenwich.

Into the green Pick up snacks and sweets at Greenwich Market (p297) to have a picnic hidden amongst Greenwich Park's (p292) 74 leafy hectares.

Hipster 'hood Cross the creek to join Londoners at Deptford's charming craft-beer bars (p297) and delightful neighbourhood restaurants (p297).

Getting There & Away

Underground & DLR Most sights can be easily reached from the Cutty Sark DLR station. The Jubilee Line stops at North Greenwich.

Train National Rail services run from London Bridge and Cannon St to Greenwich station.

Bus It's a long ride from central London. Routes 129 and 188 link to North Greenwich.

Riverboat A fun way to arrive in Greenwich. Boats run from several central London piers.

Cable car Fly over the River Thames between the O2 Arena and the Royal Docks.

Walk One of London's two under-river pedestrian-only tunnels links Greenwich to the Isle of Dogs.

PAJOR PAWEL/SHUTTERSTOCK ©

TOP EXPERIENCE

SPEND TIME AT THE ROYAL OBSERVATORY

The Royal Observatory is where the studies of the sea, stars and time converge. The prime meridian charts its line through the grounds of the observatory to divide the globe into the eastern and western hemispheres. The complex sits atop a hill within leafy and regal Greenwich Park, with iconic views of the River Thames and the skyscrapers of Canary Wharf.

Royal Observatory

The Royal Observatory was built by order of Charles II in 1675 to help solve the riddle of longitude. In 1884 Greenwich was designated as the prime meridian of the world, and Greenwich Mean Time (GMT) became the universal measurement of standard time.

Unlike other attractions in Greenwich, the Royal Observatory contains free-access areas (such as the Weller Astronomy Galleries) and others you pay for (Meridian Courtyard and Flamsteed House).

Flamsteed House & Meridian Courtyard

Charles II ordered construction of the Christopher Wren-designed **Flamsteed House**, the original observatory building, on the foundations of Greenwich Castle in 1675 after closing the observatory at the Tower of London, allegedly because the ravens were pooing on the equipment. Today it contains the magnificent **Octagon Room** and the rather simple apartment where the Royal Astronomers and their families lived. On the lower levels, you'll find the **Time Galleries**, which explain how the longitude problem – how to accurately determine a ship's east-west location – was solved through astronomical means and the invention of the marine chronometer.

DON'T MISS

- Prime meridian
- Octagon Room
- Camera obscura
- Hilltop views of Canary Wharf

PRACTICALITIES

- Map p477, D3
- 020-8312 6565
- www.rmg.co.uk/royal-observatory
- Greenwich Park, Blackheath Ave, SE10
- adult/child £16/8
- 10am-5pm Sep-Jun, to 6pm Jul & Aug
- Greenwich or Cutty Sark

TAKE A BREAK

The Astronomy Centre has a cafe, or pack a sandwich to devour in leafy Greenwich Park. Down the hill, Goddards at Greenwich (p297) dishes up traditional pie and mash in an old-school spot, or snack your way around the food stalls of Greenwich Market (p297).

It pays to plan ahead for a trip to Greenwich. If you want to enter the paid-for parts of the Royal Observatory and see the *Cutty Sark*, consider booking a combination ticket online in advance (adult/child £23.65/11.85), saving almost 25%. Planetarium shows are also cheaper if pre-booked online. If you only have time for one or the other, look for two-for-one offers on Days Out Guide (www.daysoutguide.co.uk).

WHERE TIME BEGINS

The Greenwich meridian was selected as the global prime meridian at the International Meridian Conference in Washington, DC, in 1884. Greenwich became the world's ground zero for longitude and standard for time calculations, replacing the multiple meridians that had existed before.

In the **Meridian Courtyard**, where the globe is decisively sliced into east and west, visitors can delightfully straddle both hemispheres, with one foot on either side of the meridian line. Every day, the red **Time Ball** atop the Royal Observatory drops at 1pm, as it has done since 1833. In a small brick structure next to the Meridian Courtyard, the **camera obscura** projects a live image of Queen's House – as well as the people moving around it and the boats on the Thames behind – onto a table. Enter through the thick, light-dimming curtains and close them behind you to keep the room as dark as possible.

Astronomy Centre & Peter Harrison Planetarium

The southern half of the observatory contains the informative (and free) **Weller Astronomy Galleries**, where you can touch an object as ancient as the sun: part of the Gibeon meteorite, a mere 4.5 billion years old. Other exhibits include a 1780 orrery (mechanical model of the solar system, minus the as-yet-undiscovered Uranus and Neptune), astro documentaries and the opportunity to view the Milky Way in multiple wavelengths.

The state-of-the-art **Peter Harrison Planetarium** (Map p477; 020-8858 4422; www.rmg.co.uk/whats-on/planetarium-shows; Greenwich Park, SE10; adult/child £10/5; ; Greenwich or DLR Cutty Sark) – London's only planetarium – can lay out the heavens on the inside of its roof. It runs several informative shows a day, including a program for kids, and it's best to book in advance.

Greenwich Park

Greenwich Park (Map p477; www.royalparks.org.uk/parks/greenwich-park; 6am-sunset; Greenwich or Maze Hill or DLR Cutty Sark) is one of London's loveliest expanses of green, with a rose garden, picturesque walking paths, a 6th-century Anglo-Saxon burial ground and astonishing views of Canary Wharf – the financial district across the Thames – from the crown of the hill. Covering 74 hectares, it's the oldest enclosed royal park and is partly the work of André Le Nôtre, the landscape architect who designed the palace gardens of Versailles.

If you don't want to pay to enter the Meridian Courtyard, look out for the continuation of the prime meridian line, marked in metal, just outside the fence, where you can be in two hemispheres at once for free.

BENEDEK/GETTY IMAGES ©

TOP EXPERIENCE

EXPLORE THE OLD ROYAL NAVAL COLLEGE

Home to the University of Greenwich and Trinity Laban Conservatoire of Music and Dance, the Christopher Wren–designed Old Royal Naval College is a masterpiece of baroque architecture. The grounds are open to the public, as well as a few surprising sights.

Painted Hall

Designed as a dining room for retired and disabled sailors and completed in 1726, the **Painted Hall** (020-8269 4799; adult/child £12/free; 10am-5pm) is an over-the-top space covered from floor to ceiling with the largest painting in Europe and is often called the 'Sistine Chapel of the UK'. In 2019 the £8.5 million restoration lifted nearly 300 years of grime, cigar smoke, previous poor preservation techniques and even food from the 4200 sq metres of painted surface, making the colours shine all the way up the 18m-high roof.

Sir James Thornhill was commissioned for the huge piece of work, which took 19 years and three monarchy changes to complete. The paintings celebrate Britain's naval prowess, commerce and the reigning royalty, but it's more political propaganda than historical fact. An audio guide, included in the ticket price, provides amusing stories behind the characters and the paintings.

Included in the Painted Hall admission is a worthwhile 45-minute tour of the grounds.

Chapel of St Peter & St Paul

With its mix of Greek revival and naval motifs, the beautiful **Chapel of St Peter & St Paul** (020-8269 4788; 10am-5pm) FREE, built in 1742, is decorated in an elaborate rococo style. The chapel has excellent acoustics and hosts free lunchtime concerts at 1pm on Tuesdays and Fridays.

DON'T MISS

- Painted Hall
- Chapel of St Peter & St Paul
- Tour of the grounds

PRACTICALITIES

- Map p477, C2
- www.ornc.org
- admission free
- 8am-11pm
- DLR Cutty Sark

SIGHTS

ROYAL OBSERVATORY MUSEUM

See p291.

OLD ROYAL NAVAL COLLEGE HISTORIC BUILDING

See p293.

★NATIONAL MARITIME MUSEUM MUSEUM

Map p477 (020-8312 6565; www.rmg.co.uk/national-maritime-museum; Romney Rd, SE10; 10am-5pm; ; DLR Cutty Sark) FREE Narrating the long, briny and eventful history of seafaring Britain, this excellent museum has three floors of engrossing exhibits. Highlights include JMW Turner's huge oil painting *Battle of Trafalgar* (1824), the 19m-long gilded state barge built in 1732 for the Prince of Wales, and the colourful figureheads installed on the ground floor. Families will love the children's galleries, as well as the Great Map splayed out near the upper-floor cafe.

On the 1st floor, **Atlantic Worlds** and **Traders** look back on Britain's role in the slave trade and commerce with the East in the 19th century. One floor up, **Nelson, Navy, Nation** focuses on the history of the Royal Navy during the conflict-ridden 17th century and even includes the coat in which Nelson was fatally wounded during the Battle of Trafalgar, with a musket-ball hole in the left shoulder. The **Exploration Wing**, opened in 2018, contains four galleries – Pacific Encounters, Polar Worlds, Tudor and Stuart Seafarers, and Sea Things – devoted to indigenous maritime civilisations, European exploration and human endeavour.

QUEEN'S HOUSE GALLERY

Map p477 (020-8312 6565; www.rmg.co.uk/queens-house; Romney Rd, SE10; 10am-5pm; DLR Cutty Sark) FREE Designed by architect Inigo Jones, Queen's House was the UK's first classical building, and it's as enticing for its form as for its art collection. Many pieces on display are portraits and have an unsurprising maritime bent; don't miss the iconic *Armada Portrait of Elizabeth I*, which depicts the queen in a vibrantly coloured lace and jewelled gown and commemorates the failed invasion of England by the Spanish in 1588. It's in the immaculately restored **Queen's Presence Chamber** on the 1st floor.

Side galleries radiate off from the cube-shaped **Great Hall**, which has an elaborately tiled floor laid in 1635, best viewed from the upstairs balcony. In 2016 Turner Prize–winning artist Richard Wright was commissioned to add an intricate gold-leaf design on the ceiling, the first artwork to be placed there since 1708 when the original painted panels were removed. The stunning helix-shaped (and reportedly haunted) **Tulip Stairs** in the northwest corner of the hall form England's first self-supported staircase.

The house was begun in 1616 for Anne of Denmark, wife of James I, but wasn't completed until around 1636, when it became the home of Charles I and his queen, Henrietta Maria.

RANGER'S HOUSE GALLERY

Map p477 (020-8294 2548; www.english-heritage.org.uk/visit/places/rangers-house-the-wernher-collection; Greenwich Park, Chesterfield Walk; adult/child £9.50/5.70; guided tours 11.30am & 2pm Sun-Wed late Mar-Sep; Greenwich or DLR Cutty Sark) This elegant 1723 Georgian villa once housed the ranger of Greenwich Park (p292) and now contains a collection of 700 works of art, such as medieval and Renaissance paintings, porcelain, silverware and tapestries, amassed by Julius Wernher (1850–1912), a German-born railway engineer's son who struck it rich in the diamond fields of South Africa. The Spanish Renaissance jewellery collection is one of the best in Europe. Unfortunately, the gallery is only open to visit during the summer months.

CUTTY SARK SHIP

Map p477 (020-8312 6565; www.rmg.co.uk/cuttysark; King William Walk, SE10; adult/child £15/7.50; 10am-5pm; DLR Cutty Sark) The last of the great clipper ships to sail between China and England in the 19th century, the *Cutty Sark* was launched in 1869 and carried almost 4.5 million kg of tea in just seven years of service. Nearly a century later, it was dry-docked in Greenwich and opened to the public. Films, interactive maps, illustrations and props give an idea of what life on board was like. Book online for cheaper rates.

ST ALFEGE CHURCH CHURCH

Map p477 (020-8853 0687; www.st-alfege.org; Greenwich Church St, SE10; 11am-4pm

WORTH A DETOUR

ELTHAM PALACE

The gorgeous 1930s art-deco **Eltham Palace** (www.english-heritage.org.uk/visit/places/eltham-palace-and-gardens; Court Yard, Eltham, SE9; adult/child £15.40/9.20; ⏰10am-6pm Sun-Fri Apr-Sep, to 5pm Oct-3 Nov; 🚉Eltham or Mottingham) was built by Stephen Courtauld, whose family made a fortune in the rayon (artificial silk) industry, and his wife Virginia (Ginie) as a country estate for entertaining guests. It features high-tech amenities of the time, such as telephones, electrically synchronised clocks, a built-in vacuum system and a boiler with enough hot waterto fill 12 baths at the same time, but it's also attached to the remnants of a medieval royal estate. A royal palace was built on this site in 1305 and was the boyhood home of Henry VIII before the Tudors decamped to Greenwich. Apart from the restored **Great Medieval Hall**, little of that palace remains.

Using an entertaining handheld multimedia guide on a self-paced tour, visitors view the mansion's rooms, from the built-in cage for the pet lemur purchased from Harrods to the impressive domed entrance hall panelled in veneered Australian black-bean wood, and the black marble dining room with silver-foil ceiling and heavy black doors decorated with lacquered animal figures.

The **Map Room**, where the couple plotted their extensive travels, was unveiled after 70 years of being covered by wallpaper and has wonderfully restored, if colonialist stereotyped, imagery. During the Blitz, the basement was converted to a deluxe air-raid shelter. Outside, there are 8 hectares of gardens to explore, including a rockery and moat with working bridge, so dedicate at least half a day.

Mon-Sat, from noon Sun; Ⓤ DLR Cutty Sark) Designed by Nicholas Hawksmoor to replace a 13th-century church and consecrated in 1718, baroque St Alfege features a restored mural by James Thornhill (whose work can also be found in the nearby Painted Hall and at St Paul's Cathedral), a largely wood-panelled interior and the intriguing Tallis Keyboard, a Tudor organ console with middle keyboard octaves. It is believed that Henry VIII was baptised here. Free classical music concerts take place at 1.05pm on Thursdays and Saturdays.

GREENWICH FOOT TUNNEL — TUNNEL

Map p477 (Cutty Sark Gardens, SE10; ⏰24hr; Ⓤ DLR Cutty Sark) Reached via glass-topped domes (with lifts and steps) on either side of the River Thames, this white-tiled 370m-long pedestrian tunnel opened in 1902 provides an atmospheric route to Greenwich from the Isle of Dogs; it's also an excellent diversion to get a photo of Greenwich from the north side of the river. At an average walking pace, the journey is only around 10 minutes but can be done faster, especially if you aren't keen on the feeling of the river flowingjust 15m overhead.

Look out for the WWII bomb damage at the northern end of the tunnel, which was fixed up with a steel and concrete lining. About 4000 crossings are made by pedestrians every day. There is another foot tunnel under the River Thames at Woolwich to the east.

PETER HARRISON PLANETARIUM — PLANETARIUM

Map p477 (☎020-8858 4422; www.rmg.co.uk/whats-on/planetarium-shows; Greenwich Park; adult/child £10/5; 👪; Ⓤ Greenwich or Cutty Sark) The southern half of the Royal Observatory (p103) includes this state-of-the-art, 120-seat planetarium – the only one in London. It's equipped with a digital laser projector that can lay out the heavens on the inside of its roof. It runs several informative shows a day, including a programme for kids, and it's best to book in advance.

DEPTFORD MARKET YARD — AREA

Map p477 (www.deptfordmarketyard.com; Market Yard; 🚉Deptford) The latest incarnation of this series of railway arches, originally used to store horses and carriages in the mid-1800s and later converted to WWII air-raid shelters, has seen a collection of indie shops, cocktail bars and a craft-beer taproom open up in these once derelict spaces.

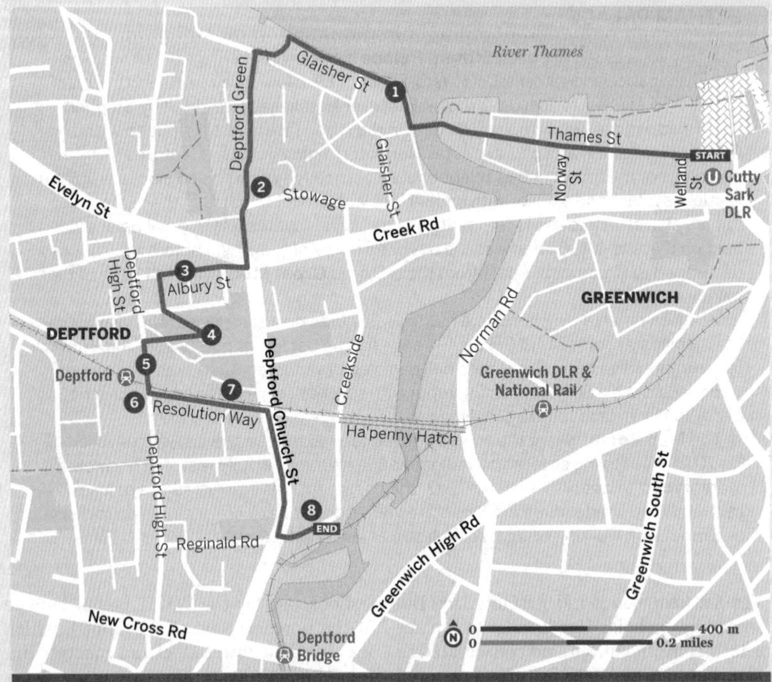

Neighbourhood Walk
Off the Beaten Track in Deptford

START DLR CUTTY SARK
END CREEKSIDE, DEPTFORD
LENGTH 2 MILES; 2½ HOURS

This walk explores the edgy neighbourhood of Deptford. Once an important and wealthy dockyard and shipbuilding centre, it's now a district in transition.

Walk west along the river and cross Deptford Creek on the swing bridge. Towards the Thames is a 1 **statue of Peter the Great** (Map p477, A2; Glaisher St, SE8; DLR Cutty Sark), recalling the Russian tsar's 1698 visit to Deptford to learn about developments in shipbuilding. Peter stayed in the home of diarist John Evelyn, and his drunken parties badly damaged the writer's house. Continue along the river and then south on Deptford Green to the late-17th-century 2 **St Nicholas Church** (www.stnicholaschurchdeptford.org; Deptford Green, SE8; Deptford), whose graveyard contains a memorial to playwright Christopher Marlowe, murdered at age 29 during a brawl in a Deptford tavern in 1593.

South across busy Creek Rd, delightful 3 **Albury Street** (Deptford) is lined with early Georgian buildings that once housed Deptford's naval officers, allegedly including Lord Nelson and his lover Lady Hamilton. To the south is the baroque 4 **St Paul's Church** (Diamond Way, SE8; Deptford), built in 1730. In the churchyard is the grave of Mydiddee, a native Tahitian who returned with Captain Bligh (of *Bounty* mutiny fame) on the HMS *Providence* and died here in 1793.

At the western end of the churchyard is Deptford High St with its thrice-weekly 5 **market**, a colourful affair with a good vintage-clothes section. Stop for a bite to eat along the High St or in 6 **Deptford Market Yard** (www.deptfordmarketyard.com; Market Yard, SE8; Deptford), which has resurrected the once abandoned railway arches. Get a taste of what's brewing in Deptford at 7 **Villages** before venturing south to sample more at 8 **Little Faith**.

STATUE OF PETER THE GREAT STATUE

Map p477 (Glaisher St; Ⓤ Cutty Sark) This strange statue recalls the Russian tsar's four-month stay in 1698 when he came to Deptford to learn more about new developments in shipbuilding.

ALBURY ST STREET

Map p477 (Ⓡ Deptford) Delightful Albury St is lined with early Georgian buildings that once housed Deptford's naval officers, allegedly including Lord Nelson and his lover Lady Hamilton. Notice the exquisite wood carvings decorating many of the doorways.

EATING

Beyond pub grub and treats from the market, decent dining options are somewhat scarce in Greenwich. The nearby neighbourhood of Deptford has a more interesting selection.

GREENWICH MARKET MARKET £

Map p477 (www.greenwichmarket.london; College Approach, SE10; ⏲10am-5.30pm; Ⓤ DLR Cutty Sark) Greenwich Market is one of London's smaller and more atmospheric covered markets. Stalls swap around depending on the day, but at least half the space is usually taken up by food vendors hawking homemade Jamaican rum cake, locally sourced oysters, Ethiopian vegetarian boxes, filled Brazilian churros and so much more. Browse handmade jewellery, cute London prints and natural beauty products while you feast.

GODDARDS AT GREENWICH BRITISH £

Map p477 (☎020-8305 9612; www.goddardsatgreenwich.co.uk; 22 King William Walk, SE10; pie & mash £4.40-8.50; ⏲10am-7.30pm Sun-Thu, to 8pm Fri & Sat; Ⓤ DLR Cutty Sark) If you're keen to try the quintessential English dish of pie and mash (minced beef, steak and kidney, or chicken in flaky pastry, served with mashed potatoes and gravy), drop into this Greenwich institution, a family business since 1890. Jellied eels, mushy peas, beans and 'liquor' (a green sauce made from parsley and vinegar) are optional extras.

JETTY CAFE £

(https://jetty.greenwichpeninsula.co.uk; Olympian Way, SE10; mains £9.50-15.50; ⏲10am-4pm Tue-Sun Jun-Sep, Thu-Sun Oct-May; Ⓤ North Greenwich) Jutting into the Thames on a disused pier, this is one of the few delightfully un-scrubbed-up parts left in North Greenwich. The overflowing plant life hints at the sustainable bent here, with urban farming initiatives, an army of volunteer gardeners and regular yoga sessions. The cafe, run by Hej Coffee, serves beans roasted down the river in Woolwich and a wonderful brunch menu.

★MARCELLA ITALIAN ££

(☎020-3903 6561; https://marcella.london; 165a Deptford High St, SE8; mains £12-16; ⏲6-10pm Mon, noon-2.30pm & 6-10pm Tue-Thu, to 10.30pm Fri & Sat, noon-4pm Sun; ✎; Ⓡ Deptford) If you avoid pasta restaurants because you think you can make it just as easily at home, Marcella is here to prove you wrong. Perfect house-made pasta comes with seasonally changing sauces in simple but delicious combinations. Starters are equally tasty (the house ricotta is creamy heaven), as are the generously large fish- and meat-based mains, made to share.

PAUL RHODES BAKERY BAKERY £

Map p477 (37 King William Walk; pastries/sandwiches from £1.80/3.50; ⏲7am-6pm; Ⓤ Cutty Sark) This handy corner bakery is a tip-top spot for a snack, baked goodies or a coffee. Delights include courgette, kale, hummus and tomato or chicken, bacon and avocado baguettes, marvellous lemon and citrus tarts, gorgeous chocolate tarts and vanilla cheesecake, served up by smiling staff. It's also open early.

DRINKING & NIGHTLIFE

Greenwich keeps it traditional, and a surplus of historic riverside pubs are strung along the water, as well as along the roads up the hills around Greenwich Park. Wonderful neighbourhood breweries can be found in Deptford.

LITTLE FAITH MICROBREWERY

Map p477 (☎020-8692 7612; https://littlefaithbeer.com; 3 Creekside, SE8; ⏲5-11pm Wed & Thu, to 1am Fri, 1pm-1am Sat, to 10pm Sun; Ⓡ DLR Deptford, Ⓤ Deptford Bridge) If it were in any other part of London, Little Faith would be unbearably busy. But in a slightly derelict corner of Deptford, this taproom serves up its own beers as well as guest pints from other London breweries. The somewhat shabby boho vibe is all part of its charm: you can even buy the art and knick-knacks straight off the walls.

VILLAGES MICROBREWERY

(www.villagesbrewery.com; 21-22 Resolution Way, SE8; ⏲5-11pm Thu & Fri, from noon Sat, 2-10pm Sun; 🚆Deptford) Down an alley off Deptford High St, this indie brewery started by two brothers pours sessionable beers and trial-run testers in its railway arch HQ. The minimalist IKEA-style decor invites drinkers to let loose and congregate at its indoor and outdoor communal tables.

OLD BREWERY PUB

Map p477 (☎020-3437 2222; www.oldbrewerygreenwich.com; Pepys House, Old Royal Naval College, SE10; ⏲10am-11pm Mon-Sat, to 10.30pm Sun; 📶; Ⓤ Cutty Sark) On the grounds of the Old Royal Naval College (p293), the Old Brewery once housed Greenwich Meantime, one of London's earliest craft breweries. Now owned by Young's pub company, it serves decent pub food and a range of beers, best enjoyed in the huge beer garden.

TRAFALGAR TAVERN PUB

Map p477 (☎020-3887 9886; www.trafalgartavern.co.uk; Park Row; ⏲noon-11pm Mon-Thu, to 1am Fri, 9am-1am Sat, to 11pm Sun; Ⓤ DLR Cutty Sark) This elegant tavern, with crystal chandeliers, nautical decor and big windows overlooking the Thames, is steeped in history. Dickens apparently knocked back a few here – and used it as the setting for the wedding-breakfast scene in *Our Mutual Friend* – and Prime Ministers William Gladstone and Benjamin Disraeli used to dine on the pub's celebrated whitebait.

★CUTTY SARK TAVERN PUB

Map p477 (☎020-8858 3146; www.cuttysarkse10.co.uk; 4-6 Ballast Quay; ⏲11.30am-11pm Mon-Sat, noon-10.30pm Sun; 📶; Ⓤ Cutty Sark or Maze Hill) Housed in a delightful bow-windowed, wood-beamed Georgian building directly on the Thames, this 200-year-old tavern is one of the few independent pubs left in Greenwich. Half a dozen cask-conditioned ales on tap line the bar, there's an inviting riverside seating area opposite and an upstairs dining room looking out on to glorious views. It's a 10-minute walk from the DLR station.

☆ ENTERTAINMENT

O2 ARENA LIVE MUSIC

(www.theo2.co.uk; Greenwich Peninsula; 📶; Ⓤ North Greenwich) One of the world's busiest arenas, the O2 has the second-largest indoor seating capacity in the country and, unsurprisingly, hosts all the big names that roll through London: Beyoncé, the Rolling Stones, BTS and Michael McIntyre, to name a few. It's also a popular venue for sporting events, and you can even climb the orange-spiked **roof** (from £30) for wide-ranging views.

Brixton, Peckham & South London

BRIXTON | LAMBETH | DULWICH & FOREST HILL | BERMONDSEY | PECKHAM | ELEPHANT & CASTLE | VAUXHALL | CLAPHAM | WANDSWORTH | TOOTING

Neighbourhood Top Five

❶ **Imperial War Museum** (p301) Hearing the challenging stories behind conflicts past and present.

❷ **Brixton Village & Market Row** (p301) Popping into food stalls, cafes, West African fabric shops, Jamaican greengrocers and craft-beer bars.

❸ **Bermondsey Beer Mile** (p306) Sampling the best of London's burgeoning craft-beer scene along more than a mile of railway arches and industrial estates.

❹ **Shad Thames** (p304) Strolling through this unique waterfront neighbourhood that still maintains authentic dockland factory facades.

❺ **Mayflower** (p309) Sipping a pint or indulging in a Sunday roast at this historic riverside pub in quaint Rotherhithe.

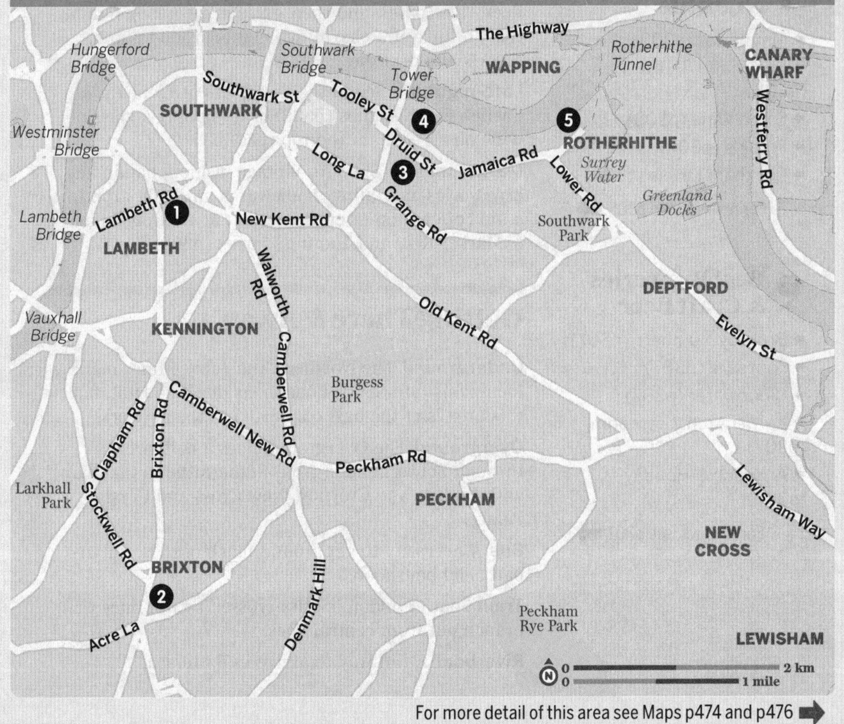

For more detail of this area see Maps p474 and p476

Lonely Planet's Top Tip

Plan your time in South London in advance. There's a lot of ground to cover, and occasionally poor public transport links can suck up a lot of time. Monday is the quietest day of the week – good for peaceful exploration but a challenge to find an open restaurant – with all neighbourhoods bursting into life from Friday to Sunday.

Best Eating

- Kudu (p304)
- Chez Bruce (p305)
- Taco Queen (p303)

For reviews, see p302.

Best Drinking & Nightlife

- Mayflower (p309)
- Shrub and Shutter (p305)
- Forza Wine (p308)
- Frank's (p307)
- Peckham Levels (p304)

For reviews, see p305.

Best Breweries & Craft Beer

- Brew by Numbers (p307)
- Fourpure (p307)
- Cloudwater (p307)
- Kernel Arch 7 Taproom (p307)
- Anspach & Hobday (p307)

For reviews, see p307.

Explore Brixton, Peckham & South London

Beyond a couple of worthwhile museums and galleries, sightseeing is not why you've come to South London. These neighbourhoods, born from leafy Victorian suburbs, retain their distinct village-like feel, with fantastic central markets – now becoming increasingly hipsterfied – and a more relaxed Londoners-at-leisure charm. Come nightfall, Brixton, Peckham and Clapham in particular are ready to stay up late, happily stealing some jewels from Shoreditch's nightlife crown. There's a fierce pride that comes with living 'saff' of the river, and an authentic sense of community that can be tapped into even on a short visit.

Things can be quiet during the week. Some must-visit markets, like the one on Maltby St, only come to life at weekends (Saturdays especially). Railways have made tracks through this part of town, and breweries, bars and restaurants have turned once dingy spaces into their hip new homes.

Local Life

Beer culture Discover London's best craft breweries hiding in the railway arches along the Bermondsey Beer Mile (p306) and then settle in for a long Sunday roast dinner at a charming neighbourhood pub to recover the next day.

Late-night life See in the wee hours at Elephant & Castle's famous clubs (p308) or by sipping a glass of wine on a Peckham rooftop (p308).

Market master Shop for vintage fashion, handmade accessories and quirky homewares until you drop into a hip coffee shop or craft-beer bar at Brixton Village & Market Row and Tooting Market (p309).

Getting There & Away

Underground The Northern and Jubilee lines make incursions into South London, as does the DLR, but this area isn't the best connected to the network.

Overground The Overground does a half-circle through South London from Rotherhithe to Clapham, with branches to Croydon, New Cross and Crystal Palace.

Bus A necessity to get around much of these suburban neighbourhoods.

Train South London is criss-crossed by rail lines that branch out from central ones.

Riverboat A fun way to arrive in Battersea.

SIGHTS

Brixton

★BRIXTON VILLAGE & MARKET ROW
MARKET

Map p474 (www.wearebrixtonvillage.co.uk; Atlantic Rd, SW9; ⏲8am-11.30pm Tue-Sun, to 6pm Mon; Ⓤ Brixton) This revitalised covered market, once the dilapidated 1930s Granville Arcade, has enjoyed an eye-catching renaissance. More than 130 traders have set up shop here, including Brixton originals **Franco Manca** (☎020-7738 3021; www.francomanca.co.uk; 4 Market Row, SW9; pizzas £5-9; ⏲noon-10pm Mon, noon-11pm Tue-Fri, 11.30am-11pm Sat, to 10.30pm Sun; 🖉) and **Honest Burgers** (Map p474; ☎020-7733 7963; www.honestburgers.co.uk; 12 Brixton Village, SW9; burgers £9-14.50; ⏲11.30am-4pm Mon, to 10.30pm Tue-Sat, to 10pm Sun), which have since successfully spiralled into mini London chains. Eclectic coffee shops, craft-beer bars, West African fabric shops and numerous restaurants cohabit with halal butchers, greengrocers and bazaars, and happily some retain the neighbourhood's Afro-Caribbean flavour.

BLACK CULTURAL ARCHIVES
CULTURAL CENTRE

Map p474 (☎020-3757 8500; https://blackculturalarchives.org; 1 Windrush Sq, SW2; ⏲10am-6pm Tue-Sat; Ⓤ Brixton) FREE The Black Cultural Archives is the only centre in the country devoted to preserving and telling the stories of African and Caribbean people in the UK. Check online to see what's happening before you visit, as the venue is primarily used for research and community meetings, but the cafe, events and rotating temporary exhibition space are open to the casual visitor.

Lambeth

BEEFEATER DISTILLERY
DISTILLERY

Map p476 (☎020-7587 0034; www.beefeaterdistillery.com; 20 Montford Pl, SE11; adult/child £15/free; ⏲10am-6.30pm Mon-Sat; Ⓤ Oval) Beefeater, established in 1863, is the oldest gin distillery still producing in London. The company opens its factory to visitors on 90-minute tours, which guide you through the gin craze of the 18th century to the cocktails and prohibition of the 1920s and '30s via interactive iPad explanations. A short talk on the production process, in the shadow

TOP EXPERIENCE

TIME HOP AT THE IMPERIAL WAR MUSEUM

Fronted by a pair of 15-inch naval guns, this riveting museum is housed in what was the Bethlem Royal Hospital, a psychiatric facility also known as Bedlam. Although the museum's focus is on military action of British or Commonwealth troops largely during the 20th century, it also covers war in the wider sense. Must-see exhibits include the state-of-the-art **First World War** galleries and **Witnesses to War** in the forecourt and atrium.

In Witnesses to War, you'll find exhibits from a Battle of Britain Spitfire and a towering German V-2 rocket to a Reuters Land Rover damaged by rocket attack in Gaza in 2006. The 1st-floor gallery **Turning Points: 1934–1945** looks at WWII through poignant objects, including the casing made for the 'Little Boy' atomic bomb and a trunk sent by Jewish parents to their children who had fled to the UK. **Peace and Security: 1945–2014** on the 2nd floor dives into more recent events. The 3rd floor hosts **Curiosities of War**, a mix of unexpected creations and artefacts from times of conflict, and temporary exhibitions.

One of the most challenging sections is the extensive, harrowing **The Holocaust** exhibition (not suitable for kids under 14); its entrance is on the 4th floor.

DON'T MISS

- First World War galleries
- The Holocaust exhibition
- Battle of Britain Spitfire

PRACTICALITIES

- Map p476, C2
- ☎020-7416 5000
- www.iwm.org.uk
- Lambeth Rd, SE1
- admission free
- ⏲10am-6pm
- Ⓤ Lambeth North

of the distillery's enormous stills, concludes with an expertly poured gin and tonic. Tours run on the hour throughout the day.

NEWPORT STREET GALLERY GALLERY

Map p476 (☎020-3141 9320; www.newportstreetgallery.com; 1 Newport St; ⊙10am-6pm Tue-Sun; Ⓤ Vauxhall) FREE Newport Street Gallery hosts artist Damien Hirst's personal collection in a series of converted industrial buildings that were once used as scenery-painting studios for theatres in the West End. The collection spans more than 3000 works, including pieces by Banksy, Jeff Koons, Pablo Picasso and Tracey Emin. Check online before you go to make sure it's open, as it's sometimes closed for weeks for new installations.

⊙ Dulwich & Forest Hill

HORNIMAN MUSEUM MUSEUM

(☎020-8699 1872; www.horniman.ac.uk; 100 London Rd, SE23; ⊙10am-5.30pm; ♿; Ⓤ Forest Hill) FREE This 1901 art-nouveau building, with its clock tower and mosaics, was specially designed to house the collection of wealthy tea merchant, Victorian gentleman and pack-rat Frederick John Horniman. The core of the museum is the **Natural History Gallery**, which contains taxidermied animals displayed in old-school glass cases, including the famous overstuffed walrus that doesn't have any wrinkles.

The **World Gallery** on the lower ground floor shows more than 3000 ancient and modern objects from civilisations around the planet, grouped by continent. The **Music Gallery** is the largest of its kind in the UK, displaying instruments from 3500-year-old Egyptian clappers to Ghanaian drums, with touchscreens so you can hear what they sound like and videos of them being played. The **Hands on Base** area, open on weekends and school holidays, is ideal for kids who want to touch and even wear part of the collection themselves. The **aquarium** (adult/child £4.50/2.50) in the basement is small but mesmerising for little ones, as jellyfish and seahorses float past. The **Butterfly House** (£6) is a tropical indoor jungle home to hundreds of free-flying insects.

The museum is set on 6.5 hectares of hillside and landscaped gardens with far-flung views of central London, perfect for a picnic on a sunny day. A number of paths circle around the gardens, including the **Horniman Nature Trail** along an abandoned railway line turned into wild woodlands and the **Animal Walk**, which goes past enclosures of alpacas, guinea pigs, rabbits and other farm critters.

DULWICH PICTURE GALLERY GALLERY

(☎020-8693 5254; www.dulwichpicturegallery.org.uk; Gallery Rd; adult/child £9/free; ⊙10am-5pm Tue-Sun; 🚆West Dulwich) The world's first purpose-built public art gallery, the small Dulwich Picture Gallery was designed by architect Sir John Soane and opened in 1817 to house nearby Dulwich College's collection of paintings by the Old Masters, including work by Rembrandt, Rubens, Gainsborough, Poussin and Canaletto. Unusually, the gallery also includes a mausoleum for its founders, lit by a moody *lumière mystérieuse* (mysterious light) created with tinted glass placed among the pictures. An audio guide is included in the ticket price.

EATING

You better have packed a second stomach because South London will satiate your appetite. Incredible restaurants cluster in the area's revitalised markets, such as Brixton Village & Market Row (p301), Tooting Market (p309) and Tooting Broadway Market (p309). The strong presence of the Afro-Caribbean community in Brixton plus Tooting's residents with roots in the Indian subcontinent have a delicious effect on the local dining options.

Brixton

POP BRIXTON MARKET £

Map p474 (☎020-3879 8410; www.popbrixton.org; 49 Brixton Station Rd, SW9; ⊙9am-11pm Sun-Wed, to midnight Thu-Sat; 📶; Ⓤ Brixton) 🍃 Pop Brixton is a brilliant community initiative that's home to 100% independently owned bars, restaurants and shops. Your taste-buds can travel the world, from Jamaican jerk chicken to Greek souvlaki and Japanese ramen. It's also home to Halo Burger, which created the UK's first plant-based 'bleeding burger'.

MAMALAN CHINESE £

Map p474 (www.mamalan.co.uk; 18 Brixton Village, SW9; mains £9.45-11.95; ⊙noon-4pm Mon, to 10pm Tue-Sun; Ⓤ Brixton) Mamalan is the place to go

WHAT'S NEW IN BATTERSEA

With its huge riverside **park** (Map p474; www.wandsworth.gov.uk/batterseapark; 8am-dusk; Battersea Park) and iconic power station, beautiful Battersea has seemingly been kept at arms length from central London because of inconvenient transport links, but now the neighbourhood is a hive of redevelopment activity that guarantees that its face will be forever changed. After lying derelict for decades, **Battersea Power Station** (Map p474; www.batterseapowerstation.co.uk; 188 Kirtling St, SW8; Battersea Power Station, Battersea Park) is getting scrubbed up into luxury flats and Apple's new London HQ, with a new district of shops, bars and restaurants at its feet – many of which are already open in a zone called Circus West Village. Some are tucked under the railway arches in true South London style. Riverboat services were extended to a pier at Battersea Power Station in 2017, and a brand-new branch of the Northern Line is scheduled to open in autumn 2021.

for authentic, handmade Beijing street food dished up in a tiny market shopfront. The eight-hour slow-cooked beef noodle soup and fried pork dumplings are menu highlights.

KRICKET INDIAN ££

Map p474 (020-3826 4090; https://kricket.co.uk; 41-43 Atlantic Rd, SW9; dishes £6-11; 5.30-10.30pm Tue-Thu, noon-10.30pm Fri & Sat, noon-5pm Sun; Brixton) Kricket has moved its Indian small plates from Pop Brixton into permanent digs in a pair of railway arches. Londoners come in droves for the KFC (Keralan fried chicken) and samphire pakora, made of a bright-green stringy sea vegetable that's lightly battered, fried and topped with tangy tamarind sauce.

THREE LITTLE BIRDS JAMAICAN ££

Map p474 (020-3910 1870; www.threelittlebirdsja.com; 412 Coldharbour Lane, SW9; dishes £5.50-10; 11am-11pm Wed, to midnight Thu, to 1am Fri & Sat, to 10pm Sun, 6-11pm Mon & Tue; Brixton) Three Little Birds combines Brixton old and new with Jamaican-inspired sharing plates. Honey jerk chicken wings, goat curry and codfish fritters are a few of the essential dishes to order, but save room for the rum-flavoured desserts and cocktail list.

NAUGHTY PIGLETS FRENCH ££

Map p474 (020-7274 7796; www.naughtypiglets.co.uk; 28 Brixton Water Lane, SW2; dishes £8-12; 6-9.45pm Mon-Thu, noon-2.30pm & 6-9.45pm Fri & Sat; Brixton) In a cosy space a short walk from central Brixton, this wonderful French bistro has an ever-changing menu of creative small plates that go well with a glass from their list of low-intervention wines. Menu standouts include the grilled pear with Jerusalem artichokes, hazelnuts and blue cheese, and blood sausage splashed with burnt apple sauce and topped with crackling.

Bermondsey

MALTBY STREET MARKET MARKET £

(www.maltby.st; Ropewalk, SE1; noon-2.30pm Fri, 10am-5pm Sat, 11am-4pm Sun; London Bridge or Bermondsey) Alongside and under railway arches leading from London Bridge, Maltby Street Market is a perfect pit stop to fuel up for a big day on the Bermondsey Beer Mile (p306) or shopping around the neighbourhood. Food stalls, serving round-the-world cuisines from Taiwanese bubble waffles to Venezuelan rainbow *arepas*, are set up in the alleyway outside the main doors of established arch restaurants and bars.

ST JOHN BAKERY BAKERY £

(https://stjohnrestaurant.com/pages/bakery; 72 Druid St; pastries/bread from £1.50/3; 9am-4pm Sat & Sun; London Bridge) During the week, this railway arch is strictly a wholesale bakery from one of London's most beloved nose-to-tail restaurants (p208), but on weekends, you can grab a few of the legendary lightly sugared jam-filled doughnuts or a loaf of bread from behind the iron shutter.

Peckham

TACO QUEEN TACOS £

(https://twitter.com/tacoqueenldn; 191 Rye Lane, SE15; tacos £3.95; noon-3pm & 6-10pm Tue-Sat, noon-3pm Sun; ; Peckham Rye) Crowd into this small shopfront for some of the best tacos in town. This former taco joint has taken Peckham by storm, all funnelled

STROLLING SHAD THAMES

For one of London's most perfect examples of time travel, step into Shad Thames, a small neighbourhood east of Tower Bridge. Once the largest warehouse complex in the city, the beige-brick converted factories, which once stored coffee, tea and spices, still line the narrow cobbled lanes, as industrial cranes and iron footbridges loom overhead. Secretive stairs provide prized and little-visited views of the river and Tower Bridge. Walk across the pedestrian-only bridge over **St Saviour's Dock** for a picturesque view of the seemingly unchanged waterside wharves.

into the loud, densely packed tables. Fantastic veg and vegan options include battered avocado, and meat-eaters should dive into the cornflake-covered baja fish and pork al pastor.

PECKHAM LEVELS INTERNATIONAL £

(https://peckhamlevels.org; 95a Rye Lane, SE15; 10am-11pm Mon-Wed, to 1am Thu-Sat, to midnight Sun; Peckham Rye) A few floors below famous Frank's (p307), Peckham Levels is the place to go if you want to drink in a former car park year-round. Head straight to the 6th floor for a delightful mix of street-food stalls and bars with enclosed weather-proof views toward London's skyscrapers.

★KUDU AFRICAN ££

(020-3950 0226; www.kuducollective.com; 119 Queen's Rd; dishes £8.50-18; 6-10pm Wed & Thu, noon-2.30pm & 6-10pm Fri, 11am-2.30pm & 6-10pm Sat, to 9pm Sun; Queens Rd Peckham) Northeast of Peckham's core, this family-run neighbourhood restaurant is worth the venture. Decorated with dusky pink and exposed-brick walls and blue velvet banquettes, Kudu presents South African flavours with inventive ingredients on delicate sharing plates. The menu can do no wrong, so order as much as you can: pig's-head tortellini, Parmesan churros with brown crab mayo and the signature pot-baked Kudu bread.

Elephant & Castle

MERCATO METROPOLITANO INTERNATIONAL £

Map p476 (020-7403 0930; www.mercatometropolitano.com; 42 Newington Causeway, SE1; 8am-11pm Mon-Wed, to midnight Thu & Fri, 11am-midnight Sat, to 10pm Sun; Elephant & Castle) Set inside a 4100-sq-metre disused paper factory, this food hall has more than 40 stalls and even its own on-site microbrewery. Mercato Metropolitano has more Italian vendors than average, but flavours range from Uzbek dumplings to Tex-Mex tacos.

PALADAR LATIN AMERICAN ££

Map p476 (020-7186 5555; www.paladarlondon.com; 4-5 London Rd, SE1; mains £12.50-19.80; noon-3pm & 5-10pm Mon-Fri, 1-10.30pm Sat; Elephant & Castle) The area between Elephant and Castle and Southwark is something of a black hole of restaurants. Fortunately, Paladar has come to the rescue with fantastic Latin American cuisine that stretches from Cuba to Colombia. It dishes up excellent-value lunch and pre-theatre set menus, too (two/three courses £17.50/21.50).

DRAGON CASTLE CHINESE ££

Map p476 (020-7277 3388; www.dragoncastlelondon.com; 100 Walworth Rd; mains £10.80-35; noon-11pm; ; Elephant & Castle) Step inside the red metal-studded doors, carefully guarded by dragon statues, into one of the better family-run Chinese restaurants south of the river. The midday dim sum service is locally loved. Don't miss the fluffy and flaky *char siu so* (roast pork puff).

Vauxhall

BRUNSWICK HOUSE BRITISH ££

Map p476 (020-7720 2926; https://brunswickhouse.london; 30 Wandsworth Rd, SW8; mains £16-22; 9.30am-midnight Mon-Fri, from 10am Sat, 10am-5pm Sun; ; Vauxhall) This boutique cafe, housed in a lone Georgian house, serves modern British fare that's simple and elegantly executed. It is wonderfully decorated with dozens of chandeliers and lengthy plant vines suspended from the ceiling.

Clapham

TRINITY BRITISH £££

Map p474 (020-7622 1199; www.trinityrestaurant.co.uk; 4 The Polygon, SW4; 3-/4-course lunch £45/55, dinner £65/75; ⏲12.30-2.30pm & 6.30-10pm; ☑; ⓊClapham Common) Named after the nearby church, this sleek Clapham restaurant boasts a Michelin star. You can't go wrong with any selection from its outstanding menu, and all courses have at least one vegetarian option. The aptly named Upstairs restaurant on the 1st floor is a more casual (and cheaper) affair.

Wandsworth

★CHEZ BRUCE FRENCH £££

(☎020-8672 0114; www.chezbruce.co.uk; 2 Bellevue Rd, SW17; 3-course lunch/dinner from £39.50/60; ⏲noon-2.30pm & 6.30-9.30pm Mon-Thu, to 10.30pm Fri, noon-3pm & 6.30-10.30pm Sat, to 9.30pm Sun; 🚆Wandsworth Common) Far off the usual tourist track, the phenomenal Chez Bruce, opposite leafy Wandsworth Common, has been in business for more than two decades. Despite its Michelin star, the atmosphere remains less pretentious than at other fine-dining establishments. Dishes rotate frequently, but duck is often the star of the menu.

Tooting

DOSA N CHUTNY INDIAN £

(☎020-8767 9200; www.dosanchutny.com; 68 Tooting High St, SW17; mains £4.95-7.95; ⏲11am-10.30pm Mon-Thu, to 11pm Fri-Sun; ⓊTooting Broadway) Along South London's curry corridor, Dosa n Chutny is the best of the South Indian restaurants in Tooting. The dining area is a slight step above no-frills, and this is one of the few places in town where you can have a filling sit-down meal for under £10. The namesake dosa, a light, crispy crepe-like piece of cooked batter, is a must-order.

KOI RAMEN BAR JAPANESE £

(☎020-8682 3888; www.koiramenbar.co.uk; Tooting Market, 21-23 Tooting High St, SW17; ramen £7-8.50; ⏲11.30am-10pm Sun-Thu, to 11pm Fri & Sat; ☑; ⓊTooting Broadway) Saddle up in one of the bar seats at this small stall in Tooting Market. The experts at Koi know their noodles, and the concise menu of just four options emphasises their speciality in *tonkotsu*, pork belly slices and al dente ramen dunked in creamy, slow-simmered pork-bone broth. Most bowls can be made meat-free with tofu.

DRINKING & NIGHTLIFE

South London's nightlife options are as diverse as its neighbourhoods. With a plethora of pop-ups and rooftops, Brixton and Peckham promise just as good a night out as Shoreditch or Soho. The Bermondsey Beer Mile (p306) is home to London's best breweries and a must for hopheads.

Brixton

★SHRUB AND SHUTTER COCKTAIL BAR

Map p474 (☎020-7326 0643; www.theshrubandshutter.com; 336 Coldharbour Lane; ⏲5pm-midnight Tue-Thu, to 2am Fri & Sat; ⓊBrixton) Drinkers come from miles around to sample the mixologist magic poured at Shrub and Shutter. As per the name, drinks often come with greenery in some form, such as a sprig of tarragon or *padrón*-pepper bitters.

BRIXTON BREWERY MICROBREWERY

Map p474 (☎020-3609 8880; www.brixtonbrewery.com; Arches 547-548, Brixton Station Rd, SW9; ⏲5-10pm Wed & Thu, to 11pm Fri, noon-11pm Sat, 2-6pm Sun; ⓊBrixton) Though its beers are now sold as far away as Hong Kong, Brixton Brewery remembers its roots in its railway-arch taproom. The names of the brews give a nod to local landmarks and history: Coldharbour Lager, Windrush Stout, Effra Ale. Limited-edition beers have been made with London-grown hops as well as ingredients found in Brixton Market (p309).

TAPROOM BY BRIXTON VILLAGE CRAFT BEER

Map p474 (www.wearetaproom.co.uk; 43-44 Brixton Village, Coldharbour Lane, SW9; ⏲5-11.30pm Tue, from noon Wed-Fri, from 11am Sat, 11am-11pm Sun; ⓊBrixton) If you don't have time to make it to all of South London's best breweries, you can get the Cliff Notes version at this small market-based taproom. Featured breweries include Canopy, Brixton Brewery, Gypsy Hill and Orbit, and there are also cocktails on tap when you're ready to switch from craft beer.

MARKET HOUSE BAR

Map p474 (☎020-7095 9443; www.market-house.co.uk; 443 Coldharbour Lane, SW9; ⏲3-11pm Mon-Wed, to midnight Thu, to 3am Fri, 1pm-4am Sat, to 11pm Sun; 📶; ⓊBrixton) Wallpapered, antique-embellished Market House makes for a good

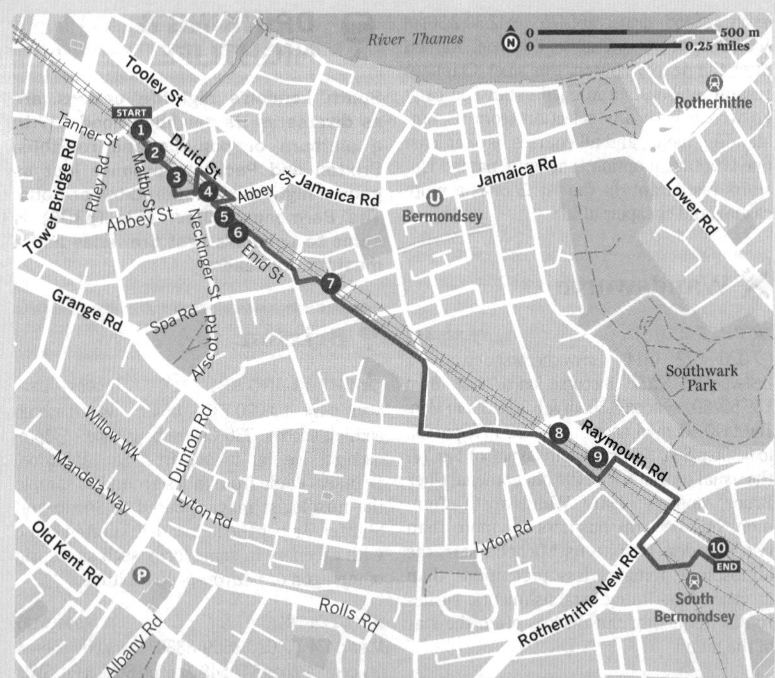

Neighbourhood Walk
Bermondsey Beer Mile

START ST JOHN BAKERY
END FOURPURE
LENGTH 1.7 MILES; FIVE HOURS

London's craft-beer revival is in full swing, with Bermondsey at its epicentre. Some two dozen breweries and taprooms have sprung along a disjointed stretch of railway arches. Most are working breweries and limit hours to the weekends.

Start your session with a legendary doughnut from ❶ **St John Bakery** (p303) before grabbing a more substantial brunch at ❷ **Maltby Street Market** (p303). At the end of the market is ❸ **Hiver** (☎020-3198 9972; www.hiverbeers.com; 56 Stanworth St, SE1; ⏰11am-6pm Sat & Sun; Ⓤ Bermondsey), which infuses IPAs, ales and blondes with local honey. Head under the railway to ❹ **Anspach & Hobday** and sample its flagship beer, a dark coffee-chocolate porter. Wind back through the arches to ❺ **Cloudwater**, the London taproom of a Manchester-based brewery. Next door is the ever-experimental ❻ **Brew By Numbers**, with its 'scientific' branding. Continue southeast on Enid St to ❼ **Kernel Arch 7 Taproom**.

It's a sobering half-mile trek through industrial estates and past taxi-repair garages to ❽ **Affinity** (www.affinitybrewco.com; 7 Almond Rd, SE16; ⏰5-8.30pm Fri, noon-8.30pm Sat, noon-6pm Sun; 🚆South Bermondsey), whose brightly coloured labels hint at its love of zingy citrus and dry-hopped brews. Pass over to ❾ **Partizan** (www.partizanbrewing.co.uk; 34 Raymouth Rd, SE16; ⏰5-11pm Fri, 11am-8pm Sat; 🚆South Bermondsey) for a heavy dose of American hops. After one last jaunt through the arches, turn left into the security-gated Bermondsey Trading Estate. The prize is at the end of the long, winding road: the revamped taproom of ❿ **Fourpure**, with much to choose from on its 43 craft-beer taps.

drinks stop on an evening's crawl around Brixton. The weekday atmosphere is laid-back, but on weekends DJs set up their decks.

FEDERATION COFFEE CAFE

Map p474 (https://federation.coffee; 77-78 Brixton Village, Coldharbour Lane, SE9; 8am-5pm Mon-Wed, to midnight Thu & Fri, 9am-midnight Sat, to 4pm Sun; Brixton) Gauge the pulse of Brixton Village over a cup of Federation's gorgeous coffee, made with beans by guest roasters from as close as a nearby market stall and as far as Sweden.

Bermondsey

★BREW BY NUMBERS BREWERY

(www.brewbynumbers.com; 75-79 Enid St, SE16; 5-10pm Wed & Thu, 4-10.30pm Fri, noon-10pm Sat, to 6pm Sun; Bermondsey) In the centre of the Bermondsey Beer Mile, this microbrewery's raison d'être is experimentation. Everything from its 'scientific' branding (the numbers refer to the type of beer – porter, pale ale etc – and recipe) to its enthusiasm for exploring new beer styles and refashioning old ones (for instance, saison – an old Belgian beer drunk by farm workers) is about broadening the definition of beer.

★CLOUDWATER BAR

(https://cloudwaterbrew.co; 73 Enid St, SE16; 3-10pm Wed-Fri, from 10am Sat, noon-8pm Sun; Bermondsey) This industrial minimalist space is the taproom of Manchester-based Cloudwater. Juicy IPAs, mouth-puckering sours and nitro stouts are all on tap, as well as collaboration and guest beers.

FOURPURE BREWERY

(020-3744 2141; www.fourpure.com; 25 Bermondsey Trading Estate, SE16; noon-8pm Tue, to 10pm Wed-Fri, 11am-8pm Sat, from noon Sun; South Bermondsey) Fourpure has the fanciest taproom on the Bermondsey Beer Mile. Revamped and reopened in 2019, the drinking area has an indoor wrap-around balcony, suspended egg chairs, trailing vines and a huge oval-shaped bar with 43 taps.

KERNEL ARCH 7 TAPROOM BREWERY

(020-7231 4516; www.thekernelbrewery.com; Arch 7, Dockley Rd Industrial Estate, SE16; 4-10pm Wed-Fri, 11am-8pm Sat, noon-6pm Sun; Bermondsey) The first brewery in this part of town, Kernel is perhaps the originator of the Bermondsey Beer Mile. It closed its taproom years ago, before relaunching in this new location in November 2019, much to the delight of hophead Londoners. Grab Kernel's beloved table beer, a surprisingly hoppy sessionable American pale ale.

ANSPACH & HOBDAY BREWERY

(020-8617 9510; www.anspachandhobday.com; 118 Druid St, SE1; 5-10pm Fri, 10.30am-10pm Sat, 1-6pm Sun; Bermondsey) Best known for its flagship deep coffee-chocolate porter, Anspach & Hobday brews that and more in its narrow railway arch along the Bermondsey Beer Mile. Drinkers pile in next to the vats and other brew kit as pints are poured from taps poking through a plywood board.

JENSEN'S DISTILLERY

(www.jensensgin.com; 55 Stanworth St, SE1; 10.30am-6pm Sat, 11am-4pm Sun; Bermondsey) This micro gin distillery at the end of Maltby Street Market (p303) provides weekend G&Ts from its railway-arch premises. Jensen's produces two kinds of gin: Bermondsey Dry, a variation of the famous London Dry gin; and Old Tom, a more intense, unsweetened opaque gin. Tours of the distillery are run on Wednesdays and Thursdays.

Peckham

FRANK'S BAR

(http://boldtendencies.com/franks-cafe; 10th fl, 95a Rye Lane, SE15; 5-11pm Tue & Wed, from 2pm Thu & Fri, 11am-11pm Sat & Sun mid-May–mid-Sep; Peckham Rye) The simple summer-only set-up at Frank's is an al fresco favourite. Drink in the views (and something from the beer taps or cocktail menu) from the top floor of a multistorey car park, where wooden pallets have been constructed into a bar and benches. Unfortunately, the no-frills approach also extends to the toilets.

BUSSEY BUILDING BAR

(020-7635 0000; www.clfartcafe.org; 133 Rye Lane, SE15; 5-11pm Tue & Wed, to 2.30am Thu, to 5am Fri, noon-5am Sat, to 11pm Sun; Peckham Rye) This former cricket-bat factory was turned into an eclectic cultural space spanning several floors that encourage exploration. The party runs until late and changes every evening, with live music, raves, theatre, a summertime rooftop film club and more. Rye Wax, an indie record shop that hosts small gigs, has taken over the basement.

FOUR QUARTERS BAR

(http://geocities.fourquartersbar.co.uk; 187 Rye Lane, SE15; ⌚5.30pm-1am Mon-Wed, to 1.30am Thu, 5pm-2am Fri, from 1pm Sat, 3.30-11pm Sun; Peckham Rye) Calling all '80s and '90s nerds: you could lose an entire evening testing out all the games in this two-level arcade bar, where you'll have to exchange your pounds for US quarters to play. There's craft beer on tap, and Mario Kart tournaments sometimes break out on the weekends.

FORZA WINE BAR

(020-7732 7500; www.forzawine.com; 5th fl, 133 Rye Lane, SE15; ⌚noon-1am Tue-Sat, to midnight Sun; Peckham Rye) The newest rooftop to open in Peckham is this Italian restaurant-bar on top of a refurbished Edwardian building. The mix of indoor and outdoor space means this spot will be in demand no matter what the weather. Food-serving hours are more limited than the drinking hours, so grab an aperitivo and enjoy the view.

Elephant & Castle

ELEPHANT & CASTLE PUB

Map p476 (020-7403 8124; https://elephantandcastlepub.com; 119 Newington Causeway, SE1; ⌚noon-midnight Sun-Wed, to 1am Thu, to 2am Fri & Sat; Elephant & Castle) Elephant and Castle almost lost the most recent incarnation of its namesake neighbourhood pub, but the council named this spot an asset of community value, and it's been injected with a dose of local love. The concrete coffered ceiling, velour banquettes and fringed table lamps set the decidedly '60s theme, and the taps offer both standard lagers and craft beers.

MINISTRY OF SOUND CLUB

Map p476 (020-7740 8600; www.ministryofsound.com; 103 Gaunt St, SE1; ⌚10.30pm-6am Fri, from 11pm Sat; ; Elephant & Castle) A veteran of London's club scene, the Ministry of Sound put four bars, three dance floors and more than 60 speakers to pump in trance, house, electro and techno in an abandoned bus garage. If you're not a night owl, sign up for yoga, spin or high-intensity interval training (HIIT) at 'London's first fitness nightclub'.

CORSICA STUDIOS CLUB

Map p476 (020-7703 4760; www.corsicastudios.com; 4/5 Elephant Rd, SE17; ⌚hours vary; ; Elephant & Castle) Tucked into two railway arches under Elephant and Castle station, Corsica Studios is where the weekend never dies: its licence extends to 3am during the week and 6am on Friday and Saturday. The sound system is usually pumping out electro, techno and house.

Vauxhall

ROYAL VAUXHALL TAVERN GAY

Map p476 (020-7820 1222; www.vauxhalltavern.com; 372 Kennington Lane, SE11; ⌚7pm-midnight Mon-Thu, to 4am Fri, 9pm-4am Sat, 4-10.30pm Sun; Vauxhall) The Royal Vauxhall Tavern is one of the city's most loved cabaret and performance venues, and there's something on every night of the week. Saturday's Duckie, dubbed a rock-and-roll honky tonk, is the club's signature performance.

EAGLE GAY

Map p476 (020-7793 0903; www.eaglelondon.com; 349 Kennington Lane, SE11; ⌚8pm-2am Tue-Thu, to 4am Fri, 9pm-4am Sat, 8pm-3am Sun; Vauxhall) This fantastic place is a haven of alternative queer goings-on. It's open six nights a week, with a different feel every evening. Big hitters are the Carpet Burn club night on Fridays and the Horse Meat Disco on Sundays.

FIRE LONDON GAY

Map p476 (020-3242 0040; www.firelondon.net; 39 Parry St, SW8; ⌚11pm-10am Thu-Sat; Vauxhall) Fire is an expansive space under Vauxhall's railway arches that also attracts hetero clubbers, and its sound system has a pronounced lean towards house and techno. Its outdoor garden is a rare gem and is good for watching the sunrise.

Clapham

TWO BREWERS GAY

Map p474 (020-7819 9539; www.the2brewers.com; 114 Clapham High St, SW4; ⌚5pm-2am Sun-Wed, to 3am Thu, to 4am Fri & Sat; Clapham Common) Two Brewers endures as one of the best London gay bars outside the LGBTIQ+ villages of Soho and Vauxhall. There's cabaret, bingo or karaoke most nights of the week, and the venue is a full-on dancing madhouse on weekends. There's often a cover charge.

WORTH A DETOUR

ROTHERHITHE

Nestled in a bend of the River Thames east of Bermondsey, the neighbourhood of Rotherhithe makes for a fascinating detour. Once an important port along the river, Rotherhithe had working docks until the 1970s, but its architectural heritage is still preserved today – you'll notice it walking down cobblestone streets past converted brick warehouses that are still fitted with dangling cranes. A stop at the 16th-century **Mayflower** (Map p462; ☎020-7237 4088; www.mayflowerpub.co.uk; 117 Rotherhithe St, SE16; ⏰11am-11pm Mon-Sat, noon-10.30pm Sun; ⓤRotherhithe) is a must; it's one of London's most atmospheric pubs. It's named after the vessel that set sail from Rotherhithe in 1620, taking the Pilgrims to North America.

ENTERTAINMENT

PRINTWORKS — LIVE MUSIC

(☎020-8498 4934; https://printworkslondon.co.uk; Surrey Quays Rd, SE16; ⓤCanada Water) This post-industrial space was once the largest printing factory in Western Europe, and much of the machinery, exposed metal- and brickwork still remain in place. The gig line-ups, announced seasonally, are generally electronic, techno and house, but there are also art shows, dinner clubs and other events.

O2 ACADEMY BRIXTON — LIVE MUSIC

Map p474 (☎020-7771 3000; https://academymusicgroup.com/o2academybrixton; 211 Stockwell Rd, SW9; ⓤBrixton) The O2 hosts club nights and gigs inside a 1920s art deco theatre with a nearly 5000-person capacity. The sloped floor guarantees good views, though if you aren't dancing enough, the ground, sticky with beer spills, may glue you into place.

KIA OVAL — SPECTATOR SPORT

Map p476 (☎020-3946 0100; www.kiaoval.com; Kennington Oval, SE11; ⓤOval) The birthplace of the Ashes, Kia Oval is South London's centre for cricket and home to the Surrey County Cricket Club. Apart from Surrey matches, it also hosts some international Test matches, the Ashes and the World Cup. The season runs from April to September, but tours are available year-round (adult/child £15/5).

BATTERSEA ARTS CENTRE — THEATRE

Map p474 (☎020-7223 2223; www.bac.org.uk; Lavender Hill, SW11; 👪; ⓡClapham Junction) Housed in a grand former town hall, the Battersea Arts Centre puts on thought-provoking stage performances and even runs 'Scratch' sessions, where the audience can watch and critique shows in their early stages. It's a true community hub, with a play space for tots and a cafe open outside show times.

SHOPPING

South London has markets galore, some of which remain delightfully old school while others have shifted wares with gentrifying neighbourhoods. Pop Brixton (p302), a cluster of businesses housed in stacked shipping containers, has shops mixed in amongst its fantastic restaurants, as does Brixton Village & Market Row (p301).

BRIXTON MARKET — MARKET

Map p474 (www.brixtonmarket.net; Electric Ave, SW9; ⏰8am-6pm Mon, Tue & Thu-Sat, to 3pm Wed; ⓤBrixton) Brixton Market showcases the richness of this neighbourhood. Jamaican fish and fruits are stacked high, and halal butchers hawk their latest cuts from permanent shops along both sides of Electric Ave, as indecisive shoppers leaf through racks of vintage and knock-off fashion set out in the middle of the thoroughfare.

TOOTING MARKET — MARKET

(☎020-8672 4760; www.tootingmarket.com; 21-23 Tooting High St, SW17; ⏰8am-6pm Mon-Thu, to 10.30pm Fri & Sat, 9am-5pm Sun; ⓤTooting Broadway) Despite facing potential demolition, this 90-year stalwart of the South London shopping scene continues to expand, most recently with a new area called **Yard Market**. Stalls range from East Asian haberdashers to purveyors of African sculptures and a Chinese medicinal clinic. Small restaurants and bars are taking over more stall spaces, making this as much a food destination as a shopping one.

A few doors southwest is **Tooting Broadway Market** (☎020-8672 6613; www.bmtooting.co.uk; 29 Tooting High St, SW17; ⏰9am-11pm Mon-Thu, to 11.30pm Fri & Sat, to 9pm Sun; ⓤTooting Broadway), which has much of the same cool atmosphere and mixture of shops, bars and restaurants.

Richmond, Kew & Hampton Court

RICHMOND & KEW | PUTNEY & BARNES | CHISWICK | TWICKENHAM | WIMBLEDON | HAMPTON COURT

Neighbourhood Top Five

❶ **Hampton Court Palace** (p312) Listening out for poltergeists along the galleries and in the vaults, before getting lost in the maze.

❷ **Kew Gardens** (p316) Plunging into luxuriant green expanses, wooded thickets and tropical foliage.

❸ **London Wetland Centre** (p320) Turning your back on urban London to discover a pristine pocket of wilderness.

❹ **White Cross** (p325) Sinking a pint of beer at this historic riverside pub while trying to avoid being cut off by the high tide.

❺ **Richmond Park** (p318) Exploring London's wild side, roaming at will.

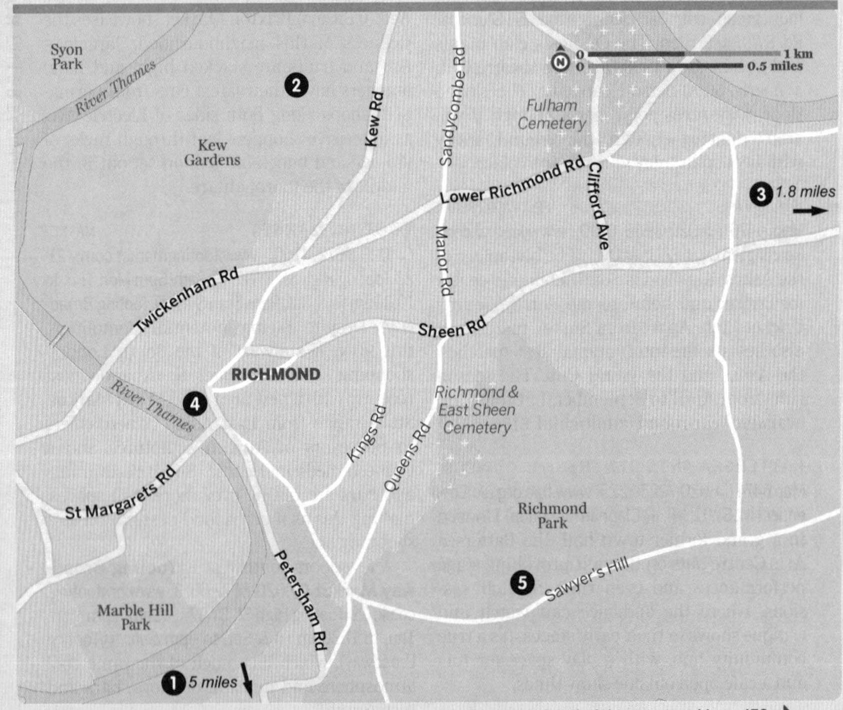

For more detail of this area see Map p478

Explore Richmond, Kew & Hampton Court

Richmond, Kew and Hampton Court is the London you barely knew existed, and you'll need a few days getting to fathom the charms of this adorable neighbourhood. The shiny city is a galaxy away: this is where the green and pleasant land of England commences. Start early in the morning with Kew Gardens, but you may find yourself there the entire day, getting magnificently lost. If you escape, head south to laze by the river in grand Richmond, Instagramming some of London's most delightful river views. Richmond Park and Wimbledon Common offer rambling opportunities galore. Several excellent hotels allow you to overnight here, if you wish, so your explorations can continue to Hampton Court Palace, the UK's most magnificent chunk of Tudor architecture; ghost hunters will want to check out this famously haunted palace to really get into the 'spirit' of things. Night-times are pretty low-key in the neighbourhood, but there's a bevy of waterside pubs to try out for a more languorous perspective of the city as it melds with pastoral England. You might not find yourself coming here exclusively to shop, but bring your wallet as there's no shortage of fine dining to fill your tummy.

Local Life

Hang-outs Get into the riverside pub-lunch mood joining locals quaffing beer at the City Barge (p324) or White Cross (p325).

Greenery Londoners from all over town bolt down to Richmond Park (p318) and Kew Gardens (p316) for weekend great escapes.

River views Join locals jogging by the river, walking their dogs or catching some sunshine north and south of Richmond Bridge (p319).

Getting There & Away

Train & Underground Both Kew Gardens and Richmond are on the District Line and London Overground; Richmond train station can be reached from Clapham Junction. Trains run to Hampton Court station from Waterloo. East Putney, Putney Bridge, Fulham Broadway and Chiswick Park are on the District Line.

Riverboat Services run several times daily from Westminster Pier to Kew and on to Hampton Court Palace (boats sometimes stop at Richmond).

Lonely Planet's Top Tip

A manageable section of the fantastic Thames Path (p324) is the 4 miles between Putney Bridge and Barnes Footbridge. Taking around 90 minutes, most of the walk is very rural and at times you will only be accompanied by birdsong and the gentle swish of the river. From the footbridge, Chiswick train station is about 0.75 miles to the northwest. For more details, see the River Thames Alliance's Visit Thames site (www.visitthames.co.uk).

Best Eating

- Glasshouse (p324)
- Petersham Nurseries Cafe (p324)
- Gelateria Danieli (p323)
- Chez Lindsay (p323)
- Orange Pekoe (p323)

For reviews, see p323.

Best Drinking & Nightlife

- White Cross (p325)
- City Barge (p324)
- White Hart (p325)
- Crooked Billet (p325)
- Tap on the Line (p325)

For reviews, see p324.

Best Guided Tours

- Kew Explorer (p317)
- Hampton Court Palace (p312)
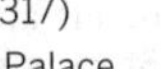
- Strawberry Hill (p321)
- Ham House (p318)

For reviews, see p312.

VLADISLAV ZOLOTOV/GETTY IMAGES ©

TOP EXPERIENCE

TIME TRAVEL AT HAMPTON COURT PALACE

Britain's most spectacular Tudor palace, this 16th-century icon concocts an imposing sense of history, from the huge kitchens and grand living quarters to the spectacular gardens, complete with a maze more than 300 years old, as well as the world's largest grapevine.

History of the Palace

Hampton Court Palace was built by Cardinal Thomas Wolsey in 1515, but he gave it to Henry VIII in an unsuccessful attempt to remain in the king's favour after failing, as his chancellor, at the impossible task of securing the king's divorce from Katherine of Aragon. It was already one of the most sophisticated palaces in Europe when, in the 17th century, Sir Christopher Wren was commissioned to build an extension. The palace was opened to the public by Queen Victoria in 1838.

Entering the Palace

Passing through the magnificent main gate, you arrive first in the **Base Court** and beyond that **Clock Court**, named after its 16th-century astronomical clock. The panelled rooms and arched doorways in the **Young Henry VIII's Story** upstairs from Base Court provide a rewarding introduction: note the Tudor graffiti on the fireplace. Off Base Court to the right as you enter, and acquired by Charles I in 1629, Andrea Mantegna's nine-painting series *The Triumphs of Caesar* portrays Julius Caesar returning to Rome in a triumphant procession.

DON'T MISS

- Great Hall
- Chapel Royal
- William III's and Mary II's apartments
- Gardens and maze
- Cumberland Art Gallery
- Henry VIII's crown
- Young Henry VIII's Story

PRACTICALITIES

- www.hrp.org.uk/hamptoncourtpalace
- adult/child £24/12
- 10am-6pm, to 4.30pm Nov-Mar
- (wi-fi)
- Hampton Court Palace, Hampton Court

Henry VIII's State Apartments

The stairs inside Anne Boleyn's Gateway lead up to Henry VIII's Apartments, including the stunning **Great Hall**. The **Horn Room**, hung with impressive antlers, leads to the **Great Watching Chamber** where guards controlled access to the king. Henry VIII's dazzling gemstone-encrusted **crown** has been recreated – the original was melted down by Oliver Cromwell – and sits in the **Royal Pew** (open 10am to 5.30pm Monday to Saturday and 12.30pm to 3pm Sunday), which overlooks the beautiful **Chapel Royal** (still a place of worship after 450 years).

Tudor Kitchens & Great Wine Cellar

Also dating from Henry's day are the delightful Tudor kitchens, used to rustle up meals for a royal household of some 1200 people. See the atmospheric Great Wine Cellar, which handled the 300 barrels each of ale and wine consumed here annually in the mid-16th century.

William III's & Mary II's Apartments

A tour of William III's Apartments takes you up the grand **King's Staircase**. Highlights include the **King's Presence Chamber**, dominated by a throne backed with scarlet hangings. During a devastating fire in 1986, staff were ready to cut the huge portrait of William III from its frame with knives, if necessary. The sumptuous **King's Great Bedchamber**, with a bed topped with ostrich plumes, and the **King's Closet** (where His Majesty's toilet has a velvet seat) should not be missed. The unique **Chocolate Kitchens** were built for William and Mary in about 1689. William's wife Mary II had her own apartments, accessible via the fabulous **Queen's Staircase** (decorated by William Kent).

Georgian Private Apartments

The Georgian Rooms were used by George II and Queen Caroline on the court's last visit to the palace in 1737. The fabulous Tudor **Wolsey Closet**, with its early-16th-century ceiling and painted panels, was commissioned by Henry VIII.

Gardens & Maze

Beyond the palace are the stunning gardens; look for the **Great Vine**, planted in 1768 and now the world's largest grapevine. Originally created for William and Mary, the **Kitchen Garden** is magnificent. Don't leave Hampton Court without losing yourself in the 800m-long **maze** (adult/child/family £4.50/3/13; ⏲10am-4.15pm, to 3.45pm Nov-Mar), also accessible to those not entering the palace.

TAKE A BREAK

There are three cafes within the grounds of the palace: the **Tiltyard Cafe**, the **Privy Kitchen** and the **Fountain Court Cafe** (open during high season only).

The gardens of the palace are huge, so pack a picnic and lie on the grass if the sun has its hat on.

Arrested for adultery and detained in the palace in 1542, Henry's fifth wife, Catherine Howard, was dragged screaming through the palace after an escape bid. Her ghost is said to do a repeat performance, uttering 'unearthly shrieks' in the Processional Gallery leading to the Royal Pew. Ghost tours can be booked in advance.

RIVER CRUISE

Thames River Boats (Map p448; ☎020-7930 2062; www.wpsa.co.uk; Westminster Pier, Victoria Embankment, SW1; adult/child Kew one way £15/7.50, return £22/11, Hampton Court one way £19/9.50, return £27/13.50; ⏲10am-4pm Apr-Oct; Ⓤ Westminster) runs services from April to October between Westminster Pier in central London and Hampton Court (via Kew). The 22-mile journey takes up to four hours (depending on the tide).

Hampton Court Palace

A DAY AT THE PALACE

With so much to explore in the palace and seemingly infinite gardens, it can be tricky knowing where to begin. It helps to understand how the palace has grown over the centuries and how successive royal occupants embellished Hampton Court to suit their purposes and to reflect the style of the time.

As soon as he had his royal hands upon the palace from Cardinal Thomas Wolsey, Henry VIII began expanding the ❶ **Tudor architecture**, adding the ❷ **Great Hall**, the exquisite ❸ **Chapel Royal**, the opulent Great Watching Chamber and the gigantic ❹ **Tudor kitchens**. By 1540 it had become one of the grandest and most sophisticated palaces in Europe. James I kept things ticking over, while Charles I added a new tennis court and did some serious art-collecting, including pieces that can be seen in the ❺ **Cumberland Art Gallery**.

PETER FIELDS / ALAMY STOCK PHOTO ©

❼ The Maze

Around 150m north of the main building

Created from hornbeam and yew and planted in around 1700, the maze covers a third of an acre within the famous palace gardens. A must-see conclusion to Hampton Court, it takes the average visitor about 20 minutes to reach the centre.

OPEN FOR INSPECTION

The palace was opened to the public by Queen Victoria in 1838.

Tudor Kitchens

These vast kitchens were the engine room of the palace, and had a staff of 200 people. Six spit-rack-equipped fireplaces ensured roast meat was always on the menu (to the tune of 8200 sheep and 1240 oxen per year).

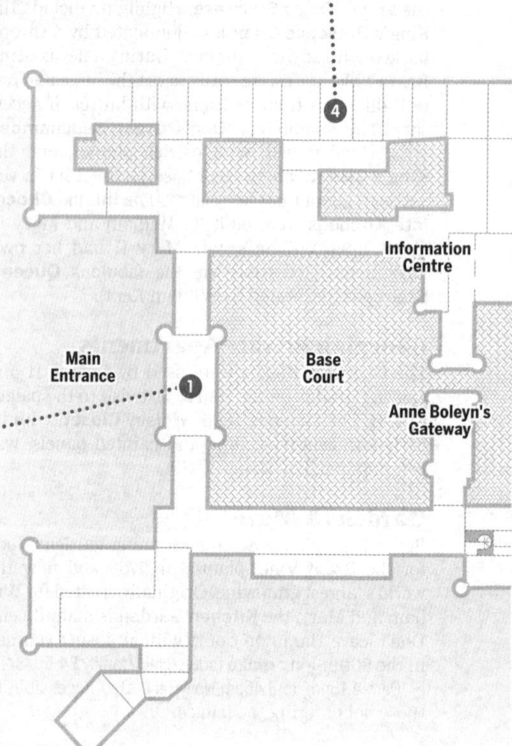

Tudor Architecture

Dating to 1515, the palace serves as one of the finest examples of Tudor architecture in the nation. Cardinal Thomas Wolsey was responsible for transforming what was originally a grand medieval manor house into a stunning Tudor palace.

KIEVVICTOR / SHUTTERSTOCK ©

After the Civil War, puritanical Oliver Cromwell warmed to his own regal proclivities, spending weekends in the comfort of the former Queen's bedroom and selling off Charles I's art collection. In the late 17th century, William and Mary employed Christopher Wren for baroque extensions, chiefly the William III Apartments, reached by the 6 **King's Staircase**. William III also commissioned the world-famous 7 **maze**.

TOP TIPS

- Ask one of the red-tunic-garbed warders for anecdotes and information.
- Tag along with a themed tour led by costumed historians or do a dusk-till-dawn sleepover at the palace.
- Grab one of the audio tours from the Information Centre.

The Great Hall

This grand dining hall is the defining room of the palace, displaying what is considered England's finest hammer-beam roof, 16th-century Flemish tapestries that depict the story of Abraham, and some exquisite stained-glass windows.

Chapel Royal

The blue-and-gold vaulted ceiling was originally intended for Christ Church, Oxford, but was installed here instead; the 18th-century oak reredos was carved by Grinling Gibbons. Books on display include a 1611 1st edition of the King James Bible, printed by Robert Barker.

The King's Staircase

One of five rooms at the palace painted by Antonio Verrio and a suitably bombastic prelude to the King's Apartments, the overblown King's Staircase adulates William III by elevating him above a cohort of Roman emperors.

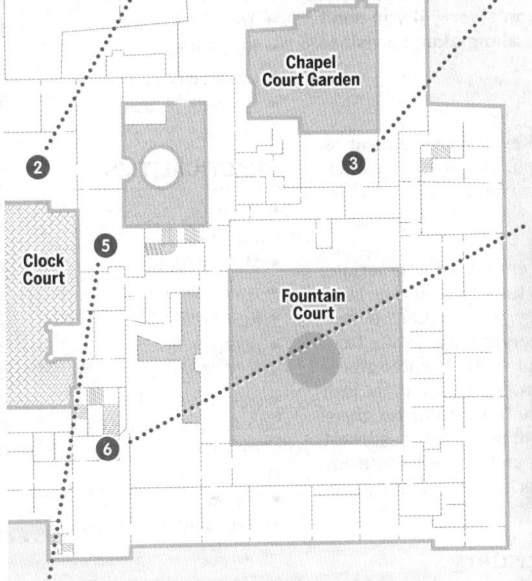

Cumberland Art Gallery

The former Cumberland Suite, designed by William Kent, has been restored to accommodate a choice selection of some of the finest works from the Royal Collection.

TOP EXPERIENCE

GO GREEN AT KEW GARDENS

Some 24% of London is a patchwork of domestic gardens, sprouting some 2.5 million trees. Combined with London's abundant parkland, this is one of the greenest cities on the planet. The 121-hectare gardens at Kew should not be missed. Don't worry if you don't know your quiver tree from your alang-alang: a visit to Kew is a discovery for all.

Botanical Collection

As well as being a public garden, Kew is a pre-eminent research centre, maintaining its reputation as the most exhaustive botanical collection in the world.

Palm House

Assuming you come by Tube and enter via Victoria Gate, you'll come almost immediately to the enormous and elaborate 700-glass-paned Palm House. This steamy, domed hothouse of metal and curved sheets of glass dating from 1848 encloses a splendid display of exotic tropical greenery; an aerial walkway offers a parrot's-eye view of the lush vegetation. The huge Jurassic cycad (*Encephalartos altensteinii*) here is the world's oldest pot plant. Just northwest of the Palm House stands the tiny and irresistibly steamy **Waterlily House** (Mar-Dec), sheltering the gigantic *Victoria cruziana* water lily.

Princess of Wales Conservatory

The angular Princess of Wales Conservatory houses plants in 10 different climatic zones – everything from a desert to a mangrove swamp. Look out for stone plants, which resemble pebbles (to deter grazing animals), carnivorous plants, gigantic water lilies, cacti and a collection of tropical orchids.

DON'T MISS

- Palm House
- Temperate House
- Treetop Walkway
- Kew Palace
- Chinese Pagoda
- Waterlily House

PRACTICALITIES

- Royal Botanic Gardens, Kew
- Map p478, C2
- www.kew.org
- Kew Rd, TW9
- adult/child £13.50/4.50
- 10am-7pm Apr-Sep, to 6pm Mar & Oct, closes earlier rest of year
- Kew Pier, Kew Bridge, Kew Gardens

Arboretum

Covering two thirds of the gardens, the arboretum refers to the more than 14,000 trees at Kew, which are often gathered together according to genus. You can find everything from eucalyptus trees to giant redwoods and ancient Japanese pagoda trees.

Kew Palace

Built in 1631 and the smallest of the royal palaces, adorable red-brick **Kew Palace** (www.hrp.org.uk/kew-palace; Kew Gardens, TW9; ⏲10.30am-5.30pm Apr-Sep; ⛴Kew Pier, 🚆Kew Bridge, ⓊKew Gardens), in the northwest of the gardens, is a former royal residence once known as Dutch House. It was the favourite home of George III and his family; his wife, Queen Charlotte, died here in 1818 (you can see the very chair in which she expired). Don't miss the **Kitchen Gardens** and **Royal Kitchens** next door.

Chinese Pagoda

Kew's 49.5m-tall eight-sided pagoda (1762), designed by William Chambers (who designed Somerset House), is one of the gardens' architectural icons. During WWII the pagoda withstood the blast from a stick of Luftwaffe bombs exploding nearby, and was also secretly employed by the Ministry of Defence to test bomb trajectories (which involved cutting holes in each floor). Recently restored, the pagoda is a colourful explosion adorned with 80 gold-detailed, roaring dragons.

Other Highlights

Several long vistas (**Cedar Vista**, **Syon Vista** and **Pagoda Vista**) are channelled by trees from vantage points within Kew Gardens. The idyllic, thatched **Queen Charlotte's Cottage** (⏲11am-4pm Sat & Sun Apr-Sep) in the southwest of the gardens was popular with 'mad' George III and his wife; the carpets of bluebells here are a draw in spring. The 320m-long **Great Broad Walk Borders** is the longest double herbaceous border in the UK. The **Marianne North Gallery** displays 833 botanical paintings by the gallery's namesake, an indomitable traveller who roamed the continents from 1871 to 1885, painting plants along the way. The vast **Children's Garden** keeps kiddos engaged across an interactive landscape.

TAKE A BREAK

Tap on the Line (p325) at Kew Gardens Tube station is a lovely setting for a pint or a pub lunch.

Inside the gardens, the **Orangery** has a restaurant and cafe.

Kew Gardens is home to its very own police force, the Kew Constabulary – one of the world's smallest police forces!

VISITING THE GARDENS

Most visitors arrive by Tube or train, but from April to October you can sail here from Westminster with Thames River Boats (p313). Kids can explore the Treehouse Towers and Climbers and Creepers (an interactive botanical zone). Summer brings concerts and the outdoor Luna Cinema (www.thelunacinema.com) to Kew.

KEW EXPLORER

For an overview of the gardens, jump aboard the Kew Explorer (☎020-8332 5648; www.kew.org/kew-gardens/whats-on/kew-explorer-land-train; tours adult/child £5/2; ⏲10.30am-3.30pm), which allows you to hop on and off at stops along the way.

SIGHTS

Hampton Court Palace, Kew Gardens, the London Wetland Centre, the sights of Richmond and charms of Wimbledon rank among London's best offerings for visitors, botanists, historians, architecture enthusiasts, river fans, tennis buffs, those in flight from the pollution of central London and hikers in search of vast, green expanses.

Richmond & Kew

KEW GARDENS — GARDENS

See p316.

★GREAT PAGODA — NOTABLE BUILDING

(Kew Gardens, TW9) This 49.5m-tall eight-sided pagoda (1762), designed by William Chambers (who designed Somerset House), is one of Kew Gardens' architectural icons. During WWII, the pagoda withstood the blast from a stick of Luftwaffe bombs exploding nearby, and was also secretly employed by the Ministry of Defence to test bomb trajectories (which involved cutting holes in each floor). Restorations in 2018 offered access to sweeping views and returned its former full colours, along with the 80 dragons that once decorated the pagoda.

The original wooden dragons vanished in the 1780s, never to return. Although almost identical to a Chinese pagoda *(tǎ),* the structure has an even number of floors (10), while pagodas in China all have an odd number. Also designed by Chambers, an 18th-century mosque with minarets stood nearby, which had disappeared by 1785. A nearby Moorish-style building, similarly designed by the indefatigable Chambers, likewise vanished, destroyed in 1820.

RICHMOND PARK — PARK

Map p478 (☎0300 061 2200; www.royalparks.org.uk/parks/richmond-park; ⊙7am-dusk; 🚆Richmond) At almost 1000 hectares (the largest urban parkland in Europe), this park offers everything from formal gardens and ancient oaks to unsurpassed views of central London 12 miles away. It's easy to flee the several roads slicing up the rambling wilderness, making the park perfect for a quiet walk or a picnic with the kids, even in summer when Richmond's riverside heaves. Coming from Richmond, it's easiest to enter via Richmond Gate or from Petersham Rd.

Herds of more than 600 red and fallow deer basking under the trees are part of the park's magic, but they can be less than docile in rutting season (September and October) and when the does bear young (May to July), so keep your distance (over 50m) during these times. Birdwatchers will love the diverse habitats, from neat gardens to woodland and assorted ponds. Floral fans should visit **Isabella Plantation** in April and May when the rhododendrons, azaleas and camellias bloom.The stunning 16-hectare woodland garden was created after WWII,

Set in a beautiful 13-hectare garden and affording great views of the city from the back terrace, **Pembroke Lodge** (Map p478; www.pembroke-lodge.co.uk; ⊙9am-5.30pm Apr-Oct, to just before dusk Nov-Mar) was the childhood home of Bertrand Russell. The Georgian tearooms can garnish your visit with warm scones and clotted cream from 9am to 5.30pm.

The pastoral vista from **Richmond Hill** has inspired painters and poets for centuries and still beguiles. It's the only view (which includes St Paul's Cathedral 10 miles away) in the country to be protected by an act of Parliament.

HAM HOUSE — HISTORIC BUILDING

Map p478 (☎020-8940 1950; www.nationaltrust.org.uk/ham-house-and-garden; Ham St, Ham, TW10; adult/child/family £13/7/33; ⊙house noon-4pm, gardens 10am-5pm; 🚌371, 🚆Richmond, Ⓤ Richmond) Known as 'Hampton Court in miniature', much-haunted red-brick Ham House was built in 1610 and became home to the first Earl of Dysart, unluckily employed as 'whipping boy' to Charles I. Inside it's grandly furnished; the Great Staircase is a fine example of Stuart woodworking. Look out for ceiling paintings by Antonio Verrio, a miniature of Elizabeth I by Nicholas Hilliard, and works by Constable and Reynolds. The grounds slope delightfully down to the Thames and lovely 17th-century formal gardens await exploration.

RICHMOND GREEN — PARK

Map p478 (🚆Richmond, Ⓤ Richmond) A short walk west of the Quadrant (the road

THAMES AT RICHMOND

The stretch of the river from Twickenham Bridge to Petersham and Ham is one of the prettiest in London. The action is mostly around five-span Richmond Bridge, built in 1777. Just before it, along one of the loveliest parts of the Thames, is tiny **Corporation Island**, colonised by flocks of feral parakeets. The gorgeous walk to Petersham can be crowded in nice weather; best to cut across pastoral Petersham Meadows and continue to Richmond Park for peace and quiet. There are several companies near Richmond Bridge, including Richmond Bridge Boathouses (p326), that rent out rowing boats.

Alternatively, walk north from Twickenham Bridge, alongside the Old Deer Park, past the two obelisks and climb onto **Richmond Lock** (Map p478; Richmond or St Margarets, Richmond) and footbridge, dating from 1894.

at the Tube exit) is Richmond Green with its mansions and delightful pubs. In the Middle Ages, jousting tournaments were held here and today it's an absolute picture on a sunny day. Cross the green diagonally for the attractive remains of **Richmond Palace** – the main entrance and red-brick gatehouse – built in 1501. On the northeast side of the green, facing Richmond Theatre (p325), is Little Green (a smaller green).

RICHMOND BRIDGE BRIDGE

Map p478 (Richmond, Richmond) This five-span bridge, built in 1777, is London's oldest surviving crossing and was only widened for traffic in 1937. According to the *Richmond Bridge Act* of 1772, vandalism of the bridge was punished with 'transportation to one of His Majesty's Colonies in America for the space of seven years'.

PETERSHAM MEADOWS PARK

Map p478 (Richmond, Richmond) Once part of the Ham House estate, pastoral Petersham Meadows – where cows still graze – is a perfectly bucolic slice of rural England, especially if you don't have time to visit the English countryside proper.

GREAT BROAD WALK BORDERS GARDENS

(Kew Gardens, TW9) Stretching north from near the Palm House in Kew Gardens, the 320m-long and well-tended Great Broad Walk Borders constitute the longest double herbaceous border in the UK. Thirty thousand plants have been planted to display a staggering variety of colour through the summer months.

Putney & Barnes

PUTNEY & BARNES VILLAGE

(Barnes or Putney) Called *Putelei* in the Domesday Book of 1086, Putney is most famous as the starting point of the annual **Oxford and Cambridge Boat Race** (www.theboatrace.org; late Mar/early Apr). Barnes is less well known and more 'villagey' in feel. The best way to approach Putney is to follow the signs from Putney Bridge Tube station for the footbridge (which runs parallel to the railway bridge crossing the river), admiring the gorgeous riverside houses, with their gardens fronting the Thames, and thereby avoiding Putney's tatty High St until the last minute.

Chiswick

CHISWICK HOUSE HISTORIC BUILDING

(020-8995 0508; www.chgt.org.uk; Burlington Lane, Chiswick Park, W4; adult/child £7.80/5, gardens free; gardens 7am-dusk, house 10am-6pm Sun-Wed Apr-Sep, to 5pm Oct; ; Chiswick, Turnham Green) Designed by the third Earl of Burlington (1694–1753) – fired up with passion for all things Roman after his grand tour of Italy – this stunner of a neo-Palladian pavilion with an octagonal dome and colonnaded portico is a delight. The almost overpoweringly grand interior includes the coffered dome of the Upper Tribunal – left ungilded, the walls below are decorated with eight enormous paintings.

Admire the stunningly painted ceiling (by William Kent) of the **Blue Velvet Room** and look out for carvings of the pagan vegetative deity, the Green Man, in the marble fireplaces of the **Green Velvet Room**.

Lord Burlington also planned the house's original gardens, now **Chiswick Park**, a huge 26-hectare expanse surrounding the house, but they have been much altered since his time and were fully restored in 2010. Children will love them – look out for the stone sphinxes near the cedar of Lebanon trees (another sphinx made of lead can be found in the Lower Tribuna).

Home to a splendid 19th-century conservatory and a gateway designed by Inigo Jones, Chiswick House also has an excellent cafe. Download an audio tour from the website.

The house is about a mile southwest of the Turnham Green Tube station and 750m northeast of Chiswick train station.

HOGARTH'S HOUSE HISTORIC BUILDING

(☎020-8994 6757; www.hounslow.info/arts/hogarthshouse; Hogarth Lane, W4; ⏲noon-5pm Tue-Sun; Ⓤ Turnham Green) FREE Home between 1749 and 1764 to artist and social commentator William Hogarth, this small house displays his caricatures and engravings, with such works as the haunting *Gin Lane* (and the less well-known, more affirmative *Beer Street*), *Marriage-à-la-Mode* and copies of *A Rake's Progress* and *The Four Stages of Cruelty*.

RUSSIAN ORTHODOX CHURCH CHURCH

(Cathedral of the Dormition of the Mother of God and the Royal Martyrs; www.russianchurchlondon.org/en; 57 Harvard Rd, W4; Ⓤ Gunnersbury) The star-speckled blue dome of this Russian Orthodox church, soaring above a quiet, residential street in Chiswick, is a slightly surreal reminder of the richness of London's cultural tapestry. The Cathedral of the Dormition of the Mother of God and the Royal Martyrs, to give it its full name, opened in 1999 and has regular services, including one with English translations on Sundays.

⊙ Twickenham

MARBLE HILL HOUSE HISTORIC BUILDING

Map p478 (☎020-8892 5115; www.english-heritage.org.uk/daysout/properties/marble-hill-house; Richmond Rd, TW1; adult/child/family £8/5/20; ⏲park 6.30am-dusk; 📶; 🚆St Margaret's or Richmond, Ⓤ Richmond) An

TOP EXPERIENCE
DISCOVER LONDON WETLAND CENTRE

One of Europe's largest inland wetland projects, this 42-hectare centre was transformed from four Victorian reservoirs in 2000 and attracts some 180 species of bird, as well as frogs, butterflies, dragonflies and lizards, plus a thriving colony of water voles.

From the visitor centre and glass-fronted observatory, meandering paths and boardwalks lead visitors around the grounds, penetrating the reedbed, marsh, fen and watery habitats. The many residents and transients here include black swans, ducks, Bewick's swans, geese, red-crested pochards, sand martins, coots and the rarer bitterns, herons and kingfishers. Don't miss the **Peacock Tower**, a three-storey hide – and magnet for serious birders – on the main lake's eastern edge; other hides are sprinkled around the reserve, including the **Headley Discovery Hide** in the west. The wetland is also well populated with eight different species of bats that feed on the abundant moths. A short walk north of the entrance, the wetland's family of sleek-coated **otters** are fed at 11am and 2pm Monday to Friday. Free daily **tours**, which are led by knowledgeable and enthusiastic staff members at 11.30am and 2.30pm, are highly recommended.

DON'T MISS

- Peacock Tower
- Headley Discovery Hide
- Otter feeding
- Daily tours

PRACTICALITIES

- ☎020-8409 4400
- www.wwt.org.uk/wetland-centres/london
- Queen Elizabeth's Walk, SW13
- adult/child/family £13/8/36
- ⏲9.30am-5.30pm, to 4.30pm Nov-Feb
- 🚆Barnes, Ⓤ Hammersmith

WORTH A DETOUR

SYON HOUSE

Just across the Thames from Kew Gardens and today owned by the Duke of Northumberland, **Syon House** (Syon Park; Map p478; ☎020-8560 0882; www.syonpark.co.uk; Brentford, TW7; adult/child £14/7, gardens only £8/5; ⊙house 11am-5pm Wed, Thu & Sun mid-Mar–Oct, gardens & conservatory 10.30am-5pm daily mid-Mar–Oct; ⓤGunnersbury) was once a medieval abbey named after Mt Zion. In 1542 Henry VIII dissolved the order of Bridgettine nuns who peacefully lived here and rebuilt it into a residence. In 1547, they say, God exacted his revenge on the king: when his lead coffin spent the night in Syon en route to Windsor for burial, his bloated body exploded, bursting the coffin open and leaving the estate's dogs to lick up the mess.

The house, from where Lady Jane Grey ascended the throne for her nine-day reign in 1553, was remodelled in the neoclassical style by Robert Adam in the 18th century and has plenty of Adam furniture and oak panelling. The interior was designed on gender-specific lines, with pastel pinks and purples for the ladies' gallery, and mock Roman sculptures for the men's dining room. Guests at the house have included the great Mohawk chieftain Thayendanegea (Joseph Brant) and Gunpowder Plot conspirator Thomas Percy.

The estate's 16-hectare gardens, with a lake and a magnificent domed Great Conservatory (1826) – the latter inspiring Joseph Paxton to design the Crystal Palace – were landscaped by Capability Brown. Syon Park is filled with attractions for children, including an adventure playground and an aquatic park. Children get free access during school holidays and bank holidays.

18th-century Palladian peach conceived as an idyllic escape from the hurly-burly of city life, this majestic love nest was originally built for George II's mistress Henrietta Howard and later occupied by Mrs Fitzherbert, the secret wife of George IV. Poet Alexander Pope had a hand in designing the park, which stretches down to the Thames. Closed for restoration at time of research, works are under way to open the house to the public for free, five days a week, in 2021.

STRAWBERRY HILL HISTORIC BUILDING

(☎020-8744 1241; www.strawberryhillhouse.org.uk; 268 Waldegrave Rd, TW1; adult/child £12.50/free; ⊙house 11am-4.30pm Sun-Wed Mar-Oct, noon-4pm Sun & Mon Nov-Feb, garden 10am-5.30pm daily; 🚉Strawberry Hill, ⓤRichmond) With its snow-white walls and Gothic turrets, this fantastical and totally restored 18th-century creation in Twickenham is the work of art historian, author and politician Horace Walpole. Studded with elaborate stained glass, the building reaches its astonishing apogee in the gallery, with its magnificent papier-mâché ceiling. For the full magic, join a twilight tour (£25). Last admission to the house is one hour before closing time.

For homemade cakes, quiche and afternoon tea (from £5), pop into the **Cloister Garden Cafe** (open 9.30am to 4pm Sunday to Wednesday) and don't overlook exploring the garden. The house is a five- to 10-minute walk from Strawberry Hill train station; otherwise take bus R68 from Richmond Tube station.

WORLD RUGBY MUSEUM MUSEUM

(☎020-8892 8877; www.worldrugbymuseum.com; Twickenham Stadium, 200 Whitton Rd, Twickenham, TW2; adult/child £12.50/7.50; ⊙10am-7pm Tue-Sat, 11am-5pm Sun; 🚉Twickenham, ⓤHounslow East) This museum at **Twickenham Stadium** (www.englandrugby.com/twickenham; tours adult/child £25/15) boasts 41,000 items of rugby memorabilia, the most extensive collection in the world. Interactive exhibitions and events include a Murder Mystery literacy workshop geared towards students, and a selection of short films on the history of rugby and more. Guided tours of the stadium take place daily (except Mondays and match days) and include entry to the museum; see the website for details on times. From Hounslow East Tube station take bus 281.

Wimbledon

WIMBLEDON COMMON PARK

(020-8788 7655; www.wpcc.org.uk; Wimbledon, Wimbledon, Wimbledon) Surging on into Putney Heath, Wimbledon Common blankets a staggering 460 hectares of southwest London. An astonishing expanse of open, wild and wooded space for walking (the best mode of exploration), nature trailing and picnicking, the common has its own windmill (p322), dating from 1817. On the southern side of the common, the misnamed **Caesar's Camp** is what's left of a roughly circular earthen fort built in the 5th century BCE. Take bus 93 from Wimbledon tube, train or tram station.

WIMBLEDON LAWN TENNIS MUSEUM MUSEUM

(020-8946 6131; www.wimbledon.com/museum; Gate 4, Church Rd, SW19; adult/child £13/8, museum & tour £25/15; 10am-5pm, last admission 4.30pm; Wimbledon, Wimbledon, Wimbledon, Southfields) This ace museum details the history of tennis – from its French precursor *jeu de paume* (which employed the open hand) to the supersonic serves of today's champions. It's a state-of-the-art presentation, with plenty of video clips and a projection of John McEnroe in the dressing room at Wimbledon, but the highlight is the chance to see Centre Court from the **360-degree viewing box**. During the championships in June/July, only those with tickets to the tournament can access the museum.

Riveting facts and figures abound: tennis clothes worn by female tennis players in 1881 weighed up to a gruelling 4.9kg! Compare this with Maria Sharapova's skimpy 2004 Ladies Singles outfit, also on display. The museum houses a cafe and a shop selling all manner of tennis memorabilia. Audio guides are available. Regular 90-minute tours of Wimbledon that take in Centre Court, No 1 Court and other areas of the All England Club also include access to the museum (best to book ahead, online or over the telephone).

From Southfields Tube station take bus 493, or it's a 15-minute walk; alternatively, take the Tube, train or tram to Wimbledon and then take bus 493.

WIMBLEDON TICKETS

For a few weeks each June and July, the sporting world's attention is fixed on the quiet southern suburb of Wimbledon, as it has been since 1877. Most show-court tickets for the Wimbledon Championships (020-8944 1066; www.wimbledon.com; Church Rd, SW19; grounds £8-25, tickets £33-225; 493, Southfields) are allocated through public ballot, applications for which usually begin in early August of the preceding year and close at the end of December. Entry into the ballot does not guarantee a ticket. A quantity of show court, outer court, ground tickets and late-entry tickets are also available if you queue on the day of play, but if you want a show-court ticket it is recommended you arrive early the day before and camp in the queue. See www.wimbledon.com for details.

Wimbledon Debenture holders can purchase guaranteed tickets for Centre Court and No1 Court in advance and during the tournament at www.wimbledondebentureholders.com.

BUDDHAPADIPA TEMPLE TEMPLE

(020-8946 1357; www.watbuddhapadipa.org; 14 Calonne Rd, SW19; 9.30am-6pm; Wimbledon, Wimbledon, Wimbledon) FREE Surrounded by trees in over 1.5 hectares of tranquil Wimbledon land, this delightful Thai Buddhist temple actively welcomes everyone. Accompanying its reflective Buddhist repose, a community feel permeates the temple grounds, with visitors invited in for coffee and a chat. The *wat* (temple) boasts a *bot* (consecrated chapel) decorated with traditional scenes by two leading Thai artists (take your shoes off before entering). Take bus 93 from Wimbledon Tube, train or tram station.

WIMBLEDON WINDMILL NOTABLE BUILDING

(www.wimbledonwindmill.org.uk; Windmill Rd, SW19; 2-5pm Sat, 11am-5pm Sun late Mar–Oct; P; Wimbledon, Wimbledon) FREE One of London's few surviving windmills, this fine smock mill (octagonal-shaped with sloping weatherboarded sides) dates from 1817. It ceased operating in 1864 and today contains a museum with working models on the history of windmills and milling. The adjacent Windmill Tearooms can supply tea, coffee and sustenance.

⊙ Hampton Court

HAMPTON COURT PALACE PALACE

See p312.

EATING

There's an excellent variety of restaurants, cafes and pubs in the area, from Michelin-starred meals to riverside gastropub lunches, gelaterias, tearooms for afternoon tea, or that classic English platter: fish and chips. Picturesque Richmond, in particular, is popular and is a diverse dining destination.

★ORANGE PEKOE CAFE £

(020-8876 6070; www.orangepekoeteas.com; 3 White Hart Lane, SW13; cream tea £9; 7.30am-5pm Mon-Fri, from 9am Sat & Sun; Barnes Bridge) This delightful Barnes teashop is a consummate haven for lovers of the tea leaf. Surround yourself with all types of tea and present all your tricky leaf-related questions to the on-site tea sommelier. There's fine coffee, too, plus tasty breakfasts and cakes, ravishing all-day cream teas (scones with clotted cream, strawberry jam and a pot of tea) and the guilty pleasure of full-on traditional afternoon teas, presented in thoroughly English fashion. Reservations recommended.

★GELATERIA DANIELI GELATERIA £

Map p478 (020-8439 9807; www.gelateriadanieli.com; 16 Brewers Lane, TW9; ice cream from £3; 10am-7pm Mon-Sat, from 11am Sun, open later in summer; Richmond, Richmond) Stuffed away down delightful narrow, pinched and flagstone-paved Brewer's Lane off Richmond Green, this tiny gelateria is a joy, and often busy. The handmade ice cream arrives in some two dozen lip-smacking flavours, from Bakewell tart pudding, pistachio, walnut and tiramisu to pine nut and chocolate, scooped into small tubs or chocolate and hazelnut cones. There are milkshakes (£5) and coffee too.

RICHMOND HILL BAKERY BAKERY £

Map p478 (54 Friars Stile Rd; pastries from £2; 8am-6pm; ; Richmond, Richmond) This dog-friendly bakery and cafe occupies a popular and welcoming niche along the marvellously named Friars Stile Rd, supplying Richmond Park ramblers with fine coffee, teas, strawberry tarts, quiches, croissants and cakes. Suncatchers can aim for one of the tables out the front, or sit behind one of the bay windows. Order your coffee from the front till and collect from the rear.

PIER 1 FISH & CHIPS £

Map p478 (020-8332 2778; www.pier1richmond.com; 11-13 Petersham Rd, TW10; mains from £10; 11.30am-11pm Mon-Sat, to 10pm Sun; ; Richmond, Richmond) The ambience at this fish-and-chip restaurant is a stylish cut above the rest and the fish – fried or grilled – is delightfully succulent. The fish, served with chips, tartare sauce and a small dish of mushy peas, comes in at £14 and is prodigiously sized. The menu also nets a haul of non-fish dishes, from sirloins to vegetable lasagne and steak and merlot pie.

The kids menu gets the nippers a small main, with chips, drink and ice cream for £7.45.

★CHEZ LINDSAY FRENCH ££

Map p478 (020-8948 7473; www.chez-lindsay.co.uk; 11 Hill Rise, TW10; mains from £20, 2-/3-course set lunch £14/17; noon-11pm Mon-Sat, to 10pm Sun; ; Richmond, Richmond) This appetising slice of Brittany at the bottom of Richmond Hill serves wholesome Breton cuisine with a side serving of comfortable ambience and river views. There's an accent on seafood, and house specialities include adorable galettes (buckwheat pancakes; from £4.25) with countless tasty fillings (or plain), washed down with a variety of hearty (and very dry) Breton ciders.

The set lunch is available from Monday to Friday.

MA GOA INDIAN ££

(020-8780 1767; www.magoaputney.co.uk; 242-244 Upper Richmond Rd, SW15; mains £11-16; 6.30-10.30pm Tue-Thu, to 11pm Fri & Sat, 5-9.30pm Sun; ; Putney, Putney Bridge) This much-loved family-run restaurant specialises in the subtle cuisine of Portugal's former colony of Goa on India's west coast. Winning dishes include the fantastic *achari raan* (pot-roasted lamb shank with tomato and spices) and the *murgh makhini* (charcoal-grilled chicken in a creamy masala sauce), plus excellent

THAMES PATH

The entire **Thames Path National Trail** is a 184-mile walk stretching from the river's source at Thames Head, near Kemble in the Cotswolds, to the Thames Barrier. It's truly magnificent, particularly in its upper reaches, but tackling the entire course is for the truly ambitious and will need a couple of weeks. Most visitors walk sections of it, such as the 16-mile chunk from Battersea to the barrier, which takes about 6½ hours. There is also a short, but lovely riverside walk from Putney to Barnes (4 miles), and the gorgeous stretch of river from Twickenham Bridge to Petersham and Ham (1.5 miles).

seafood mains. Vegetarian options are also available.

★PETERSHAM NURSERIES CAFE MODERN EUROPEAN £££

Map p478 (020-8332 8665; www.petershamnurseries.com; Church Lane, off Petersham Rd, TW10; mains £24-30; cafe noon-5pm Tue-Sun; Richmond, Richmond, 65) In a greenhouse at the back of the fabulously located Petersham Nurseries is this award-winning cafe straight out of the pages of *The Secret Garden*. The confidently executed cuisine includes organic ingredients harvested from the nursery gardens and produce adhering to Slow Food principles. Seasonal dishes include chargrilled monkfish, sage pork chops and veggie tagine. Booking in advance is essential.

There's also a **teahouse** (9am to 5pm, from 11am Sunday) for coffee, tea and cakes through the day and a lunch menu with a small selection of soups, salads, pies and pastas. Because of local residents', and council concerns about traffic increasing with the cafe's popularity, patrons are asked to walk here via the picturesque river towpath from Richmond, or to use public transport.

★GLASSHOUSE MODERN EUROPEAN £££

Map p478 (020-8940 6777; www.glasshouserestaurant.co.uk; 14 Station Pde, TW9; 3-course lunch/dinner from £40/57.50; noon-12.30pm & 6.30-9.30pm Tue-Thu, noon-2.30pm & 6.30-10.30pm Fri & Sat, 12.30-4pm Sun; ; Kew Gardens) A day at Kew Gardens finds a perfect conclusion at this Michelin-starred gastronomic highlight. The glass-fronted exterior envelops a delicately lit, low-key interior, where the focus remains on divinely cooked food. Diners are rewarded with a seasonal, consistently accomplished menu from chef Gregory Wellman that combines English mainstays with modern European innovation.

The menu is constantly in flux, depending on which sublime ingredients the chef has sourced that day. The relaxed atmosphere is complimented with friendly and attentive service.

DRINKING & NIGHTLIFE

Richmond may not be on everyone's alcohol radar, but it should be: some of the capital's best, most charming and historic riverside pubs can be found on either side of the Thames. Some of them are lapped by waters at high river tide, or even cut off!

★CITY BARGE PUB

(020-8994 2148; www.metropolitanpubcompany.com/our-pubs/the-city-barge; 27 Strand on the Green, W4; noon-11pm Mon-Thu, to midnight Fri, 10am-midnight Sat, 10am-10.30pm Sun; ; Gunnersbury) In a line of small riverside cottages facing wooded Oliver's Island (where Cromwell is alleged to have taken refuge), this excellent pub looks straight onto the muddy Thames. Its lineage to the 14th century would make it one of London's most ancient pubs. There are three open fires, drinkers spill outside in clement weather and a fine gastropub menu has taken hold.

Once known as the Navigators Arms, there has been a pub here since the Middle Ages, although the Luftwaffe gave it a dramatic facelift (as has an attractive refurb). A scene from the Beatles' film *Help!* was shot here, celebrated in framed photo stills. The hefty steel door clangs shut during high tides, which inundate the towpath.

★WHITE CROSS PUB

Map p478 (☎020-8940 6844; www.thewhitecrossrichmond.com; Water Lane, TW9; ⏰10am-11pm Mon-Sat, to 10.30pm Sun; 📶; 🚆Richmond) The riverside location and fine food and ales make this bay-windowed pub – on the site of a former friary – a winner. There are entrances for low and high tides, but when the river is at its highest, Cholmondeley Walk along the Thames floods and the pub is out of bounds to those not willing to wade. Wellies are provided.

Very occasionally boats have to pick up stranded boozers: a chalkboard lists high-tide times and depths (you can also check the website). Originally called the Waterman's Arms, the pub dates from 1748 and was rebuilt in 1838. Quirky detail: there's a tiny working fireplace *under* the window on your right as you enter.

TAP ON THE LINE PUB

Map p478 (☎020-8332 1162; www.taponthe line.co.uk; Station Approach, TW9; ⏰8am-11pm Mon-Fri, from 9am Sat, 10am-10.30pm Sun; 📶; Ⓤ Kew Gardens) Right by the platform at Kew Gardens station (the only London Tube platform with its own pub), this lovingly restored Victorian yellow-brick boozer is well worth a visit. With outside seating surrounded by foliage and twinkling fairy lights in the courtyard at the front, it's a fine haven for a pub lunch. There's live music on Saturdays from 7pm.

WHITE SWAN PUB

Map p478 (☎020-8744 2951; www.whiteswan twickenham.co.uk; Riverside, TW1; ⏰11am-11pm Tue-Sat, to 10.30pm Sun & Mon; 📶; 🚆Twickenham) This traditional pub in Twickenham overlooks a quiet stretch of the Thames from what must be one of the most English-looking streets in London. It boasts a fantastic riverside location, a great selection of beer, a loyal crowd of locals and roaring fires in winter. Check the tide chart out front to dine outside on the paved garden with Thames water lapping at your table.

CROOKED BILLET PUB

(☎020-8946 4942; www.thecrookedbillet wimbledon.com; 14-15 Crooked Billet, SW19; ⏰11am-11pm Mon-Thu, to midnight Fri & Sat, to 10.30pm Sun; 📶; 🚊Wimbledon, 🚆Wimbledon) This historic Young's boozer south of Cannizaro Park, just off Wimbledon Common, is brim-full of character, with flagstone floors, open fires and a cosy village-pub personality. Drinkers collapse on the green opposite in summer, while home-cooked food, award-winning ale and seasonal drinks welcome weary ramblers and Wimbledon wayfarers. The Hand in Hand pub next door is another snug option, packed at weekends.

WHITE HART PUB

(☎020-8876 5177; www.whitehartbarnes.co.uk; The Terrace, SW13; ⏰11am-11pm Mon-Thu, to midnight Fri & Sat, from noon Sun; 📶; 🚆Barnes Bridge) This riverside Young's pub in Barnes was formerly a Masonic lodge. It's huge, traditional and welcoming downstairs, but the temptation in warmer months is to head to the balcony upstairs for Thames views, or to plonk yourself down at one of the riverside tables. When Boat Race (p319) day arrives, the pub is deluged with beer-toting spectators.

☆ ENTERTAINMENT

RICHMOND THEATRE THEATRE

Map p478 (☎0844 871 7651; www.atgtickets.com/venues/richmond-theatre; Little Green, TW9; 🚆Richmond, Ⓤ Richmond) A magnificent old Victorian building facing Little Green (next to Richmond Green), Richmond Theatre opened in 1899. Designed by architect Frank Matcham, the theatre stages a variety of popular plays, operas, ballets, musicals, live music performances and comedy.

SHOPPING

This is sightseeing rather than shopping territory, but Richmond has a good selection of retail choices for window-shoppers, browsers and shopaholics.

Richmond High St is full of chains, but there are some independent stores around. In an enclave of cobbled streets you'll find jewellery shops tucked away down Brewers Lane en route to, or away from, Richmond Green.

TEDDINGTON CHEESE FOOD

Map p478 (☎020-8977 6868; www.teddington cheese.co.uk; 74 Hill Rise, TW10; ⏰10am-6pm Wed-Sat, from 11am Sun; 🚆Richmond, Ⓤ Richmond) As you come down – or head up – Richmond Hill, stop by this cheesemongers that packs a veritable smorgasbord of cheesy delights into a small space. Over 130 different English and international varieties contribute to the aroma and the helpful owner can point you in the right direction, whether it's Garrotxa from Catalonia, Vacherin Fribourgeois from Switzerland or Capria from Worcester.

OPEN BOOK BOOKS

Map p478 (☎020-8940 1802; https://theopenbook0.wixsite.com/theopenbook-richmond; 10 King St, TW9; ⊙9.30am-6pm Mon-Sat, from 11am Sun; Richmond, Richmond) Helena Richardson's charming bookshop – fighting off a leviathan Waterstones around the corner – is a mainstay of Richmond reading life. With a terrific range compressed into a small space, this is excellent, unhurried browsing territory and full of surprises; but if you're after something specific, ask Helena – she knows her stock inside out.

TOKO JEWELLERY

(☎020-8332 6620; www.tokojewellery.co.uk; 18 Brewers Lane, TW9; ⊙10am-6pm Mon-Sat, noon-5pm Sun; Richmond) This small jewellery shop down charming Brewers Lane sells an intriguing and eye-catching collection of necklaces, rings, bracelets and earrings, elegantly styled from silver, gold and precious and semiprecious stones.

SPORTS & ACTIVITIES

RICHMOND BRIDGE BOAT HIRE BOATING

Map p478 (☎020-8948 8270; www.richmondboathire.co.uk; Richmond Bridge; adult/child £10/5; Richmond, Richmond) Rents out a variety of rowing boats, including big 12-seaters, for journeys along the Thames. Day rates are £18 for an adult and £9 for a child.

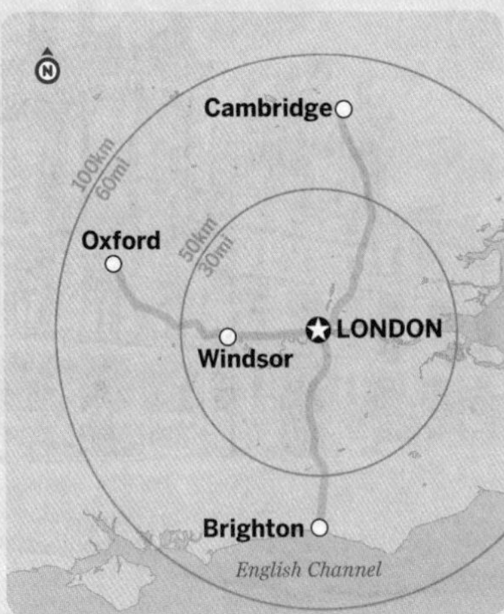

Day Trips from London

Windsor Castle p328

The bastion of British royalty, Windsor Castle overlooks the affluent town of Windsor, picturesquely located along the River Thames.

Harry Potter Studio Tour p331

A self-guided tour through this massive Warner Brothers complex offers a glimpse of the magic behind the beloved film series.

Oxford p333

The world's oldest university town, Oxford boasts more than three dozen prestigious (and eye-catching) colleges, but also some world-class museums.

Cambridge p337

Awash in exquisite architecture, steeped in history and tradition, and renowned for its quirky rituals, Cambridge is the quintessential English university town.

Brighton p341

This seaside enclave with a history of royal revelry is home of off-kilter culture, hedonistic nightlife and a thriving LGBTIQ+ scene.

KIEV.VICTOR/SHUTTERSTOCK ©

TOP EXPERIENCE

VISIT ROYAL WINDSOR CASTLE

Windsor Castle is not only the world's largest fortress, it's been continuously occupied longer than any other. A redoubtable mass of towers, turrets and battlements, it dominates the riverside town of Windsor, 25 miles west of London. British monarchs have holed up here for more than 900 years, and it remains the Queen's favourite of her several official residences.

History

The story of Windsor Castle began in 1071, when William the Conqueror ordered the construction of a hilltop, earth-and-timber fortress. A century later, his great-grandson Henry II replaced it with a stone round tower. Edward III added a Gothic palace; Elizabeth I, the sturdy North Terrace; and Charles II gave the State Apartments a baroque makeover, creating an 'English Versailles'. George III stuck on turrets and battlements, to make it look more medieval, while George IV inserted a modern palace into the ancient ensemble. After a thousand years of rebuilding, the 951-room castle thus displays an amazing range of architectural styles, from half-timbered fired brick to Gothic stonework.

Inner Hall

Created by George IV in the 1820s as a welcoming area for heads of state and official guests, this hall was later closed by Queen Victoria in 1866 – its entry sealed by a stone wall – and used primarily for storage space for 150 years. Reopened to the public in 2019, restoration works included chipping off layers of paint to reveal the intricate Regency

DON'T MISS

- Grand Vestibule
- St George's Hall
- St George's Chapel
- Queen Mary's Dolls' House
- Changing of the Guard

PRACTICALITIES

- ☎03031-237304
- www.royalcollection.org.uk
- Castle Hill, Windsor
- adult/child £23.50/13.50
- ⏰10am-5.15pm, to 4.15pm Nov-Feb
- 👪
- 🚌702 from London Victoria, 🚆London Waterloo to Windsor & Eton Riverside, dLondon Paddington to Windsor & Eton Central via Slough

ceiling bosses created by stuccoist Francis Bernasconi, and linking the visitor entrance on the **North Terrace** with the **State Entrance Hall** on the south side, which offers an uninterrupted view of the **Long Walk**. Also on display are stone remnants believed to be part of the buildings constructed by Henry I around 1110.

State Apartments

The State Apartments, in the castle's Upper Ward, reverberate with history and style. Around two dozen rooms are usually open to the public, with the crossed swords, suits of armour and banners of the initial **Grand Staircase** setting the tone.

A seated statue of Queen Victoria presides over the **Grand Vestibule** at the top, which displays tribute and trophies from the British Empire. Highlights include a life-sized tiger's head of gold with crystal teeth, seized from Tipu, sultan of Mysore, and the musket ball that killed Lord Nelson. The **Waterloo Chamber** beyond, commemorating the 1815 battle, is festooned with portraits of triumphant generals and diplomats.

Two self-guided routes – ceremonial and historic – take in the fabulous **St George's Hall**, the headquarters of the 24-strong order of the Knights of the Garter, which is still used for state banquets. Its ornate ceiling, recreated following a devastating fire in 1992 – it began in the adjoining **Lantern Lobby** – holds the shields of knights past and present. Blank shields record 'degraded' knights expelled from the order; most are foreign royals who declared war on Britain.

Beyond the **Grand Reception Room**, where the Queen hosts state visits, lie 10 chambers designated as the **King's Rooms** and **Queen's Rooms**. Largely created by Charles II, they're bursting with opulent furniture, tapestries, frescoed ceilings and carved wall panels, as well as paintings by Hans Holbein, Bruegel, Rembrandt, Peter Paul Rubens, Van Dyck and Gainsborough. The **Queen's Guard Chamber**, bristling with pistols and swords, holds statues and busts of military leaders including Sir Winston Churchill.

Queen Mary's Dolls' House

This incredible dolls' house, to the left as you enter the State Apartments, was designed by Sir Edwin Lutyens for Queen Mary, the wife of George V, and completed in 1924. The attention to detail is spellbinding: it has running water, electricity and lighting, tiny Crown Jewels, vintage wine in the cellar and unique miniature books by Sir Arthur Conan Doyle and Rudyard Kipling.

ROYAL RESIDENCE

Windsor is used for state occasions and is one of the Queen's principal residences; if she's at home, the Royal Standard, not the Union Flag, flies from the Round Tower.

A disastrous fire in 1992 nearly wiped out the State Apartments. Fortunately the damage, though severe, was limited and a £37-million, five-year restoration returned the rooms to their former glory.

TAKE A BREAK

A la Russe (☎01753-833009; www.alarusse.co.uk; 6 High St, Windsor; mains £13-23, 2-/3-course lunch menus £12.50/16.50; ⏲6-9.30pm Mon, noon-2.30pm & 6-9.30pm Tue-Sat) serves tip-top French cuisine a mere hop-and-skip from the castle.

Two Brewers (☎01753-855426; www.twobrewerswindsor.co.uk; 34 Park St, Windsor; mains £15-26; ⏲11.30am-11pm Mon-Thu, to 11.30pm Fri & Sat, noon-10.30pm Sun) is a great place to wind down, be it by the flower-decked exterior in summer or the roaring fire in winter.

St George's Chapel

Moving westward through the Middle Ward and past the distinctive **Round Tower**, rebuilt in stone from the original Norman keep in 1170, you enter the Lower Ward. Begun by Edward IV in 1475 but not completed until 1528, St George's Chapel has a superb nave fashioned in the uniquely English style of Perpendicular Gothic, with gorgeous fan vaulting and massive 'gridiron' stained-glass windows. Now familiar the world over from the May 2018 wedding of Prince Harry and Meghan Markle, it also serves as a royal mausoleum, containing the tombs of 10 monarchs. Both Henry VIII and Charles I lie beneath the magnificent Quire, while the Queen's father (King George VI) and mother (Queen Elizabeth) rest in a side chapel.

St George's Chapel closes on Sundays, and otherwise at 4pm, though visitors can attend choral evensong at 5.15pm every day except Wednesday.

Albert Memorial Chapel

Originally built by Henry III in 1240 and dedicated to Edward the Confessor, this small and highly decorated chapel was the place of worship for the Order of the Garter until St George's Chapel was built alongside and snatched away that honour. After Prince Albert died at Windsor Castle in 1861, Queen Victoria ordered the chapel to be redecorated in honour of her husband. A major feature of the elaborate restoration is the magnificent vaulted roof – the gold mosaic pieces were crafted in Venice.

Windsor Great Park

South of the castle, **Windsor Great Park** (☎01753-860222; www.windsorgreatpark.co.uk; Windsor; ⏲dawn-dusk) FREE ranges over a staggering area of 7.7 sq miles. The **Long Walk** is a 2.7-mile jaunt along a tree-lined path from King George IV Gate to the Copper Horse statue (of George III) on Snow Hill, the park's highest point. The **Savill Garden** (Wick Lane, Englefield Green; adult/child £12/6; ⏲9.30am-6pm, to 4.30pm Nov-Feb; P) is particularly lovely, and located just over 4 miles south of Windsor Castle. By car, take the A308 out of town and follow the brown signs.

Changing of the Guard

Replete with pomp and pageantry, the Changing of the Guard usually takes place at 11am on Tuesdays, Thursdays and Saturdays, weather permitting. Although the Household Troops march through the streets of Windsor, the actual handover happens in the Lower Ward or, when the Queen is in official residence, the Quadrangle in the Upper Ward.

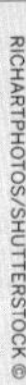
RICHARTPHOTOS/SHUTTERSTOCK ©

TOP EXPERIENCE

EXPLORE THE WORLD OF HARRY POTTER

Whether you're a fair-weather fan or a full-on Potterhead, this magical, self-guided studio tour is well worth a visit. Authentic sets, costumes, props and behind-the-scenes exhibitions on spellbinding animatronics and visual effects are spread across two massive hangars and an outdoor lot, requiring at least three hours to fully appreciate. Interactive exhibits let you test your wand-waving and broom-riding skills, while themed seasonal events like 'Dark Arts' in autumn and 'Hogwarts in the Snow' in winter add to the wonder.

Entering the World of Harry Potter

Awe is instantaneous upon entering the complex, where a gargantuan model of the **Ukrainian Ironbelly** dragon from 2011's *Harry Potter and the Deathly Hallows – Part 2* is suspended from the ceiling of the Studio Tour Hub. Here you'll also find the **Hub Café**, the **Chocolate Frog Café** and the **Food Hall**, plus a counter to pick up an optional digital guide (£4.95) and a complementary activity passport to collect stamps throughout the tour.

At the tour entrance, a curved hallway emblazoned with JK Rowling quotes takes you past the **Cupboard Under the Stairs** set to a holding room where you'll hear housekeeping rules and video testimonials from real fans. From there, a small cinema with a short film screening takes place before you're ushered through giant doors into the actual set of Hogwarts' enormous Great Hall – just the first of many 'wow' moments.

DON'T MISS

- Platform 9¾ and Hogwarts Express
- Forbidden Forest
- Dumbledore's office
- Butterbeer
- Gryffindor common room
- Diagon Alley
- Gringotts Wizarding Bank

PRACTICALITIES

- ☎ 0345 084 0900
- www.wbstudiotour.co.uk
- Studio Tour Dr, Leavesden
- adult/child £47/38
- 🕗 8.30am-10pm, hours vary Oct-May
- P 🚻

FORBIDDEN FOREST

Fans unperturbed by the dark will revel in this spooky set. Flashing lights and animatronics abound, including **Buckbeak** the hippogriff and **Aragog**, the 1-tonne spider, whose 5.5m leg span incited authentic terror in arachnophobic actor Rupert Grint's Ron Weasely character.

The Backlot features vehicles seen throughout the series, including the triple-decker Knight Bus, the Weasleys' Ford Anglia, and Sirius Black's motorbike, ridden by Hagrid. It also features Hogwarts Bridge and the set of 4 Privet Drive.

HOGWARTS CASTLE MODEL

The final stretch of the tour features a shimmering, gasp-inducing 1:24 scale **model of Hogwarts**, used for exterior shots. With a landscape inspired by the Highlands of Scotland, the model was meticulously hand-constructed by an 86-person team and contains more than 2500 fibre optic lights, and real gravel and plants for rocks and trees.

The Great Hall

The setting for key scenes like the Yule Ball and the Battle of Hogwarts, the Great Hall houses an abundant dinner feast across two long tables, student costumes from each house, **Dumbledore's lectern** and the **House Points Counter**, which contains thousands of Indian glass beads.

Iconic Interiors

One large hangar contains the most familiar interior sets, such as the **Gryffindor boys' dormitory** and cosy **common room**. **Dumbledore's office** contains shelves stocked with old microscopes, star charts and other astronomical devices, and the glittering **memory cabinet**, containing more than 800 hand-labelled vials.

Platform 9¾ & Hogwarts Express

Prior to its life as the Hogwarts Express, the 5972 Olton Hall steam engine was a working passenger locomotive from 1937 to 1963. While most of the series' scenes that take place on Platform 9¾ were shot at King's Cross Station in London, part of the station platform, complete with the track and train, was recreated on a soundstage during *Harry Potter and the Deathly Hallows – Part 2*.

Gringotts Wizarding Bank

Flanked by imposing marble pillars, this 5000-sq-metre goblin-run banking hall is illuminated by opulent chandeliers. Tellers' desks are topped with inkwells, quills, ledgers, and stacks of **Galleons**, **Sickles** and **Knuts** – the prop department created more than 210,000 of the coins for the final two films alone. The **Lestrange vault** holds 38,000 pieces of rubber treasure, including Death Eater masks, and 7010 Hufflepuff Cups. Beyond the vault is another set of the hall – ensure you linger long enough for the startling cameo.

A Stroll Down Diagon Alley

The set of the cobbled, Dickens-inspired Diagon Alley, with its gravity-defying lean, features storefronts like **Gringotts Bank** and **Ollivanders Wand Shop**, where you'll see stacks of dusty wand boxes, plus broomsticks at **Quality Quidditch Supplies**, baby Pygmy Puffs at **Magical Menagerie**, and Hogwarts robes at **Madame Malkin's**. Standing out in bright orange, the three-storey **Weasleys' Wizard Wheezes** was designed to favour an 18th-century joke shop.

Oxford

Explore

With its honey-coloured colleges arrayed in splendour beside the river, the university town of Oxford is a seductive vision of medieval learning and modern charm.

The Best...

Sight Christ Church

Place to Eat Vaults & Garden (p336)

Place to Drink Turf Tavern (p337)

Getting There & Away

Bus Buses run from London's Victoria station to Oxford's busy city-centre **bus station** (Gloucester Green). Fares are between £9 and £15, and the journey takes 1¾ to two hours.

Train Oxford's main train station is a 10-minute walk west of the city centre. Services run from London Marylebone (£6 to £22) and London Paddington (£13 to £39), and take 1¼ hours. Oxford Parkway station is less conveniently located 4 miles north of the centre; it also has trains to London Marylebone (£7 to £26, one hour).

Need to Know

Area Code ☎01865

Location 52 miles northwest of London.

SIGHTS

★CHRIST CHURCH COLLEGE

(☎01865-276492; www.chch.ox.ac.uk; St Aldate's; adult/child £15/14; ⏲10am-5pm, from 2pm Sun) With its compelling combination of majestic architecture, literary heritage and double identity as (parts of) Harry Potter's Hogwarts, Christ Church attracts tourists galore. Among Oxford's largest colleges – *the* largest, if you include its bucolic meadow – and proud possessor of its most impressive quad, plus a superb art gallery and even a cathedral, it was founded in 1525 by Cardinal Wolsey. It later became home to Lewis Carroll, whose picnic excursions with the then-dean's daughter gave us *Alice's Adventures in Wonderland*.

The main entrance to Christ Church, Tom Gate, stands immediately below the imposing 17th-century **Tom Tower**. Sir Christopher Wren, who studied at Christ Church, was responsible for its topmost portions. Pass by at 9.05pm, and you'll hear 101 chimes from its 6-tonne bell, **Great Tom**, to commemorate the curfew inflicted on the college's original students.

All visitors, however, enter further south along St Aldate's, walking through the gardens to reach Meadow Gate (where there may be queues). From there, the self-guided tour route leads to the Renaissance **Great Hall**, the college's jaw-dropping dining room, with its hammer-beam roof and portraits of past scholars including Lewis Carroll and an entire troop of British prime ministers who studied here. It's often closed to visitors at lunchtime, between noon and 2pm and visitors must pre-book tickets.

If the Great Hall looks awfully familiar, that may be because it starred as Hogwarts' dining hall in the *Harry Potter* films. Although the movie-screen hall was mocked up in the studio, the fan-vaulted staircase via which you enter it appeared in *Harry Potter and the Philosopher's Stone*, as the spot where Professor McGonagall welcomes Harry.

The route then crosses one side of **Tom Quad** – Oxford's largest and most impressive quadrangle, overlooked by Tom Tower and with a statue of Mercury adorning its pond – to reach **Christ Church Cathedral** (☎01865-276150; www.chch.ox.ac.uk/cathedral; St Aldate's; ⏲10am-5pm Mon-Sat, from 2pm Sun) FREE. It stands on the site where the shrine of St Frideswide, Oxford's patron saint, was erected during the 8th century. The cathedral itself was built as the priory church during the 12th century, and became the college chapel when Cardinal Wolsey established what he called Cardinal College in 1525.

Long one of Oxford's wealthiest colleges, Christ Church has amassed an exceptional art collection. Displayed in the small **Christ Church Picture Gallery** (☎01865-276172; www.chch.ox.ac.uk/gallery; Oriel Sq; adult/child £4/2; ⏲10.30am-5pm Mon-Sat, from 2pm Sun Jul-Sep, shorter hours rest of year), added during the 1960s, it includes paintings and

Oxford

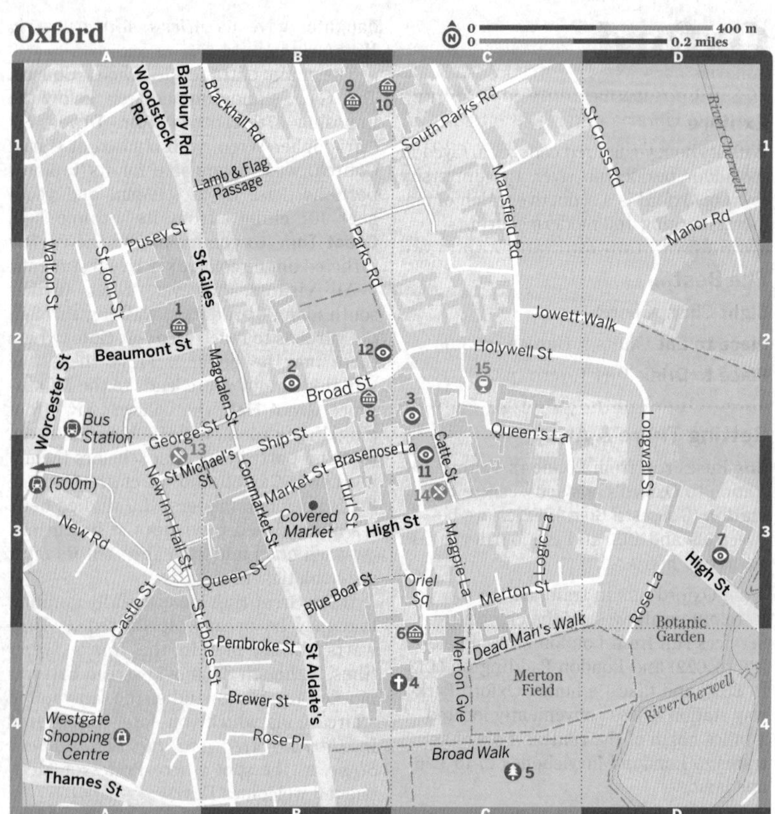

Oxford

Sights

1 Ashmolean Museum A2
2 Balliol College B2
3 Bodleian Library C2
Christ Church .... (see 4)
4 Christ Church Cathedral C4
5 Christ Church Meadow C4
6 Christ Church Picture Gallery C4
7 Magdalen College D3
8 Museum of the History of Science B2
9 Oxford University Museum of Natural History B1
10 Pitt Rivers Museum B1
11 Radcliffe Camera C3
12 Weston Library B2

Eating

13 Handle Bar A3
14 Vaults & Garden C3

Drinking & Nightlife

15 Turf Tavern C2

drawings by Tintoretto, Michelangelo and other Renaissance masters.

Stretching away south and east of the college, and accessible free of charge, **Christ Church Meadow** (www.chch.ox.ac.uk; St Aldate's; ⏲dawn-dusk) FREE, a verdant expanse bordered by the rivers Cherwell and Thames (or Isis), is ideal for a leisurely half-hour walk. Look out for the college's own herd of longhorn cattle.

★**BODLEIAN LIBRARY** LIBRARY

(☎01865-287400; www.bodleian.ox.ac.uk/bodley; Catte St; ⏲9am-5pm Mon-Sat, from 11am

Sun) At least five kings, dozens of prime ministers and Nobel laureates, and luminaries such as Oscar Wilde, CS Lewis and JRR Tolkien have studied in Oxford's Bodleian Library, a magnificent survivor from the Middle Ages. Wander into its central 17th-century quad, and you can admire its ancient buildings for free. Both Blackwell Hall and the exhibition rooms in the Weston Library can be visited free of charge, though Covid-19 restrictions meant only students and staff can were permitted inside during the initial reopening plans.

All tours, including the two most popular daily options – the 'mini-tour' (30 minutes, £6) and the 'standard tour' (one hour, £9) – start in the ornate medieval **Divinity School**, the university's earliest teaching room. A superb specimen of English Gothic architecture, it was founded around 1423. Inspect its fan-vaulted ceiling closely and you'll spot the initials of benefactors, including Thomas Kemp, who features 84 times, who worked on it, as well as three 'Green Men'. In the *Harry Potter* films, the Divinity School served as the Hogwarts hospital wing.

Every tour also includes on the upper level, which dates from 1488. Visitors are not allowed to enter this magnificently decorated medieval room, or peruse the ancient tomes that it contains, just admire it from the adjoining 17th-century extension. It too featured in the *Harry Potter* films, as Hogwarts' library.

The standard tours additionally take in two grand chambers at the far end of the Divinity School – **Convocation House**, which hosted the English Parliament three times, once under Charles I and twice under Charles II, and the **Chancellor's Court**, in which Oscar Wilde and Romantic poet Percy Bysshe Shelley went on trial (for debt and promoting atheism, respectively).

Less frequent 'extended tours' cover the same ground while also offering the only public access to the nearby Radcliffe Camera (p336), which houses part of the Bodleian's collection.

Check tour times online or at the information desk; tickets for all tours can be purchased up to two weeks in advance. Note also that a selection of 'Bodleian Treasures' is displayed in the nearby **Weston Library** (☎01865-287400; www.bodleian.ox.ac.uk/weston; Broad St; ⊙10am-5pm Mon-Sat, from 11am Sun) FREE.

★PITT RIVERS MUSEUM MUSEUM

(☎01865-270927; www.prm.ox.ac.uk; South Parks Rd; ⊙10am-4.30pm Tue-Sun, from noon Mon; 🚻) FREE If exploring an enormous room full of eccentric and unexpected artefacts sounds like your idea of the perfect afternoon, welcome to the amulets-to-zithers extravaganza that is the Pitt Rivers museum. Tucked behind Oxford's **natural-history museum** (☎01865-272950; www.oum.ox.ac.uk; Parks Rd; ⊙10am-5pm; 📶🚻) FREE, and dimly lit to protect its myriad treasures, it's centred on an anthropological collection amassed by a Victorian general, and revels in exploring how differing cultures have tackled topics like 'Smoking and Stimulants' and 'Treatment of Dead Enemies'.

Wandering its three balconied floors, you may come across anything from Mesopotamian temple receipts to Japanese Noh-theatre masks or a warrior's helmet made from the skin of a porcupine fish. There's even an entire case of lamellaphones (wait and see!).

★ASHMOLEAN MUSEUM MUSEUM

(☎01865-278000; www.ashmolean.org; Beaumont St; ⊙10am-5pm Tue-Sun, to 8pm last Fri of month; 🚻) FREE Britain's oldest public museum, Oxford's wonderful Ashmolean Museum is surpassed only by the British Museum in London. It was established in 1683, when Elias Ashmole presented Oxford University with a collection of 'rarities' amassed by the well-travelled John Tradescant, gardener to Charles I. You could easily spend a day exploring this magnificent neoclassical building, and family-friendly pamphlets draw kids into select exhibits.

Each bright, spacious gallery across its four floors seems to hold some new marvel, be that a dazzling fresco from the palace of Knossos; artwork from Renaissance Italy to Japan, taking in Goya, van Gogh and JMW Turner; or, famously, the Anglo-Saxon Alfred Jewel, a glorious, golden 9th-century gem, thought to have been a sort of bookmark, that was crafted for Alfred the Great. There's a strong connection throughout with Oxford and its heritage. Tickets must be pre-booked.

★**MAGDALEN COLLEGE** COLLEGE

(☎01865-276000; www.magd.ox.ac.uk; High St; adult/child £7/6; ⊙10am-7pm late Jun-late Sep, 1pm-dusk rest of year) Guarding access to a breathtaking expanse of private lawns, woodlands, river walks and even its own deer park, Magdalen ('mawd-lin'), founded in 1458, is one of Oxford's wealthiest and most beautiful colleges. Beyond its elegant Victorian gateway, you come to its medieval chapel and glorious 15th-century tower. From here, move on to the remarkable 15th-century **cloisters**, where the fantastic grotesques (carved figures) may have inspired CS Lewis' stone statues in *The Chronicles of Narnia*.

Behind the cloisters, lovely **Addison's Walk** loops for just under a mile around the ravishing **Water Meadow**, a wedge-shaped island in the River Cherwell that's renowned for its glorious wildflowers. You can extend that walk by continuing to the **Angel and Greyhound Meadow** – the lush green tract visible from Magdalen Bridge – smaller **Bat Willow Meadow**, home to Mark Wallinger's tree-shaped sculpture *Y*, and the secluded **Fellows' Garden** slightly upstream.

Magdalen's herd of deer usually browse the bucolic **Deer Park**, north of the main college buildings, in winter and spring, and spend the summer in the riverside meadows.

Notable Magdalen students have included writers CS Lewis, John Betjeman, Seamus Heaney and Oscar Wilde, while other alumni range from Edward VIII, TE Lawrence 'of Arabia' and Cardinal Wolsey to Dudley Moore.

The college also boasts a fine choir, which as part of the annual **May Day** (1 May) festivities sings *Hymnus Eucharisticus* at 6am on top of the 44m bell tower.

Tickets for Magdalen College must be pre-booked.

RADCLIFFE CAMERA LIBRARY

(☎01865-287400; www.bodleian.ox.ac.uk; Radcliffe Sq; tours £15; ⊙tours 9.15am Wed & Sat, 11.15am & 1.15pm Sun) Surely Oxford's most photographed landmark, the sandy-gold Radcliffe Camera is a beautiful, light-filled, circular, columned library. Built between 1737 and 1749 in grand Palladian style, as 'Radcliffe Library', it's topped by Britain's third-largest dome. It's only been a 'camera', which simply means 'room', since 1860, when it lost its independence and became what it remains, a reading room of the Bodleian Library. The only way for nonmembers to see the interior is on an extended 1½-hour tour of the Bodleian (p334).

BALLIOL COLLEGE COLLEGE

(☎01865-277777; www.balliol.ox.ac.uk; Broad St; adult/child £3/1; ⊙10am-5pm, to dusk in winter) Dating its foundation to 'about' 1263, Balliol College claims to be the oldest college in Oxford, though its current buildings are largely 19th-century. Scorch marks on the huge Gothic wooden doors between its inner and outer quadrangles, however, supposedly date from the public burning of three Protestant bishops, including Archbishop of Canterbury Thomas Cranmer, in 1556.

Notable alumni include Prime Minister Boris Johnson, writers Gerard Manley Hopkins and Aldous Huxley, and three former British prime ministers.

MUSEUM OF THE HISTORY OF SCIENCE MUSEUM

(☎01865-277293; www.mhs.ox.ac.uk; Broad St; ⊙noon-5pm Tue-Sun) FREE Students of science will swoon at this fascinating museum, stuffed to the ceilings with awesome astrolabes, astonishing orreries and early electrical apparatus. Housed in the lovely 17th-century building that held the original Ashmolean Museum, it displays everything from cameras that belonged to Lewis Carroll and Lawrence of Arabia to a wireless receiver used by Marconi in 1896 and a blackboard that was covered with equations by Einstein in 1931, when he was invited to give three lectures on relativity.

EATING & DRINKING

★**VAULTS & GARDEN** CAFE £

(☎01865-279112; www.thevaultsandgarden.com; University Church of St Mary the Virgin, Radcliffe Sq; mains £9-10.50; ⊙9am-6pm; 📶🅟) This beautiful lunch venue spreads from the vaulted 14th-century Old Congregation House of the University Church into a garden facing the Radcliffe Camera. Come early, and queue at the counter to choose from wholesome organic specials such as carrot and nutmeg soup, chicken *panang* curry, or slow-roasted lamb shoulder with red currant. Breakfast and afternoon tea (those scones!) are equally good.

HANDLE BAR CAFE £

(☎01865-251315; www.handlebaroxford.co.uk; Bike Zone, 28-31 St Michael's St; dishes £8-13; ⌚8am-6pm Mon & Tue, to 11pm Wed-Fri, 9am-11pm Sat, 9am-5pm Sun; 📶🌶) Upstairs above a bike shop, this chatty, friendly cafe has bikes galore, including penny-farthings, dangling from its ceiling and white-painted brick walls. It's usually packed with students, professionals and lucky tourists, all here for luscious, health-focused bites, like avocado and beetroot hummus toast, pan-fried tofu salad and granola breakfast 'pots', plus tasty cakes, smoothies, teas and coffees.

Across from the bike shop downstairs is a coffee and cocktail bar serving the same menu.

★TURF TAVERN PUB

(☎01865-243235; www.turftavern-oxford.co.uk; 4-5 Bath Pl; ⌚11am-11pm; 📶) Squeezed down an alleyway and subdivided into endless nooks and crannies, this medieval rabbit warren dates from around 1381. The definitive Oxford pub, this is where Bill Clinton famously 'did not inhale'; other patrons have included Oscar Wilde, Stephen Hawking and Margaret Thatcher. Home to a fabulous array of real ales and ciders, it's always pretty crowded, but there's outdoor seating, too.

Cambridge

Explore

With its exquisite architecture, its history and tradition, and renowned for its quirky rituals, Cambridge is a university town extraordinaire. The tightly packed core of ancient colleges, the picturesque riverside 'Backs' (college gardens) and the leafy meadows surrounding the city give it a more tranquil appeal than its historic rival Oxford.

Like 'the Other Place', as Oxford is known locally, it's possible to wander around the colleges and experience them as countless prime ministers, poets, writers and scientists have done. Sheer academic achievement seems to permeate the very walls: cyclists loaded down with books negotiate cobbled passageways, students relax on manicured lawns and great minds debate life-changing research in historic pubs. First-time punters zigzag erratically across the river, and those long past their student days wonder what it would have been like to study in such splendid surroundings.

The Best...

Sight King's College Chapel

Place to Eat Midsummer House (p340)

Place to Drink Eagle (p341)

Getting There & Away

Bus There are nine buses daily from London Victoria (£4.70, 2½ hours), dropping you at Parkside just east of Cambridge's city centre.

Train The train station is 1.5 miles southeast of the centre. There are two to four trains per hour to London King's Cross (£13) and the journey takes one hour.

Need to Know

Area Code ☎01223

Location 49 miles north of London.

Tourist Office (☎01223-791500; www.visitcambridge.org; The Guildhall, Peas Hill; ⌚9.30am-5pm Mon-Sat Nov-Mar, plus 11am-3pm Sun Apr-Oct)

SIGHTS

★KING'S COLLEGE CHAPEL CHURCH

(☎01223-331212; www.kings.cam.ac.uk; King's Pde; adult/child £9/6; ⌚9.30am-3.15pm Mon-Sat, 1.15-2.30pm Sun term time, 9.30am-4.30pm rest of year) In a city crammed with show-stopping buildings, this is a scene-stealer. Grandiose 16th-century King's College Chapel is one of England's most extraordinary examples of Gothic architecture. Its inspirational, intricate 80m-long fan-vaulted ceiling is the world's largest and soars upwards before exploding into a series of stone fireworks. This hugely atmospheric space is a fitting stage for the chapel's world-famous choir; hear it sing during the free and magnificent

Cambridge

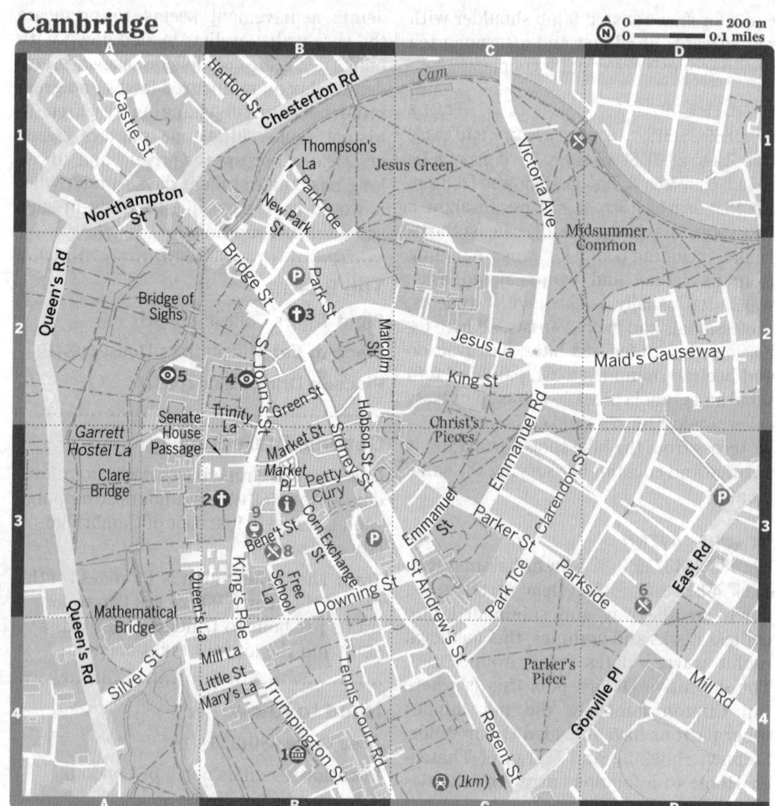

Cambridge

Sights

1 Fitzwilliam Museum B4
2 King's College Chapel B3
3 Round Church B2
4 Trinity College B2
5 Wren Library A2

Eating

6 Espresso Library D3
7 Midsummer House C1
8 Smokeworks B3

Drinking & Nightlife

9 Eagle B3

evensong in term time (5.30pm Monday to Saturday; 10.30am and 3.30pm Sunday).

King's **steeples** have long been a magnet for student night climbers, and today images of the chapel adorn thousands of postcards, tea towels and choral CDs. But it was begun in 1446 as an act of piety by Henry VI and was only finished by Henry VIII around 1516.

The lofty **stained-glass windows** that flank the chapel's sides ensure it's remarkably light. The glass is original, a rare survivor of the excesses of the 17th-century Civil War in this region. It's said that these windows were ordered to be spared by Oliver Cromwell, who knew of their beauty from his own studies in Cambridge.

The antechapel and the choir are divided by a superbly carved **wooden screen**, designed and executed by Peter Stockton for Henry VIII. The screen bears his master's initials entwined with those of Anne Boleyn. Look closely and you may find an angry human face (possibly Stockton's) amid the elaborate jungle of mythical beasts and symbolic flowers. Above is the magnificent bat-wing **organ**, originally constructed in 1686, though much altered since.

Beyond the thickly carved dark-wood choir stalls, light suffuses the high **altar**, which is framed by Rubens' masterpiece *Adoration of the Magi* (1634) and the magnificent east window. To the left of the altar in the side chapels, an **exhibition** charts the construction stages and methods.

Note the chapel itself (but not the grounds) is open during the exam period (April to June).

Each Christmas Eve, King's College Chapel stages the **Festival of Nine Lessons & Carols**. It's broadcast globally by the BBC, and to around 300 US radio stations. You can also queue for a place – if you arrive early enough (often by around 9am), you could well get in.

★**TRINITY COLLEGE** COLLEGE

(☎01223-338400; www.trin.cam.ac.uk; Trinity St; adult/child £3/1; ⏰10am-4.30pm, to 3.30pm Nov-Jun) The largest of Cambridge's colleges, Trinity offers an extraordinary Tudor gateway, an air of supreme elegance and a sweeping Great Court – the largest of its kind in the world. It also boasts the renowned and suitably musty **Wren Library** (☎01223-338400; www.trin.cam.ac.uk; Trinity St; ⏰noon-2pm Mon-Fri, plus 10.30am-12.30pm Sat term time) FREE, containing 55,000 books published before 1820 and more than 2500 manuscripts. Works include those by Shakespeare, St Jerome, Newton and Swift – and AA Milne's original *Winnie the Pooh;* both Milne and his son, Christopher Robin, were graduates.

As you enter Trinity through the part-gilded gate, have a look at the **statue** of the college's founder, Henry VIII, that adorns it. His left hand holds a golden orb, while his right grips not the original sceptre but a table leg, put there by student pranksters and never replaced. It's a wonderful introduction to one of Cambridge's most venerable colleges, and a reminder of who really rules the roost.

In the **Great Court** beyond, scholastic humour gives way to wonderment, thanks to its imposing architecture and sheer size. To the right of the entrance is a small tree, planted in the 1950s and reputed to be a descendant of the apple tree made famous by Trinity alumnus Sir Isaac Newton. Other alumni include Francis Bacon, Lord Byron, Tennyson, HRH Prince Charles (legend has it his bodyguard scored higher in exams than he did), at least nine prime ministers (British and international) and more than 30 Nobel Prize winners.

The college's vast **hall** has a dramatic hammer-beam roof and lantern; beyond lie the dignified cloisters of **Nevile's Court**. Henry VIII would have been proud to note, too, that his college would eventually come to throw the best party in town, the lavish **May Ball** in early June, though you will need a fat purse, and a friend on the inside, to get an invitation.

★**FITZWILLIAM MUSEUM** MUSEUM

(www.fitzmuseum.cam.ac.uk; Trumpington St; by donation; ⏰10am-5pm Tue-Sat, from noon Sun) FREE Fondly dubbed 'the Fitz' by locals, this colossal neoclassical pile was one of the first public art museums in Britain, built to house the fabulous treasures that the seventh Viscount Fitzwilliam bequeathed to his old university. Expect Roman and Egyptian grave goods, artworks by many of the great masters and some quirkier collections: banknotes, literary autographs, watches and armour.

The building's unabashedly over-the-top appearance sets out to mirror its contents; this ostentatious jumble of styles mixes mosaic with marble, and Greek with Egyptian. The **lower galleries** are filled with priceless treasures spanning the ancient world; look out for a Roman funerary couch, an inscribed copper votive plaque from Yemen (c 100–200CE), a figurine of Egyptian cat goddess Bastet, splendid Egyptian sarcophagi and mummified animals, plus dazzling illuminated manuscripts. The **upper galleries** showcase works by Leonardo da Vinci, Titian, Rubens, the impressionists, Gainsborough, Constable, Rembrandt and Picasso; standout works include the tender *Pietà* by Giovanni del Ponte and Salvator Rosa's dark and intensely personal *L'Umana Fragilita*.

The Fitz has a tragic footnote: although begun by George Basevi in 1837, he didn't live to see its completion. While working on Ely Cathedral he stepped back to admire his handiwork, slipped and fell to his death.

One-hour guided tours (£8) of the museum are held at 2.30pm on Saturdays.

ROUND CHURCH CHURCH

(☎01223-311602; www.christianheritage.org.uk; Bridge St; £3.50; ⊙11am-4.30pm Mon-Fri, from 10am Sat) Cambridge's intensely atmospheric Round Church is one of only four such structures in England. It was built by the mysterious Knights Templar in 1130 and shelters an unusual circular nave ringed by chunky Norman pillars. The carved stone faces crowning the pillars bring the 12th century vividly to life. Guided walks take place Monday to Saturday at 2.15pm.

The church's position on Bridge St reminds you of its original role – that of a chapel for pilgrims crossing the river.

EATING & DRINKING

ESPRESSO LIBRARY CAFE £

(☎01223-367333; www.espressolibrary.com; 210 East Rd; mains £7.50-11; ⊙7.30am-5pm Mon-Sat, from 8.30am Sun;) A chilled soundtrack and customers with laptops at almost every table signal that this industrial-chic cafe is a student favourite. That's partly down to the wholesome food – dishes might include frittata with sweet potatoes and spinach, or juicy portobello mushrooms in brioche buns – and partly down to some cracking coffee.

SMOKEWORKS BARBECUE ££

(www.smokeworks.co.uk; 2 Free School Lane; mains £11-20; ⊙11.30am-10pm Mon-Thu, to 10.30pm Fri & Sat, to 9.30pm Sun;) This dark, industrial-themed dining spot draws discerning carnivores with its melt-in-your-mouth ribs, wings and wonderfully smoky pulled pork. The service is friendly and prompt, and the salted-caramel milkshakes come in a glass the size of your head.

★MIDSUMMER HOUSE MODERN BRITISH £££

(☎01223-369299; www.midsummerhouse.co.uk; Midsummer Common; 3/8 courses £55/145; ⊙noon-1.30pm & 6.30-9.15pm Wed-Sat;) At the region's top table, chef Daniel Clifford's double-Michelin-starred creations are distinguished by depth of flavour and immense technical skill. Savour buttermilk-poached Cornish cod with vanilla and champagne beurre blanc, or pot-roasted Anjou pigeon with braised cabbage purée and crispy mushroom before a sesame and white-chocolate pyramid, served with guava sorbet, coconut, chilli and garlic.

Unusually, there are vegetarian, vegan and pescatarian versions of the eight-course menu.

FANCY A PUNT?

Gliding a self-propelled punt along the Backs is a blissful experience – once you've got the hang of it. It can also be a manic challenge for beginners. If you wimp out, you can always opt for a relaxing chauffeured punt.

Punt hire costs around £24 to £30 per hour; 45-minute chauffeured trips of the Backs cost about £18 to £24 per person. One-way trips to Grantchester (1½ hours) start at around £30 per person.

Punting looks pretty straightforward but, believe us, it's not! So here are some tips to stop you zigzagging wildly across the river, losing your pole and falling in.

➡ Standing at the back end of the punt, lift the pole out of the water at the side of the punt.

➡ Let the pole slide through your hands to touch the bottom of the river.

➡ Tilt the pole forward (that is, in the direction of travel of the punt) and push down to propel the punt forward.

➡ Twist the pole to free the end from the mud at the bottom of the river, and let it float up and trail behind the punt. You can then use it as a rudder to steer.

➡ If you haven't fallen in yet, raise the pole out of the water and into the vertical position to begin the cycle again.

➡ Hold on to the pole, particularly when passing under Clare Bridge, as students sometimes snatch them for a giggle.

EAGLE PUB

(☎01223-505020; www.eagle-cambridge.co.uk; Bene't St; ⏰11am-11pm Sun-Thu, to midnight Fri & Sat; 📶👪) Cambridge's most famous pub has loosened the tongues and pickled the grey cells of many an illustrious academic, among them Nobel Prize–winning scientists Crick and Watson, who discussed their research into DNA here (note the blue plaque by the door). Fifteenth-century, wood-panelled and rambling, the Eagle's cosy rooms include one with WWII airmen's signatures on the ceiling.

The food (mains £10 to 15), served all day, is good too; it includes some thoughtful options for children.

Brighton

Explore

Raves on the beach, Graham Greene novels, mods and rockers in bank-holiday fisticuffs, naughty weekends for Mr and Mrs Smith, and the UK's biggest gay scene – this coastal city evokes many images for the British. But one thing is certain: with its bohemian, hedonistic vibe, Brighton is where England's seaside experience goes from cold to cool.

Brighton is Britain's most colourful and outrageous city. Here burlesque meets contemporary design, microbrewed ales share bar space with 'sex on the beach' and stags watch drag. The city returned the UK's first Green Party MP, and according to the 2001 census, it has the UK's highest Jedi population.

The highlight for sightseers is the Royal Pavilion, a 19th-century party palace built by the Prince Regent, who kicked off Brighton's love of the outlandish.

The Best...

Sight Royal Pavilion

Place to Eat Terre à Terre (p343)

Place to Drink Black Dove (p343)

Getting There & Away

Bus Services run between Brighton and London Victoria at least every two hours (from £9, 2½ hours).

Train There are three trains hourly to London Victoria (£25.30, one hour), and half-hourly trains to London St Pancras (£19.10, 1¼ hours). London-bound services pass through Gatwick Airport (£8.50, 25 to 35 minutes, up to five hourly).

Need to Know

Area Code ☎01273

Location 57 miles south of London.

Tourist Office (☎01273-290337; www.visitbrighton.com)

SIGHTS

★ROYAL PAVILION PALACE

(☎03000 290900; http://brightonmuseums.org.uk/royalpavilion; Royal Pavilion Gardens; adult/child £15/9; ⏰9.30am-5.45pm Apr-Sep, 10am-5.15pm Oct-Mar; 📶) The Royal Pavilion is the city's must-see attraction. The glittering party pad and palace of Prince George, later Prince Regent and then King George IV, it's one of the most opulent buildings in England, and certainly the finest example of early-19th-century chinoiserie anywhere in Europe. It's an apt symbol of Brighton's reputation for decadence. An unimpressed Queen Victoria called the Royal Pavilion 'a strange, odd Chinese place', but for visitors to Brighton it's an unmissable chunk of Sussex history.

The entire palace is an eye-popping spectacle, but some interiors stand out even amid the riot of decoration. The dragon-themed banqueting hall must be the most incredible in all of England. More dragons and snakes writhe in the music room, with its ceiling of 26,000 gold scales, and the then-state-of-the-art kitchen must have wowed Georgians with its automatic spits and hot tables. Prince Albert carted away all of the furniture, some of which has been loaned back by the present queen.

I360 TOWER TOWER

(☎03337 720360; www.britishairwaysi360.com; Lower King's Rd; adult/child £17/8; ⏰10am-7.30pm Sun-Thu, to 9.30pm Fri & Sat) Brighton's newest attraction opened in 2016, at the point the now defunct West Pier used to make landfall. The world's most slender tower is a brutal, 162m-tall

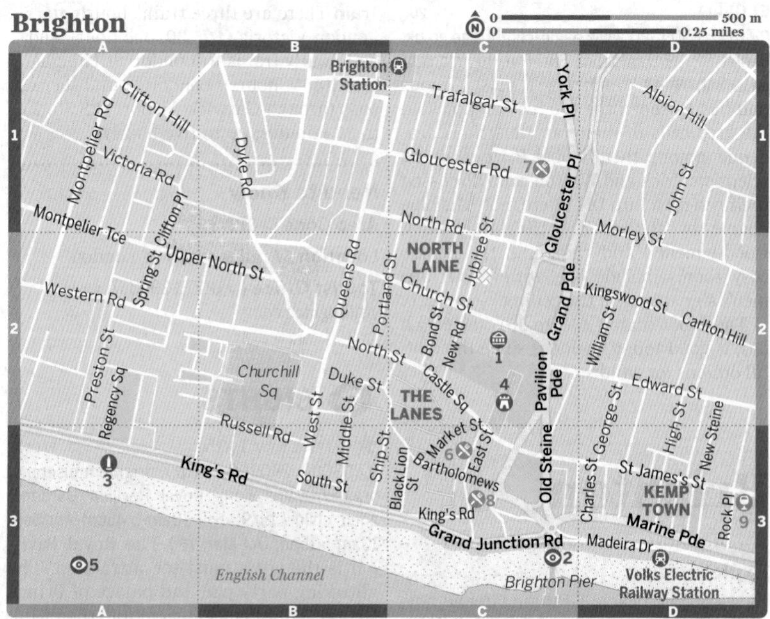

Brighton

Sights

1 Brighton Museum & Art Gallery........C2
2 Brighton Pier........C3
3 i360 Tower........A3
4 Royal Pavilion........C2
5 West Pier........A3

Eating

6 English's of Brighton........C3
7 Isaac At........C1
8 Terre à Terre........C3

Drinking & Nightlife

9 Black Dove........D3

column of reinforced steel and concrete rising like a space-age phallus (this is Brighton after all) from the seafront, with a huge, impaled, glass doughnut taking 'passengers' 138m above the city for some gob-smacking vistas of the Sussex coast.

The i360 is the world's tallest moving observation tower and the vistas from it are truly spectacular – certainly much better than the views of it, especially as it rises incongruously near the architectural purity that is Regency Sq. A fancy restaurant and bars huddle at the base. The idea is that profits from the i360, a 21st-century 'vertical pier', will one day be used to rebuild the horizontal West Pier.

BRIGHTON PIER LANDMARK

(www.brightonpier.co.uk; Madeira Dr) This grand old Edwardian pier is the place to experience Brighton's tackier side. There are plenty of stomach-churning fairground rides and noisy amusement arcades to keep you entertained, and candy floss and Brighton rock to chomp on while you're doing so. Just west are the sad remains of the **West Pier** (www.westpier.co.uk), a skeletal iron hulk that attracts flocks of starlings at sunset.

BRIGHTON MUSEUM & ART GALLERY MUSEUM, GALLERY

(https://brightonmuseums.org.uk; Royal Pavilion Gardens; adult/child £6/3; ⏲10am-5pm Tue-Sun) Set in the Royal Pavilion's renovated stable block, this museum and art gallery has a glittering collection of 20th-century art and design, including a crimson Salvador Dalí sofa modelled on Mae West's lips. There's also an enthralling gallery of world art, an impressive collection of Egyptian artefacts, and an 'Images of Brighton' multimedia

STONEHENGE

Stonehenge (EH; ☎0370 333 1181; www.english-heritage.org.uk; near Amesbury; adult/child £21/13, advance booking £19/11; ⏰9am-8pm Jun-Aug, 9.30am-7pm Apr, May & Sep, 9.30am-5pm Oct-Mar; P) is one of Britain's great archaeological mysteries: despite countless theories about the site's purpose, from a sacrificial centre to a celestial timepiece, no one knows for sure what drove prehistoric Britons to expend so much time and effort on its construction, although recent archaeological findings show the surrounding area was sacred for hundreds of years before work began.

An ultramodern makeover at ancient Stonehenge has brought an impressive visitor centre and the closure of an intrusive road (now restored to grassland). The result is a strong sense of historical context, with dignity and mystery returned to an archaeological gem.

A pathway frames the ring of massive stones. Although you can't walk in the circle, unless on a recommended **Stone Circle Experience** (☎0370 333 0605; www.english-heritage.org.uk; adult/child £47/28) tour, you can get fairly close. Admission is through timed tickets – secure a place well in advance.

Trains run from London Waterloo to Salisbury station (£25, 1½ hours, every half-hour), 9 miles from Stonehenge. **Stonehenge Tour** (☎01202-338420; www.thestonehengetour.info; adult/child £31.50/21) buses (£16) depart from Salisbury station half-hourly from June to August, and hourly between September and May.

exhibit containing a series of oral histories and a model of the defunct West Pier.

EATING & DRINKING

★TERRE À TERRE VEGETARIAN ££
(☎01273-729051; www.terreaterre.co.uk; 71 East St; mains from £17; ⏰noon-10pm Tue-Sun;) Take your taste buds around the world without any meat in sight. In this vegetarian restaurant, inventive and flavourful dishes are meticulously plated and the ambience is casual and friendly. For the unconverted, there are nods to nonvegetarian favourites, including battered halloumi and chips, and steamed Szechuan buns. A daily afternoon tea service includes a vegan option.

ENGLISH'S OF BRIGHTON SEAFOOD ££
(☎01273-327980; www.englishs.co.uk; 29-31 East St; mains £15-34; ⏰noon-10pm) A 75-year-old institution and celebrity haunt, this local seafood paradise dishes up everything from Essex oysters to locally caught lobster and Dover sole. It's converted from fishers' cottages, with shades of the elegant style of the Edwardian era inside, and has alfresco dining on the pedestrian square outside.

ISAAC AT BRITISH £££
(☎07765 934740; www.isaac-at.com; 2 Gloucester St; set menu £40, tasting menu £60; ⏰6.30-10.30pm Tue-Fri, 12.30-2.30pm & 6.30-10.30pm Sat) Tucked on a street corner is this intimate fine-dining restaurant run by a small team of culinary talent, all aged under 30. Every ingredient is locally sourced, including the wines, with food miles for each ingredient noted on the menu. It's probably the homeliest high-end dining experience in the area. First-class, fresh and thoughtful food.

BLACK DOVE PUB
(www.blackdovebrighton.com; 74 St James's St; ⏰4pm-late) Eclectic hang-out with shabby-chic furnishings, huge antique ceiling fans, a bar stocked with unusual tipples and a quirky basement snug. Live acoustic music and local DJs provide the soundtrack for evening quaffing that spills out onto the pavements when the mercury is high.

Sleeping

Accommodation in London can be painfully expensive, and you'll almost always need to book well in advance. Decent hostels are easy to find but aren't as cheap as you might hope. Hotels range from no-frills chains to the world's ritziest establishments, such as the Ritz itself. B&Bs are often better value and more atmospheric than hotels.

Hotels

London has a grand roll call of stately hotels, and many are experiences in their own right. Standards at the top end are very high, as are the prices. Quirkiness and individuality can be found in abundance, alongside dyed-in-the-wool traditionalism. While a rung or two down in overall quality and charm, mid-range chains generally offer good location and dependable comfort. Something new is the smart hotels with tiny but well-designed rooms and larger communal spaces; prices often start extremely reasonably but rise sharply for last-minute bookings. Demand can often outstrip supply – especially at the bottom of the market – so book ahead, particularly during holidays and in summer.

B&Bs

Bed and breakfasts generally fall in at a level below hotels, often promising boutique-style charm and a more personal service. Handy clusters appear in Paddington, South Kensington, Victoria, Pimlico and Bloomsbury.

Hostels

Generally the cheapest option, hostels can be an affordable and a sociable option. They vary widely in quality, so choose carefully. Those with a reputation as party hostels can be a lot of fun, but don't expect to get much sleep. As well as dorm rooms, many hostels also offer twin and double rooms, sometimes with en suite bathrooms. These private rooms are often better than what you'd get for the same price at a budget hotel.

Apartments

If you're here for a week or more, a short-term or serviced apartment may make sense. They usually come with cooking and laundry facilities, and rates at the bottom end can be comparable to a B&B. At the top end are luxurious pads you may never want to leave.

Rates & Booking

Deluxe hotel rooms cost from around £350 per double, but there's good variety at the top end, so you should find a room from about £200 offering superior comfort without the prestige. Some boutique hotels also occupy this bracket. There's a noticeable dip in quality below this price, with notable exceptions. Under £100 and you're at the more serviceable, budget end of the market. Look out for weekend deals that can put a better class of hotel within your reach. Rates often slide in winter. Book through the hotel website for the best deals. Hostelling International (HI) members net discounts on YHA hostels.

Booking Services

Visit London (www.visitlondon.com) Huge range of listings; official tourism portal.

London Town (www.londontown.com) Last-minute offers on boutique hotels and B&Bs.

London Bed & Breakfast (www.londonbb.com) B&B in private homes across the city.

Lonely Planet (lonelyplanet.com/england/london/hotels) Recommendations.

Lonely Planet's Top Choices

CitizenM Tower of London (p351) Designer digs at reasonable prices with extraordinary views.

Hoxton Shoreditch (p354) Cool location, nifty looks and very cheap rooms.

Hazlitt's (p350) A step back into the Georgian era in the middle of Soho.

St Ermin's Hotel (p348) From nest of spies to luxury hotel.

40 Winks (p356) Two gorgeously designed rooms in the historic East End.

Best by Budget

£

Qbic (p356) Well-designed little rooms available at a steal if booked early enough.

London House Hotel (p358) Good-value in a rather grand Regency building.

YHA London Oxford Street (p347) Centrally positioned hostel with excellent shared facilities.

££

CitizenM Tower of London (p351) Small but perfectly formed rooms, some with killer views.

Hoxton Shoreditch (p354) Outstanding value for its location and design.

Twenty Nevern Square (p359) Affordable elegance and style.

£££

Brown's Hotel (p351) Luxury in London's oldest hotel.

St Ermin's Hotel (p348) Enviable location, back stories for days.

Hazlitt's (p350) Old-world elegance in a terrific location.

Best Hostels

Clink78 (p357) Excellent facilities in an unusual courthouse setting.

Safestay Holland Park (p358) A bright addition to the only surviving wing of a Jacobean mansion.

St Christopher's Village (p352) Large, newly renovated party hostel.

Sohostel (p347) Bright, friendly, unbeatable location

Park Villa (p355) New boutique hostel in the old East End

Best Heritage Hotels

Hazlitt's (p350) Immerse yourself in the 1718 ambience and modern comforts.

The Ned (p351) Bank palace transformed into 5-star hotel.

Brown's Hotel (p351) London's oldest hotel still remains near the top of the heap.

Rookery (p355) Original Georgian features in Clerkenwell.

Great Northern Hotel (p357) World's first railway hotel.

Best B&Bs

Kennington B&B (p360) Tasteful rooms in a Georgian house.

40 Winks (p356) Two eccentrically furnished designer rooms.

Barclay House (p358) Ticks every box – and a few more.

Aster House (p353) Great location with charming hosts.

Windermere Hotel (p353) Family-owned in a mid-Victorian town house.

NEED TO KNOW

Price Ranges

The following price ranges refer to a double room with bathroom.

£	less than £100
££	£100–£200
£££	more than £200

Reservations

➡ For the best prices, book as far in advance as possible, especially for weekends and holidays.

➡ Prices for business-oriented City hotels often drop at weekends.

➡ Most hotels match booking-site prices if you book directly, and may add perks such as free breakfast or late checkout.

Tax

Value-added tax (VAT; 20%) is added to hotel rooms. Hotels almost always include VAT in their advertised rates.

Checking In & Out

Check-in is usually 2pm, though most places will let you check in earlier if your room is available, or at least let you leave your luggage. Check-out is usually between 10am and noon.

Breakfast

Breakfast may be included in the room rate. Often this is a continental breakfast; a cooked breakfast usually costs extra.

Where to Stay

NEIGHBOURHOOD	FOR	AGAINST
West End	Close to main sights; great transport links; wide range of accommodation in all budgets; good restaurants.	Busy tourist areas; expensive.
The City	Near sights like St Paul's and Tower of London; good transport links; handy central location; quality hotels; some cheaper weekend rates.	Very quiet at weekends; a business district so high prices during the week.
The South Bank	Near Tate Modern, London Eye and Southbank Centre; cheaper than West End; excellent pubs and views.	Many chain hotels; choice limited.
Kensington & Hyde Park	Excellent for South Kensington museums and shopping; great accommodation range; stylish area; good transport.	Quite expensive; drinking and nightlife options limited.
Clerkenwell, Shoreditch & Spitalfields	Hip area with great bars and nightlife; excellent for boutique hotels.	Few notable sights.
East London	Markets, multicultural feel; great restaurants and traditional pubs.	Limited sleeping options; some areas less safe at night.
North London	Leafy; vibrant nightlife; pockets of village charm; excellent boutique hotels and hostels; great gastropubs; quiet during the week.	Noncentral and away from main sights.
West London	Good shopping, markets and pubs; excellent boutique hotels; good transport.	Pricey; light on top sights.
Greenwich & South London	Great boutique options; leafy escapes; near top Greenwich sights.	Sights spread out beyond Greenwich; transport limited.
Richmond, Kew & Hampton Court	Smart riverside hotels; semirural pockets; quiet; fantastic riverside pubs.	Sights spread out; a long way from central London.

West End

SOHOSTEL HOSTEL £

Map p440 (020-8821 5154; www.sohostel.co.uk; 91 Dean St, W1; dm/tw £25/80; ; Tottenham Court Rd) Offering an unbeatable location in the middle of Soho, this brightly painted, friendly establishment offers spacious, clean dorm rooms with four to 18 beds as well as twins and triples in five colour-coded sections. Communal areas include a Hawaiian-themed roof garden and bar, where you can find locally brewed beer, and a large basement games room.

YHA LONDON OXFORD STREET HOSTEL £

Map p440 (020-7734 1618; www.yha.org.uk/hostel/yha-london-oxford-street; 14 Noel St, W1; dm £18-36, tw £50-90; ; Oxford Circus) The most central of London's seven YHA hostels is also one of the most intimate with just 104 beds in 36 rooms. The excellent shared facilities include a fuchsia-coloured kitchen and a bright, funky lounge. Dormitories have two solid bunk beds, and there are doubles and twins. The in-house shop sells coffee and beer. Free wi-fi in common areas.

The hostel offers free daily walking tours at 9.30am.

GENERATOR LONDON HOSTEL £

Map p444 (020-7388 7666; https://staygenerator.com/hostels/london; 37 Tavistock Pl, WC1; dm/r from £11/61; ; Russell Sq) With its industrial lines and funky decor, the huge Generator (it has more than 870 beds) is one of central London's grooviest budget spots. The bar, complete with pool tables, stays open until 3am and there are frequent themed parties. Dorm rooms have between four and 13 beds; backing it up are twins and triples.

There is no kitchen, but breakfast is provided and the large canteen serves bargain dinners till 10.30pm. Public areas are a delight, especially the large TV lounge, with comfy theatre-style seating.

HOXTON HOLBORN HOTEL ££

Map p438 (020-7661 3000; https://thehoxton.com/london/holborn/hotels; 199-206 High Holborn, WC1; r £90-300; ; Holborn) This enlarged branch of the Hoxton hotel chain continues the tradition of offering stylish yet affordable accommodation in 220 rooms that vary enormously in size and comfort. At the lowest end is the aptly named 12-sq-metre Shoebox (from as low as £90) through Snug and Cosy to the top-end Biggy, which has a king-size bed. Note the Dickens-themed wallpaper.

The buzzy lobby has maps, newspapers and the Hubbard & Bell, a convivial cafe, bar and grill.

FIELDING HOTEL BOUTIQUE HOTEL ££

Map p438 (020-7836 8305; www.thefieldinghotel.co.uk; 4 Broad Ct, Bow St, WC2; s/d/q from £120/180/200; ; Covent Garden) Hidden away in a pedestrianised court in the heart of Covent Garden, this pretty and desirable 25-room hotel (named after the novelist Henry Fielding, who lived nearby) has been furnished to a very high standard: bathrooms have lovely walk-in showers, and rooms, while small, are beautifully done up and fully air-conditioned. There's no breakfast but the area is full of cafes.

RIDGEMOUNT HOTEL B&B ££

Map p444 (020-7636 1141; www.ridgemounthotel.co.uk; 65-67 Gower St, WC1; s/d/tr/q £81/122/156/176, without bathroom £66/102/138/152; @; Goodge St) This traditional-style family hotel dispenses a warmth and consideration that can be hard to find in London these days. About half of its 32 utilitarian rooms have bathrooms (others have wash basin only), and there are a number of triples and quadruples, plus laundry service.

No lift but there is a small, pretty garden in the back.

GEORGE HOTEL B&B ££

Map p444 (020-7387 8777; www.georgehotels.co.uk; 58-60 Cartwright Gardens, WC1; s/tw/tr from £110/160/185, without bathroom £70/90/160; @; Russell Sq) Housed in three crescent town houses dating to around 1810, the George is a friendly chap, if a tad old-fashioned. There's no lift and little air-conditioning, but there are fans in each of the 40 rooms. Lone travellers might consider room 26 or 103 with views of the leafy square.

MIMI'S HOTEL SOHO BOUTIQUE HOTEL ££

Map p440 (020-8017 9100; http://mimishotelsoho.com; 56-57 Frith St, W1; r £100-250; P; Tottenham Court Rd) The location couldn't be any more central. The lobby has a great bar, a working fireplace and reclaimed oak flooring. We love the Trump-style gold lift. But, boy, are the rooms tiny – some as small as 7 sq metres without a window! The 58 rooms are spread over six floors; there are an additional seven apartments on nearby Greek St.

Room types range from the smallest 'Tiny' and 'Mini' ones to 14-sq-metre 'Cosy' rooms, and 'Lux' ones that are a cat-swinging 22 sq metres. Still, you get what you pay for in uber central London.

JESMOND HOTEL B&B ££

Map p444 (020-7636 3199; www.jesmondhotel.org.uk; 63 Gower St, WC1; s/d/tr/q from £80/105/140/160; ; Goodge St) The 15 guest rooms at this popular, family-run Georgian-era B&B in Bloomsbury are basic but clean and cheerful (four are with shared bathroom): there's a small, pretty garden out back, and the prices are very attractive indeed. There's also laundry service and good breakfasts for kicking off your London day. Location is highly central.

Room 2 on the ground level looks to the street and sleeps five.

MORGAN HOTEL B&B ££

Map p444 (020-7636 3735; www.morganhotel.co.uk; 24 Bloomsbury St, WC1; s/d/tr/ste from £120/145/165/215; ; Tottenham Court Rd) In a delightful row of 18th-century Georgian houses an artefact's toss from the British Museum, the 21-room Morgan offers fine service, breakfast fit for a king, and excellent value for central London. Room decor may be somewhat dated, but cleanliness is a strong point. There's no lift, and the top floor might be a scramble for some. Reception is below ground floor.

Larger suites are worth the extra outlay, but they don't have air-con.

AROSFA HOTEL B&B ££

Map p444 (020-7636 2115; www.arosfalondon.com; 83 Gower St, WC1; s/d/tw/tr/f from £100/140/145/165/210; ; Goodge St) The modern look in the lounge is more lavish than the decor in the 17 small guest rooms, with cabin-like bathrooms in many of them. Fully refurbished, this was once the home of the Pre-Raphaelite artist John Everett Millais. There are a couple of family rooms; room 4 looks on to a small but charming garden in the back.

HARLINGFORD HOTEL HOTEL ££

Map p444 (020-7387 1551; www.harlingfordhotel.com; 61-63 Cartwright Gardens, WC1; s/d/tr £105/145/160; ; Russell Sq) With a modern interior with lashings of mauve and royal blue and green-tiled bathrooms, this stylish 43-room Bloomsbury hotel is arguably the best on a street where competition is fierce. The welcome is always warm and the price unbeatable, but there are lots of stairs and no lift. Room 10 looks on to the tranquil courtyard, room 12 to the main garden.

★ST ERMIN'S HOTEL LUXURY HOTEL £££

Map p448 (020-7222 7888; www.sterminshotel.co.uk; 2 Caxton St, SW1; r £250-300; ; St James's Park) One of our favourite West End hotels, St Ermin's not only has 331 super-comfortable rooms and an enviable location in Westminster, it also has back stories for days. In the 1930s its Caxton Bar was a centre of espionage activities (MI6 being close by), and there's a Division Bell to call back supping MPs to Parliament – by secret tunnel!

Superior rooms like 227 are quite small; go for deluxe room 456 that looks out to Broadway. There's a lovely rooftop garden with vegetables and beehives and a wonderful and very leafy forecourt.

ACADEMY BOUTIQUE HOTEL £££

Map p444 (020-7631 4115; www.theacademyhotel.co.uk; 21 Gower St, WC1; s/d/ste from £190/250/290; ; Goodge St) This beautiful, terribly English hotel ranges through five Georgian townhouses in Bloomsbury. The 50 refurbished rooms are kitted out with fluffy feather duvets, elegant furnishings and the latest in creature comforts. A conservatory overlooks a leafy back garden (choose smallish room 42 for the view), and there's a cosy breakfast room. No lift.

★ZETTER TOWNHOUSE MARYLEBONE BOUTIQUE HOTEL £££

Map p446 (020-7324 4577; www.thezettertownhouse.com/marylebone; 28-30 Seymour St, W1; d from £275, studio £300-580; ; Marble Arch) We've always loved the Zetter group of hotels and this new boutique number with two dozen rooms only increases our passion. The comfy back rooms on the ground floor and above are dressed in black and burgundy, superior rooms have four-poster beds with canopies and Lear's Loft is a suite reached by its own staircase.

Check out Seymour's Parlour, a kind of library/lounge lobby named after a fictional 'wicked' uncle. It's all a blend of fusty style, kitsch and good humour.

★BEAUMONT HOTEL £££

Map p446 (020-7499 1001; www.thebeaumont.com; Brown Hart Gardens, W1; d/studio/ste from £550/865/1475; Bond St) A stylish and handsome smaller-scale luxury hotel, the 73-room Beaumont is all art deco opulence. Fronted by an arresting stainless-steel-and-oak cuboid sculpture by British artist Antony Gormley called *Room* (which encompasses part of a £1260-per-night suite on the 3rd floor), the striking white building dates from 1926. Rooms – 104 has fab views – and suites are swish and elegant.

Don't miss the American-style Magritte Bar (p126) off the main lobby with paintings and original posters from the 1920s and 1930s. Room prices include local drop-offs.

★ROSEWOOD LONDON HOTEL £££

Map p438 (020-7781 8888; www.rosewoodhotels.com/en/london; 252 High Holborn, WC1; d/ste from £440/1100; Holborn) What was once the grand Pearl Assurance building (dating from 1914) houses the stunning Rosewood hotel, where an artful marriage of period and modern styles, thanks to designer Tony Chi, can be found in its 262 rooms and 45 suites. British heritage is carefully woven throughout the bar, restaurant, lobby and even the housekeepers' uniforms.

We love Swedish artist Agnetha Sjögren's dog sculpture in the lobby, the caged birds on the landings and the little metal roosters on the guest-room doors. The Manor House Suite, with its own separate street entrance and postal code, has a huge dining room and circular marble bath that has to be seen to be believed.

★HAYMARKET HOTEL HOTEL £££

Map p438 (020-7470 4000; www.firmdalehotels.com/hotels/london/haymarket-hotel; 1 Suffolk Pl, off Haymarket, SW1; r/ste £350/550; Piccadilly Circus) With the trademark colours and lines of hotelier/designer duo Tim and Kit Kemp, in a converted building designed by John Nash, the Haymarket is scrumptious, with hand-painted Gournay wallpaper, signature fuchsia and green designs in the 50 different guest rooms – 206 has windows on two sides – a sensational 18m pool, an exquisite library lounge, and original artwork.

We love the dog silhouettes on the chairs and bar stools in the Brumus Bar, which takes its name from the owner's late pooch.

★RITZ LONDON LUXURY HOTEL £££

Map p448 (020-7493 8181; www.theritzlondon.com; 150 Piccadilly, W1; r/ste from £650/1500; Green Park) What can you say about a place that has lent its name to the English lexicon? This 136-room hotel, opened by the eponymous César in 1906, has a spectacular position overlooking Green Park and is supposedly the Royal Family's home away from home. (It is very close to the palace.) All rooms have Louis XVI–style interiors and antique furniture.

Various formal-dress and smart-casual codes (shirt and tie) apply in some of the hotel's outlets. For stunning cocktails in art deco opulence, take a seat in the Rivoli Bar (p121).

★COVENT GARDEN HOTEL BOUTIQUE HOTEL £££

Map p438 (020-7806 1000; www.firmdalehotels.com/hotels/london/covent-garden-hotel; 10 Monmouth St, WC2; d/ste from £360/550; Covent Garden) This gorgeous and discreet 58-room boutique hotel housed in a former French hospital features antiques, bright fabrics and quirky bric-a-brac to mark its individuality. There's an excellent bar-restaurant off the lobby and two stunning guest lounges with fireplaces (note the beautiful marquetry desk) on the 1st floor, which come into their own in the winter.

Rooms on the ground floor (like rooms 3, 5 and 8) are larger and have higher ceilings. The Asian touches in room 4 are fetching.

ME LONDON HOTEL £££

Map p438 (020-7395 3400; www.mebymelia.com/hotels/me-london; 336-337 The Strand; d £285-375, ste from £525; Temple, Covent Garden) The Foster & Partners–designed ME London, at the southwestern curve where the Strand meets Aldwych, is all sophisticated and natty cool. All 157 rooms are super-neat, ultramodern and classy, with dizzy-making floor-to-ceiling windows; room 310 is a corner one with two. The 10th-floor Radio Rooftop Bar (p124) also has some of the best views in town from its alfresco terrace.

Terrace rooms on the 8th and 9th floors come with balcony. The light shows on the 1st-floor atrium lobby are wonderful.

HARD ROCK HOTEL HOTEL £££

Map p446 (0800 330 8089, 020-3808 0431; www.hardrockhotels.com/london; Great Cumberland Pl, W1; s/d/ste from £250/300/400;

; Marble Arch) Let the inner guitarist in you strum loud and free in this hotel refashioned from the landmark Cumberland that is 100% dedicated to rock and roll. Part of the eponymous bar/restaurant/shop chain, the 900-room hotel has a hangar-sized lobby crammed with rock artefacts – including Freddie Mercury's piano, a Jimi Hendrix guitar, a frock worn by Taylor Swift and Madonna's jacket.

And the guitar for that inner guitarist? They're available to borrow – complete with headsets, of course.

GRAZING GOAT
HOTEL £££

Map p446 (020-7724 7243; http://thegrazinggoat.co.uk; 6 New Quebec St, W1; d £210-250; ; Marble Arch) On an attractive little street lined with boutiques and cafes and a shopping bag's throw from Oxford St, this upmarket pub/restaurant has eight tasteful rooms in a contemporary country style with wood-panelled walls painted teal. All rooms have king-size beds, vintage-style DAB radios and iPod docks. Superior rooms are larger with bigger beds, bathtubs and fans.

NADLER SOHO
BOUTIQUE HOTEL £££

Map p440 (020-3697 3697; www.nadlerhotels.com/the-nadler-soho; 10 Carlisle St, W1; s/d/ste from £180/190/400; ; Tottenham Court Rd) In the heart of Soho, this 78-room boutique hotel is a sleek mix of creams, tans and blacks, with a good range of rooms, all with mini kitchens complete with microwave and fridge. (Room 14 has a bathtub.) Service is welcoming and smooth; guests are offered discounts at some two-dozen nearby bars and restaurants.

Hew Locke's winged sculpture *Selene* above the hotel entrance represents, appropriately enough, 'sleep'.

W LONDON LEICESTER SQUARE
LUXURY HOTEL £££

Map p440 (020-7758 1000; www.marriott.co.uk/hotels/travel/lonhw-w-london-leicester-square; 10 Wardour St, W1; r from £300; ; Leicester Sq) Everything at zany W has been designed to within an inch of its life – from the disco balls spelling out the floor numbers to the curved walls and furniture, to the cartoon cushions and the desk-cum-double-sink at the guest room entrance. The bold, retro red-and-gold themed decor is camp, but the 192-room W is more sophisticated than that.

There's a great in-house spa called Away and the fabulous Revolve Bar overlooking Leicester Sq and boasting the world's largest disco ball. 'Normal gets you nowhere', the neon sign above tells us.

★HAZLITT'S
HERITAGE HOTEL £££

Map p440 (020-7434 1771; www.hazlittshotel.com; 6 Frith St, W1; s/d/ste from £200/230/600; ; Tottenham Court Rd) Built in 1718 and comprising four original Georgian houses, this Soho gem was the one-time home of essayist William Hazlitt (1778–1830). The 30 guest rooms are furnished with original antiques from the appropriate era and boast a profusion of seductive details, including panelled walls, mahogany four-poster beds, antique desks, Oriental carpets, sumptuous fabrics and fireplaces in every room.

CLARIDGE'S
LUXURY HOTEL £££

Map p446 (020-7629 8860; www.claridges.co.uk; Brook St, W1; r/ste from £450/780; ; Bond St) Claridge's, with 203 rooms, is one of London's iconic five-star hotels. Celebrated for its sumptuous art-deco features (including 1930s vintage furniture that once graced the staterooms of the decommissioned SS *Normandie*), it has a series of more modern rooms and suites designed by David Linley, the Queen's nephew. The result is muted colours and elegant, classic furniture designs.

SOHO HOTEL
HOTEL £££

Map p440 (020-7559 3000; www.firmdalehotels.com/hotels/london/the-soho-hotel; 4 Richmond Mews, W1; r/ste from £380/585; ; Oxford Circus) The hipper-than-hip Soho Hotel has all the hallmarks of the eclectically chic duo Tim and Kit Kemp writ large over 94 individually fashioned guest rooms, each light-filled with floor-to-ceiling windows. Colours are soft, yet vivacious and creative, and the loving attention to design extends to a stunning black cat sculpture by Fernando Botero at the entrance.

45 PARK LANE
BOUTIQUE HOTEL £££

Map p446 (020-7493 4545; www.dorchestercollection.com/en/london/45-park-lane; 45 Park Lane, W1; r £600-900; ; Hyde Park Corner) Part of the upscale Dorchester Collection, this luxurious hotel's address alone is sufficiently evocative as a name, enjoying as it does one of the most prestigious locations in London. Staring down upon Hyde

Park, the 46 boutique rooms, suites and penthouse over nine floors come with king-size beds and marble bathrooms, and the hotel itself hosts art exhibitions.

BROWN'S HOTEL HISTORIC HOTEL £££

Map p448 (020-7493 6020; www.roccofortehotels.com/hotels-and-resorts/browns-hotel; 30 Albemarle St, W1; r/ste from £500/2000; ; Green Park) London's oldest hostelry, this landmark hotel was created in 1837 from 11 town houses. Each of the 115 rooms has been individually decorated by designer Olga Polizzi, and many feature antiques and original artworks. The public areas are lovely: the traditional **English Tea Room** is all Edwardian oak panelling and working fireplaces while the **Donovan Bar** has a stunning 19th-century stained-glass window.

The City

LONDON ST PAUL'S YHA HOSTEL £

Map p450 (020-7236 4965; www.yha.org.uk; 36 Carter Lane, EC4; dm/d from £20/70; ; St Paul's) Housed in the former boarding school for St Paul's Cathedral choir boys, this 213-bed hostel has notable period features, including Latin script in a band around the exterior. There's no kitchen, no lift and no en-suite rooms, but there is a comfortable lounge, a licensed cafe and all new beds with USB ports.

★CITIZENM TOWER OF LONDON DESIGN HOTEL ££

Map p450 (020-3519 4830; www.citizenm.com/destinations/london/tower-of-london-hotel; 40 Trinity Sq, EC3; r from £170; ; Tower Hill) Downstairs it looks like a rich hipster's living room, with well-stocked bookshelves, kooky art like Warhol's *Reigning Queens* and Beefeater bric-a-brac. The 370 rooms are compact but well-designed, with an iPad controlling curtains, the TV and even the shower lighting. It's worth paying an extra £20 for the extraordinary Tower views, although they're even better from the two-level 7th-floor bar.

APEX LONDON WALL HOTEL ££

Map p450 (020-7562 3030; www.apexhotels.co.uk; 7-9 Copthall Ave, EC2; r from £152; ; Bank) Given its position right in the heart of the financial district, it's unsurprising that this upmarket hotel – one of three Apexes in London – feels a tad corporate. On the upside, the staff are delightful, the 89 renovated rooms extremely comfortable, there's a small gym, prices drop substantially on the weekends, and you even get to take home a rubber ducky.

Room 226 looks to the rear of the building but is quite large. Some rooms have bathtubs.

MOTEL ONE LONDON-TOWER HILL HOTEL ££

Map p450 (020-7481 6420; www.motel-one.com; 24-26 Minories, EC3; s/d from £99/114; ; Aldgate) Part of a German chain, this almost budget option is just a short hop from the Tower of London. The 290 rooms are small but fully equipped, with a sleek contemporary design; room 311 has views of the City and two windows. If you feel a bit cramped, there's a large, stylish lounge bar downstairs.

★SOUTH PLACE HOTEL £££

Map p450 (020-3503 0000; www.southplacehotel.com; 3 South Pl, EC2; d/ste from £232/740; ; Moorgate) A hip, design-led hotel, South Place impresses at every turn. From the art-filled lobby and espionage-inspired theme (a Russian spy ring was once located in this area) to the Michelin-starred **Angler** (Map p450; 020-3215 1260; www.anglerrestaurant.com; L7, 3 South Pl, EC2; mains £32-38; noon-2.30pm & 6-10pm Mon-Sat, 6-10pm Sun) seafood restaurant and 80 beautifully laid-out rooms – every detail has been carefully considered. There are even cheeky hangover cures and sex kits alongside the British products in the luxurious minibar.

★THE NED HERITAGE HOTEL £££

Map p450 (020-3828 2100; www.thened.com; 27 Poultry, EC2; r £230-400;) What was until recently the Midland Bank, designed by Sir Edwin 'Ned' Lutyens in 1924, has metamorphosed into a splendid butterfly with 250 rooms over nine floors. Choose a 'Cosy' room (there are a dozen different types) facing Queen Victoria St. The Ned counts a full seven restaurants in the erstwhile Grand Banking Hall, where there is daily live music.

The spa with enormous swimming pool, sauna and hammam in the basement is a delight. Beg, borrow or steal to get into the Vaults lounge and its adjacent bar with 3000 original safe-deposit boxes.

CHEVAL THREE QUAYS APARTMENT £££
Map p450 (020-3725 5333; www.chevalresidences.com; 40 Lower Thames St, EC3; apt from £300; ; Tower Hill) Right at the doorstep of the Tower of London, these 97 spacious, modern apartments available for short stays have all the comforts of home, including full kitchen and laundry facilities. Those facing south – a total of 76 – have small balconies, providing the perfect perch for afternoon gin and tonics with the most extraordinary river views. Fitness room too.

South Bank

ST CHRISTOPHER'S VILLAGE LONDON BRIDGE HOSTEL £
Map p452 (020-7939 9710; www.st-christophers.co.uk; 161-165 Borough High St, SE1; dm/r incl breakfast from £10.50/60; ; London Bridge) This 349-bed party-zone hostel has modern bathrooms, pod beds with privacy curtains, reading lights, power sockets (British and European) and USB ports, and great common areas. Dorms have four to 33 beds (following the introduction of triple bunks); breakfast and linen are included. Oasis, the female-only wing of the hostel, is very popular, with dorms of up to 14 beds.

Its ground-floor pub, Belushi's, is a perennial favourite. The rooftop (3rd-floor) chill-out space is another magnet.

WALRUS HOSTEL £
Map p452 (020-7928 4368; www.thewalrusbarandhostel.com; 172 Westminster Bridge Rd, SE1; dm/d incl breakfast from £15/60; ; Waterloo) This little hostel with 68 beds gets top marks for trying so hard (and succeeding!) at creating a welcoming, individual, friendly and cosy place to stay. The corridors and stairs are on the shabby side, but the dorms (sleeping from four to 22) and bathrooms are spick and span. The downside is the noise from the street and railway.

★**CITIZENM LONDON BANKSIDE** BOUTIQUE HOTEL ££
Map p452 (020-3519 1680; www.citizenm.com/destinations/london/london-bankside-hotel; 20 Lavington St, SE1; r £109-325; ; Southwark) If citizenM had a motto, it would be 'Less fuss, more comfort'. The hotel has done away with things it considers superfluous like room service and reception and instead has gone all out on mattresses and bedding, and state-of-the-art technology (everything from mood lighting to TV is controlled through a tablet computer and you unlock the door with your phone).

★**HOXTON SOUTHWARK** HOTEL ££
Map p452 (020-7903 3000; https://thehoxton.com/london/southwark; Blackfriars Rd, SE1; r £140-300;) This latest feather in the now three-plumed Hoxton cap counts 192 retro-styled rooms (antique radios, rotary telephones) and fabulous artwork displayed in every nook and cranny. Like its sisters, the Hoxton Southwark offers stylish yet affordable accommodation in rooms that vary enormously in size and comfort; try Cosy room 419 or the even bigger Roomy 408 looking onto a churchyard.

The lobby bar is always buzzy but the destination outlet here is the rooftop Seabird bar and restaurant, with unmatchable views.

SHANGRI-LA HOTEL AT THE SHARD HOTEL £££
Map p452 (020-7234 8000; www.shangri-la.com/london/shangrila; 31 St Thomas St, SE1; d/ste from £500/1000; ; London Bridge) Unsurprisingly for a hotel occupying levels 34 to 52 of the Shard, there are breathtaking views everywhere you look in the 202-room Shangri-La: be it the floor-to-ceiling windows in the bedrooms, the panoramic bathrooms (you've never had such a good view while taking a bath), the Skypool, the bar or the restaurant. The decor is a stylish blend of Chinese influence and modern.

Kensington & Hyde Park

MEININGER HOSTEL £
Map p456 (020-3318 1407; www.meininger-hostels.com; Baden Powell House, 65-67 Queen's Gate, SW7; dm/s/tw from £16/60/72; ; Gloucester Rd, South Kensington) Housed in a 1959 building opposite the Natural History Museum, this 48-room German-run 'urban travellers' home' has spick-and-span rooms – most are dorms of between four and 12 beds, with podlike showers. There is also a handful of private rooms. It has

good security and nice communal facilities, including a bar and a big garden terrace on the 2nd floor.

ASTOR HYDE PARK HOSTEL £

Map p456 (☎020-7581 0103; www.astorhostels.com; 191 Queen's Gate, SW7; dm/d from £15/60; @📶; Ⓤ Gloucester Rd or High St Kensington) Wood-panelled walls, bay windows with leaded lights, plus a 19th-century vibe and a posh address just over from the Royal Albert Hall. This one-time hospital has 150 beds in rooms over five floors (no lift), including dorms with four to 15 beds, and a good kitchen and dining area and spacious lounge. The hostel only accepts guests over age 18.

All-you-can-eat breakfast is £1.

CHERRY COURT HOTEL B&B £

Map p456 (☎020-7828 2840; www.cherrycourthotel.co.uk; 23 Hugh St, SW1; s/d/tr/f £65/75/110/135; ❄📶👪; Ⓤ Victoria) The dozen brightly coloured rooms may be pocket-sized, but they're clean and tidy at this five-floor Victorian house hotel (no lift) with excellent rates for this part of town. The heartfelt welcome from the Patel family is a real bonus, as is the handy breakfast basket (fresh fruit, cereal bar and fruit juice), which you can eat in or take away.

Room 1 on the ground floor has a double and a single bed.

LUNA SIMONE HOTEL B&B ££

Map p456 (☎020-7834 5897; www.lunasimonehotel.com; 47-49 Belgrave Rd, SW1; s/d/tr/q from £85/100/165190; @📶👪; Ⓤ Pimlico) This central and very welcoming 36-room hotel is an excellent choice among the hotels along Belgrave Rd. Compact rooms come with clean showers, double-glazed windows and innocuous blonde-wood furniture. Twin room 7 has a balcony and looks to the street; quieter (and smaller) room 8 faces the back.

Luggage storage is free, but there is no lift. English breakfast included.

WINDERMERE HOTEL B&B ££

Map p456 (☎020-7834 5163; www.windermere-hotel.co.uk; 142-144 Warwick Way, SW1; s/d/tw/ from £145/175/185; ❄📶; Ⓤ Victoria) In a sparkling-white, mid-Victorian town house (with lift and renovated **Pimlico Grid** brasserie), the Windermere has 19 small but bright and individually designed rooms, all refurbished, and named (eg the Busby) with shower or bathroom. The hotel has been family-owned for more than three decades, service is exemplary and an English breakfast is included in the price.

★**LIME TREE HOTEL** BOUTIQUE HOTEL £££

Map p456 (☎020-7730 8191; www.limetreehotel.co.uk; 135-137 Ebury St, SW1; s/d/tr incl breakfast from £120/195/250; @📶; Ⓤ Victoria) Family-run for over three decades, this beautiful 28-room Georgian town house hotel is all comfort, British design and understated elegance. Rooms are individually decorated, many with open fireplaces, sash windows and lovely wooden floors. There is a delightful back garden for late-afternoon rays (picnics encouraged on summer evenings). Rates include a hearty full English breakfast. No lift.

★**NUMBER SIXTEEN** HOTEL £££

Map p456 (☎020-7589 5232; www.firmdalehotels.com/hotels/london/number-sixteen; 16 Sumner Pl, SW7; s/d from £200/300; ❄@📶👪🐾; Ⓤ South Kensington) With uplifting splashes of colour, choice art and a sophisticated-but-fun design ethos, Number Sixteen is simply ravishing. There are 41 individually designed rooms, a cosy drawing room, library and honesty bar. And wait till you see the idyllic, long back garden set around a pond stocked with koi, or sit down for breakfast in the light-filled conservatory.

ASTER HOUSE B&B £££

Map p456 (☎020-7581 5888; www.asterhouse.com; 3 Sumner Pl, SW7; s/d from £180/240; ❄@📶👪; Ⓤ South Kensington) The trump cards of this Victorian town house in South Kensington are its location and the charming welcome of its hosts. The plant-filled Orangerie is an atmospheric place for breakfast, and the decor is cosy and comfortable rather than overwhelming. Continental buffet breakfast included.

Room 5 looks onto the pretty back garden, room 17 to the quiet street.

ARTIST RESIDENCE BOUTIQUE HOTEL £££

Map p456 (☎020-3019 8610; www.artistresidencelondon.co.uk; 52 Cambridge St, SW1; r/ste from £185/540; ❄📶; Ⓤ Pimlico or Victoria) It's not cheap, but this superbly distinctive boutique Pimlico hotel elevates the concept of shabby chic to new heights: sporadic bare brick and each piece of furniture and decor individually sourced and crafted, from the reclaimed parquet floors and vintage furniture to retro Smeg fridges. All 10 rooms have rainforest showers – for grand free-standing baths, upgrade to the suites.

Room 5 faces to the back. The acme is the stunner Club Suite (room 4). No lift.

AMPERSAND HOTEL DESIGN HOTEL £££

Map p456 (☎020-7589 5895; https://ampersandhotel.com; 10 Harrington Rd, SW7; s/d from £170/£216; ; South Kensington) It feels light, fresh and bubbly in the Ampersand, where smiling staff wear denims, waistcoats and ties rather than impersonal dark suits. The common rooms are colourful and airy, and the 111 stylish guest rooms are decorated with wallpaper designs celebrating the nearby arts and sciences of South Kensington's museums.

Deluxe studio 117 has two large windows looking to the street and a separate shower and toilet.

GORE HOTEL £££

Map p456 (☎020-7584 6601; www.gorehotel.com; 190 Queen's Gate, SW7; r from £220; ; Gloucester Rd) With obliging staff in tails, twinkling chandeliers, walls crowded with framed portraits and prints, and enough wood-panelling to put paid to a sizeable chunk of prime woodland, this fantastic 50-room hotel wallows in old England charm. The suites are especially lavish (Judy Garland aficionados can sleep on her bed – shipped over from the US – in the namesake suite).

BLAKES HOTEL £££

Map p456 (☎020-7370 6701; www.blakeshotels.com; 33 Roland Gardens, SW7; d from £500; ; Gloucester Rd or South Kensington) Five Victorian houses cobbled into one hotel and incomparably designed by Anouska Hempel, Blakes oozes panache. Each of its 45 guest rooms is elegantly decked out in a distinctive, flamboyant style: expect four-poster beds (with and without canopies), rich fabrics, plenty of Asian influences, and antiques set on bleached hardwood floors.

Clerkenwell, Shoreditch & Spitalfields

DICTIONARY HOSTEL £

Map p458 (☎020-7613 2784; www.thedictionaryhostel.com; 10-20 Kingsland Rd, E2; dm/tw incl breakfast from £20/90; ; Shoreditch High St) Dressed in apian black, white and yellow, this none-too-salubrious 150-bed hostel sits right in the heart of Shoreditch's nightlife action. The four- to 12-bed dorms, sporting red metal bunks with lockable cages for storage, are pretty cramped; most are en suite or, if not, facilities are on the same landing. The location means that things can get noisy.

There's a female-only dorm on the 5th floor with eight beds per room, and a well-equipped kitchen in the basement. Guests get a 20% discount at the bar next door.

★HOXTON SHOREDITCH HOTEL ££

Map p458 (☎020-7550 1000; https://thehoxton.com/london/shoreditch/hotels; 81 Great Eastern St, EC2; r £109-260; ; Old St) In the heart of hip Shoreditch, this sleek hotel takes the low-cost airline approach to selling its rooms – book long enough ahead and you might pay just £109. The 210 renovated rooms are small but stylish, with flat-screen TVs, desks, fridges with complimentary bottled water and milk, and breakfast (orange juice, granola, yoghurt and banana) in a bag delivered to your door.

★CITIZENM LONDON SHOREDITCH DESIGN HOTEL ££

Map p458 (www.citizenm.com/destinations/london/london-shoreditch-hotel; 6 Holywell Lane, EC2; r £119-300; ; Shoreditch High St) CitizenM's winning combination of awesome interior design and a no-nonsense approach to luxury (yes to king-sized beds and high-tech pod rooms; no to pillow chocolates and room service) is right at home in Shoreditch. Rates at the 216 rooms are just right, and the convivial 24-hour lounge/bar/reception on the ground floor always seems to be on the right side of busy.

MALMAISON BUSINESS HOTEL ££

Map p458 (☎020-3750 9402; www.malmaison.com; 18-21 Charterhouse Sq, EC1; r £109-400; ; Farringdon) Facing a leafy square in Clerkenwell, this chic 97-room hotel in a converted nurses' residence revels in understated 1970s chic. The cocktail bar in the lobby is a centre of continental cool and the luminous subterranean restaurant is a delight. Prices vary considerably and can be much cheaper at weekends so check the web.

FOX & ANCHOR BOUTIQUE HOTEL ££

Map p458 (☎020-7250 1300; www.foxandanchor.com; 115 Charterhouse St, EC1; r/ste from £139/199; ; Farringdon or Barbican) A characterful option in a handy location above a glorious pub,

STUDENT DIGS

During university holidays (generally mid-March to late April, late June to September, and mid-December to mid-January), many student dorms and halls of residence are open to paying visitors. Choices include **LSE Vacations** (☎020-7955 7676; www.lsevacations.co.uk;), whose eight halls include **Bankside House** (Map p452; ☎020 7107 5750; www.lsevacations.co.uk/Accommodation/Bankside-House/Bankside-House.aspx; 24 Sumner St, SE1; s/tw/tr/q incl breakfast from £68/89/119/133; late Jun–Sep; ; Southwark) and **High Holborn Residence** (Map p438; ☎020-7107 5737; www.lsevacations.co.uk/Accommodation/High-Holborn/High-Holborn.aspx; 178 High Holborn, WC1; s/d from £50/90; ; Holborn). **King's Venues** (☎020-7848 1700; www.kingsvenues.com) handles six residences, including the centrally located **Great Dover Street Apartments** (☎020-7407 0068; www.kingsvenues.com; 165 Great Dover St, SE1; s from £55; Jul & Aug; ; Borough) and **Stamford Street Apartments** (Map p452; ☎020-7848 4664; www.kingsvenues.com; 127 Stamford St, SE1; s incl breakfast £57; Jun-Aug; ; Waterloo).

this delightful hotel offers just six small but sumptuous rooms, each individually decorated and many with roll-top zinc bathtubs. For the ultimate luxury, choose the Market Suite, which has a king-sized bed and its own private rooftop terrace.

ACE HOTEL DESIGN HOTEL ££

Map p458 (☎020-7613 9800; www.acehotel.com/london; 100 Shoreditch High St, E1; r £175-600; ; Shoreditch High St) Part of a small, seriously hip US chain, this 258-room hotel prides itself on creating a relaxed atmosphere while maintaining exacting standards. From the guitars, turntables and vinyl-record libraries in the deluxe rooms to the Pot Noodles and Yorkshire tea in the open minibar, there's a real sense of fun here. Sauna and gym too and four free-to-use bikes.

Choose room 121 for a view to the street, room 134 for a tub in the bathroom. The hotel's restaurant (Hoi Polloi), cafe (Bulldog Edition) and basement club (Miranda) are destinations in their own right, and the popular lobby offers a space to sit, with free wi-fi available to all.

★ROOKERY HERITAGE HOTEL £££

Map p458 (☎020-7336 0931; www.rookeryhotel.com; 12 Peter's Lane, Cowcross St, EC1; d/ste from £249/650; ; Farringdon) This charming warren of 33 rooms has been built within a row of 18th-century Georgian town houses and fitted out with period furniture (including a museum-piece collection of Victorian baths, showers and toilets), original wood panelling shipped over from Ireland and artwork selected by the owner. Highlights include the small courtyard garden and the library with its honesty bar and working fireplace.

ZETTER HOTEL BOUTIQUE HOTEL £££

(☎020-7324 4444; www.thezetter.com; St John's Sq, 86-88 Clerkenwell Rd, EC1; d from £210, studio £300-438; ; Farringdon) The Zetter Hotel is a temple of cool minimalism with an overlay of colourful kitsch on Clerkenwell's main thoroughfare. Built using sustainable materials on the site of a derelict office block, its 59 rooms are spacious for this area. The rooftop studios are the real treat, with terraces commanding superb views. There is a hot-drink station on every floor for guests' use.

East London

PARK VILLA HOSTEL £

Map p462 (☎020-8980 1439; www.parkvilla.co.uk; 51 Grove Rd, E3; dm/d from £21/57; ; Mile End) Styling itself as a 'new boutique hostel in the old East End', the 42-bed Park Vila (established 2014) is neither of the first two things, but it is clean, comfortable and is two minutes from Mile End Tube. It's in a three-storey Georgian villa; dorms, with sturdy wooden bunks and floors, have four to eight beds and there's a double.

We love the 'History of the East End' mural in the reception lobby. Breakfast, parking and towels cost extra (£3/10/1).

WOMBAT'S LONDON HOSTEL £

Map p462 (☎020-7680 7600; www.wombats-hostels.com/london; 7 Dock St, E1; dm/d from £17/90; ; Tower Hill) An ideal base from which to explore London's East End, this 700-bed hostel offers light and airy budget accommodation in a historical setting. With its vaulted brick ceiling, the enormous bar has a cosy atmosphere; the terrace, complete with hammocks, is ideal for lazy summer evenings.

EAST LONDON HOTEL HOTEL £

Map p462 (020-3146 1960; www.theeastlondonhotel.com; 309-317 Cambridge Heath Rd, E2; d £85-93; Undergound Bethnal Green) This excellent budget option with 161 rooms is a hop, skip and trampoline jump to/from London's hippest areas. Rooms are compact and not meant for lounging around; do that downstairs at the Due East cafe/bar. Some 10 of the rooms are windowless (eg room 111) but are sensitively designed and lighted.

Service is hands-off but efficient and mega-friendly.

QBIC DESIGN HOTEL £

Map p462 (020-3021 3300; https://qbichotels.com/london-city; 42 Adler St, E1; r £54-100; ; Aldgate East) There's a modern feel to this snappy hotel, with white tiling, neon signs, vibrant art and textiles and a pool table in the lobby. Its 171 rooms are sound-insulated, mattresses excellent and rainforest showers powerful. Prices vary widely depending on when you book, and the cheapest rooms are windowless.

AVO HOTEL £

Map p462 (020-3490 5061; www.avohotel.com; 82 Dalston Lane, E8; r from £69; ; Dalston Junction) Positioned above an Indian restaurant on busy Dalston Lane, this family-run boutique hotel is a surprising find. It has just six rooms, all with mango-wood furnishings, gleaming black-and-grey bathrooms, memory-foam mattresses, iPod docks and Elemis toiletries. Double-glazing keeps things quiet.

The only room on the ground floor – there is no lift – has a kitchenette.

★40 WINKS B&B ££

Map p462 (020-7790 0259; www.40winks.org; 109 Mile End Rd, E1; s/d/ste £115/185/280; ; Stepney Green) Short on space but not on style, this 300-year-old town house in Stepney Green oozes quirky charm. There are just two bedrooms (a double and a compact single) that share a bathroom – or you can book both as a spacious suite. Owned by a successful designer, the rooms are uniquely and extravagantly decorated with an expert's eye.

North London

★CLINK78 HOSTEL £

Map p466 (020-7183 9400; www.clinkhostels.com/london/clink78; 78 King's Cross Rd, WC1; dm/r from £16/65; ; King's Cross St Pancras) This fantastic 630-bed hostel is housed in a 19th-century magistrates' courthouse where Charles Dickens once worked as a scribe and members of the Clash stood trial in 1978. It features pod beds (including overhead storage space) in four- to 16-bed dormitories. There's a top kitchen with a huge dining area and a busy bar – Clash – in the basement.

Parts of the hostel are heritage listed, including six cells that have been converted

FEW-FRILLS CHAINS

London has various discount hotel chains that offer clean and modern – if somewhat institutional – accommodation for reasonable rates.

Days Hotel (www.wyndhamhotels.com) Just two branches in central London.

easyHotel (www.easyhotel.com) Functional, with orange-moulded-plastic rooms, some without windows; seven branches in London, including Luton and Heathrow airports.

Express by Holiday Inn (www.hiexpress.com) One of the more upmarket chains on this list, with 20 London branches.

Premier Inn (www.premierinn.com) Excellent local chain with 40 properties and generally high standards; also runs the **Hub** (www.hubhotels.co.uk) chain of even smaller rooms.

Travelodge (www.travelodge.co.uk) Serviceable rooms in dozens of properties but few public facilities.

into bedrooms and a pair of wood-panelled courtrooms used as a cinema and internet room. There are all-female dorms. You'll find an ATM in the lobby. Linen is included but breakfast (toast and spreads, cereal, juice, tea and coffee) costs £4 (£3 booked online).

LONDON ST PANCRAS YHA HOSTEL £
Map p466 (020-7388 9998; www.yha.org.uk; 79-81 Euston Rd, NW1; dm/tw from £16/80; ; King's Cross St Pancras) This hostel with 190 beds spread over eight floors has modern, clean dorms sleeping four to six (nearly all with private facilities) and some private rooms, including four en-suite doubles. The downside is the noise from busy Euston Rd, but it is convenient to everything. There's a small bar and cafe, but no self-catering facilities.

MEGARO BOUTIQUE HOTEL ££
Map p466 (020-7843 2222; www.themegaro.co.uk; 1 Belgrove St, WC1; d/f from £120/195; ; King's Cross St Pancras) Now under new management, the Megaro has 49 indulgently large rooms, lovely decor, in-room creature comforts (espresso machines, fresh milk, rainforest showerheads), attentive service and an excellent bar-restaurant. There is some noise from the street, so if you're a light sleeper, go high (eg room 603) or towards the back (room 310).

GYLE BOUTIQUE HOTEL ££
Map p466 (020-3301 0333; www.thegyle.co.uk; 16-18 Argyle Sq, WC1; d/ste from £159/220; ; King's Cross St Pancras) This lovely boutique hotel in a Georgian terrace house overlooking leafy Argyle Sq feels almost as if it had been dropped into the countryside yet it's seconds from King's Cross and St Pancras stations. The public areas are zany, with a light-filled bar with a textured green baize ceiling and walls, and Archie the Scottish terrier (real or imagined?) is everywhere.

GREAT NORTHERN HOTEL HISTORIC HOTEL £££
Map p466 (020-3388 0800; www.gnhlondon.com; King's Cross Station, Pancras Rd, N1; r from £180; ; King's Cross St Pancras) Built as the world's first railway hotel in 1854, the GNH is now an 88-room boutique hotel in a classic style reminiscent of luxury sleeper trains. Exquisite artisanship is in evidence everywhere. And in addition to the two lively bars and a restaurant, there's a 'pantry' on every floor, from which you can help yourself to hot or cold drinks and snacks.

Rooms come in three categories: the small Couchette (room 305); Wainscot (room 515) with dark mahogany panelling; and the bright Cubitt (room 322) with views of King's Cross Station. Guests have access to a nearby gym with large swimming pool.

YORK & ALBANY BOUTIQUE HOTEL £££
Map p468 (020-7387 5700; www.gordonramsayrestaurants.com/york-and-albany; 127-129 Parkway, NW1; d/ste incl breakfast from £175/305; ; Camden Town) Luxurious yet cosy, the York & Albany, owned by TV chef Gordon Ramsay, oozes Georgian charm. Many of the nine rooms have feature fireplaces, antique furniture, beautiful floor-to-ceiling windows, lush bathrooms (with underfloor heating) and Egyptian-cotton bed linen. We love the four-poster bed and sunken bathroom in room 5.

ST PANCRAS RENAISSANCE HOTEL LONDON LUXURY HOTEL £££
Map p466 (020-7841 3540; www.stpancrasrenaissance.co.uk; Euston Rd, NW1; d from £250; ; King's Cross St Pancras) Housed in the former Midland Grand Hotel, a red-brick Gothic Victorian marvel designed by Sir George Gilbert Scott in 1873, the St Pancras Renaissance counts 245 rooms but only 38 of them are in the original building, and only one, the architect's namesake suite, is restored to its Victorian design. The rest are in an extension at the back and rather bland.

West London

SAFESTAY HOLLAND PARK HOSTEL £
Map p472 (020-7870 9626; www.safestay.com/london-kensington-holland-park; Holland Walk, W8; dm/r from £11/70; ; High St Kensington, Holland Park) This upbeat and well-run place has taken over a long-serving YHA hostel with more than 300 beds. With a bright (fuchsia) and bold design, the hostel has dorm rooms with four to 21 bunk beds and twins with a single bunk, free wi-fi in the lobby and a fabulous location in the Jacobean east wing of Holland House in Holland Park (p274).

There's a large and very comfortable bar and restaurant downstairs with mains from £6, a pool room and garden.

LONDON HOUSE HOTEL HOTEL £

Map p470 (020-7243 1810; www.londonhousehotels.com; 81 Kensington Gardens Sq, W2; d £80-160; Bayswater) This good-value, snappy-looking hotel in a rather grand Regency-style building looks over Kensington Gardens Sq. The 103 rooms may be on the small side, but each is clean and pleasantly furnished, while the setting is peaceful if not terribly convenient. The best rooms have views out to the leafy square.

YHA EARL'S COURT HOSTEL £

Map p472 (0345 371 9114; www.yha.org.uk/hostel/london-earls-court; 38 Bolton Gardens, SW5; dm/tw/tr/q from £17/59/69/119; Earl's Court) There's some lovely original tiling on the floor as you enter this fine old property on a quiet, leafy street in Earl's Court, although most other period detailing has disappeared. Most accommodation (186 beds) is in clean, airy dormitories of between four and 10 metal bunk beds. Common areas are spacious, showers and toilets clean and staff helpful.

POINT A HOTEL HOTEL £

Map p470 (020-7258 3140; www.pointahotels.com; 41 Praed St, W2; r £70-150; Paddington) This 137-room budget hotel offers super-duper rates for early birds who book in advance. Everything is clean as a whistle, and staff are efficient (if a titch officious). Check-out time is 11am. There are extras if you want them, such as daily room cleaning, early check-in (from noon) and late check-out (till 2pm; £20). There are six other branches in London.

ST JAMES BACKPACKERS HOSTEL HOSTEL £

Map p472 (07450 645573; www.saint-james-hostel.co.uk; 21 Longridge Rd, SW5; dm/d £20/70; Earl's Court) One of the oldest hostels in London, the 11-bed St James Backpackers has been providing budget accommodation in the Earl's Court neighbourhood for almost 50 years. There are both private rooms and shared dormitories of four to eight beds, as well as a communal kitchen. Friendly reception.

GARDEN COURT HOTEL HOTEL £

Map p470 (020-7229 2553; www.gardencourthotel.co.uk; 30-31 Kensington Gardens Sq, W2; s/d/tr/q from £40/50/65/75; Bayswater) The very tidy 40-room Garden Court is a reliable choice for its price and location. The decor is simple, with decorative wallpaper and basic furniture. Prices can dip as low as £40 per night during the slack season. The three cheapest singles are quite small and not en suite, but have a private shower room outside the room.

NEW LINDEN HOTEL BOUTIQUE HOTEL ££

Map p470 (020-7221 4321; www.newlinden.co.uk; 59 Leinster Sq, W2; s/d from £90/128; Bayswater) The Buddha bust in the lobby sets the zen tone for this light, airy and beautifully designed option located between Westbourne Grove and Notting Hill. Some of the 50 rooms (eg room 108 with a small balcony) are on the small side due to the Georgian building's quirky layout, but they feel cosy rather than cramped. Staff are charming too.

Check out the gorgeous wooden door leading to the lounge. There's a lift.

★**MAIN HOUSE** GUESTHOUSE ££

Map p470 (020-7221 9691; www.themainhouse.co.uk; 6 Colville Rd, W11; ste £130-150; Ladbroke Grove, Notting Hill Gate, Westbourne Park) The four delightful suites at this peach of a Victorian mid-terrace house make the Main House a superb choice. The bright and spacious rooms come with large bathrooms and endless tea and coffee. Cream of the crop is the uppermost suite, occupying the entire top floor. There's no sign, but look for the huge letters 'SIX'. Minimum three-night stay.

★**BARCLAY HOUSE** B&B ££

Map p472 (07767 420943; www.barclayhouselondon.com; 21 Barclay Rd, SW6; s/d from £125/140; Fulham Broadway) The three dapper, thoroughly modern and comfy bedrooms in this shipshape Victorian house are a dream, from the Philippe Starck showers, walnut furniture, double-glazed sash windows and underfloor heating to the thoughtful details (fumble-free coat hangers, drawers packed with sewing kits, plasters and maps). The cordial, music-loving owners – bursting with tips and handy London knowledge – concoct an inclusive, homely atmosphere.

STYLOTEL HOTEL ££

Map p470 (020-7723 1026; www.stylotel.com; 160-162 Sussex Gardens, W2; s/d/tr/q £85/120/140/160, ste from £165; Paddington) The crisp industrial design – scored aluminium treads, opaque coloured glass, riveted stainless steel, metal bed frames – of this 50-room niche hotel is contemporary and upbeat. Elbow room is at a premium in some: 'stylorooms' are small, but the largely carpet-free floor surfaces help keep things dapper. The larger fully automated 'awesome stylorooms' in the new wing have fabulous bathrooms.

Still more spacious and swish are the eight 'stylosuites' above the Sussex Arms pub around the corner. Free tea and coffee in the lounge, and the location near Paddington train station is excellent.

MELROSE GARDENS B&B ££

Map p472 (020-7603 1817; www.staylondonbandb.co.uk; 29 Melrose Gardens, W6; s/tw/d £80/105/120; ; Goldhawk Rd) Ideal for those seeking peace and a sedate tempo, this charming B&B is run from a typical Victorian family home. Everything is in its right place. It's overseen by cordial hosts Su and Martin, who are quick to dispense handy London info. The only room with its own bathroom is the Master Double at the very top (no lift).

The other two rooms – a twin and a single – share one bathroom and look out over the small back garden.

SPACE APART HOTEL HOTEL ££

Map p470 (020-7908 1340; www.aparthotel-london.co.uk; 36-37 Kensington Gardens Sq, W2; apt £120-220; ; Bayswater or Royal Oak) Light, bright, spic-and-span double and triple studio apartments with kitchenette at eye-catching rates. This converted 30-room Georgian building is neatly designed and provides a handy and affordable stay not far from the Notting Hill action. The studios are not big, but for around £20 you can upgrade to a roomier double studio. Rather reserved staff.

TWENTY NEVERN SQUARE HOTEL ££

Map p472 (020-7565 9555; www.20neversquare.co.uk; 20 Nevern Sq, SW5; r incl breakfast from £90; ; Earl's Court) Each of the 20 rooms is different at this elegant and stylish four-floor brick hotel overlooking a lovely square. Cosy, but not especially large, rooms like room 6 (with its own staircase) are decorated with Asian-style woodwork, imposing carved-wood beds (some four-poster), venetian blinds and heavy fabrics. Some rooms have bath, others shower; suite 5 has both.

There is a gorgeous conservatory where breakfast is served and a tiny patio and (gratefully) a lift.

VANCOUVER STUDIOS APARTMENT ££

Map p470 (020-7243 1270; www.vancouverstudios.co.uk; 30 Prince's Sq, W2; apt £97-350; ; Bayswater) Everyone will feel at home in this appealing terrace of stylish and affordable studios, with a restful and charming walled garden. Some 47 well maintained rooms contain kitchenettes but otherwise differ wildly – ranging from tiny but well-equipped singles and smallish twins (eg room 14) to seven family rooms and a spacious three-bedroom apartment that sleeps up to six.

LA SUITE WEST DESIGN HOTEL ££

Map p470 (020-7313 8484; www.lasuitewest.com; 41-51 Inverness Tce, W2; r £129-279; ; Bayswater) The black-and-white foyer of the Anouska Hempel–designed La Suite West – bare walls, a minimalist slit of a fireplace, a stark white-marble reception desk – presages the OCD neatness of 79 rooms hidden down dark corridors. The straight lines, spotless surfaces and sharp angles are accentuated by impeccable bathrooms and softened by comfortable beds and warm service.

Downstairs suites have gardens and individual gated entrances.

K + K HOTEL GEORGE BOUTIQUE HOTEL £££

Map p472 (020-7598 8700; www.kkhotels.com; 1-15 Templeton Pl, SW5; s/d from £200/230; ; Earl's Court) From the niftily designed, wide-open foyer to the joyfully huge garden with its glorious lawn, this tidy 154-room boutique hotel just round the corner from Earl's Court Tube station has smallish rooms, but they are attractively presented, comfy and come with neat shower or bath. It has a snazzy bar, helpful service throughout, and soft colours.

Greenwich & South London

SAFESTAY LONDON ELEPHANT & CASTLE HOSTEL £

Map p476 (020-7703 8000; www.safestay.com/london-elephant-castle; 144-152 Walworth Rd, SE17; dm/d from £15/75; ; Elephant & Castle) The one-time Labour Party headquarters in an 18th-century Georgian building has been stunningly renovated: inside, it's all purple and magenta stripes and bright lights, though the 91 rooms are more sober. Most dorms (sleeping four to 12) are en suite as are the private rooms for up to three. There's an enormous bar/lounge with parties most nights.

MITRE B&B ££

Map p477 (020-8293 0037; www.themitregreenwich.co.uk; 291 Greenwich High Rd, SE10; d £119-149; Cutty Sark) This centrally located pub in Greenwich next door to the landmark St Alfege Church (1718) counts two-dozen large rooms and suites on the upper floors, with modern bathrooms but limited furnishings. Public areas for residents are no great shakes but there's a little garden and the pub with a large range of brews, decent food and live music some nights.

BERMONDSEY SQUARE HOTEL BOUTIQUE HOTEL ££

(020-7378 2450; www.bermondseysquarehotel.co.uk; Bermondsey Sq, Tower Bridge Rd, SE1; r/ste from £107/300; London Bridge or Borough) Just the ticket for Bermondsey is this hip purpose-built 90-room design hotel. Rooms are spacious and comfortable, if a little simple in decor. The terrace rooms on the 1st floor, featuring large terraces, and the pricier suites on the top floor, with their colour themes, king-sized beds and balconies, have the wow factor.

CHURCH STREET HOTEL HOTEL ££

(020-7703 5984; www.churchstreethotel.com; 29-33 Camberwell Church St, SE5; s/d/tr from £88/128/188; Denmark Hill) One of London's more unusual themed hotels, this vibrant (though somewhat chaotically run) 28-room establishment is a much-needed shot of tequila into the dull hotel landscape of south London. Done up in a Latin American theme, the hotel brims with colour; the tiled bathrooms will perk up anyone's day. The smallest rooms are 'off suite' (share bathrooms). Be warned: it's very off-the-beaten track.

KENNINGTON B&B B&B ££

Map p476 (020-7735 7669; stay@kenningtonbandb.com; 103 Kennington Park Rd, SE11; d £120-150; Kennington) With gorgeous bed linen, well-preserved Georgian features and just seven rooms and a suite, this lovely B&B in an 18th-century house is tasteful in every regard, from the shining, tiled shower rooms and Georgian shutters to the fireplaces and cast-iron radiators. Not all rooms are en suite, but each has a private shower room. Pretty back garden.

Richmond, Kew & Hampton Court

★PETERSHAM HOTEL ££

Map p478 (020-8940 7471; www.petershamhotel.co.uk; Nightingale Lane, TW10; s/d £120/175, riverview ste from £270; Richmond, Richmond) Neatly perched on sloping Richmond Hill leading across Petersham Meadows towards the Thames, the impressive four-star Petersham offers stunning Arcadian views at every turn. And its restaurant, with its voluminous windows gazing down to the river, offers some choice panoramas. The 58 rooms are classically styled but those with good river views are dearer. Take bus 65 from Richmond train or tube stations.

BINGHAM RIVERHOUSE BOUTIQUE HOTEL £££

Map p478 (020-8940 0902; www.binghamriverhouse.com; 61-63 Petersham Rd, TW10; s/d £195/210; Richmond, Richmond) Just upriver from Richmond Bridge, this lovely Georgian-style town house dating from 1865 is an enticing escape from central London, with 15 very elegant and well-presented rooms – all of them recently restyled. Riverside rooms are naturally pricier, but worth it, as roadside rooms (although deliciously devised and double-glazed) look out over busy Petersham Rd.

PHOTO.UA/SHUTTERSTOCK ©

Understand London

History

London's history is a long and turbulent journey spanning more than two millennia. Along the way there have been good times (the arrival of the Romans, for example, with their wine, law and order, and road-building skills and the expansion of London as the capital of an empire) and bad times (apocalyptic plagues, the Great Fire of 1666 and the Blitz carpet bombing of WWII). But even when down on its knees, London has always been able to get up, dust itself off and move on, constantly reinventing itself along the way.

Londinium

London was settled by the Romans, and the area, particularly the City of London, has been inhabited continuously ever since. As a result, archaeologists have had to dig deep to discover the city's past, relying more often than not on redevelopment such as the Crossrail high-frequency railway line to allow excavations.

But the Romans were not the first on the block here. The Iron Age Celts had arrived in Britain sometime in the 4th century BCE and settled around a ford in the Thames. The river was twice as wide as it is today and probably served as a barrier separating tribal groups.

When the Romans first visited in the 1st century BCE, they traded with the Celts. In 43 CE, an invasion force led by Emperor Claudius established the port of Londinium, the first real settlement at what is now London, and used it as a springboard to subdue Celtic strongholds. They constructed a wooden bridge across the Thames near today's London Bridge, and this became the focal point for a network of roads fanning out around the region.

The settlement's development as a trading centre was interrupted in 60 or 61 CE when an army led by Boudica, queen of the Celtic Iceni tribe based in East Anglia, exacted violent retribution on the Romans, who had attacked her kingdom, flogged her and raped her daughters. The Iceni overran Camulodunum (now Colchester in Essex), which had become the capital of Roman Britannia, and then turned on Londinium,

TIMELINE

55–54 BCE

Roman Emperor Julius Caesar makes a fast-paced and poorly planned visit to Britain and returns empty-handed – though the Senate declares a celebration that lasts 20 days.

43 CE

The Romans, led by Emperor Claudius, invade Britain; they mix with the local Celtic tribespeople and will stay for almost four centuries.

47–50

A defensive fort at Londinium is built. The name Londinium was probably taken from a Celtic place name (a common Roman practice), but there is no evidence as to what it actually means.

massacring its inhabitants and razing the settlement before the Romans defeated them.

The Romans rebuilt Londinium around Cornhill, the highest elevation north of the bridge, between 80 and 90 CE. About a century later they wrapped a defensive wall some 2.7m thick and 6m high around it. Towers were added to strengthen it, and the four original gates – Aldgate, Ludgate, Newgate and Bishopsgate – are remembered as place names even today in London. By then Londinium, a centre for business and trade but not a fully fledged *colonia* (settlement), was an imposing city with a massive basilica where official functions took place, an amphitheatre, a forum and a governor's palace.

By the middle of the 3rd century, Londinium was home to some 30,000 people of various ethnic groups, with temples dedicated to a large number of cults. When Emperor Constantine converted to Christianity in 312, the fledgling religion became the empire's – and London's – official cult, seeing off its closest rival, Mithraism.

In the 4th century, the Roman Empire in Britain began to decline, with increasing attacks by the Picts and Scotti in the north, and the Saxons, Germanic tribes originating from north of the Rhine, in the east and southeast. In 410, when the embattled Emperor Honorius cut off their military aid, the Romans abandoned Britain, and Londinium was reduced to a sparsely populated backwater.

They say that if you dig deep enough in the City of London you'll find a layer of rubble and soft red ash dating from the great conflagration brought about by Boudica's attack on Roman Londinium.

Lundenwic

What happened to Londinium after the Roman withdrawal remains the subject of much historical debate. While there is no written record of the town between 457 and 604, most historians now think that Romano-Britons continued to live here even as Saxon settlers established farmsteads and small villages in the area.

Lundenwic (or 'London settlement') was established outside the city walls west of Londinium and around present-day Aldwych and Charing Cross as a Saxon trade settlement. By the early 7th century the Saxons had been converted to Christianity by the pope's emissary St Augustine. Lundenwic was an episcopate and the first St Paul's Cathedral was established on Ludgate Hill.

This infant trading community grew in importance and attracted the attention of the Vikings in Denmark. They launched a vicious attack in 842 and again nine years later, burning Lundenwic to the ground. Under the leadership of King Alfred the Great of Wessex, the Saxon population fought back, driving the Danes out in 886.

Saxon London grew into a well-organised and prosperous town divided into 20 wards, each with its own alderman, and resident colonies

122

Emperor Hadrian pays a visit to Londinium and many impressive municipal buildings are constructed. Roman London reaches its peak, with temples, bathhouses, a fortress and a port.

190–225

London Wall is constructed around Londinium after outsiders breach Hadrian's Wall to the north. The wall encloses an area of just 132 hectares and is 6m high.

London Wall (p380)

597

Ethelbert, the first English monarch to convert to Christianity, welcomes St Augustine and his 40 missionaries to Canterbury, ensuring that city's religious supremacy.

of German merchants and French vintners. But attacks by the Danes continued apace, and the Saxon leadership was weakening; in 1016 Londoners were forced to accept the Danish leader Knut (or Cnut) as king of England.

With the death of Knut's brutal son Harthacanute in 1042, the throne passed to the Saxon Edward the Confessor, so named for his piety, who went on to found the palace and abbey at Westminster. When Edward moved his court to Westminster, a division of the city's labour began that would continue to this day: the port (or City) became the trading and mercantile centre of London, with Westminster its seat of justice and administration.

The Normans

Hidden London (http://hidden-london.com) explores and brings London's obscure attractions, curiosities, districts and localities out into the open, with some fascinating historical nuggets and details thrown in.

The year 1066 marks the real birth of England as a unified nation state. After the death of Edward the Confessor in January, a dispute over who would take the English throne spelled disaster for the Saxon kings. Harold Godwinson, the Earl of Wessex, was anointed successor by Edward on his deathbed, but this enraged William, the Duke of Normandy, who claimed that Edward had promised him the throne. William mounted a massive invasion of England from France and on 14 October defeated Harold at the Battle of Hastings, before marching on London to claim his prize. The newly dubbed 'William the Conqueror' was crowned king of England in the new Westminster Abbey on 25 December 1066, ensuring the Norman conquest was complete.

William distrusted the 'vast and fierce populace' of London, and to overawe and intimidate his new subjects (as well as protect himself from them), he built 10 castles within a day's march of each other, including the White Tower, the core of the Tower of London, and a motte and bailey castle at Windsor. Cleverly, he kept the prosperous merchants on side by confirming the City's independence in exchange for taxes. London, counting about 18,000 people, would soon become the principal town of England.

Medieval London

The last of the Norman kings, the ineffectual Stephen, died in 1154, and the throne passed to Henry II, founder of the powerful House of Plantagenet, which would rule England for the next two centuries. Henry's successors were happy to let the City of London keep its independence as long as its merchants continued to finance their wars and building projects. When his son Richard I (known as 'the Lionheart'), a king who spent a mere six months of his life in England, needed funds for

c 600

The Saxon trade settlement of Lundenwic (literally 'London settlement') is formed to the west of Roman Londinium.

604

The first Christian cathedral dedicated to St Paul is built on Ludgate Hill, the site of the current (and fifth) cathedral; it burns down in 675 and is rebuilt a decade later.

842

Vikings attack and burn London to the ground; a period of great struggle between the kingdoms of Wessex and the Danes begins for control of the Thames.

886

King Alfred the Great, first king of all England, reclaims London for the Saxons from the Vikings and founds a new settlement within the walls of the old Roman town.

his crusade to the Holy Land, he recognised the city as a self-governing commune in return for cash.

A city built on trade and commerce, London would always guard its independence fiercely, as Richard's brother and successor, King John, learned the hard way. In 1215 John was forced to cede power to his barons, and to curb his arbitrary demands for pay-offs from the City. Among those pressing him to put his seal to the watershed Magna Carta, which effectively diluted royal power, was the by then powerful lord mayor of the City of London; the first holder of this position, Henry FitzAylwin, had taken office just a quarter-century before.

Fire was a constant hazard in the cramped and narrow houses and lanes of 14th-century London, but disease caused by unsanitary living conditions and impure drinking water sourced from the Thames was the greater threat. In 1348 rats on ships from Europe brought the Black Death, a bubonic plague that wiped out almost half the population of about 70,000 over the next year and a half.

With their numbers down, there was growing unrest among labourers, for whom violence became a way of life, and rioting was commonplace. In 1381, miscalculating – or just disregarding – the mood of the nation, the young Richard II tried to impose another poll tax on everyone in the realm four years after the first. Tens of thousands of peasants in Kent and Essex, led by the ex-soldier Wat Tyler and the prelate Jack Straw, marched in protest on London. The Archbishop of Canterbury, Simon Sudbury, was dragged from the Tower and beheaded, several ministers were murdered and many buildings were razed before the Peasants' Revolt ran its course and its leaders were executed.

London gained wealth and stature under the Houses of Lancaster and York in the 15th century, but their struggle for ascendancy led to the catastrophic Wars of the Roses. The century's greatest episode of political intrigue occurred during this time: in 1483 the 12-year-old Edward V of the House of York reigned for only two months before vanishing with his younger brother into the Tower of London, never to be seen again. Whether or not their uncle, Richard III – who became the next king – murdered the boys has been the subject of much conjecture over the centuries. (Shakespeare would have us believe Richard committed the evil deed.) In 1674, workers found a chest containing the skeletons of two children near the White Tower, which were assumed to be the princes' remains, and they were reburied in Westminster Abbey.

Richard III didn't have long in the driver's seat: he was killed in 1485 at the Battle of Bosworth by Henry Tudor, who as Henry VII became the first monarch of the House of Tudor. In September 2012, Richard's remains, confirmed by rigorous DNA tests, were excavated beneath a

The winds of change were still blowing a quarter of a century after the Norman Conquest when the Great London Tornado of 1091 swept through the town, destroying much of the original church of St Mary-le-Bow, the wooden London Bridge and countless houses.

1016

The Danes return to London, and Knut is crowned king of England, ushering in two decades of relative peace.

1066

After defeating King Harold at the Battle of Hastings, William, Duke of Normandy (later William the Conqueror), is crowned king in Westminster Abbey.

1078

William builds 10 castles within a day's march of London (including the Tower of London and Windsor), first in earth and timber and later in stone.

1097

William Rufus, son of William the Conqueror, begins the construction of Westminster Hall. The hall, possibly the largest in Europe at the time, is completed in two years.

car park in central Leicester. They were laid to rest with great ceremony in that city's cathedral in March 2015.

The Tudor Dynasty

Though the House of Tudor lasted less than 120 years and just three generations, it is the best-known English dynasty. London became one of the largest and most important cities in Europe under its kings and queens, the Americas were discovered and colonised, and world trade thrived.

Henry's son and successor, Henry VIII, was the most extravagant of the clan, constructing new palaces at Whitehall and St James's, and bullying his lord chancellor, Cardinal Thomas Wolsey, into handing over Hampton Court.

The first stone London Bridge was completed in 1209, although it was frequently too crowded to cross and most people traversed the river on a small boat called a wherry. The current bridge was completed in 1972.

Henry's life was dominated by the need to produce a male heir, which indirectly led to his split with the Roman Catholic Church. This occurred in 1534 after the Pope refused to annul his marriage to Catherine of Aragon, who had borne him only a daughter after 25 years of marriage. Turning his back on Rome, he made himself the supreme head of the church in England and married Anne Boleyn, the second of his six wives. He 'dissolved' (abolished) London's monasteries, seized the church's vast wealth and property, and smashed ecclesiastical culture. Many of the religious houses disappeared, leaving only their names in such areas as Whitefriars, Blackfriars and Greyfriars (after the colour of the robes worn by Carmelite, Dominican and Franciscan monks).

Despite his penchant for settling differences with the axe (two of his six wives and Wolsey's replacement as lord chancellor, Thomas More, were beheaded, along with 32 other leaders and up to 72,000 others) and his persecution of both Catholics and fellow Protestants who didn't toe the line, Henry VIII remained a popular monarch until his death in 1547. The reign of Mary I, his daughter by Catherine of Aragon, saw a brief return to Catholicism, during which time the queen sanctioned the burning to death of 200 Protestants at Smithfield and earned herself the nickname 'Bloody Mary'. By the time Elizabeth I, Henry VIII's daughter with Anne Boleyn, took the throne, Catholicism was a waning force, and hundreds of people who dared to suggest otherwise were carted off to the gallows at Tyburn near today's Marble Arch.

Elizabethan London

The 45-year reign (1558–1603) of Elizabeth I is still looked upon as a 'golden age' in England, and it was just as significant for London. During these four and a half decades, English literature reached new and still unbeaten heights, and religious tolerance gradually became

1170

Archbishop of Canterbury Thomas Becket, born in Ironmongers Lane and known as Thomas of London in his lifetime, is murdered by four of Henry II's knights.

HULTON ARCHIVE/GETTY IMAGES ©

1215

King John signs the Magna Carta (literally 'Great Charter'), an agreement with his barons that forms the basis of constitutional law in England.

1290

King Edward I issues an edict expelling all Jews from England; the banishment will remain in effect until Oliver Cromwell comes to power more than 360 years later.

accepted doctrine, although Catholics and some Protestants still faced persecution. After defeating the Spanish Armada in 1588, England became a naval superpower, and the city established itself as the premier world trade market with the official opening of the Royal Exchange by Elizabeth in 1570.

London was blooming economically and physically: by the end of the 16th century the population had more than doubled to 200,000. The first recorded map of London was published in 1558, and John Stow produced *A Survey of London*, the first history of the city, in 1598.

This was also the golden era of English drama, and the works of William Shakespeare, Christopher Marlowe and Ben Jonson packed new playhouses like the Rose (built in 1587), the Swan (1596) and the Globe (1599). They were in Southwark, a notoriously ribald place at the time, teeming with 'stews' (vapour baths but brothels in reality) and bawdy taverns. Most importantly, they were outside the jurisdiction of the City, which frowned upon such pursuits and even banned theatre.

When Elizabeth died without an heir in 1603, she was succeeded by her second cousin, who was crowned James I. Although the son of the Catholic Mary, Queen of Scots (not to be confused with Elizabeth's half-sister Mary I), whom Elizabeth had executed for supposedly plotting against her, James was slow to improve conditions for England's Catholics and drew their wrath. He narrowly escaped death when the alleged plot by Guy Fawkes and his co-conspirators to blow up the Houses of Parliament on 5 November 1605 was uncovered. The discovery of the audacious plan is commemorated on this date each year with bonfires and fireworks.

In order to raise money to build ships and develop England's ports, Elizabeth I held the world's first national lottery in 1567, with an unheard-of top prize of £5000 (equivalent to £2.6 million today). Tickets cost 10 shillings, and the draw took place next to Old St Paul's Cathedral.

The Civil Wars & Restoration

When James I's son, Charles I, came to the throne in 1625, his intransigent personality and total belief in the 'divine right of kings' set the monarchy on a collision course with an increasingly confident parliament at Westminster and a City of London tiring of extortionate taxation. The crunch came when Charles tried to arrest five antagonistic members of parliament, who had fled to the City. By 1642 the country had slid into civil war.

The Puritans (extremist Protestants) and the city's expanding merchant class threw their support behind Oliver Cromwell, leader of the Parliamentarians nicknamed 'Roundheads', who battled the Royalist troops (called the Cavaliers). London firmly backed the Roundheads, and Charles I was defeated in 1646, although a Second Civil War (1648–49) and a Third Civil War (1649–51) continued to wreak havoc on what had been a stable and prosperous nation.

1348

Rats on ships from Europe bring the so-called Black Death, a bubonic plague that wipes out up to half of the city's population of about 70,000 and returns several times until 1375.

1455

The Wars of the Roses between two houses of the Plantagenet Dynasty – Lancaster (red rose) and York (white rose) – erupts and rages on for more than three decades.

1476

William Caxton, a prominent merchant from Kent, establishes his press near Westminster Abbey, printing more than 90 volumes of works.

1558

The first detailed map of London is produced by land surveyor and cartographer Ralph Agas; a golden age of peace, art and literature begins as Queen Elizabeth I ascends the throne.

Charles I was beheaded for treason outside Banqueting House in Whitehall on 30 January 1649, famously asking for a second shirt on the cold morning of his execution so as not to shiver and appear cowardly. Cromwell ruled the country as a quasi-republic for 11 years, during which time Charles' son, Charles II, continued fighting for the restoration of the monarchy. During this period Cromwell banned theatre, dancing, Christmas and just about anything remotely fun.

After Cromwell's death in 1658, parliament decided that the royals weren't so bad after all, refused to recognise the authority of Cromwell's successor, his son Richard, and restored the exiled Charles II to the throne in 1660.

Plague & Fire

Crowded, filthy London had suffered from recurrent outbreaks of bubonic plague since the 14th century, but nothing had prepared it for the Great Plague of 1665, which dwarfed all previous outbreaks.

As the plague spread, families affected were forced to stay inside for 40 days' quarantine, until the victim had either recovered or died. Previously crowded streets were deserted, churches and markets were closed, and an eerie silence descended. To make matters worse, the mayor believed that dogs and cats were the spreaders of the plague and ordered them all killed, thus ridding the disease-carrying rats of their natural predators. Over a period of just eight months, an estimated 100,000 people perished, their corpses collected and thrown into vast 'plague pits'.

The plague finally began to wane in November 1665. But Londoners scarcely had a year to recover before another disaster struck. The city had for centuries been prone to fire, as nearly all buildings were constructed from wood and roofed with thatch, but the mother of all blazes broke out on 2 September 1666 in a bakery in Pudding Lane close to London Bridge.

It didn't seem like much to begin with – the mayor himself dismissed it as 'something a woman might piss out' before going back to bed – but the unusual autumn heat combined with rising winds meant the fire raged out of control for four days, reducing 80% of London to ash. Only eight people died (officially at least), but most of medieval London was obliterated. The fire finally stopped at Pye Corner in Smithfield, on the very edge of London, but not before destroying 89 churches, including St Paul's Cathedral, and more than 13,000 houses, leaving tens of thousands of people homeless.

Historical Reads

A Short History of London (Simon Jenkins)

London: The Biography (Peter Ackroyd)

London: A History in Maps (Peter Barber)

A Traveller's History of London (Richard Tames)

London: The Illustrated History (John Clark & Cathy Ross)

1599

The Globe opens in Southwark, alongside other London theatres such as the Rose and the Swan; most of Shakespeare's plays written after 1599 are staged here, including *Macbeth* and *Hamlet*.

1605

A Catholic plot to assassinate James I by hiding gunpowder under the House of Lords is foiled; eight of the alleged plotters, including Guy Fawkes, are executed the following year.

1613

The Globe Theatre catches fire and burns to the ground; it is rebuilt the following year but closed by the Puritans and demolished in 1642.

1649

King Charles I is executed at Whitehall at the height of the English Civil Wars, a series of armed conflicts over nine years between Royalists and Parliamentarians.

Wren's London

The inferno created a blank canvas upon which master architect Christopher Wren could rebuild 51 magnificent churches and a cathedral. Wren's plan for redesigning the entire city – much of it on a grid pattern – was deemed too expensive, and many landlords opposed it; the familiar pattern of streets that had grown up over the centuries since the time of the Romans quickly reappeared. However, new laws stipulated that brick and stone designs should replace the old timber-framed, overhanging thatched houses and that many roads be widened. The fire accelerated the movement of the wealthy away from the City and into what is now the West End.

By way of memorialising the blaze – and the rebuilding of London – the Monument, designed by Wren, was erected in 1677 near the site of the fire's outbreak. At the time, the 62m-tall column was by far the highest structure in the city, visible from everywhere in the capital.

Following the revocation of the Edict of Nantes in 1685, effectively ending religious tolerance in Catholic France, the trickle of Huguenot (Protestant) refugees arriving in London over the previous century became a mass exodus of 30,000. Mainly artisans, many began manufacturing luxury goods such as silks and silverware in and around Spitalfields and Clerkenwell, which would later welcome Irish, Jewish and Italian immigrants. London was fast becoming one of the world's most cosmopolitan places.

The Glorious – ie bloodless – Revolution in 1688 brought the Dutch King William of Orange to the English throne after the Catholic James II had fled to France. King William III and Queen Mary II, who ruled jointly, relocated from Whitehall Palace to a new palace in Kensington Gardens and, in order to raise finances for the war with France, established the Bank of England in 1694.

London's growth continued unabated, and by 1700 it was Europe's largest city, with some 600,000 people. The influx of foreign workers brought expansion to the east and south, while those who could afford it headed to the more salubrious environs of the north and west.

The crowning glory of the 'Great Rebuilding', Wren's St Paul's Cathedral opened in 1711 during the reign of the last Stuart monarch, Queen Anne. A masterpiece of English baroque architecture, it remains one of the city's most prominent and beautiful landmarks.

For superb city views from London's most iconic piece of ecclesiastical architecture, climb the 528 stairs (no lift) to the Golden Gallery, 85m up in the dome of Sir Christopher Wren's opus magnum: the three-centuries-old St Paul's Cathedral.

Georgian London

Queen Anne died in 1714 without leaving an heir (despite 17 pregnancies). Although there were some 50 Catholic relatives with stronger claims to the throne, a search was immediately launched to find a

1661

Oliver Cromwell's body is dug up from Westminster Abbey three years after his death and given a posthumous 'execution' by hanging.

1665

The Great Plague ravages London, wiping out almost a quarter of the estimated population of 460,000 people.

1666

The Great Fire of London burns for four days, destroying medieval London and leaving 13,200 houses and 89 churches, including St Paul's Cathedral, destroyed.

1702

The *Daily Courant*, London's first daily newspaper, is published by printer Elizabeth Mallet in Fleet St, consisting of a single page of news.

Protestant relative, since the 1701 Act of Settlement forbade Roman Catholics from becoming monarch. Eventually George of Hanover, a great-grandson of James I, arrived from Germany and was crowned King of England, though he never learned to speak English.

Robert Walpole's Whig Party controlled parliament during much of George I's reign, and as 'First Lord of the Treasury', Walpole effectively became Britain's first prime minister. He was presented with 10 Downing St, which remains the official residence of the prime minister today.

London grew at a phenomenal pace during this time, and measures were taken to make the city more accessible. The Roman wall surrounding the City of London was torn down, and a second span over the Thames, Westminster Bridge, opened in 1750.

Georgian London saw a great creative surge in music, art and architecture. Court composer George Frederick Handel wrote *Water Music* (1717) and *Messiah* (1741) after settling here at age 27, and in 1755 Dr Johnson published the first English-language dictionary. William Hogarth, Thomas Gainsborough and Joshua Reynolds produced some of their finest paintings and engravings, and many of London's most elegant buildings, streets and squares were erected or laid out by architects such as John Soane, his pupil Robert Smirke and the prolific John Nash.

You may worry about today's vehicle emissions, but at the end of the 19th century 1000 tonnes of horse manure would fall on the streets of London every day. Crossing sweepers, often young boys, made meagre earnings clearing a path for pedestrians.

All the while, though, London was becoming ever more segregated and lawless. Indeed, King George II himself was relieved of 'purse, watch and buckles' during a stroll through Kensington Gardens. This was Hogarth's London, in which the wealthy built fine mansions in attractive squares and gathered in fashionable new coffee houses while the poor huddled together in appalling slums and drowned their sorrows with cheap gin. To curb rising crime, two magistrates, the writer Henry Fielding and his half-brother John, established the Bow Street Runners in 1749. This voluntary group was effectively a forerunner to the Metropolitan Police Force, which would be established in 1829.

In 1780 parliament proposed to lift the law preventing Catholics buying or inheriting property. One MP, Lord George Gordon, led a 'No Popery' demonstration that turned into the so-called Gordon Riots. A mob of 30,000 went on a rampage, attacking Irish labourers and burning prisons, 'Papish dens' (chapels) and several law courts. As many as 700 people died during five days of rioting.

As George III, forever remembered as the king who lost the American colonies, slid into dementia towards the end of the 18th century, his son, the Prince Regent (and future George IV), set up an alternative and considerably more fashionable court at Carlton House in Pall Mall. By this time London's population had mushroomed to just under a million.

1707

The first-ever sitting of the parliament of the Kingdom of Great Britain occurs in London as the Act of Union brings England and Scotland together under one parliament.

1711

Sir Christopher Wren's masterpiece, St Paul's Cathedral, is officially completed, just over 35 years after it was started.

St Paul's Cathedral (p143)

1812

Charles Dickens, Victorian England's greatest novelist, is born in Portsmouth; many of his novels portray London in all its Victorian squalor.

Victorian London

In 1837 George IV's 18-year-old niece, Victoria, ascended the throne. During her long reign London would become the nerve centre of the largest and richest empire the world had ever known, covering a quarter of the globe's surface and ruling over more than 500 million people.

New docks in East London were built to facilitate the booming trade with the colonies, and railways began to fan out from the capital. The world's first underground railway opened between Paddington and Farringdon in 1863 and was such a success that other lines quickly followed. Many of London's most famous buildings and landmarks were built at this time, including what is now officially named Elizabeth Tower but popularly known as Big Ben (1859), the Royal Albert Hall (1871) and the iconic Tower Bridge (1894).

The city, however, heaved under the burden of its vast size, and in 1858 London was in the grip of the 'Great Stink', when the population explosion so overtook the city's sanitation facilities that raw sewage seeped in through the floorboards of wealthy merchants' houses and the Houses of Parliament were draped with sheets soaked in lime chloride to allay the stench from the river. Leading engineer Joseph Bazalgette tackled the problem by creating an underground network of sewers in the late 1850s.

At the same time, intellectual achievement in the arts and sciences was enormous. The greatest chronicler of the Victorian age was Charles Dickens, whose *Oliver Twist* (1837) and other works explored the themes of poverty, hopelessness and squalor among the working classes. In 1859 Charles Darwin published his seminal and immensely controversial *On the Origin of Species* here, in which he outlined the theory of evolution.

Some of Britain's most capable prime ministers served during Victoria's 64-year reign, most notably William Gladstone (four terms between 1868 and 1894) and Benjamin Disraeli (who served in 1868 and again from 1874 to 1880). And with the creation of the London County Council (LCC) in 1889, the capital had its first-ever directly elected government.

Waves of immigrants, from Irish and Jews to Chinese and Indian sepoys, arrived in London during the 19th century, when the population exploded from one million to well over six million people. This breakneck expansion was not beneficial to everyone – inner-city slums housed the poor in atrocious conditions of disease and overcrowding, while the affluent expanded to the leafy suburbs.

Queen Victoria (of 'We are not amused' fame) is often seen as a dour, humourless old curmudgeon, but was in reality an intelligent, progressive

The night of 29/30 December 1940 has been called the 'Second Great Fire of London', when 136 German bombers dropped more than 24,000 high-explosive bombs and 100,000 incendiary devices on London in a few hours, starting 1500 fires raging across the City and up to Islington.

1829

London's first regular bus service – the horse-drawn 'omnibus' – begins, running from Paddington to Bank. The fare is 1 shilling (now 5p).

1838

The coronation of Queen Victoria at Westminster Abbey ushers in a new era for London; the British capital becomes the economic centre of the world.

1843

Connecting Wapping to the north with Rotherhithe to the south, Marc Isambard Brunel opens his Thames Tunnel, the first to be constructed under a navigable river.

1851

The Great Exhibition, the brainchild of Victoria's consort, Prince Albert, who would die a decade later, opens in the purpose-built steel-and-glass Crystal Palace in Hyde Park.

and passionate woman. While her beloved husband and consort, Prince Albert, died prematurely of what is believed to have been typhoid in 1861, she lived on to celebrate her Diamond Jubilee in 1897 and died four years later at the age of 81. Her reign is considered the climax of British world supremacy.

From Empire to World War

Victoria's self-indulgent son Edward, the Prince of Wales, was already 60 by the time he was crowned Edward VII in 1901. London's belle époque was marked with the introduction of the first public-service motorised double-decker buses in 1904 on the Peckham to Oxford Circus route, which replaced the horse-drawn versions that had plodded their trade since 1829. And a touch of glamour came in the form of luxury hotels, such as the Ritz in 1906, and department stores, such as Selfridges, in 1909. The first London Olympics were held at White City Stadium in 1908.

What became known as the Great War (or WWI) broke out in August 1914, and the first German bombs fell from zeppelins near the Guildhall a year later, killing 39 people. In all, some 670 Londoners were killed by bombs (half the national total of civilian casualties) and another 2000 were wounded.

For an upfront view of WWI and its unspeakable devastation, visit the interactive First World War Galleries (www.iwm.org.uk/exhibitions/iwm-london/first-world-war-galleries) at the Imperial War Museum.

The Interwar Years

After the war ended in 1918, London's population continued to rise, reaching nearly 7.5 million in 1921. The LCC busied itself clearing slums and building new housing estates, while the suburbs spread further into the countryside, especially to the west.

Unemployment rose steadily, and in May 1926 a wage dispute in the coal industry escalated into a nine-day general strike, in which so many workers downed tools that London virtually ground to a halt. The army was called in to maintain order and to keep the buses and the Underground running, but the stage was set for more than half a century of industrial strife.

Intellectually the 1920s were the heyday of the Bloomsbury Group, which counted writers Virginia Woolf and EM Forster and the economist John Maynard Keynes among its ranks. The spotlight shifted westwards to Fitzrovia in the following decade, when George Orwell and Dylan Thomas raised glasses with contemporaries at the Fitzroy Tavern on Charlotte St. Cinema, TV and radio arrived: the BBC aired its first radio broadcast from the roof of Marconi House on the Strand in 1922, and the first TV program from Alexandra Palace 14 years later.

The monarchy took a knock when Edward VIII abdicated in 1936 to marry a woman who was not only twice divorced but an American to

1884

Greenwich Mean Time is established, making Greenwich Observatory the centre of world time, according to which all clocks around the globe are set.

1901

Queen Victoria dies after reigning 63 years, seven months and two days – the longest reign in British history until Elizabeth II surpassed that record in September 2015.

1908

London hosts its first Olympic Games in the now-demolished White City Stadium; some 22 teams take part and the entire budget is £15,000.

1926

London all but closes down for nine days during the nationwide General Strike, with little violence and ultimately almost no impact on trade-union activity or industrial relations.

boot. The same year Oswald Mosley attempted to lead the black-shirted British Union of Fascists on an anti-Jewish march through the East End but was repelled by a mob of around half a million at the famous Battle of Cable St.

WWII & the Blitz

Prime Minister Neville Chamberlain's policy of appeasing Adolf Hitler during the 1930s eventually proved misguided as the Führer's appetite for expansion appeared insatiable. When Germany invaded Poland on 1 September 1939, Britain declared war, having signed a mutual-assistance pact with that nation a few days before. WWII had begun.

The first year of the war was one of anxious waiting. Some 600,000 women and children had been evacuated to the countryside from London and the Battle of Britain raged elsewhere, primarily around Royal Air Force bases elsewhere in England, but no bombs fell to disturb the blackout in the capital. On 7 September 1940 that all came to a devastating end when the Luftwaffe, the German Air Force, dropped hundreds of bombs on the East End, killing 430 people and injuring 1600 more.

The Blitz (from the German '*Blitzkrieg*' or 'lightning war') lasted for 57 nights, and then continued intermittently until mid-May 1941. Some Underground stations were turned into giant bomb shelters, although one bomb rolled down the escalator at Bank station and exploded on the platform, killing more than 100 people. Londoners largely responded with resilience and stoicism. To the great admiration and respect of the people, the King and Queen refused to leave London during the bombing (their daughters Elizabeth and Margaret remained at Windsor). Buckingham Palace took a direct hit during a bombing raid early in the campaign, famously prompting Queen Elizabeth (the present monarch's late mother) to pronounce: 'Now I can look the East End in the face'. Winston Churchill, prime minister from 1940, orchestrated much of Britain's war strategy from the subterranean Cabinet War Rooms at Whitehall, and it was from here that he made several of his stirring wartime speeches.

London's spirit was tested again in June 1944, when Germany launched pilotless V-1 bombers (known as doodlebugs) over East London. By the time Nazi Germany capitulated in May 1945, up to a third of the East End and the City had been flattened, almost 30,000 Londoners killed and a further 50,000 seriously wounded.

For an idea of the scale of the devastation brought about by the Blitz on London, visit the website of the Bomb Sight (http://bombsight.org) project, which has mapped the WWII bomb census between October 1940 and June 1941.

Postwar London & the '60s

Once the Victory in Europe (VE) celebrations were over, the nation began to assess the war's appalling toll and to rebuild. The years of austerity had begun, with rationing of essential items and the building of high-rise

1936 The 'Year of Three Kings': George VI ascends the throne following the death of his father, George V, and abdication of his brother, Edward VIII, who gave up his throne for an American divorcée.

1940–41 London is devastated by the Blitz, although landmarks like St Paul's Cathedral and the Tower of London escape the bombing for the most part unscathed.

1945 Big Ben is illuminated again in April and full street lighting restored after the Blackout is downgraded to a dim-out over London; 'Victory in Europe' is declared in May.

1951 King George VI opens the Festival of Britain, marking the centenary of the Great Exhibition and aiming to lift the national mood after the devastation of of WWII.

residences on bomb sites in areas like Pimlico and the East End to solve the chronic housing problem. To help boost morale, London hosted the 1948 Olympics (dubbed 'the austerity Games') and the feel-good Festival of Britain in 1951.

The gloom returned, quite literally, on 6 December 1952 in the form of the Great Smog. A lethal blend of fog, smoke and pollution descended, and some 4000 people died of respiratory-related disorders. This prompted the promulgation of the Clean Air Act of 1956, which introduced zones to central London where only smokeless fuels could be burned.

The current queen was crowned Elizabeth II in 1953 following the death of her much-loved father King George VI the year before. Rationing of most goods ended in July 1954, 14 years after it had begun.

Immigrants from around the world – particularly from the former colonies – flocked to London, where a dwindling population had led to acute labour shortages. However, despite being officially encouraged to come, new immigrants weren't always welcomed on the streets, as was proved in the Notting Hill race riots of 1958.

Some economic prosperity returned in the late 1950s, and Prime Minister Harold Macmillan told Britons they'd 'never had it so good'. London became the place to be during the 1960s, when the bottled-up creative energy of the postwar era was spectacularly uncorked. London found itself the epicentre of cool in fashion and music: the streets were awash with colour and vitality, the iconic Mini car (1959) and skirt became British icons, and the Jaguar E-type (1961) was launched to adoring crowds.

For trivia, little-known facts and endless specialist information on the history of the East End and its personalities, head to East London History (www.eastlondon-history.co.uk).

Social norms underwent a revolution: the introduction of the contraceptive pill, the partial decriminalisation of homosexuality, and the popularisation of drugs such as marijuana and LSD through the hippy movement created an unprecedentedly permissive and liberal climate. Popular music in the mid-1960s onward became increasingly linked with drug use, political activism and a counter-cultural mindset. The Beatles recording at Abbey Road and the Rolling Stones performing free in front of half a million people in Hyde Park were seminal moments. Carnaby St and the King's Rd were the most fashionable places on earth, and pop-culture figures from Twiggy and David Bailey to Marianne Faithfull and Christine Keeler became the faces of the new era.

The Punk Era

London returned to the doldrums in the harsh economic climate of the 1970s. The city's once-important docks never recovered from the loss of empire, the changing needs of modern container ships and poor labour relations, and disappeared altogether between 1968 and 1981. Shipping moved 25 miles east to Tilbury, and the Docklands declined to a point

1952

London is brought to a virtual standstill for four days in December by a thick, 'pea-souper' smog that smothers the city, contributing to the deaths of thousands of people.

1953

Queen Elizabeth II's coronation is held at Westminster Abbey, the first major event to be broadcast live around the world on TV.

1959

The Notting Hill Carnival is launched to promote better race relations after the riots of 1958 when white and Afro-Caribbean communities clashed.

of decay, until they were rediscovered by property developers a decade later. In 1973 a bomb went off at the Old Bailey (the Central Criminal Court), signalling the arrival of the Irish Republican Army (IRA) in London and its campaign for a united Ireland.

Post-1960s music became more formulaic as glam rock ruled, even as glam rock ruled with the blossoming of London legends Marc Bolan and David Bowie. Economic stagnation, cynicism and the superficial limits of disco and glam rock spawned a novel London aesthetic: punk. Largely white, energetic, abrasive and fast, punk transformed popular music and fashion in one stroke as teenagers traded in denim bell-bottoms for black drainpipes, and long hair for spiked Mohicans. The late 1970s were exhilarating times for London youth as punk opened the door for new wave, a punchy mod revival and the indulgent new romantics.

Meanwhile, torpor had set into Britain's body politic. Seen as weak and in thrall to the all-powerful trade unions, the brief and unremarkable Labour premiership of James Callaghan (1976–79) was marked by crippling strikes in the late 1970s, most significantly the 'Winter of Discontent' of 1978–79 when Leicester Sq became a rubbish tip after waste-collection workers walked off the job.

The Thatcher Years

In 1979 the Conservative leader Margaret Thatcher became the UK's first female prime minister. In power for all of the 1980s and embarking on an unprecedented program of privatisation, Margaret Thatcher – aka the 'Iron Lady' – is arguably the most significant of Britain's postwar leaders. While her critics decry her approach to social justice and the large gulf that developed between the haves and have nots during her time in office, her defenders point to the massive modernisation of Britain's infrastructure (until then in the grip of trade unions) and the vast wealth creation her policies generated.

In the beginning, her monetarist policy sent unemployment skyrocketing; an inquiry following the Brixton riots of 1981 found that an astonishing 55% of men aged under 19 in that part of London were jobless. Meanwhile the Greater London Council (GLC), under the leadership of 'Red' Ken Livingstone, proved to be a thorn in Thatcher's side. County Hall, which faces the Houses of Parliament across the Thames, was hung with a giant banner recording the number of unemployed in the capital and goading the prime minister to do something about it. Thatcher responded in 1986 by abolishing the GLC, leaving London the only European capital without a unified central government.

While poorer Londoners suffered under Thatcher's significant trimming of the welfare state, things had rarely looked better for the business

The Iron Lady (2011) starring Meryl Streep is a very watchable biopic of the late Margaret Thatcher. It seamlessly traces the former prime minister's life and career from politically astute grocer's daughter to grieving widow suffering from dementia. Thatcher died two years after the film's release.

1966

England beat Germany to win the World Cup at Wembley – possibly the greatest day in the history of British sport and one seared into the consciousness of many Britons.

1979

Margaret Thatcher is elected prime minister. Her policies will change Britain beyond recognition – part vital modernisation, part radical right-wing social policy.

1981

Brixton sees the worst race riots in London's history; Lord Scarman, delivering his report on the events, puts the blame squarely on 'racial disadvantage that is a fact of British life'.

1990

Britain erupts in civil unrest, culminating in the poll-tax riots in Trafalgar Sq; the deeply unpopular tax ultimately proves to be Thatcher's undoing and she resigns in November.

community. Riding a wave of confidence partly engendered by the deregulation of the stock exchange in 1986, London underwent explosive economic growth. Property developers proved to be only marginally more discriminating than the Luftwaffe, though some outstanding modern structures, including the Lloyd's of London building, went up.

Like previous booms, the one of the late 1980s proved unsustainable. As unemployment started to rise again and people found themselves living in houses worth much less than they had paid for them, Thatcher introduced a flat-rate poll tax. Protests around the country culminated in a 1990 march on Trafalgar Sq that ended in a fully fledged riot. Thatcher's subsequent resignation after losing a confidence vote in parliament brought to an end this divisive era. Her successor, the former Chancellor of the Exchequer, John Major, employed a far more collective form of government.

In 1992, to the amazement of most Londoners, the Conservatives were elected for a fourth successive term in government, without the inspiring leadership of Thatcher. The economy went into a tailspin shortly after, and the IRA detonated two huge bombs, one in the City in 1992 and another in the Docklands four years later. The writing was on the wall for the Conservatives, as the Labour Party re-emerged with a new face.

For a fascinating review of the social, musical and cultural history of 20th-century London, take a look at Another Nickel in the Machine (www.nickelinthemachine.com), a blog covering everything from suffragettes and Charlie Chaplin's homecoming to vintage David Bowie.

Blair's Britain

Desperate to return to power after almost two decades in opposition, the Labour Party selected the telegenic Tony Blair to lead it. The May 1997 general election overwhelmingly returned a Labour government to power, but it was a much changed 'New Labour' party, one that had shed most of its socialist credo and supported a market economy, privatisation and integration with Europe.

Most importantly for London, Labour recognised the legitimate demand the city had for local government, and created the London Assembly and the post of mayor. The former leader of the GLC, Ken Livingstone, stood as an independent candidate and won handily. Livingstone introduced a successful congestion charge to limit road traffic in central London and sought to bring London's backward public transport network into the 21st century.

London's resurgence as a great world city seemed to be going from strength to strength, culminating in its selection in July 2005 to host the Olympic Games in 2012. London's buoyant mood was, however, shattered the very next morning when extremist Muslim terrorists detonated a series of bombs on the city's public transport network, killing 52 people. Triumph turned to terror, followed quickly by anger and then defiance. Just two weeks later the attempted detonation of several more bombs on London's public transport system sent the city into a state

1997

Labour sweeps to victory after almost two decades of Conservative government. Tony Blair's centrist 'New Labour' party wins a majority of 179 in the House of Commons.

2000

Ken Livingstone is elected mayor of London as an independent 14 years after Margaret Thatcher dissolved his Greater London Council.

2003

London's congestion charge is introduced by Livingstone, a scheme that sees traffic volume reduced by 10% in its first decade.

2005

A day after London is awarded the 2012 Olympics on 6 July, 52 people are killed by terrorists in a series of suicide bombings on London's transport network.

of severe unease, which culminated in the tragic shooting by the Metropolitan Police of an innocent Brazilian electrician, Jean Charles de Menezes, who was mistaken for one of the failed bombers.

Boris and the Olympic Games

Ken Livingstone's campaign to win a third term as London mayor in 2008 was fatally undermined when the Conservative Party fielded maverick MP and popular TV personality Boris Johnson as its candidate. Even more of a populist than Livingstone, Eton-educated Johnson, portrayed by the media as a gaffe-prone toff, actually proved to be a deft political operator and surprised everyone by sailing past Livingstone to become the first Conservative mayor ever of London.

Johnson was popularised in the media as an almost eccentric, oddball figure, with his wild mop of blond hair, shapeless suits and in-your-face eagerness. It was a persona Londoners warmed to. He disagreed with Livingstone on many issues, but continued to support several of his predecessor's policies, including the congestion charge and the expansion of bicycle lanes. A keen cyclist himself, Boris is forever associated with the bicycle-hire scheme sponsored by Barclays, now underwritten by Santander Bank and nicknamed 'Boris Bikes' (though Livingstone proposed it first). Johnson pledged to replace Livingstone's unloved 'bendy buses' with remodelled Routemasters, which were introduced on some routes in 2012.

Johnson's first mayoral term coincided with London's transformation for the 2012 Olympic Games. Neglected areas of the recession-hit city were showered with investment and a vast building program in East London took shape. Danny Boyle's Olympics Opening Ceremony treated the world to an extravagant potted history of London and the UK, football superstar David Beckham drove the Olympic Torch down the Thames and into the Olympic Park in a speedboat, and James Bond (in the form of Daniel Craig) jumped out of a helicopter into the Olympic Stadium accompanied by none other than Her Majesty, 'the Queen'.

The Millennium Dome on the Greenwich Peninsula failed to impress when it opened in 2000. Designed by Richard Rogers and sometimes mockingly referred to as the Millennium Tent, the dome eventually succeeded. when rebranded as the O2 in 2007. It is now one of the most successful live-entertainment venues in the world.

London's Year

The year 2012 promised to be London's year, and few people – at home or abroad – were disappointed.

A four-day holiday in June marked the Queen's Diamond Jubilee – the 60th anniversary of her ascension to the throne. As celebratory and joyous as the Jubilee was, it was but a prelude to *the* London event of the year: the all-singin', all-dancin' Olympics and Paralympics that welcomed some 15,000 athletes competing in almost 50 sports for 800 medals. Over the course of 29 days there were many expected highs (Britain took 65 Olympic and 120 Paralympic medals, to rank third in each games) and

2008

Boris Johnson, a Conservative MP and journalist famed for both his gaffes and eccentric appearance, beats Ken Livingstone to become London's new mayor.

2010

Labour is defeated in the general elections, which results in a hung Parliament and a Conservative–Liberal Democrat coalition government with David Cameron as prime minister.

2012

Boris Johnson narrowly beats Ken Livingstone again to win his second mayoral election; London hosts the 2012 Olympics and Paralympics.

2015

The Conservatives defeat Labour in the general election, emerging with a narrow majority and abandoning their coalition government with the Liberal Democrats.

some surprising ones (London's transport system did not just cope but excelled).

But nothing came close to Danny Boyle's Olympics Opening Ceremony in which the world was treated to an extravagant potted history of London and the UK, football superstar David Beckham drove the Olympic Torch down the Thames and into the Olympic Park in a speedboat, and James Bond (in the form of Daniel Craig) jumped out of a helicopter into the Olympic Stadium accompanied by none other than Her Majesty, 'the Queen'.

Brexit & Big Change

In less than a decade, the nation has changed leadership twice (Boris Johnson victorious in the December 2019 general election after having replacing Theresa May as prime minister who had taken over from David Cameron) and the city once, with Sadiq Khan taking over as mayor from Boris Johnson. At the same time, scores of new high-rise buildings have transformed the London skyline, most notably in the City and South Bank. Countless construction sites throughout London have reduced traffic to a crawl and the price of a pint is now well over £5.

But the issue that has dominated all media since mid-2016 has been so-called Brexit, after the people of the UK voted, by 52% to 48%, in a hastily called referendum, to leave the EU. After much dickering and divisive posturing, the UK's departure from 'Europe' after almost half a century came into effect on 31 January 2020. But it was hardly a clean break. Although the UK agreed to the terms of its departure, the post-Brexit UK-EU relationship remained fraught. Thorny issues included disagreement over the terms of the Brexit arrangements for Northern Ireland and tussling over fishing rights, while the COVID-19 pandemic added further complications.

2016

Sadiq Khan is elected mayor, the first Muslim to hold such a position in a major Western capital; the UK electorate votes 52% to 48% to leave the EU, approving a withdrawal that becomes known as Brexit.

2017

The Conservative Party scrapes home in a national election, and Theresa May forms a new minority government; London is hit by Islamic terrorist attacks in March and in June.

2019

Theresa May is replaced as prime minister by Boris Johnson, whose Conservative Party defeats Labour in the general election; another Islamic terrorist attack leaves three dead.

2020

The UK's first cases of COVID-19 are confirmed as two people test positive for the virus on 31 January.

Architecture

Unlike some cities, London has never been methodically planned. Instead, it has developed in an almost haphazard fashion. As a result, London retains architectural reminders from every period of its long history, but they are often hidden: part of a Roman wall enclosed in the lobby of a modern building near St Paul's Cathedral, say, or a galleried coaching inn from the Restoration in a courtyard off Borough High St. As you'll soon discover, this is a city for explorers. Remember that and you'll be surprised at every turn.

Laying the Foundations

London's architectural roots lie below the walled Roman settlement of Londinium, established in 43 CE on the northern banks of the River Thames where the City of London is located. Few Roman traces survive outside museums, though a Temple of Mithras (or Mithraeum), built in 240 CE and excavated and moved in 1954, has been returned to its

Above: 30 St Mary Axe (The Gherkin); (p385) by architect Norman Foster

original location on Walbrook at the eastern end of Queen Victoria St. Stretches of the Roman wall remain as foundations to a medieval wall outside Tower Hill Tube station and to the north and in a few sections below Bastion Highwalk just south of the appropriately named London Wall.

The Saxons, who moved into the area after the Romans decamped around 410, found Londinium too small, so they all but ignored what the Romans had left behind and built their communities further up the Thames. Excavations carried out during renovations at the Royal Opera House in the late 1990s uncovered extensive traces of the Saxon settlement of Lundenwic, including some wattle-and-daub houses. All Hallows-by-the-Tower, northwest of the Tower of London, shelters an important archway, and the walls of a 7th-century Saxon church.

With the arrival of William the Conqueror in 1066, the country received its first example of Norman architecture with the White Tower, the sturdy keep at the heart of the Tower of London. The church of St Bartholomew-the-Great at Smithfield also has Norman arches and columns supporting its nave. The west door and elaborately moulded porch at Temple Church (shared by Inner and Middle Temple), the Pyx Chamber at Westminster Abbey and the crypt at St-Mary-le-Bow are other outstanding examples of Norman architecture.

The London Festival of Architecture (www.londonfestivalofarchitecture.org) is an annual month-long event in June celebrating the capital's buildings with some 500 events, walks, talks, tours and debates.

Medieval London

Enlarged and refurbished in the 13th century by 'builder king' Henry III, Westminster Abbey is a splendid reminder of the work of master masons in the Middle Ages. Perhaps the finest surviving medieval church in the city is the 13th-century church of St Ethelburga-the-Virgin near Liverpool St station, heavily restored after Irish Republican Army (IRA) bombing in 1993. The 15th-century Church of St Olave, northwest of Tower Hill, is one of the City's few remaining Gothic parish churches, while the crypt at the largely restored Church of St Etheldreda, north of Holborn Circus, dates from about 1250. Southwark Cathedral includes some remnants from the 12th and 13th centuries.

Secular medieval buildings are even scarcer than ecclesiastical ones, although the ragstone Jewel Tower, opposite the Houses of Parliament, dates from 1365, and much of the Tower of London goes back to the Middle Ages. Staple Inn in Holborn dates from 1378, but the half-timbered shopfront facade is mostly Elizabethan from about 1580, and was heavily restored in the mid-20th century after WWII bombing. Parliament's Westminster Hall was originally built at the end of the 11th century; the hammerbeam roof came 300 years later. The splendid hammerbeam roof at Middle Temple Hall dates from 1573; the one in St George's Hall in Windsor Castle was rebuilt after a fire in 1992.

A Trinity of Architects

The finest London architect of the first half of the 17th century was Inigo Jones (1573–1652), who spent a year and a half in Italy and became a convert to the Renaissance-style architecture of Andrea Palladio. His *chefs d'œuvre* include Banqueting House (1622) in Whitehall and Queen's House (1635) in Greenwich. Often overlooked is his much plainer church of St Paul's in Covent Garden, which Jones designed in the early 1630s.

The greatest architect to leave his mark on London was Christopher Wren (1632–1723), responsible for St Paul's Cathedral (1710). Wren oversaw the building (or rebuilding) of more than 50 churches, many replacing medieval ones lost in the Great Fire, as well as the Royal Hospital Chelsea (1692) and the Old Royal Naval College, begun in 1694 at Greenwich. His English baroque buildings and churches are taller and lighter

Christ Church Spitalfields (p207)

than their medieval predecessors, with graceful steeples taking the place of solid square medieval towers.

Nicholas Hawksmoor (1661–1736) was a pupil of Wren and worked with him on several churches before going on to create his own masterpieces. The restored Christ Church (1729) in Spitalfields, St George's Bloomsbury (1731), St Anne's Limehouse (1730), and St George-in-the-East (1726) at Wapping are among the finest of his half-dozen churches in London.

Georgian Manners

Among the greatest exponents of classicism (or neo-Palladianism) was Scotsman Robert Adam (1728–92), whose surviving work in London includes Kenwood House (1779) on Hampstead Heath and some of the interiors of Apsley House (1778) at Hyde Park Corner.

A row of four houses at 52–55 Newington Green, N16, makes up London's oldest surviving brick terrace houses. Predating the Great Fire of London, they were built in 1658.

Adam's fame has been eclipsed by that of John Nash (1752–1835), whose contribution to London's architecture can almost be compared to that of Christopher Wren. Nash was responsible for the layout of Regent's Park and its surrounding elegant crescents. To give London a 'spine', he created Regent St as an axis from the new park south to St James's Park. This grand project also involved the formation of Trafalgar Sq and the development of the Mall and the western end of the Strand. Nash refashioned the old Buckingham House into Buckingham Palace (1830) for George IV.

Nash's contemporary, John Soane (1753–1837), was the architect of the Bank of England, completed in 1833 (though much of his work was lost during the bank's rebuilding by Herbert Baker between 1925 and 1939), as well as the Dulwich Picture Gallery (1814). Robert Smirke (1780–1867) designed the British Museum, completed in 1823; it's one of the finest expressions of the so-called Greek Revivalist style.

Albert Memorial (p188)

A Gothic Rethink

In the 19th century, the highly decorative neo-Gothic style, also known as Gothic Revival or Victorian High Gothic, was very much in vogue. Champions were the architects George Gilbert Scott (1811–78), Alfred Waterhouse (1830–1905) and Augustus Pugin (1812–52). Scott was responsible for the elaborate Albert Memorial (1872) in Kensington Gardens and the Midland Grand Hotel (1873), now fully restored as the St Pancras Renaissance Hotel. Waterhouse designed the flamboyant Natural History Museum (1881), while Pugin worked from 1840 with the designer Charles Barry (1795–1860) on the Houses of Parliament after the Palace of Westminster burned down in 1834. The last great neo-Gothic public building to go up in London was the Royal Courts of Justice, designed by George Edmund Street in 1882.

Charles Dickens referred to the Church of St Olave as 'St Ghastly Grim' because of the macabre ornamentation of skulls that can still be seen above the entrance.

The emphasis on the artisanship and materials required to create these elaborate neo-Gothic buildings led to the formation of the Arts and Crafts movement, of which William Morris (1834–96) was the leading exponent. Morris' work can be seen in the Morris (or Green Dining) Room of the Victoria & Albert Museum; at his Red House in Bexleyheath; at the William Morris Gallery in Walthamstow; and at Kelmscott House (headquarters of the William Morris Society) and Emery Walker's House, both in Hammersmith.

Flirting with Modernism

Relatively few notable public buildings emerged from the first 15 years of the 20th century, apart from Admiralty Arch (1910), which was done in the 'Edwardian baroque' style by Aston Webb (1849–1930). Webb also designed the Queen Victoria Memorial (1911) in front of Buckingham Palace. County Hall, designed by Ralph Knott in 1909, was not completed until 1922. More modern imagination is evident in commercial design: for example, the superb art nouveau design (with a little art deco in there too) of Michelin House on Fulham Rd, designed by François Espinasse and completed in 1911.

In the period between the two world wars, English architecture was barely more creative, though Edwin 'Ned' Lutyens (1869–1944) designed the Cenotaph (1920) in Whitehall as well as the Midland Bank Building (1924) on Poultry in the City – now the Ned hotel and restaurant complex. Displaying the same amount of Edwardian optimism is the former Port of London Authority (1922), designed by Edwin Cooper and now a hotel and apartment block.

Designed by US architect Harvey Wiley Corbett (1873–1954), Bush House, at the southern end of Kingsway and until 2012 the home of the BBC World Service, was built between 1923 and 1935. It's now part of King's College London. The black-and-chrome curves of the Daily Express Building (1932, Ellis Clarke with Owen Williams) at 120 Fleet St are a splendid example of Modernist architecture with an art deco foyer. Other art deco classics are St Olaf House, an office block on Tooley St that fronts the Thames (1928, HS Goodhart-Rendel); 55 Broadway, a listed block above St James's Tube station (1929, Charles Holden); and Michelin House.

Given its somewhat foreboding appearance (it is very black), the art deco Daily Express building on Fleet St was nicknamed 'the Black Lubyanka' by the satirical magazine *Private Eye* in reference to the KGB headquarters in Moscow.

Postwar Reconstruction

Hitler's bombs during WWII wrought the worst destruction on London since the Great Fire of 1666, and the immediate postwar problem was a chronic housing shortage. Low-cost developments and ugly high-rise housing were thrown up on bomb sites and many of these blocks still scar London's horizon today.

The Royal Festival Hall, designed by Robert Matthew (1906–75) and J Leslie Martin (1908–2000) for the 1951 Festival of Britain, attracted as many bouquets as brickbats when it opened as London's first major public building in the modernist style. Even today, hardly anyone seems to have a good word to say about the neighbouring National Theatre, a brutalist structure by Denys Lasdun (1914–2001), which was begun in 1966 and finished a decade later.

The 1960s saw the ascendancy of the workaday glass-and-concrete high-rises exemplified by the mostly unloved (but Grade II listed) Centre Point (1967) by Richard Seifert (1910–2001). The 1964 BT Tower, formerly known as the Post Office Tower and designed by Eric Bedford (1909–2001), has also received the same listed status.

Little building was undertaken in the 1970s apart from roads, and the recession of the late 1980s and early 1990s brought much development and speculation to a standstill. Helping to polarise traditionalists and modernists still further was Prince Charles, who described a proposed (but never built) extension to the National Gallery as being like 'a

OPEN HOUSE LONDON

If you want to see the inside of buildings whose doors are normally shut tight to visitors, come to London on the third weekend in September. That's when the charity **Open House London** (020-7383 2131; https://openhouselondon.open-city.org.uk; Sep) arranges for the owners of more than 800 private and public buildings to let the public in free of charge. Major buildings (eg the Gherkin, City Hall, Lloyd's of London building, Royal Courts of Justice, BT Tower etc) have participated in the past; the full program (£7 to £10 depending on when you order it) becomes available in mid-August. Its affiliate, Open City (p417), offers architect-led tours year-round.

monstrous carbuncle on the face of an elegant and much loved friend'. Prince Charles is not an architect.

Postmodernism Lands

London's contemporary architecture was born in the City and the revitalised Docklands in the mid-1980s. The City's centrepiece was the 1986 Lloyd's of London building, Richard Rogers' 'inside-out' *chef d'œuvre* of ducts, pipes, glass and stainless steel. Taking pride of place in the Docklands was Cesar Pelli's 244m-high One Canada Square (1991), commonly known as Canary Wharf and easily visible from central London. But London's very first postmodern building (designed in the late 1980s by James Stirling but not completed till 1998) is considered to be No 1 Poultry, a playful, shiplike landmark in the City faced with yellow and pink limestone. The graceful British Library (Colin St John Wilson, 1998), with its warm red-brick exterior, Asian-like touches and wonderfully bright interior, initially met a very hostile reception but has now become a popular landmark.

At the end of the 1990s, attention turned to public buildings, including several new landmarks. From the disused Bankside Power Station (Giles Gilbert Scott, 1947–63), the Tate Modern (Herzog & de Meuron, 1999) was refashioned as an art gallery that scooped international architecture's most prestigious prize, the Pritzker. The stunning Millennium Bridge (Norman Foster and Anthony Caro, 2000), the first new bridge to cross the Thames in central London since Tower Bridge went up in 1894, is much loved and much used. Even the white-elephant Millennium Dome (Richard Rogers), the class dunce of 2000, won a new lease of life as the O2 and is now the world's most successful entertainment venue.

Situated above St James's Park Underground station, 55 Broadway was highly controversial when it opened in 1929 due to a pair of sculptures, *Day* and *Night*, by Jacob Epstein on the exterior. The generous anatomy of the figures caused an outcry and Epstein had to snip 4cm from the penis of the smaller figure *Day*.

Here Today & Tomorrow

Early in the millennium such structures as the 2002 glass 'egg' of City Hall and the ever-popular, ever-present 2003-built 30 St Mary Axe – or 'Gherkin' – gave the city the confidence to continue planning more heady buildings.

By the middle of the noughties, London's biggest urban development project ever was under way: the 200-hectare Olympic Park in the Lea River Valley near Stratford, where most of the events of the 2012 Summer Olympics and Paralympics would take place. But the park would offer few architectural surprises, with the exception of the late Zaha Hadid's stunning Aquatics Centre, Hopkins Architects' award-winning Velodrome and the *ArcelorMittal Orbit*, a zany 115m-tall public work of art with viewing platforms designed by the sculptor Anish Kapoor.

Although the 2008 recession undermined, for several years, what was the most ambitious building program in London since WWII, an improved economic climate at the start of the following decade saw those buildings under construction completed and 'holes in the ground' filled in with the beginnings of new structures.

Topped out in 2010 were the 230m-tall Heron Tower in the City, then London's third-tallest building, and the very distinctive Strata (150m) south of the river, with three wind turbines embedded in its roof. But nothing could compare with the so-called Shard, at 310m the UK's tallest building, completed in 2012. The glass-clad upturned icicle, dramatically poking into Borough skies and visible from across London, houses offices, apartments, a five-star hotel, restaurants and, on the 72nd floor, London's highest public viewing gallery. Not as high but twice as pleasant are the restaurants and cafe-bar in the junglelike Sky Garden on levels 35 to 37 of bulbous 20 Fenchurch St, better known as the 'Walkie Talkie'.

Economic recovery in the 21st century's second decade and the rise in population (largely through immigration) sparked a building

BROKEN GLASS & RAZOR SHARP

Londoners have a predilection for nicknaming new towers, and many of them go on to replace the original name. Here are some of the popular ones, inspired, of course, by the building's shape and form:

Cheese Grater Opened in mid-2014, the recession-delayed 50-storey, 224m-tall Leadenhall Building in the form of a stepped wedge faces architect Richard Rogers' other icon, the Lloyd's of London building.

Gherkin The 180m-tall bullet-shaped tower that seems to pop up at every turn has also been known as the Swiss Re Tower (after its first major tenants), Cockfosters (after its architect, Norman Foster), the erotic pickle, the suppository etc. Its official name merely reflects its address: 30 St Mary Axe.

Razor (Strata; Map p476; 8 Walworth Rd, SE1; ⓤElephant & Castle) This 43-storey, turbine-topped tower (officially the Strata SE1 building), rising 148m over Elephant & Castle in South London, (sort of) resembles an electric razor. It's one of the tallest residential buildings in London.

Scalpel (Map p450; 52 Lime St, EC3; ⓤBank, Aldgate) The nickname of this 39-storey tower completed in 2018 in the City was so apt it dislodged the skyscraper's official name: 52 Lime St.

Shard (p164) This needlelike 95-storey tower by Italian architect Renzo Piano is one heck of a splinter. Views from the top floors are awesome. Originally called London Bridge Tower, it is now officially the Shard.

Stealth Bomber (p157) French architect Jean Nouvel's office block and shopping mall next to St Paul's Cathedral was built to bring new life to the City, especially at the weekend. Its nickname, only occasionally used, comes from its distinctive low-slung design. Its real name is One New Change.

Vase (Map p452; 1-16 Blackfriars Rd, SE1; ⓤBlackfriars) The bulbous 52-storey One Blackfriars is called 'the Vase' by some for its unusual shape while others prefer 'the Tummy' or 'the Pregnant Tower'.

Walkie Talkie (p146) This 37-storey, 160m-tall tower bulges in and bulges out, vaguely resembling an old-fashioned walkie-talkie. The popular Sky Garden, with its cafe and restaurants at the top, is said to be the world's highest public park.

To see how London's built environment looks and will look in the future visit New London Architecture just north of Oxford Circus (and don't miss the ever-updated scale model).

boom unseen since the reconstruction of London after WWII. When completed, the proposed 290m-tall 1 Undershaft, dubbed 'the Trellis' for its external cross-hatch bracing, will be the City's tallest building and the second highest in the UK after the Shard. Also piercing the skyline of the City, the 190m-tall 'Scalpel' (52 Lime St) was completed in 2018. South London, in particular, has become one giant building site, at Vauxhall (50-storey Vauxhall Square towers; Allies & Morrison), Nine Elms (twin-towered One Nine Elms; Kohn Pedersen Fox) and especially around Bankside (52-storey One Blackfriars, or 'the Vase'; SimpsonHaugh & Partners). Indeed, at the close of the decade, nearby Bankside Yard, site of unloved Sampson and Ludgate House, was being cleared for nine new buildings, including a series of mixed-use towers, the highest of which will reach 49 storeys. And many people (ourselves included) are calling the 62,300-seat Tottenham Hotspur Stadium, completed in 2019, the Eighth Wonder of the World.

Literary London

It's hard to reconcile the bawdy portrayal of London in Geoffrey Chaucer's *Canterbury Tales* with Charles Dickens' bleak hellhole in *Oliver Twist,* let alone Daniel Defoe's plague-ravaged metropolis in *Journal of the Plague Year* with Zadie Smith's multiethnic romp *White Teeth.* Ever-changing, yet somehow eerily consistent, London has left its mark on some of the most influential writing in the English language.

Top Literary Sights

Shakespeare's Globe (p162; South Bank)

Charles Dickens Museum (p97; Bloomsbury)

Keats House (p255; Hampstead)

Carlyle's House (p192; South Kensington)

Sherlock Holmes Museum (p109; West End)

British Library (p246; King's Cross & Euston)

Literary London until 1900

Chaucerian London

The first literary reference to London appears in Chaucer's *Canterbury Tales,* written between 1387 and 1400: the 29 pilgrims of the tale (plus narrator) gather for their trip to Canterbury at the Tabard Inn in Talbot Yard, Southwark, and agree to share stories on the way there and back. The inn burnt down in 1676; a plaque marks the site of the building next to the popular George Inn (p170) pub today.

Shakespeare's London

Born in Warwickshire, William Shakespeare spent most of his adult life as an actor and playwright in London around the turn of the 17th century. He trod the boards of several theatres in both Shoreditch and Southwark, and wrote his greatest tragedies, including *Hamlet, Othello, Macbeth* and *King Lear,* for the original Globe theatre (now reconstructed as Shakespeare's Globe) on the South Bank. Although London was his home for most of his life, Shakespeare set nearly all his plays in foreign or imaginary lands. Only *Henry IV: Parts I & II* include a London setting – a tavern called the Boar's Head in Eastcheap (though he came close to home with *The Merry Wives of Windsor*).

Defoe & 18th-Century London

Daniel Defoe might be classified as the first true London writer, both living in and writing about the city during the early 18th century. He is most famous for his novels *Robinson Crusoe* (1719–20) and *Moll Flanders* (1722), which he wrote while living in Church St in Stoke Newington in northeast London. Defoe's *Journal of the Plague Year* is his most absorbing account of London life, documenting the horrors of the Great Plague during the summer and autumn of 1665.

Dickensian & 19th-Century London

Two early-19th-century Romantic poets drew inspiration from London. John Keats, born above a Moorgate public house in 1795, wrote 'Ode to a Nightingale' while living in Hampstead in 1819 and 'Ode on a Grecian Urn' reportedly after viewing the Parthenon frieze in the British Museum the same year. William Wordsworth discovered inspiration for the poem 'Upon Westminster Bridge' while passing through London in 1802.

Charles Dickens was the quintessential London author. When his father was interned at Marshalsea Prison in Southwark for not paying his debts, the 12-year-old Charles was forced to fend for himself on the streets. That grim period provided a font of experiences on which to draw for his writing. His novels most closely associated with London are *Oliver Twist,* with its gang of Clerkenwell thieves led by Fagin, and *Little Dorrit,* whose heroine was born in the Marshalsea Prison. The house in Bloomsbury where Dickens wrote *Oliver Twist* and two other novels now houses the Charles Dickens Museum (p97).

Built in 1567, the half-timbered Old Curiosity Shop (13–14 Portsmouth St, WC2) may have been the inspiration for Charles Dickens' novel. (It's now a shoe shop.) His close friend and biographer, John Forster, did live at nearby 57–58 Lincoln's Inn Fields.

Sir Arthur Conan Doyle portrayed a very different London, with his pipe-smoking, cocaine-injecting sleuth, Sherlock Holmes, coming to exemplify a cool and unflappable Englishness. Letters to the mythical hero and his admiring friend, Dr Watson, still arrive at 221b Baker St, where there's a museum (p109) to the fictitious Victorian detective.

London at the end of the 19th century appears in many books. Jerome K Jerome inserted a memorably witty description of visiting the maze at Hampton Court Palace into his *Three Men in a Boat.* At the turn of the 20th century Joseph Conrad chose Greenwich as the setting for *The Secret Agent;* HG Wells' *War of the Worlds* has wonderful descriptions of the London of that epoch. Somerset Maugham's first novel, *Liza of Lambeth,* was based on his experiences as an intern in the slums of South London, while *Of Human Bondage* provides a portrait of late-Victorian London.

Modern Literary London

American Writers & London

Among Americans who lived in and wrote about London at the turn of the 20th century, Henry James stands supreme with his *Daisy Miller* and *The Europeans. The People of the Abyss,* by socialist writer Jack London, is a sensitive portrait of poverty and despair in the East End. And who could forget Mark Twain's *Innocents Abroad* in which the inimitable humorist skewers both the Old and New Worlds? St Louis–born poet TS Eliot moved to London in 1915, where he published his poem 'The Love Song of J Alfred Prufrock' almost immediately and moved on to his groundbreaking epic 'The Waste Land', in which London is portrayed as an 'unreal city'.

The sternly modernist Senate House (1937) on Malet St in Bloomsbury contained offices of the Ministry of Information, where George Orwell's wife Eileen worked in the Censorship Department during WWII. It is thought to have been the inspiration for the Ministry of Truth in his classic dystopian 1949 novel *Nineteen Eighty-Four*.

Interwar Developments

The 1920s were the heyday of the so-called Bloomsbury Group, among them the writers Virginia Woolf (*Mrs Dalloway,* 1925) and Lytton Strachey (*Eminent Victorians,* 1918). Between the world wars, PG Wodehouse depicted London high life with his hilarious lampooning of the English upper classes in the Jeeves stories. Quentin Crisp, the self-proclaimed 'stately homo of England', provided the flipside, re-

LITERARY BLUE PLAQUES

The very first of London's Blue Plaques (p98) was put up in 1867, identifying the birthplace of the poet Lord Byron at 24 Holles St, W1, off Cavendish Sq, but the house was demolished in 1889. Since then a large percentage – some 25% of the 900-odd in place – have honoured writers and poets. The locations include everything from the offices of publisher Faber & Faber at 24 Russell Sq, where TS Eliot worked, to the Primrose Hill residence of Irish poet and playwright WB Yeats at 23 Fitzroy Rd, NW1 (where, incidentally, the US poet Sylvia Plath also briefly lived and committed suicide in 1963).

counting in his ribald and witty memoir *The Naked Civil Servant* (not published until 1968) what it was like to be openly gay in sexually repressed prewar London. George Orwell's experience of living as a beggar and manual labourer in London's East End coloured his book *Down and Out in Paris and London* (1933).

Postwar Literary London

The End of the Affair, Graham Greene's novel chronicling a passionate and doomed romance, takes place in and around Clapham Common just after WWII, while Elizabeth Bowen's *The Heat of the Day* is a sensitive, if melodramatic, account of living through the Blitz.

Colin MacInnes described the bohemian, multicultural world of 1950s Notting Hill in *Absolute Beginners,* while Doris Lessing captured the political mood of 1960s London in *The Four-Gated City,* the last of her five-book *Children of Violence* series. Lessing also provided some of the funniest and most vicious portrayals of 1990s London in *London Observed.* Nick Hornby, nostalgic about his days as a young football fan in *Fever Pitch* and obsessive about vinyl in *High Fidelity,* found himself the voice of a generation.

A larger-than-life statue of John Betjeman gazing up in wonder above the departures hall at St Pancras International Station recalls the former poet laureate's campaign in the 1960s to save the Victorian neo-Gothic structure.

Hanif Kureishi explored London from the perspective of ethnic minorities, specifically young Pakistanis, before it became fashionable. His best-known novels include *The Black Album* and *The Buddha of Suburbia.* He also wrote the screenplay for the groundbreaking film *My Beautiful Laundrette.* Author and playwright Caryl Phillips won plaudits for his description of the Caribbean immigrant's experience in *The Final Passage,* while Timothy Mo's *Sour Sweet* is a poignant and funny account of a Chinese family in the 1960s trying to adjust to British life.

The decades leading up to the turn of the third millennium were great ones for British literature, bringing a dazzling new generation of writers to the fore, including Martin Amis *(Money, London Fields),* Julian Barnes *(Metroland, Talking it Over),* Ian McEwan *(Enduring Love, Atonement),* Salman Rushdie *(Midnight's Children, The Satanic Verses),* AS Byatt *(Possession, Angels & Insects)* and Alan Hollinghurst *(The Swimming Pool Library, The Line of Beauty).*

Millennial London

Helen Fielding's *Bridget Jones's Diary* and its sequels, *Bridget Jones: The Edge of Reason* and the much later *Bridget Jones: Mad About the Boy,* launched the 'chick lit' genre, one that transcended the travails of a young single Londoner to become a worldwide phenomenon. Enfant terrible and incisive social commentator Will Self's *Grey Area* is a superb collection of short stories focusing on skewed and surreal aspects of the city. *The Book of Dave* is his hilarious, surreal story of a bitter, present-day London cabbie burying a book of his observations, which are later discovered and regarded as scripture by the people on the island of Ham. Britain in the distant future is an archipelago due to rising sea levels.

Peter Ackroyd names the city as the love of his life. *London: the Biography* is his inexhaustible paean to the capital, while *The Clerkenwell Tales* brings to life the 14th-century London of Chaucer. His more recent *The Canterbury Tales: A Retelling* renders Chaucer's timeless tales in lucid, compelling modern English. *Thames: Sacred River* is Ackroyd's fine monument to the muck, magic and mystery of the river through history.

Iain Sinclair is the bard of Hackney who, like Ackroyd, has spent his life obsessed with and fascinated by the capital. His acclaimed and ambitious *London Orbital,* a journey on foot around the M25, London's mammoth motorway bypass, is required London reading, while

LITERARY READINGS, TALKS & EVENTS

Covent Garden's Poetry Café (p127) is a favourite for lovers of verse, with almost daily readings and performances by established poets, open-mic evenings and writing workshops.

Both the British Library (p246) and the Institute of Contemporary Arts (p100) have excellent talks and lectures monthly, with well-known writers from all spectrums.

Bookshops, particularly Waterstones (p131), Foyles (p131) and the London Review Bookshop (p130), often stage readings and talks. Some major authors also now appear at the Southbank Centre (p165). Many such events are organised on an ad-hoc basis, so keep an eye on the freebie *Time Out* listings guide available every Tuesday or any of the weekend newspaper supplements, including the *Guide* distributed with the *Guardian* newspaper on Saturday.

Rodinsky's Room, coauthored with Rachel Lichtenstein, recounts the true story of a Jewish mystic-hermit whose room on Princelet St in Spitalfields is opened up after nearly two decades. *Hackney, That Rose-Red Empire* is an exploration of a borough that was once among London's most notorious but is now increasingly trendy.

Current Scene

Home to most of the UK's major publishers and its best bookshops, London remains a vibrant place for writers and readers alike. But the frustrating predominance of several powerful corporations within publishing can occasionally limit pioneering writing. It is often left to smaller houses to discover and groom new and as yet unproven writing talent.

This state of affairs has, however, stimulated an exciting literary fringe, which, although tiny, is very active and passionate about good writing. London still has many small presses where quality and innovation are prized over public-relations skills, and events kick off in bookshops and in the back rooms of pubs throughout the week.

Back in the mainstream, the big guns of the 1980s and 1990s, such as Martin Amis, Ian McEwan, Salman Rushdie and Julian Barnes, are still going strong, although new voices have broken through in the last decades, including Monica Ali, who brought the East End to life in *Brick Lane;* Zadie Smith, whose groundbreaking novel *White Teeth* was followed by *Swing Time,* the tale of two mixed-race girls from North London; and Elif Shafak, whose *Honour* tells of how traditional practices shatter and transform the lives of Turkish immigrants in 1970s East London. Jake Arnott's *The Long Firm* is an intelligent Soho-based gangster yarn.

'Rediscovered' author Howard Jacobson, variously called the 'Jewish Jane Austen' and the 'English Philip Roth', won the Booker Prize in 2010 for *The Finkler Question,* the first time the prestigious award had gone to a comic novel in a quarter-century. Literary titan and huge commercial success Hilary Mantel, author of *Wolf Hall,* won the same award for her historical novel *Bring up the Bodies* two years later. In 2019, in an exceptional move, the jury awarded the prize to two authors: Canadian novelist Margaret Atwood for *Testaments,* her long-awaited sequel to the dystopian *The Handmaid's Tale,* and Bernadine Evaristo, the first black woman to win the award, for *Girl, Woman, Other,* which tells the separate but linked stories of a dozen British women of colour.

Literary Pubs

- *George Inn (South Bank)*
- *Museum Tavern (West End)*
- *French House (West End)*
- *Prospect of Whitby (East London)*
- *Dove (West London)*

Theatre & Dance

London has more theatrical history than almost anywhere else in the world, and it's still being made nightly on the stages of the West End, South Bank and the vast London fringe. No visit to the city is complete without taking in a show, and just walking among the theatre-bound throngs in the evening in the West End is an electrifying experience. If dance is on your list, take your pick from the capital's various and varied world-class companies.

Above: Graham Butler as Christopher in Mark Haddon's *The Curious incident of the Dog in the Night-Time* at the National Theatre (p174)

Theatre

Elizabethan Period

Little is known about London theatre before the Elizabethan period, when a series of 'playhouses', including the aptly named Theatre, were built in Shoreditch and later on the south bank of the Thames. Although the playwrights of the time – Shakespeare, his great rival Ben

Jonson *(The Alchemist. Bartholomew Fair)* and Christopher Marlowe *(Doctor Faustus, Edward II)* – are now considered timeless intellectual geniuses, theatre was then a raucous popular entertainment, where the crowd drank and heckled the actors. The Puritans responded by shutting the playhouses at the start of the Civil War in 1642.

Restoration Theatre

Three years after the return of the monarchy in 1660, the first famous Drury Lane theatre was built, and a particularly dynamic period began under the patronage of the rakish King Charles II. Borrowing influences from Italian and French theatre, 'Restoration theatre' incorporated drama (such as John Dryden's *All For Love,* 1677) and comedy (John Vanbrugh's *The Provoked Wife*). The first female actors appeared – in Elizabethan times men played female roles – and Charles II is recorded as having had an ongoing affair with at least one, Nell Gwyn.

If innovation and change are too much for you, drop by St Martin's Theatre, where the same production of *The Mousetrap* has been running since 1952. Or there's the monolithic musicals that show no sign of letting up anytime soon: *Phantom of the Opera, Lion King, Les Miserables, Wicked, Mamma Mia!* et al.

Victorian Period

Despite the success of John Gay's *The Beggar's Opera* (1728), Oliver Goldsmith's farce *She Stoops to Conquer* (1773) and Richard Sheridan's *The Rivals* and *The School for Scandal* (1777) at Drury Lane, popular music halls replaced serious theatre under the Victorians. Light comic operetta, as defined by Gilbert and Sullivan *(HMS Pinafore, The Pirates of Penzance, The Mikado),* was all the rage. A sea change only arose with the emergence at the end of the 19th century of such compelling playwrights as George Bernard Shaw *(Pygmalion, The Apple Cart)* and Oscar Wilde *(An Ideal Husband, The Importance of Being Earnest).*

The 20th Century

In their footsteps appeared such comic wits as Noël Coward *(Private Lives, Design for Living)* and earnest dramatists like Terence Rattigan *(The Winslow Boy, The Browning Version)* and JB Priestley *(An Inspector Calls).* However, it wasn't until the 1950s and 1960s that English drama yet again experienced such a fertile period as it had in the Elizabethan era.

Perfectly encapsulating the social upheaval of the time, John Osborne's *Look Back in Anger* at the Royal Court Theatre in 1956 heralded a rash of new writing there, including Harold Pinter's *The Homecoming,* Joe Orton's *Loot,* Edward Bond's *Saved* and Arnold Wesker's *Roots.* During the same period, many of today's leading theatre companies were formed, including the National Theatre.

Though somewhat eclipsed by the National Theatre, today's Royal Court Theatre (p199) retains a fine tradition of new writing. In the past

SHAKESPEARE ON OFFER

Shakespeare's legacy is generously honoured on the city's stages, most notably by the Royal Shakespeare Company (RSC) and at the reconstructed Globe theatre. The RSC stages one or two of the bard's plays in London annually, although it has no London home. (Its productions are based in Stratford-upon-Avon and usually transfer to the capital later in their run.)

Shakespeare's Globe (p174) on the South Bank attempts to recreate an Elizabethan open-air theatre experience. Its indoor **Sam Wanamaker Playhouse**, which opened in 2014 and seats just 340 spectators, is a unique place to savour Shakespeare's words, with an intimate candlelit atmosphere. Shakespeare's plays remain at the core of the Globe's programming, but other classic and contemporary plays do get a look-in from time to time.

CHILDREN'S THEATRE

If you've got junior culture-vultures in tow, make sure to scan the theatre listings for kid-friendly West End smashes such as *Matilda the Musical*, based on the book by Roald Dahl, and *School of Rock*, the stage version of Jack Black's film with music by Andrew Lloyd Webber. It's also worth checking out what's on at the Little Angel Theatre (www.littleangeltheatre.com) in Islington, which specialises in puppetry, and the Unicorn Theatre (www.unicorntheatre.com) in Southwark, which stages productions for infants, children and young adults.

decade, it has nurtured such talented playwrights as Jez Butterworth *(Jerusalem, Ferryman)*, Caryl Churchill *(Top Girls)*, Ayub Khan-Din *(East Is East)*, Conor McPherson *(The Weir, Shining City)*, Joe Penhall *(Dumb Show)*, Richard Bean *(The Heretic)*, Lucy Kirkwood *(The Children)*, Laura Wade *(Posh)*, Bruce Norris *(Clybourne Park)* and Debbie Tucker Green *(Ear for Eye)*.

London's Best Theatres

- *National Theatre (South Bank)*
- *Royal Court Theatre (Kensington & Hyde Park)*
- *Donmar Warehouse (West End)*
- *Old Vic (South Bank)*
- *Shakespeare's Globe (South Bank)*
- *Young Vic (South Bank)*

Today's Scene

London remains a thrilling place for theatre lovers. Nowhere else, with the possible exception of New York, offers such a diversity of high-quality drama, first-rate musical theatre and a sizzling fringe. Whether it's Hollywood A-listers gracing tiny stages and earning Equity minimum wage for their efforts or lavish West End musicals, London remains an undisputed theatrical world leader and innovator.

While the West End's 'Theatreland' gets most of the attention, some of London's hottest theatre tickets are for a trio of innovative venues south of the river: the National Theatre, the Old Vic and the Young Vic. Former National Theatre director Sir Nicholas Hytner's 900-seat Bridge Theatre, which opened beside Tower Bridge in Borough in 2017, might also be added to this list. Other innovative off–West End theatres include the Almeida in Islington, the Bush Theatre in Shepherd's Bush, the Hampstead Theatre, the Theatre Royal Stratford East and the Southwark Playhouse. Many successful off–West End plays eventually make their way to the West End for a longer theatrical run.

In recent years, the mainstream West End has re-established its credentials, with extraordinary hits by the likes of the Donmar Warehouse, while the smarter end of the fringe continues to shine with risky, controversial and newsworthy productions.

Big names can often be seen treading Theatreland's hallowed boards – think Bradley Cooper playing *The Elephant Man* at the Haymarket Theatre Royal; Helen Mirren and then Kristen Scott Thomas playing the Queen in *The Audience* at the Apollo Shaftesbury; Imelda Staunton belting it out in *Gypsy* at the Savoy Theatre or being both witty and malicious in *Who's Afraid of Virginia Woolf?* at the Harold Pinter Theatre; or David Tennant being filthy in *Don Juan in Soho* at Wyndham's Theatre. Over the last few decades a troupe of American stars have taken hefty pay cuts to tread the London boards, including Glenn Close, Gwyneth Paltrow, Gillian Anderson, Christian Slater and Danny DeVito.

There's something for all dramatic tastes in London, from contemporary political satire to creative reworking of old classics, and all shades in between. Recent productions that have won critical acclaim include the children's musical *Matilda*, the adaptation of Mark Haddon's novel *The Curious Incident of the Dog in the Night-Time*, David Grieg's *Charlie and the Chocolate Factory* directed by Sam Mendes, Conor McPherson's

Girl from the North Country with music by Bob Dylan, feel-good musical *Everybody's Talking About Jamie* by Tom MacRae and Dan Gillespie Sells and the latest money-minter from JK Rowling, *Harry Potter and the Cursed Child*.

Dance

Whether contemporary, classical or crossover, London will have the right moves for you. As one of the world's great dance capitals, London's artistic environment has long created and attracted talented choreographers with both the inspiration and aspiration to fashion innovative productions.

London's most celebrated choreographer is award-winning Sir Matthew Bourne – *Play Without Words, Edward Scissorhands, Dorian Gray, Oliver!, Cinderella, Swan Lake* (with male swans), and *Romeo and Juliet* with 80 new dancers – who has been repeatedly showered with praise for his reworking of classics. Another leading London-based talent is Wayne McGregor, who worked as movement director on *Harry Potter and the Goblet of Fire* and is a Professor of Choreography at the acclaimed Trinity Laban Conservatoire of Music and Dance in Greenwich.

The Place (p128) in Bloomsbury is one of the most important modern dance venues in London and the home of the edgy Richard Alston Dance Company. Sadler's Wells (p218) – the birthplace of English classical ballet in the 19th century – continues to deliver exciting programming covering many styles of dance. Its roster of 17 'associate artists' includes such luminaries as Matthew Bourne, Russell Maliphant, Sidi Larbi Cherkaoui, Wayne McGregor, Crystal Pite, Nitin Sawhney, Christopher Wheeldon, Sylvie Guillem, Kate Prince and Hofesh Shechter. **Sadler's Wells East**, a purpose-built branch seating 500, will open in Stratford in 2022.

Covent Garden's Royal Opera House (p127) is the impressive home of London's leading classical-dance troupe, the world-famous Royal Ballet. The company largely sticks to the traditional – *Giselle, Romeo and Juliet, Sleeping Beauty* – but more contemporary influences occasionally seep into productions.

One of the world's best companies, the **English National Ballet** (Map p462; ☎020-7581 1245; www.ballet.org.uk; 41 Hopewell Sq, E14; ⓤCanning Town), is a touring ballet company. You may be fortunate enough to catch it at one of its various venues in London – principally at the London Coliseum in Soho.

For more cutting-edge work, the innovative **Rambert Dance Company** (Map p452; ☎020-8630 0600; www.rambert.org.uk; 99 Upper Ground, SE1; ⓤWaterloo) is the UK's foremost contemporary dance troupe and arguably the most creative force in UK dance.

Another important venue for experimental dance is the Barbican (p156) in the City, which is particularly good at presenting new works exploring the crossover of dance, theatre and music.

Consult London's weekly *Time Out* (available on Tuesday) for theatrical listings. Even if you've heard that a hot new play is completely sold out for months ahead, it's often possible to secure a ticket via standby lists and the like. Check individual theatre websites, apps such as TodayTix or visit Tkts Leicester Square.

UG WILSON/CORBIS VIA GETTY IMAGES ©

Art & Fashion

When it comes to both visual art and fashion, London has traditionally been overshadowed by other European capitals. Yet many of history's greatest artists have spent time in London (Monet, Van Gogh, Whistler), and London is at the helm of contemporary art and trailblazing street fashion. Of London's 1500-strong art galleries, most of the established ones are in Mayfair, but for more cutting-edge work head for Hackney in East London and Bermondsey south of the river.

Art

Holbein to Turner

Above: *The Ambassadors* by Hans Holbein the Younger

It wasn't until the Tudors came to power that art began to take off in London. The German Hans Holbein the Younger (1497–1543) was court painter to Henry VIII, and one of his finest works, *The Ambassadors* (1533), hangs in the National Gallery. A batch of great portrait artists worked at court during the 17th century, the best being Anthony van Dyck (1599–1641), who painted the *Equestrian Portrait of Charles I* (1637–38), which is also in the National Gallery. Charles I was a keen collector of art, and it was during his reign that the Raphael Cartoons (1515–16), now in the Victoria & Albert Museum, came to London.

Local artists began to emerge in the 18th century, including portrait and landscape painter Thomas Gainsborough (1727–88); William Hogarth (1697–1764), whose social commentary *A Rake's Progress* (1732–34) hangs in Sir John Soane's Museum; and poet, engraver and watercolourist William Blake (1757–1827). A superior visual artist to Blake, John Constable (1776–1837) studied the clouds and skies above Hampstead Heath, sketching hundreds of scenes that he would later match with subjects in his landscapes. George Stubbs' iconic *Whistlejacket* (1762) is a singular and iconic portrait of an Arabian thoroughbred horse.

JMW Turner (1775–1851), equally at home with oils and watercolours, represented the pinnacle of 19th-century British art. Through innovative use of colour and gradations of light, he created a new atmosphere that seemed to capture the wonder, sublimity and terror of nature. His later works, including *The Fighting Temeraire* (1839), *Snow Storm: Steam-Boat off a Harbour's Mouth* (1842), *Peace – Burial at Sea* (1842) and *Rain, Steam and Speed – the Great Western Railway* (1844), now in the Tate Britain and the National Gallery, were increasingly abstract, and although widely vilified at the time, later inspired the Impressionist works of Claude Monet.

Arguably the greatest artworks on display in London include *The Fighting Temeraire* (JMW Turner, National Gallery); *A Bar at the Folies-Bergère* (Edouard Manet, Courtauld Gallery); *Sunflowers* (Vincent Van Gogh, National Gallery); *The Virgin of the Rocks* (Leonardo da Vinci, National Gallery); *Three Studies for Figures at the Base of a Crucifixion* (Francis Bacon, Tate Britain); *Metamorphosis of Narcissus* (Salvador Dalí, Tate Modern); and *The Seagram Murals* (Mark Rothko, Tate Modern).

The Pre-Raphaelites to Hockney

The brief but splendid flowering of the Pre-Raphaelite Brotherhood (1848–53) took its inspiration from the Romantic poets, abandoning the pastel-coloured rusticity of the day in favour of big, bright and intense depictions of medieval legends and female beauty. The movement's main proponents were William Holman Hunt, John Everett Millais and Dante Gabriel Rossetti; artists Edward Burne-Jones and Ford Madox Brown were also strongly associated with the Pre-Raphaelites. Works by all can be found at Tate Britain, with highlights being Millais' *Christ in the House of His Parents* (1849–50) and *Ophelia* (1851–5), Rossetti's *Ecce Ancilla Domini!* (The Annunciation, 1849–50), John William Waterhouse's *The Lady of Shalott* (1888) and William Holman Hunt's *The Awakening Conscience* (1853). Don't miss John Singer Sargent's *Carnation, Lily, Lily, Rose* (1885–6).

In the early 20th century, cubism and futurism helped generate the short-lived Vorticists, a modernist group of London artists and poets, led by the dapper Wyndham Lewis (1882–1957), that sought to capture dynamism in artistic form. Sculptors Henry Moore (1898–1986) and Barbara Hepworth (1903–75) both typified the modernist movement in British sculpture. You can see examples of their work in the gardens of Kenwood House (p249) in Hampstead Heath. Walter Richard Sickert (*La Hollandaise,* 1906), a member of the Camden Town Group of post-impressionist artists, was an important influence on distinctively British styles of avant-garde art.

After WWII, art transformed yet again. In 1945 the tortured, Irish-born painter Francis Bacon (1909–92) caused a stir when he exhibited his contorted *Three Studies for Figures at the Base of a Crucifixion* – now on display at the Tate Britain – and afterwards continued to spook the art world with his repulsive yet mesmerising visions. Also owned by the Tate is Bacon's *Triptych – August 1972,* painted in the aftermath of his lover George Dyer's suicide.

Carnation, Lily, Lily, Rose by John Singer Sargent

The late art critic Robert Hughes once eulogised Bacon's contemporary, Lucian Freud (1922–2011), as 'the greatest living realist painter'. Freud's early work was often surrealist, but from the 1950s the bohemian Freud exclusively focused on pale, muted portraits – often nudes, and frequently of friends and family (although he also painted the Queen).

Also prominent in the late 1950s was painter and collage artist Peter Blake, whose work includes the cover design of the Beatles' 1967 album *Sgt Pepper's Lonely Hearts Club Band*. London in the swinging '60s was perfectly encapsulated by pop art, its vocabulary best articulated by David Hockney, born in 1937 and still active today. Hockney gained a reputation as one of the leading pop artists through his early use of magazine-style images, but after a move to California, his work became increasingly naturalistic. Two of his most famous works are the Tate-owned *A Bigger Splash* (1967) and *Mr and Mrs Clark and Percy* (1970–1).

Gilbert & George were quintessential English conceptual artists of the 1960s. The Spitalfields odd couple are still at the heart of the British art world, having now become a part of the establishment. Likewise Bridget Riley (*Nataraja,* 1993), is celebrated for her colourful Op art.

Brit Art

Despite its incredibly rich art collections, Britain had never led, dominated or even really participated in a particular artistic epoch or style as Paris had in the 1920s or New York in the 1950s. That all changed in the twilight of the 20th century, when 1990s London became the beating heart of the art world.

Brit Art sprang from a show called *Freeze,* which was staged in a Docklands warehouse in 1988, organised by artist and showman

Damien Hirst and largely featuring his fellow graduates from Goldsmiths' College. Influenced by pop culture and punk, this loose movement was soon catapulted to notoriety by the advertising guru Charles Saatchi, who bought an extraordinary number of works and came to dominate the local art scene.

Brit Art was brash, decadent, ironic, easy to grasp and eminently marketable. Hirst chipped in with a cow sliced in half and preserved in formaldehyde; flies buzzed around another cow's head and were zapped in his early work *A Thousand Years*. Another notable Hirst work is *Saint Bartholomew, Exquisite Pain* in the Church of St Bartholomew the Great. Chris Ofili provoked with *The Holy Virgin Mary*, a painting of the black Madonna made partly with elephant excrement; brothers Jake and Dinos Chapman produced mannequins of children with genitalia on their heads; and Marcus Harvey created a portrait of notorious child-killer Myra Hindley, made entirely with children's handprints, whose value skyrocketed when it was repeatedly vandalised by the public.

The areas of Shoreditch, Hoxton, Spitalfields and Whitechapel – where many artists lived, worked and hung out – became the epicentre of the movement, and a rash of galleries opened up. For the 10 years or so that it rode the wave of publicity, the defining characteristics of Brit Art were notoriety and shock value. Its two biggest names, Damien Hirst and Tracey Emin, inevitably became celebrities.

Some critics argued the hugely hyped movement was the product of a cultural vacuum, an example of the emperor's new clothes, with people afraid to criticise the works for fear they'd look stupid. Others praised its freshness and ingenuity.

The biggest date on the art calendar is the controversial Turner Prize at the Tate Britain. Any British visual artist is eligible to enter, although there is a strong preference for conceptual art.

Since 1999 the Fourth Plinth Commission has offered a platform in Trafalgar Sq for novel, and frequently controversial, works by contemporary artists, including Antony Gormley and Marc Quinn.

LONDON ARTISTS TODAY

London continues to generate talent across a range of artistic media, keeping critics on their toes. These are some of the biggest-name artists working in contemporary London today:

Antony Gormley Sculptor best known for the 22m-high *Angel of the North*, beside the A1 trunk road near Gateshead in northern England. In London, look for *Planets* outside the British Library (p246), *Quantum Cloud* below the Emirates Air Line (p416) in the Docklands, and *Room* above the entrance of the Beaumont (p349).

Anish Kapoor Indian-born sculptor working in London since the 1970s. His *ArcelorMittal Orbit* (p229) towers over Queen Elizabeth Olympic Park; *Ishi's Light* is in the Tate Modern.

Marc Quinn *Self* is a sculpture of the artist's head made from his frozen blood, which Quinn recasts every five years. It's owned by the National Portrait Gallery (p42).

Banksy The anonymous street artist whose work is a worldwide phenomenon hails from Bristol, but you'll find many of his most famous works on London's streets.

Chantal Joffe London-based artist well known for naive, expressionist large-scale portraits of women and children; Saatchi Gallery (p191) owns many of her works.

Yinka Sonibare British-Nigerian artist explores cultural identity, colonialism and post-colonialism; his hallmark material is brightly coloured Dutch wax fabric (*The Swing after Fragonard*, 2001).

Mona Hatoum Dalston-based Palestinian multimedia and installation artist (*Present Tense*, 1996).

Fashion

The British fashion industry has always been about younger, directional and more left-field designs. London fashion focuses on streetwear and the 'wow' factor, with a few old reliables keeping the frame in place and mingling with hot new designers, who are often unpolished through inexperience, but bursting with ideas, talent and creativity. As a result, London is exciting in a global sense, and nobody with an interest in street fashion will be disappointed.

London weathered a tough decade after the economic downturn at the end of the millennium's first decade, and its status as an international fashion centre suffered. But the city has returned to the heart of the fashion universe, boasting a bright new firmament of young stars.

Find high-street fashion at Oxford St and Westfield Stratford City; new designers at Shoreditch and Spitalfields boutiques; luxury brands at Old Bond St and Mayfair; men's tailoring on Savile Row and Jermyn St; high-end department stores in Knightsbridge and Oxford St; vintage in Spitalfields and Dalston; and jewellery in Hatton Garden.

London's Who's Who

The biggest names in London fashion need little introduction. They include long-enduring punk maven Vivienne Westwood, menswear designer Paul Smith and ethical fashionista Stella McCartney, who has transcended the connection to her famous father (former Beatle, Sir Paul) to become world famous in her own right. Making a splash on both sides of the Atlantic is the eponymous label of one Victoria Beckham, erstwhile Spice Girl and wife of ex-footballer David.

Other big international names include Riccardo Tisci (chief creative at Burberry, late of Givenchy), Sarah Burton (royal wedding dress designer for Kate Middleton and creative director at Alexander McQueen) and Clare Waight Keller, artistic director of Givenchy who designed Meghan Markle's wedding dress.

With his witty designs and eclectic references, St Martin's graduate Giles Deacon has taken London fashion by storm with his own eponymous label. Gareth Pugh is also someone to look out for, another St Martin's alumnus who took the underground club fashions of Shoreditch and transposed them onto the shop floor. Other designers making a buzz are Erdem Moralıoğlu, Henry Holland, Jonathan Saunders and Christopher Kane.

London Fashion Abroad

The high point on the London fashion calendar is London Fashion Week (www.londonfashionweek.co.uk), held in February and September each year at various venues throughout the city including Somerset House on the Strand.

The influence of London's designers continues to spread well beyond the capital. The 'British Fashion Pack' still work at, or run, many of the major Continental fashion houses. Houses such as Alexander McQueen retain design studios in London, and erstwhile defectors to foreign catwalks such as Luella Bartley and Matthew Williamson have returned to London to show their collections.

Fame & Celebrity

London fashion appears eccentric when compared to the classic feel of the major Parisian and Milanese houses or the cool street-cred of New York designers, and this spirit was best exemplified by Isabella Blow. This legendary stylist discovered McQueen, Stella Tennant and Sophie Dahl (among many others) during her career at *Vogue* and *Tatler*. Blow sadly committed suicide in 2007. A further shock for the industry was the tragic suicide of McQueen three years later at the age of 40.

British fashion's 'bad girl' Kate Moss has been in and out of the news since the start of her career – for both her sense of style and Topshop clothes line and her off-runway antics. The fashion world thrives on notoriety, but former Wilson's grammar school pupil John

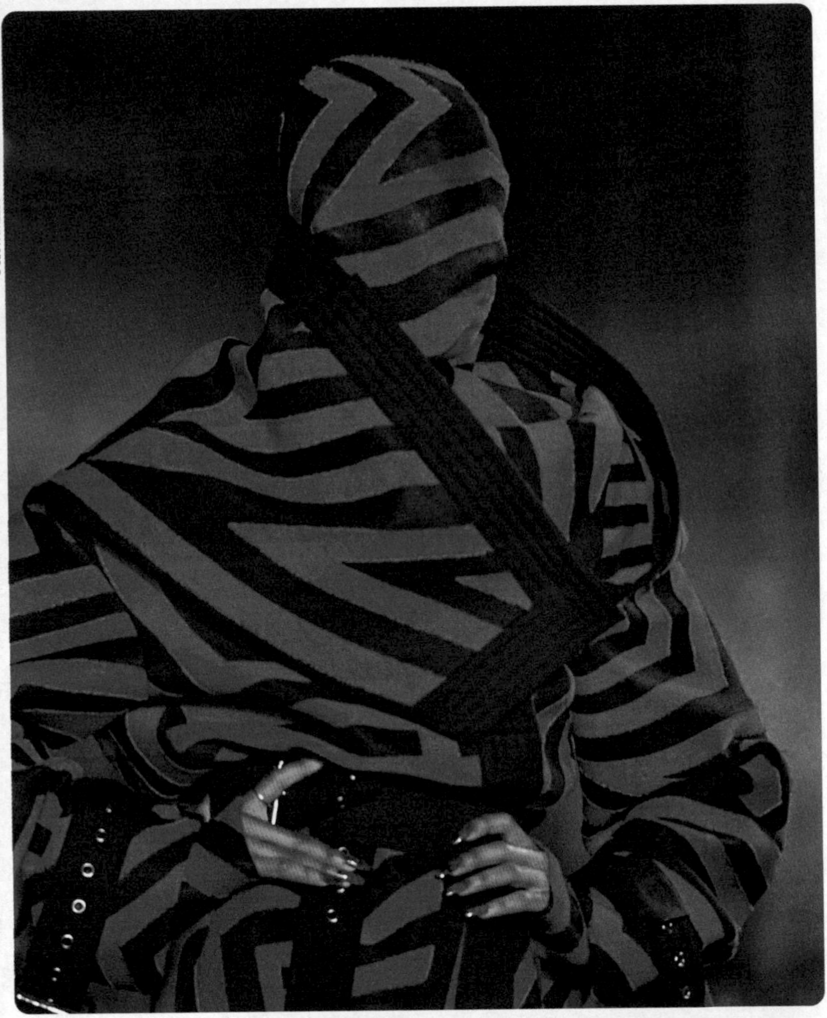

VICTOR VIRGILE/GAMMA-RAPHO VIA GETTY IMAGES ©

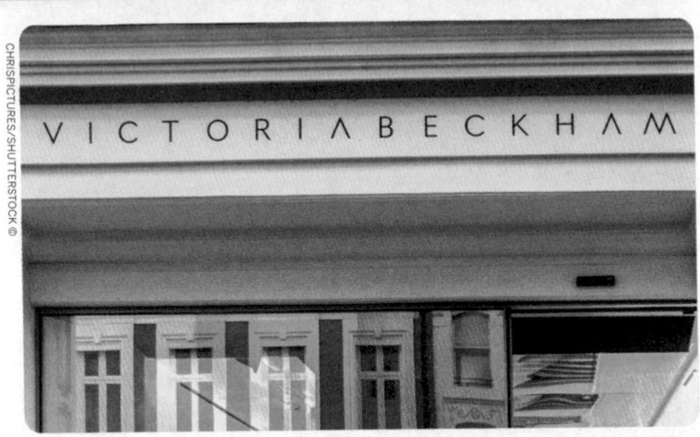

CHRISPICTURES/SHUTTERSTOCK ©

Top: Model in runway show, London Fashion Week
Bottom: Victoria Beckham store, Mayfair

Oxford Circus junction at Oxford St and Regent St (p101)

Galliano's much-publicised arrest in 2011 for an anti-Semitic rant against a couple in a Paris cafe was a nadir for Dior's chief designer, who was consequently dropped by the fashion house. He has since joined Maison Margiela, where he is employed as creative director and has unveiled a new perfume for the house called Mutiny.

Despite these tragic losses and moments of scandal, London retains all the innovative ingredients for exhilarating developments in fashion, today and tomorrow.

The Music Scene

Drawing upon a deep reservoir of talent, London's modern music scene is one of the city's greatest sources of artistic power and is a magnet for bands and hopefuls from all musical hemispheres. Periodically a world leader in musical fashion and innovative soundscapes, London blends its home-grown talent with a continuous influx of styles and cultures, keeping currents flowing and inspiration percolating.

The Swinging '60s

In the early 1960s, London was emerging from the coffee bar and skiffle era. Bethnal Green's teenage wonder, sugar-coated Helen Shapiro, was voted Britain's top singer. Shoreditch's mellifluous Matt Monroe crooned his way to national stardom, soundtracking 'From Russia With Love' and 'Born Free' along the way.

At around the same time that The Beatles from Liverpool were making their first recordings with George Martin at Abbey Road Studios in St John's Wood, a group of London lads were appearing on stage together for the first time at the Marquee Club in Oxford St. An R&B band with frequent trajectories into blues and rock and roll, the Rolling Stones quickly set up as a more rough-edged counterpoint to the cleaner, boys-next-door image of the Fab Four.

In the musical explosion that followed, there was one band that chronicled London life like no other. Hailing from Muswell Hill in North London, the Kinks started out with a garage R&B sound not dissimilar to that of the Stones, but eventually began to incorporate elements of the Victorian music hall tradition into their music while liberally seeding their lyrics with London place names (eg 'Waterloo Sunset').

The Who, from West London, attracted attention to their brand of gritty rock by smashing guitars on stage, propelling TVs from hotel windows and driving cars into swimming pools. Struggling to be heard above the din was inspirational mod band the Small Faces, formed in 1965 in East London. They burned brightly before splintering and partially reforming as Faces, a band featuring Ronnie Wood and Rod Stewart on vocals.

Seattle-born Jimi Hendrix came to London, lived on Brook St in Soho and took guitar playing to unseen

LONDON MAKES TRACKS

1967

'Waterloo Sunset' (The Kinks) Unimpeachable classic from the '60s.

1978

'(I Don't Want to Go to) Chelsea' (Elvis Costello) Punchy Costello from the early years.

1978

'Baker Street' (Gerry Rafferty) With an iconic and spine-tingling saxophone riff.

1979

'London Calling' (The Clash) Raw and potent punk anthem.

1984

'West End Girls' (Pet Shop Boys) Smooth and glossy first chart success from the British pop duo.

1989

'Twenty-Four Minutes from Tulse Hill' (Carter the Unstoppable Sex Machine) SW2 finds fame in this throbbing indie track.

1993

'Buddha of Suburbia' (David Bowie) One of the Thin White Duke's most sublime songs.

2004

'Round Here' (George Michael) Moving song drawing on the singer's recollections of his first day at school.

heights before tragically dying in a flat in the Samarkand Hotel in Notting Hill in 1970. Meanwhile West Hampstead's Dusty Springfield crossed the pond, signed to Motown and became one of the decade's biggest female singers. In July 1969 the Stones famously staged their free concert in Hyde Park in front of more than 250,000 adoring fans.

'60s Songs

- *'Play with Fire' (The Rolling Stones)*
- *'Eight Miles High' (The Byrds)*
- *'The London Boys' (David Bowie)*
- *'Waterloo Sunset' (The Kinks)*
- *'Sunny Goodge Street' (Donovan)*

The '70s

A local band called Tyrannosaurus Rex had enjoyed moderate success throughout the '60s. In 1970 they changed their name to T.Rex, frontman Marc Bolan donned a bit of glitter and the world's first 'glam' band was born. Glam rock encouraged the youth of uptight Britain to be whatever they wanted to be. Baritone-voiced Brixton boy David Jones (aka David Bowie) then altered the rock landscape with his astonishing *The Rise and Fall of Ziggy Stardust and the Spiders from Mars* in 1972, one of the decade's seminal albums. Genre-spanning Roxy Music blended art rock and synth pop into a sophisticated glam sound.

Back at the rock face, a little band called Led Zeppelin (formed in 1968) were busy cultivating the roots of heavy metal. Two years later Zanzibar-born Farrokh Bulsara, by then known as Freddie Mercury, led Queen to become one of the greatest rock-and-roll stars of all time. British-American band Fleetwood Mac left blues for pop rock and stormed the charts in the US as well as in Britain; their landmark *Rumours* became the eighth-highest-selling album in history.

'70s Songs

- *'Do the Strand' (Roxy Music)*
- *'London Boys' (T.Rex)*
- *'Baker Street' (Gerry Rafferty)*
- *'(I Don't Want to Go to) Chelsea' (Elvis Costello)*
- *'London Calling' (The Clash)*

Meanwhile, in the back rooms of pubs like the Half Moon in Putney, the Bull and Gate in Kentish Town and the Dublin Castle in Camden, reaction against the excesses of the big stadium rock bands began to foment. A stripped-back version of R&B, this new 'pub rock' laid the foundations of the revolution to follow. Small venues, independent record companies and easy-to-master licks were the blueprint. Soon-to-be-known names like Joe Strummer, Ian Dury, the Stranglers, Dr Feelgood and Eddie and the Hot Rods emerged from this scene.

Suddenly it seemed everyone in London could start a band. Stoke Newington's arch impresario Malcolm McLaren was never far away from the action; his Sex Pistols was the most notorious of a wave of so-called punk bands that began playing to pogoing and spitting crowds around London in 1976 to anthems like 'Anarchy in the UK'.

The Clash, also Londoners, harnessed the raw anger of the time into a collar-grabbing brand of political protest that would see them outlast their peers, treading the fine line between angry punks and great songwriters. The disillusioned generation finally had a plan and a leader in frontman Joe Strummer; London Calling is a spirited call to arms. And it wasn't just a guy thing. Chrissie Hynde, the Slits, X-Ray Spex and Siouxsie Sioux brought a vital and sometimes skewed sensibility to London's post-punk scene.

'80s Songs

- *'Driving in My Car' (Madness)*
- *'Electric Avenue' (Eddy Grant)*
- *'West End Girls' (Pet Shop Boys)*
- *'London Girl' (The Pogues)*
- *'London' (The Smiths)*

Punk cleared the air and into the oxygen-rich atmosphere swarmed a gaggle of late-'70s acts. The Damned sought out an innovative niche as goth-punk pioneers. The Jam deftly vaulted the abyss between punk and mod revivalism (lead singer and 'Modfather' Paul Weller followed up with a hugely successful solo career after sophisti-pop hits with the Style Council) and Madness put the nutty sound on the London map.

Perhaps a reaction to a shabby and underpopulated London, kids started to party like it was 1933 Berlin. New Wave and the New Romantics quickly shimmied into the fast-changing music scene, ushering in the '80s with the likes of Boy George, Adam Ant and Spandau Ballet.

The '80s

Guitars disappeared, swiftly replaced by keyboard synthesisers and drum machines. Fashion and image became indivisible from music. Thin ties, winklepickers, Velcro-fastening white sneakers, spandex, densely pleated trousers and heavy make-up dazzled at every turn. Hair was big. Overpriced, oversexed and way overdone, '80s London was a roll call of hair-gelled pop: Spandau Ballet, Culture Club, Wham! and Bananarama. Wham!'s Georgios Kyriacos Panayiotou changed his name to George Michael and gained massive success as a solo artist.

While the late '80s brought blond boy band Bros and the starlets of the Stock Aitken Waterman hit factory (including Londoners Mel & Kim and Samantha Fox), relief had already been assured from up north with the arrival of the Smiths and their alternative-rock innovations. In the closing years of the decade, fellow Mancunians the Stone Roses and the Happy Mondays devised a new sound that had grown out of the recent acid-house raves. Dance exploded in 1988's summer of love, with Soul II Soul, dilated pupils and a stage set for rave anthems such as the KLF's mighty 'What Time is Love?'. A generation was gripped by dance music and a new lexicon ruled: techno, electronica, hip hop, garage, house and trance.

Britpop & the '90s

The early 1990s saw the explosion of yet another new scene: Britpop, a genre broadly defined as a punky take on The Beatles. A high-profile battle between two of the biggest bands, Blur from London and Oasis from Manchester, drew a line in the musical sand.

Weighing in on the London side were the brilliant Suede and Elastica, not to mention Sheffield defectors to the capital, Pulp (with their irrepressible lead man, Jarvis Cocker). Skirting around the edges, doing their own thing, were Radiohead from Oxford.

But other musical styles were cooking. London's Asian community made a big splash in the early 21st century, with Talvin Singh and Nitin Sawhney fusing dance with traditional Indian music, and Asian Dub Foundation bringing their unique mix of rapcore, dub, dancehall, ragga, and political comment to an ever-widening audience.

Arguably the greatest global fame in this period was attained by the London-based boy and girl bands Take That, All Saints, East 17 and the Spice Girls. Their enduring popularity is reflected in the reunions of some of these bands decades later and the Spice Girls' appearance in the London Olympics closing ceremony in 2012, which cemented them as an inherent part of British music culture.

As Britpop ebbed in the late '90s, other currents were flowing into town, and drum 'n' bass and electronica found an anthem-packed sound with DJs like Goldie and London band Faithless seeing in the millennium.

2006

'LDN' (Lily Allen) Catchy ska-beat hit from the London popster.

2007

'Hometown Glory' (Adele) Exquisite celebration of West Norwood from the Tottenham-born songster.

2007

'London Town' (Kano) London rapper on his hometown.

2008

'Warwick Avenue' (Duffy) The beautiful voice of this Welsh starlet puts Warwick Ave Tube station on the musical map.

2011

'The City' (Ed Sheeran) Folkie Sheeran has a cynic's eye for the joys and trials of London.

2013

'Goin' Crazy' (Dizzee Rascal & Robbie Williams) Rascal and Williams meet up in Dalston on souped-up mobility scooters.

2013

'My Name is London Town' (Reg Meuross) Sweeping, bittersweet take on the capital recorded at Abbey Road Studios.

2015

'River Lea' (Adele) Much-lauded singer's paean to the river flowing through her North London stomping grounds.

2019

'Take Me Back to London' (Ed Sheeran & Stormzy) Megastar's grime-inspired single with Croydon-born rapper.

The Noughties

London band Coldplay – melodic rockers led by falsetto front man Chris Martin – first made a big splash in the UK at the dawn of the new millennium, before finding international fame. After eight best-selling studio albums – the latest a double – their position as one of the world's biggest rock bands appears unshakeable.

Pete Doherty and Carl Barât of the Libertines renewed interest in punky guitar music following its post-Britpop malaise. Their 2002 debut single 'What a Waster' created a huge splash and their first album, *Up the Bracket,* went platinum. Doherty went on to form Babyshambles and Barât released albums with Dirty Pretty Things and The Jackals.

Fronted by eponymous Alison, Goldfrapp brought a seductive and sensual electronica to the fore on the albums *Black Cherry* and *Supernature,* before abruptly departing in a mystical pastoral-folk direction on the band's much-applauded *Seventh Tree* (2008).

The decade also saw the rise of grime and its successor genre, dubstep – two indigenous London musical forms born in the East End out of a fusion of hip hop, drum 'n' bass and UK garage. Dizzee Rascal and Kano are the best-known rappers working in the genre.

Other London talents from the 2000s that won both awards and enormous success on both sides of the Atlantic include the bellowing Florence and the Machine, quirky West London singer-songwriter Lily Allen and the extraordinary but tragic Southgate-born and Camden-resident chanteuse Amy Winehouse, who died in 2011 at age 27..

'90s Songs

- *'Piccadilly Palare' (Morrissey)*
- *'Parklife' (Blur)*
- *'Mile End' (Pulp)*
- *'Babylon' (David Gray)*

Noughties Songs

- *'Tied Up Too Tight' (Hard-Fi)*
- *'Me & Mr Jones' (Amy Winehouse)*
- *'LDN' (Lily Allen)*
- *'Warwick Avenue' (Duffy)*
- *'Dirtee Cash' (Dizzee Rascal)*

London Music Today

While it's never really lost its position at the top rung of popular-music creativity, the London sound is once again riding a wave of international commercial success. Boy bands continue to come and go, most notably London-based One Direction, who clocked up the sales before going the way of all boy bands and splitting up in acrimonious fashion.

Singer-songwriters are also a strong point. Tottenham-born soulster-songwriter Adele's clean sweep at the 2017 Grammys, including both Album (*25*) and Song of the Year ('Hello') cemented her success of six years earlier when she spent 10 weeks at number one in the US album charts with *21* (2011) and won Album of the Year at the 2012 Grammys. At the same time Ed Sheeran has taken the world by storm; his third album *(÷)* was released in 2017 and notched up 10 Top 10 hit singles (a British record) as well as two singles in the US Top 10, becoming the first artist in history to do so. To date, Sheeran has sold more than 150 million records, putting him in the top tier of the world's most successful (and richest) artists.

Other Londoners at the helm of the new British invasion of the US include indie folk-rock ensemble Mumford & Sons, rapper Tinie Tempah and angel-faced (and -voiced) soul singer Sam Smith, who took out four Grammys in 2015 for his debut *In the Lonely Hour*.

Meanwhile London band The xx have been busy creating their own genre of stripped-back electronic pop, Brixton-based Jessie Ware has won the hearts of soul- and electro-loving audiences worldwide, and the ethereal singer James Blake won critical acclaim for his soulful post-dubstep sound. Westminster's Dua Lipa has already garnered three Brits and two Grammys with her singular brand of 'dark pop'.

Other London-born or -based talent to keep an ear out for are Mercury Prize–winning Skepta, probably the hottest grime artist of the moment; soul soloist Michael Kiwanuka; alternative singer-songwriter Bat for Lashes (AKA Natasha Khan); North London indie band Girl Ray; and London Grammar, whose music mixes melancholy guitar with soaring vocals and plaintive lyrics.

2010s Songs

- *'The City' (Ed Sheeran)*
- *'Under the Westway' (Blur)*
- *'Ill Manors' (Plan B)*
- *'Dirty Boys' (David Bowie)*
- *'River Lea' (Adele)*

Film & Media

The UK punches well above its weight in its standing on the international film scene, but London is far from the glittering hub of the film industry that it might be, despite notable celluloid triumphs. Nonetheless, the city forms the backdrop to a riveting array of films. The nation's media sphere has had its share of crises in recent years, but there's still a wide variety of newspapers and magazines filling the shelves of London newsagencies.

London & Film

The Local Cinematic Industry

Despite frequent originality and creative novelty, British films can be hit and miss, certainly at the box office. Commercial triumphs have been Oscar-winners *Shakespeare in Love* (1998) and *The King's Speech* (2010), and Oscar nominees *Four Weddings and a Funeral* (1994) and *The Queen* (2006). Unfortunately, however, a frustrating inconsistency persists, despite the disproportionate influence of Britons in Hollywood.

Film fans nostalgically dwell on the golden – but honestly rather brief – era of Ealing comedies, when the West London–based Ealing Studios turned out a steady stream of hits. Between 1947 and 1955 (after which the studios were sold to the BBC), it produced enduring classics such as *Passport to Pimlico, Kind Hearts and Coronets, Whisky Galore, The Man in the White Suit, The Lavender Hill Mob* and *The Ladykillers*. This was also the time of legendary film-makers Michael Powell and Emeric Pressburger, the men behind *The Life and Death of Colonel Blimp* and *The Red Shoes*.

If you're interested in James Bond, especially the various vehicles the superspy drove or was pursued by in his many films, head for the 'Bond in Motion' exhibition at the London Film Museum in Convent Garden in West End.

Today the industry finds itself habitually stuck in a deep groove of romantic comedies, costume dramas and gangster pics, while setting periodic benchmarks for horror. Producers, directors and actors complain about a lack of adventurousness in those holding the purse strings, while film investors claim there are not enough scripts worth backing.

Recently, however, there has been a run of notable British films based on real events, including biopics of Elton John (*Rocketman,* 2019), Judy Garland (*Judy,* 2019), Winston Churchill (*The Darkest Hour,* 2017), Stephen Hawking (*The Theory of Everything,* 2014) and Alan Turing (*The Imitation Game,* 2014). *Pride* (2014) tells the true story of gay activists supporting striking miners in the 1980s. *Legend* (2015) is yet another film celebrating the identical twin gangsters Reggie and Ronnie Kray. *Lady in the Van* (2015) is based on Alan Bennett's play about a transient woman who lives in a van in his Camden Town driveway for 15 years.

Where Brits are at the very top of the world is in the field of acting, with British stars taking out numerous Oscars in recent years, including Gary Oldman, Olivia Colman, Eddie Redmayne, Dame Helen Mirren, Sir Daniel Day-Lewis, Colin Firth, Kate Winslet, Mark Rylance, Christian Bale, Julianne Moore, Tilda Swinton and Rachel Weisz. Other notable names include Dame Judi Dench, Dame Maggie Smith, Sir Ian McKellen, Benedict Cumberbatch, Ewan McGregor, Ralph Fiennes,

Jude Law, Liam Neeson, Hugh Laurie, Keira Knightley, Emily Watson, Catherine Zeta-Jones and Phoebe Waller-Bridge.

Well-known British directors include Steve McQueen *(12 Years a Slave)*, Tom Hooper *(The King's Speech)*, Danny Boyle *(Slumdog Millionaire)*, Ridley Scott *(Blade Runner, Alien, Thelma & Louise, Gladiator, Black Hawk Down)*, Sam Mendes *(American Beauty, 1917)*, Stephen Frears *(Dirty Pretty Things, The Queen)* and Mike Leigh *(Another Year, Vera Drake)*.

London on the Screen

From the seedy South Kensington and Earl's Court of Roman Polanski's *Repulsion* (1965) to the impressions of an interwar Harley St in *The King's Speech* (2010), London remains a hugely popular location to make films. That most die-hard of New Yorkers, Woody Allen, has made four films – *Match Point, Scoop, Cassandra's Dream* and *You Will Meet a Tall Dark Stranger* – in the capital since 2005.

The city's blend of historic and modern architecture works massively to its advantage: Ang Lee's *Sense and Sensibility* (1995) retreated to historic Greenwich for its wonderful parkland and neoclassical architecture. Merchant Ivory's costume drama *Howard's End* (1992) and the biopic *Chaplin* (1992) feature the neo-Gothic St Pancras Station, while David Lynch's *The Elephant Man* (1980) took advantage of the moody atmosphere around the then-undeveloped Shad Thames. *Withnail & I* (1987) remains a quintessential classic of offbeat British comedy, partly set in Camden. Camden also features prominently in spy romp *Kingsman: The Secret Service* (2014), as does Savile Row and Kennington's Black Prince pub.

Outdoor cinema is rolled out at Film4 Summer Screen at Somerset House just south of Covent Garden, where films projected on the city's largest screen can be enjoyed in a sublime setting.

London also serves as an effective backdrop to the horror genre and dystopian cinema. Battersea Power Station and then-derelict Shoreditch and Docklands provided background for Michael Radford's adaptation of *1984* (1984) by George Orwell. Danny Boyle's shocking *28 Days Later* (2002) haunted viewers with images of an entirely deserted central London in its opening sequences, scenes rekindled in the gore-splattered sequel *28 Weeks Later* (2006). Much of Stanley Kubrick's controversial and bleak *A Clockwork Orange* (1971) was filmed in London, while Alfonso Cuarón's *Children of Men* (2006) forged a menacing and desperate vision of a London to come. Further dystopian visions of a totalitarian future London coalesce in James McTeigue's *V for Vendetta* (2005).

Other parts of town to look out for include *Notting Hill* (1999), which put the eponymous West London neighbourhood on the world map; Joel Hopkins' *Hampstead* (2017) tried (and failed) to do the same thing for North London. The Dickensian backstreets of Borough feature in such opposites as chick-flick *Bridget Jones's Diary* (2001) and Guy Ritchie's

BEST CINEMATIC FESTIVALS

A host of London festivals ranging across the film spectrum entertains cinema enthusiasts, from the popcorn crowd to art-house intelligentsia, and those in between.

London Film Festival (p60) The highlight of London's many festivals celebrating the silver screen. Held in October.

Raindance Festival (www.raindance.co.uk; ⏲late Sep) Europe's leading independent film-making festival. It's a celebration of independent, nonmainstream cinema from across the globe, screening for 12 days just before the London Film Festival.

Portobello Film Festival (www.portobellofilmfestival.com; ⏲Aug-Sep) Features some 700, largely independent works by London film-makers and international directors. It's the UK's largest independent film competition, and it's free to attend. Held over three weeks in August and September.

gangster-romp *Lock, Stock and Two Smoking Barrels* (1998). Smithfield conveys a certain bleak glamour in *Closer* (2004) and Brick Lane finds celluloid fame in its namesake drama (2007). Farringdon and other parts of town north of the Thames provide the backdrop to David Cronenberg's ultraviolent *Eastern Promises* (2007), while Crouch End and New Cross Gate are overrun by zombies in the hilarious *Shaun of the Dead* (2004). Ealing makes an appearance outside its famous studios in the coming-of-age film *An Education* (2009).

Sam Mendes' well-received *Skyfall* puts London into action-packed context in James Bond's 2012 outing, while the MI6 headquarters is spectacularly destroyed in the sequel *Spectre* (2015). Awkward British monster movie *Attack the Block* (2011) sees a South London council-estate gang fighting off an alien invasion. British director Terence Davies' critically acclaimed dramatic adaptation of Terence Rattigan's *The Deep Blue Sea* (2011) conjures up a tragic portrait of post-WWII London. *Mary Poppins Returns* (2018), filmed entirely on location, puts London landmarks like Big Ben, the Bank of England and Buckingham Palace in centre frame while *Spider-Man: Far from Home* (2019) does the same for the Tower of London and Tower Bridge.

Set in Poplar in London's desperately poor East End in the 1950s, the period drama *Call the Midwife* has been the BBC's most successful TV series since it first aired in 2012, having been sold to almost 200 territories. It's made an international celebrity out of much-loved British comedian Miranda Hart.

Media

Television

When it comes to televisual output, London plays with a stronger hand than it does in film: a huge amount of global TV content originates in Britain, from the *Teletubbies* and *Top Gear* to the extraordinary films of the BBC natural history unit, to cutting-edge comedy and drama across the channels – including smash hits like *Downton Abbey, Doctor Who, Call the Midwife* and *The Crown*. British TV shows adapted to localised versions garnering huge followings include *The X Factor, Who Wants to Be a Millionaire?* and *MasterChef*. There are five free-to-air national TV stations: BBC1, BBC2, ITV1, Channel 4 and Channel 5. Publicly owned broadcaster the BBC has the advantage of being commercial-free.

Radio

As with television, BBC Radio is commercial-free: BBC Radio London (94.9 FM) is largely a talk-fest; Radio 4 (93.5 FM) has news; Radio 2 (88.8 FM) has adult-oriented music and entertainment; and Radio 1 (98.5 FM) has youth-focused pop. Capital FM (95.8 FM) is Radio 1's commercial equivalent. Then there's Radio X (104.9 FM) for indie music, Kiss 100 (100 FM) for dance and Classic FM (100.9 FM) for abridged highbrow stuff.

Newspapers & Magazines

National newspapers in England and London are almost always financially independent of any political party, although their political leanings are often self-evident. There are two broad categories of newspapers, most commonly distinguished as broadsheets (or 'quality papers') and tabloids (or 'red-tops'). Nowadays the distinction is more about content than format as many erstwhile full-size papers now appear in tabloid size.

Daily Papers

The main London newspaper is the (currently) centre-right *Evening Standard*, a free tabloid published between Monday and Friday and handed out around mainline train stations, Tube stations and some shops. At the helm as editor is George Osborne, Chancellor of the Exchequer for six years under David Cameron. *Metro* (also published

London Twitter Accounts

@Londonist – London news, events, features, personalities.

@Secret_London – Londoners' secret places and finds.

@lecool_London – London's best gigs, clubs, art, film, theatre, food and shops.

@SkintLondon – things to see and do for free or for under £10.

@stephenfry – actor, intellect and fabulous Londoner Stephen Fry is one to follow.

weekdays) is a skimpy morning paper, a rehash of the previous night's *Standard* and designed to be read in about 20 minutes.

Readers are extremely loyal to their paper and rarely switch from one to another. Liberal and middle-class, *The Guardian* has excellent reporting, an award-winning website and a progressive agenda. A handy small-format entertainment supplement, *The Guide,* comes with Saturday's paper. The right-wing *Daily Telegraph,* dubbed the 'Torygraph', is the unofficial Conservative party paper; it has exceptionally good foreign news coverage. *The Times* is a stalwart of the British press, despite now being part of Australian mogul Rupert Murdoch's media empire; it's a decent read with a wide range of articles and strong foreign reporting. Not aligned with any political party, *The Independent* is a left-leaning serious-minded (some say earnest) tabloid with a focus on lead stories that other papers ignore. It is rabidly anti-royalist. The *Financial Times* is a heavyweight business paper with a weekend edition offering some of the best journalism in Britain.

For sex and scandal over your eggs and bacon, turn to the *Mirror,* a working-class and 'Old Labour' tabloid; *The Sun* – the UK's bestseller – a gossip-hungry Tory-leaning tabloid legendary for its sassy headlines; or the lowbrow *Daily Star*. Other tabloid reads include the mid-level *Daily Express* and the centre-right *Daily Mail.*

London Websites

Londonist (https://londonist.com) 'Things to Do' section is tops.

Urban 75 (http://www.urban75.org/blog/tag/london) Outstanding community website.

London on the Inside (http://londontheinside.com) What's so-hot-right-now.

London Eater (https://london.eater.com) Still one of the better food blogs.

Spitalfields Life (https://spitalfieldslife.com) Unmissable daily take on the life and culture of East London by 'the Gentle Author'.

Sunday Papers

Most dailies have Sunday equivalents, and (predictably) the tabloids have bumper editions of trashy gossip, star-struck adulation, fashion extras and mean-spirited diatribes. *The Observer,* established in 1791, is the oldest Sunday paper and stablemate of *The Guardian,* with a great Sunday arts supplement called *The New Review*. The *Sunday Telegraph* is as serious and politically conservative as its weekly sister-paper, while *The Sunday Times* is brimful of fashion and scandal, but a good deal of it (supplements, advertising extras etc) can be comfortably tossed in the recycle bin upon purchase.

Magazines

An astonishing range of magazines is published and consumed in London, from celebrity gossip to ideological heavyweights.

Political magazines are particularly strong. The satirical *Private Eye* has no political bias and lampoons everyone equally, although those in positions of power are preferred. The excellent weekly 'newspaper' *The Economist* cannot be surpassed for international political and business analysis. Claiming to be Britain's oldest-running magazine, the right-wing weekly *The Spectator* is worshipped by Tory voters, but its witty articles are often loved by left-wingers too. The *New Statesman* is a stalwart left-wing intellectual weekly news magazine.

A freebie available from Tube stations, big museums and galleries, *Time Out* is an entertainment listings guide available every Tuesday; it's great for taking the city's pulse and offers strong arts coverage. The *Big Issue,* sold on the streets by the homeless, is not just an honourable project, but can be a decent read too.

London loves celebrities and *Heat, Closer* and *OK!* are the most popular purveyors of the genre. Top women's glossies include *Elle* and *Vogue;* competitors like the UK editions of *Glamour* and *Marie Claire* are now digital only. The thinking-man's glossies include *GQ* and *Esquire*. A slew of style magazines is published here, including *i-D,* an ubercool London fashion and music biweekly, and rival *Dazed,* published every other month.

PHOTOCREO MICHAL BEDNAREK/SHUTTERSTOCK ©

Survival Guide

Transport

ARRIVING IN LONDON

Most visitors arrive in London by air, although train travel has experienced a surge in popularity as the carbon impact of air travel is better understood. Long-haul buses are another (low-cost) option for getting to the capital.

Eurostar travels between London and Paris, Brussels, Amsterdam and Marseilles, with more connecting services coming on board, including to Nordic destinations. Most long-haul flights land at Heathrow. Europe and the Middle East flights also land at Gatwick and Stansted. Luton and London Southend service budget airlines only.

Flights, cars and tours can be booked online at lonelyplanet.com/bookings.

Heathrow Airport

Heathrow (www.heathrowairport.com) is one of the world's busiest international airports and has four passenger terminals (numbered 2 to 5 – Terminal 1 closed in 2015). It's Britain's main airport for international flights.

Left luggage Facilities are in each terminal and open from 5am (5.30am at T4) to 11pm. The charge per item is £7.50 for up to three hours, £12.50 for up to 24 hours, and £20 for 48 hours.

Hotels There are four international-style hotels that can be reached on foot from the terminals, and more than 20 nearby. The **Hotel Hoppa** (www.hotelhoppa.co.uk; adult/family £5.50/10.50) bus links to more than 25 hotels in the surrounding area with the airport's terminals, and has 900 services around the clock every day.

Train

The Piccadilly Line serves Heathrow: one for Terminals 2 and 3, another for Terminal 4, and the terminus for Terminal 5. The Tube is the cheapest way to get to Heathrow. Purchase an Oyster Card to pay for journeys (these cost £5, refunded when you return the card) or use a contactless payment card to board.

Trains depart every three to nine minutes from just after 5am to 11.45pm (11.28pm Sunday). Heading to the airport, they run from 5.47am to 12.32am (11.38pm Sunday); the Piccadilly line runs all night Friday and Saturday, with reduced frequency. The journey is approximately 45 minutes to central London.

Heathrow Express (www.heathrowexpress.com; one-way/return £25/37; children free; wi-fi) Links Heathrow with Paddington train station in a mere 15 minutes; handy if you're staying near there. Trains run from 5am to 11pm/midnight. You can use an Oyster or contactless card, or pre-purchase tickets online for a cheaper fare. Children travel for free.

Bus

National Express (www.nationalexpress.com) Coaches (one-way from £6, 40 to 90 minutes, every 30 minutes to one hour) link Heathrow Central bus station with Victoria coach station. The first bus leaves Heathrow Central bus station (at Terminals 2 and 3) at 4.20am, with the last departure at 10.05pm. The first bus leaves Victoria at 1am, the last at around midnight.

N9 bus If you arrive very late, the N9 bus (£1.50, 1¼ hours, every 20 minutes) connects Heathrow Central bus station (and Heathrow Terminal 5) with central London, terminating at Aldwych.

Taxi

A metered black-cab trip to/from central London will cost between £50 and £100 and take 45 minutes to an hour, depending on traffic.

Ride-share services, such as Uber, require organising a meeting point near the airport exit directly with your driver; problematic if you're relying on airport wi-fi.

Gatwick Airport

Gatwick (www.gatwickairport.com) is smaller than Heathrow and is Britain's

CLIMATE CHANGE & TRAVEL

Every form of transport that relies on carbon-based fuel generates CO_2, the main cause of human-induced climate change. Modern travel is dependent on aeroplanes, which might use less fuel per kilometre per person than most cars but travel much greater distances. The altitude at which aircraft emit gases (including CO_2) and particles also contributes to their climate change impact. Many websites offer 'carbon calculators' that allow people to estimate the carbon emissions generated by their journey and, for those who wish to do so, to offset the impact of the greenhouse gases emitted with contributions to portfolios of climate-friendly initiatives throughout the world. Lonely Planet offsets the carbon footprint of all staff and author travel.

number-two airport for international flights. The North and South Terminals are linked by a 24-hour shuttle train (three minutes).

Left luggage Facilities in both terminals; open 24 hours in the South Terminal and from 5am to 10pm in the North Terminal. The charge is £6/11 per item for three/24 hours (or part thereof), up to a maximum of 90 days. You can pre-book left luggage online (www.gatwickairport.com/at-the-airport/passenger-services/luggage).

Train

National Rail (www.nationalrail.co.uk) Regular train services to/from London Bridge (30 to 45 minutes, every 15 to 30 minutes), London King's Cross (55 minutes, every 15 to 30 minutes) and Victoria (30 to 50 minutes, every 10 to 15 minutes) run almost all night. Fares vary depending on the time, route, company (Southern or Thameslink) and class you take. Ticket machines are near the airport exit to the train station or pay with an Oyster Card, or contactless payment card.

Gatwick Express (www.gatwickexpress.com; one-way/return adult £19.90/36.70, child £9.95/18.35, under 5yrs free) Trains run every 15 minutes from the station near the Gatwick South Terminal to Victoria. From the airport, there are services between 5.41am and 11.11pm. From Victoria, they leave between 5am and 10.44pm. The journey takes 30 minutes; book online for the slightly cheaper fares.

Bus

National Express (www.nationalexpress.com) Coaches run throughout the day from Gatwick to Victoria coach station (one-way from £10). Services depart hourly around the clock. Journey time is between 80 minutes and two hours, depending on traffic.

EasyBus (www.easybus.com) Runs 13-seater minibuses to Gatwick every 15 to 20 minutes on several routes, including from Earl's Court/West Brompton and Victoria coach station (one way from £2 if you book ahead online). The service runs around the clock. The journey time averages 75 minutes; it must be booked in advance.

Taxi

A metered black-cab trip to/from central London costs around £100 and takes just over an hour. Minicabs or ride-share taxis are usually, but not always, cheaper.

Stansted Airport

Stansted (www.stanstedairport.com) is 35 miles northeast of central London in the direction of Cambridge. An international airport, Stansted serves mainly European destinations and is used primarily by low-cost carriers such as Ryanair and EasyJet, but bigger players like Emirates also fly from here.

Train

Stansted Express (☎0345 600 7245; www.stanstedexpress.com; one-way/return £19.40/30.70) This rail service (45 minutes, every 15 to 30 minutes) links the airport with Liverpool St station via Tottenham Hale (which also has good Tube connections). From the airport, the first train leaves at 5.30am, the last at 12.30am. Trains depart Liverpool St station from 4.40am (on some days at 3.40am) to 11.25pm.

Bus

National Express (www.nationalexpress.com) Coaches run around the clock, offering 200 services per day.

Airbus A6 (☎0871 781 8181; www.nationalexpress.com; one-way from £10) Runs to Westminster (around one hour to 1½ hours, every 20 minutes) via Marble Arch, Paddington, Baker St and Golders Green. **Airbus A7** (one-way from £10) also runs to Victoria coach station (around one hour to 1½ hours, every 20 minutes), via Waterloo and Southwark. **Airbus A8** (one-way from £7) runs to Liverpool St station (60 to 80 minutes, every 30 minutes), via Bethnal Green and Shoreditch

High St. **Airbus A9** (one way from £7, 50 minutes) goes to London Stratford.

Airport Bus Express (www.airportbusexpress.co.uk; one-way from £8) Runs every 30 minutes to Victoria coach station, Baker St, Liverpool St and London Stratford.

EasyBus (www.easybus.com) Runs services to Victoria coach station via Waterloo station every 15 minutes, or Liverpool St station via London Stratford. The total journey to central London (one-way from £2) takes 1¾ hours.

Terravision (www.terravision.eu) Coaches link Stansted to Liverpool St station (one-way from £7, 75 minutes) and Victoria coach station (from £7, two hours) every 20 to 40 minutes between 6am and 1am.

Taxi

A metered black-cab trip to/from central London costs around £130. Minicabs and ride-share taxis are cheaper.

Luton Airport

A smallish, single-runway airport 32 miles northwest of London, Luton (www.london-luton.co.uk) generally caters for cheap charter flights and discount airlines and serves almost 15 million passengers a year.

Train

National Rail (www.nationalrail.co.uk) Has 24-hour services (one way from £16.70, 35 to 50 minutes, regular departures during peak times) from London St Pancras International to Luton Airport Parkway station, from where an airport shuttle bus (one-way/return £2.40/3.80, half-price for five- to 15-year-olds, kids under five ride for free) will take you to the airport in 10 minutes. Cash or contactless payment cards are accepted on the shuttle bus.

Bus

Airbus A1 (www.nationalexpress.com; one way if booked online from £7) Runs over 60 times daily around the clock to Victoria coach station, via Portman Sq, Baker St, St John's Wood, Finchley Rd and Golders Green. It takes around one to 1½ hours.

Green Line Bus 757 (☎0344 800 4411; www.greenline.co.uk; one-way/return £11.50/17.50) Runs to Luton Airport from Victoria coach station every 30 minutes on a 24-hour service via Marble Arch, Baker St, Finchley Rd and Brent Cross.

Taxi

A metered black-cab trip to/from central London costs about £110.

London City Airport

Its proximity to central London, which is just 6 miles to the west, as well as to the commercial district of the Docklands, means **London City Airport** (☎020-7646 0088; www.londoncityairport.com; Hartmann Rd, E16; 📶; Ⓤ London City Airport) is predominantly a gateway airport for business travellers.

Train

Docklands Light Railway (DLR; www.tfl.gov.uk/dlr) Stops at the London City Airport station (zone 3). Trains depart every eight to 10 minutes from just after 5.30am to 12.15am Monday to Saturday, and 7am to 11.15pm Sunday. The journey to Bank takes just over 20 minutes.

Taxi

A metered black-cab trip to the City/Oxford St/Earl's Court costs about £30/40/60 depending on traffic.

London Southend Airport

Consistently rated as a good airport experience by budget travellers, London's overlooked sixth airport, **London Southend** (https://southendairport.com), is less busy than most. It's 39 miles from central London but is well serviced by regular trains to Liverpool St making it a good option if you're staying in East London. Budget airlines fly here from domestic and European cities.

Train

Trains run to/from a purpose-built station at the airport (adult/child £17.80/8.90), making connecting to London Liverpool St or Stratford station an easy one-hour journey. Six trains run per hour during peak times, fewer off-peak. The first train from Liverpool St leaves at 4.30am to meet early-morning flight departures, and the last train leaves at 11.59pm.

Taxi

Flight delays or any procrastinating will mean you're in a fix after midnight. It's either an expensive taxi ride (£110, but can be split with others, of course) or an airport hotel. Phone **Andrews Taxis** (☎01702 200 000), currently the only option at this hour.

Train

Main national rail routes are served by a variety of private train-operating companies. Tickets are not cheap, but if you book ahead you can get better deals. If you're planning to do a lot of train travel, look into the cost of a Rail Card and how much you may save, especially if travelling in a family group. Check the website of **National Rail** (www.nationalrail.co.uk) for timetables, fares and Rail Cards.

Eurostar (www.eurostar.com) High-speed passenger rail service linking London St Pancras International with Paris, Brussels, Amsterdam and Marseilles, with up to 19 daily departures. Fares vary greatly, from £29 for a one-way standard-class ticket to around £245 each way for a fully flexible business premier ticket (prices based on return journeys). Sign up to Eurostar social media channels or email to get notifications of special deals and sales.

GETTING AROUND LONDON

Both **Transport for London** (TfL; https://tfl.gov.uk/plan-a-journey) and **Citymapper** (https://citymapper.com/london) will give you route options for trip planning with up-to-date information on departures and delays.

The cheapest way to get around London is with an **Oyster Card** (https://oyster.tfl.gov.uk/oyster/entry.do) or a UK contactless card (foreign cardholders should check for extra international transaction charges first) with a daily fare cap.

Tube (London Underground) The fastest and most efficient way of getting around town, but you won't see anything. First/last trains operate from around 5.30am to 12.30am and 24 hours on Friday and Saturday on five lines.

Train The DLR and Overground networks are ideal for connecting between distant parts of the city. The route from Peckham to Shoreditch is fondly called 'the hipster line'.

Bus The London bus network is very extensive and efficient and, best of all, above ground; in heavy traffic it can be quicker to walk.

Taxis Black cabs are ubiquitous and available around the clock. Although not cheap, they're an experience.

Bicycle Santander Cycles are good for shorter journeys around central London, but you need to be fairly road-wise.

OYSTER CARD

The Oyster Card is a smart card on which you can store credit towards 'prepay' fares, as well as Travelcards valid for periods from a day to a year. Oyster Cards are valid across the entire public transport network in London.

All you need to do when entering a station is touch your card on a reader (which has a yellow circle with the image of an Oyster Card on it) and then touch again on your way out. The system will then deduct the appropriate amount of credit from your card, as necessary. For bus journeys, you only need to touch *once* when boarding. Note that some train stations don't have exit turnstiles, so you will need to tap out on the reader (which will bleep) before leaving the station; if you forget, you will be hugely overcharged.

The benefit lies in the fact that fares for Oyster Card users are lower than standard ones. If you are making many journeys during the day, you will never pay more than the appropriate Travelcard (peak or off-peak) once the daily 'price cap' has been reached.

Oyster Cards can be bought (£5 refundable deposit required) and topped up at any Underground station, travel information centre or shop displaying the Oyster logo. To get your deposit back along with any remaining credit, simply return your Oyster Card at a ticket booth. Contactless cards (which do not require chip and pin or a signature) can be used directly on Oyster Card readers and are subject to the same Oyster fares. The advantage is that you don't have to bother with buying, topping up and then returning an Oyster Card, but foreign visitors should bear in mind the cost of card transactions!

Bus

London's ubiquitous red double-decker buses afford great views of the city, but be aware that the going can be slow, thanks to traffic jams and dozens of commuters getting on and off at every stop.

There are excellent bus maps at every stop detailing all routes and destinations served from that particular area (generally a few bus stops within a two- to three-minute walk, shown on a local map).

Bus services normally operate from 5am to 11.30pm. Many bus stops have LED displays listing bus arrival times, but downloading an app such as Citymapper to your smartphone is the most effective way to keep track of when your next bus is due.

Almost all buses are now wheelchair- and pram-accessible, lowering to the pavement with an automated ramp facility – you'll need to board at the middle doors and touch on with your Oyster Card when you can. Other passengers are mostly patient and courteous when assisting people on and off the bus with items like prams or large suitcases.

Night Bus

➡ More than 50 night-bus routes (prefixed with the letter 'N') run from around 11.30pm to 5am.

➡ There are also another 60 bus routes operating 24 hours; the frequency decreases between 11pm and 5am.

➡ Oxford Circus, Tottenham Court Rd and Trafalgar Sq are the main hubs for night routes.

➡ Night buses can be infrequent and stop only on request, so remember to ring for your stop.

Fares

Cash cannot be used on London's buses. You must pay with an Oyster Card, Travelcard or a contactless payment card. Bus fares are a flat £1.50, no matter the distance travelled. If you don't have enough credit on your Oyster Card for a £1.50 bus fare, you can make the journey (and go into the black) but must top up your credit before your Oyster Card will work again.

Children aged under 11 travel free; 11- to 15-year-olds travel half-price if registered on an accompanying adult's Oyster Card on the Young Visitor Discount (register at Zone 1 or Heathrow Tube stations).

Bicycle

Tens of thousands of Londoners cycle to work every day, and it is generally a good way to get around the city, although traffic can be intimidating for less confident cyclists and it's important to keep your wits about you. The city has tried hard to improve the cycling infrastructure, by opening new 'cycle superhighways' for commuters, while the public bike-hire scheme **Santander Cycles** (☎0343 222 6666; www.tfl.gov.uk/modes/cycling/santander-cycles) is particularly useful for visitors.

Transport for London (www.tfl.gov.uk) publishes 14 free maps of London's cycle routes, and the online TfL Journey Planner maps display 'easy', 'moderate' and 'fast' route options.

Bicycles on Public Transport

Bicycles can be taken on the Overground and DLR except at peak times (7.30am to 9.30am and 4pm to 7pm Monday to Friday). Folding bikes can be taken on a handful of Underground lines.

Pedicabs

Three-wheeled cycle rickshaws seating two or three passengers have been a regular part of the West End scene for over a decade. They're less a mode of transport than a gimmick for tourists and the occasional drunk on a Saturday night. Expect to pay from £10 for a short trip; it's worth confirming the rate before you get in as there have been some high-profile incidents of overcharging. Their carbon-neutral tours of London are available from £80 per person for a pub tour. For more information visit www.londonpedicabs.com.

Taxi

Although expensive, taxis can be a very useful way to get about town. Black-cab drivers can be hailed on the street and are generally very friendly and knowledgable.

Black Cabs

The black cab is as much a feature of the London cityscape as the red double-decker bus. Licensed black-cab drivers have The Knowledge, acquired over three to five years of rigorous training and a series of exams. They are supposed to know 25,000 streets within a 6-mile radius of Charing Cross/Trafalgar Sq and the 100 most-visited spots of the moment, including clubs and restaurants.

➡ Cabs are available for hire when the yellow sign above the windscreen is lit; just stick your arm out to signal one.

➡ All are supposed to be wheelchair-accessible but experiences reported on the ground belie this claim.

➡ Fares are metered, with the flagfall charge of £2.60 (covering the first 235m during a weekday), rising by increments of 20p for each subsequent 117m.

➡ Fares are more expensive in the evening and overnight.

➡ You can tip taxi drivers up to 10%, but most Londoners simply round up to the nearest pound.

➡ Apps such as **Gett** (https://gett.com/uk/city/london) use your smartphone's GPS to locate the nearest black cab. You only pay the metered fare.

➡ **ComCab** (☎020-7908 0271; www.comcab-london.co.uk) operates one of the largest fleets of black cabs in town.

Minicabs

➡ Minicabs, which are licensed, are (usually) cheaper competitors of black cabs.

➡ Unlike black cabs, minicabs cannot legally be hailed on the street; they must be hired by phone or directly from one of the minicab offices (every high street has at least one and some nightclubs work with a minicab firm to send revellers home promptly).

➡ Don't accept unsolicited offers from individuals claiming to be minicab drivers – they are just guys with cars.

➡ Minicabs don't have meters; there's usually a fare set by the dispatcher. Make sure you ask before setting off.

➡ Your hotel or host will be able to recommend a reputable minicab company in the neighbourhood; every Londoner has the number of at least one company. Alternatively, phone a large 24-hour operator such as **Addison Lee** (www.addisonlee.com).

➡ Ride-share apps such as **Uber** (www.uber.com) allow you to book a ride easily, but at the time of research Uber's licence to operate in London was under review (again).

Boats

Several companies operate along the River Thames; only **Thames Clippers** (Map p477; www.thamesclippers.com; one-way adult/child £8.70/4.35) really offers commuter services, however. It's fast, pleasant and you're almost always guaranteed a seat and a view. All boats are fully wheelchair-accessible and all piers are wheelchair-accessible apart from Cadogan Pier, Wandsworth Riverside Quarter Pier and London Bridge City Pier.

Thames Clippers boats run regular services between Embankment, Waterloo (London Eye), Blackfriars, Bankside (Shakespeare's Globe), London Bridge, Tower Bridge, Canary Wharf, Greenwich, North Greenwich and Woolwich piers from 6.28am to 11.38pm (from 8.10am to 11.20pm on weekends).

Thames Clippers River Roamer tickets (adult/child £17.80/8.90) give the freedom to hop on and off boats on most routes all day. Book online for the discounted fare; only piers with a ticket booth accept cash payments.

You can also get a discount if you're a pay-as-you-go Oyster Card holder or Travelcard holder (paper ticket or on Oyster Card). Children under five travel free on most boats.

Between April and October, Hampton Court Palace can be reached by boat on the 22-mile route along the Thames from Westminster Pier in central London (via Kew and Richmond). The trip can take up to four hours, depending on the tide. Boats are run by **Westminster Passenger Services Association** (www.wpsa.co.uk; one-way/return adult £19/27, child £9.50/13.50).

The **London Waterbus Company** (Map p470; ☎07917 265114; www.londonwaterbus.com; Browning's Pool, Warwick Cres W2; tours adult/child one-way £12/9; ⏲hourly 10am-5pm Apr-Oct, weekends only & less frequent departures other months; Ⓤ Warwick Ave, Camden Town) runs canal boats between Camden Lock and Little Venice.

CYCLE-HIRE SCHEMES

London's main cycle-hire scheme is called **Santander Cycles** (☎0343 222 6666; www.tfl.gov.uk/modes/cycling/santander-cycles). The bikes have proved as popular with visitors as with Londoners.

The idea is simple: pick up a bike from one of the 750 (and counting) docking stations dotted around the capital; cycle; drop it off at another docking station. The access fee is £2 for 24 hours. All you need is a credit or debit card. The first 30 minutes are free; it's £2 for any additional period of 30 minutes, to keep you regularly docking the bikes.

You can take as many bikes as you like during your access period (24 hours), leaving five minutes between each trip.

The pricing is designed to encourage short journeys rather than longer rentals; for those, go to a hire company. You'll also find that although easy to ride, the bikes only have three gears and are quite heavy. You must be aged 18 to buy access and at least 14 to ride a bike.

Alternatively, Uber's bike-share scheme **Jump** (www.jump.com) has entered London with bright orange e-bikes seemingly abandoned on pavements anywhere.

Car & Motorcycle

As a visitor, it's very unlikely you'll need to drive in London. Much has been done to encourage Londoners to get out of their cars and onto public transport (or on their bikes), and the same disincentives should keep you firmly off the road: the additional congestion and Ultra Low Emission Zone (ULEZ) charges, extortionate parking fees, the high price of fuel, fiendishly efficient traffic wardens, and ubiquitous CCTV cameras recording cars parked (even momentarily) on double yellow lines or not giving way when they should… It's not worth it.

Congestion Charge

London has a congestion charge in place to reduce the traffic and pollution in the city centre. The charge zone begins at Euston and Pentonville Rds to the north, Park Lane to the west, Tower Bridge to the east, and Elephant and Castle and Vauxhall Bridge Rd to the south. As you enter the zone, you will see a large white 'C' in a red circle on signs and painted on the road.

If you enter the zone between 7am and 6pm Monday to Friday (excluding public holidays), you must pay the £11.50 charge (payable in advance or on the day) or £14 on the first charging day after travel to avoid receiving a fine (£160, or £80 if paid within 14 days).

In addition, if your car is not a new cleaner greener model, the Ultra Low Emission Zone (ULEZ) charge needs to be paid in the same zone 24/7. You can pay online or over the phone. For full details, see the TFL website (www.tfl.gov.uk).

Hire

There is no shortage of car rental agencies in London, including several branches of major brands such as Avis, Europcar and Hertz. Book in advance for the best fares, especially at weekends.

Road Rules

➡ Drive on the left side of the road.

➡ Get a copy of the *Highway Code* (www.gov.uk/highway-code), available at Automobile Association (AA) and Royal Automobile Club (RAC) outlets, as well as some bookshops and tourist offices.

➡ A foreign driving licence is valid in Britain for up to 12 months from the time of your last entry into the country.

➡ If you bring a car from continental Europe, make sure you're adequately insured.

➡ All drivers and passengers must wear seatbelts, and motorcyclists must wear a helmet.

➡ It is illegal to use a mobile phone to call or text while driving (using a hands-free device to talk on your mobile is permitted).

➡ Pedestrians have right of way at zebra crossings (black and white stripes on the road); some assume they have the right of way everywhere else. Be careful.

➡ The speed limit on many urban roads is now 20mph, with speed cameras everywhere.

Fines

If you get a parking ticket or your car gets clamped, call the number on the ticket. If the car has been removed, ring the free 24-hour service called **TRACE** (%0845 206 8602; https://trace.london) to find out where your car has been taken. It will cost you a minimum of £200 to get your vehicle back on the road.

Cable Car

The **Emirates Air Line** (Map p462; www.emiratesairline.co.uk; 27 Western Gateway, E16; one-way adult/child £4.50/2.30, with Oyster Card £3.50/1.70; ⏲7am-9pm Mon-Thu, to 11pm Fri, 8am-11pm Sat, 9am-9pm Sun; 🚇Royal Victoria DLR, Ⓤ North Greenwich) is a cable car linking the Royal Docks in East London with North Greenwich some 90m above the Thames. The journey is brief, and rather pricey, but the views are stunning. The Air Line is step-free and the cable cars can accommodate most motorised wheelchairs.

Tram

South London has a small tram network called **London Tramlink** (☎0343 222 1234; https://tfl.gov.uk/modes/trams/). There are three routes running along 17 miles of track, including Wimbledon to Elmers End via Croydon; Croydon to Beckenham; and Croydon to New Addington. Single tickets cost £2.60 (£1.50 with an Oyster Card).

Walking

You can't beat walking for neighbourhood exploration, though a good map or GPS is recommended as London's winding streets can quickly disorientate even the best of us. Bridges cross the Thames at regular intervals, and there are two pedestrian tunnels beneath the river: one at **Greenwich** (Map p477; Cutty Sark Gardens, SE10; ⏲24hr; Ⓤ Cutty Sark) and one at Woolwich.

It's worth noting that some Tube stations can be closer to each other on the ground than they may appear on the Tube map, and in busy central London it can be quicker to walk than catch the Tube or bus for a short distance.

TOURS

Hop-On/Hop-Off Sightseeing Buses

Big Bus Tours (☎020-7808 6753; www.bigbustours.com; tours adult/child/family £39/29/107; ⏲every 5-20min 8.30am-6pm Apr-Sep, to 5pm Oct & Mar, to 4.30pm Nov-Feb) Globally recognised bus touring group with informative commentaries in 12 languages. Hop-on hop-off along four bus routes. The ticket includes a free river cruise with City Cruises and three thematic walking tours. The ticket is valid for 24 hours; for an a small additional charge you can upgrade to the 48-hour 'premium' ticket.

Original Tour (www.theoriginaltour.com; tours adult/child/family £34/16/84; ⏲8.30am-8.30pm; 👪) Hop-on/hop-off bus service in 11 languages (plus kids' commentary) on six routes, and includes discounts on a host of London attractions. Buses run every five to 15 minutes; you can buy tickets on the bus or online. Also available: 48-hour tickets (adult/child/family £44/21/109) and 72-hour tickets (adult/child/family £54/26/134).

Special-Interest Tours

★**Guide London** (Association of Professional Tourist Guides; ☎020-7611 2545; www.guidelondon.org.uk; half-/full-day tours £176/288) Hire a prestigious Blue Badge Tourist Guide, know-it-all guides who have studied for two years and passed a dozen written and practical exams to do their job. They can tell you stories behind the sights that you'd only hear from them or whisk you on a themed tour (eg Royalty, The Beatles, museums, parks). Go by car, public transport, bike or on foot.

For private tours by car, driver guides typically charge £405 for a half-day and £585 for a full day.

Hidden London (☎020-7565 7298; www.ltmuseum.co.uk/whats-on/hidden-london; tours £35-85) Get under the skin of London on an incredible insider-access tour run by the **London Transport Museum** (Map p438; ☎020-7379 6344; www.ltmuseum.co.uk; Covent Garden Piazza, WC2; adult/child £18/free; ⏰10am-6pm; 🚸; Ⓤ Covent Garden). Excursions take you to the depths of the city's abandoned Tube stations, which have been film sets for a number of flicks including *Skyfall* and *V for Vendetta*, and to the heights of London's first skyscraper at 55 Broadway, Transport for London's art deco HQ. Sign up for email alerts to get notice of when the next tours are going on sale, and book early.

Alternative London (www.alternativeldn.com; per person from £20) Avoiding the obvious headline London sites, these small-group cycling and walking tours cover themes such as street art, culinary experiences and craft-beer spots, mainly around East London.

Black History Walks (www.blackhistorywalks.co.uk; 2hr tours £10) Learn a little of London's 2000 years of black history in Soho, St Paul's and Notting Hill, to name a few locations where these informative, paradigm-shifting tours are run.

Look Up London (https://lookup.london; per person £15-30) Walking tours include secrets of Bermondsey, Soho, Greenwich and The City plus a Feminist Jack the Ripper tour that tells the stories of the women involved in this bloody chapter of London's history. Group sizes are kept small. Tours go for one to two hours.

Unseen Tours (☎07514 266774; www.sockmobevents.org.uk; tours £15) See London from an entirely different angle on one of these award-winning neighbourhood tours led by the London homeless (60% of the tour price goes to the guide). Tours cover Covent Garden, Soho, Brick Lane, Shoreditch and London Bridge.

Derelict London (www.derelictlondon.com; tours £16) Writer and photographer Paul Talling hosts these popular tours of abandoned buildings, lost rivers, industrial streetscapes, and the recent social history of London. The time estimates can be rather loose depending on questions and the tales that ensue. Most tours end at a brewery or pub for some socialising with your fellow walkers afterwards.

Strawberry Tours (☎020-7859 4996; www.strawberrytours.com/london) These guided walking tours are offered for free, but with the hope (or expectation) punters will be sufficiently impressed so they generously tip their host. Thematic tours include London Landmarks (split into West, East and South), Harry Potter, Street Art, Soho, Jack the Ripper, Ghosts and a London Pub Crawl.

London Beatles Walks (☎07958 706329; www.beatlesinlondon.com; tours adult/child £10/8) Public and private tours following in the footsteps of the Fab Four. Most tours are just over two hours and can be pre-booked online.

Open City (☎020-3006 7008; https://open-city.org.uk; 2½-3hr tours from £25.50) This not-for-profit organisation focusing on the built environment organises architectural tours to various parts of London, including King's Cross, Battersea, Stratford and Canary Wharf on foot, on bicycle or by boat, sometimes with a photography focus. Tours include well-informed commentary.

London Walks (☎020-7624 3978; www.walks.com; adult/child £10/free) A huge choice of themed walks, including those on Foodie London, Oscar Wilde, Sherlock Holmes, Harry Potter and major sites like Portobello Market and the British Museum. Check the website for schedules – there are walks every day; you just need to turn up on time.

Capital Taxi Tours (☎07970 911223, 020-8590 3621; www.capitaltaxitours.co.uk; 3hr daytime tour per taxi (up to 5 people) £299-325) A variety of tailored tours on everything from shopping to TV and film locations with Blue Badge, City of London and City of Westminster registered guides/drivers. Foreign-language guides are also available.

London Mystery Walks (☎07957 388280; www.tourguides.org.uk; per person from £15) Get spooked with London's ghost stories or serial killer Jack the Ripper–themed walking tours. For something more nourishing, try VIP chocolate or gelato tours (£40). Book in advance.

Sandeman's New Europe (www.neweuropetours.eu/london) Offers a 'free' walking tour (the guides work for tips), along with themed Old City, Street Art and Grim Reaper tours. Check online for times and departure points. The company runs tours across Europe.

Directory A–Z

Accessible Travel

For travellers with access needs, London is a frustrating mix of occasional user-friendliness and head-in-the-sand disinterest. New hotels and modern tourist attractions are legally required to be wheelchair-accessible, but many historic buildings, B&Bs and guesthouses are in older buildings, which are hard (or prohibitively expensive) to adapt to meet contemporary expectations.

Since hosting the 2012 Olympics and Paralympics, and thanks to an inclusivity-minded tourist board in Visit England, there have been some noticeable improvements in services. Visitors with vision, hearing or cognitive impairments will find their needs met in a piecemeal fashion.

Download Lonely Planet's free Accessible Travel guides from http://lptravel.to/AccessibleTravel.

Resources

Various websites offer useful information.

AccessAble London (www.accessable.co.uk) Excellent professionally audited information online that can be searched by neighbourhood.

Accessible Travel Online Resources (https://shop.lonelyplanet.com/categories/accessible-travel) Lonely Planet has a strong accessible-travel offering with many more useful links to get the best out of your trip.

Disability Rights UK (www.disabilityrightsuk.org/shop/official-and-only-genuine-radar-key) Umbrella organisation for voluntary groups for people with disabilities. Many wheelchair-accessible toilets can be opened only with a special Royal Association of Disability & Rehabilitation (Radar) key, which can be obtained via the website prior to travel for £8.75.

Transport for London (www.tfl.gov.uk/transport-accessibility) All the information you'll need to get around London on public transport, including 'how to' videos and a live Twitter feed keeping you up to date on transport access issues such as out-of-order lifts. Several organisations have a UK-wide remit.

Action on Hearing Loss (www.actiononhearingloss.org.uk) The main organisation working with deaf and hard-of-hearing people in the UK. Many ticket offices are fitted with hearing loops by them to help the hearing-impaired; look for the ear symbol.

Royal National Institute for the Blind (www.rnib.org.uk) The UK's main charitable institution for people with sight loss.

Transport

➡ Around a quarter of Tube stations, half of Overground stations, most piers, all tram stops, the Emirates Air Line (cable car) and all DLR stations have step-free access. However, even if your starting and destination Tube stations have step-free access, stations where you interchange may not and there is always the dreaded gap between train and platform to mind – careful planning and notification of a

PRACTICALITIES

Smoking Forbidden in all enclosed public places. Pubs sometimes have a designated smoking spot outside, often on the pavement. A lot of venues also have no-vaping policies. Vaping is not allowed on public transport either.

Weights & Measures The UK uses a confusing mix of metric and imperial systems.

staff member are recommended before you board a train.

➡ Buses are a much better bet: all can be lowered to street level when they stop and wheelchair users travel free. A recent court case has confirmed that wheelchair users have priority use of the wheelchair space over pram (stroller) users, and bus drivers should back you up if a buggy is blocking the space.

➡ All black cabs are wheelchair-accessible, but power wheelchair users should note that the space is tight and sometimes headroom is insufficient.

➡ Guide dogs are universally welcome on public transport and in hotels, restaurants and attractions.

➡ Pavements are generally in good repair, pedestrian crossings relatively frequent and well placed, and kerb cuts sufficient not to leave you stranded. The further you get from the centre of London, the more likely it is that you'll have the occasional issue with a missing kerb cut.

Customs Regulations

The UK distinguishes between goods bought duty-free outside the EU and those bought in another EU country, where taxes and duties will have already been paid.

If you exceed your duty-free allowance, you will have to pay tax on the items. For European goods, there is officially no limit to how much you can bring but customs use certain guidelines to distinguish between personal and commercial use. In the initial post-Brexit period there is (temporarily) no change to this arrangement.

Import Restrictions

Item	Duty-free
Tobacco	200 cigarettes, 100 cigarillos, 50 cigars or 250g tobacco
Spirits & liqueurs	1L spirit or 2L fortified wine (eg sherry or port)
Beer & wine	16L beer & 4L still wine
Other goods	Up to a value of £390

Discount Cards

London Pass (www.londonpass.com; 1/2/3/6/10 days £75/99/125/169/199) Only worthwhile if you plan to visit lots of paid sights in a short time (and start early in the day). It offers free entry and queue-jumping to all major attractions plus a hop-on/hop-off bus. It can be adapted to include use of the Underground and buses too. A discounted child pass is also available. You can download the app to your smartphone or collect your pass from the **London Pass Redemption Desk** (Map p438; ☎020-7293 0972; www.londonpass.com; 11a Charing Cross Rd, WC2; ⊙10am-4.30pm; ⓤLeicester Sq), near Leicester Sq.

Historic Royal Palaces (☎020-3166 6000; www.hrp.org.uk; individual/joint membership £53/82, 1-/2-adult family £76/108) If you're a royalty, history or palace buff, taking out a membership allows you to jump the queues and visit the Tower of London, Kensington Palace, Banqueting House, Kew Palace and Hampton Court Palace, which saves on individual entry to each – plus you can go as often as you like over a year, if you're staying. Temporary membership cards are issued immediately so you can get visiting while you're in town.

Electricity

Type G
230V/50Hz

Emergency

London area code	☎020
International access code	☎00
Police, fire or ambulance emergency	☎999
Non-emergency police	☎101

Health

Medical Services

Until the UK formally leaves the EU at the end of 2020, EU nationals can still obtain free emergency treatment on presentation of a **European Health Insurance Card** (www.ehic.org.uk). At the time of research, plans for the EHIC card after Brexit were not confirmed.

Reciprocal arrangements with the UK allow Australians, New Zealanders and residents and nationals of several other countries to receive free emergency medical treatment and subsidised dental care through the **National Health Service** (NHS; www.nhs.uk). They can use hospital emergency departments, GPs and dentists. For a full list, visit the 'Services near you' section of the NHS website.

The NHS non emergency number is 111 if you require medical advice and help. It is free of charge and available 24 hours a day, every day of the year. This is not the number to call for life-threatening situations; for that call ☎999.

Taking out a travel insurance policy that covers medical expenses is strongly advised. You will have more flexibility over where, when and how you're treated (the NHS is currently underfunded and waiting lists for treatment can be long). Make sure you are covered for any expenses such as ambulances and repatriation if required.

Dental Services

For emergency dental care, visit the NHS website (www.nhs.uk) to find listed dentists who are primary practitioners, even out of hours. If the situation involves severe pain, heavy bleeding or injuries to the face, mouth or teeth, you're advised to attend a hospital's accident and emergency department.

University College London Hospital (Map p444; ☎020-3456 7890; www.uclh.nhs.uk; 235 Euston Rd, NW1; ⓊWarren St or Euston Sq) offers dental care but only when referred by a dentist. Note that many travel insurance policies do not cover emergency dental care, so check the fine print before you take out coverage as services can be expensive.

Hospitals

A number of London hospitals have 24-hour accident and emergency departments. However, in an emergency just call an ambulance.

Charing Cross Hospital (Map p472; ☎020-3311 1234; www.imperial.nhs.uk/charingcross; Fulham Palace Rd, W6; ⓊHammersmith) Hammersmith.

Chelsea & Westminster Hospital (Map p472; ☎020-3315 8000; www.chelwest.nhs.uk; 369 Fulham Rd, SW10; 🚌14 or 414, ⓊSouth Kensington, Fulham Broadway) Fulham.

Guy's & St Thomas' Hospital (☎020-7188 7188; www.guysandstthomas.nhs.uk; Westminster Bridge Rd, SE1; ⓊWaterloo or Westminster) Waterloo.

Royal Free Hospital (☎020-7794 0500; www.royalfree.nhs.uk; Pond St, NW3; ⓊBelsize Park, Hampstead Heath) Hampstead.

Royal London Hospital (Map p462; ☎020-7377 7000; www.bartshealth.nhs.uk; Whitechapel Rd, E1; ⓊWhitechapel) Whitechapel (includes children's hospital).

University College London Hospital (Map p444; ☎020-3456 7890; www.uclh.nhs.uk; 235 Euston Rd, NW1; ⓊWarren St or Euston Sq) Euston.

Pharmacies

The main pharmacy chains in London are Boots and Superdrug; a branch of either – or both – can be found on virtually every high street. If you need prescription drugs such as antibiotics, sleeping pills or Ventolin, you will need to see a doctor for a prescription.

The Boots store in Piccadilly Circus is one of the biggest and most centrally located and has extended opening times.

Tap Water

London tap water is drinkable and is generally of good quality. Diners at restaurants often ask for tap water.

Vaccinations

No vaccinations are required for visits to London, but check with your personal medical provider about any preventive actions you may need to take before you travel.

Insurance

There are myriad insurance policies to choose from these days, most underwritten by larger well-known firms. Do your research and choose what best suits your needs.

Pre-existing conditions (including depression and anxiety) are rarely covered without talking to the insurers first.

The cheaper the premiums, the higher your excess if you do need to make a claim. Always read the fine print.

Legal Matters

Should you face any legal difficulties while in London, contact your home country's embassy for advice.

Driving Offences

Drink-driving is treated very seriously in the UK. Currently the limit is 80mg of alcohol in 100mL of blood, but did you know you are 37% more likely to be involved in a fatal road accident with just 10mg per 100mL of blood than when sober? Probably best not to risk it. The consequences if caught driving under the influence: a driving ban, £2500 fine or a short prison sentence. It is also illegal to use a mobile phone while driving.

Drugs

Non-prescription drugs are quite widely available in London despite pretty heavy penalties for possessing or dealing drugs (see www.gov.uk/penalties-drug-possession-dealing). If you're caught smoking pot, expect an on-the-spot fine of £90. The punishment for possession of other illegal drugs, such as cocaine, will depend on where you and the drugs were found, your criminal history and any other aggravating or mitigating factors. Drug searches before entering clubs are not unusual.

Maps

If you want to go 'old school' and ditch the GPS on your phone, you'll need to find a *London A–Z* at a WHSmith and then work out how to read it.

Money

Increasingly most purchases are made via electronic payments, but a few places will have a sign saying 'cash only'.

Notes come in denominations of £5, £10, £20 and £50, while coins are 1p (penny), 2p, 5p, 10p, 20p, 50p, £1 and £2. A dual-metal, hologram-decorated, 12-sided £1 coin entered circulation in 2017 after counterfeit £1 coins flooded the market.

Cashpoints

ATMs (cashpoints) are everywhere and will generally accept Visa, MasterCard, Cirrus or Maestro cards. Check with your home bank about transaction charges for cash withdrawals while overseas; there are good transaction-fee-free alternatives available now.

There are also non-bank-run ATMs normally found inside shops charging £1.50 to £2 per transaction on all withdrawals (mostly used when people are desperate, drunk or short of time), making them particularly expensive for foreign-bank-card holders. Look for nearby ATMs promising 'Free Cash' instead.

Some supermarkets will give you 'cashback' (extra money added to the purchase), but not many in London.

Credit Cards & Smartphones

Londoners have embraced contactless or pay-wave card payments (which do not require PIN or a signature) and are increasingly making transactions using mobile phones through Apple and Google Pay. Contactless payments can be made on transactions up to £30.

Card transactions are generally also subject to additional charges for foreign cardholders; check what these are with your bank to determine the best way to access your money when travelling. American Express and Diners Club are far less widely accepted than Visa and MasterCard.

Exchange Rates

Australia	A$1	£0.51
Canada	C$1	£0.58
Euro	€1	£0.84
Japan	¥100	£0.70
New Zealand	NZ$1	£0.50
USA	US$1	£0.76

For current exchange rates, see www.xe.com.

Tipping

Hotels Pay a porter £1 per bag; gratuity for room staff is at your discretion.

Pubs Not expected unless table service is provided, then £1 for a round of drinks is sufficient. If you tip at the bar, staff will assume you must be American.

Restaurants Service charge is always included in the bill. If not (it pays to check!), 10% is fine for decent service, but 15% is best for good service.

Taxis Londoners generally round the fare up to the nearest pound only.

Opening Hours

The following are standard opening hours.

Banks 9am–5pm Monday–Friday

Post offices 9am–5.30pm Monday–Friday and 9am–noon Saturday

Pubs & bars 11am–11pm (but many are open later)

Restaurants noon–2.30pm and 6–11pm

Sights 10am–6pm

Shops 9am–7pm Monday–Saturday, noon–5pm Sunday (sometimes 11am–6pm)

Post

The **Royal Mail** (www.royalmail.com) is generally very reliable. To find your nearest post office, consult www.postoffice.co.uk/branch-finder.

Postcodes

The unusual London postcode system dates back to WWI. The whole city is divided up into districts denoted by a letter (or letters) and a number.

For example, W1, the postcode for Mayfair and Soho, stands for 'West London, district 1'. EC1, on the other hand, stands for 'East Central London, district 1'. The number a district is assigned has nothing to do with its geographic location, but rather its alphabetical listing in that area.

For example, in North London N1 and N16 are right next to each other, as are E1 and E14 in East London.

Public Holidays

Most attractions and businesses close for a couple of days over Christmas and sometimes Easter. Places that normally shut on Sunday will often close on bank-holiday Mondays. The transport network shuts down in London on Christmas Day, apart from Santander Cycles (pre-book a taxi if you want to get somewhere).

New Year's Day 1 January

Good Friday Late March/April

Easter Monday Late March/April

May Day Holiday First Monday in May

Spring Bank Holiday Last Monday in May

Summer Bank Holiday Last Monday in August

Christmas Day 25 December

Boxing Day 26 December

Safe Travel

London is a fairly safe city for its size, but exercise common sense.

➡ Occasional terror attacks have afflicted London over the last few decades, but risks to individual visitors are remote.

➡ Keep a hand on your handbag/wallet, especially in bars and nightclubs, and in crowded areas such as the Underground.

➡ Be discreet with your tablet/smartphone – snatch and run happens all too often.

➡ When crossing the road look out for silent high-speed cyclists.

➡ Victims of rape and sexual abuse can contact Rape Crisis England & Wales (0808 802 9999, www.rapecrisis.org.uk); anyone in emotional distress contact Samaritans (116 123 toll-free, 24 hours; www.samaritans.org).

➡ For the latest government regulations on COVID-19, check www.gov.uk/coronavirus.

➡ At the time of writing, you are required to wear a face covering on public transport.

➡ If using public transport, plan ahead to travel at less busy times.

➡ Check ahead with venues for information on entry requirements regarding COVID-19.

Taxes & Refunds

Value-added tax (VAT) is a 20% sales tax levied on most goods and services. Restaurants must always include VAT in prices, but the same requirement doesn't apply to hotel-room prices.

It's possible for visitors to claim a refund of VAT paid on goods while on holidays. You must live outside the EU and be heading back home, though this is likely to change in the post-Brexit period.

Select shops participate in what is called either the VAT Retail Export Scheme or Tax Free Shopping, with different minimum purchase conditions (normally around £75) to be eligible.

On request, the shop will give you a special form (VAT 407) which is presented with the goods and receipts to customs when you depart the UK. VAT-free goods can't be posted or shipped home. After customs has certified the form, you usually get a refund on the spot. Otherwise, the form is sent back to the shop, which then processes your refund (minus an administration or handling fee). It's worth the red tape if you're spending up big.

Telephone

British Telecom's famous red phone boxes survive in conservation areas only (notably Westminster). Some people use them as shelter from the rain while using their mobile phones. Pay phones are largely a thing of the past, but you will seem them on occasion; most accept coins and credit cards.

Calling London

London's area code is ☎020, followed by an eight-digit number beginning with 7 (central London), 8 (Greater London) or 3 (non-geographic).

You need to dial the ☎020 code when you are calling London from elsewhere in the UK or from a mobile.

To call London from abroad, dial your country's international access code (usually ☎00 but ☎011 in Canada and the USA), then ☎44 (the UK's country code), then 20 (dropping the initial 0), followed by the eight-digit phone number.

Mobile Phones

Unless your international roaming charges are good, buy a local SIM card once in the UK. Once Britain leaves the EU, it's likely international roaming charges will return for EU providers.

Time

London is on GMT/UTC; during British Summer Time (BST; late March to late October) clocks are one hour ahead of GMT/UTC.

Toilets

You'll find public toilets of varying standards across the city; some are automated. Typically there is a charge (50p) for access, though this seems to be changing as the world goes cashless. Train stations and bus terminals generally have good facilities, providing for people with disabilities and those with young children. Department stores, museums and art galleries also generally have easy-to-find and well-maintained toilets. To locate your nearest toilet, consult the **Great British Public Toilet Map** (www.toiletmap.org.uk), or download one of several toilet-finding apps to your smartphone. By the way, it's an offence to urinate in the street.

Tourist Information

Visit London (www.visitlondon.com) has info on special events, tours, accommodation, eating, theatre, shopping etc.

Key locations:

Heathrow Airport (www.visitlondon.com/tag/tourist-information-centre; Terminal 1, 2 & 3 Underground station concourse; ⌚7.30am-8.30pm)

King's Cross St Pancras Station (www.visitlondon.com/tag/tourist-information-centre; Western Ticket Hall, Euston Rd, N1; ⌚8am-6pm)

Liverpool Street Station (Map p450; www.visitlondon.com/tag/tourist-information-centre; Liverpool St Underground station, EC2; ⌚8.30am-5pm Sun-Wed, to 6.30pm Thu-Sat; ⓤLiverpool St)

Victoria Station (Map p456; www.visitlondon.com/tag/tourist-information-centre; Victoria Station; ⌚9am-5pm; ⓤVictoria)

Visas

There are several different short-stay visas, depending on the nature of your visit. For stays of up to six months, EU, Australian, Canadian, NZ and US visitors, among others, don't need visas.

Entry & Exit Formalities

Immigration to the UK is becoming tougher, particularly for those seeking to work or study.

After the exit of the UK from the EU, visitors from the EU can still, in most cases, come to the UK as a visitor without a visa for stays of up to six months

Check the website of the UK Border Agency (www.gov.uk/check-uk-visa) or with your local British embassy or consulate for the most up-to-date information.

Visa Extensions

Tourist visas can be extended as long as the total time spent in the UK is less than six months, or in clear emergencies (eg an accident, death of a relative). Contact the UK Visas & Immigration Contact Centre (0300 790 6268) for details. Note: if you break the conditions of your visa, you may not be able to return to the UK again.

Women Travellers

Women will find there is nothing out of the ordinary about being female and travelling, dining or even having a drink out alone in London. Street harassment or unwelcome body contact in crowded places is less of an issue than in many other major cities of the world. This said, crime is on the increase in London, so take the usual precautions to avoid being mugged or worse.

Both men and women usually leave an empty Tube carriage and prefer not to sit alone on the top deck of a bus. Be aware of your surroundings, who you are with, and have a plan for getting home at night (that taxi app won't work if your phone battery has died, so have a solid plan B).

If you're a woman travelling solo hoping to meet up with others, consider staying in a hotel or hostel with communal spaces. London has a bunch of new ones like **Mama Shelter** (www.mamashelter.com), **Qbic** (Map p462; ☎020-3021 3300; https://qbichotels.com/london-city; 42 Adler St, E1; r £54-100; P❄📶🐾; ⓤAldgate East) 🌿, **Hoxton** (Map p452; ☎020-7903 3000; https://thehoxton.com/london/southwark; Blackfriars Rd, SE1; r £140-300; ❄@📶🐾) and **Ace Hotel** (Map p458; ☎020-7613 9800; www.acehotel.com/london; 100 Shoreditch High St, E1; r £175-600; ❄📶🐾; ⓤShoreditch High St), to name a few. Look for classes, talks and experiences via websites such as **Eventbrite** (www.eventbrite.co.uk), **Airbnb Experiences** (www.airbnb.co.uk/s/experiences) and **Meetup** (www.meetup.com); friending apps like **Bumble BFF** (https://bumble.com/bff); plus small-group and specialist walking tours (p416) where you've got a good chance of meeting like-minded people.

Behind the Scenes

SEND US YOUR FEEDBACK

We love to hear from travellers – your comments keep us on our toes and help make our books better. Our well-travelled ed team reads every word on what you loved or loathed about this book. Although we cannot reply individually to your submissions, we always guarantee that your feedback goes straight to the appropriate authors, in time for the next edition. Each person who sends us information is thanked in the next edition – the most useful submissions are rewarded with a selection of digital PDF chapters.

Visit **lonelyplanet.com/contact** to submit your updates and suggestions or to ask for help. Our award-winning website also features inspirational travel stories, news and discussions.

Note: We may edit, reproduce and incorporate your comments in Lonely Planet products such as guidebooks, websites and digital products, so let us know if you don't want your comments reproduced or your name acknowledged. For a copy of our privacy policy visit lonelyplanet.com/privacy.

WRITER THANKS

Steve Fallon

Many thanks to my fellow London writers, in particular Damian Harper. Kevin Bond read the Music Scene chapter and made valuable suggestions. Fellow Blue Badge Tourist Guides who vetted the Understand chapters for mistakes and/or omissions include David Thompson (Architecture), Diane Burstein Lynch (Theatre & Dance), Sarah Ciacci (Art & Fashion) and Pepe Martinez (Film & Media). I am very grateful for their assistance. As always, I'd like to state my admiration, gratitude and great love for my now husband Michael Rothschild, as much a Londoner as I.

Damian Harper

Many thanks to everyone who helped and offered tips, including my co-authors, the ever-helpful staff at the Natural History Museum, Amaya Wang, Polly Bussell, Freya Barry, Tania Patel, Norman MacDonald, Penny Aikens, Bill Moran, Hollie and the excellent staff at Japan House, Shannon and James Peake. And big thanks to Tim Harper for his fine suggestions and Emma Harper too.

Lauren Keith

Cheers to Megan for the pints, pep talks and expert 'souf' London advice; to GG for always being up for one more sharing plate; to Tasmin and MaSovaida for eternal immoral support and heading into the future wearing red lippy; to Thomas for being a Sunday-night rooftop bar yes-man; to Sandie for allowing me to explore more; and to my own silly heart for leading me to this beautiful city 10 years ago in the first place.

MaSovaida Morgan

Deepest thanks to the wonderful souls who made this dream assignment the delight that it was. Love and gratitude are due in particular to James Thorpe, Osi and Mat; Anna Castelaz, Travis Levius, Shirin Beheshti; Nazanin Shahnavaz, Austin Milne, Rosaline Shahnavaz, Maman Simin & Baba Reza; Ali Lemer, Jo & Al; Megan Eaves, Dan, Angus; Mike, Debbie & B; Max & Ro; and Russ. Big hugs and love to my fellow former SheDEs, Tasmin and Lauren, for the immoral support and insightful feedback through frenzied WhatsApp chats. Finally, heartfelt thanks to Sandie for allowing me to return, once again, to my heart's home.

Tasmin Waby

First thanks to Sandie for this amazing opportunity, and the amazing Lonely Planet team for making it happen. Big thanks to my co-writers for their advice, insights and feedback, especially Lauren who kept me sane and

MaSovaida who kept me company. Thanks to everyone who's ever helped me out in London, making sense (and softening the edges) of this chaotic, historic capital: you know who you are (that includes you Dane). Cheers to my two fabulous little ladies, Willa and Maisie (and their brave mate, Rosa) who accompanied me on some of my research trips to identify the best places to eat, shop, rest, and play. And finally to Hugh: thank you for, well, everything.

ACKNOWLEDGEMENTS

Climate map data adapted from Peel MC, Finlayson BL & McMahon TA (2007) 'Updated World Map of the Köppen-Geiger Climate Classification', Hydrology and Earth System Sciences, 11, 163344.

Illustrations: pp74-5, pp82-3, pp140-1, pp180-1, pp314-5 by Javier Zarracina, River Thames alterations by Michael Weldon.

Cover photograph: Tower Bridge, London Massimo Ripani/4Corners Images©

THIS BOOK

This 12th edition of Lonely Planet's *London* guidebook was researched and written by Steve Fallon, Damian Harper, Lauren Keith, MaSovaida Morgan and Tasmin Waby. The previous edition was also written by Steve and Damian.

This guidebook was produced by the following:

Commissioning Editor Kate Chapman

Cartographers Mark Griffiths, Valentina Kremenchutskaya

Product Editor Gary Quinn, Fergus O'Shea

Book Designers Catalina Aragón, Clara Monitto

Assisting Editors Janet Austin, Judith Bamber, Kate James, Anne Mulvaney, Kirsten Rawlings, Brana Vladisavljevic, Simon Williamson

Cover Researcher Brendan Dempsey-Spencer

Thanks to Ronan Abayawickrema, Imogen Bannister, Georgia Barrett, Luke Busuttil, Doug Heather, Genna Patterson, Abby Ross, Kathryn Rowan, Peter Rubers, Ambika Shree, Vicky Smith

See also separate subindexes for:
EATING P429
DRINKING & NIGHTLIFE P431
ENTERTAINMENT P432
SHOPPING P433
SPORTS & ACTIVITIES P434
SLEEPING P434

Index

Sights 000
Map Pages **000**
Photo Pages **000**

M

N

O

P

Q

R

S

Sights 000
Map Pages **000**
Photo Pages **000**

EATING

ENTERTAINMENT

SHOPPING

SPORTS & ACTIVITIES

SLEEPING

London Maps

Sights

- Beach
- Bird Sanctuary
- Buddhist
- Castle/Palace
- Christian
- Confucian
- Hindu
- Islamic
- Jain
- Jewish
- Monument
- Museum/Gallery/Historic Building
- Ruin
- Shinto
- Sikh
- Taoist
- Winery/Vineyard
- Zoo/Wildlife Sanctuary
- Other Sight

Activities, Courses & Tours

- Bodysurfing
- Diving
- Canoeing/Kayaking
- Course/Tour
- Sento Hot Baths/Onsen
- Skiing
- Snorkelling
- Surfing
- Swimming/Pool
- Walking
- Windsurfing
- Other Activity

Sleeping

- Sleeping
- Camping
- Hut/Shelter

Eating

- Eating

Drinking & Nightlife

- Drinking & Nightlife
- Cafe

Entertainment

- Entertainment

Shopping

- Shopping

Information

- Bank
- Embassy/Consulate
- Hospital/Medical
- Internet
- Police
- Post Office
- Telephone
- Toilet
- Tourist Information
- Other Information

Geographic

- Beach
- Gate
- Hut/Shelter
- Lighthouse
- Lookout
- Mountain/Volcano
- Oasis
- Park
- Pass
- Picnic Area
- Waterfall

Population

- Capital (National)
- Capital (State/Province)
- City/Large Town
- Town/Village

Transport

- Airport
- Border crossing
- Bus
- Cable car/Funicular
- Cycling
- Ferry
- Metro station
- Monorail
- Parking
- Petrol station
- S-Bahn/Subway station
- Taxi
- T-bane/Tunnelbana station
- Train station/Railway
- Tram
- U-Bahn/Underground station
- Other Transport

Routes

- Tollway
- Freeway
- Primary
- Secondary
- Tertiary
- Lane
- Unsealed road
- Road under construction
- Plaza/Mall
- Steps
- Tunnel
- Pedestrian overpass
- Walking Tour
- Walking Tour detour
- Path/Walking Trail

Boundaries

- International
- State/Province
- Disputed
- Regional/Suburb
- Marine Park
- Cliff
- Wall

Hydrography

- River, Creek
- Intermittent River
- Canal
- Water
- Dry/Salt/Intermittent Lake
- Reef

Areas

- Airport/Runway
- Beach/Desert
- Cemetery (Christian)
- Cemetery (Other)
- Glacier
- Mudflat
- Park/Forest
- Sight (Building)
- Sportsground
- Swamp/Mangrove

Note: Not all symbols displayed above appear on the maps in this book

MAP INDEX

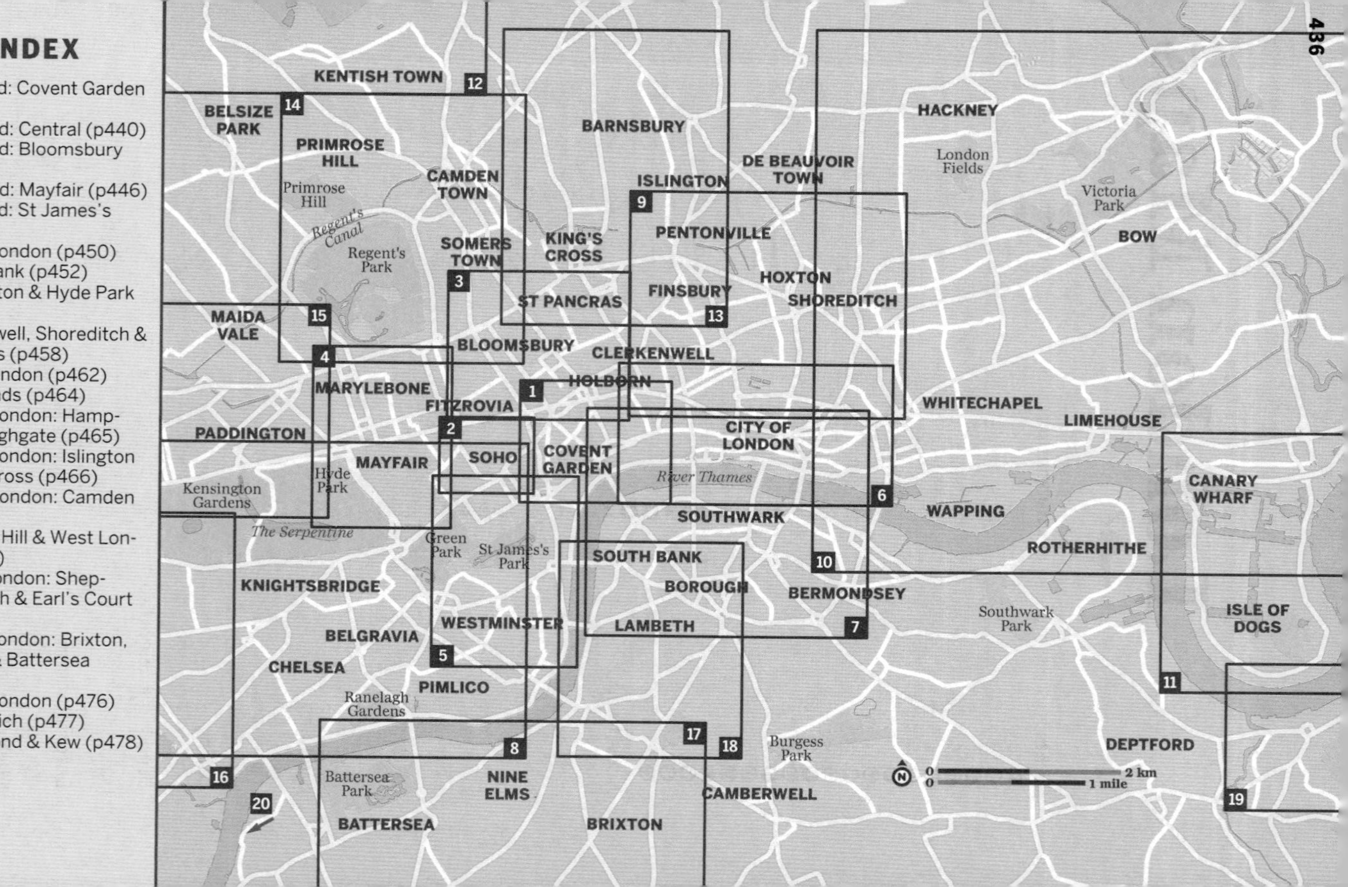

KENTISH TOWN
BELSIZE PARK
PRIMROSE HILL
Primrose Hill
CAMDEN TOWN
Regent's Canal
Regent's Park
BARNSBURY
ISLINGTON
DE BEAUVOIR TOWN
HACKNEY
London Fields
Victoria Park
BOW
SOMERS TOWN
KING'S CROSS
PENTONVILLE
HOXTON
SHOREDITCH
FINSBURY
ST PANCRAS
MAIDA VALE
BLOOMSBURY
CLERKENWELL
HOLBORN
MARYLEBONE
FITZROVIA
WHITECHAPEL
LIMEHOUSE
PADDINGTON
CITY OF LONDON
MAYFAIR
SOHO
COVENT GARDEN
Hyde Park
Kensington Gardens
River Thames
CANARY WHARF
WAPPING
SOUTHWARK
The Serpentine
Green Park
St James's Park
ROTHERHITHE
SOUTH BANK
KNIGHTSBRIDGE
BOROUGH
BERMONDSEY
Southwark Park
ISLE OF DOGS
WESTMINSTER
LAMBETH
BELGRAVIA
CHELSEA
PIMLICO
Ranelagh Gardens
Burgess Park
DEPTFORD
Battersea Park
NINE ELMS
CAMBERWELL
BATTERSEA
BRIXTON
0
2 km
0
1 mile
N
1
2
3
4
5
6
7
8
9
10
11
12
13
14
15
16
17
18
19
20

WEST END: COVENT GARDEN *Map on p438*

Top Experiences (p91)

1 National Gallery............ B7
2 National Portrait Gallery........................ B6
3 Sir John Soane's Museum......................E2
4 Somerset House............E5
5 Trafalgar Square........... B7

Sights (p101)

6 Covent Garden Piazza......................... D4
7 Gray's Inn.......................G1
8 Inner Temple................. H4
9 Lincoln's Inn F2
10 London Film Museum..................... D5
11 London Transport Museum..................... D5
12 Middle Temple G4
13 Royal Courts of Justice........................ G3
14 St Clement Danes..........F4
15 St Giles-in-the-Fields.......................... B3
16 St Martin-in-the-Fields.......................... B6
17 St Paul's Church........... C5
18 Staple Inn........................G1
19 Temple Church............. H4
20 The Strand..................... C6
21 Two Temple Place........ G5

Eating (p116)

22 Balthazar....................... D4
23 Barrafina C6
24 Battersea Pie Station... C5
25 Delaunay E4
Delaunay Counter ....(see 25)
Holborn Dining Room .... (see 64)
26 Ivy Market Grill.............. C5
27 J Sheekey....................... B5
28 Kanada-Ya B3
29 National Café................. B6
30 Rules.............................. C5
31 Seven Dials Market....... B4
Spring.....................(see 4)

Drinking & Nightlife (p124)

32 American Bar D5
33 Bar Polski.......................E2
34 Craft Beer Co................ B3
35 Gordon's Wine Bar........ C7
36 Heaven C7
37 Holborn Whippet............D1
38 Lamb & Flag................... C5
39 Princess Louise............. D2
Radio Rooftop Bar .... (see 63)
40 Salisbury B5
41 Terroirs C6

Entertainment (p126)

42 Donmar Warehouse B4
43 English National Opera.......................... B6
44 Poetry Café................... C3
45 Royal Opera House....... D4

Shopping (p132)

46 Apple Store.................... C5
47 Benjamin Pollock's Toyshop D5
48 Cambridge Satchel Company..................... C4
49 Forbidden Planet B3
50 James Smith & Sons Umbrellas......... B2
51 Molton Brown................ D4
52 Neal's Yard Dairy B3
53 Stanfords....................... C4
54 Stanley Gibbons............ D5
55 Ted Baker........................ C4
56 Twinings......................... G4
57 Watkins B6

Sleeping (p347)

58 Covent Garden Hotel B3
59 Fielding Hotel D4
60 Haymarket Hotel........... A7
61 High Holborn Residence C3
62 Hoxton Holborn............ D2
63 ME London......................E5
64 Rosewood London.........E2

Key on p437

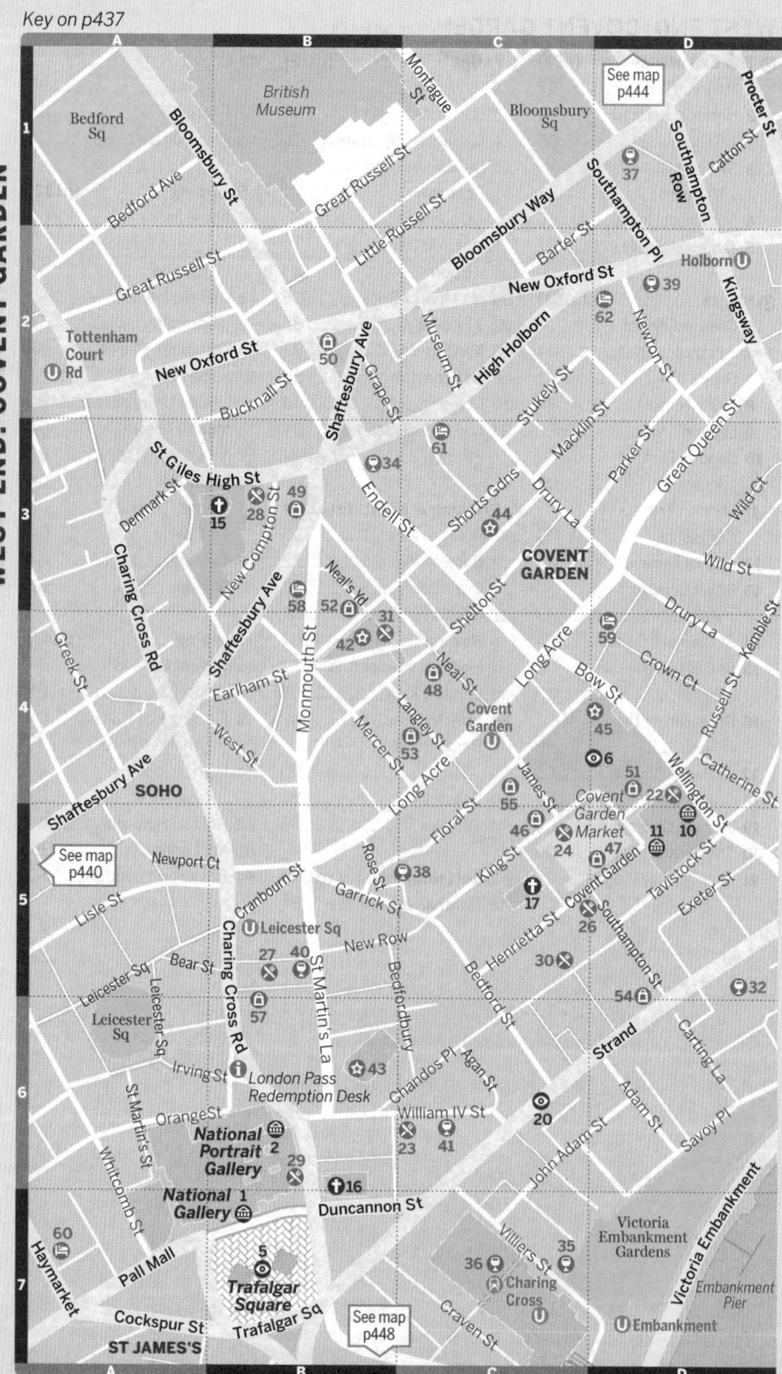
WEST END: COVENT GARDEN
See map p444
See map p440
See map p448
British Museum
Bedford Sq
Bloomsbury Sq
Tottenham Court Rd
Holborn
Leicester Sq
Covent Garden
Charing Cross
Embankment
Embankment Pier
Victoria Embankment Gardens
National Portrait Gallery
National Gallery
Trafalgar Square
London Pass Redemption Desk
Covent Garden Market
COVENT GARDEN
SOHO
ST JAMES'S
Bloomsbury St
Bedford Ave
Great Russell St
Little Russell St
Montague St
Bloomsbury Way
Southampton Pl
Southampton Row
Procter St
Catton St
Barter St
New Oxford St
High Holborn
Kingsway
Newton St
Museum St
Shaftesbury Ave
Grape St
Bucknall St
St Giles High St
Denmark St
New Compton St
Charing Cross Rd
Endell St
Shorts Gdns
Stukely St
Macklin St
Parker St
Great Queen St
Drury La
Wild Ct
Wild St
Neal's Yd
Monmouth St
Earlham St
Greek St
West St
Neal St
Shelton St
Long Acre
Bow St
Crown Ct
Kemble St
Russell St
Langley St
Mercer St
James St
Floral St
Catherine St
Wellington St
Newport Ct
Lisle St
Cranbourn St
Garrick St
Rose St
King St
Covent Garden
Tavistock St
Exeter St
New Row
Bear St
Leicester Sq
St Martin's La
Bedfordbury
Henrietta St
Southampton St
Bedford St
Strand
Carting La
Irving St
Chandos Pl
Agan St
Adam St
Savoy Pl
John Adam St
Orange St
William IV St
St Martin's St
Whitcomb St
Duncannon St
Villiers St
Craven St
Victoria Embankment
Haymarket
Pall Mall
Cockspur St
Trafalgar Sq

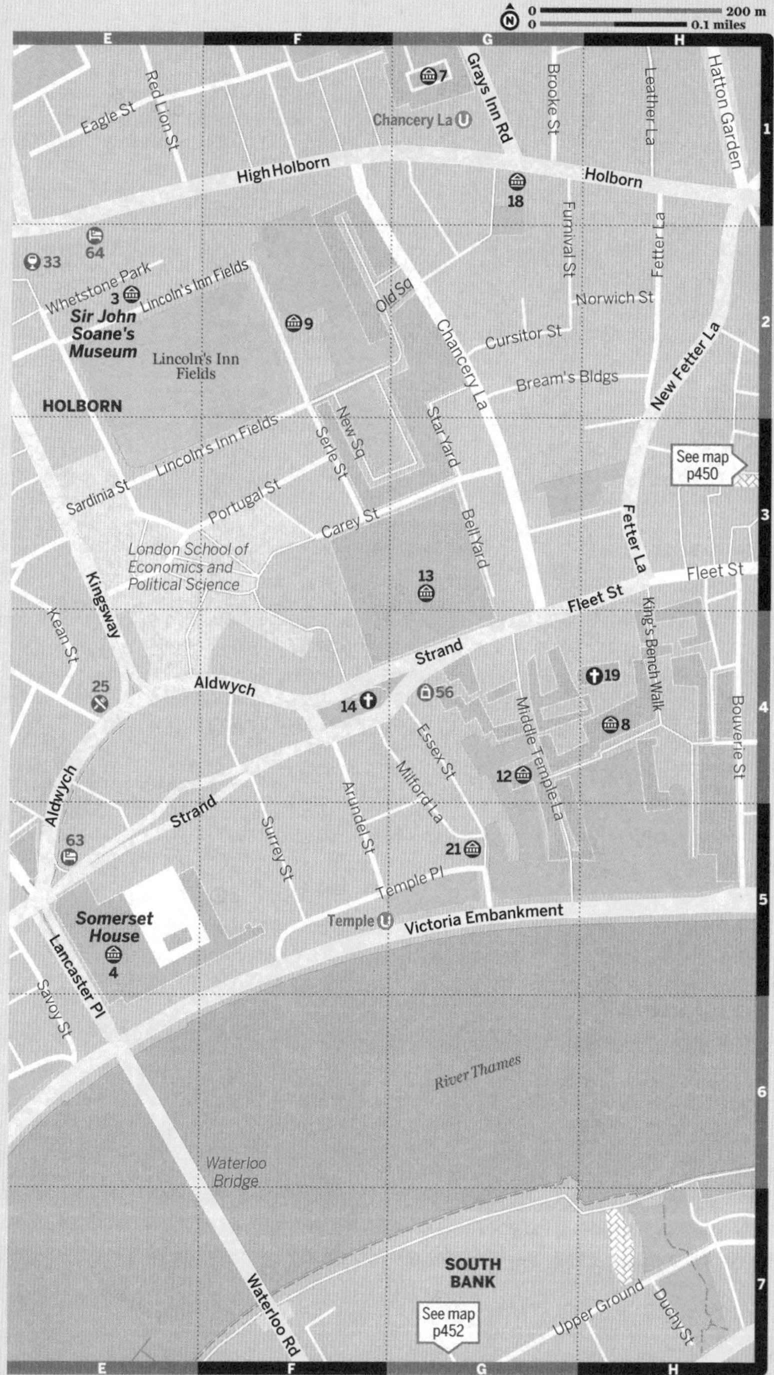
200 m
0.1 miles
E
F
G
H
1
2
3
4
5
6
7
Red Lion St
Eagle St
Chancery La
Grays Inn Rd
Brooke St
Leather La
Hatton Garden
High Holborn
Holborn
Furnival St
Fetter La
7
18
64
33
Whetstone Park
Lincoln's Inn Fields
3
Sir John Soane's Museum
9
Old Sq
Chancery La
Norwich St
Cursitor St
New Fetter La
Lincoln's Inn Fields
Bream's Bldgs
HOLBORN
Lincoln's Inn Fields
New Sq
Serle St
Star Yard
See map p450
Sardinia St
Portugal St
Carey St
Bell Yard
Fetter La
London School of Economics and Political Science
13
Fleet St
Fleet St
Kingsway
Kean St
King's Bench Walk
Strand
Aldwych
25
14
56
19
Middle Temple La
8
Bouverie St
Essex St
12
Milford La
Arundel St
Surrey St
Aldwych
Strand
63
21
Temple Pl
Temple
Victoria Embankment
Somerset House
4
Lancaster Pl
Savoy St
River Thames
Waterloo Bridge
SOUTH BANK
Waterloo Rd
See map p452
Upper Ground
Duchy St

Key on p442

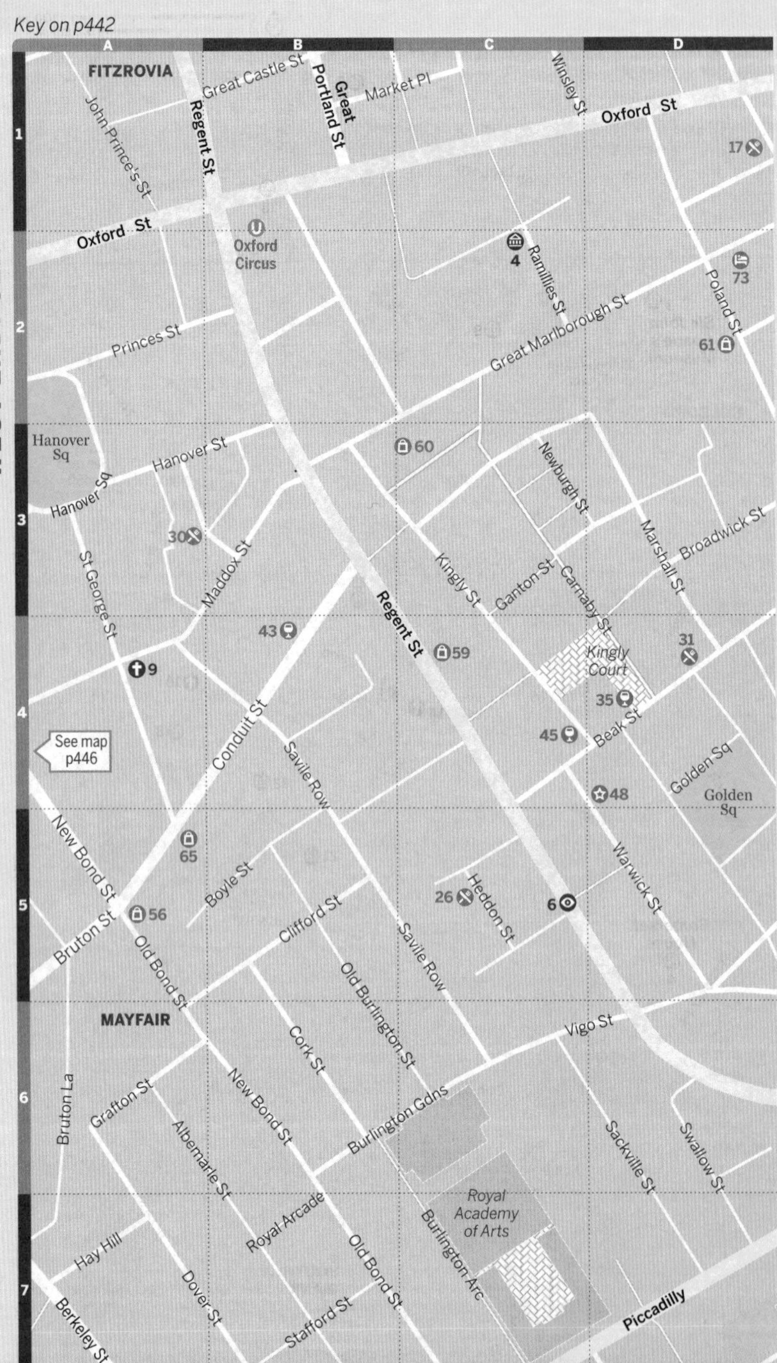
FITZROVIA
MAYFAIR
Oxford St
Regent St
Great Castle St
Great Portland St
Market Pl
Winsley St
John Prince's St
Oxford Circus
Ramillies St
Poland St
Great Marlborough St
Princes St
Hanover Sq
Hanover St
Newburgh St
Marshall St
Broadwick St
Maddox St
Kingly St
Ganton St
Carnaby St
St George St
Kingly Court
Beak St
Conduit St
Savile Row
Golden Sq
See map p446
New Bond St
Boyle St
Heddon St
Warwick St
Bruton St
Clifford St
Old Bond St
Old Burlington St
Vigo St
Cork St
Bruton La
Grafton St
Albemarle St
Burlington Gdns
Sackville St
Swallow St
Royal Academy of Arts
Royal Arcade
Burlington Arc
Hay Hill
Dover St
Stafford St
Berkeley St
Piccadilly

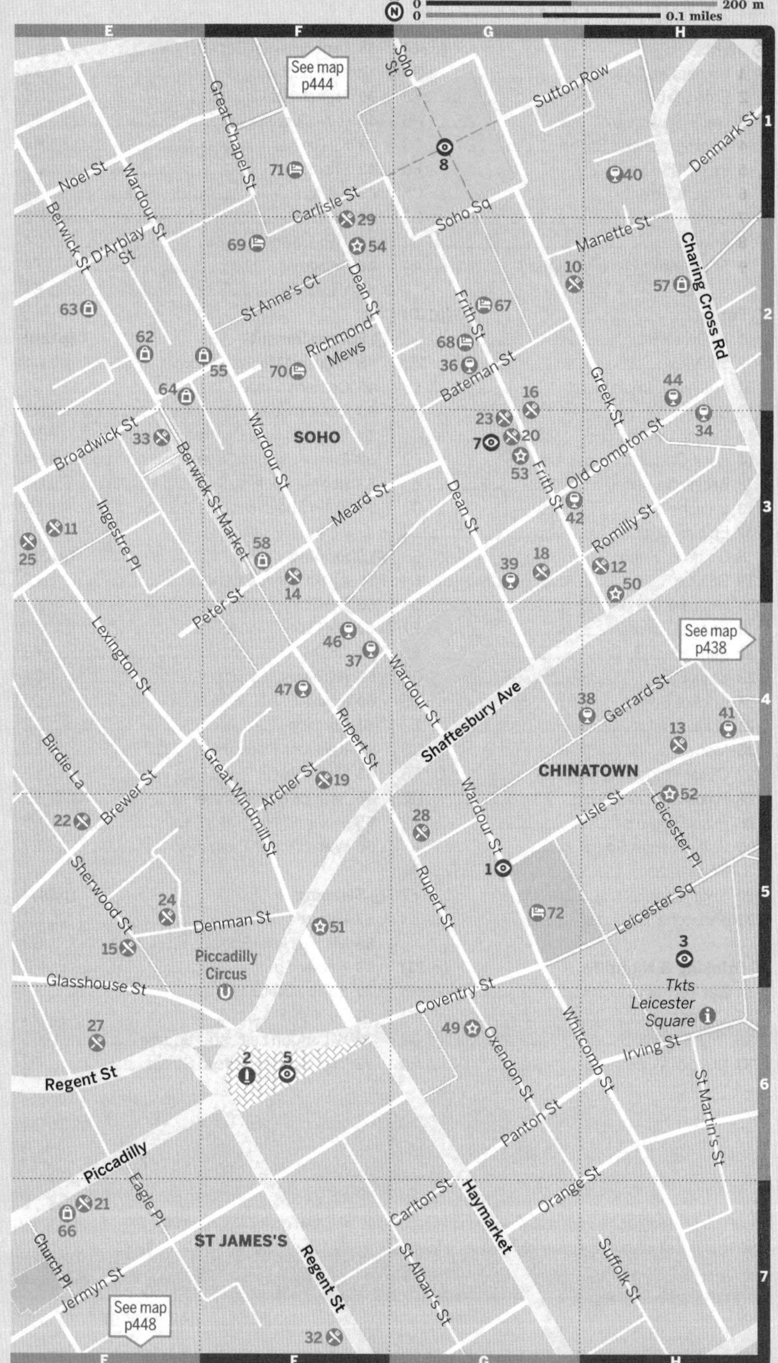
WEST END: CENTRAL
0
200 m
0
0.1 miles
See map p444
See map p438
See map p448
SOHO
CHINATOWN
ST JAMES'S
Piccadilly Circus
Tkts Leicester Square
Soho St
Sutton Row
Denmark St
Noel St
Wardour St
Great Chapel St
Carlisle St
Soho Sq
Berwick St
D'Arblay St
Manette St
Charing Cross Rd
St Anne's Ct
Dean St
Frith St
Richmond Mews
Bateman St
Greek St
Broadwick St
Berwick St Market
Old Compton St
Meard St
Ingestre Pl
Romilly St
Peter St
Lexington St
Shaftesbury Ave
Gerrard St
Rupert St
Birdie La
Brewer St
Great Windmill St
Archer St
Lisle St
Leicester Pl
Sherwood St
Denman St
Leicester Sq
Glasshouse St
Coventry St
Oxendon St
Whitcomb St
Irving St
Regent St
Panton St
St Martin's St
Piccadilly
Eagle Pl
Carlton St
Haymarket
Orange St
Church Pl
Jermyn St
St Alban's St
Suffolk St

WEST END: CENTRAL *Map on p440*

WEST END: BLOOMSBURY *Map on p444*

Key on p443

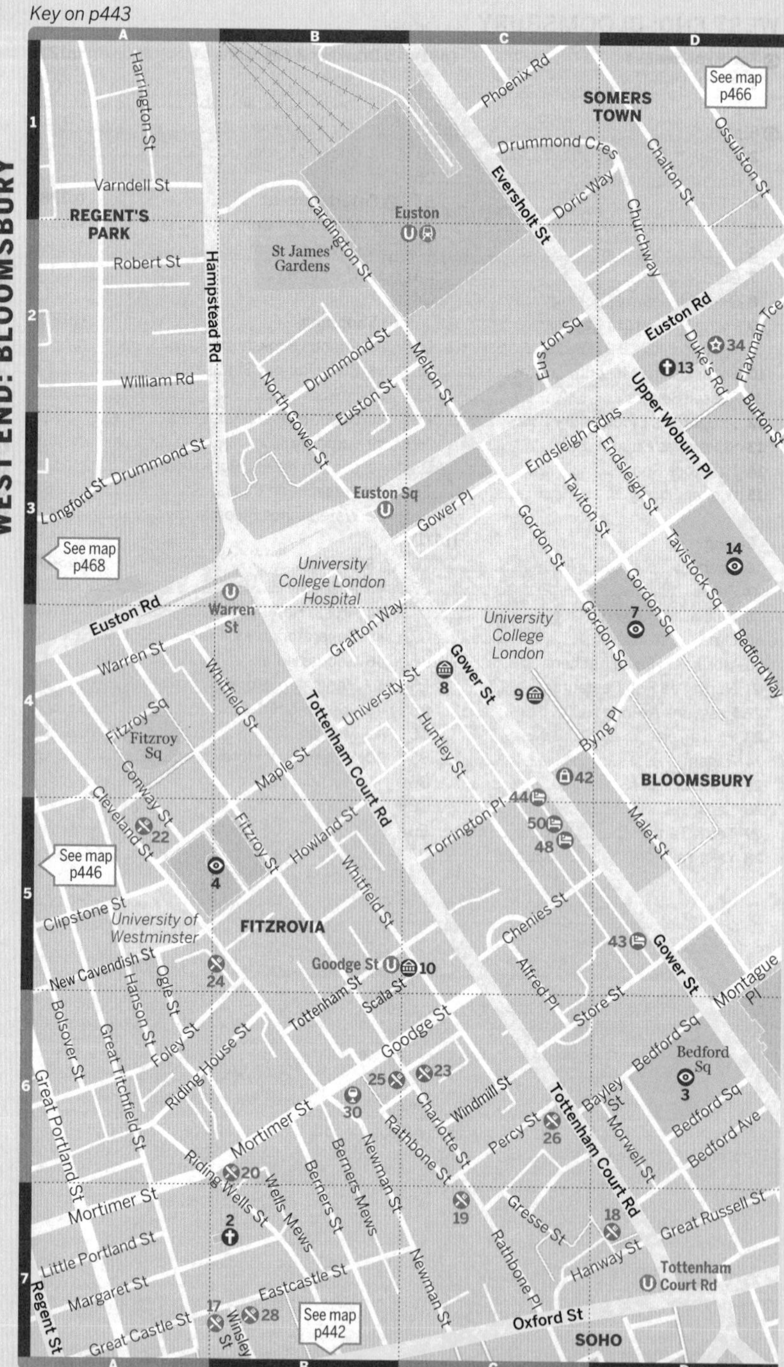

SOMERS TOWN
See map p466
Phoenix Rd
Drummond Cres
Harrington St
Varndell St
REGENT'S PARK
Robert St
William Rd
Hampstead Rd
Euston
St James' Gardens
Cardington St
Eversholt St
Doric Way
Chalton St
Ossulston St
Churchway
Euston Rd
Euston Sq
Drummond St
Melton St
North Gower St
Euston St
Duke's Rd
Flaxman Tce
Burton St
Upper Woburn Pl
Endsleigh Gdns
Endsleigh St
Taviton St
Longford St
Drummond St
Euston Sq
Gower Pl
Gordon St
Tavistock Sq
See map p468
University College London Hospital
Euston Rd
Warren St
Grafton Way
University College London
Gordon Sq
Bedford Way
Warren St
Whitfield St
Tottenham Court Rd
University St
Gower St
Huntley St
Byng Pl
Fitzroy Sq
Maple St
BLOOMSBURY
Conway St
Cleveland St
Fitzroy St
Howland St
Torrington Pl
Malet St
See map p446
FITZROVIA
Clipstone St
University of Westminster
Whitfield St
Chenies St
New Cavendish St
Goodge St
Gower St
Montague Pl
Hanson St
Ogle St
Tottenham St
Scala St
Alfred Pl
Store St
Bolsover St
Great Titchfield St
Foley St
Riding House St
Goodge St
Bedford Sq
Great Portland St
Mortimer St
Charlotte St
Windmill St
Bayley St
Morwell St
Percy St
Bedford Ave
Rathbone St
Riding Wells St
Wells Mews
Berners St
Berners Mews
Newman St
Mortimer St
Gresse St
Rathbone Pl
Great Russell St
Little Portland St
Newman St
Hanway St
Tottenham Court Rd
Margaret St
Eastcastle St
Regent St
Great Castle St
Winsley St
See map p442
Oxford St
SOHO

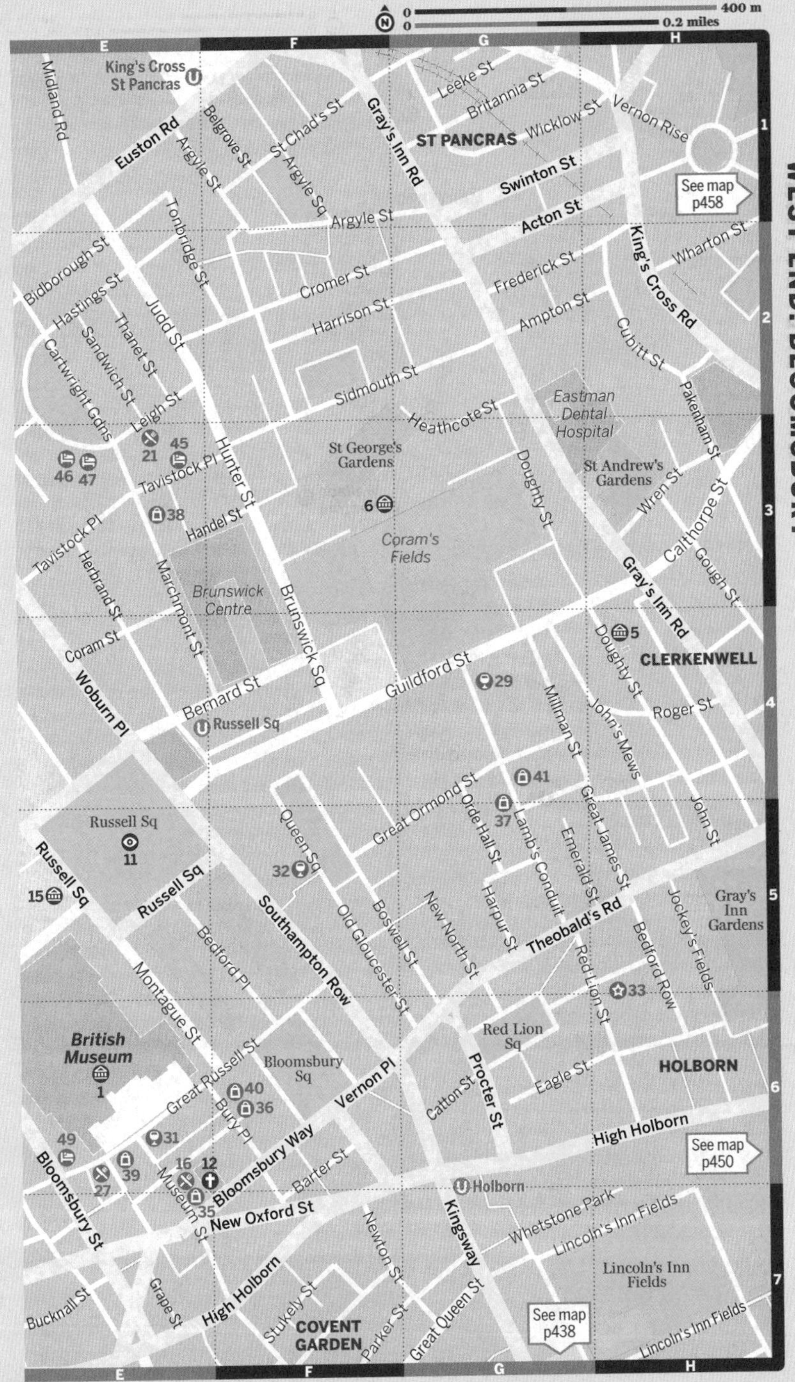
0
400 m
0
0.2 miles
E
F
G
H
King's Cross St Pancras
Midland Rd
Euston Rd
Belgrove St
Argyle St
St Chad's St
Argyle Sq
Gray's Inn Rd
Leeke St
Britannia St
ST PANCRAS
Wicklow St
Vernon Rise
Swinton St
See map p458
Acton St
Argyle St
Tonbridge St
Bidborough St
Hastings St
Cromer St
Frederick St
King's Cross Rd
Wharton St
Judd St
Harrison St
Ampton St
Thanet St
Sandwich St
Cartwright Gdns
Cubitt St
Sidmouth St
Leigh St
Pakenham St
Eastman Dental Hospital
Heathcote St
St George's Gardens
St Andrew's Gardens
Hunter St
Tavistock Pl
Doughty St
Wren St
Handel St
Calthorpe St
Tavistock Pl
Herbrand St
Coram's Fields
Gough St
Marchmont St
Brunswick Centre
Brunswick Sq
Coram St
Doughty St
CLERKENWELL
Woburn Pl
Bernard St
Guildford St
Millman St
John's Mews
Roger St
Russell Sq
Great Ormond St
Orde Hall St
Lamb's Conduit
Great James St
John St
Russell Sq
Queen Sq
Emerald St
Russell Sq
Russell Sq
Southampton Row
Old Gloucester St
Boswell St
New North St
Harpur St
Theobald's Rd
Gray's Inn Gardens
Bedford Pl
Red Lion St
Bedford Row
Jockey's Fields
Montague St
British Museum
Red Lion Sq
Bloomsbury Sq
Great Russell St
Procter St
Eagle St
HOLBORN
Bury Pl
Vernon Pl
Catton St
Bloomsbury Way
High Holborn
See map p450
Barter St
Holborn
Bloomsbury St
Museum St
New Oxford St
Newton St
Kingsway
Whetstone Park
Lincoln's Inn Fields
Lincoln's Inn Fields
Grape St
High Holborn
Bucknall St
Stukely St
Parker St
Great Queen St
COVENT GARDEN
See map p438
Lincoln's Inn Fields
1
2
3
4
5
6
7
1
5
6
11
12
15
16
21
27
29
31
32
33
35
36
37
38
39
40
41
45
46
47
49

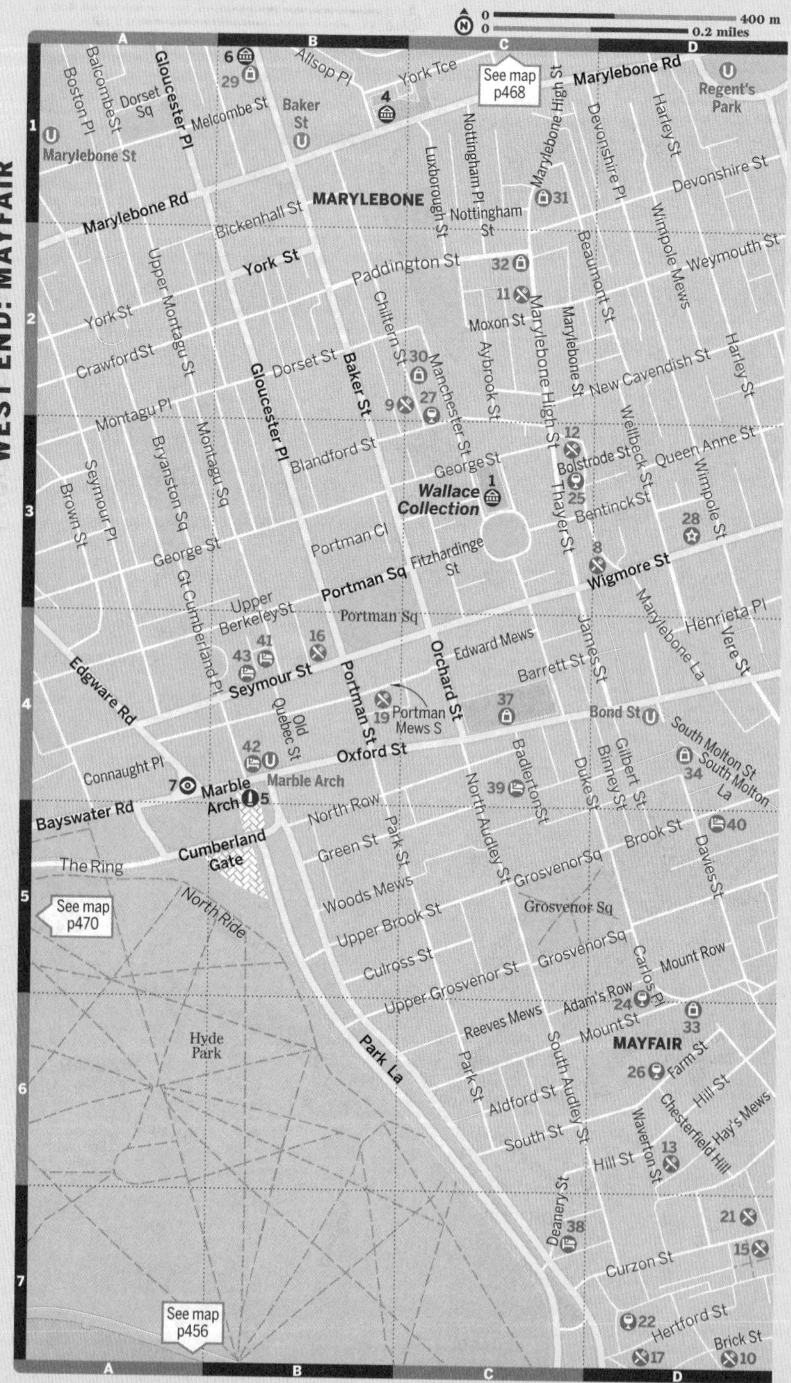
0 400 m
0 0.2 miles
A
B
C
D
1
2
3
4
5
6
7
See map p468
See map p470
See map p456
Marylebone Rd
Regent's Park
Baker St
Marylebone St
MARYLEBONE
Boston Pl
Balcombe St
Dorset Sq
Gloucester Pl
Melcombe St
Allsop Pl
York Tce
Nottingham Pl
Luxborough St
Marylebone High St
Devonshire Pl
Harley St
Devonshire St
Bickenhall St
Nottingham St
Beaumont St
Wimpole Mews
Weymouth St
York St
Paddington St
Upper Montagu St
Chiltern St
Moxon St
Marylebone St
New Cavendish St
Crawford St
Dorset St
Baker St
Manchester St
Aybrook St
Montagu Pl
Bryanston Sq
Montagu Sq
Blandford St
Welbeck St
Bolstrode St
Queen Anne St
Wimpole St
George St
Seymour Pl
Brown St
Wallace Collection
Thayer St
Bentinck St
George St
Portman Cl
Fitzhardinge St
Wigmore St
Gt Cumberland Pl
Upper Berkeley St
Portman Sq
Henrietta Pl
Vere St
Marylebone La
Edgware Rd
Seymour St
Portman St
Orchard St
Edward Mews
James St
Barrett St
Old Quebec St
Portman Mews S
Bond St
South Molton St
South Molton La
Oxford St
Connaught Pl
Marble Arch
Badlerton St
North Audley St
Duke St
Binney St
Gilbert St
Bayswater Rd
North Row
Park St
Brook St
Davies St
The Ring
Cumberland Gate
Green St
Grosvenor Sq
Woods Mews
North Ride
Upper Brook St
Grosvenor Sq
Culross St
Carlos Pl
Mount Row
Upper Grosvenor St
Adam's Row
Reeves Mews
Mount St
Hyde Park
Park La
MAYFAIR
South Audley St
Farm St
Park St
Aldford St
Hill St
Chesterfield Hill
Hay's Mews
South St
Waverton St
Hill St
Deanery St
Curzon St
Hertford St
Brick St
1 2 4 5 6 7 8 9 10 11 12 13 15 16 17 19 21 22 24 25 26 27 28 29 30 31 32 33 34 37 38 39 40 41 42 43

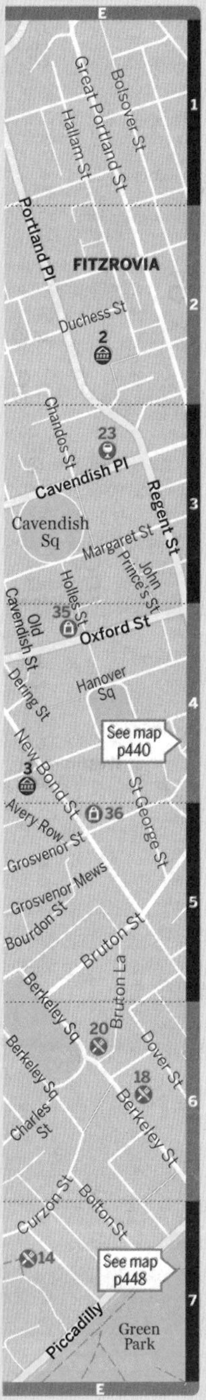

Top Experiences (p107)

1 Wallace Collection C3

Sights (p109)

2 Broadcasting House.............E2
3 Handel & Hendrix in London E4
4 Madame Tussauds B1
5 Marble Arch B4
6 Sherlock Holmes Museum B1
7 Tyburn Tree Memorial Plaque A4

Eating (p119)

8 28-50 ....D3
9 Chiltern Firehouse C2
10 El Pirata D7
11 Fishworks.............................C2
Foyer & Reading Room at Claridge's ..(see 40)
12 Golden Hind C3
13 Greenhouse D6
14 Kitty Fisher's.........................E7
15 Le Boudin Blanc D7
16 Locanda Locatelli..................B4
17 Nobu D7
18 Park Chinois E6
19 Roti Chai...............................B4
20 Sexy Fish..............................E6
21 Tamarind D7
Wallace Restaurant ....(see 1)

Drinking & Nightlife (p126)

22 10° at Galvin at Windows D7
23 Artesian E3
24 Connaught Bar......................D5
25 Golden Eagle C3
Magritte Bar ....(see 39)
26 Punchbowl............................D6
27 Purl C2

Entertainment (p127)

28 Wigmore Hall........................D3

Shopping (p133)

29 Beatles Store B1
30 Cadenhead's Whisky Shop & Tasting Room..................................C2
31 Cath Kidston C1
32 Daunt Books.........................C2
33 Gina D6
34 Grays Antiques D4
35 John Lewis............................E4
36 Mulberry E5
37 Selfridges C4

Sleeping (p347)

38 45 Park Lane C7
39 Beaumont..............................C4
40 Claridge's..............................D5
41 Grazing Goat B4
42 Hard Rock Hotel B4
43 Zetter Townhouse Marylebone B4

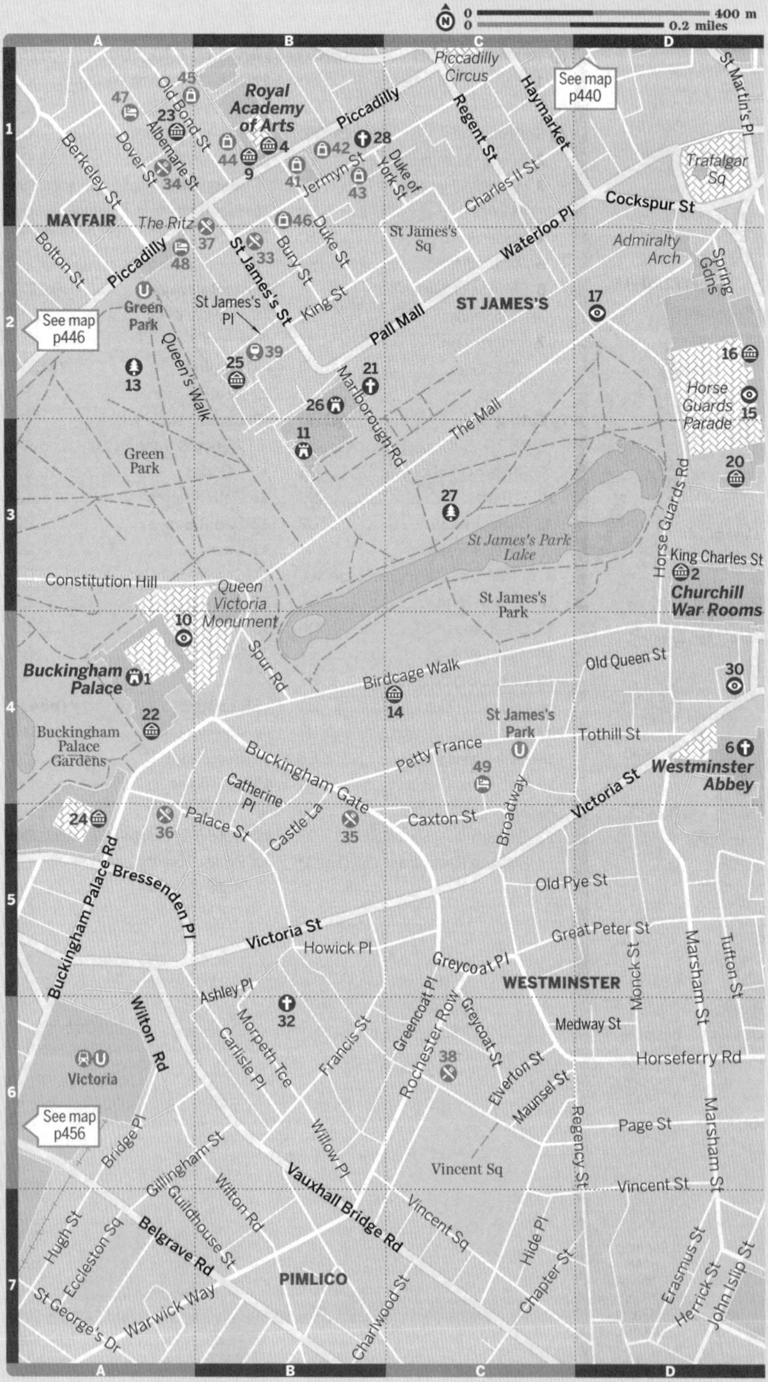

Piccadilly Circus
Royal Academy of Arts
Piccadilly
Regent St
Haymarket
See map p440
St Martin's Pl
Trafalgar Sq
Old Bond St
Albemarle St
Dover St
Berkeley St
Jermyn St
Duke of York St
Charles II St
Cockspur St
MAYFAIR
The Ritz
Bolton St
Piccadilly
St James's St
Bury St
Duke St
St James's Sq
Waterloo Pl
Admiralty Arch
Spring Gdns
Green Park
See map p446
St James's Pl
King St
Pall Mall
ST JAMES'S
Queen's Walk
Marlborough Rd
The Mall
Horse Guards Parade
Green Park
Horse Guards Rd
St James's Park Lake
King Charles St
Churchill War Rooms
Constitution Hill
Queen Victoria Monument
St James's Park
Buckingham Palace
Spur Rd
Birdcage Walk
Old Queen St
Buckingham Palace Gardens
St James's Park
Tothill St
Petty France
Buckingham Gate
Catherine Pl
Palace St
Castle La
Caxton St
Broadway
Victoria St
Westminster Abbey
Buckingham Palace Rd
Bressenden Pl
Old Pye St
Victoria St
Howick Pl
Great Peter St
Greycoat Pl
WESTMINSTER
Monck St
Marsham St
Tufton St
Ashley Pl
Wilton Rd
Morpeth Tce
Carlisle Pl
Francis St
Greencoat Pl
Rochester Row
Greycoat St
Medway St
Horseferry Rd
Victoria
Elverton St
Maunsel St
Regency St
Page St
Marsham St
See map p456
Bridge Pl
Gillingham St
Wilton Rd
Willow Pl
Vauxhall Bridge Rd
Vincent Sq
Vincent Sq
Vincent St
Guildhouse St
Hugh St
Eccleston Sq
Belgrave Rd
PIMLICO
Charlwood St
Hide Pl
Chapter St
Erasmus St
Herrick St
John Islip St
St George's Dr
Warwick Way

0 — 400 m
0 — 0.2 miles

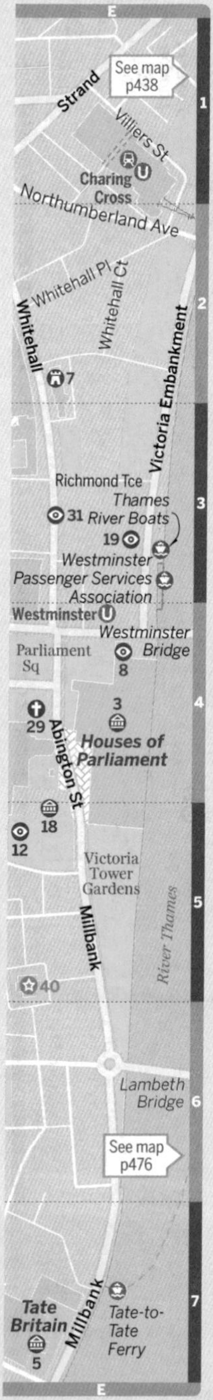

E
Strand
See map p438
Villiers St
Charing Cross
Northumberland Ave
Whitehall Pl
Whitehall Ct
Whitehall
7
Victoria Embankment
Richmond Tce
31 Thames River Boats
19
Westminster Passenger Services Association
Westminster
Westminster Bridge
Parliament Sq
8
3
29
Abingdon St
Houses of Parliament
18
12
Victoria Tower Gardens
Millbank
River Thames
40
Lambeth Bridge
See map p476
Tate Britain
5
Millbank
Tate-to-Tate Ferry
E

Top Experiences (p78)

1 Buckingham Palace A4
2 Churchill War Rooms D3
3 Houses of Parliament E4
4 Royal Academy of Arts B1
5 Tate Britain E7
6 Westminster Abbey D4

Sights (p98)

7 Banqueting House E2
8 Big Ben E4
9 Burlington Arcade B1
10 Changing the Guard A4
11 Clarence House B3
12 College Garden E5
13 Green Park A2
14 Guards Museum C4
15 Horse Guards Parade D2
16 Household Cavalry Museum D2
17 Institute of Contemporary Arts D2
18 Jewel Tower E5
19 New Scotland Yard Building E3
20 No 10 Downing Street D3
21 Queen's Chapel B2
22 Queen's Gallery A4
23 Royal Arcade A1
24 Royal Mews A5
25 Spencer House B2
26 St James's Palace B2
27 St James's Park C3
28 St James's Piccadilly B1
29 St Margaret's Church E4
30 Supreme Court D4
31 The Cenotaph E3
32 Westminster Cathedral B6

Eating (p110)

33 Cafe Murano B2
34 Gymkhana A1
35 Quilon B5
36 The Other Naughty Piglet A5
37 The Wolseley B2
38 Vincent Rooms C6

Drinking & Nightlife (p121)

39 Dukes London B2
Rivoli Bar .... (see 48)

Entertainment (p128)

40 St John's, Smith Square E5

Shopping (p129)

41 Fortnum & Mason B1
42 Hatchards B1
43 Paxton & Whitfield B1
44 Penhaligon's B1
45 Stella McCartney A1
46 Taylor of Old Bond Street B1

Sleeping (p348)

47 Brown's Hotel A1
48 Ritz London A2
49 St Ermin's Hotel C4

CITY OF LONDON

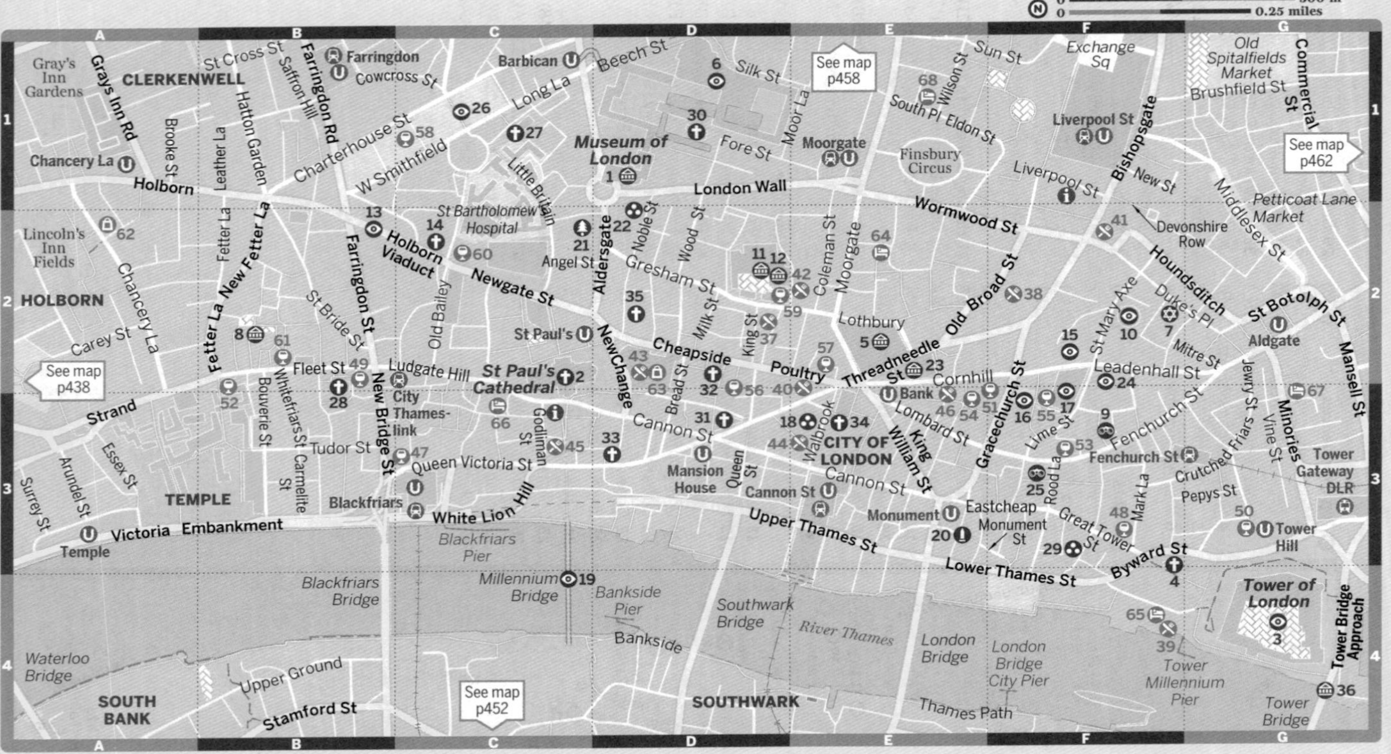

THE CITY

Top Experiences **(p137)**
1 Museum of London D1
2 St Paul's Cathedral C2
3 Tower of London G4

Sights **(p146)**
4 All Hallows by the Tower F3
5 Bank of England Museum E2
6 Barbican D1
Barbican Art Gallery .... (see 6)
Barbican Conservatory .... (see 6)
7 Bevis Marks Synagogue F2
Curve .... (see 6)
8 Dr Johnson's House B2
9 Garden at 120 .... F3
10 Gherkin F2
11 Guildhall D2
12 Guildhall Art Gallery D2
13 Holborn Viaduct B2
14 Holy Sepulchre C2
15 Leadenhall Building F2
16 Leadenhall Market F3
17 Lloyd's Building F3
18 London Mithraeum E3
19 Millennium Bridge C4
20 Monument to the Great Fire of London E3
21 Postman's Park C2
22 Roman Fort & City Wall D2
23 Royal Exchange E2
24 Scalpel F2
25 Sky Garden F3
26 Smithfield Market C1
27 St Bartholomew the Great C1
28 St Bride's B2
29 St Dunstan in the East F3
30 St Giles' Cripplegate D1
31 St Mary Aldermary D3
32 St Mary-le-Bow D2
33 St Nicholas Cole Abbey D3
34 St Stephen Walbrook E3
35 St Vedast-alias-Foster D2
36 Tower Bridge Exhibition G4

Eating **(p151)**
Angler .... (see 68)
Bob Bob Cité .... (see 15)
Café Below .... (see 32)
37 City Càphê D2
38 City Social F2
39 Coppa Club F4
40 Coq d'Argent E3
41 Duck & Waffle F2
Fortnum's Bar & Restaurant .... (see 23)
42 Hawksmoor Guildhall E2
43 Ivy Asia D2
44 Kym's E3
45 Miyama C3
46 Simpsons Tavern E3
Sushi Samba .... (see 41)

Drinking & Nightlife **(p153)**
14 Hills .... (see 9)
Black Parrot .... (see 49)
47 Blackfriar C3
48 BrewDog Tower Hill F3
49 City of London Distillery B2
50 cloudM G3
51 Counting House F3
52 El Vino B2
53 Gobpsy F3
54 Jamaica Wine House E3
55 Lamb Tavern F3
56 Merchant House D2
57 Nickel Bar E2
58 Oriole C1
Searcys at the Gherkin .... (see 10)
59 Trading House D2
60 Viaduct Tavern C2
61 Ye Olde Cheshire Cheese B2

Entertainment **(p156)**
Barbican Centre .... (see 6)

Shopping **(p157)**
62 London Silver Vaults A2
63 One New Change D2

Sleeping **(p351)**
64 Apex London Wall E2
65 Cheval Three Quays F4
CitizenM Tower of London .... (see 50)
66 London St Paul's YHA C3
67 Motel One London-Tower Hill G3
68 South Place E1
The Ned .... (see 57)

Key on p454

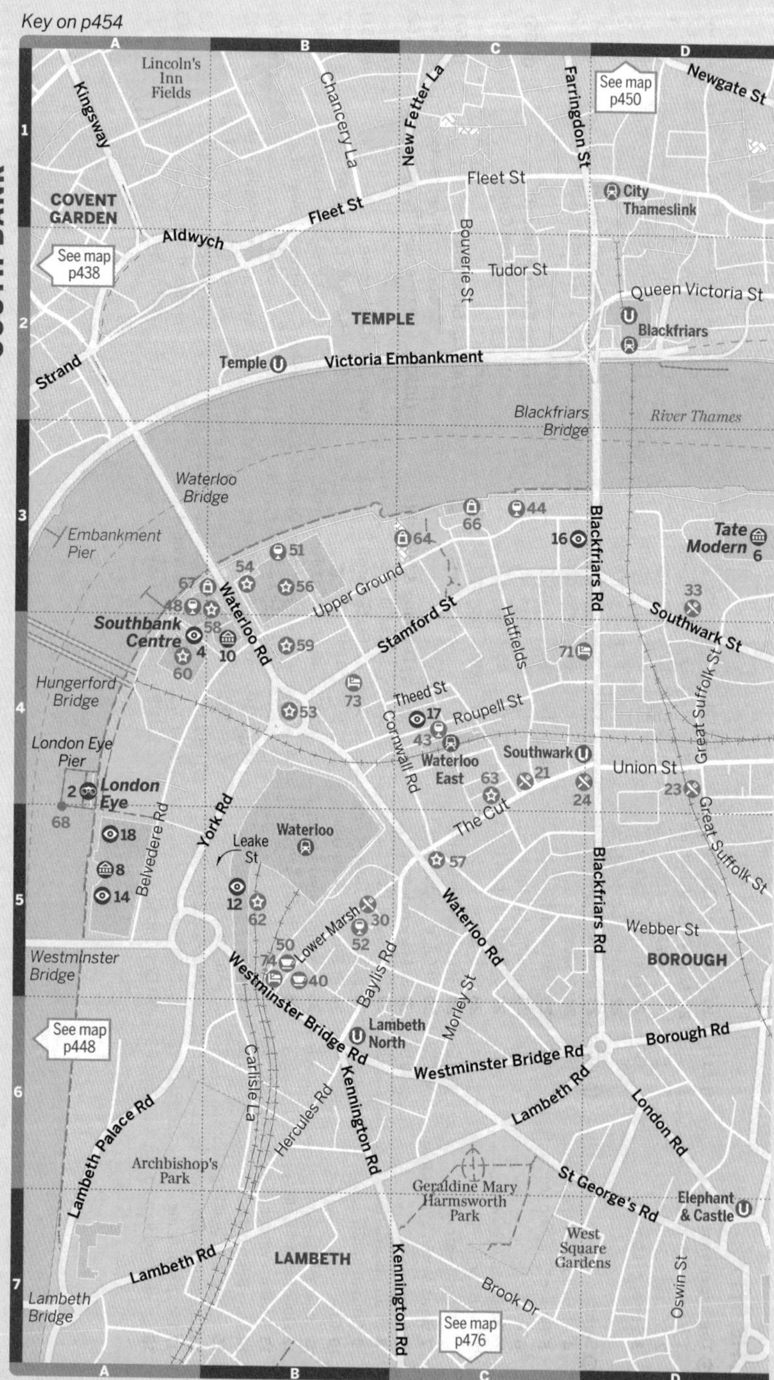

A
B
C
D
1
2
3
4
5
6
7
Lincoln's Inn Fields
Kingsway
Chancery La
New Fetter La
Farringdon St
See map p450
Newgate St
Fleet St
City Thameslink
COVENT GARDEN
Aldwych
See map p438
Bouverie St
Tudor St
Queen Victoria St
TEMPLE
Blackfriars
Strand
Temple
Victoria Embankment
Blackfriars Bridge
River Thames
Waterloo Bridge
Embankment Pier
Tate Modern
Blackfriars Rd
Upper Ground
Stamford St
Hatfields
Southwark St
Southbank Centre
Waterloo Rd
Hungerford Bridge
Great Suffolk St
Theed St
Roupell St
Cornwall Rd
London Eye Pier
Southwark
Waterloo East
Union St
London Eye
The Cut
York Rd
Belvedere Rd
Leake St
Waterloo
Lower Marsh
Webber St
Westminster Bridge
BOROUGH
Baylis Rd
Morley St
See map p448
Westminster Bridge Rd
Lambeth North
Borough Rd
Carlisle La
Kennington Rd
Lambeth Rd
London Rd
Lambeth Palace Rd
Hercules Rd
Archbishop's Park
St George's Rd
Geraldine Mary Harmsworth Park
Elephant & Castle
West Square Gardens
LAMBETH
Lambeth Bridge
Brook Dr
Oswin St
See map p476

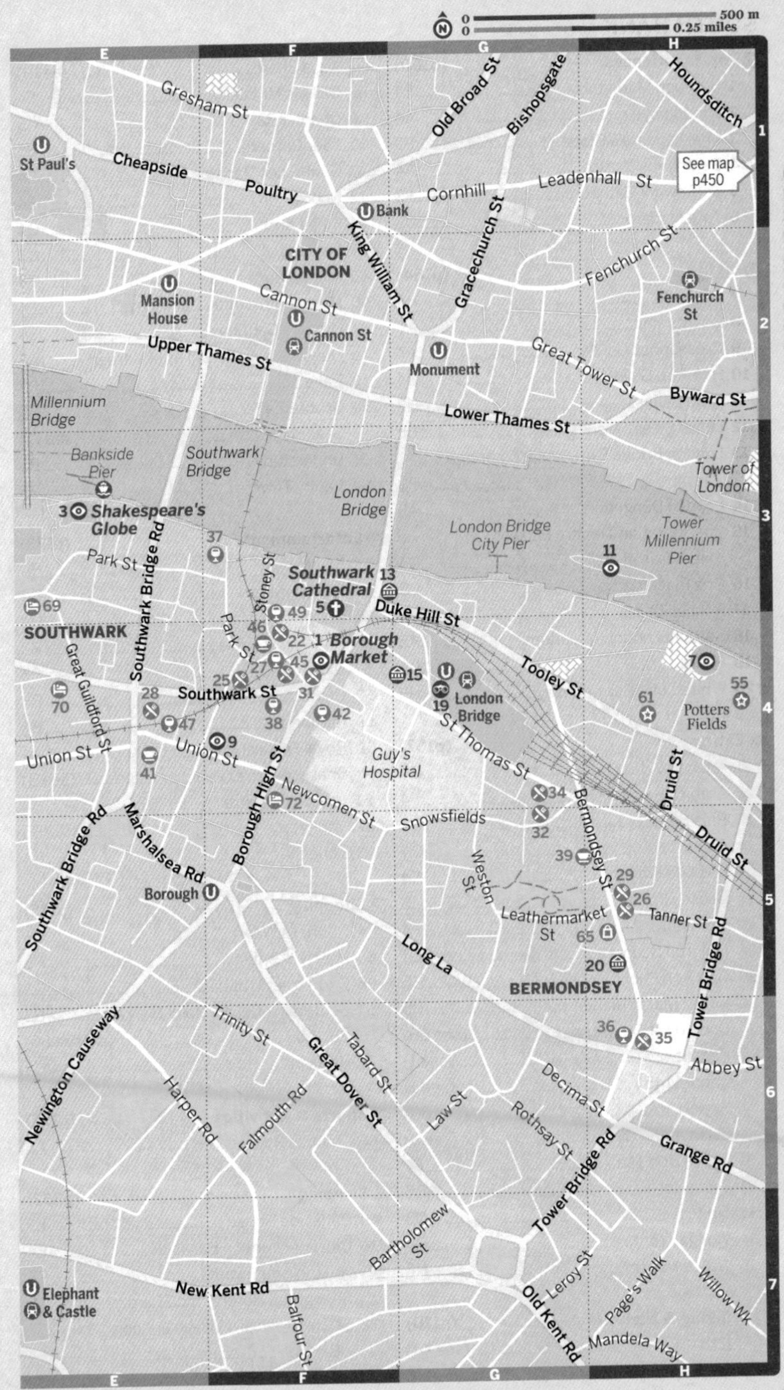

0 500 m
0 0.25 miles
Gresham St
Old Broad St
Bishopsgate
Houndsditch
St Paul's
Cheapside
Poultry
Cornhill
Leadenhall St
See map p450
Bank
King William St
Gracechurch St
CITY OF LONDON
Fenchurch St
Fenchurch St
Mansion House
Cannon St
Cannon St
Monument
Great Tower St
Upper Thames St
Byward St
Lower Thames St
Millennium Bridge
Bankside Pier
Southwark Bridge
London Bridge
Tower of London
3 Shakespeare's Globe
London Bridge City Pier
Tower Millennium Pier
Southwark Bridge Rd
Park St
Stoney St
Southwark Cathedral
Duke Hill St
SOUTHWARK
Great Guildford St
1 Borough Market
Tooley St
Southwark St
London Bridge
Potters Fields
St Thomas St
Union St
Union St
Guy's Hospital
Druid St
Borough High St
Newcomen St
Snowsfields
Bermondsey St
Druid St
Southwark Bridge Rd
Marshalsea Rd
Weston St
Borough
Leathermarket St
Tanner St
Long La
Tower Bridge Rd
BERMONDSEY
Newington Causeway
Trinity St
Tabard St
Great Dover St
Abbey St
Decima St
Harper Rd
Falmouth Rd
Law St
Rothsay St
Grange Rd
Tower Bridge Rd
Bartholomew St
Elephant & Castle
New Kent Rd
Leroy St
Page's Walk
Willow Wk
Old Kent Rd
Balfour St
Mandela Way
SOUTH BANK

SOUTH BANK *Map on p452*

KENSINGTON & HYDE PARK *Map on p456*

Top Experiences (p178)

1 Apsley House F3
2 Hyde Park D2
3 Kensington Palace A3
4 Natural History Museum C4
5 Science Museum C4
6 Victoria & Albert Museum C4

Sights (p187)

7 Albert Memorial B3
8 Brompton Oratory C4
9 Carlyle's House D7
10 Chelsea Old Church C7
11 Chelsea Physic Garden E7
12 Diana, Princess of Wales Memorial Fountain C2
Elfin Oak ..... (see 67)
13 Holocaust Memorial Garden E3
14 Italian Gardens C1
15 Kensington Gardens B2
16 King's Road D6
17 Michelin House D5
18 National Army Museum E6
19 Peter Pan Statue C2
20 Rose Garden E3
21 Royal Albert Hall B3
22 Royal College of Music Museum B4
23 Royal Hospital Chelsea E6
24 Saatchi Gallery E5
25 Serpentine Gallery C3
26 Serpentine Lake D2
27 Serpentine Sackler Gallery C2
28 Speakers' Corner E1
29 The Arch C2
30 Wellington Arch F3
Wildlife Photographer of the Year ..... (see 4)

Eating (p192)

31 A Wong G5
32 Bar Boulud E3
33 Cambio de Tercio B6
34 Comptoir Libanais C5
35 Dinner by Heston Blumenthal E3
36 Five Fields E5
37 Gordon Ramsay E7
38 Kazan G5
39 Kensington Palace Pavilion A2
40 Launceston Place A4
41 Market Hall Victoria G4
42 Medlar C7
43 Pimlico Fresh G5
44 Rabbit D6
V&A Cafe ..... (see 6)
45 Wulf & Lamb E5
46 Zuma D3

Drinking & Nightlife (p197)

47 Anglesea Arms C6
48 Coffee Bar D4
49 Drayton Arms B6
50 K Bar B5
51 Queen's Arms B4
52 Tomtom Coffee House F5

Entertainment (p198)

53 Cadogan Hall E5
54 Pheasantry D6
Royal Albert Hall ..... (see 21)
55 Royal Court Theatre E5

Shopping (p199)

56 Church's D4
Conran Shop ..... (see 17)
57 Harrods D4
58 Harvey Nichols E3
59 Jo Loves F5
60 John Sandoe Books E5
61 Penhaligon's E5
62 Peter Harrington C6
63 Peter Jones E5
64 Pickett E5
65 Pylones G5
66 V&A Shop C4

Sports & Activities (p200)

67 Diana, Princess of Wales Memorial Playground A2
68 Pure Gym C5
Royal Albert Hall Behind the Scenes Tours ..... (see 21)
Royal Albert Hall Tour ..... (see 21)
69 Serpentine Boathouse D2
70 Serpentine Lido C3
Serpentine SolarShuttle Boat ..... (see 69)
71 Will to Win (Hyde Park Tennis & Sports Centre) C3
72 Winter Wonderland E2

Sleeping (p352)

73 Ampersand Hotel C5
74 Artist Residence G5
75 Aster House C5
76 Astor Hyde Park B3
77 Blakes B6
78 Cherry Court Hotel G5
79 Gore B4
80 Lime Tree Hotel F5
81 Luna Simone Hotel H5
82 Meininger B5
83 Number Sixteen C5
84 Windermere Hotel G6

Key on p455

KENSINGTON & HYDE PARK

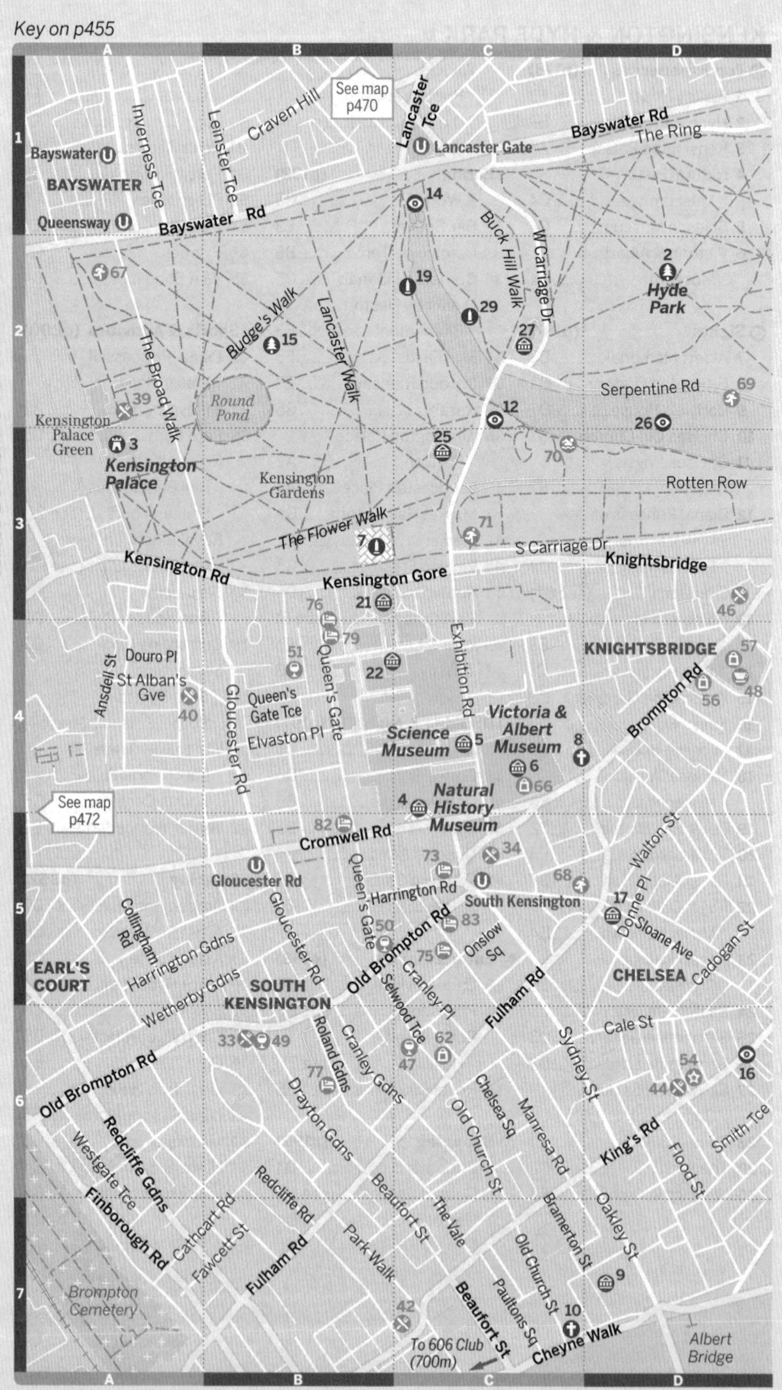

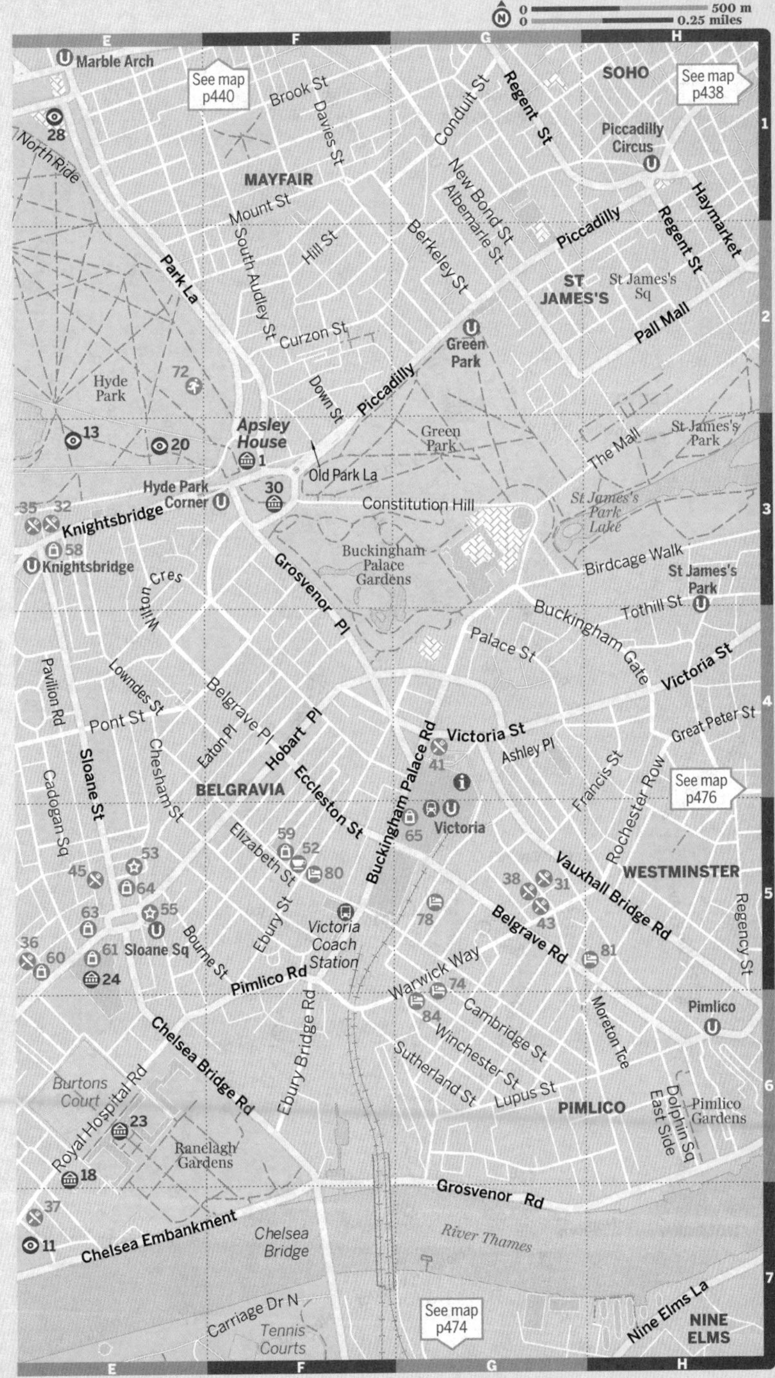

0 500 m
0 0.25 miles
Marble Arch
See map p440
See map p438
See map p476
See map p474
SOHO
MAYFAIR
ST JAMES'S
BELGRAVIA
WESTMINSTER
PIMLICO
NINE ELMS
Piccadilly Circus
Green Park
Hyde Park
Apsley House
Hyde Park Corner
Knightsbridge
St James's Park
Victoria
Victoria Coach Station
Sloane Sq
Pimlico
Buckingham Palace Gardens
St James's Park Lake
Burtons Court
Ranelagh Gardens
Chelsea Bridge
River Thames
Tennis Courts
Pimlico Gardens
St James's Sq
Brook St
Davies St
Conduit St
Regent St
New Bond St
Albemarle St
Haymarket
Piccadilly
Mount St
South Audley St
Hill St
Berkeley St
Park La
Curzon St
Pall Mall
Down St
Old Park La
The Mall
Constitution Hill
Birdcage Walk
Tothill St
Buckingham Gate
Palace St
Grosvenor Pl
Wilton Cres
Lowndes St
Belgrave Pl
Pont St
Pavilion Rd
Sloane St
Cadogan Sq
Chesham St
Eaton Pl
Hobart Pl
Eccleston St
Buckingham Palace Rd
Victoria St
Great Peter St
Ashley Pl
Francis St
Rochester Row
Vauxhall Bridge Rd
Regency St
Elizabeth St
Ebury St
Bourne St
Belgrave Rd
Warwick Way
Pimlico Rd
Ebury Bridge Rd
Cambridge St
Winchester St
Sutherland St
Lupus St
Moreton Tce
Dolphin Sq
East Side
Chelsea Bridge Rd
Royal Hospital Rd
Grosvenor Rd
Chelsea Embankment
Carriage Dr N
Nine Elms La
North Ride

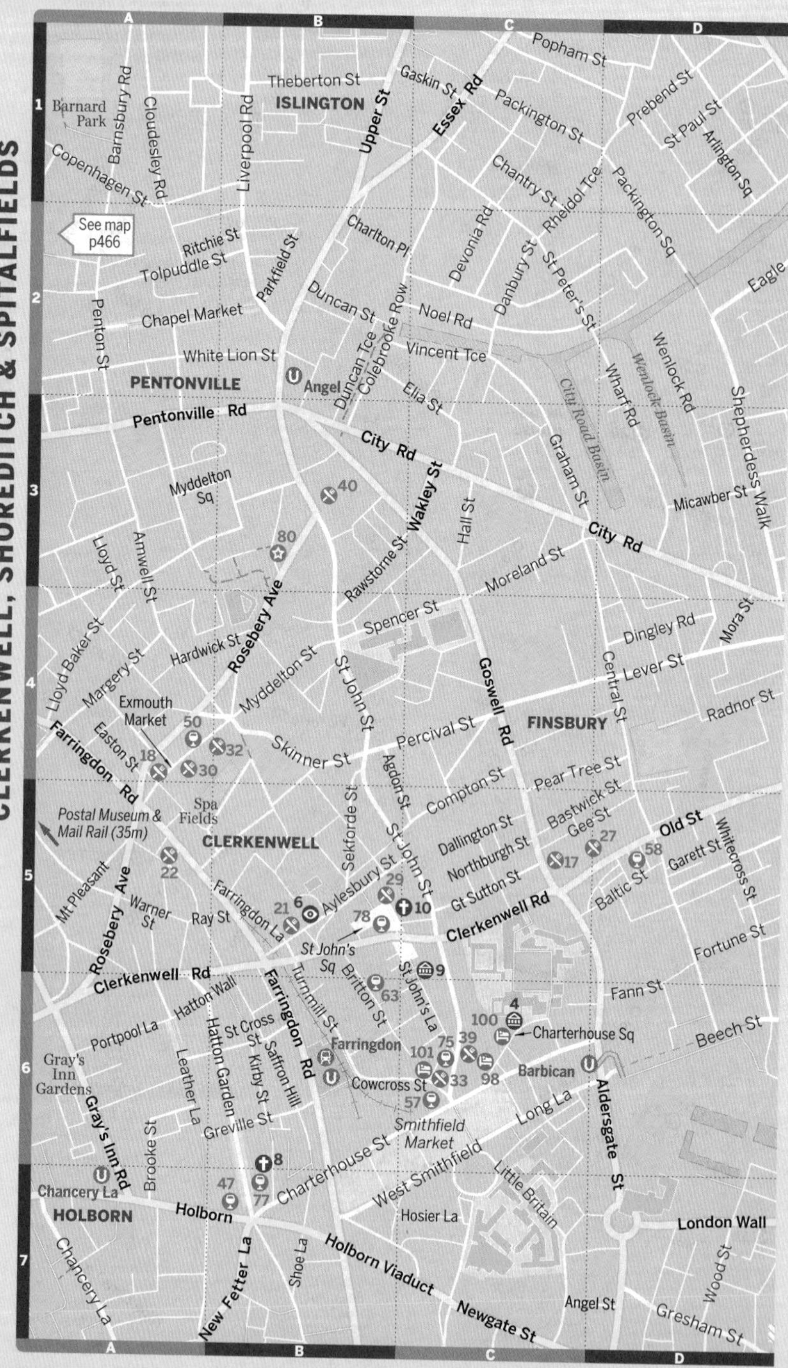
ISLINGTON
PENTONVILLE
CLERKENWELL
FINSBURY
HOLBORN
See map p466
Angel
Farringdon
Barbican
Chancery La
City Rd
Pentonville Rd
Goswell Rd
Clerkenwell Rd
Farringdon Rd
Rosebery Ave
St John St
Old St
Holborn
Holborn Viaduct
Newgate St
London Wall
Aldersgate St
Charterhouse Sq
Smithfield Market
Postal Museum & Mail Rail (35m)
City Road Basin
Wenlock Basin

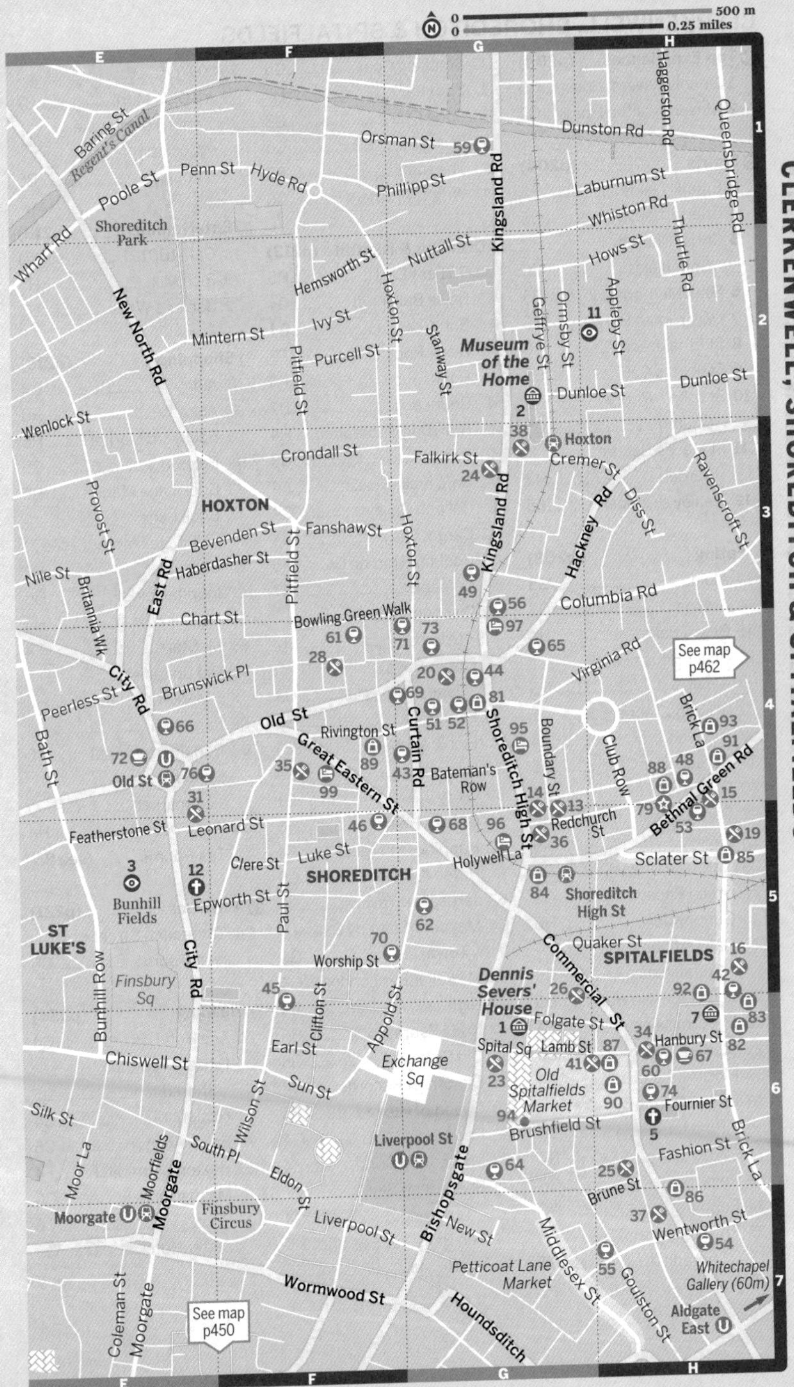
CLERKENWELL, SHOREDITCH & SPITALFIELDS
500 m
0.25 miles
HOXTON
SHOREDITCH
SPITALFIELDS
ST LUKE'S
Museum of the Home
Dennis Severs' House
Old Spitalfields Market
Shoreditch Park
Bunhill Fields
Finsbury Sq
Finsbury Circus
Exchange Sq
Petticoat Lane Market
Whitechapel Gallery (60m)
See map p462
See map p450
Hoxton
Old St
Shoreditch High St
Liverpool St
Moorgate
Aldgate East

CLERKENWELL, SHOREDITCH & SPITALFIELDS

EAST LONDON *Map on p462*

Top Experiences (p226)
1 Whitechapel Gallery B5

Sights (p224)
2 ArcelorMittal Orbit....... F2
3 Blind Beggar C5
4 Cable Street Mural C6
5 Columbia Road Flower Market B4
6 Dalston Eastern Curve Garden....................... H2
7 East London Mosque ..B5
8 Emirates Air Line H6
9 Hackney City Farm B3
10 Hackney Museum C2
11 House Mill F4
12 London Fields B2
13 London Stadium F2
14 Mile End Park D4
15 O2 Arena G7
16 Queen Elizabeth Olympic Park E2
17 Ragged School Museum D5
18 Ridley Road Market H2
19 St Anne's Limehouse ..E6
20 St Augustine's Tower .. C1
21 St George-in-the-East B6
22 St Katharine Docks..... B6
23 Sutton House C1
24 Tower Bridge A7
25 Tower Hamlets Cemetery Park E4
26 Tower House B5
27 Trinity Buoy Wharf H6
28 Trinity Green Almshouses...............C5
29 V&A Museum of Childhood C4
30 Victoria Park D3
31 Viktor Wynd Museum of Curiosities, Fine Art & Natural History..........B3
32 Whitechapel Road B5
33 William Booth Statue ..C5

Eating (p230)
34 Barge East E2
35 Berber & Q A3
36 Bistrotheque C3
37 Brawn B4
38 Café Spice Namasté B6
39 Chick 'n' Sours G3
40 Climpson & Sons B3
41 Corner Room.................. C3
42 E Pellicci B4
43 Empress.......................... C3
44 Formans..........................E2
45 Gallery Cafe C4
46 Green Papaya................. C2
47 Lardo B2
48 L'Atelier..........................G1
49 Laxeiro B4
50 Little Georgia.................. B3
51 Mangal Ocakbasi H1
52 Mare Street Market........ B3
53 Randy's Wing Bar E1
54 Silo..................................E2
55 Smith's B7
56 Tayyabs.......................... B5
57 Temple of Seitan............ C2
58 Towpath A3

Drinking & Nightlife (p236)
59 Bethnal Green Working Men's Club B4
60 Captain Kidd................... C7
61 Carpenter's Arms B4
62 Cat & Mutton.................. B3
Crate Brewery .... (see 54)
Dalston Roof Park .... (see 86)
63 Dalston Superstore G1
64 Dove B3
65 Draughts G2
66 Farr's School of Dancing........................ H2
67 Grapes............................ D6
68 High Water.......................G1
69 Howling Hops E2
Last Tuesday Society .... (see 31)
70 Martello Hall B2
71 Mayflower C7
Netil360 ....(see 52)
72 No 90...............................E2
73 Old Ship.......................... D5
74 People's Park Tavern D2
75 Prospect of Whitby C6
76 Ridley Road Market Bar H2
77 Royal Inn on the Park ... D3
78 Royal Oak....................... B4
79 Ruby's.............................G1
80 Sager + Wilde A3
81 Satan's Whiskers C4
82 Shacklewell Arms H1
83 Town of Ramsgate........ B7
84 White Swan.................... D6

Entertainment (p240)
85 Arcola Theatre G2
86 Cafe Oto H2
87 Copper Box Arena E2
88 Dalston Jazz Bar G2
89 English National Ballet.......................... G5
90 Genesis.......................... C5
91 Hackney Empire............ C2
O2 Arena .... (see 15)
92 Rio Cinema G1
93 Vortex Jazz Club G2
94 Wilton's B6

Shopping (p241)
95 Artwords B3
96 Beyond Retro B4
97 Beyond Retro G1
98 Broadway Market B3
99 Burberry Outlet Store........................... C2
100 Traid G2

Sports & Activities (p242)
Alfred Le Roy .... (see 54)
101 Lee & Stort Boats F2
102 Lee Valley VeloPark....... F1
103 London Fields Lido B2
104 Secret Adventures........ B2
Up at the O2.......... (see 15)

Sleeping (p355)
105 40 Winks C5
106 Avo H2
107 East London Hotel C4
108 Park Villa D4
109 Qbic............................... B5
110 Wombat's London B6

Key on p461

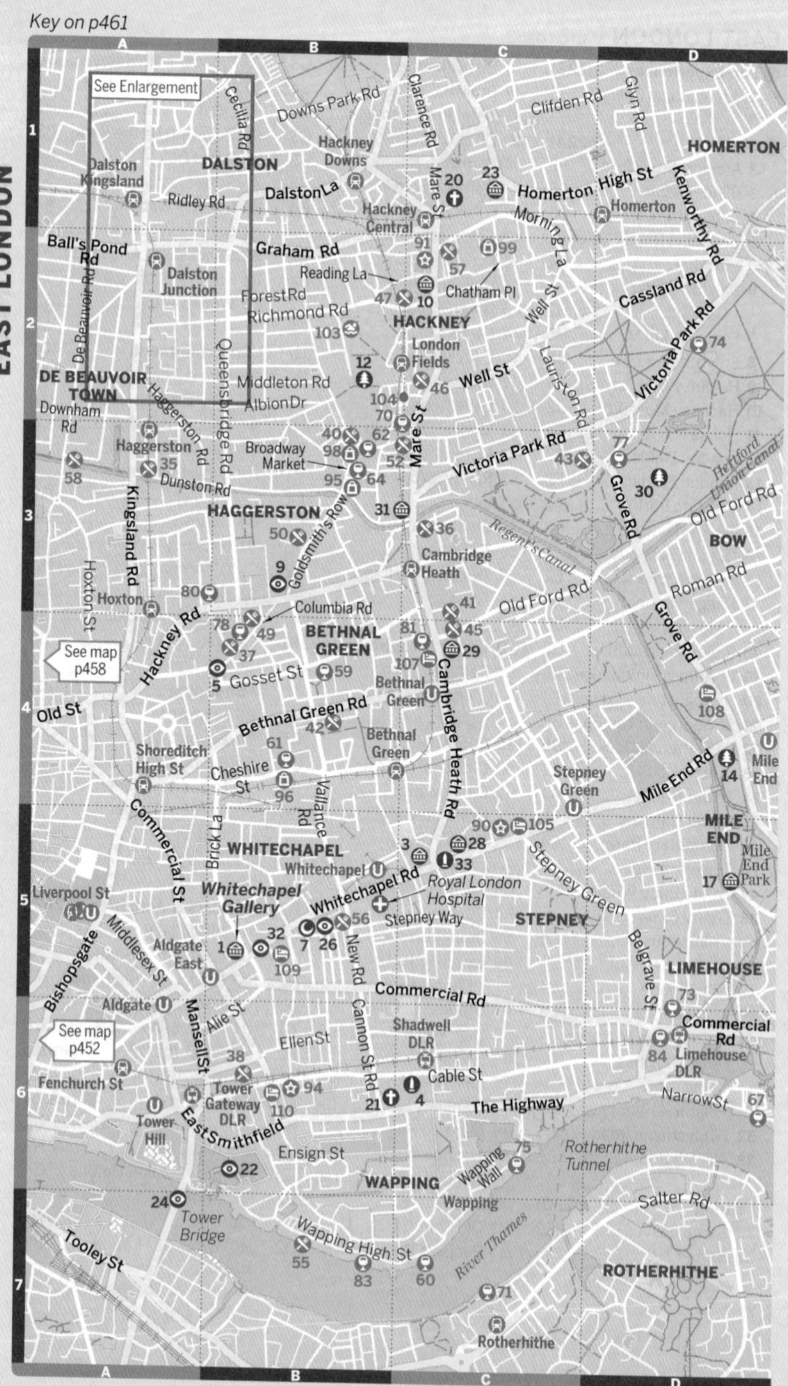
See Enlargement
DALSTON
Dalston Kingsland
Ridley Rd
Dalston La
Downs Park Rd
Hackney Downs
Cecilia Rd
Clarence Rd
Mare St
Clifden Rd
Glyn Rd
HOMERTON
Homerton High St
Homerton
Kenworthy Rd
Hackney Central
Morning La
Ball's Pond Rd
Graham Rd
Reading La
Chatham Pl
Dalston Junction
Forest Rd
Richmond Rd
HACKNEY
London Fields
Cassland Rd
Well St
Lauriston Rd
Victoria Park Rd
De Beauvoir Rd
Queensbridge Rd
Middleton Rd
Albion Dr
DE BEAUVOIR TOWN
Downham Rd
Haggerston Rd
Haggerston
Broadway Market
Dunston Rd
Kingsland Rd
HAGGERSTON
Goldsmith's Row
Grove Rd
Hertford Union Canal
Old Ford Rd
BOW
Regent's Canal
Cambridge Heath
Hoxton St
Hoxton
Columbia Rd
Roman Rd
Hackney Rd
BETHNAL GREEN
See map p458
Gosset St
Bethnal Green
Cambridge Heath Rd
Old St
Bethnal Green Rd
Shoreditch High St
Cheshire St
Vallance Rd
Stepney Green
Mile End Rd
Mile End
MILE END
Commercial St
Brick La
WHITECHAPEL
Whitechapel
Whitechapel Rd
Royal London Hospital
Stepney Way
STEPNEY
Mile End Park
Liverpool St
Whitechapel Gallery
Middlesex St
Bishopsgate
Aldgate East
New Rd
Belgrave St
LIMEHOUSE
Commercial Rd
Aldgate
Mansell St
Alie St
Ellen St
Cannon St Rd
Shadwell DLR
See map p452
Limehouse DLR
Fenchurch St
Tower Gateway DLR
Cable St
Narrow St
Tower Hill
East Smithfield
The Highway
Ensign St
Wapping Wall
Rotherhithe Tunnel
WAPPING
Wapping
Salter Rd
Tower Bridge
Tooley St
Wapping High St
River Thames
ROTHERHITHE
Rotherhithe

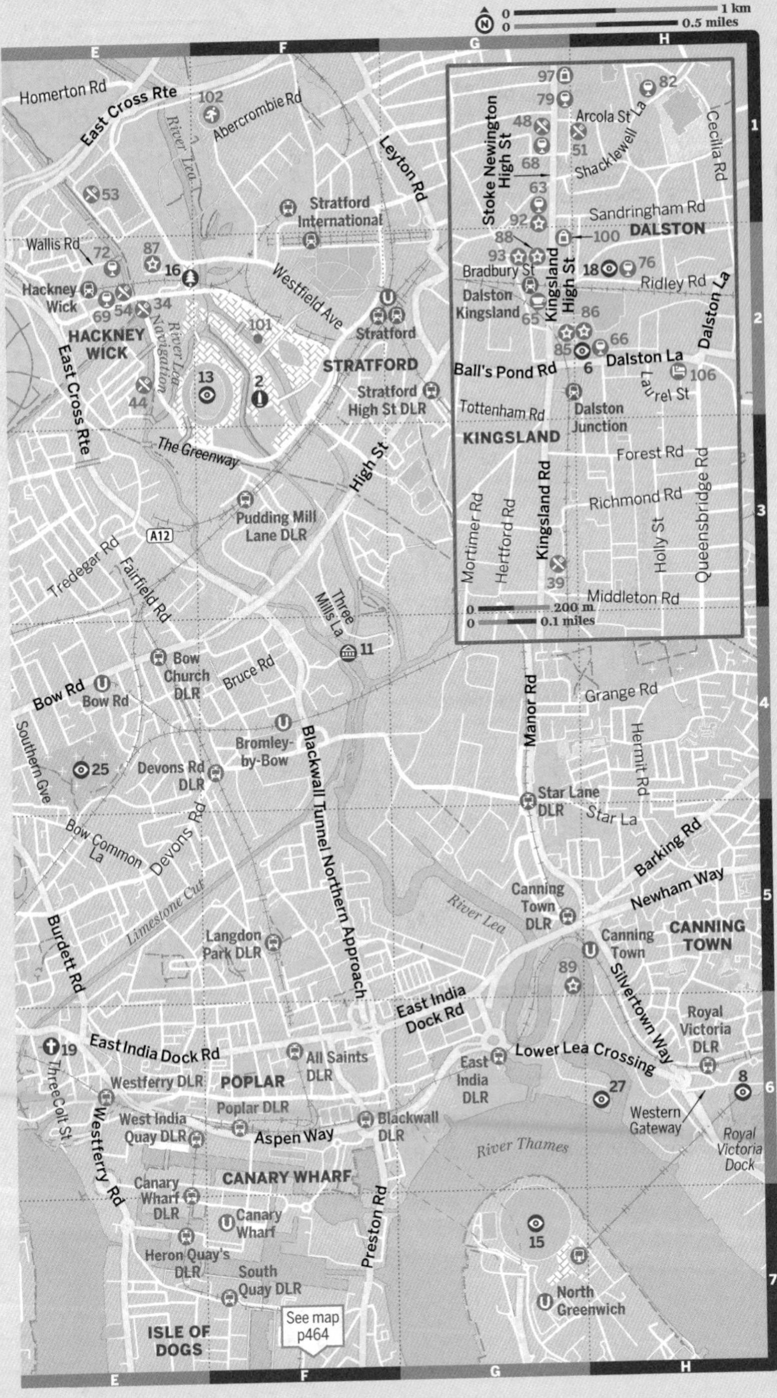
EAST LONDON
0 1 km
0 0.5 miles
Homerton Rd
East Cross Rte
Abercrombie Rd
River Lea
Leyton Rd
Stratford International
Wallis Rd
Hackney Wick
HACKNEY WICK
River Lea Navigation
Westfield Ave
Stratford
STRATFORD
Stratford High St DLR
East Cross Rte
The Greenway
High St
Pudding Mill Lane DLR
A12
Tredegar Rd
Fairfield Rd
Three Mills La
Bow Church DLR
Bruce Rd
Bow Rd
Bow Rd
Southern Gve
Bromley-by-Bow
Blackwall Tunnel Northern Approach
Devons Rd DLR
Devons Rd
Bow Common La
Limestone Cut
Burdett Rd
Langdon Park DLR
East India Dock Rd
East India Dock Rd
All Saints DLR
Westferry DLR
POPLAR
Three Colt St
Westferry Rd
Poplar DLR
West India Quay DLR
Aspen Way
Blackwall DLR
CANARY WHARF
Canary Wharf DLR
Canary Wharf
Preston Rd
Heron Quay's DLR
South Quay DLR
See map p464
ISLE OF DOGS
Stoke Newington High St
Arcola St
Shacklewell La
Cecilia Rd
Sandringham Rd
DALSTON
Bradbury St
Dalston Kingsland
Kingsland High St
Ridley Rd
Dalston La
Ball's Pond Rd
Dalston La
Laurel St
Tottenham Rd
Dalston Junction
KINGSLAND
Forest Rd
Richmond Rd
Mortimer Rd
Hertford Rd
Kingsland Rd
Holly St
Queensbridge Rd
Middleton Rd
0 200 m
0 0.1 miles
Manor Rd
Grange Rd
Hermit Rd
Star Lane DLR
Star La
Barking Rd
Newham Way
Canning Town DLR
River Lea
Canning Town
CANNING TOWN
Silvertown Way
Royal Victoria DLR
Lower Lea Crossing
East India DLR
Western Gateway
Royal Victoria Dock
River Thames
North Greenwich
E
F
G
H
1
2
3
4
5
6
7
102
53
72
87
16
69
54
34
101
13
2
44
11
25
19
97
79
48
51
68
63
92
88
93
100
18
76
82
65
86
85
66
6
106
39
89
27
8
15

DOCKLANDS

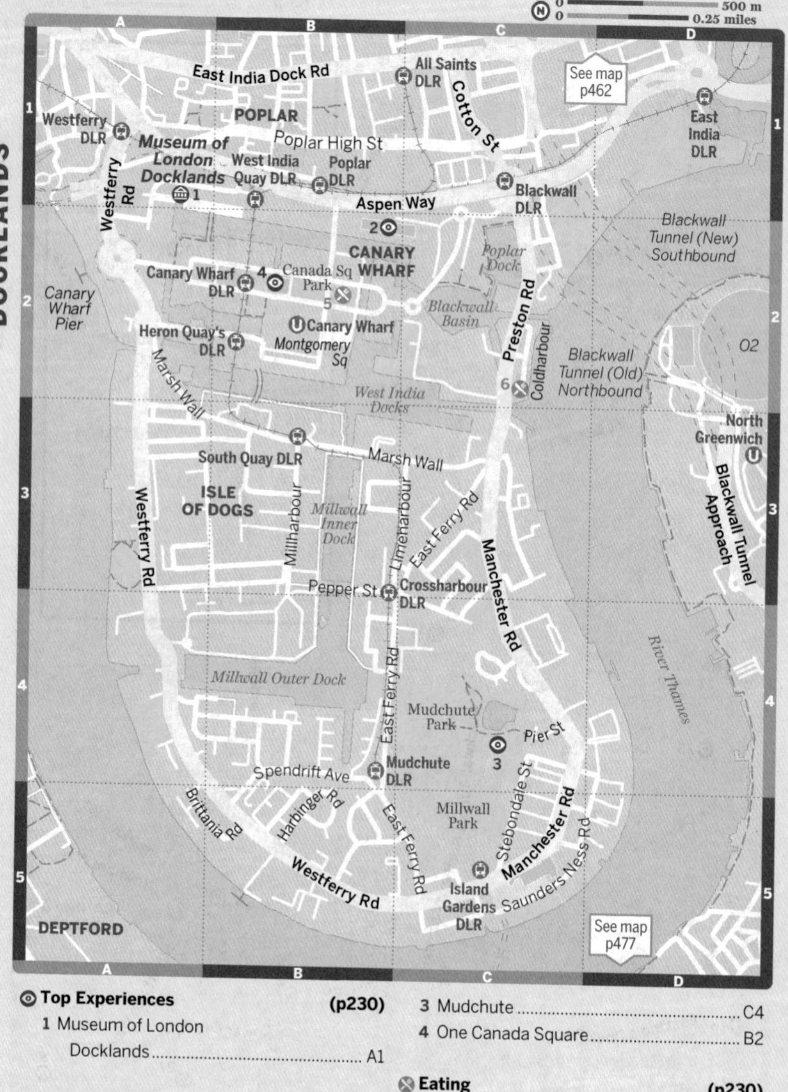

Top Experiences (p230)

1 Museum of London Docklands A1
3 Mudchute C4
4 One Canada Square B2

Sights (p224)

2 Billingsgate Fish Market B2

Eating (p230)

5 Plateau B2
6 The Gun C2

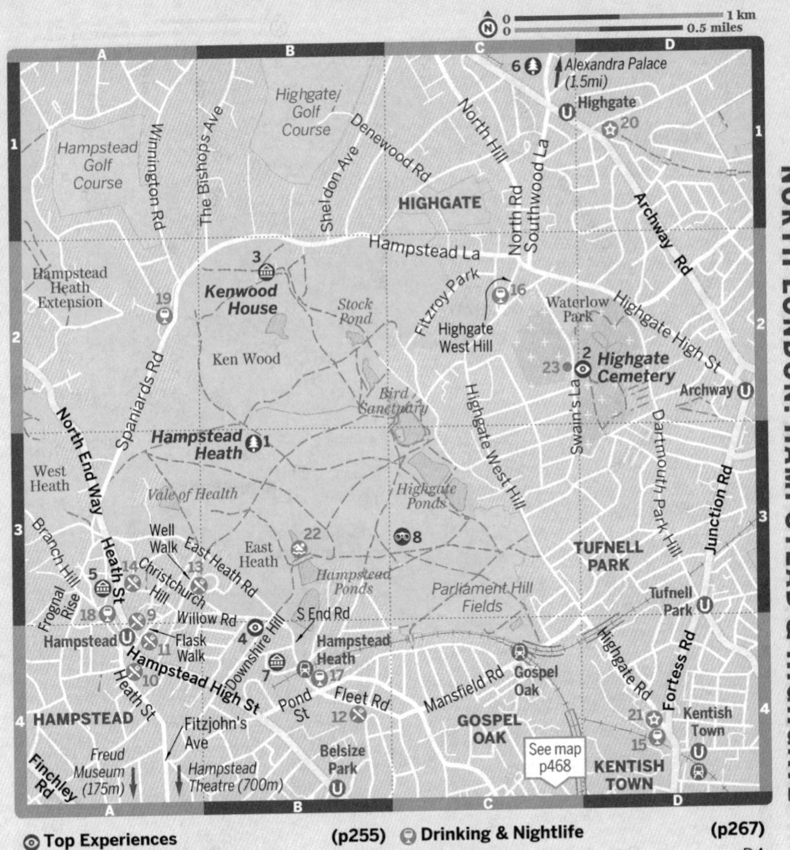

Top Experiences (p255)

1 Hampstead Heath ... B3
2 Highgate Cemetery ... D2
3 Kenwood House ... B2

Sights (p254)

4 2 Willow Road ... B3
5 Fenton House ... A3
6 Highgate Wood ... C1
7 Keats House ... B4
8 Parliament Hill ... C3

Eating (p262)

9 Gaucho ... A3
10 Ginger & White ... A4
11 La Cage Imaginaire ... A4
12 Stag ... B4
13 Wells Tavern ... A3
14 Woodlands ... A3

Drinking & Nightlife (p267)

15 Bull & Gate ... D4
16 Flask ... C2
17 Garden Gate ... B4
18 Holly Bush ... A3
19 Spaniard's Inn ... A2

Entertainment (p268)

20 Boogaloo ... D1
21 O2 Forum ... D4

Shopping (p270)

Exclusivo ... (see 11)

Sports & Activities (p271)

22 Hampstead Heath Ponds ... B3
23 Highgate West Cemetery Tour ... C2

500 m
0.25 miles
TUFNELL PARK
LOWER HOLLOWAY
BARNSBURY
ISLINGTON
KING'S CROSS
PENTONVILLE
SOMERS TOWN
CLERKENWELL
Holloway Rd
Caledonian Rd
Highbury & Islington
Caledonian Rd & Barnsbury
Angel
King's Cross
King's Cross St Pancras
St Pancras International (Eurostar)
British Library
King's Cross Visitor Centre
Caledonian Park
Barnard Park
Chapel Market
St Andrew's Gardens
Spa Fields
Regent's Canal
Parkhurst Rd
Camden Rd
Hornsey Rd
Holloway Rd
Drayton Park
Brecknock Rd
York Way
Camden Park Rd
Mackenzie Rd
Sheringham Rd
Liverpool Rd
Madras Pl
Furlong Rd
Roman Way
Bride St
Market Rd
Brewery Rd
Blundell St
Laycock St
Offord Rd
Belitha Villas
Barnsbury Park
Bewdley St
Brooksby St
Huntingdon St
Agar Gve
St Paul's Cres
College Cross
Carnoustie Dr
Lofting Rd
Barnsbury St
Ripplevale Gve
Hemingford Rd
Bingfield St
Matilda St
Camley St
Twyford St
Copenhagen St
Gibson Sq
Barnsbury Rd
Cloudesley Rd
Pancras Rd
King's Blvd
Wynford Rd
Wharfdale Rd
Upper St
Penton St
White Lion St
Killick St
Calshot St
Rodney St
Pentonville Rd
St John St
Ossulston St
Chalton St
King's Cross Rd
Anwell St
St Chad's St
Eversholt St
Churchway
Euston Rd
Bidborough St
Argyle St
Judd St
Cromer St
Harrison St
Regent Sq
Gray's Inn Rd
Cubitt St
Wharton St
Lloyd Baker St
Margery St
Rosebery Ave
Myddelton St
Skinner St
See map p468
See map p444

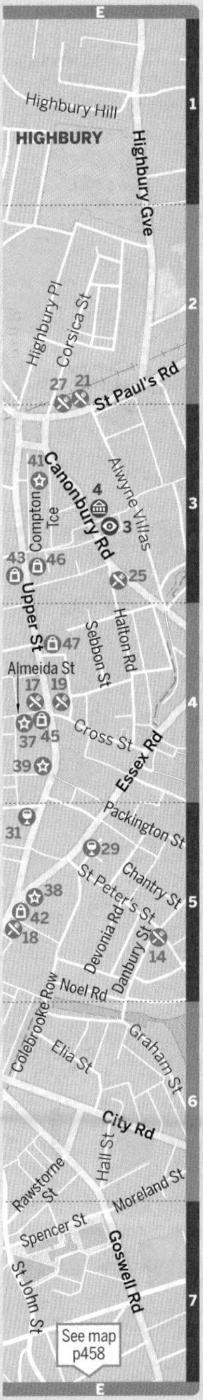
E
1
Highbury Hill
HIGHBURY
Highbury Gve
2
Highbury Pl
Corsica St
27
21
St Paul's Rd
3
41
Canonbury Rd
Compton Tce
Alwyne Villas
4
3
43
46
25
Upper St
47
Sebbon St
Halton Rd
4
Almeida St
17
19
37
45
Cross St
Essex Rd
39
31
Packington St
29
Chantry St
St Peter's St
5
38
42
18
Devonia Rd
Danbury St
14
Noel Rd
Colebrooke Row
Elia St
Graham St
6
City Rd
Hall St
Rawstorne St
Moreland St
Spencer St
Goswell Rd
St John St
7
See map p458
E

Top Experiences (p246)

1 British Library A6

Sights (p257)

2 Arsenal Emirates Stadium .. D1
3 Canonbury Square E3
4 Estorick Collection of Modern Italian Art........E3
5 Gasholder Park A5
6 Granary Square........B5
7 House of Illustration B5
8 King's Cross Station........B6
9 London Canal Museum........B5
10 St Pancras Station & Hotel B6

Eating (p258)

11 Addis........B6
12 Bar Pepito B6
Caravan........(see 6)
13 Chilango D5
14 Duke of Cambridge E5
15 Ekachai........B5
16 Iberia........C4
Kipferl........(see 42)
17 Le Mercury........E4
18 Oldroyd E5
19 Ottolenghi E4
20 Piebury Corner........B6
21 Prawn on the Lawn........E2
22 Real Food Market........B6
23 Ruby Violet B5
24 Sambal Shiok D2
25 Smokehouse E3
26 Terrace Cafe & Restaurant........A6
27 Trullo E2
28 Yipin China........D5

Drinking & Nightlife (p267)

29 69 Colebrooke Row E5
30 Big Chill B6
Booking Office Bar & Restaurant........(see 53)
31 Bull........E5
32 Camino........B6
33 Castle D6
34 Craft Beer Co D6
35 Egg LDN B4
36 Origin Coffee Roasters B7

Entertainment (p268)

37 Almeida........E4
38 Angel Comedy E5
39 King's Head Theatre E4
40 Scala........B6
41 Union Chapel........E3

Shopping (p270)

Annie's Vintage Costume & Textiles........(see 42)
42 Camden Passage Market........E5
43 Gill Wing Gifts........E3
44 Harry Potter Shop at Platform 9¾ B6
Housmans ....(see 20)
45 Mary's Living & Giving Shop E4
46 Sampler E3
47 Twentytwentyone........E4

Sleeping (p356)

48 Clink78........C7
49 Great Northern Hotel........B6
50 Gyle B7
51 London St Pancras YHA B7
52 Megaro........B6
53 St Pancras Renaissance Hotel London........B6

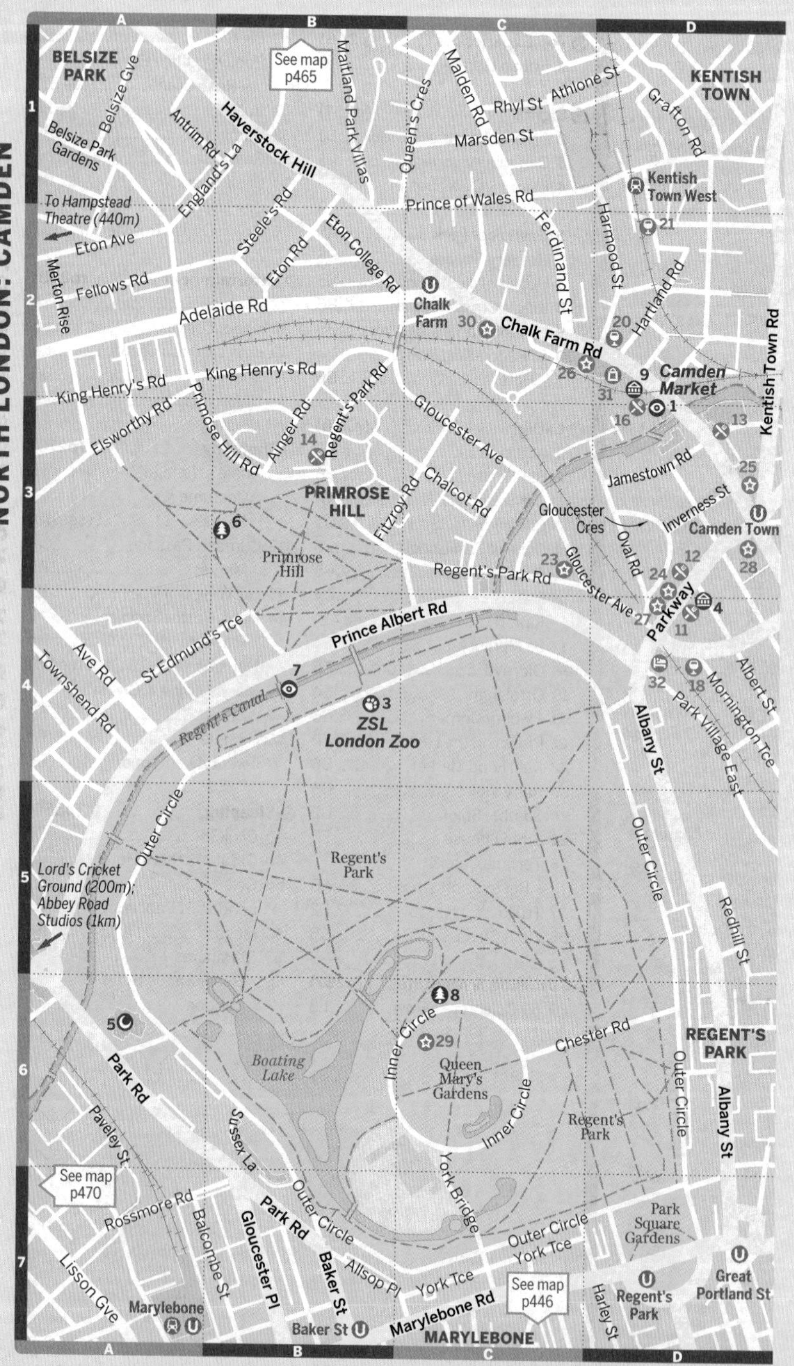
A
B
C
D
BELSIZE PARK
See map p465
KENTISH TOWN
Belsize Gve
Belsize Park Gardens
Antrim Rd
Haverstock Hill
Maitland Park Villas
Queen's Cres
Malden Rd
Rhyl St
Athlone St
Grafton Rd
Marsden St
England's La
To Hampstead Theatre (440m)
Steele's Rd
Prince of Wales Rd
Kentish Town West
Eton Ave
Eton College Rd
Ferdinand St
Harmood St
21
Merton Rise
Fellows Rd
Eton Rd
Chalk Farm
Hartland Rd
Adelaide Rd
30
Chalk Farm Rd
20
Kentish Town Rd
King Henry's Rd
Regent's Park Rd
26
9
Camden Market
King Henry's Rd
Primrose Hill Rd
31
Elsworthy Rd
Ainger Rd
Gloucester Ave
16
1
13
14
Jamestown Rd
25
PRIMROSE HILL
Chalcot Rd
Fitzroy Rd
Gloucester Cres
Inverness St
6
Oval Rd
Camden Town
Primrose Hill
23
Gloucester Ave
12
28
Regent's Park Rd
24
4
27
Parkway
11
Prince Albert Rd
St Edmund's Tce
Ave Rd
Townshend Rd
7
3
ZSL London Zoo
32
18
Mornington Tce
Albert St
Park Village East
Albany St
Regent's Canal
Outer Circle
Outer Circle
Regent's Park
Lord's Cricket Ground (200m); Abbey Road Studios (1km)
Redhill St
8
5
Inner Circle
29
Chester Rd
REGENT'S PARK
Boating Lake
Queen Mary's Gardens
Inner Circle
Regent's Park
Outer Circle
Albany St
Park Rd
Paveley St
Sussex La
York Bridge
See map p470
Rossmore Rd
Balcombe St
Gloucester Pl
Park Rd
Outer Circle
Outer Circle
York Tce
Park Square Gardens
Baker St
Allsop Pl
York Tce
Harley St
Great Portland St
Lisson Gve
See map p446
Regent's Park
Marylebone
Marylebone Rd
Baker St
MARYLEBONE
1
2
3
4
5
6
7

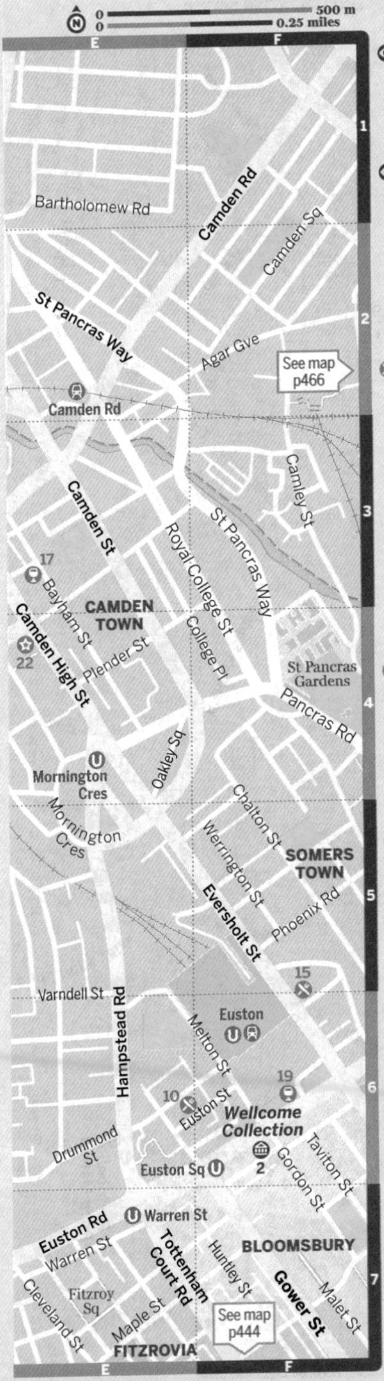

See map p466

See map p444

Top Experiences (p246)
1 Camden Market ... D3
2 Wellcome Collection ... F6
3 ZSL London Zoo ... B4

Sights (p250)
4 Jewish Museum London ... D4
5 London Central Mosque ... A6
6 Primrose Hill ... B3
7 Regent's Canal ... B4
8 Regent's Park ... C6
9 Vagina Museum ... D2

Eating (p258)
Chin Chin Labs ... (see 1)
10 Diwana Bhel Poori House ... E6
11 Hook Camden Town ... D4
12 Namaaste Kitchen ... D3
13 Poppies ... D3
14 Queen's ... B3
15 Roti King ... F5
16 Shaka Zulu ... D3
West Yard Market ... (see 1)
York & Albany ... (see 32)

Drinking & Nightlife (p265)
17 BrewDog Camden ... E3
18 Edinboro Castle ... D4
19 Euston Tap ... F6
20 Lock Tavern ... D2
21 Tapping the Admiral ... D2

Entertainment (p268)
22 Blues Kitchen ... E4
23 Cecil Sharp House ... C3
24 Dublin Castle ... D3
25 Electric Ballroom ... D3
26 FEST Camden ... C2
27 Green Note ... D4
28 Jazz Cafe ... D3
29 Regent's Park Open Air Theatre ... C6
30 Roundhouse ... C2

Shopping (p270)
Camden Lock Market ... (see 1)
31 Stables Market ... D2

Sleeping (p357)
32 York & Albany ... D4

NOTTING HILL & WEST LONDON

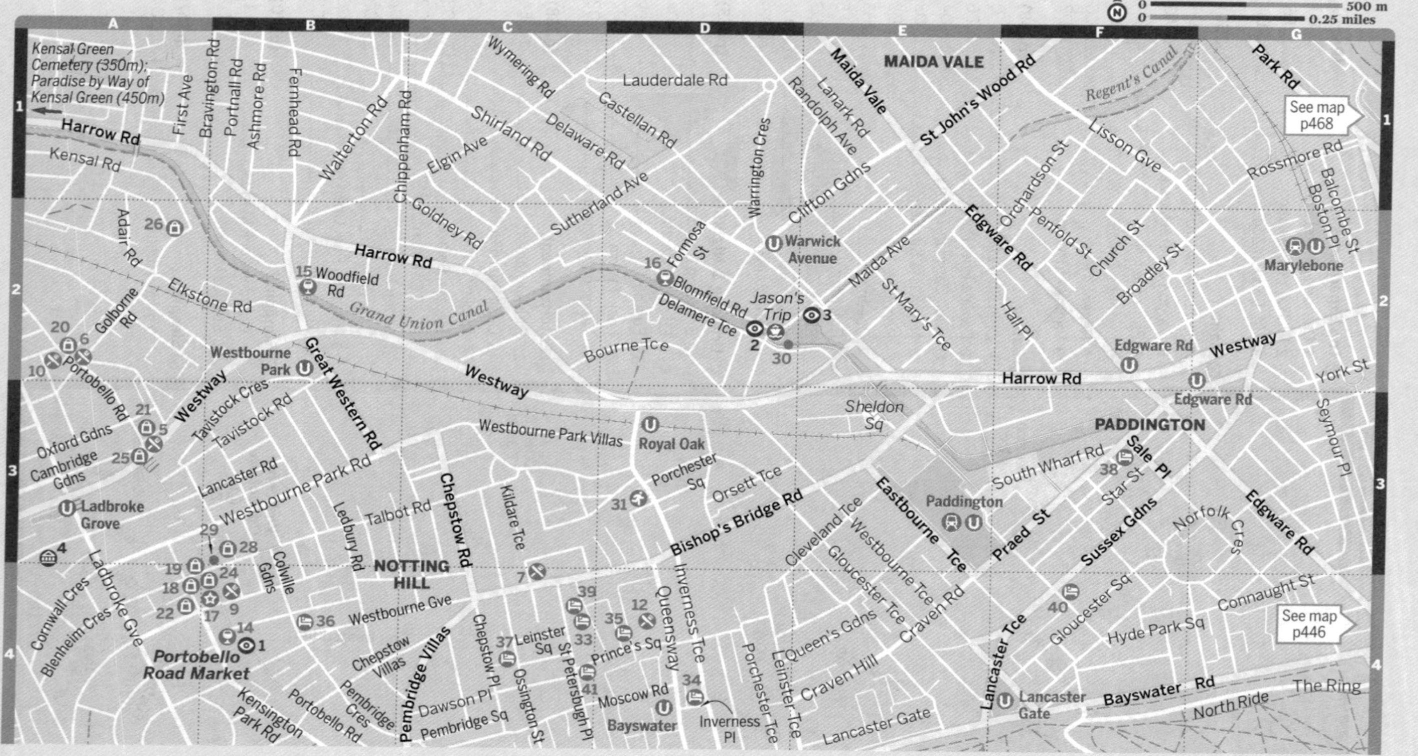

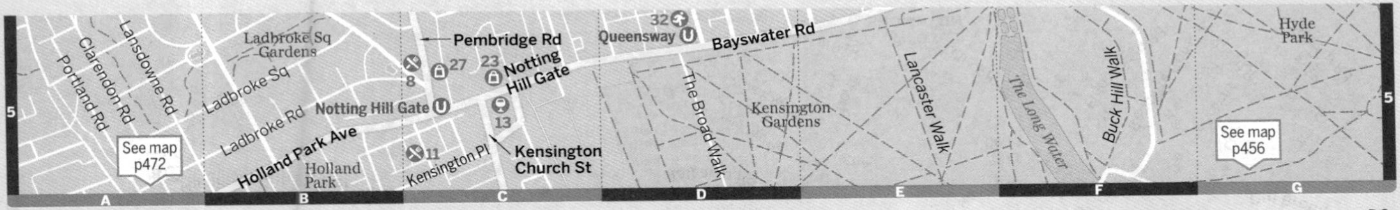

Top Experiences (p276)
1 Portobello Road Market B4

Sights (p274)
2 Grand Union Canal D2
3 Little Venice E2
4 Museum of Brands A3

Eating (p278)
5 Acklam Village Market A3
Arancina (see 8)
6 Cockney's Pie and Mash A2
7 Farmacy C4
8 Fish House C5
9 Honest Burgers B4
10 Lowry & Baker A2
11 Mazi C5
12 Urban Social D4

Drinking & Nightlife (p282)
13 Notting Hill Arts Club C5
14 Portobello Star B4
15 Union Tavern B2
16 Waterway D2

Entertainment (p284)
17 Electric Cinema B4
Puppet Theatre Barge (see 3)

Shopping (p285)
Adam (see 25)
18 Biscuiteers A4
19 Ceramica Blue A4
Chinese Tea Company (see 25)
20 Found and Vision A2
21 Honest Jon's A3
22 Lutyens & Rubinstein A4
23 Music & Video Exchange C5
24 Notting Hill Bookshop B4
25 Portobello Green Arcade A3
26 Rellik A2
27 Retro Woman Clothing Exchange C5
28 Rough Trade West B3

Sports & Activities (p287)
29 Ginstitute B3
30 London Waterbus Company D2
31 Porchester Spa D3
32 Queens Ice & Bowl D5

Sleeping (p357)
33 Garden Court Hotel C4
34 La Suite West D4
35 London House Hotel D4
36 Main House B4
37 New Linden Hotel C4
38 Point A Hotel F3
39 Space Apart Hotel C4
40 Stylotel F4
41 Vancouver Studios C4

WEST LONDON: SHEPHERD'S BUSH & EARL'S COURT

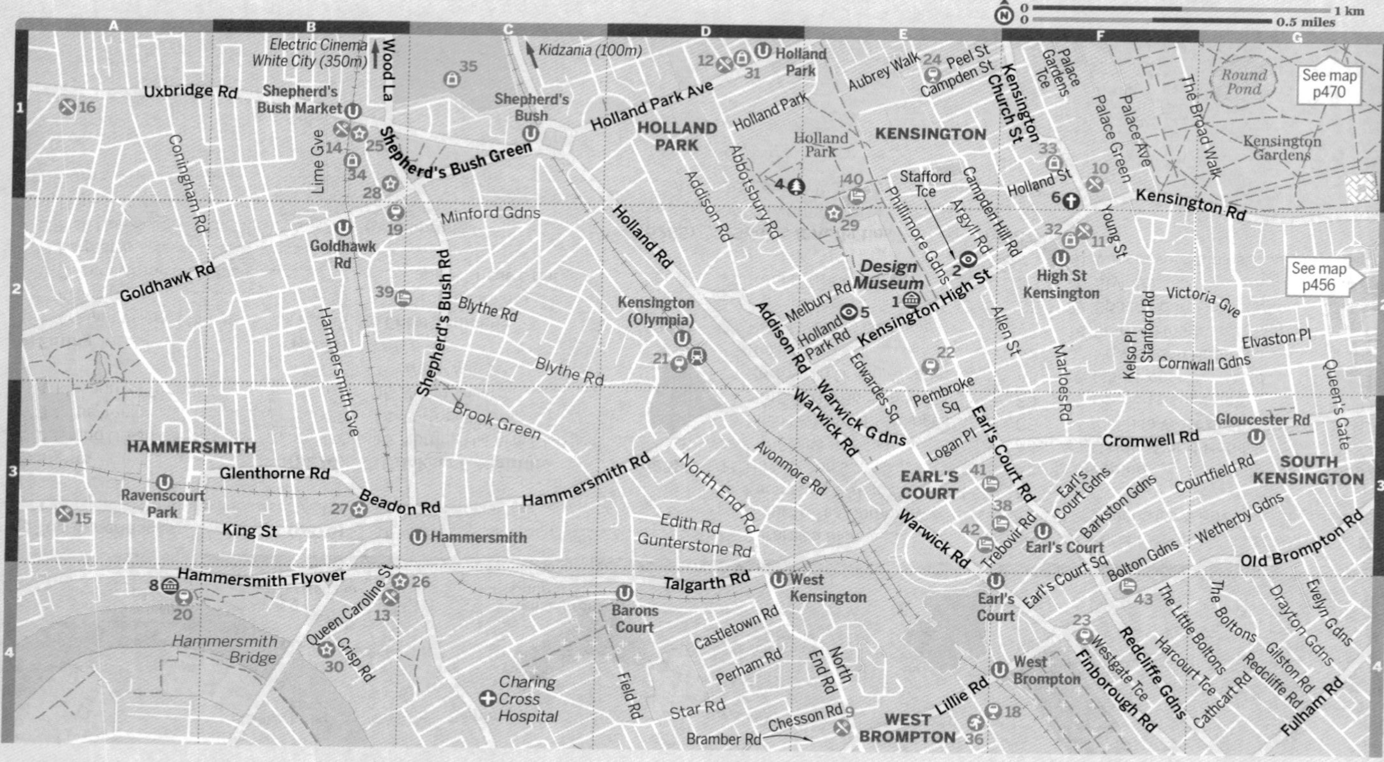

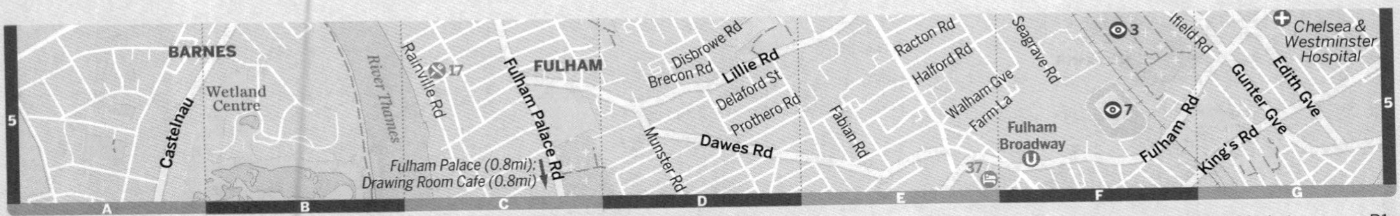

BARNES
Castelnau
Wetland Centre
River Thames
Rainville Rd
FULHAM
Fulham Palace Rd
Fulham Palace (0.8mi); Drawing Room Cafe (0.8mi)
Disbrowe Rd
Brecon Rd
Lillie Rd
Delaford St
Prothero Rd
Munster Rd
Dawes Rd
Fabian Rd
Racton Rd
Halford Rd
Walham Gve
Farm La
Seagrave Rd
Fulham Broadway
Fulham Rd
King's Rd
Ifield Rd
Gunter Gve
Edith Gve
Chelsea & Westminster Hospital

Top Experiences (p275)
1 Design Museum ... E2

Sights (p276)
2 18 Stafford Terrace ... E2
3 Brompton Cemetery ... F5
4 Holland Park ... D1
5 Leighton House ... E2
6 St Mary Abbots ... F1
7 Stamford Bridge ... F5
8 William Morris Society ... A4

Eating (p281)
9 222 ... E4
10 Dirty Bones ... F1
11 Dishoom ... F2
12 Flat Three ... D1
13 Gate ... B4
14 Mr Falafel ... B1
15 Potli ... A3
16 Princess Victoria ... A1
17 River Cafe ... C5

Drinking & Nightlife (p283)
18 Atlas ... F4
19 Brew Dog ... B2
20 Dove ... A4
Library Bar ... (see 25)
21 Pergola Olympia ... D2
22 Scarsdale Tavern ... E2
23 Troubadour ... F4
24 Windsor Castle ... E1

Entertainment (p284)
25 Bush Theatre ... B1
26 Eventim Apollo ... C4
27 Lyric Hammersmith ... B3
28 O2 Shepherd's Bush Empire ... B1
29 Opera Holland Park ... E2
30 Riverside Studios ... B4

Shopping (p285)
31 Daunt Books ... D1
32 Japan House ... F2
33 Royal Trinity Hospice ... F1
34 Shepherd's Bush Market ... B1
35 Westfield ... C1

Sports & Activities (p288)
36 Roberson Wine ... E4

Sleeping (p357)
37 Barclay House ... E5
38 K + K Hotel George ... F3
39 Melrose Gardens ... B2
40 Safestay Holland Park ... E1
41 St James Backpackers Hostel ... E3
42 Twenty Nevern Square ... E3
43 YHA Earl's Court ... F4

SOUTH LONDON: BRIXTON, CLAPHAM & BATTERSEA

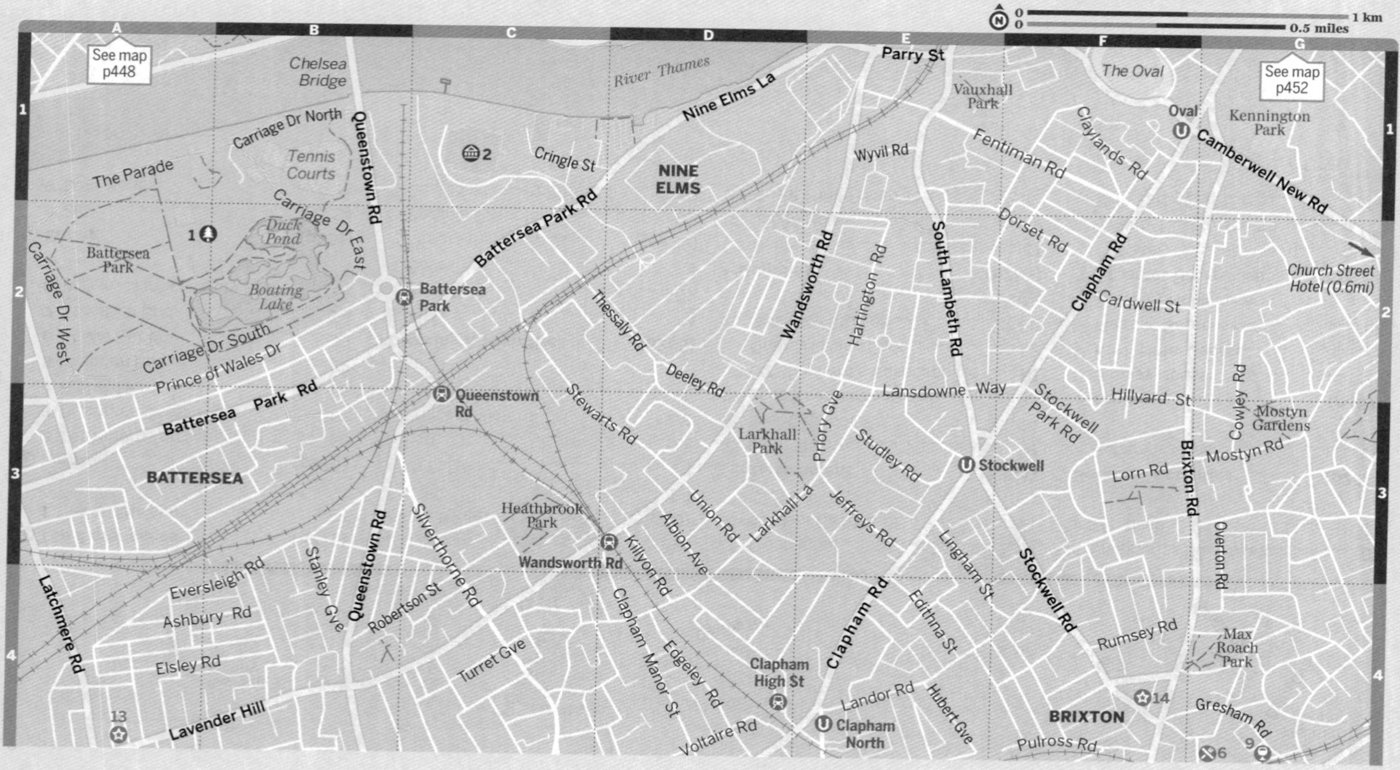

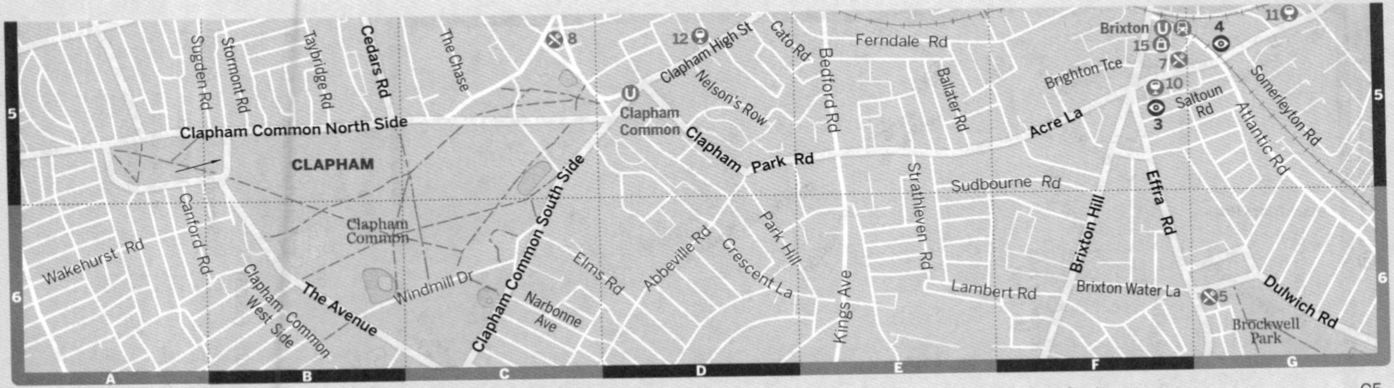

Sights (p301)

1 Battersea Park A2
2 Battersea Power Station C1
3 Black Cultural Archives F5
4 Brixton Village & Market Row G5

Eating (p302)

Franco Manca .... (see 15)
Honest Burgers .... (see 4)
Kricket .... (see 4)
Mamalan .... (see 4)
5 Naughty Piglets G6
6 Pop Brixton G4
7 Three Little Birds F5
8 Trinity C5

Drinking & Nightlife (p305)

9 Brixton Brewery G4
Federation Coffee .... (see 4)
10 Market House F5
11 Shrub and Shutter G5
Taproom by Brixton Village .... (see 4)
12 Two Brewers D5

Entertainment (p309)

13 Battersea Arts Centre A4
14 O2 Academy Brixton F4

Shopping (p309)

15 Brixton Market F5

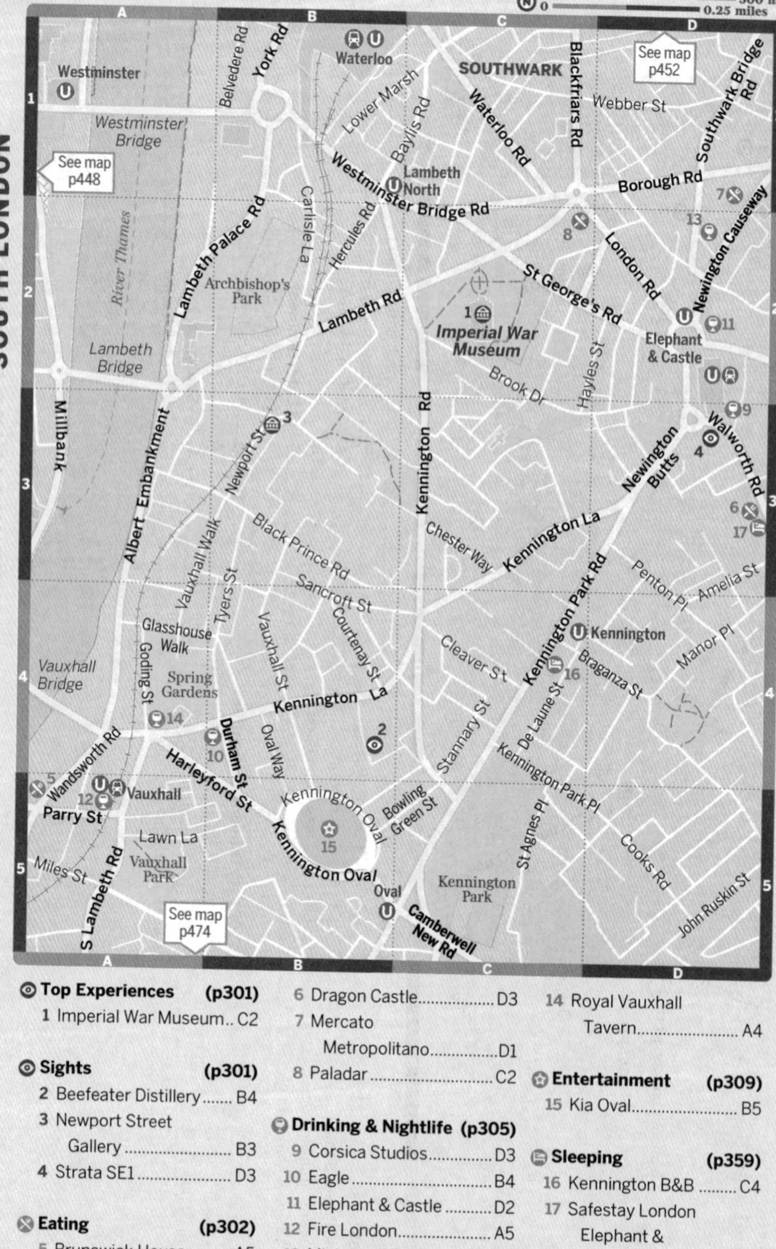

Top Experiences (p301)
1 Imperial War Museum.. C2

Sights (p301)
2 Beefeater Distillery....... B4
3 Newport Street Gallery........................ B3
4 Strata SE1..................... D3

Eating (p302)
5 Brunswick House.......... A5
6 Dragon Castle................. D3
7 Mercato Metropolitano................D1
8 Paladar............................ C2

Drinking & Nightlife (p305)
9 Corsica Studios.............. D3
10 Eagle.............................. B4
11 Elephant & Castle D2
12 Fire London..................... A5
13 Ministry of Sound D2
14 Royal Vauxhall Tavern........................ A4

Entertainment (p309)
15 Kia Oval........................ B5

Sleeping (p359)
16 Kennington B&B C4
17 Safestay London Elephant & Castle....................... D3

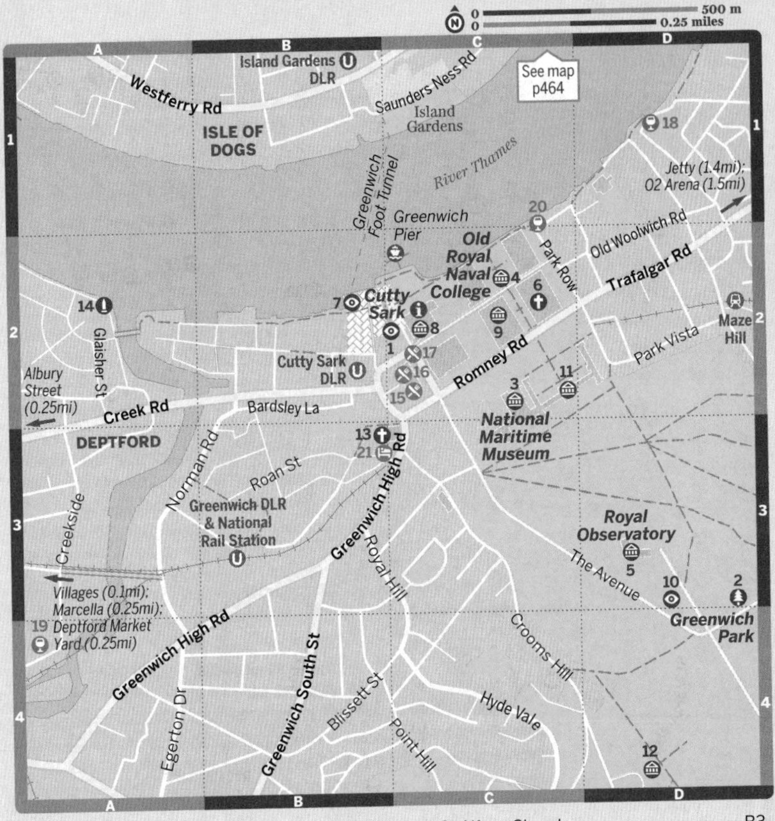

Top Experiences (p291)

1 Cutty Sark ... C2
2 Greenwich Park ... D3
3 National Maritime Museum ... C2
4 Old Royal Naval College ... C2
5 Royal Observatory ... D3

Sights (p294)

6 Chapel of St Peter & St Paul ... C2
7 Greenwich Foot Tunnel ... B2
8 Old Royal Naval College Visitor Centre ... C2
9 Painted Hall ... C2
10 Peter Harrison Planetarium ... D3
11 Queen's House ... C2
12 Ranger's House ... D4
13 St Alfege Church ... B3
14 Statue of Peter the Great ... A2

Eating (p297)

15 Goddards at Greenwich ... C2
16 Greenwich Market ... C2
17 Paul Rhodes ... C2

Drinking & Nightlife (p297)

18 Cutty Sark Tavern ... D1
19 Little Faith ... A4
Old Brewery ... (see 8)
20 Trafalgar Tavern ... C1

Sleeping (p359)

21 Mitre ... B3

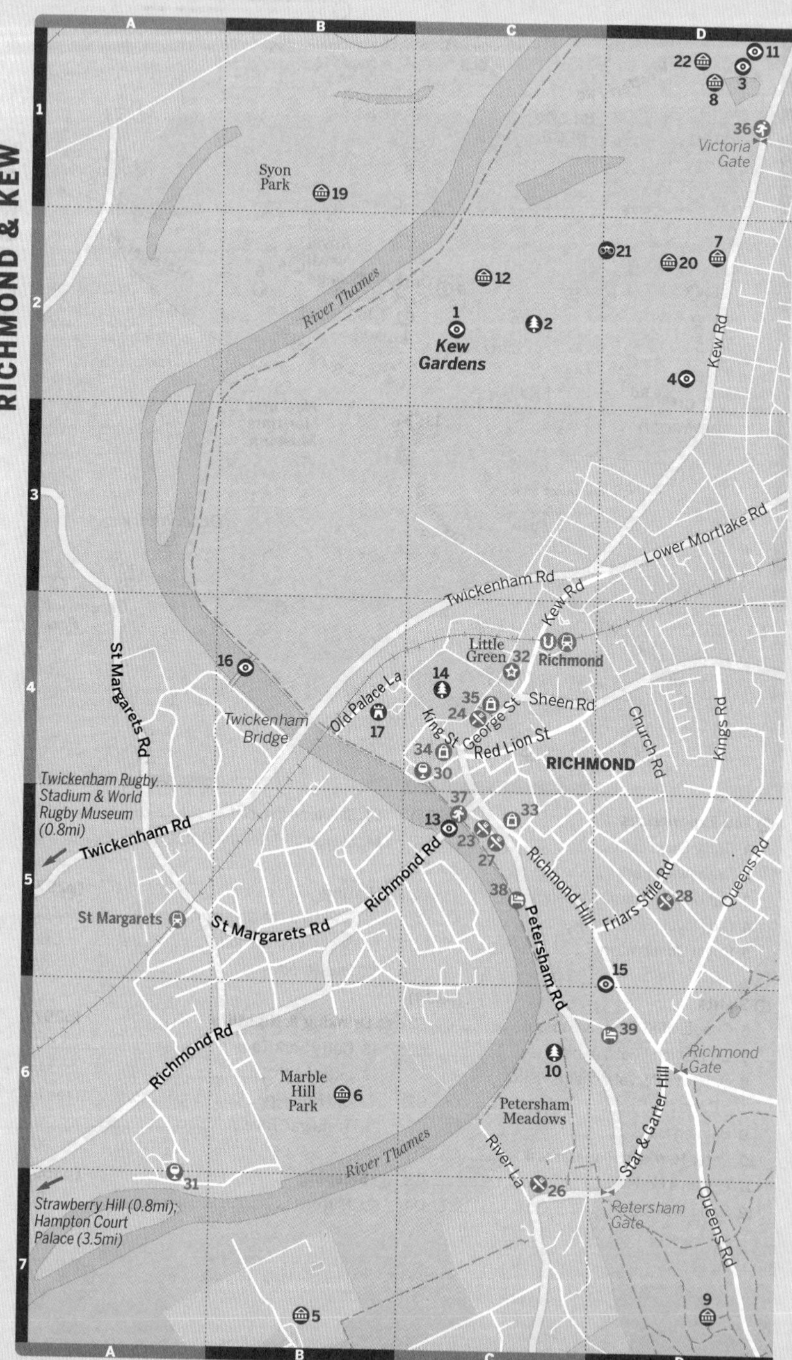

Syon Park
River Thames
Kew Gardens
Victoria Gate
Kew Rd
Lower Mortlake Rd
Twickenham Rd
Little Green
Richmond
Old Palace La
King St
George St
Sheen Rd
Red Lion St
RICHMOND
Church Rd
Kings Rd
Twickenham Bridge
St Margarets Rd
Twickenham Rugby Stadium & World Rugby Museum (0.8mi)
Richmond Rd
Richmond Hill
Friars Stile Rd
Queens Rd
St Margarets
Petersham Rd
Richmond Gate
Marble Hill Park
Petersham Meadows
Star & Garter Hill
River La
Petersham Gate
Strawberry Hill (0.8mi); Hampton Court Palace (3.5mi)

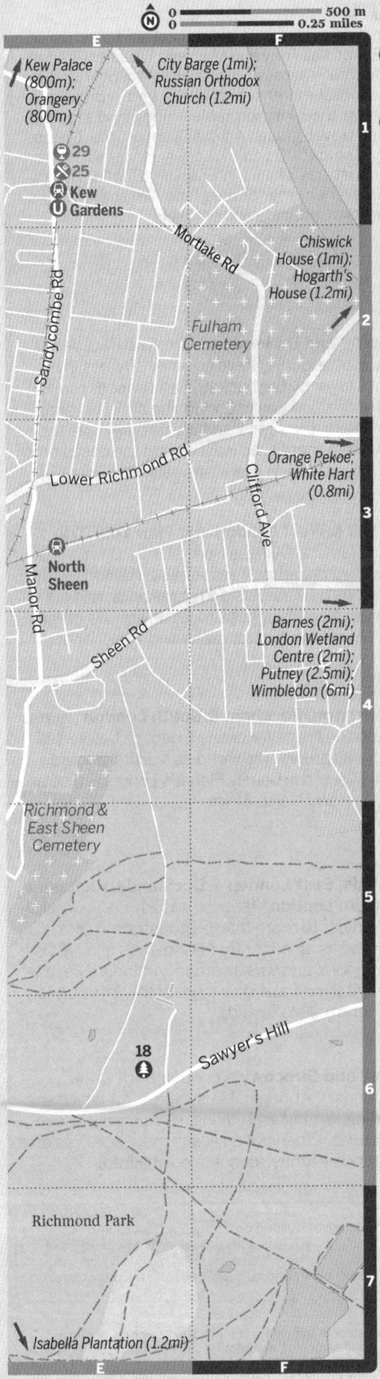

0 500 m
0 0.25 miles

E F

Kew Palace (800m); Orangery (800m)
City Barge (1mi); Russian Orthodox Church (1.2mi)
29
25
Kew Gardens
Mortlake Rd
Chiswick House (1mi); Hogarth's House (1.2mi)
Sandycombe Rd
Fulham Cemetery
Lower Richmond Rd
Orange Pekoe; White Hart (0.8mi)
Clifford Ave
North Sheen
Manor Rd
Sheen Rd
Barnes (2mi); London Wetland Centre (2mi); Putney (2.5mi); Wimbledon (6mi)
Richmond & East Sheen Cemetery
18
Sawyer's Hill
Richmond Park
Isabella Plantation (1.2mi)

1 2 3 4 5 6 7

Top Experiences (p316)
1 Kew Gardens C2

Sights (p318)
2 Arboretum C2
3 Great Broad Walk Borders D1
4 Great Pagoda D2
5 Ham House B7
6 Marble Hill House B6
7 Marianne North Gallery D2
8 Palm House D1
9 Pembroke Lodge D7
10 Petersham Meadows C6
11 Princess of Wales Conservatory D1
12 Queen Charlotte's Cottage C2
13 Richmond Bridge C5
14 Richmond Green C4
15 Richmond Hill D5
16 Richmond Lock B4
17 Richmond Palace Remains B4
18 Richmond Park E6
19 Syon House B1
20 Temperate House D2
21 Treetop Walkway D2
22 Waterlily House D1

Eating (p323)
23 Chez Lindsay C5
24 Gelateria Danieli C4
25 Glasshouse E1
26 Petersham Nurseries Cafe C7
27 Pier 1 .... C5
28 Richmond Hill Bakery D5

Drinking & Nightlife (p324)
29 Tap on the Line E1
30 White Cross C4
31 White Swan A7

Entertainment (p325)
32 Richmond Theatre C4

Shopping (p325)
33 Teddington Cheese C5
34 The Open Book C4
35 Toko C4

Sports & Activities (p326)
36 Kew Explorer D1
37 Richmond Bridge Boat Hire C5

Sleeping (p360)
38 Bingham Riverhouse C5
39 Petersham D6

E F

Our Story

A beat-up old car, a few dollars in the pocket and a sense of adventure. In 1972 that's all Tony and Maureen Wheeler needed for the trip of a lifetime – across Europe and Asia overland to Australia. It took several months, and at the end – broke but inspired – they sat at their kitchen table writing and stapling together their first travel guide, *Across Asia on the Cheap*. Within a week they'd sold 1500 copies. Lonely Planet was born.

Today, Lonely Planet has offices in Franklin, Dublin, Beijing and Delhi, with a network of over 2000 contributors in every corner of the globe. We share Tony's belief that 'a great guidebook should do three things: inform, educate and amuse'.

Our Writers

Steve Fallon

Hampstead & North London, Sleeping and Understand After two decades of living in the centre of the universe – East London – Steve cockney-rhymes in his sleep, eats jellied eel for brekkie, drinks lager by the bucketful and dances round the occasional handbag. As always, for this addition of London he did everything the hard/fun way: walking the walks, seeing the sights, sniffing through hotels, digesting lots and taking (some) advice from friends, colleagues and the occasional taxi driver. Steve is also a London-qualified Blue Badge Tourist Guide (www.steveslondon.com).

Damian Harper

Kensington & Hyde Park, Notting Hill & West London and Plan Your Trip With two degrees (one in modern and classical Chinese from SOAS), Damian has been writing for Lonely Planet for over two decades. A seasoned guidebook writer, Damian has penned articles for numerous newspapers and magazines, and currently makes Surrey, England, his home. A self-taught trumpet novice, his other hobbies include collecting modern first editions, photography and Taekwondo. Follow Damian on Instagram (damian.harper).

Lauren Keith

The City, South Bank, Greenwich, Brixton, Peckham & South London Lauren is a writer and journalist who called London home for nearly a decade before selling everything she owned in 2019 to travel around the world as a digital nomad. Before hitting the road, she previously worked in Lonely Planet's London office as the Destination Editor for the Middle East and North Africa.

MaSovaida Morgan

Clerkenwell, Shoreditch & Spitalfields, East London & Docklands, Richmond, Kew & Hampton Court, Day Trips from London MaSovaida is a travel journalist whose wayfaring tendencies have taken her to more than 55 countries across all seven continents. Previously, she worked as an editor for newspapers and NGOs in New York, Israel, and the United Kingdom, and was awarded a Fulbright Fellowship in 2012 to study publishing and digital media at University of the Arts London, where she earned a master's degree. Follow her on Instagram @MaSovaida.

Tasmin Waby

West End, Plan Your Trip, Transport and Directory A London-born writer, Tasmin was raised on the traditional lands of Aboriginal Australians, for which she will always be grateful. As well as reading, writing and editing, she's madly in love with cartography, deserts, and starry skies. When not on assignment she lives on a narrowboat in the UK, raising two hilariously funny school-aged children.

Published by Lonely Planet Global Limited
CRN 554153
12th edition – May 2022
ISBN 978 1 787017061

10 9 8 7 6 5 4 3 2 1
Printed in China